THE CHIEF EXECUTIVE

REVISED EDITION

THE CHIEF EXECUTIVE

REVISED EDITION

Louis W. Koenig

New York University

HARCOURT, BRACE & WORLD, INC.

New York / Chicago / San Francisco / Atlanta

Library of Congress Catalog Card Number: 68-54953

Printed in the United States of America

TO   *Juliana, Fred, and David*

Preface

This is a revision of the book that first appeared in 1964. In this second chance that I have had to examine the American Presidency, I have, in the luxury of hindsight, amended some of my earlier judgments. I have endeavored to reflect the growing scholarship in the field and to bring into these chapters material provided by the past four years of the administration of Lyndon B. Johnson, which one may predict—if prediction is possible in this year of 1968—will stand as one of the most interesting of Presidencies.

In response to suggestions offered by gentle, and not so gentle, readers, I have added material comparing the Presidency with the American state and local executives. I have also included a new chapter on Presidential personality, in the belief that if we are to understand why the Chief Executive decides, speaks, and acts as he does, we must examine his personality, especially his values, goals, and stylistic traits. The bibliography has been enlarged, and citations have been provided throughout the book.

It is a pleasure to acknowledge my gratitude to Professors Murray Havens of the University of Texas and James Barber of Yale University for careful and thoughtful readings of the manuscript. Their suggestions, warnings, and encouragements have been most valuable. Joseph Willard of the Executive Seminar Center of the U.S. Civil Service Commission at Kings

Point, New York, has also been a rewarding critic. My views on the Chief Executive have continued to profit from the perceptive scrutiny of students in my university classes on the American Presidency. My mother, the late Pauline Graef Koenig, helped with the original edition, and to my wife, Eleanor, and daughter, Juliana, I am once again genuinely grateful.

Louis W. Koenig

New York University
July 11, 1968

Contents

THE CHIEF EXECUTIVE

REVISED EDITION

Perspectives 1
on Presidential Power

"I do have disappointments and moments of distress, as I think every President has had," observed Lyndon B. Johnson in an off-the-cuff stock-taking of his experience, at the annual Presidential Prayer Breakfast in 1967.[1] Like other Chief Executives before him, President Johnson worked in a world of limitations.

The biggest and most critical problems he struggled with are problems that cannot be solved. The most that a President can accomplish or hope for are some tenuous, largely inadequate solutions that American society and the world at large can learn to live with. Some of his gravest problems may be tantalizingly long in reaching even this modest equilibrium. Since the mid-1950's, American Presidents have wrestled with the conflict in Vietnam, with spiraling commitment of their energies and reputations and the nation's resources. But neither President Johnson nor his shrewdest counselors nor his most persevering critics were able to devise by that most critical of deadlines —the commencement of the 1968 Presidential campaign—what American society, the Southeast Asian nations, and the world were willing to accept as a realistic solution for that dark and slippery problem.

The American President, to be sure, has impressive power, but it is seldom fully available or appropriate for the worst problems he must cope with. He has at hand an awesome arsenal of atomic and hydrogen bombs and other weaponry. Yet President Kennedy could do little more than watch the wall go up in Berlin in 1961, and President Johnson chose to limit himself to cautious response in the face of that rarest of outrages, the seizure of an American naval vessel, the *Pueblo*, by the North Koreans in 1968. Johnson could have retaliated immediately with military force, but he chose to use not his greater powers but his lesser powers. He resorted to diplomatic action and limited defensive measures. He could have bombed and invaded North Korea and possibly retrieved the *Pueblo*.[2] But to do so would have committed the nation's power and reputation and opened the gates to another major war. As Presidents nowadays so often find, their lesser powers in foreign affairs may be more appropriate and more useful than their greater powers.

Johnson was engaged in yet another kind of conflict, the urban war, which too has had its moments of violence that increasingly and alarmingly resemble certain patterns of the warfare between nations. Presidential effort in the urban war is chiefly directed to lifting the great body of the poor, among whom Negro citizens are heavily concentrated, up to levels of economic security and even equality. In the 1960's this goal has evoked large governmental expenditure, imaginative public and private programs, new laws, and abundant political rhetoric. But the net results reveal the urban war as another war that eludes victory and solution. If anything, the gulf between the races widens. White prosperity increases faster than Negro prosperity; the unemployment rate among Negroes compares more and more unfavorably with that of the whites. Despair and rioting mount in the cities, and urban blight creeps steadily onward.[3]

Presidential power, both now and in the foreseeable future, is frustrated by the Negro ghettos and the urban problem. The urban problem is so complex and overwhelming that it far outstrips the available resources of Presidential power. The President can deal at most with only a small segment of the problem. In a federal system of government, he shares power with the states and cities and a hodgepodge of other local political structures. The fate of the Negro citizen is largely a matter of private economic and social decision. Decisions affecting his chance for employment, the kind of job he is to hold, and his possibilities of advancement do not repose in Presidential hands, but in private hands.

What the President can do with the urban problem and the Negro ghettos also depends heavily upon what Congress is willing to do. Upon Congress he depends for new laws and annual appropriations. But, as any President would gladly testify, his prospects on Capitol Hill, most of the time, are highly uncertain. In 1966 and 1967, most urgent years for the ghetto problem, Johnson was not able to secure the passage of a substantial civil rights bill. When the rioting and pillaging in cities across the country were at a high point in 1967, the President did not come forward, as circumstances seemed to warrant, with bold new initiatives and programs. His existing proposals at that critical moment in the hot month of August wallowed in the lowest of ebbs in Congress. Appropriations for the important model cities program were cut by one-third. The House of Representatives refused to provide any funds for the rent supplement program, which carried the highest Presidential priority. A rat control program, addressed to one of the worst problems of the ghettos, originally drew only merriment and jest.[4] It was, plainly, the wrong political time to launch new attacks on the urban problem despite its soaring urgency. Again, the outbreaks after Martin Luther King's assassination in 1968 evoked no special measures beyond the enactment of a long-delayed civil rights bill. The President and the nation were the victims of, in the phrase of James MacGregor Burns, "the deadlock of democracy."[5]

The President also lives within the limits of his own political skills and personality, within the limits of his own vision and goals and his ability to lead, inspire, and administer. Whenever he acts, his confidence and assertion suffer restraints that afflict all mortals, as Johnson recalled at the Presidential Prayer Breakfast. "We know," he said, "that at the hour of decision in public and private life, faced with the tormenting choices that are always a part of man's destiny, none of us can ever be certain that we are right."[6]

The Imagined Presidency

Most American Chief Executives are the victims of the chasm between the Presidency as it appears, or is imagined, and the Presidency of reality. The imagined Presidency is vested in our minds with more power than the Presidency really has. The real Presidency is what the Presidency effectively is in the present, what it can do in a given situation. The imagined Presidency is a euphoric impression of its past, present, and future and is grounded partly in reality and partly in fancy. It exaggerates the office's strength, encouraged by the substantial power it actually possesses, the prestige built in its past, and the pomp that surrounds it. The imagined Presidency underestimates the limitations of power and environment that the office suffers. It equates past Presidential success, the nation's might, and expectations of how the world should go with available Presidential power.

The Chief Executive of the world's most advanced technological nation, which produces far more of the world's wealth than any other nation and sustains a military establishment of unsurpassed destructive capabilities, is bound to bask in an aura of reflected power, no matter what the inherent power of his office may be. Our view of what the Presidency can do is shaped by what it has done. It is an office whose finest triumphs are remembered better than its failures. It is a gallery of our heroes: Washington launching the republic despite economic weakness and foreign hostility; Andrew Jackson asserting union against nullification and implanting political and economic democracy; Abraham Lincoln leading the Union through the crucible of civil war; Theodore Roosevelt, Woodrow Wilson, and Franklin D. Roosevelt raising high the banner of economic and social reform; and Wilson and the second Roosevelt leading the nation through two wars. The Presidency is a place where men faced with horrendous challenge have achieved unexpected growth and responded with unexpected effectiveness. Lincoln, James K.

Polk, and others, held in poor esteem when they took up their duties, grew enormously in stature after brief exposure to the trials of office. "Go thou and do likewise," we are ready to instruct any incumbent.

The Presidency appears all the more imposing because it is the center of our expectations. Just as he is to the Sioux Indians, the President is in a sense the Great Father to us all. We look to him because he has unlimited power to make proposals for action. He can, if he chooses, espouse any cause, from simplified spelling to the soil bank, and whatever he says will be heard and noticed. Since he is elected by and responsible to a national constituency, he better than anyone can bring problems forward, define the possible solutions, and advocate the one most likely to achieve the chosen end. But woe to him if trouble does not fade and the clouds do not roll back. He often will fail because some of us expect him to do things he cannot do: to maintain a posture of victory in any war the country is associated with, to secure from the investment of foreign aid a return of friendship and loyalty, and to organize an administration of invariable efficiency. The President cannot extract conformity to United States objectives with absolute success from traditional allies whose wealth, and therefore independence, is on the rise. He cannot, merely by his own acts, keep the economy whirring at high speed, puncture ballooning unemployment, and fasten tight the lid on inflation. He cannot, by a wave of his hand, assure Americans a life of peace, contentment, and security. He does not, as Sidney Hyman has suggested, "have God's autonomous powers to make mountains without valleys as the mood strikes him."[7] The difference between what some of us imagine the Presidency to be and what it really is leads to disappointment, frustration, and attack.

The appearance of Presidential power is enhanced by the color and pageantry of the office, the adaptation to American needs of the monarchical principle. The President reigns as well as rules. Like the flag, he is the symbol of national unity, a focal point of loyalties, and the ceremonial chief of the nation. He approaches with the accompaniment of "Hail to the Chief"; he decorates war heroes, dedicates parks and post offices, and performs prodigious social feats on the scale of Theodore Roosevelt's hand-shaking with eight thousand people on New Year's Day in 1902.

The appearance of Presidential power is increased by the sweeping appreciations that are accorded it, like Harry S. Truman's when he declared that "the Presidency of the United States of America has become the greatest and most important office in the history of the world." Its might is inherent in the epithets sometimes flung at Presidents in midtenure like "that man in the White House" Franklin D. Roosevelt and "Mad Tom" Jefferson. The appearance of power glows more strongly when a hero-figure like Dwight D. Eisenhower and a hero-glamour-figure like John F. Kennedy occupy the White House. The appearance of power is conveyed in Johnson's astounding electoral victory margin of nearly sixteen million votes in 1964 and by the astounding popularity of Eisenhower and Kennedy in the public opinion polls. But mere popularity, those Presidents would testify, does not achieve policy.

The appearance of the Presidency as an office more powerful than it really is has led to ill-advised attempts to reduce its presumed effectiveness by drastic surgery. One of the most menacing of these attempts has succeeded, the Twenty-second Amendment, adopted in 1951, which was hawked with cries that it was imperative to prevent the President from becoming a dictator, even though no such dictator had appeared in the long experience of the American Presidency. In actuality, as public discussion made clear, the amendment was a reflection upon Franklin D. Roosevelt, who was driven by the urgencies of World War II into accepting, and by no means willingly, an incumbency of four terms. The amendment is a tragedy whose full dimensions are yet to be known; it greatly inhibits the President's power in his second term and shifts the balance in the legislature's favor.

Spurred by the success of the Twenty-second Amendment, the foes of Presidential power launched the Bricker amendment, also of the 1950's. Appearing in its long career in several forms and pushed by tireless promoters, the amendment would in effect have prevented the Chief Executive from making treaties and executive agreements with foreign governments. It would have largely shut down the Presidency in foreign affairs. Other amendments are floated periodically by those afflicted with the high fever of the imagined Presidency. They propose to limit income tax assessments to 25 per cent, to transfer federal welfare functions to the states, and other such things, all of which either directly or indirectly could do the Presidency great harm.

The glory and power of the Presidency have been a favorite theme of those who, over the decades, have been charged with the task of introducing the Chief Executive on great occasions to make an address. Former President William Howard Taft recalled one day in a lecture at Columbia University how those who once had presented him, by way of exalting the occasion, frequently cited him as one "who exercised greater governmental power than any monarch in Europe." This of course was a time when monarchs still were thriving. Taft declared to his university audience,

> I need hardly point out the inaccuracies of this remark, by comparing the powers of the President of the United States with those of the rulers of countries in which there is not real popular legislative control. The powers of the German Emperor, of the Emperor of Austria, and the Emperor of Russia are far wider than those of the President of the United States.[8]

The Real Presidency

Those who introduced President Taft on the public platform were confused by the difference between the appearance and the reality of Presidential power. The real Presidency exists in a world of circumscribed powers whose limits are becoming increasingly confining. That the Presidency should be a tightly limited office was part of its original conception. Distrustful of power and fearful of tyranny, the Founding Fathers instilled the principles of checks and balances and separation of powers into the Constitution. The arrangement of the executive and Congress, as Woodrow Wilson put it, reflected "the Whig Theory of political dynamics, which was a sort of unconscious copy of the Newtonian Theory of the universe."[9] Neither Congress nor the executive was to become the dominant force, but each shared the power of the other, whether making laws, appointments, or treaties, and each therefore could check the other's assertion.

From the beginning and throughout Presidential history, the Chief Executive has been able to maintain no important policy, domestic or foreign, without Congressional support in the form of laws and money. Neither is there any dependable way under the Constitution in which the President can bring Congress to provide this wherewithal against its will. A complex of forces that prompts Congress to resist or oppose the President much of the time prevails. Because the method of electing the President differs from the method of electing Congress, their constituencies, concerns, and viewpoints differ. The President and Vice President alone are chosen by the nation. Senators and Congressmen, in contrast, are essentially local officers responsible to the voters of a single state or Congressional district. Congress does not choose the President and is therefore not beholden to him and cannot be bullied by him. Only once in four years are the President and members of the House of Representatives elected simultaneously, and even on that occasion only one-third of the Senate is elected. At the President's midterm the House and another one-third of the Senate are chosen, usually with local issues predominating. The outcome more often than not reduces the President's own party support in both Congressional houses. At no point in his four-year span does the President face a Senate wholly elected during his tenure, owing to the Senate's six-year term and system of staggered elections. Presidents come and go, but the most powerful legislators—the chairmen of the standing committees—stay on, often rolling up tenure of a third of a century and more.

The likelihood is that a President who seeks legislation promoting social and economic reforms will face a hard wall of opposition from the legislative leaders of his own party. These are the committee chairmen who have risen by seniority because they come from "safe" districts, which are situated chiefly in Southern or rural Northern areas. Both areas tend toward conservative outlooks and therefore produce conservative legislators. Theodore Roosevelt, advancing the reforms of his Square Deal, had to work principally through conservative Senators Eugene Hale and Nelson Aldrich in the Senate and Speaker "Uncle Joe" Cannon in the House, who "distrusted anything that was progressive." "We succeeded in working together," Roosevelt wrote of their relationship, "I pushing forward and they hanging back," not a promising juxtaposition, on its face, for cooperative endeavor. Speaker Cannon's estimate of his dealings with Theodore Roosevelt is an admirable indication of the President's common plight in legislative relations. "He was a good sportsman," said Cannon, "and accepted what he could get so long as legislation conformed even in part to his recommendations."[10]

Although the Founding Fathers did not foresee political parties, their rise has in no significant way hampered the intended effect of checks and balances. Parties are not a dependable force for cooperation between the legislative and executive branches. The party functions effectively as a national organization only once every four years, when control of the White House is at stake. Otherwise, the party is a confederation of largely autonomous state and local organizations, where sectional cleavages and factional differences are commonplace. The President, in fact, invests much time maintaining unity between the squabbling factions. The President and the legislators, although they wear the same party label, are nominated by different party organizations and are chosen by different electorates, an arrangement that is hardly conducive to unity. There is no known common standard of party loyalty and no party caucus, as in Great Britain, which joins the executive with the legislators of his party in the enterprise of an accepted policy program. Indeed the Presidency and Congress may simply be vantage points of the party's rival factions. Thus Eisenhower in the Presidency was faced with an array of standing committee chairmen, holders of the supreme legislative policy posts, who were identified overwhelmingly with the Taft wing of his party, which had fought his nomination unremittingly. Eisenhower may have beaten Robert Taft for the nomination, but Taft got the enormous consolation prize of the United States Congress.

The President is checked by the opinion of the people in general or, when they organize, by their opinion as pressure groups. American pressure groups possess enormous economic, ethnic, and sectional diversity. What pleases the Democratic Italian voters of New York may be anathema to Democratic Negro voters of Los Angeles or Democratic Protestants of the Middle West. A policy that delights Republican hard-money bankers in New York may disgruntle Republican wheat-farmers in Kansas. The President has the Solomon-like task of mediating between the groups with all their hopes and fears, of weighing the political situation as a whole, and of safeguarding the public interest. He is both a great and good engine of the aspirations of the groups and a brake upon them when they seek too much at the expense of the nation and other groups. The relationship is also, to a degree, reciprocal. A President, particularly a Democratic President, must pay heed to groups that because of their voting power function as veto groups. Pressuring for new advantage and meaning to keep gains already achieved, they weigh and criticize his plans and act according to their lights. He earns their votes only if they judge him to be sufficiently the vehicle of their purposes. Among Lyndon Johnson's

earliest callers after his accession to the Presidency were the leaders of organized labor and Negro civil rights groups, the two veto groups on whose
favor his political future most depended.

Practical Politics

Impressed by his own full and intimate knowledge of the limitations the
Chief Executive toils under, Harry S. Truman once observed, "The principal
power that the President has is to bring people in and try to persuade them
to do what they ought to do without persuasion. That's what I spend my time
doing. That's what the powers of the President amount to."[11] Given the interdependence of its powers, the Presidency is an intensive experience in
practical politics. To lead, to win support, to achieve, the President must practice with skill and ardor the arts of political persuasion. Woodrow Wilson
noted before taking up the Presidency, "We have all been the disciples of
Montesquieu, but we have also been practical politicians."[12] The President
must woo, cajole, threaten, and even wage war on party leaders, legislators,
and chieftains of the veto groups. He must bring the several parts of government and the private groups into harmonious effort to accomplish shared
objectives. He alone in our political life can do it.

George Washington discovered the necessity for practical politics promptly
upon taking up the Presidential office. The new government, he wrote, was to
be one "of accommodation as well as a government of laws."[13] The President's
political means cover a wide gamut: blandishments, favors, bargains, compromises, and the assertion, when necessary, of naked pressure. Herbert Hoover,
aiming to secure tariff reform legislation, met with the legislative leaders
and made public appeals. When these proved unavailing, he granted a rare
recognition by entertaining Senator William E. Borah alone at dinner to woo
him, and, varying his attack, dispatched a sharp message to Senator Reed
Smoot, who was guiding the bill in the Senate: "No flexible tariff, no tariff
bill." Again failure on both counts, whereupon Hoover entertained all the
Republican leaders at breakfast, but without success. When he learned that
the House-Senate conference committee had watered down the flexible provisions nearly to the point of drowning them, Hoover responded with equal
ferocity. "I wrote out the provision I wanted," he said, "I sent word that unless
my formula was adopted the bill would be vetoed. The result was a complete
victory."[14]

To get his controversial measures enacted, whether in foreign or domestic affairs, the President, because of the unreliability of his own party,
must build a special coalition for his purpose from both major parties. Lyndon
Johnson, this is to say, could not have secured civil rights legislation in 1964
and 1965 without Republican support. The coalitions keep forming and
breaking up as their purpose is achieved. Moving on to new objectives, the

President must develop a new combination of support. To make his way, the President must know when to spend and when to hoard his influence and how to build it. He must realize, as Richard Neustadt has suggested, that the essence of his persuasive task is to convince the legislators whose support he courts "that what the White House wants of them is what they ought to do for their sake and on their authority."[15] In playing the political game, the President occupies certain of the best vantage points in the political system. His power of publicity, his veto, his power over budget and expenditure, his power of appointment are means that exist nowhere else in the political structure. For all the limits upon his power, he is the supreme unifying force in our diffuse political system and pluralistic society. He better than anyone else can act affirmatively and flexibly. But his great rival, Congress, also enjoys distinction. No other body can cast the negative so readily, so conclusively, and in so many ways.

But the President, if he shall write his name large on the pages of history, must do more than excel at practical politics. He must use political power to advance great ends. His shining hours occur in the Fourteen Points of Wilson, in the social purposes of Lincoln and the Roosevelts, and in the assertion of principle by Grover Cleveland against the test of events. He must rise to moments as Cleveland did when pressing the House Speaker to support an administration measure; Cleveland found him hesitant and fearful of the consequences to his future. "Mr. Speaker," Cleveland exclaimed, "what is your political future weighed in the balance against the fortunes of the country? Who are you and I compared with the welfare of the whole American people?"[16] The Speaker surrendered. But the President who, like Cleveland, chooses to enter the roaring furnace where political necessity and principle converge, subjects himself to the burning anguish that reaches its highest intensity in the Presidency itself. One day Cleveland invited a visitor, Dr. Wilton M. Smith, to listen to the draft of a speech. Cleveland, as he read on, worked up into a high pitch of emotion. He exclaimed, turning suddenly on his visitor,

> Doctor, I suppose at times you won't approve of many things I do, but I want you to know that I am trying to do what is right. . . . Sometimes the pressure is most overwhelming, and a President cannot always get at the exact truth; but I want you to know that I am trying to do what is right. *I am trying to do what is right.*[17]

Tears welled in the big President's eyes; he blew his nose hard, and paced the room.

Limitations of the Office

The President wears many chains. Since there are no more hours in the President's day than in any other man's, the President needs aides and assistants for the massive affairs of the executive branch. Upon their information, skill, initiative, and loyalty much of his administration's success depends. But the vast executive bureaucracy, as Presidents have found, can be a slumbering giant, slow to act, unimaginative and uncreative, and disloyal to his purposes in its alliance with pressure groups that oppose him. Aides who earn his confidence acquire in time influence of their own and become, to a degree, independent of their chief.

Certain of the machinery of the Presidency has had little or no repair since the Founding Fathers originally constructed it in 1787. The electoral college is a creaky affair from whose capacity for disaster the country has already had narrow escapes, and given the law of probabilities, we are due for further crises. And Congress—the source of laws without which he often cannot act—has never undergone any substantial modernization.

The President and the Presidency, in a word, are in a race without letup against change and emergency. The office has indeed adjusted, too, and remarkably so, but the nice question remains: Has it been adapted sufficiently to stay with the race; can it give the nation, the world, and mankind creative and forceful responses for the towering problems of the 1960's and 1970's?

Presidential Types

Without undue violence to history, it is possible to divide the Presidents the United States has had into three recurrent types with a view to assessing their suitability as models for the contemporary Chief Executive in all his rugged circumstances.

The most numerous type is one that might be styled a "literalist" President. James Madison, James Buchanan, Taft, and, to a degree, Eisenhower are of this school. The mark of the literalist President, as his title suggests, is close obedience to the letter of the Constitution. Taft, who with Buchanan was the most literal of the Presidents, formulated its operative belief:

> The true view of the Executive function is . . . that the President can exercise no power which cannot be fairly and reasonably traced to some specific grant of power or justly implied and included within such express grant as proper and necessary to its exercise. Such specific grant must be either in the Federal Constitution or in an act of Congress passed in pursuance thereof. There is no undefined residuum of power which he can exercise because it seems to him to be in the public interest.[18]

The Taft-like President tends also to live by the Whig assumption that the legislative power is popular and the executive monarchical. He is respectful, even deferential, to Congress. "My duty," James Buchanan was prone to say, "is to execute the laws . . . and not my individual opinions."[19] When Congress did nothing in the face of gathering rebellion, Buchanan too did nothing. In a later day, President Eisenhower is reported sometimes to have remarked privately to his aides that he felt called upon to "restore" to Congress powers that Franklin Roosevelt had "usurped." In public pronouncement and personal act, Eisenhower was respectful of Congressional prerogative and the doctrine of separation of powers. "Our very form of Government," he declared to the Convention of the National Young Republican Organization in 1953, "is in peril unless each branch willingly accepts and discharges its own clear responsibilities—and respects the rights and responsibilities of the others."[20]

The Taft-like President makes little use of his independent powers or prerogative (his powers, for example, as Commander-in-Chief and as implied in the executive power clause). He exerts political pressure sparingly. Symptomatic of his approach is James Bryce's observation that the typical nineteenth-century President's communications to Congress were so perfunctory that "the expression of his wishes . . . in messages has not necessarily any more effect on Congress than an article in a prominent party newspaper."[21]

The literalist President has little taste for innovation in social policy. He is nostalgic for the past and urges it be used as a blueprint for the future. He feels, as Taft did, that the bane of government is "ill-digested legislation" and that "real progress in government must be by slow stages."[22] It is a view that Theodore Roosevelt found upheld in society by "most able lawyers who are past middle age" and "large numbers of well-meaning, respectable citizens."[23]

The Presidency in the manner of Taft and Buchanan is, on its face, inadequate for the necessities of the contemporary Presidency. The past, which it venerates, can be only a partial and imperfect guide to the present and future. It excessively neglects the President's independent powers, which again and again have been a mighty sword in times of crisis and change. Its neglect of politics abdicates action to passivity and, as the experience of several nineteenth-century Presidents proves, can thoroughly reduce the President from leader to clerk. The best proof of the inadequacy of the literalist model is the abandonment of its key concepts by Presidents who once had taken them up. Cleveland at first proposed to be a literalist President, spurning to use patronage and pressure upon Congress and declaring, "I did not come here to legislate."[24] But when Congress blocked the bills he was driven to sponsor, his attitude changed, and he went furiously to work to win votes by promising jobs. Dwight Eisenhower, for all his professed deference to Congress and distaste for politics, in time did push his legislative program, and his campaigning in the 1954 Congressional elections was on a scale comparable to Franklin Roosevelt's.

At the opposite end of the spectrum from the literalist President is the "strong" President, typified by Washington, Jackson, Lincoln, Wilson, and the Roosevelts. He generally, although not exclusively, flourishes in times of crisis and change—during a war or a depression—and when political movements such as liberalism or social progressivism are at their crests. He interprets his powers with maximum liberality; he is a precedent-maker and -breaker to the point where the legality of his acts is questioned and attacked.

His legal bible is the "stewardship theory" of Theodore Roosevelt, who felt that it was the President's "duty to do anything that the needs of the nation demanded unless such action was forbidden by the Constitution or by the laws." "I acted for the public welfare," Roosevelt said, "I acted for the common well-being of all our people."[25]

The strong President provides leadership, in Franklin Roosevelt's words, "alert and sensitive to change," which in the Jefferson-Jackson tradition means that the government must act positively in promoting a good life, and in the Wilson tradition means that the nation cannot shun or escape its obligations of world leadership. His orientation is less to the past than to the future, which he approaches with hope and plan. He is skillful politically and is concerned more with substance than with form. When necessary, he resorts to bold action, whether economic, social, or military, which he does not avoid for the sake of lowering the national debt. He accepts and abides a strong Congress but purposefully uses the lawmaking process. He has the gift of inspiring and rallying the people with messages that mix practicality and prophecy. In his view, the President as a person must dominate the Presidency as an institution. He, a fleeting political figure, must bend, divert, and lead the cumbrous bureaucratic executive branch according to his purpose.

Between the strong and literalist Presidents is a middle ground that many Chief Executives have occupied; it unites elements of both extremes. This middle ground need not now detain us. The urgencies of the 1960's and beyond make emphatically clear that only one of the three available Presidential types is suitable for the future. The United States' world responsibilities and domestic urgencies require a Presidency that is continuously strong. The great, if not the foremost, task of American politics is to convert the strong Presidency, which has appeared only intermittently, into an assured and constant feature of our government. To be sure, particular actions of past strong Presidents have to a degree been institutionalized over the years. Theodore Roosevelt's "stewardship" in the 1902 coal strike is regularized in the Taft-Hartley Act; Wilson's and Franklin Roosevelt's venturings into world affairs set precedents for our many routine commitments to alliances and especially to the United Nations. But, as John Kennedy's experience as Chief Executive testifies, many pieces in the mosaic of the strong President lack a coating of permanence. The President is weak as party chief, legislative leader, and general manager of the executive branch. His weaknesses there spawn further weaknesses in his capacities as chief diplomat, Commander-in-Chief, and decision-maker. Because of his plight as legislative and party leader, he must suffer drastic cuts in appropriations for his foreign aid bill or carry on with weapons systems he would prefer to drop. Charles de Gaulle, beholding the American Presidential system in 1964, concluded that it was functioning in a limping way.[26] Our task is to see where weakness eats upon strength, to discover what combination of arrangements will satisfy our most urgent governmental need: a Presidency with continuous strength in all its parts.

Creation of the Presidency 2

A year before the Constitutional Convention of 1787, John Jay, in a letter to George Washington recounting the inadequacies of the existing government, moved boldly to the inevitable question: "Shall we have a king?"[1] It was indeed a question stirring in many influential minds, but few men dared ask it openly. The propagandists of the Revolution had done their work too well in portraying that enterprise as a struggle against a tyrannical monarch, although their description of that monarch was much more appropriate for the earlier James I or Charles I than for the monarch of their day, the unfortunate, ineffective George III. The general revulsion from monarchy had produced in the states a prevailing pattern of the weak executive and in the Articles of Confederation almost no executive at all. But the weak executive was maintained at a high price. The event that drove Jay to his writing desk was Shays's Rebellion in Massachusetts, an upheaval exposing the impotence of government and foreshadowing for the young nation a desperate existence of anarchy, confiscation of property, possible military dictatorship, and foreign intervention.

Hard questions pounded like hailstones upon responsible men's thoughts. How could the strong executive that circumstances required be best provided? Should there be a monarch, as Jay suggested? Or could some other form of strong executive be discovered or created, untainted with the tyranny that the country dreaded yet endowed with sufficient authority? In the interlude before the Convention, men carried on the search, and at Philadelphia they struggled with it under the pressure of decision.

The states, and before them the colonies, provided the major domestic experience with executive power. The colonial governor initially was a strong executive: commander-in-chief of the provincial forces and representative of the crown, embodying the several kingly prerogatives. He was the fountain of honor and privilege and thus created offices and filled them. With little exception he shared power with a council, usually of twelve members appointed by the crown at the governor's recommendation. The council functioned as the legislative upper house, advised and influenced the governor, and was his ally in local political struggles.[2]

As relations with the mother country deteriorated, the governorship passed under the increasing influence and direction of the assembly, the lower and more popular legislative house. Particularly in the French and Indian War, when the governor was constantly in need of money for the army, the assembly employed its control over supplies to pare down the governor's power. The American view of George III as the tyrant over Parliament spurred the hostility against his agent, the local governor.

The animus against executive power carried into the early state constitutions of the Revolutionary period. Power rushed to the legislature. The governor, or president as he was called in several states, was reduced almost to a cipher. His term was for one year, except in South Carolina where it was two and in Delaware where it was three. His reeligibility was strictly limited. He was chosen by, and was therefore the creature of, the legislature. The executive branch was deliberately disunified. The governor was saddled with a council chosen by the legislature, except in Pennsylvania. Most of the enumerated executive powers and functions were subject to council control. In Maryland the council was a "board" in which the executive had one vote "for the transacting of business." In Virginia Governor Edmund Randolph viewed himself as "a member of the executive."[3] The power that the legislature did not have by direct grant it could get by bold assertion against the other branches, which were endowed with little power to defend themselves. Thomas Jefferson observed of the Virginia as he might have of most state constitutions, "All the powers of government, legislative, executive and judiciary, result to the legislative body."[4]

The governor's drab plight was relieved only in Massachusetts, where he possessed the veto power (subject to overriding by two-thirds of the legislature) and was indefinitely reeligible, and in New York, where he could fairly be termed a strong executive.

The New York Governor

The New York constitution was established late, in 1777, sometime after the creation of other state constitutions, and it profited from their imperfections. The folly of the weak chief executive characteristic of those constitutions was daily revealed in the urgencies of the Revolution, which demanded the summoning of effective executive power. New York's situation, exceedingly roughened by the onmarching British, made strong executive power imperative. The state convention that drafted the constitution was literally chased up the state by the British army. It was a convention on the run, which moved from Harlem to Kingsbridge and then successively to Philipse Manor, Fishkill, Poughkeepsie, and finally Kingston, as the British pressed relentlessly northward.

The New York constitution rejected the ascendancy that the legislature enjoyed in other state constitutions. In language instilled in the future federal Constitution "the supreme executive power and authority of the state" was vested in the governor. The New York governor, in contrast to the governors of other states, served a substantial term—three years—with no limit upon his reeligibility. He was chosen not by the legislature, the prevailing pattern elsewhere, but by a constitutionally identified electorate, a popular suffrage that for the time was generously defined. His electoral independence from the legislature was a giant step toward making the governor the strongest officer of his kind in the Confederation.

His further powers all foreshadowed the Presidency. The governor was commander-in-chief and admiral of the navy; he could convene the legislature on extraordinary occasions; and he could grant reprieves and pardons. His duty was to inform the legislature of the condition of the state, recommend matters for their consideration, and take care that the laws were faithfully executed. He did not escape altogether the restraints commonly imposed upon other governors. His power of appointment was shared with a Council of Appointment of four senators elected by the assembly from each of the four senatorial districts. The governor was president of the council and possessed a casting vote. The governor shared his otherwise strong veto power with a Council of Revision, consisting of the governor, the chancellor, and the judges of the Supreme Court. They, or any three of them, always including the governor, could veto legislative measures inconsistent with the spirit of the constitution or the public good. A two-thirds vote in both houses could override the veto.[5]

But the offices a constitution creates cannot live on the written document alone. They thrive upon skilled and vigorous incumbents. The New York governorship, by rare good fortune, had as its first occupant a skillful and courageous chief executive, George Clinton. Clinton's reign was rich and memorable; Clinton used fully his store of power and became the dominant political figure of his state. Particularly impressive to the federal Founding Fathers was Clinton's ability, as a strong executive, to maintain public order. He put down the savage Doctors' Riots in New York City with the militia and routed out the remnants of Shays's men who fled to New York after springing their rebellion in Massachusetts.[6] The New York governorship's influence was further assured by the circumstance that a Founding Father who was to be most influential in creating the Presidency was a principal draftsman of the New York constitution; Gouverneur Morris engaged in this double enterprise.

The Philadelphia Convention

The Constitution-makers who gathered in Philadelphia in 1787, hailed by Thomas Jefferson as "an assembly of demi-gods," organized themselves by electing George Washington their "president" and Major William Jackson their secretary. Rules of procedure were adopted and precautions taken to keep the proceedings secret. In the weeks of lengthy, intense, and often disheartening deliberations, no single problem was more perplexing in building the new government than the office of President. The President must be endowed with impressive powers yet must not appear to the people as another king and incipient tyrant. He must have sufficient but not dangerous independence. He must be dependent but not, as state governors commonly were, the mere creature of the legislature.

The Convention began its hard grapple with specifics when it resolved itself on May 29 into a Committee of the Whole to consider several competing plans and proposals submitted by state delegations and individual members. Each plan dealt with the whole structure of a federal government, including the question of executive power.

The Virginia plan, which had been prepared chiefly by James Madison before the Convention assembled, called for a "national executive" to be chosen by the "National Legislature." The executive would be eligible only for a single term, and "besides a general authority to execute the National laws, [he] ought to enjoy the Executive rights vested in Congress by the Confederation." The Committee of the Whole at the Convention added certain features to the Virginia plan: The term of the executive would be seven years, he could make appointments "in cases not otherwise provided for," and he would be removable "on impeachment and conviction of malpractice, or neglect of duty." He could "negative" any legislative act unless overriden "by two third parts" of each branch of the legislature. With certain "members" of the judiciary, he could exercise the veto power. The Virginia plan was bold in conception. Instead of simply revising or altering the Articles, it aimed to enlarge them and proposed a national executive, legislature, and judiciary to do what was done, or should have been done, by the Continental Congress.[7]

The New Jersey plan, offered by William Paterson on June 15, was the response of the small states to the power of the large states that would have resulted from the Virginia plan. Whereas the Virginia plan undertook to replace the Articles with a document for a truly national government, the New

Jersey plan merely revised them. It would endow the central government with powers to levy import duties and regulate foreign and domestic trade. The states were to collect taxes, but Congress could act if the states defaulted. The New Jersey plan called for a plural executive chosen by Congress, removable on the application of a majority of the state executives, ineligible for a second term, and empowered to direct all military operations though in no case to take command in the field.[8]

In addition to the rival plans of the large and small states, comprehensive plans of two Convention members dealt with the executive. One plan, by Alexander Hamilton, presented in a five-hour speech on June 18, was the most extreme proposal to be offered at the Convention for a strong executive and central government. Hamilton announced himself as "unfriendly" to both the Virginia and the New Jersey plans, terming the former, the stronger of the two, "pork still, with a little change of the sauce." The severity of the crisis required a central government of highest competence. "The general power whatever be its form if it preserves itself, must swallow up the State powers, otherwise it will be swallowed up by them." For the substance of the new government, Hamilton's probing gaze fell upon the British structure, "the best in the world"; he doubted "whether any thing short of it would do for America." Monarchy and Parliament he unreservedly admired. No good government could exist without a good executive, and no good executive could ever be established "on Republican principles." The hereditary monarch, endowed with great wealth, was above corruption from abroad and was "both sufficiently independent and sufficiently controlled, to answer the purpose of the institution at home."

The Hamilton plan called for a monarch and nobles, a single executive and a Senate for life or good behavior, and an inferior popular house. The states would have no powers except over local affairs. So extreme was the plan that it was supported by no other delegate and was not even discussed. Days later, on June 29, Hamilton left Philadelphia, despairing that the Convention would fail to recommend a strong central government and would "let slip the golden opportunity of rescuing the American empire from disunion, anarchy, and misery. No motley or feeble measure can answer the end or will finally receive the public support." The Virginia plan was "motley" and the New Jersey plan "feeble."[9]

Still another plan was advanced by Charles Pinckney of South Carolina, member of a congressional committee charged with recommending amendments to the Articles. His plan, most of it now lost, seems from its several surviving parts to have attempted to revise the Articles rather than supplant them. In drawing his executive, Pinckney relied heavily upon the New York constitution. The powers and duties of the executive and the contingencies of his death and removal all followed the New York arrangement. His election and term, however, did not. Pinckney's executive would be elected by Congress annually.[10]

Decisions at Philadelphia

The Committee of the Whole debated the several plans with their conflicting conceptions. The issue of Virginia's proposed single executive versus New Jersey's plural executive quickly came to a head when James Wilson of Pennsylvania moved and Charles Pinckney seconded that the executive consist of one person. In the debate the principal argument made against the single executive was that it would constitute a standing invitation to the very kind of monarchy that the Revolution was intended to overcome. Randolph typified this opinion, according to Madison's *Journal*, when he "strongly opposed a unity in the Executive magistracy. He regarded it as the foetus of monarchy. We had, he said, no motive to be governed by the British Government as our prototype." Randolph also objected that a single magistrate could never evoke confidence and that the appointment would generally be in favor of some inhabitant near the "center of the Community," and the "remote parts" consequently "would not be on an equal footing." He preferred an executive department of three persons "drawn from different portions of the Country."[11]

James Wilson answered. Randolph, he contended, was less concerned with merit than with the popularity of the Convention's handiwork. Wilson, for his part, believed that the people well knew that "a single magistrate is not a King." All thirteen states, although agreeing upon almost nothing else in their constitutions, had established a single head as governor or president. "The idea of three heads," which promised neither "vigor" nor "tranquillity," "has taken place in none." Other Fathers viewed the single executive not as an "absolute" monarch like the propagandized image of George III but as a kind of "limited" monarch, the most desirable of all executives. "A firm Executive," as John Dickinson of Delaware put it, "could only exist in a limited monarchy."[12] While the Convention analyzed the monarchy, stories circulated in the world outside that the Fathers, in their love for that brand of executive, were bent upon importing a Hanoverian bishop to be king of the United States. Fortunately, the stories quickly subsided.[13]

A lengthy struggle centered upon two further questions, viewed as inseparable: the source of the executive's election and the length of his term. Three major types of election were advanced. James Wilson and Gouverneur Morris, friends of a strong executive, urged election, as Morris put it, "by the people at large, by the freeholders of the Country." When practical administrative difficulties were cited, Morris retorted that these had been overcome in New York and could be likewise in other states. The people, the doubters said, would be uninformed and misled by designing men. Morris preferred to be optimistic: "If the people should elect, they will never fail to prefer some man of distinguished character, or services; some man, if he might so speak, of continental reputation."[14] A second method was election by the legislature. That body's handling of the task, Morris contended, would be the work "of intrigue, of cabal, of faction." The final method, and the one ultimately adopted, was choice by electors. Advocates of an electoral system felt that it would best give effect to the dominant popular choice whose direct expression was barred for practical reasons. Many Fathers feared that citizens would blindly favor local candidates and would be ignorant of able men in other states.

Linked with method of choice were the questions of length of term and reeligibility. Elbridge Gerry of Massachusetts argued that the longer the term the less would the executive depend upon the legislature that chose him. Oliver Ellsworth of Connecticut likewise proposed a long term of six years. If elections were too frequent, the executive would not "be firm enough." (He said, "There must be duties which will make him unpopular for the moment.") Without a long term (seven years), Hugh Williamson of North Carolina argued, "The best men will not undertake the service and those of an inferior character will be liable to be corrupted."[15]

Proposals of six- or seven-year terms were predicated upon the assumption that the legislature would choose the President. A long term plus ineligibility for reelection, a common feature of such proposals, appeared the best means to safeguard executive independence of the legislature. Reeligibility would prompt the executive to court the legislature to win another term. The alternative of a shorter term and reeligibility came to the fore when selection by electors was ultimately settled upon.

The Fathers considered long and anxiously the question of annexing a council to the chief executive. A council would diminish the monarchical tendency and the danger of tyranny. Collective advice was deemed safer and more competent than the assorted individual advice that might befall the President. Various kinds of councils were proposed. The Pinckney plan vested in the executive "a Right to advise with the Heads of the different Departments as his Council." Ellsworth, rather fearful of personal government, would add to the council the President of the Senate and the Chief Justice. George Mason preferred a council representative of the chief sections of the country, the East, the Middle States, and the South. James Madison, a strong exponent of the council, proposed that it possess initiative to advise the President and to record its sentiments. But the floor discussion proved inconclusive, and ultimately the council idea was dropped.[16] The prospect that the venerated Washington would serve as first President drained much of the interest from the council proposal. Indeed many Fathers feared that a council of some power might harass the position of future President Washington.

In its final draft the Constitution not only failed to provide a council, it did not even call for the "cabinet" that appeared early in Washington's Presidency. The Constitution merely specified that the Chief Executive could require the "opinions of the heads of his departments in writing." Hamilton, for one, considered even this provision redundant as the right "would result of itself from the office." Other critics were haunted to the very end by monarchical fears. George Mason, crying doom, warned that a Presidency without a council was an "experiment" that even "the most despotic governments" had never undertaken. Benjamin Franklin, ordinarily optimistic, beheld a melancholy prospect, seeing only "caprice, the intrigues of favorites and mistresses, etc." in the absence of a council.[17]

The Fathers debated a score of issues in establishing the substantive powers of the executive. These were resolved with a tendency toward generosity to the executive, sparked by the prospect that Washington would become President. The veto power, remembered as an arbitrary instrument of the royal governors, was critically scrutinized. The Declaration of Independence's first indictment of George III was his refusal to "Assent to Laws, the most wholesome and necessary for the public good." But excesses by the state legislatures since Revolutionary days made the Fathers receptive to a strong veto power. The Virginia plan's coupling of the judiciary with the executive in the veto was dropped. The variant proposals for a Council of Revision met a like fate, and the President emerged as the solitary executive possessor of the veto power.

The appointing power was one of the knottier issues. James Wilson, constant friend of a strong Presidency, opposed the eventual arrangement, a power shared between the President and the Senate. "There can be no good Executive," he argued, "without a responsible appointment of officers to execute." Responsibility was impaired by involving the Senate. Wilson's view was respected to a degree when the President was given an exclusive appointing power "in all cases not otherwise provided for."[18]

Treaty and war powers and the President's pay, removal, and disability also evoked considerable discussion. "What is the extent of the term 'disability' and who is to be the judge of it?" Dickinson asked, questions that remained unanswered almost to this day. Debate waxed over the respective powers of Congress and the executive to "declare" and to "make" war.[19] One motion on the subject shocked Gerry, who "never expected" to hear in a republic a proposal to empower the executive alone to declare war. Madison contended that the war power could not be safely entrusted to the President or the Senate. He was for "clogging" rather than "facilitating" war.[20]

Drafting the Presidential Article

The work of the Committee of the Whole was supplemented by two drafting committees, the Committee of Detail and the Committee of Style. After discussion of some weeks the Convention established the Committee of Detail—the members being Edward Rutledge (South Carolina), Randolph (Virginia), Nathaniel Gorham (Massachusetts), Ellsworth (Connecticut), and Wilson (Pennsylvania)—to reduce the delegates' ponderings to a systematic Constitution draft. The work of the Committee of Detail, a long stride toward the strong Presidency, was aided by Convention-adopted resolutions providing for a single executive empowered to execute national laws, to veto national legislation, and to appoint to offices in cases not otherwise provided for. The executive was also made subject to impeachment. The Committee of Detail adapted these resolutions to its draft and, with an eye on the New York constitution, further elaborated the President's powers. The committee made it the President's duty to give information to the legislature, to recommend measures, to convene Congress into extraordinary session, and, in disagreement between the two houses on the subject, to adjourn them. The President would also receive ambassadors, grant pardons and reprieves, and act as Commander-in-Chief.[21]

The Convention debated intensively for five weeks, section by section, the draft of the Committee of Detail. On September 8 a Committee of Style headed by Gouverneur Morris was appointed to "revise the style of and arrange the articles which had been agreed to by the house." This committee too was innovative. It installed the plan for choosing the President through electors and empowered him to make treaties, provided two-thirds of the Senators present concurred, and to nominate and, with the advice and consent of the Senate, appoint ambassadors, other public ministers and consuls, and justices of the Supreme Court. The President's term was put at four years with indefinite reeligibility. The Presidential Article II began with a sentence, attributed to Morris, of vast future significance: "The executive Power shall be vested in a President of the United States of America."

On September 13 the Committee of Style presented a draft of the Constitution to the Convention in the handwriting of Gouverneur Morris. Two days later the Constitution was adopted, and in another two days the Convention adjourned. The Presidency, as it finally emerged, admirably fulfilled the ideal of a strong but responsible Chief Executive. The President would be a single, not a plural, executive, with no council but presumably heads of departments, although these were not specifically provided for. His election and identity were distinct and separate from Congress. His term of four years was longer than the state governors', and he was reeligible for an indefinite number of terms. His powers were generous and both specific and general. The opening language of Article II, "The executive Power shall be vested in a President," was clearly broader than the investiture of Article I, "All legislative Powers herein granted shall be vested in a Congress," or Article III, "The judicial Power shall extend to all cases, in Law and Equity, arising under this Constitution, the Laws of the United States, and Treaties."[22]

Makers of the Presidency

In any listing of Founding Fathers who played a heroic part in creating a strong Chief Executive, the name of James Wilson of Pennsylvania would take an honored place. Forty-five years of age, Wilson was a Scotsman by birth and education, tall, large-featured, and afflicted with nearsightedness, which with his glasses added a touch of sternness to his appearance. Endowed with a tough, perceptive mind, Wilson contributed more than anyone else to the concept of the Presidency: He laid it persuasively before the Convention and was an instrumental member of the Committee of Detail that worked out the final revision. Wilson's success, although impressive, was not total. His chief defeat was the rejection of his proposal that the executive be chosen by the people.

Gouverneur Morris, chairman of the committee that wrote the final draft of the Constitution, is another hero. Draftsman of the New York constitution, member of the Continental Congress, and hardy *bon vivant*, he illuminated the Convention's deliberations with insights from the instructive New York experience. Eloquent, caustic, dynamic, and aggressive, Morris steadily championed the strong executive. James Madison spoke afterward of the "brilliancy of his genius." Madison too stands among the heroes. He began conservatively on the question of executive power but gradually came around to Wilson's views.

The indispensable presence at the Convention was the presiding officer, the nation's future first Chief Executive, George Washington. Elected unanimously to his Convention post, his tall, heavy, ruddy presence, grave mien, his very embodiment of the young country's agony and triumph, marked him as the most conspicuous and the most influential delegate. Although he spoke but once, his commitment to strong central government was well known. "My wish is," he wrote to Madison, prior to Philadelphia, "that the convention may adopt no temporizing expedients, but probe the defects of the constitution to the bottom, and provide a radical cure, whether they are agreed to or not."[23] The prevailing assumption, candidly articulated in the Convention, was that he would become the first President. Pierce Butler of South Carolina expressed Washington's significance in the creation of the Presidency when he wrote, "Entre nous, I do [not] believe they [the executive powers] would have been so great had not many members cast their eyes toward General Washington as President; and shaped their Ideas of the Powers to be given the President, by their opinions of his Virtue."[24]

Structural Concepts

The making of the Presidency adhered to two overarching structural concepts: the separation of powers and checks and balances. Mutually contradictory, one posed division and independence, the other interaction and dependence.

The separation of powers was a basic principle in the works of several major political writers well known to the Fathers. Although the writers differed in the ways these powers should be separated, they shared a common view of the nature and purpose of separated powers. John Locke's *Two Treatises of Government*, probably the most powerful philosophic influence at the Convention, Montesquieu's *Esprit des lois*, and William Blackstone's *Commentaries on the Laws of England* all viewed the concentration of power as an invitation to tyranny. Liberty was best preserved if power were distributed between several branches. Locke, for instance, divided governmental power between the legislative or lawmaking power, the executive or law-enforcing power, and the "federative" power of war and peace, leagues and alliances, and other foreign relations. Locke did not specify the judicial power but presumably intended to safeguard its independence by the Act of Settlement.

Although the Founding Fathers repeatedly and reverently invoked separation of powers, the doctrine fared unevenly at their hands. As Charles C. Thach has rightly observed, few governments exceed the functional overlapping of that created by the American Constitution.[25] Lawmaking is shared between the two-house Congress and the President, treaty-making and appointments between the President and the Senate, and so on. The Fathers did meticulously observe the doctrine in the sense of arranging a personal separation of powers in contrast to functional separation. The memberships of the three branches executive, legislative, and judicial were separated. An officer of one could not serve in another, except for the Vice President, who had minor duties in the Senate but a general identity with the executive.

Checks and balances, the second overarching doctrine, was also well articulated by influential writers. The theory of balanced government reached back to the Greeks and enjoyed vogue in the eighteenth century among English and continental writers. Montesquieu and Blackstone interpreted the English constitution as a complex of checks: the Lords against the Commons and both against the crown. Government was viewed not as a cooperative enterprise between its several parts but as an enduring conflict of opposite interests.

The leading American exponent of balanced government was John Adams, whose *Defence of the Constitutions of the United States of America Against the Attack of Mr. Turgot* was well known to the Founding Fathers. For liberty to be preserved and property safeguarded, Adams argued, government must be poised in an equilibrium. Governments, like the populations they govern, divide into three distinct entities: the one, the few, and the many; or the leader, the aristocracy of birth or property, and the mass of people. Each part is capable of abuse—of jealousy, encroachment, and folly. The wellspring of disequilibrium, in the words of Thucydides, is "thirst of power, from rapacious and ambitious passions." The art of constitution-making, as Adams perceived it, was the establishment of "a multitude of curious and ingenious inventions to balance in their turn, all those powers [legislative, executive, and judicial], to check the passions peculiar to them, and to control them from rushing into the exorbitancies to which they are most addicted." The stability and purposes of a government, in a word, were best achieved by a delicate balance between more or less equal powers vital-ized by mutual jealousies.

The Founding Fathers were much preoccupied with the problem of balance. "It is [the] most difficult of all rightly to balance the Executive," Gouverneur Morris observed: "Make him too weak: the Legislature will usurp his power. Make him too strong: he will usurp on the Legislature." The leading analyst of balanced power was Madison, whose views are most fully stated in the *Federalist* paper Number 51. "The great security against a gradual concentration of the several powers in the same department," he wrote, "consists in giving to those who administer each department the nec-essary constitutional means and personal motives to resist encroachments of the others. Ambition must be made to counteract ambition."

The Presidency Begins

The final phase of the creation of the Presidency was Washington's nearly impeccable workmanship as the office's first incumbent. His strong and good hands imparted to the Presidency a form and substance that have forever remained with it. In confronting his duties, Washington knew well that what he did possessed both present and future significance, that his every act was a potential precedent, and that the body of his conduct was creating an entire executive system. He wrote,

> Many things appear of little importance in themselves and at the begin-ning may have great and durable consequences from their having been established at the commencement of a new general government. It will be much easier to commence the administration, upon a well adjusted system, built on tenable grounds, than to correct errors or alter incon-veniences after they shall have been confirmed by habit.[26]

Washington did not take up his task gladly. In the weeks before his election he allowed himself to hope that he might not be elected and that, if he were, he might somehow contrive to decline. His longings were deep-ened by seizures of pessimism about the future. "May Heaven assist me in forming a judgment," he wrote to Jonathan Trumbell, "for at present I see nothing but clouds and darkness before me."[27] But the electors, whom the Constitution left free to exercise their own choice in voting for the President, were carefully selected for their probable support of Washington. The electors in casting their ballots unanimously lived up to their promise.*

The Vice-Presidency was contested. Washington interested himself in the struggle in an interval when he hoped that if he had to accept the Presidency, he might resign once the new governmental machinery had swung into operation. The Vice-Presidency stirred a quick, intense party struggle. The Anti-Federalists, who accepted Washington as President, put forward one of their own, George Clinton, for Vice President. Although Washington enjoyed sturdy wartime ties with Clinton, the future President was troubled by the governor's hostility to the new federal Constitution. Clinton had promoted the well-known "New York circular," urging the Constitution's severe amendment, or "suicide" as Madison termed it. To avoid the danger of Clinton, Washington quietly and privately supported the Federalist candidacy of John Adams. Alexander Hamilton, the general's arranger and emissary, worked closely with Benjamin Lincoln, an Adams leader, and Henry Knox, a major political figure in Massachusetts. The emissaries did their work well. Washington was soon pleased to hear that "the votes have run in favor of Mr. Adams."[28]

On April 16, 1789, Washington set out for New York, the national capital, with heavy heart. "I bade adieu to Mount Vernon, to private life, and to domestic felicity," he wrote in his diary, "and with a mind oppressed with more anxious and painful sensations than I have words to express." He added that he left "with the best disposition to render service to my country in obedience to its call, but with less hope of answering its expectations."[29] Washington's distress was soon overwhelmed by the acclaim showered upon him on his journey northward.

On Inauguration Day, April 30, 1789, the joint inaugural committee of Congress arrived at the President-elect's temporary residence to escort him to Federal Hall in New York. Shortly after midday the general started out in a grand coach drawn by four horses, preceded by troops and the Senators of the joint committee and followed by his secretaries, the Representatives of the committee, Chancellor Robert Livingston, who would administer the oath, the heads of the federal departments, and a handful of eminent citizens. When the procession reached Federal Hall, Washington passed with simple dignity into the building and mounted the stairs to the Senate chamber, where members of the two houses of Congress, foreign diplomats, and other dignitaries had assembled. The general passed through an arched central door leading onto a small, half-enclosed portico overlooking Wall and Broad Streets. Cheers rolled up from the vast multitude below. Samuel Otis, Secretary of the Senate, lifted the Bible reposing on a red cushion on a small table. Washington placed his hand on the Bible, Livingston pronounced the oath, and Washington repeated it and kissed the Book. "It is done," Livingston

* The nature of the electoral college is discussed in Chapter 3.

declared, and, turning to the crowd, made a broad sweep with his hand and shouted, "Long live George Washington, President of the United States." The crowd roared back Livingston's words and "God bless our President"; church bells rang, the flag was run up in the cupola of Federal Hall, and guns were fired from the Battery and a Spanish sloop of war in the harbor. The Presidency was now in being.[30]

Presidential Strength: George Washington

In two terms of office Washington launched the Presidency on a high note of success. Weathering times that were full of crisis, he left the republic stronger, more purposeful, and more confident than when he had begun his task. A string of measures, highly impressive by twentieth-century standards in their number and scope, steadily emerged from the Washington administration: a national currency was issued and the Bank of the United States was established to provide credit; manufacture and trade were fostered by tariffs and bounties; inventions were protected by patent and copyright laws; neutrality was preserved in the face of an enlarging European war; and the national security was enhanced by reorganization of the army and navy, the founding of West Point, and the building of fortifications in the East and West.

Washington exercised the powers of his office in a fashion that permitted vigorous and innovative administration, but he respected the necessities of legitimacy and responsibility. Midway in his term Washington wrote,

> The powers of the Executive of the United States are more definite, and better understood perhaps than those of almost any other Country; and my aim has been and will continue to be, neither to stretch nor relax from them in any instance whatever, unless imperious circumstances should render the measure indispensable.[31]

In "gray" areas, where the Constitution did not state whether Congress or the President was to act, Washington asserted executive authority. The establishment of the nation's neutrality in the Franco-British war, a cardinal foreign policy, was a Presidential rather than a legislative act. (Later in the nation's history the roles altered, and neutrality policy was one of the areas that became the province of Congress.)

Where authority was clearly his, Washington maintained his mastery. He truly dominated the executive branch. He was not long in office when he requested the heads of departments to provide "a full, precise and general *idea*" of the work entrusted to them.[32] With few exceptions he prescribed the duties of his department heads and kept abreast of daily detail. He read incoming and outgoing communications of the executive branch and passed upon important plans and actions that the departments submitted in writing.

All loan and debt transactions were subject to his approval. Each use of the seal of the United States required his consent. No lighthouse keeper, customs collector, or captain of a cutter could be appointed without his consideration. So confident was he of his mastery that he brought into the leading posts of his administration two of the most gifted department heads the nation has ever known, Thomas Jefferson as Secretary of State and Alexander Hamilton as Secretary of the Treasury.

Washington triumphed in an area where many of his successors have floundered: relationships with Congress. Washington converted his popularity into major laws without tarnishing his prestige in the inevitable struggle. In his deportment toward Congress he was the essence of constitutional propriety. He stayed officially aloof from most major struggles, leaving the heat and dust of battle to his subordinates, chiefly Hamilton.

Washington was careful to respect Congress. Following his Annual or State of the Union Address, the Senate and House prepared addresses in response. The great throng of lawmakers of both chambers, led by the Speaker and the bearer of the mace, symbol of Congressional authority, gathered before the President. The Vice President and the Speaker spoke for their respective houses. The President, for his part, was also attentive to Congress with social and ceremonial gesture. Shortly before the inauguration, he visited the members of Congress, and his manner was agreeable. "He made us complaisant bows," Senator William Maclay of Pennsylvania noted, "one as he mounted and the other as he went away on horseback."[33] He regularly tendered dinners with a dozen and more guests from the Senate, the House, and his own administration.

The close work of researching and drafting legislative proposals and the chores of advocating them, rallying votes, and working out compromises were left to his lieutenant, Alexander Hamilton, Secretary of the Treasury and field leader of the Federalist party. Hamilton drafted the Great Reports, presenting with detail and justification the major legislation of the administration: public credit, the Bank, manufactures, and the like. Washington engaged in no public advocacy of these measures. He seems, however, to have been a behind-the-scenes influence when Jefferson and Hamilton arranged their famous compromise, the location of the future capital in Washington in exchange for federal assumption of state debts. The observant Senator Maclay confided to his diary, "The President of the United States has (in my opinion) had a great influence in this business. The game was played by him and his adherents . . . his name goes to wipe away blame and silence all murmuring."[34]

Washington was a resolute defender of the integrity of Presidential power against all trespass, even when Congress was the offender. A most momentous challenge was the call by the Republican-controlled House of Representatives for the instructions and pertinent papers of John Jay's mission to negotiate the treaty bearing his name. The House's bold intrusion into an enterprise allotted by the Constitution to the President and Senate gripped the capital with tension. "Anxiety is on the tiptoe . . . our galleries have been crowded," Representative Francis Preston of Virginia noted. Washington's response was strong and forthright. Foreign relations by their very nature, the President wrote, required secrecy; disclosure of the requested papers would be "impolitic" and "a dangerous precedent." The fundamental law did not require the House's assent to a treaty. "A just regard to the Constitution and to the duty of my Office . . . forbids a compliance with your request." The House opposition thundered and maneuvered, but all in vain. "What firmness does this great man display!" Senator William Plumer rejoiced.[35]

Washington was no slave to literal constitutional prescription but a resourceful innovator. The Constitution said little of how the President might secure advice in the daily business of decision- and policy-making. Washington exploited the freedom this silence permitted and instituted practices that Presidents since his time have followed. He founded the cabinet. In the autumn of 1791 he began bringing his department Secretaries—Jefferson, Hamilton, his Secretary of War Henry Knox, and his Attorney General Edmund Randolph—together for a joint consideration of policy. The cabinet meeting with a timesaver over individual consultation with the Secretaries and permitted the testing of the opinions of his counselors in the presence of their peers. Washington believed that advice should be competitive, that one man's views should be checked against other sources. Repeatedly he ranged beyond the cabinet for counsel, to Congressman James Madison, for example, and Chief Justice John Jay, from whom he invited "ideas . . . not confined to matters judicial, but extended to all other topics which have occurred, or may occur to you, as fit subjects for general or private communications."[36] Washington also believed that advice should be broadly representative. He recruited his cabinet from the three principal sections of the country, the North, the South, and the Middle States. A close student of grass-roots opinion, he maintained correspondents in all the sections and instituted the grand tour, traveling the length and breadth of the republic to gather impressions first-hand.

Washington prized and jealously maintained the intrinsic dignity of the Presidential office. He wanted, he said, to make the Presidency "respectable." His natural taste for regal display was freely indulged. He ventured forth in a handsome coach drawn by six cream-colored horses or on a white steed mounted with leopard-skin housing and saddlecloth with gold binding. The Presidential household operated on a large scale, with fourteen white servants, seven slaves, and frequent elaborate dinners done with a high formality conveyed by the presence of powdered lackeys in the entrance hall. The President conducted two levees a week and made no visits. His birthday continued to be, as it had been since the Revolution, the occasion of celebrations in the larger towns. Inevitably these practices provoked criticism. "Even Cincinnatus received no adulations of this kind," the National Gazette observed, "Surely the office [the President] enjoys is a sufficient testimony of the people's favor, without worshipping him likewise."[37]

Throughout this period the Presidency was sustained by the unfailing magnificence of Washington's character. Judgment, vision, skill in managing men, integrity, infinite patience, self-discipline—all were his marks. He "always walked," his biographer Douglas Southall Freeman observed, "on a straight line." "Let honor and probity be your polar star," the President counseled his nephew Bushrod Washington.[38] The President valued "the candid and cautious line of conduct" and abided by the principle that "without virtue and without integrity, the finest talents or the most brilliant accomplishments can never gain the respect or conciliate the esteem of the truly valuable part of mankind."[39] In 1794 Washington perhaps was too cautious, however. He gave Hamilton precious little backing when the Anti-Federalists, who had wrested control of the House of Representatives, drove the Secretary of the Treasury, by a process of studied harassment, from the administration. Yet Washington's virtues were steadily seen by his contemporaries. "His integrity was most pure," Thomas Jefferson observed, "his justice the most inflexible I have ever known. . . . He was indeed, in every sense of the words, a wise, a good and a great man. . . ."[40]

Presidential Weakness: John Adams

But the Presidency was not all strength, achievement, and glory; it also harbored weakness. Ironically, it was the leading American theoretician of checks and balances, the second President of the United States, who provided the earliest illustration of the weakness his ideas had helped create. John Adams was not long in the Presidency when he demonstrated where the provision for the strong executive left off. He proved by his own experience the far depths of trouble in which the President can wallow as party chief, as legislative leader, and as general manager of the executive branch. For the first of these the Founding Fathers had made no provision; for the others, very little. The Presidency was in several large particulars an unfinished office.

Adams the President was only the nominal leader of his Federalist party; its real leader was an outsider who held no public office at the time, the talented, driving, ubiquitous Alexander Hamilton. The contrast was exaggerated by a growing break between the two men. Thomas Jefferson, leader of the Anti-Federalists, noted that the Congressional Federalists were only "a little less hostile" to the President than to himself. The Jefferson men and disaffected legislative Federalists were unstinting in demonstrating the President's weakness as legislative leader. When relations with France crumbled and war threatened, Adams, anxious to maintain peace, recommended to Congress a defensive policy based upon expanded naval power. Hamilton, the covert influence, reputedly eager to drive the French out of North America, instructed his Congressional followers to vote appropriations for an expanded army, which they did. Congress, in another defiance of Presidential leadership, passed in succession the Alien and Sedition Acts, which empowered the President to deport undesirable aliens and made it a crime to criticize the federal government or its officials. Adams neither requested nor wanted either law.

But Adams drank his bitterest draft as chief administrator of the civil and military affairs of the executive branch. Yielding to Congress's enthusiasm for an army in an act designed to win the popular acclaim he so badly lacked, he drew George Washington out of retirement to command the provisional forces. This seemingly splendid triumph was suddenly jeopardized when Washington requested the appointment as his generals of the following in order of rank: Hamilton, Pinckney, and Knox. Adams disputed the order, holding that Knox rightfully should come first, followed by Pinckney and then Hamilton. Ironically, Washington, creator of the strong Presidency, now became the agent of its degradation. In a forceful letter to Adams he insisted upon his listing; otherwise, he strongly implied, he would resign. The President, in all his political feebleness, could hardly afford the storm of Washington's resignation. The Commander-in-Chief yielded to his commanding general. Adams staggered on through a full agenda of woe. When upon his own initiative he nominated W. Vans Murray to be minister to the French Republic, his cabinet displayed unconcealed resentment at his failure to consult it. Other times the cabinet concentrated upon its major preoccupation of leaking secrets to Hamilton to assist his campaign against the President. Adams, the man of large talents and rich public experience, ultimately crowned his failure and abandoned his misery by sustaining defeat for re-election.

The Founding Fathers, the Washington-Adams experience reveals, had created a Presidency of both strength and weakness. The first two Presidencies were the beginning of a continuing dilemma in American history between the people's fear of executive power and their confidence in its necessity and capacity for good.

Selection 3

The American Presidency can be no better or stronger than the caliber of its incumbents. Being a highly personal office, it is foredoomed to an interlude of mediocrity if the Chief Executive who fills it can boast no more than middling talents. Being an intensely political office, it faces deadlock and futility, unless the processes of selecting its holders can screen out men lacking in the high order of political talent required to function successfully in a governmental system where power is much divided. In the modern era, the incumbent needs to be both a man of action and a man of thought, one who "can get things done" and one who is alert to new ideas, one who is adept at the practical politics of getting bills through Congress and one who can engage in dialogue with the universities and other incubators of thought, all to the end of producing policies of depth and sophistication, fit for times of revolutionary change.

The processes of selection that will somehow produce this human paragon must make the widest possible search. If Presidential hopefuls are heavily concentrated in the wealthy classes or dependent upon them for support, the recruiting base is obviously and practically too narrow, and it violates the democratic ideal of a widely available citizenry for office-holding. It is all too evident that the fast-rising costs of modern campaigning serves more and more to limit candidacy to those possessing wealth or with access to it. The processes of selection are patently awry if their cumulative burdens would crumple an athlete or wilt a truck horse. There is a useful warning in Robert Kennedy's observation, made several months after his brother's inauguration, that John Kennedy's quest for the Presidency was more arduous than the office itself.

The selection process can be judged by still other standards. To contribute to the strength of the Presidency, it must pass certain objective tests of mechanical performance. The election results must have legitimacy; they must produce a winner whose victory is undoubted by the standards of established law. To invite or permit an unfair or obscure result, to tolerate delay in the ultimate decision, is to court the very worst trouble.

There can be no strong President if the selection process fails to produce or reflect a social and political consensus that will sustain a constructive program for major public problems. Thus, the function of the selection process is not only to choose the incumbent but to build political union among disparate interests and sections.

It is not altogether clear when the selection of a President actually begins. In a sense he selects himself; in a sense the party selects him; in a sense—and here the final decision lies—the people do the selecting themselves. To win the Presidency, the aspirant must travel a long, hard, treacherous road abounding in bumps and quicksand and divisible into three distinct segments: the preconvention buildup, the national nominating convention, and the postconventional electoral campaign.

The Preconvention Struggle

The preconvention phase is the longest, often the severest, part of the journey, and it may engage the candidate in fiercer struggles with his rival contenders for the nomination than his later race with the opposing nominee. In this phase the candidate surrounds himself with an entourage of helpers of assorted skills. The entourage has expanded from less than a handful in the nineteenth century to well-nigh a score for the serious modern candidate. Several standard types of helpers are distinguishable. There are the early sponsors and supporters, the launchers of the candidacy. The founding fathers of the Woodrow Wilson-for-President movement were two editors, George Harvey of *Harper's Weekly* and Henry Watterson of the Louisville *Courier Journal*, who began work two years before the 1912 convention. Three years before the 1896 convention William McKinley's indefatigable sponsor, Mark Hanna, wisely rented a house in Thomasville, Georgia, imported the William McKinleys for a three-week visit, and invited prominent Southern Republicans to meet the rising Ohio governor. The Southerners enjoyed the social approach, at which McKinley shone, and Hanna took a long first step toward lining up the Southern delegations. Some early supporters, such as Hanna, become the managers of the long campaign. The managers are political craftsmen who supply broad leadership to the entire enterprise. If they are victorious, they are hailed as "kingmakers."

In modern day, John Kennedy's preconvention staff demonstrates the lengths to which specialization is resorted to in staging the candidate's effort. His brother Robert was general manager of operations, Lawrence F. O'Brien, placid, stocky, and hard-working, commanded the organizational base, a great phalanx of young men who had done their political teething in the Senator's home state of Massachusetts. Kenneth O'Donnell, a taciturn former Harvard football captain and veteran of Kennedy's Massachusetts wars, was Kennedy's link with the organization and transmitted Kennedy's reflections and directives to O'Brien. Theodore C. Sorensen was the candidate's "idea man" and star draftsman—"my intellectual blood bank,"[1] Kennedy called him. Stephen Smith, the candidate's brother-in-law, discreet and business-trained, opened the Washington headquarters for the Kennedy staff and eventually became the general manager in charge of mobilizing scores of thousands of volunteers and employees. Pierre Salinger, a former California newspaperman, Congressional investigator, and a big-cigar man, presided with joviality and shrewdness over press relations. Louis Harris, public opinion analyst and market research entrepreneur, was the candidate's personal polltaker. His findings were the basis of key campaign decisions. John Bailey, Connecticut Democratic chairman, coordinated the Northeastern bosses.

On the preconvention landscape are several other standard political types. Not the least important, of course, are the several species of opposing candidates: the serious contenders, the dark horses, and the favorite sons. In 1968, at the outset, these several species resulted in a full field of possible Republican nominees: Richard Nixon of New York and California, Nelson Rockefeller of New York, Ronald Reagan of California, George Romney of Michigan, and Charles Percy of Illinois.

The landscape is also dotted with prestigious political figures who are not candidates but whose support is cherished and whose favor is courted: governors above all, Senators, Congressmen, party patriarchs, and labor, business, nationality, and racial leaders who hover at the party's fringes. Beyond Washington and into the American hinterland stretches the intricate continental tangle of party machinery, manned by a varied body of functionaries, known collectively as "organization politicians," the state and local party officialdom. Many a Presidential aspirant has run aground from want of support from the organization politicians. A formidable obstacle to Wilson's 1912 candidacy was his cold rejection by the generality of organization politicians. "They have an impression of you," Wilson's manager, William F. McCombs, wrote with frankness, "in a large degree that you are austere and dictatorial and that you will not have a due appreciation of what is to be done for you. . . . Another thing I hear much of, particularly throughout the East, is that you are unreliable."[2]

Not the least importance of the organization politicians is their large hand in selecting the delegates, the official decision-makers, of the future convention. Most candidates run with the delegates of their home states pledged to them. Franklin Roosevelt was denied this common privilege in 1932 when Tammany Hall and its upstate allies decided upon an uninstructed delegation. When the Presidential nomination is being seriously contested, the specific commitments of state delegations may be in great disarray.

Preconvention Strategies

The preconvention campaign is a time of hard choices between alternative strategies. Franklin Roosevelt and his managers at the outset of his preconvention candidacy perceived a choice between two major and opposite courses. They could sit back and conduct a passive campaign, limited to building friendly contacts and issuing press statements extolling Roosevelt's virtues. The risk of antagonizing the rather numerous favorite son candidates would be avoided, at least until the campaign began in earnest. Or the pressure could be turned on immediately, Roosevelt's candidacy announced, and the job begun of rounding up delegates to clinch the nomination. History provided not a few grisly illustrations of the outstanding candidate who declared early and subsequently was trampled into the dust by opponents who ganged up on him. William G. McAdoo's disastrous experience in 1924 is a monumental reminder of the hazard. Democratic candidates in Roosevelt's day, because of the party's convention rule requiring a two-thirds vote to nominate, were highly susceptible to the deadly danger. Another risk was that a candidacy begun too early might wither and die from public apathy. This species of political blight is known in the trade as the "morning-glory" candidacy. Roosevelt ultimately decided to run early and to run fast, notwithstanding the risks. Candidates as a rule back away from the Roosevelt pattern by carefully avoiding any announcement of their candidacy for as long as possible, all the while, however, pursuing the grail with might and main.

Tours, visits, and speeches—the chief preconvention activities—involve basic strategic and tactical choices. Woodrow Wilson was so impressed by the potentialities of the tour that in his first eight months of serious preconvention campaigning he made a nine thousand-mile transcontinental journey and campaigned besides in New York, Pennsylvania, Virginia, North Carolina, South Carolina, Georgia, Texas, and Wisconsin. Tours not merely display the candidate to the populace but enable him to visit, and hopefully to impress, key local leaders and personalities. Wilson, in one rewarding sojourn in Atlanta, Georgia, met the leading progressive Democrats of the state, converted the editors of the Savannah *Evening Press*, the Atlanta *Journal*, and the Atlanta *Georgian* to his cause, and conferred at length with Governor Hoke Smith, who became the first important political figure to support Wilson's candidacy openly.

Tours and speeches lead the candidate onto some of the most treacherous terrain of his preconvention effort—taking a stand on issues. Worst of all is the unavoidable issue on which any position the candidate takes will alienate support he needs. Franklin Roosevelt in 1932 was bedeviled by a momentous question he could not avoid—his attitude toward United States membership in the League of Nations. Almost anything he said on this burning subject would offend supporters on whom his success at the convention depended. His foes, of course, trumpeted the League issue constantly. William Randolph Hearst in his transcontinental newspaper chain attacked the candidate unmercifully as an "internationalist," quoting abundantly in front-page editorials Roosevelt's pro-League statements in his Vice-Presidential campaign of 1920.

Roosevelt at first hoped to fend off Hearst by maintaining silence but to no avail. The attacks continued; a statement was necessary. In a carefully devised release Roosevelt acknowledged that in 1920 he had worked for American participation in the League. He said,

> But the League of Nations today is not the League conceived by Woodrow Wilson. . . . Too often through these years its major function has been not the broad overwhelming purpose of world peace, but rather a mere meeting place for the political discussion of strictly European political national difficulties. . . . Because of these facts, therefore, I do not favor American participation.[3]

Fortunately for Roosevelt, the statement accomplished its immediate purpose. Hearst ceased his attacks. But there were costs, which presumably the candidate and his managers had anticipated and weighed. The statement stretched to the uttermost the loyalty of the Wilsonians, a compact and powerful band of associates of the last Democratic President. Colonel Edward N. House, Wilson's former confidant, wrote to Farley that Roosevelt's position "created something akin to panic among the devoted Wilson followers." Intellectuals of the school of Walter Lippmann were sorely distressed. Roosevelt swabbed the disgruntled with a remedy that his secretary Louis Howe called "soothing syrup." One body of opinion Roosevelt could not allay was the cynics, a not uncommon breed among political professionals. Senator William E. Borah, eying Roosevelt's statement, muttered sarcastically, "Repent ye, for the kingdom of heaven is at hand."[4]

The candidate in the preconvention period is confronted with the possibility, and sometimes the necessity, of "deals" on issues and offices. The deals presumably will strengthen his chances for the nomination if, on balance, they gain more support than they lose. In the fall of 1895, with the future convention well in sight, Mark Hanna sat down with two great political dictators of the day, Senator Matt Quay of Pennsylvania and former

Senator Tom ("Boss") Platt of New York. Both ruled their respective state machines absolutely and were grand masters of the arts of venality. Hanna met with the dark, cynical Quay and the scrawny, secretive Platt to bargain for the huge electoral votes of their respective states. With these William McKinley's nomination would be assured. The bosses' terms came high. Probably more than one cabinet seat was involved, and Platt wanted the Secretaryship of the Treasury for himself, in writing, please. Hanna rushed back to Ohio to report the terms of incipient victory to the candidate. He fortified McKinley first with a choice cigar. As Hanna spoke, McKinley listened in silence, pulled on his cigar, got up, and paced the floor. "There are some things in this world that come too high," he said at last. "If I cannot be President without promising to make Tom Platt Secretary of the Treasury, I will never be President." McKinley thus took a long stride toward sainthood.[5]

PRIMARIES.   The candidate makes a major strategic decision in choosing among the several Presidential primaries in which to make his race. Kennedy, in his 1960 strategy, battled a leading rival, Senator Hubert Humphrey, in the Wisconsin and West Virginia primaries and in the latter succeeded in putting the Senator out of the race. In 1968 fifteen primaries were held, which chose less than half of the convention delegates. The selection of delegations to national conventions began in Wisconsin in 1903, an innovation of "Battling Bob" La Follette, who hoped to chase away the bosses and return politics to the people. Although the Presidential primary is at best only moderately successful as a predictive plebiscite, it has enjoyed bursts of importance in this century's elections. Kennedy's primary victories were indispensable for his 1960 nomination. Eugene McCarthy's powerful showing in 1968 against Lyndon Johnson in New Hampshire both gave a great lift to the Senator's candidacy and brought Robert Kennedy into the race. Ironically, the capacity of New Hampshire, a small state with fewer than one-third of 1 per cent of the national vote, to snuff out a candidacy defeats the democratic ideal envisioned by La Follette in championing the primary idea.

Presidential contenders rightly complain of the inhuman strain upon their health caused by existing primaries that force them to wage full-scale campaigns in a succession of states. "There were days when I just didn't think I could last out until Chicago," Estes Kefauver said of his 1952 primary ordeal of fierce struggles in fifteen states.[6] For office-holders such as governors, primaries, with their weeks of intensive effort, mean neglect of official duties.

A large-scale primary campaign is also enormously expensive. Eisenhower's preconvention effort in 1952 cost an estimated $2.5 million and Taft's was even more. Given the astronomical expense and the absence of public or party financing, the well-heeled candidate enjoys enormous advantage over his poorer competitor. Hubert Humphrey, fighting the 1960 West

Virginia primary in a battered bus, scraping desperately to muster the price of a half-hour's local radio time, and literally throwing the family grocery money into the breach, was a picture of pathos.[7]

The National Nominating Convention

The national nominating convention itself, the final arbiter, is as uniquely American as the hot dog and salt-water taffy. Everyone knows its spirit of carnival, the marching, shouting delegates, the frothy oratory, the grating brass bands. Like most citizens, H. L. Mencken, sage and cynic, viewed the nominating convention with mixed sentiments. "One sits through long sessions wishing heartily that all the delegates and alternates were in hell," he wrote, "—and then suddenly there comes a show so gaudy and hilarious, so melodramatic and obscene, so unimaginably exhilarating and preposterous that one lives a gorgeous year in an hour."[8]

The convention poses for the top contender and his managers two vitally important tasks, failure in either one of which might spell the difference between victory and defeat. The first is to keep the bloc of pledged or promised delegates "nailed fast" to prevent their straying "off the reservation" to another candidate. The second is to control the convention machinery to permit its manipulation for, rather than against, the candidate. In a contested convention these undertakings are a high-tension ordeal. Jim Farley wrote of the 1932 Democratic convention,

> The nervous strain during this period of suspense was very close to the limit of physical endurance. . . . I was working eighteen or nineteen hours a day, conversing with hundreds of people, constantly consulting with other leaders, receiving reports from every delegation, and meeting at least twice daily with several hundred newspapermen. I . . . slept a few hours just before dawn if the opportunity offered. . . . Hundreds of other men were caught in the same dizzy whirl and were trying to keep up the same maddening pace.[9]

In facing their convention tasks, the managers of the modern candidate resort to specialization, as they do in the preconvention phase. In 1932 Farley operated the main Roosevelt reception center at Chicago, where he greeted the Roosevelt delegates and tried mightily to win others over from the opposition. One of Farley's props was a huge map of the United States on which the Roosevelt states were blocked out in red. So vividly and convincingly did the map demonstrate that Roosevelt was the choice of a big majority that the worried opposition took pains to deride it as "Field Marshal Farley's Map." In negotiations with delegates in his hotel suite, Ed Flynn, the suave and astute Bronx boss, supplemented Farley's efforts to build Roosevelt's strength. Louis Howe, too, wooed the delegates, and he had installed in his suite a microphone attached to a direct wire from Albany. Roosevelt's exhilarating voice would come booming into the room full of visitors, "My friends from Iowa," and launch into a personal message. Roosevelt would expound his views, answer questions, and delight and impress the delegates. Thanks to the direct wire, Roosevelt, remaining at home, could electioneer and share in nearly every important decision at Chicago. The Roosevelt floor manager was Arthur Mullen of Nebraska, an old hand at conventions and one well-liked by all factions.[10]

The managers of a serious modern candidate coordinate their far-flung effort through an internal communications network at the convention itself. One of the most elaborate of these was Kennedy's in 1960. From the Kennedy liaison post, a cottage outside the Los Angeles Sports Arena, ran a net of direct communication lines to special telephone posts fixed on the chairs of friendly delegations. Eight of Kennedy's forty "state shepherds" who roved the convention floor carried walkie-talkie sets that were linked to a communications control at the cottage. From there the floor managers, Governor Abraham Ribicoff and Robert Kennedy, directed the whole body of shepherds. Another set of lines ran to Room 8315 at the Biltmore Hotel, the strategic center of the candidate's top command. Other lines were connected with Kennedy's private hideaway in Hollywood and his public Presidential suite.[11]

In 1964 Barry Goldwater's communications system at the Republican convention surpassed Kennedy's, which he had admired and studied. The consoles of a telephone board and quantities of walkie-talkies and telephone lines enabled the convention managers to range freely over the floor, to reach the several delegate headquarters and points across the convention city of San Francisco. A devoted amateur radio operator fascinated by electronics, Goldwater later regretfully acknowledged that with just a few more weeks of preparation his managers could have installed a miniature telephone in the shirt pocket of every delegate on the floor.[12]

To control the convention machinery, the candidate and his managers must concentrate upon several key parts. Much of their effort occurs before the convention begins and centers upon the national committee and the national chairman who decide when and where the convention is to be held and make the local arrangements. The national committee selects the temporary chairman of the convention, who delivers the keynote address. Since the tone and tendency of this oration shape the convention's initial and sometimes decisive mood, the selection of the temporary chairman may touch off a fierce struggle. His further power to hand down parliamentary rulings helpful to the candidate he favors adds zest to the combat.

In 1932 the Roosevelt camp had to maneuver forcefully to prevent Jouett Shouse from becoming temporary chairman. Shouse, who fiercely opposed the Roosevelt candidacy, had powerful support. The Roosevelt emissaries were able to install their own nominee, Alben Barkley, for temporary chairman when the New York governor agreed that the arrangements sub-committee of the national committee might "commend" (Roosevelt's word) rather than "recommend" Shouse for a second major convention post, the permanent chairmanship.

Well before the convention, however, the Roosevelt forces decided to oppose Shouse for permanent chairman as well and advance their own candidate, Senator Thomas J. Walsh of Montana. Following Roosevelt's agreement to commend him, Shouse had campaigned ardently against the New York governor in Massachusetts and Pennsylvania and had convinced Roosevelt's managers that a loyal permanent chairman was imperative. Cries of "unfair" greeted disclosure of the Rooseveltians' decision. The fight grew so furious and the outcome so unpredictable that Charles Michelson, the party's stellar ghost writer, carried in one pocket an acceptance speech for Shouse and, in another, one for Walsh. Roosevelt's candidate, Walsh, was elected 626 to 528, the convention high-water mark for the opposition. The Roosevelt forces rounded out their control of convention machinery by installing Cordell Hull as chairman of the committee on resolutions and Bruce Kremer of Montana as chairman of the rules committee. Roosevelt chose no nominees for two other committee chairmanships to leave Farley free to dangle them before wavering delegations.[13]

The fine art of winning and keeping delegations, like any other art, defies exact description. It is a blend of grand strategy, nice detail, human psychology, luck, and hard work. The candidate himself may take on front-line duty at the convention in the battle for delegates. Kennedy and his chief rivals all were on hand at the Los Angeles convention in 1960. He was literally in the thick of the fight. On July 11, between 8:30 A.M. and 1:30 P.M., for instance, he addressed the caucuses of Nevada, Pennsylvania, Michigan, North Carolina, Arkansas, New York, South Carolina, Florida, and Alaska. The afternoon was equally crowded. On the morning of July 12 he addressed North Carolina again, a collective New England breakfast, Wyoming, South Dakota, a nationality group, and California. On July 13, balloting day, he spoke to Indiana, a farm-state caucus, Virginia, Colorado, and Hawaii.[14] The amount of effort a candidate and his camp lavish upon a delegation is roughly proportionate to its importance.

A race's outcome is often determined by "deals" arranged by the candidates' convention representatives. Franklin Roosevelt was eventually put across in 1932 by a bargain for the Vice-Presidency, which not a few times in the nation's history has determined the choice of the Presidential nominee. Farley suggested to Garner's representative, Sam Rayburn, that if Texas threw its support to Roosevelt, Garner could have the Vice-Presidency. Rayburn answered crustily that he and his co-workers had come to Chicago to nominate Garner for President, although they did not want a stalemate. Eventually Garner made the decision. Fearful that an ugly convention deadlock might damage public confidence and cost the Democrats the election,

Temp.   Resolutions
Perm.   Credentials

Garner released his delegates and reluctantly exchanged his proud Speaker-ship for the quietude of the Vice-Presidency. Texas and California went over to Roosevelt and the nomination was clinched.[15]

The Convention Decides

The convention can also be viewed as a series of decisions, climbing, by phases, to the climax of the Presidential nomination. The proceedings of the convention committees—credentials, rules, permanent organization, and plat-form or resolutions—are often the harbinger of things to come. The com-mittees' reports to the whole convention often provide an early test of strength of the rival candidates. The credentials committee, for instance, acts as a kind of court to decide which one of two or more contesting delegations from a given state is entitled to be seated. At the Republican national convention of 1952 nearly a hundred delegates were involved in seating contests. Supporters of Robert A. Taft controlled the credentials committee and reported favorably on delegations pledged to his candidacy from Louisiana, Georgia, and Texas. The Eisenhower camp carried the fight to the convention floor, waved the banner of "fair play," won the uncommitted delegations over to their side, seated their own delegations from the contested states, and opened the way for a first-ballot nomination.

The convention's balloting may simply be a routine ratification of the candidate's success constructed in the previous months of careful effort. The first-ballot nominations of Kennedy and Nixon in 1960 were no surprise. A succession of ballotings, which is not uncommon, reflects the continuing struggle for delegates and requires adroit maneuvers. As the balloting pro-ceeds, the serious candidate must demonstrate a steadily increasing strength. To satisfy this psychological necessity, Farley at the 1932 convention held on to a meager reserve of delegates and doled them out sparingly with each new ballot to maintain the appearance of gathering vigor. He also had the task of keeping his disclosed strength intact, of preventing delegates com-mitted to Roosevelt from abandoning him on the next ballot. Disaster almost engulfed the Roosevelt forces on the third ballot, when Mississippi threat-ened to crack. The delegates were polled with intense pressures beating upon them from the several camps. Roosevelt squeaked through by 10½ votes to 9½. Since the "unit rule" was operating, by which a majority of the delega-tion controls the state's entire vote, all twenty of Mississippi's votes went to Roosevelt.[16]

When at last the balloting has produced a nomination, a double for-mality remains: the notification of the candidate and his acceptance. Prior to 1932 the notification procedure was a musty affair, done by a committee weeks after the event. Franklin Roosevelt in 1932 smashed precedent and thrilled the nation by flying to Chicago to accept the nomination and setting forth his position in confident generalities and a ringing voice. Roosevelt's innovation has since become standard practice in both major parties.

It may seem that the prize of the nomination goes to the man with the best organization and the most compelling political personality. But actually nominees are weeded out in advance to some extent; not all able men are eligible in practice. One of America's favorite candidates has been the military hero. Of the thirty-five men who have been elected President, twelve have been military veterans. Both parties have thrice nominated former military men in the same year. The Republicans tapped no less than four Civil War generals; Theodore Roosevelt was the glamorous Rough Rider of the Spanish-American War; and Dwight Eisenhower achieved international military renown in World War II. John Kennedy's valor in that war was not forgotten, either. In this century governors have been the leading source of Presidential candidates, sixteen of them having been nominated between 1900 and 1956. Nowadays being governor of any large state almost automatically puts one in the running, and for a New York governor not to crave the White House would be downright pathological. The United States Senate, once a liability, is fast becoming a factory of Presidential candidates. The chief Democratic contenders in 1960—Kennedy, Johnson, Humphrey, and Stuart Symington—were all Senators, and the Republican standard-bearer—Richard Nixon—was a former Senator. In 1964 both major candidates had served in the Senate. The Senator's importance has been enhanced in recent years by television and the dominance of foreign affairs, a subject that traditionally receives heavy attention in the upper chamber.

The Mountain States did not provide a candidate until Barry Goldwater in 1964, nor did the South for more than a century until Lyndon Johnson's nomination in 1964. Of the fifty-seven men nominated by the two parties since 1856, forty-one have come from either New York State or the Middle West. Religion, race, and sex have also been selective factors for the nomination. Kennedy's breakthrough in 1960 as the first Catholic to become President may, before many more elections come to pass, throw the gates open to all. Before this only a white Anglo-Saxon Protestant male was considered eligible.

After the Presidential nomination comes the usually anticlimactic selection of the Vice President. This decision is ordinarily governed by the tradition of "balancing the ticket" geographically. (Among the exceptions is the Truman-Barkley, Missouri-Kentucky, border state ticket of 1948.) After Wilson's nomination in 1912, his manager, A. S. Burleson, telephoned to say that the convention was leaning toward Thomas R. Marshall of Indiana. "But, Burleson," Wilson remonstrated, "he is a very small caliber man." Burleson did not argue the point but noted that Marshall was from the Middle West and a doubtful state. His candidacy would ideally supplement Wilson's. "All right, go ahead," Wilson said, not too agreeably.[17] Wilson notwithstanding, the opinion of the Presidential nominee is also weighty in choosing the Vice President. The degree to which the choice is specific varies. Eisenhower in 1952 wrote down five names he considered acceptable as running mates. In 1960 Kennedy induced Lyndon Johnson of Texas to become the Vice-Presidential nominee, a choice that proved an invaluable asset toward the ultimate victory. Johnson picked Hubert Humphrey as his running mate in 1964, after considering various possibilities, and the convention ratified his choice. Humphrey seems to have been chosen less for geographic reasons than because he was a "Johnson man."

The Campaign

The Presidential nominee of the mid-nineteenth century campaigned with luxurious ease and calm compared with the fiery involvement of his mid-twentieth-century counterpart. James Buchanan, Democratic nominee of 1856, tarried on his comfortable estate, Wheatland, near Lancaster, Pennsylvania, receiving visitors and answering mail with the help of a clerk. The bulk of the work was done by the state organizations supplemented by a quartet of Congressional managers. Nearly a century later Harry S. Truman, in an unstinting "whistle-stop" campaign, traveled 31,700 miles and delivered 356 speeches over a thirty-five day stretch, once making sixteen speeches in a single day.

Radio and television, broadened press coverage, and a burgeoning transportation technology have made campaigning strenuous for the candidate and have driven him to enlarge his staff. His increased exposure reduced the utility of that ancient standby, the set speech. The modern candidate must make many and varied speeches respectably adorned with an array of ideas. For this phase of his needs, Franklin Roosevelt's innovation, copied and adapted by his successors, was the brain trust, a body of professors and researchers who dealt with policies and issues for the candidate's speeches and other statements. A second distinct group, comprising Farley, Flynn, and others who had marshaled delegates for the convention, redirected their talents to gathering popular votes in the campaign. Kennedy's postconvention campaign organization in 1960 enlarged upon the Roosevelt pattern. There were new brain-trusters, professors recruited largely from Harvard through Archibald Cox of the university's law school. Ideas and speech drafts spewed from the group that followed Cox to Washington. In addition, Kennedy's idea-generators included his personal brain trust, Sorensen and Richard Goodwin, who dealt with high affairs and pronouncements.

For the political management phases, each member of Kennedy's prenomination entourage adapted his special skill to the new environment of the postconvention campaign. O'Donnell handled campaign scheduling, a difficult art concerned with allocating every minute of the candidate's time, with due regard for transportation and speech schedules, the necessities and feuds of local leaders, and the shepherding of newsmen following hard on the candidate's heels. O'Brien became Director of Organization for the National Committee and Byron (Whizzer) White, Director of the Kennedy-Johnson Volunteers Organization. Robert Kennedy presided over the entire enterprise—idea men and political managers—aided and abetted by Richard Donahue, Ralph Dungan, and other personal Kennedy lieutenants and a half-dozen members of the Kennedy family. The vast realm of the communications media was handled by Salinger, polltaker Harris, and a speech coach brought in to pare away the candidate's regional accent.[18]

The postconvention campaign, like other phases of the route to the Presidency, requires a series of major strategic decisions. Strategy on one level is the selection of an array of voter entities, which when pieced together will provide an electoral majority. Kennedy's 1960 strategy focused upon nine large states (New York, Pennsylvania, California, Michigan, Texas, Illinois, Ohio, New Jersey, and Massachusetts) comprising 237 of the 269 electoral votes required to elect a President. These plus sixty more electoral votes added by Lyndon Johnson in the deep South or by several New England and Middle Western states would make victory certain.

A further phase of strategy is the welding of groups—national, racial, and economic—into a winning coalition. Negro citizens, for instance, since the elections of the 1940's, have been wooed by both parties. A powerful political fact, not overlooked, is the large Negro population in big Northern cities that are a key to capturing the states with imposing electoral votes. Both Nixon and Kennedy courted the Negro vote in 1960, the latter, as it proved in a dramatic test, more energetically. Late in the campaign Martin Luther King, a hero of the Negro struggle, was arrested during an Atlanta sit-in, sentenced on a technicality to four months of hard labor, and thrust into the state penitentiary. The King situation coupled with the Southern white vote, which both parties were also courting, put the two candidates in the middle of a predicament. At least three Southern governors informed Kennedy that if he threw support behind King, the South would be lost to the Democratic ticket. Nixon eventually chose to keep silent in the King episode. Kennedy, on the other hand, telephoned Mrs. King, assuring her of his concern and, if necessary, his intervention. Word of this act spread through the Negro leadership. Robert Kennedy next telephoned to the sentencing judge a plea for King's release. The reverend was soon freed on bail, pending an appeal. Negro leaders across the nation praised Kennedy's action, and his organization printed a million pamphlets recounting the episode. These were distributed on the Sunday before the election outside Negro churches everywhere. The importance of Kennedy's action in the King situation is illuminated by the electoral data of 1960. In Illinois, carried by 9,000 votes, approximately 250,000 Negroes voted for Kennedy; in Michigan, carried by 67,000 votes, 250,000 Negroes voted for Kennedy; in South Carolina, carried by 10,000 votes, 40,000 Negroes voted for Kennedy.[19]

The candidate must also make several basic organizational choices. He can choose between relying heavily upon the regular party machinery or supplementing it with "independent" citizens' committees. In 1952 the independent Citizens for Eisenhower organization figured importantly in the Republican victory, particularly in drawing dissatisfied Democrats over to support the Eisenhower candidacy. A perpetual organizational problem is the relating of national and local efforts. In John Kennedy's campaign local organization implemented a major strategy of voter registration. If a massive registration drive could be mounted and ten million new names added to the voting lists, the Kennedy managers reasoned, seven million more Democratic votes would result. Congressman Frank Thompson of New Jersey, an experienced hand at registration drives, directed fifty state registration chairmen, two hundred key county registration chairmen, and a paid staff of eight specially trained leaders.[20] The Kennedy drive and a corresponding Nixon effort brought the 1960 popular vote to 6,800,000 beyond the 1956 total.

Another strategic problem concerns the candidate's personal involvement in the campaign. How much of the campaign emphasis should be on issues and how much on personality? Eisenhower, national hero and international personage in 1952, was under less pressure to emphasize issues than the lesser known Kennedy in 1960, whose campaign stressed issues. Should the candidate concentrate on mass appeal via radio, television, and big rallies? Or should he do the whistle-stop routine, as Harry Truman did in 1948, with folksy talks to hundreds of small audiences across the nation? For all of the magic of radio and television, candidates still heavily invest their time and treasure in going out to the voters. Although in 1960 the four television debates supplied the candidates with an audience of unsurpassed size, both Kennedy and Nixon traveled by rail and air to give brief talks in hundreds of communities and to shake thousands of hands. A powerful inducement for whistle-stopping is Truman's extraordinary success at it in 1948 in achieving a victory unpredicted by the public opinion polls or by any reputable politician save Truman himself.

Truman made his whistle-stop speeches from the back of a reconstructed Pullman car, the *Ferdinand Magellan*, purchased in 1942 for one dollar from the Association of American Railroads. According to the 1948 routine, the local high school band blared out "Hail to the Chief" upon Truman's arrival. Then came a gift for the President, his expression of thanks, his welcome to local Democratic leaders, and compliments to the citizenry for their new highway or factory. Hereupon Truman ripped into the Republicans and the

Eightieth Congress with wild ridicule. His Republican listeners heard their party brethren referred to as "gluttons of privilege" and "bloodsuckers with offices in Wall Street." ("Ridicule is a wonderful weapon," Truman told his aides.) After his political talk, Truman asked the crowd, "Howja like to meet my family?" and he proceeded to introduce Mrs. Truman as "the boss" and his daughter Margaret as "my baby" and "the boss's boss." The family bit delighted the crowds.[21]

The opposite of the whistle-stop tour is the "front porch" campaign, perfected by William McKinley and the organizing genius of his manager, Mark Hanna. Instead of the candidate going to the people, as in the whistle-stop, the people, in the front porch campaign, come to the candidate. Delegations visited McKinley from all parts of the country, thanks to the low excursion rates of the cooperating railroads. The trip to McKinley's base at Canton, the Cleveland *Plain Dealer* complained, was "cheaper than staying at home." Sporting campaign badges, caps, and neckties, the delegations poured off the trains and into the arms of committees of greeters. They marched through the town, passing beneath an elaborate plastic structure—the McKinley Arch—which supported a huge portrait of the candidate, and finally poured onto his lawn. After a short, suspenseful wait the door opened, and McKinley, appearing on the front porch, was greeted with a roar.

A spokesman of the delegation stepped forward to deliver an address of dedication to the Republican party and its illustrious candidate, mixed with acclaim for the visitors' locality or organization. Despite the seeming informality, a copy of the remarks had been cleared beforehand with McKinley, who sometimes edited them. Then the candidate mounted a chair, bade the crowd welcome, treated the campaign issues briefly, and complimented his audience. Concluding, he shook hands with his visitors in an informal reception on the porch steps.[22]

In 1960 Presidential campaigning took a new turn when the traditional political debate of Congressional and local elections was adapted to the Presidential canvass and the idiosyncracies of television. The resulting Kennedy-Nixon TV debates had enormous impact upon the electoral outcome. An audience of 120 million viewed one or more of the Kennedy-Nixon encounters. When the debates began, Nixon appeared the likely electoral winner, with Kennedy rather well behind; when they ended, the contestants' positions were reversed. The result will hardly prompt future candidates who are leading at the outset of a campaign to take on TV debates gladly.

Debates between Presidential candidates will probably reappear in future elections, with further evolutions of format. The debates helpfully provide the voters with a close-up of the candidates without their props of speechwriters and idea men. The candidates can be seen thinking and speaking under stress, a situation that casts a great shaft of light upon character. In 1960 the debates undeniably quickened voter interest in the campaign.

But the debate system is not without flaws. The Presidency has a limited need of forensic talent; the office is far more than a great debate. No President, fortunately, is expected to formulate in a matter of seconds answers to great questions of foreign policy. The 1960 debates, while they revealed the candidates' personalities in sharp topographical relief, added little to public understanding of issues. Indeed a built-in drawback of TV debates may be overattention to personality and superficial examination of the issues.

THE COSTS OF CAMPAIGNING.   The age of television is also an age of rocketing campaign costs. In his study *Financing the 1964 Election*, Herbert E. Alexander finds that the two major parties spent a combined total of $29 million on the election, of which $11 million was devoted to radio and television alone. The specter of exorbitant costs has stirred both proposals and action from executive and legislative quarters.

In 1967 President Johnson urged Congress to provide for each Presidential election a substantial fund to finance party expenses incurred in bringing "issues before the public"; that is, for radio and television, newspaper and periodical advertising, preparation and distribution of literature, and travel costs. The fund would not cover staff salaries, telephones, administration, and the like. For these expenditures, as well as for outlays in the years between elections, the national party committees would still rely on private contributions. Primary and convention expenses also would not be chargeable to the fund, and only official party candidates could partake of the subsidy. Minor parties would also share in it. Parties would be limited in the amount they could spend in any one state.

Johnson's plan raised a wide outcry of opposition on Capitol Hill by those rightly concerned that it would work a drastic redistribution of power in the party structures by centralizing political power in the hands of Presidential candidates and national committees at the expense of state and local party organizations. The plan also lacks any provision for controlling radio and television rates for political broadcasts financed by the election fund. Another gaping loophole results from the inability of government, because of constitutional limitations, to control the expenditures of private committees and individuals working independently of the political parties.

As an alternative to the President's plan, various legislators advanced proposals for a tax allowance for the taxpayer who contributes to the party of his choice. This plan would help all candidates. One possibility is a tax credit, which, like charitable contributions, is deductible from taxable income. If, say, a 50 per cent credit were allowed, a credit of $5 could be given on contributions up to $10. A tax credit would make political giving attractive to the entire body of taxpayers and encourage broader participation in campaign financing. It would avoid the centralization of campaign funds and preserve the federal character of the party structure.

The Electoral College

The final stage of selecting the President—his actual election—was a very knotty, much debated issue at the Constitutional Convention. Eventually the electoral college method of choosing the President emerged as a compromise. In actuality, there are fifty electoral colleges, one in each state. The number of electors in a given state equals the number of its Senators and Representatives in Congress.

Each elector has one vote, and a majority of the whole number of electors appointed is required to choose the President. If no Presidential candidate receives a majority, the Constitution directs the House of Representatives to complete the election of the President. The House is limited in choice to the three candidates receiving the greatest number of the electors' votes.

The Constitution authorizes each state to appoint its electors "in such manner as the legislature thereof may direct." In the first three Presidential elections the electors were chosen chiefly by the state legislatures. Thereafter, popular choice gradually took hold. By 1824 electors were chosen by popular vote in all but six states, and in 1832 in all states but South Carolina, which clung to legislative election until 1864. Popular choice has been registered through two main systems—election of electors by districts and election of electors on a "general ticket." Each system spawned numerous variations. In the former method, the people would vote in districts relatively equal in population, each district choosing one elector. Districts often coincided with Congressional districts. The district system was widely employed in the early days of the Constitution; indeed, according to Madison, most of the Founding Fathers strongly preferred it. In practice, electors were pledged to particular candidates. Whichever candidate's elector then carried a district was the official elector of that district. Since, in a given state, the elector of one candidate might triumph in one district, and the elector of a different candidate might win in another district, the total electoral vote of a state might be divided among several candidates. The division tended to follow the pattern of the Congressional elections in the House districts.

In time a political party, having gained control of a state, would sniff an opportunity to avoid the division of its electoral strength by introducing the general ticket system, which applies an ancient principle of gamesmanship— "winner take all." The party carrying the state, by however small a popular plurality, wins all the state's electors and the minority party or parties get none. Since 1836 all states have used the general ticket system, except for a brief relapse in Michigan to the district system following the 1892 election.

Although the states determine the method of choosing their electors, the timetable of a Presidential election is set by national law. On the first Tuesday after the first Monday in November, every fourth year, the qualified popular voters of the several states choose the Presidential electors. On the first Monday after the second Wednesday in December the electors meet in their respective states to cast their votes for President. On January 6 the electoral votes are counted in the presence of the two houses of Congress and the results are announced by the presiding officer—the Vice President, if there is one. Vice President Nixon, consequently, had the privilege of declaring Kennedy's victory and his own defeat.

The Founding Fathers' expectation that the electors would exercise an element of free judgment in choosing the President was quickly crushed by the appearance of political parties, the Federalists and the Anti-Federalists, the latter soon becoming the Republican-Democratic party. George Washington's two Presidential candidacies were untouched by electoral vote politics. Following his departure from the Presidential scene, the electors took to party-line voting in choosing John Adams as President in 1796 over his chief rival, Thomas Jefferson. Thereafter, with rare individual exceptions, the electors have functioned as the automatons of their parties. Only rarely has an elector violated his pledge to vote for a particular Presidential candidate. In 1820 William Plumer voted for John Quincy Adams instead of Monroe. In 1956 a Democratic elector in Alabama, though pledged to vote for whomever the Democratic national convention nominated, voted for a leading segregationist judge. In 1960 Senator Harry F. Byrd of Virginia, who was not a candidate on any ticket, received six of Alabama's eleven Democratic electoral votes, all eight of Mississippi's votes, one vote in Oklahoma, or a total of fifteen electoral votes. But none of these lapses affected the outcomes.

Such departures from standard electoral college practice are founded on the notion that if enough electoral votes are withheld from the two major Presidential candidates, the required majority might be denied to either. In that event, the House of Representatives, under constitutional procedure, would decide the election. Each state would have one vote, and the eleven Southern states, each now as powerful as New York or California, would enjoy an imposing bargaining position. They could commit their votes to the Presidential candidate who offered them the greatest concessions, particularly on the paramount issue of civil rights.

Custom, which dictates the electors' voting conduct, has been reinforced by legislation and court opinion. State statutes range from those calling for a party nomination of electors, which itself is a presumption of pledged electors, to the laws of two states prescribing that electors vote for the party nominees, regardless of personal preference. In *Ray v. Blair* (343 U.S. 214, 1952) the Supreme Court gave its blessing to these arrangements, upholding a state law empowering party organizations to fix the qualifications of candidates for nomination as electors. The state law, the Court said, simply converted custom into legal obligation. Anticipating the 1964 elections, Mississippi and Georgia in 1961 passed laws permitting the election of unpledged electors. In Alabama, electors, although identified with a major party, are not required to vote for its Presidential nominee. In 1963 Governor Wallace of Alabama disclosed that his 1964 efforts would be devoted to spreading the unpledged elector movement in lieu of launching a third party. Unpledged elector slates were entered in Alabama and Mississippi in the 1964 election, but they were foiled when the popular vote in both states chose electors committed to the Republican candidate, Senator Barry Goldwater.

The selection of electors has also been altered by revisions of the Presidential ballot that confronts the popular voter in the polling booth. One is the requirement, first adopted in Nebraska in 1917, that electors be listed and voted for as a party group rather than individually. Another change brought the names of the Presidential nominees on the ballot with those of the electors. The latest evolutionary step is the Presidential short ballot, on which only the names of the Presidential and Vice-Presidential nominees appear, an innovation speeded by the use of voting machines, which impose severer limitations of space than the paper ballot does. Each popular vote cast by the Presidential short ballot counts for the elector whose name, although unknown to the voters, is on file with the state secretary of state.

Originally, under the Constitution, each elector cast two votes for President, one of which had to be for a candidate who was not an inhabitant of the elector's state. This provision, coupled with the necessity of an electoral vote majority for victory, barred even the largest state from choosing by itself a President from among its own inhabitants. The double-vote feature virtually compelled the selection of a candidate of national reputation. The candidate receiving the second highest number of electoral votes became Vice President, a method that brought into the number-two post men of Presidential caliber like John Adams and Thomas Jefferson. The double-voting system, for all of its seeming merit, was abandoned in 1804 with the adoption of the Twelfth Amendment. The double vote had crashed on the rocks in the election of 1800, when a deadlock developed between the Republican candidates, Jefferson and Aaron Burr. The election passed into the House of Representatives, where the rival Federalist party, which controlled the outcome, favored Burr but was pressured by Alexander Hamilton, its national chieftain, into backing Jefferson. Snatched from a disaster they wished never to encounter again, the Republicans championed the Twelfth Amendment, establishing separate electoral votes for the President and the Vice President.[23]

Defects of the Electoral College System

The existing electoral vote arrangements have long been the object of heavy criticism and dire warnings. The critics hold that the electoral system violates basic tenets of democracy and that its many mechanical flaws invite breakdown and the eruption of a Presidential election into a nightmare of civil strife.[24]

The electoral college system has been employed in forty-five elections and has failed three times to elect a President: in 1800, 1824, and 1876. Three elections are also often indicted for flaunting the voice of the people, for electing Presidents who received fewer popular votes than their opponents. The suspected elections are John Quincy Adams' triumph over Jackson in 1824, Rutherford B. Hayes's over Samuel J. Tilden in 1876, and Benjamin Harrison's over Cleveland in 1888. Jackson's showing in 1824 is clouded by the fact that no popular votes were cast in six of the twenty-four states. In 1876 Tilden received some two hundred thousand more popular votes than Hayes. Since fraud and violence marked the popular voting in the South, North, and West, Tilden's popular margin is not unblemished. Harrison's victory by a popular minority over Cleveland cannot be gainsaid.

In *Gray v. Saunders* (372 U.S. 368, 1963) the Supreme Court stated that the electoral college philosophy violated the constitutional concept of "we the people," which, the Court said, "can mean only one thing—one person, one vote." The electoral college system, by this standard, is a kind of gigantic gerrymander. It grossly exaggerates the value of the individual popular vote in the less populous states in contrast to the large states. Thus in the 1956 election each electoral vote in Illinois represented 163,235 popular voters, in Mississippi 31,018 voters.

Of all the features of electoral college practice the general ticket system has raised the severest criticism. The general ticket, as Lucius Wilmerding demonstrates, puts the Presidency on a federative rather than a national basis. It has taken "the choice of the President from the people of the nation at large and given it, in effect, to the people of the large states."[25] The principle of winner take all serves to disenfranchise a substantial minority of popular votes or even more outrageously transfers them to the use of the candidate against whom they were cast. Charles Evans Hughes in 1916, for instance, carried Minnesota by a popular plurality of only 359 but received all twelve of that state's electoral votes. A large part of those electoral votes were made possible by thousands of Minnesotans who voted against Hughes. On a national scale, John W. Davis received six million popular votes in 1924 that earned him no electoral votes at all—or in reality were transferred to the use of his rival, Calvin Coolidge—while two million others brought him 136 electoral votes.

The general ticket system's rough handling of minority popular votes extravagantly favors the large states. The pluralities of the twelve largest states control 281 electoral votes. If these states should vote for a single candidate, he would be elected regardless of the strength of his opposition in those states and in the remaining thirty-eight states. The general ticket system, this is to say, enables the popular voter in the large states to participate in the choice of a larger number of electors than the voter of a small state. In 1964 a popular voter in New York shared in the choice of forty-three electors, and in Nevada only three. The candidate of the popular majority of the nation is far from certain to prevail in an electoral college where the representation of each state is not that of its people but of its plurality. The likelihood of minority Presidents will surely increase in our present era of close Presidential elections.

The general ticket system, with its winner-take-all principle that rewards the victor more lavishly than any other system, wreaks other distortions. It prods parties into seeking out their candidates in big states such as New York and Ohio, while ignoring the small states, whose sons may be equally talented. The general ticket system has also encouraged the historic one-party solid South. The Republican party, faced with a hopeless minority position, for years maintained no serious organization in Southern states. The general ticket system also causes party campaigning to be concentrated in doubtful states and in large states. New York, Ohio, and Illinois are regularly showered with relatively more campaign dollars and rhetorical fervor than states such as Maine, Nevada, or Georgia, which are safe or small. In 1960 Kennedy was hailed for his political wisdom in concentrating on the large industrial states.

The general ticket system is also attacked for grossly inflating the bargaining power of pressure groups and minority parties in large doubtful states. A well-organized national, racial, religious, or economic group whose votes are concentrated upon a Presidential candidate can more powerfully exact his commitment if the group is situated in a large state.

Defenders of the existing electoral system argue that its distortions serve the cause of social justice, that the system enables smaller masses of people to strike bargains that unshackle their oppressions. A more perfect system, presumably, would afford fewer liberating opportunities. Yet a standard that judges the quality of the electoral system in terms of whether the bargains struck are good or bad is of dubious merit. Wilmerding argues in *The Electoral College,*

> If the President is to be the man of the people, if all the people are to stand on the same footing, equal masses of people must be given equal votes, equal bargaining power. Their weight in the electoral count must be proportional to their numbers and not to the rightness or wrongness of their causes.[26]

The pretension of distinguishing good groups from bad and of assigning greater electoral weight to the former than to the latter cannot be justified in democratic theory, nor can it long be asserted satisfactorily in practice.

Alternatives to the Electoral College

Hardly a session of Congress passes when legislators, distressed by the flaws of the electoral college system, do not introduce proposals, embodied in drafts of constitutional amendments, to reform it. Although differing in detail, the proposals that perennially appear can be grouped into several broad categories:

A NATIONAL POPULAR VOTE.   According to this proposal, the President would be chosen by the majority of the national popular vote. Electors and electoral votes would be tossed upon the political scrap heap.

The plan of national popular election offers powerful attractions. It is the only plan extant that assures against the election of a President receiving fewer popular votes than his opponent. Every voter, be he a New Yorker or a Nevadan, would have one vote of equal weight. Majoritarian democracy would be cleanly applied, in which 51 per cent and above would rule. The several evils of the general ticket system would be banished at one fell swoop. The principle of Presidential selection would be national rather than federative; minority votes of states would at least be counted; large states would be barred from consolidating their votes to the disadvantage of the small. The power of pressure groups and minor parties would be more nearly proportionate to their numbers. Political activity in safe states would rise and be meaningful.

The national popular election of the President best harmonizes with the Supreme Court's ideal of one man, one vote voiced in its apportionment decisions. The new reapportionment plans required by the courts for the state legislatures and the national House of Representatives have deflated the traditional argument that the electoral college system, operated by the general ticket principle, is the only sure defense of large urban areas against rural-dominated state legislatures, malapportioned Congressional districts, and a United States Senate weighted in behalf of the small states.

The national popular vote carries several formidable defects. It would jeopardize our two-party system by encouraging minor parties, giving them a weight in the national popular vote that they lack in the electoral college system. It violates the federal principle by redistributing political power among the states: The proposal would shift power from the smaller to the larger states; from the South to the North, East, and West; from states that are politically passive to those politically active.

From 1966 onward, the proposal for the popular election of Presidents has enjoyed a quickened momentum after endorsement by the American Bar Association, by Senator Birch Bayh, Democrat of Indiana and chairman of a constitutional amendments subcommittee, by Everett Dirksen of Illinois, Senate Republican leader, and by Mike Mansfield of Montana, Senate Democratic leader. The bipartisan liberal-conservative support augurs a glittering future for the proposal.

Individual plans for popular elections introduced in Congress over the years have offered different provisions for the eventuality wherein no candidate wins a majority. Some would permit a plurality to elect; others would hold a run-off election limited to the two or three candidates polling the highest initial vote. Still others would throw the election into the House of Representatives, with each member having one vote.

The two plans most discussed in 1967 and after, those of the American Bar Association and Senator Bayh, would require a President to win a minimum of 40 per cent of the popular vote for election. If no candidate won 40 per cent, Bayh would have all 535 members of Congress choose a President from the two high men, by majority vote.[27] The Bar Association proposal calls for a national run-off election between the two high candidates.* Both arrangements are vulnerable. Congress might not be controlled by the party of the top Presidential vote-getter, in which case it might be prone to choose the second or third man. A narrowly divided Congress would put a premium on promises and deals, and a President who emerged from such a process would probably have mortgaged much of his future incumbency.

The Bar Association's run-off plan would prolong campaigns that already are overlong. It would enormously increase the already exorbitant costs of Presidential elections. It would encourage a third candidate with a devoted following to throw his support as leverage to one of the front-runners for a price, perhaps a key cabinet post. Furthermore, experience in state run-off elections reveals that the total vote tends to decline in the run-off, with the front-runner suffering most from apathy and defection. An alternative, of course, would be to have no run-off and thus avoid these garish consequences. But election by plurality raises another specter—the fear that in a field of several candidates a President would be elected with too weak a mandate to govern effectively.

PROPORTIONAL VOTING.   The leading modern advocate of this century-old plan is Henry Cabot Lodge, Jr., who while Senator, and with Congressman Ed Gossett of Texas as cosponsor, incorporated it into a constitutional amendment in 1950. In the early 1960's its champions included Senators George Smathers, Thomas Kuchel, and Leverett Saltonstall, but later in the decade, the plan attracted little backing in Congress.

Under the plan, which has many variations, each candidate who polled a fraction of a state's popular votes would win the same fraction of its electoral votes. The candidate's national electoral vote would be the sum of his electoral votes in all fifty states. The President would continue to be chosen by electoral, not popular, votes. If no candidate received 40 per cent of the entire electoral vote, the contest would be decided between the two highest candidates by the House and Senate jointly, with each member having one vote. The state legislatures would lose their present freedom to decide the methods of choosing electors and of voting.

Lodge and his fellow advocates contend that their plan is "fair, accurate,

---

* Bayh's 1967 bill incorporates the Bar Association Proposals, although he is reported still to prefer his own plan. See Tom Wicker, "Graduating from the Electoral College," New York *Times*, January 12, 1967.

and democratic." The minority popular vote in each state would be accurately reflected in the electoral vote. The plan would abolish the evil of the one-party state and diminish the disproportionate influence of local pressure groups and the dread possibility that a candidate with a minority of the popular vote will win a majority of the electoral vote. The plan harmonizes with the federal structure by preserving the interests of the small states.

But proportional voting has heavy disadvantages. It would encourage the development of minor parties and would in time weaken or destroy the two-party system. The Presidential constituency would cease to be primarily geographical and would become, instead, primarily mathematical or ideological. Groups rather than areas would be the focus of appeal. The geographical constituency encourages the candidate to be moderate in view and balanced in appeal to its diverse groups. To win an ideological constituency, the candidate must tend to extremes and subordinate himself to its special purposes. Proportional voting would increase rather than reduce the danger of electing minority Presidents. If, for example, proportional voting rather than the present electoral system had operated in the elections of 1880 and 1896, their outcomes would have been reversed. In 1880 James A. Garfield received more popular votes than Winfield Scott Hancock, and in 1896 McKinley more than Bryan. The Lodge-Gossett formula, however, would have converted Hancock and Bryan from losers into victors because of the way their popular votes were distributed among the states.

THE SINGLE-MEMBER DISTRICT SYSTEM.   Modern critics have revived interest in the single-member district system, beloved by Madison and other Founding Fathers. Its contemporary sponsors include Senators Karl Mundt, Strom Thurmond, Thruston Morton, and Congressman Thomas Hale Boggs.

Each state would be divided by the state legislature into districts equal to the number of Representatives the state is entitled to in Congress. Ideally, the districts would comprise contiguous and compact territory and, as nearly as possible, equal numbers of inhabitants. (Ideally, also, the electoral college districts would correspond with the districts of the House of Representatives.) Each district's voters would choose one elector. In addition, two electors would be chosen from the state at large. The candidate winning a majority of the electoral votes (some proposals require only 40 per cent) would be deemed elected. If no candidate qualified, the House and Senate would jointly choose the President.

Like other proposals, the district system would take the method of electing the President out of the hands of the state legislatures and more nearly make the President the man of the people. It would end the power of large states, or their dominant party, to override the dominant party in the country at large. It would hamper minor parties and pressure groups in doubtful states from defeating, for their own ends, the will of the nation. Finally, it would force the parties to lift their eyes beyond the big states and into the country at large in their quest for candidates.

The district system has several forbidding weaknesses. It is vulnerable to the gerrymander. Its champions face the gerrymander evil by incorporating into their proposed constitutional amendment precise standards concerning population and territory by which districts would be made up. These the courts presumably would enforce. The districts still would not be equal in each state; large states would have districts with more populous constituencies than small states. Worst of all, the district plan would probably convert the present system, by which the American people engage in a national act focused upon national problems, into a series of petty campaigns in local districts. The district system would encourage minor parties by giving them a stronger opportunity to choose an elector in a district than the traditional system permits in a state. In a close election, a minor party might hold the balance in the national tally of electors. The district system would decrease the power of Northern Democrats, who, under the present system, have been able to capture all the electoral votes despite the substantial numbers of popular votes cast by Republican minorities. Northern Democrats would be driven to rely increasingly upon Southern votes. (This would also be the case with the national popular vote and proportional voting proposals.) By the late 1960's the district plan still enjoyed significant support in Congress. Its chief political effect is to siphon off support from the national popular vote plan, a tendency that the growing momentum of the latter plan may soon overcome.

KEEPING THE ELECTORAL VOTE BUT DROPPING THE ELECTORS.   In 1801 Jefferson wrote to Albert Gallatin of an "amendment which I know will be proposed, to wit, to have no electors, but let the people vote directly, and the ticket which has a plurality of the votes of any state to be considered as receiving the whole vote of the state." Senators George Norris in 1934 and John Kennedy in 1957 proposed similar amendments geared to the general ticket system. President Johnson urged the step in a 1967 message, and it is contained in a proposed twenty-sixth amendment. The accompanying argument is undeniable. If the elector is faithful to the popular vote, he is useless; if he is not, he is dangerous.

ALTERING THE PROCEDURES OF THE HOUSE OF REPRESENTATIVES.   The Twelfth Amendment specifies that if no candidate receives a majority of the electoral votes, the House of Representatives, voting by states, shall immediately choose the President by ballot "from the persons having the highest numbers not exceeding three on the list of those voted for as President." A majority of all the states is necessary for election. The present system of a single vote for each state is unjust in making one Representative from Nevada equal to forty-one Representatives from New York.

Critics from George Mason to Henry Cabot Lodge would avoid the House altogether simply by making the candidate with the greatest number of electoral votes the victor. Most proposals would have the Representatives vote by heads rather than by states, patently a fairer procedure. Still others would have the Senate and House sit jointly and vote by heads. Including the Senate would be a sop to the small states, who would lose strength if the House shifted from voting by the states as units to voting by heads.

The proposed twenty-sixth amendment, whose supporters include Senator Bayh and Republican Congressman William McCulloch of Ohio, calls for each member of the House and Senate to cast one vote in a joint session, with a simple majority of those voting required for victory. The proposal preserves the advantage of the populous states in the electoral college and carries it into a possible multicandidate Presidential election in which no one candidate received a majority. The advantage, of course, would not have the solid impact of the general ticket system. Most state delegations in Congress would divide on party lines, although New York with forty-three members would still wield more power than Mississippi with seven. The amendment would also make a deadlock impossible by limiting the Congressional voting to the two leading candidates.

The Future Presidency

In the interest of strengthening the Presidency, several innovations might advantageously be made in its selection procedures.

1. We ought, at the very least, to abolish the electoral college, which is a standing invitation to trouble. Even if we abolished the college, we could retain the electoral vote, which should automatically reflect the plurality of the popular vote. The proposed amendment carries this feature and deserves our support.

2. We ought to review periodically the question of whether we might advantageously abandon both the electoral college and the electoral vote and substitute a plan for selecting the President on the basis of a national popular vote. A national popular vote is most in accord with democratic principle, and it would apply a standard of absolute fairness of "one American, one vote," which is badly violated by the present system. It would avoid the dread possibility, under the present electoral vote system, that the candidate winning a national popular majority will not prevail because he does not command a majority of the electoral votes. A serious drawback of the national popular vote plan is the possible necessity of a run-off election. But this is better in the bargain than the present danger that the popular vote winner will lose in the

electoral college. There is, however, a formidable difficulty that to this writer makes prohibitive the adoption of the national vote system now. The system would encourage minor parties by affording them a recognition in the national popular vote that they do not have in the present electoral vote. The fact that their votes would count under the national popular vote plan would induce them to extend themselves nationally. Such a development would further weaken our already much too weak major parties. But if the new Conservative party makes substantial inroads into the Republican party, and if former Governor George C. Wallace of Alabama and others continue to encourage individual states to adopt a plan of unpledged electors, who presumably would vote for a local "Dixiecrat" Presidential candidate—if our major parties suffer these and other deteriorations on a growing scale in the future, then we ought to consider all the more seriously the adoption of a plan of national popular election.

3. When the House of Representatives is called upon to choose a President, it should vote by heads rather than by states. A vote by heads clearly would better approximate the popular vote than the existing system. Best of all would be a combined Senate-House vote by heads, since Senators are chosen by the states at large and therefore reflect state-wide opinion. Fortunately this arrangement is included in the proposed twenty-sixth amendment.

4. The assassination of President Kennedy should teach us for all time that the only valid criterion for choosing a Vice-Presidential candidate is his suitability for the Presidency. The folly of the traditional formula of "balancing the ticket"—the North-South tandem of the Democrats and East-West one of the Republicans—is exposed by the stark statistic that four out of our eleven Presidents in the twentieth century were brought into the highest office from the Vice-Presidency by the death of the President.

5. The most promising response to the ever more monstrous problem of the soaring campaign costs of Presidential elections is the tax credit. It would have the democratizing effect of extending the base of party financing to include innumerable small contributors, and it would avoid centralizing political power at the expense of state and local party organizations. We depend heavily upon these organizations as incubators of political talent with Presidential potential.

6. Although television debates between the Presidential candidates are not without flaw, it is not likely that they should be discarded after their importance in the 1960 elections. In an era of public relations slickness that is moving rapidly into the political arena, the television debates are a strong antidote, affording the nation a better view of the real candidate than it would

get in any other way. But with television taking such a great chunk of campaign costs, is it not time to ask this medium to donate a goodly quantity of hours to the task of choosing a President?

7. Modern America is a nation on the move, with millions changing their residences, often leaving one state for another annually. Antiquated residence laws bring wholesale disenfranchisement to millions of citizens in a Presidential election year. Since Presidential election issues have little to do with local residence, the requirements should be scaled down to the barest minimum.

Tenure 4

Tenure is power. Whether the Presidency is a center of energy and direction or of weakness and futility depends in no small way upon the length and security of the Chief Executive's term of office, his eligibility for reelection, and the adequacy of arrangements available to bolster the office if his health, physical or mental, should falter. Tenure, therefore, depends partly upon the structuring of the office and partly upon the President's ability to escape the afflictions of biological frailty. If he does succumb to serious illness, the office, to function adequately, requires provision beforehand for a substitute President to take over with adequate preparation and authority.

Tenure is hollow if the President and his administration follow the departing administration in an abrupt transition that does not afford the new Chief Executive and his aides adequate opportunity to learn the status of ongoing policy and the central facts of current problems and adequate time to prepare the legislative and budget messages through which the new administration speaks. If the incoming Chief Executive lacks these opportunities he flounders in ignorance, at least at the beginning of his term, in undue dependence upon the civil service and labors excessively at learning his job as he does it.

The Founding Fathers, aware of the importance of tenure to the strong Executive, debated the President's term and his reeligibility long and anxiously. The most formidable attacks upon the office since then have concentrated upon the same question. The worst assault—the impeachment trial of Andrew Johnson—was at bottom a question of tenure. In 1951 those who could not abide the Presidency's swift enlargement of power and function during the 1930's and 1940's also struck at the conditions of tenure, inserting into the Constitution the Twenty-second Amendment, limiting the Presidential incumbent to two terms.

The Founding Fathers' anxiety about the President's term of office was reflected in their consideration at successive junctures of a term first of seven, then of six, and finally of four years. If Congress chose the President, as many favored, a long term without eligibility for reelection seemed best, because a President otherwise might become a Congressional yes-man in courting reelection. But once the electoral college system had been adopted, a shorter term with unlimited eligibility was agreed upon.

The Founding Fathers expected that George Washington would become the first President and would willingly serve the rest of his days. Their acceptance of the principle of indefinite eligibility ran counter to another American political principle deeply ingrained since Revolutionary times—that rotation in executive office is essential to liberty.

The principle of unlimited eligibility for reelection was innocently but irreparably undermined in practice by the man in whose behalf it had been established, George Washington himself. Washington announced upon completing his second Presidential term that it was his personal wish not to serve another. Thomas Jefferson brought the weakened principle crashing to the ground when, after admiring state legislatures earnestly asked him to continue for a third term, he declared he would not. He said that if there were no limitation on office, understood if not required, the office would be held "for life" and would degenerate "into an inheritance." "Truth also requires me to add," Jefferson continued, "that I am sensible of that decline which advancing years bring on, and feeling their physical I ought not to doubt their mental effect."[1] By the Civil War, Presidential observance had established the two-term principle in the core of American political doctrine.

The two-term practice has occasionally been under siege, however. One assault is the proposal that a President be limited to a single term. Such a doctrine was preached, for example—though certainly not practiced—by Andrew Jackson. And as late as 1912 the Democratic platform endorsed a single Presidential term, a pledge that its nominee, Woodrow Wilson, quickly repudiated. This was by no means the last to be heard of the subject. Dwight D. Eisenhower, both before and after assuming office, found the notion intriguing. Convinced that he could establish in a span of four years his cherished concepts of moderate government, a free economy, and a balanced budget, and mindful of his own advanced years, he proposed to hand over the reins after a single term to a younger man. Eisenhower came within an eyelash of incorporating this proposal into his first inaugural address. At the last minute he was talked out of it, but as his term wore on he often reverted to it in private conversation.[2]

A second major assault upon the two-term principle has been leveled by the President who seeks a third or even a fourth term. Although Franklin D.

Roosevelt alone exceeded the two-term limitation, he was far from the first to try. In the decades between Lincoln and Franklin D. Roosevelt, there was seldom a period when the third-term fever did not seize the Chief Executive. So menacing in fact did the third-term boom of Ulysses S. Grant become in 1875 that the House of Representatives felt duty-driven to resolve, by a vote of 234 to 18, that departure from the two-term tradition would be "unwise, unpatriotic and fraught with peril to our free institutions."[3]

Theodore Roosevelt, like Grant before him and Calvin Coolidge at a later day, took the pragmatic view that the two-term limitation applied only to a third consecutive term. He had sworn fealty to the two-term custom in the exuberance of his electoral victory of 1904, a pledge his foes gleefully recalled when he entered the Presidential race of 1912. But Roosevelt was a supreme rationalizer and saw no contradiction between his words in 1904 and his actions in 1912. If he were to decline "a third cup of coffee," he explained, no one would suppose he meant never to take another cup. By his 1904 pledge, he said, "I meant, of course, a third consecutive term."[4]

Franklin D. Roosevelt's distinction in achieving reelection to a third and a fourth term was prevented by the Twenty-second Amendment from becoming more than a personal triumph. The amendment inscribes in the nation's fundamental law the prohibition, "No person shall be elected to the office of the President more than twice." For anyone like Ulysses S. Grant, who after two terms and an interlude of retirement strains to possess the office a third time, the amendment would provide a clear and unequivocal negative. For Presidents such as Theodore Roosevelt, Calvin Coolidge, and Lyndon Johnson, whose incumbencies stretched across a partial and a full term, the amendment continues in a fashion too clear to be misinterpreted: ". . . and no person who has held the office of President, or acted as President, for more than two years of a term to which some other person was elected President shall be elected to the office of the President more than once." Admirers of former President Eisenhower, the first casualty of the amendment, concluded after reading its text that he could well be restored as Chief Executive by the route of succession by electing him Vice President and having the President elected with him step down in his favor.

The Twenty-second Amendment demonstrates how vulnerable the Presidency is to stealthy emasculation by amendment. For all of its controversial character, the amendment emerged from the House of Representatives with but a single day's debate. Its four-year journey through the state legislatures stirred a minimum of public discussion. Only by untiring alertness could the diligent citizen keep up with the amendment's progress, disclosed in microscopic news items in the back pages of the New York *Times*. And if he read another paper even diligence would have been unrewarded.

The Constitution provides that amendments be ratified either by state legislatures or by special state conventions. Backers of the Twenty-second Amendment skillfully avoided action by state conventions; conventions would be more closely attuned to popular opinion than the legislatures. From the voters' repudiation of the two-term tradition by electing Roosevelt to third and fourth terms it was clear that popular opinion could not be trusted. In sending the amendment to the state legislatures, moreover, Congress was relying upon bodies endowed with impressive experience in trammeling executive authority. Curbing the terms of chief executives is old hat to state legislatures. In fourteen states governors can serve only one term, and in six states not more than two. Of the thirty states that permit their own governors to serve without limitation, all but five recoiled from according the same privilege to the President. New York and California, for example, voted for limitation of the tenure of the Presidency at a time when they had as their governors Thomas E. Dewey and Earl Warren (the Republican national ticket in 1948), both of whom were to be reelected for third consecutive four-year gubernatorial terms in 1950.

The Twenty-second Amendment is a mixture of political motivations, partisan and personal. It was a posthumous revenge against Franklin Roosevelt for breaking the two-term tradition. It was a desperate attempt to push back the rushing flood of Executive authority. It was a psychological release for legislators who find joy in curbing the Executive. And to the career politician it was an assurance that the foremost prize of American politics would be available at regular intervals.

The amendment also instills certain weaknesses into the office of the Presidency, however. It can gravely weaken the President's influence during the entire span of his second, and final, term. In 1957, the first year of Eisenhower's second term, the President was hampered by a noticeable weakening of his grip on Republican legislators and a softening of his hitherto staunch support from the press and business. Yet Eisenhower had been returned to power only a year earlier with a fresh and overwhelming mandate. Even worse is the amendment's potential mischief in a foreign affairs crisis. The nation could conceivably be deep in war, or on the brink of it, when the tenure of its Chief Executive was suddenly cut off. The amendment would require the nation to violate that wise old adage warning against changing horses in midstream. The electorate would be wrenched into choosing new leadership at a time when national unity was imperative; it would be deprived of a Chief Executive whose experience and knowledge of the ongoing crisis could not be duplicated. The crisis of war kept Franklin Roosevelt in office because the electorate concluded that the continuity of leadership and policy could not be safely shattered midway without peril. Had the Twenty-second Amendment then been in force, Roosevelt would automatically have been disbarred and new leadership imposed contrary to the electorate's judgment. The Twenty-second Amendment, whatever may be said in its favor, is antidemocratic in spirit, a frustration of the will of the people out of fear that the people might choose unwisely.[5]

Resignation and Impeachment

The Presidential tenure can be interrupted not only by restriction on reelection but by others means—resignation, for example, a means for which the Constitution provides. No President has ever resigned, but Woodrow Wilson came closest of all to committing that final act of voluntary separation. An admiring student of British governmental practice, which turns upon the Prime Minister's periodic resignation to seek a vote of public confidence for his party, Wilson twice as President contemplated resigning. If his rival in the 1916 Presidential race, Charles Evans Hughes, had won, he proposed to resign to avoid a lame-duck Presidency in the midst of world crisis. His plan was first to ask his Secretary of State, Robert Lansing, to resign so he could appoint President-elect Hughes as his successor. Thereupon President Wilson and Vice President Marshall would both resign, permitting Hughes's ascent to the Presidency under the existing succession law.[6] Wilson's electoral victory rendered the novel plan unnecessary. In a later crisis, the fight for the Versailles peace treaty in 1919, Wilson briefly weighed the tactic of resigning and then immediately running again in a special Presidential election permitted by the Succession Act of 1886 then in force. His election presumably would have expressed a national desire for membership in the League and sustained confidence in him. Wilson dropped this plan. The approaching elections of 1920 seemed to him to promise to be "a great and solemn" referendum on the treaty.[7] In 1946, following the Congressional elections in which the Democrats lost control of Congress for the first time in sixteen years, Senator J. William Fulbright of Arkansas, presumably in a spirit of helpfulness, proposed that President Truman resign.[8] Truman rejected the suggestion crustily and marched on to reelection in 1948 and the restoration of full Democratic control of Congress. President Eisenhower, after his stroke in 1957, considered resigning, driven by doubts that he could bear the burdens of the office. To test his capacity, he attended, against his doctors' protests, a NATO conference in Paris. Intending to resign if the results proved unsatisfactory, Eisenhower participated successfully in the strenuous activities of the conference and was sufficiently enheartened to stay on in office.[9]

The President can also leave office involuntarily. If he can be "hired," he can also be fired, for causes enumerated in Article II of the Constitution: "treason, bribery, or other high crimes and misdemeanors." Imitating existing state constitutions, the Founding Fathers empowered the House of Representatives to impeach the President, and the Senate, sitting as a law court with the Chief Justice of the United States presiding, to conduct the trial. A two-thirds vote of the Senators present is necessary for conviction. The penalties that the Constitution brings down upon the convicted President are removal from office, disqualification for "any office of honor, trust, or profit under the United States," and liability to "indictment, trial, judgment, and punishment, according to law." Although the introduction of impeachment resolutions is a favorite indulgence of Congressmen embittered by the spectacle of activist Presidents, only once has the necessary support developed. Andrew Johnson enjoys distinction as the only President who has walked the impeachment gangplank. Far more important, he, and the Presidency with him, came out of it alive. By a single vote Johnson missed conviction and the Presidency was spared.

Johnson's impeachment is memorable not merely as supreme drama but as an enduring object lesson to those who, seeking to improve the American governmental system, propose to link Congress more intimately with the Presidency. The Johnson case demonstrates the capacity of legislators to convert a solemn judicial function into what Gideon Welles, Johnson's Secretary of the Navy, termed "a deed of extreme partisanship."[10]

The impeachment was built upon the rotten foundation of the Tenure of Office Act of 1867, which denied the President the right to remove civil officials, including members of his cabinet, without Senatorial consent. Presidents had been removing cabinet Secretaries since the days of Washington. By the act of 1867 Congress was contravening precedent and stripping Johnson of control of his administration. Convinced that the Tenure Act was unconstitutional, Johnson requested and then ordered Secretary of War Edwin M. Stanton to resign and appointed General Lorenzo Thomas his successor. When Thomas appeared at the War Department, Stanton barricaded himself behind his office door.[11]

On February 28, 1868, the House voted to impeach the President for "high crimes and misdemeanors." Eleven articles of impeachment were drawn, ten centering upon Stanton's removal. The remaining article, contrived from garbled newspaper accounts of the President's speeches, charged, among other things, that he used unseemly language and spoke in a loud voice. Johnson meanwhile expected to knock the props from under the impeachment proceedings by obtaining a ruling from the Supreme Court endorsing his views on the Tenure of Office law. But the Court, in a spasm of "judicial restraint," declined to act.

The ensuing impeachment enterprise reeked with self-serving politics. If Johnson were convicted and deposed, the new President of the United States, owing to the Vice-Presidential vacancy and the line of succession in the applicable law of 1792, would be Ben Wade of Ohio, the vulgar and vituperative President pro tempore of the Senate. When Wade's participation in the trial was objected to because of his not inconsiderable personal stake, the Senator replied with simple finality that he saw nothing wrong with serving as a judge. He would do impartial justice, he said, and was sworn. Chief Justice

Salmon P. Chase, who presided, also wanted to be President, having for the office a craving that Lincoln once likened to insanity. By day Chase conducted the trial and by night he wrote letters building his claim to the next Democratic Presidential nomination. That the trial would ooze with low politics was instantly apparent when after the President's counsel requested forty days to prepare their case, with its numerous intricacies of law and fact, they were permitted ten.

The trial itself was a garish extravaganza lasting eleven and a half weeks. The thousand tickets printed for each day, and valid only for that day, were furiously competed for. Diplomats and Senators' wives and daughters, blooming with finery, crammed the galleries, along with scores of reporters, including Anthony Trollope, the distinguished novelist, who came from Britain to cover the proceedings, and Henry Adams, who described the scene as a national nightmare of unspeakable crudity.

Of forty-one witnesses, only sixteen appeared for the defense. Johnson proposed to testify in his own behalf but in view of his tendency to outlandish statement was fortunately dissuaded. The Chief Justice, empowered within narrowly defined limits to rule on points of law, heroically put political ambition aside and rose to the full height of his responsibilities. According to the Senate rules specially adopted for the trial, if one Senator objected to the Chief Justice's holding, the matter was voted by the entire body. The Chief Justice was overruled seventeen times, in most instances for the purpose of suppressing evidence favorable to the President.

President Johnson, for all of his reputation for wild epithet and the big blunder, was a model of decorum. He bore patiently the lengthy conferences with his counsel on tactics and fine points of fact and law. At night he read books on immortality and Joseph Addison's dramatization of the last days of Cato the Younger, who chose to die by his own hand rather than submit to Julius Caesar's dictation. At Johnson's direction, a White House secretary researched the trial and execution of Charles I of England. The President's chief act of self-assertion lay in putting his case before the people in interviews with several friendly reporters. Said the President,

> Suppose Congress should pass a bill abolishing the veto power. . . . Suppose it should pass a dozen bills of this character—would the President be constitutionally bound to execute them as laws? Would it not be his duty, as in the present instance, to seek immediately judgment in the Supreme Court?[12]

When the President was told that the Radicals were not above using money to obtain his conviction, and that perhaps he, too, should stoop to that expedient, he refused.

The Radicals indeed were desperate. The vote on Article XI, the first impeachment article to be disposed of, fell short of the two-thirds majority necessary for conviction. To revive their wilting plot, the Radicals maneuvered the Senate into an adjournment of ten days for the known but carefully unacknowledged purpose of lining up votes for Johnson's conviction. The adjournment occurred only after the Chief Justice's ruling against it was overridden. During the ten-day interlude a massive machinery of pressures and intrigue was unloosed upon Senators who were still on the fence or who conceivably might be lured or bullied into abandoning Johnson and voting for his conviction. After some days of effort the machinators discovered from their tally sheets that the issue's outcome turned upon the vote of Edmund G. Ross, a Radical soldier-journalist of Kansas who was believed to oppose Johnson. To make certain, the Radicals swung their cannonade full-square upon the Senator. The low character of their pressures led Ross to see through the Radicals' flimsy case. But the dread consequences of resisting it gave him pause. "Almost literally," he wrote of his moment of truth, he was looking down into his "open grave." "Friends, position, fortune, everything that makes life desirable to an ambitious man," he said, "were about to be swept away by the breath of my mouth, perhaps forever."[13] Ross's tough moral fiber ultimately prevailed. He voted for Johnson, and the Presidency was saved. Senator Lyman Trumbull, who also sided with the President, captured the significance of the lamentable episode in explaining his vote:

> Once set the example of impeaching a President for what, when the excitement of the hour shall have subsided, will be regarded as insufficient cause, and no future President will be safe who happens to differ with the majority of the House and two-thirds of the Senate on any measure deemed by them important, particularly if of a political character.[14]

Disability

The President, as the Constitution anticipates and history demonstrates, may on occasion fall victim to crushing illness or to death. Seven Presidents (one out of five) have died in office, four by assassination. A sick President may be unable to discharge the duties of his office. According to Richard Hansen's computations, the cumulative periods of actual Presidential disability add up to a full year in which the country was "without a President." Such periods unfortunately occurred during difficult times, when large issues demanded the Chief Executive's full vigor and skill. Until the Twenty-fifth Amendment was adopted in 1967, the problem of disability was treated by provisions in Article II whose language was a quagmire of ambiguity.[15] Article II reads,

> In case of [the President's] inability to discharge the powers and duties of the said office, the same shall devolve on the Vice President, and the Congress may by law provide for the case of . . . inability, both of the President and Vice President, declaring what officer shall then act as

President, and such officer shall act accordingly, until the disability be removed or a President shall be elected.

Neither here nor elsewhere in the Constitution were the following questions answered: Who is authorized to say whether a President is unable to discharge the powers and duties of his office? If he is unable, does the office become vacant? To what does the Vice President succeed when the President is disabled—to the "powers and duties of the said office" or to the office itself? What is the election referred to—the next regular Presidential election or a special election called by Congress?

Twice in American experience Presidents have been incapacitated for extended periods. President Garfield lay stricken after July 2, 1881, when he was shot just before leaving Washington by train for a class reunion at Williams College. The assassin's bullet struck a vertebra of his spinal column and became deeply embedded in the muscles of his back. The White House was converted into a hospital, and fans in the President's sickroom blew cool breezes over ice cubes to provide relief from the capital's broiling summer.[16]

The President, a large, rugged man who faced his ordeal with unflagging heroism, rallied through most of July. In August he passed through cycles of decline and improvement. Despite several surgical probes, the President's doctors failed to locate the bullet. Alexander Graham Bell assisted in the vain search by devising a special detecting electrical device. Meanwhile the wound became infected and the bullet encysted. As the President's fever rose and fell, his great form wasted and his strength ebbed. On September 6 he was transported by rail with maximum precautions to Elberon on the New Jersey coast, where it was hoped the sea air would by some miracle rally him. But his strength only dwindled, and in a few days he died.

During his entire illness, President Garfield committed only one official act. He signed an extradition paper, prepared in the State Department, after a physician read it aloud. He saw only Mrs. Garfield and his doctors and had no visitors except one day at Elberon, when members of his cabinet filed in for brief interviews. The President had been fretting over the lapse of cabinet meetings, and by prearrangement the Secretaries assured him that all was well and nothing required his attention.[17]

In reality this was not so. The Star Route frauds,* inherited from the previous Hayes administration, still bedeviled the Post Office Department, and the gush of illicit dollars from the United States Treasury into corrupt hands continued. The President's isolation brought to a standstill Secretary of State James G. Blaine's effort to modify the existing Clayton-Bulwer Treaty in the interest of the proposed Nicaraguan canal. (Blaine's ultimate purpose

---

* These frauds occurred in the carriage of mails over roads marked by asterisks in the official records and popularly known as "star routes." The Post Office scandalously overpaid certain persons operating such lines, including the chairman of the Republican National Committee.

in this complex maneuver was to establish an isthmian canal under United States control.) A conference of American republics that the President had called was postponed.[18]

As the neglected problems accumulated, demands spiraled in the press, in Congress, and among the cabinet that Vice President Arthur take over the duties of the incapacitated President. The cabinet, which was most distressed by the ravages of neglect, earnestly discussed the Vice President's possible assumption of Presidential authority, a prospect that repelled them. Agitated meetings in the Secretaries' offices and homes quickly revealed disagreement on a thorny issue of constitutional interpretation. Four of the seven Secretaries believed that Arthur's exercise of Presidential power would make him President for the remainder of the existing term and would immediately and permanently oust Garfield from the office. The Attorney General, Wayne MacVeagh, the chief law interpreter of the executive branch, reportedly took this view. A minority of the Secretaries held that Arthur could occupy the Presidency only for the duration of Garfield's illness, and that the latter, upon his recovery, would resume the office. In time the cabinet concluded that since the decision was of such large consequence, it ought to be discussed with the President first. But as the President's condition worsened, the consultation was deferred in the fear that its shock might speed his death.

Legalistic interpretation was not the only bond joining those in the cabinet in opposition to the Vice President's assumption of Presidential duties. Arthur, in their view, belonged to a low order of politicians—the "Stalwart" Republicans—who had wished Grant to be nominated for a third term and fought Garfield with waspish oratory and savage deed ever since the onset of his Presidency. Indeed Stalwart rancor had inflamed the President's crazed assassin, who shouted in emptying his pistol, "I am a Stalwart and now Arthur is President!" Arthur was not helped either by his friendship with the notorious Roscoe Conkling, the Stalwart leader, upon whose advice he was known to depend. Should Arthur become President, it was feared, Conkling would come along too.

Chester Arthur, for his part, was facing the question of his assumption of the Presidency with characteristic prudence. He stayed out of public view, dodged the press, and remained in New York as much as possible. When on occasion he had to venture to Washington, he avoided his own residence and found seclusion in the home of his friend Senator John P. Jones of Nevada. The most painful element in Arthur's situation was the cold suspicion with which the President's friends beheld him. Arthur felt the full bite of the frosty atmosphere when he called one night at the White House, shortly after the attack, as a courteous demonstration of concern for the stricken President. The Vice President was ushered to an office where the full cabinet sat gathered in vigil. He paused uncertainly in the doorway, waiting for an invitation to enter. None came; no one moved to greet him. The cabinet stared with unanimous hostility. Arthur was about to withdraw in painful confusion when another visitor who came along greeted him cordially and drew him into the room. Several cabinet Secretaries then extended the Vice President the minimum amenities.[19]

For all of their revulsion toward Arthur, the cabinet in the later days of Garfield's illness again considered the question of the Vice President's succession. To the harried Secretaries the mounting pile of neglected problems left no choice. Postmaster General Thomas L. James was dispatched to New York to ascertain Arthur's views. The Vice President's answer was swift and categorical. Under no circumstances would he assume the responsibilities of the Presidency while Garfield was alive. The Vice President held to his point and public problems drifted. Not until his own formal investiture in the Presidency after Garfield's death did Arthur touch the power of the office.[20]

The other occasion of extended Presidential incapacity occurred during the second administration of Woodrow Wilson, at a time immeasurably more serious than Garfield's. During the ailing Wilson's taxing Western trip in September 1919, to rally the people behind the League of Nations, the President collapsed and was rushed back by train to Washington. Conflicting versions persist of the onset of the President's illness. One, by Mrs. Wilson and Rear Admiral Cary T. Grayson, the President's physician, contends that Wilson "collapsed" in the West, returned to Washington, and three days later suffered a stroke described by Mrs. Wilson as "paralyzing the left side of his body. An arm and one leg were useless."[21] A contrasting version by Joe Tumulty, the President's trusted secretary, holds that the stroke occurred in Colorado, during the Western journey. At 4 A.M. September 26 in Pueblo, where the Presidential train had stopped, Tumulty was aroused by a knock on the door of his sleeping compartment. It was Dr. Grayson with word that the President was seriously ill. Tumulty rushed to the train's drawing room where the President, fully dressed, was seated in a chair. Tumulty stood transfixed by the spectacle. "His face was pale and wan," the secretary later described it. "One side of it had fallen, and his condition was indeed pitiful to behold. . . . His left arm and leg refused to function. I then realized that the President's whole left side was paralyzed."[22]

The White House was again transformed into a hospital. The President, who was not expected to live long, somehow clung to the edge of existence. Although his body was broken, his mind was clear. "Physically he was very weak," observed Grayson, "but mentally very alert."[23] Meanwhile, the nation was caught up in the cumbrous transition from warmaking to peacemaking. The peace treaty, with its controversial League of Nations provision, was before the Senate at midcourse, where it faced the hostility of the President's archrival, Henry Cabot Lodge. On the autumn agenda were scheduled visits of European dignitaries with the President. Domestically the economy was demobilizing to peacetime footing. In the din and lash of public business, the President lay crippled, his true condition known only to his wife, his physician, and the little ring of medical specialists who surrounded him and desperately administered their skills. The President, in their general opinion, was hopelessly beyond recovery. A year and a half of his term stretched ahead. What was to be done?

Dr. Francis X. Dercum, the eminent nerve authority, told Mrs. Wilson, "Madam, it is a grave situation, but I think you can solve it. Have everything come to you; weigh the importance of each matter, and see if it is possible by consultations with the respective heads of the Departments to solve them without the guidance of your husband. In this way you can save him a great deal. But always keep in mind that every time you take him a new anxiety or problem to excite him, you are turning a knife in an open wound. His nerves are crying out for rest, and any excitement is torture to him."

"Then," replied Mrs. Wilson, "had he better not resign, let Mr. Marshall [the Vice President] succeed to the Presidency and he himself get that complete rest that is so vital to his life?"

"No, not if you feel equal to what I suggested," Dr. Dercum said. "For Mr. Wilson to resign would have a bad effect on the country, and a serious effect on our patient."[24]

The *modus operandi* suggested by Dr. Dercum was quickly instituted for the remainder of Wilson's term. Officials coming to the White House took up with Mrs. Wilson business that hitherto they had discussed with the President. The brave First Lady applied herself conscientiously to understanding the intricacies that poured upon her and to reporting them in as precise a language as possible to her husband. Mrs. Wilson said in describing her stewardship,

> I studied every paper, sent from the different Secretaries or Senators, and tried to digest and present in tabloid form the things that, despite my vigilance, had to go to the President. I, myself, never made a single decision regarding the disposition of public affairs. The only decision that was mine was what was important and what was not, and the *very* important decision of when to present matters to my husband.[25]

In deciding what was important, Mrs. Wilson, of course, was making a vital kind of policy decision.

Even the trusted Tumulty, who had been accustomed to seeing the President whenever he chose, bent to the new procedure. Colonel Edward M. House, the President's intimate adviser and confidant, was cut off from all access. He was not invited and never ventured to the White House; his several letters to the President were neither answered nor acknowledged. Only Mrs. Wilson and Dr. Grayson saw the President.

Somehow the public business limped forward. The hurdle of the State of the Union message, an annual and unalterable constitutional requirement, was managed when cabinet Secretaries, acting in accordance with the traditional procedure, submitted paragraphs reflecting their departmental concerns to the White House. There Tumulty received them and pursued further procedures for which no tradition existed. The Presidential secretary wove the paragraphs together into a single document of reasonable coherence. It was read to Wilson and, with a few changes, the President approved it. On his better days, the President read state papers or listened as Mrs. Wilson read. He signed documents and in bursts of strength dictated notes for Senator Gilbert Hitchcock's guidance in the treaty fight.

But the President's dedicated helpers and his own valiant effort could not tame the mounting suspicion and unrest in the world outside. Colonel House reported that the cabinet Secretaries, cut off from all direct contact with the President, were "greatly exercised over the President's inability to transact executive business." To House, Secretary of State Robert Lansing confided his suspicion that the President was not really writing the papers purporting to come from him. Senator Hitchcock, curious and anxious for the President's guidance in the League fight, was permitted an interview of an hour and five minutes with Wilson. The stricken President was full of fight. "I am a sick man, lying in this bed, but I am going to debate this issue with these gentlemen," he said of his Senatorial obstructors, "in their respective states whenever they come up for reelection if I have breath enough in my body to carry on the fight."[26] On December 4 the Senate, collectively overcome by curiosity, appointed Hitchcock and Albert B. Fall, soon destined for exposure in the muck of Teapot Dome, as a committee to inquire into the condition of the President. After a visit with Wilson, they reported publicly that his mind was clear and that he was recovering. The baseless and misleading character of the latter finding appalled Mrs. Wilson. Nor did the Senators' reassurances deter several sensational newspapers from contending that the President was tightly secluded because he was insane, or that he was dead and his death was being kept secret. Several Republican Senators, according to the New York Times, were studying Wilson's signature on Presidential communications to the upper chamber for the possibility of forgery. One of these Senators eventually declared that either two of the signatures under study were not Wilson's, or, if they were, he had been assisted in signing his name.[27]

The cabinet Secretary most concerned over the leaderless state of affairs was the head of the senior executive department, Secretary of State Robert Lansing. A responsible man of granitic integrity, he decided it was time to act. He arranged a private meeting with Presidential secretary Tumulty in the cabinet room. As diplomatically as possible, Lansing said he wished to suggest that in view of Wilson's incapacity the Vice President be called in to act in lieu of the President. To reinforce his suggestion, he cited the disability provisions of the Constitution. Tumulty was outraged at this seeming invitation to mutiny, and candidly vented his displeasure. Who, he asked, could authoritatively determine the fact of the President's disability? Those having the best information of it, answered Lansing—Dr. Grayson and Tumulty himself. Dr. Grayson, when he learned of the proposal, helped Tumulty to kill it quickly. If "anyone outside the White House," Tumulty warned Lansing, attempted to certify that the President was unable to carry on his duties, the President's physician and secretary would jointly repudiate the notion.[28]

Tumulty's rebuff did not quiet Lansing's conscience, agonized by the drift of affairs. The Secretary of State tried another tactic. The cabinet, the President's chief body of counselors, had not met since the commencement of Wilson's illness. If the cabinet were to meet occasionally on its own initiative, Lansing reasoned, the country's confidence would be buoyed. He placed this new inspiration before his fellow Secretaries. Their response was favorable, and Lansing as senior Secretary began calling and holding meetings of his fellow department heads in his office. That Lansing took the venture seriously is attested by the fact that in the first four months of Wilson's illness twenty-one cabinet meetings were called. When Wilson ultimately learned of them, he promptly wrote to Lansing pointing out that under established Constitutional procedure only the President could convene the department heads into conference and no one but he and Congress were entitled to request their views, collectively or individually, on public questions. Wilson's letter blazed with implications that Lansing's resignation would not be unwelcome. It was quickly forthcoming.[29]

Goaded by Lansing's initiative, Wilson rallied his feeble strength sufficiently some two months later to meet with the cabinet. It was a brief and sad affair. "The President looked old, worn, and haggard," Secretary of Agriculture David Houston said of the event. "It was enough to make one weep to look at him. One of his arms was useless. [In speaking] his jaw tended to drop on one side, or seemed to do so. His voice was very weak and strained. . . . He put up a brave front and spent several minutes cracking jokes." Several more cabinet meetings, each brief, were subsequently held, with Mrs. Wilson looking in regularly and signaling their close.[30]

In contrast to the venturesome Lansing, Vice President Thomas R. Marshall was a study in monumental caution. He shrank from every suggestion that he take over any of Wilson's duties. The Vice President, according to the New York *Times,* said he would not act unless Wilson or the cabinet requested it, and then only at the express approval of both houses of Congress. When legislators proposed that a federal court writ be secured directing the Vice President to act as President, he retorted that he would "never do such a thing in a thousand years." The Vice President's instinctive caution was stiffened by ugly forebodings. If he acted as President, he told Ira E. Bennett, editor of the Washington *Post,* he would surely be assassinated and the country thrown "into civil war." In discussing the predicament with his secretary one day, the Vice President said, "I am not going to seize the place and then have Wilson— recovered—come around and say, 'Get off, you usurper.' "[31] Marshall rode out the crisis by doing nothing, and history remembers him only for articulating an aspiration long since dashed by inflation—"What this country needs is a good five-cent cigar."

In the spring of 1920 Wilson made some gain. He could sit in his wheel chair, in the White House garden or on the South Portico, dictate to a secretary, and take up business with Mrs. Wilson. But his improvement was only tentative. When James M. Cox and Franklin D. Roosevelt, the Democratic Presidential and Vice-Presidential candidates of 1920, visited Wilson in the summer of that year, Roosevelt reported afterward that Wilson was unable to speak except to mumble a few broken words.[32]

The several illnesses of Dwight D. Eisenhower, although fortunately less severe than those of his predecessors, stirred national and world concern. In 1955 President Eisenhower sustained a coronary thrombosis, in 1956 an ileitis attack and operation, and in 1957 a mild stroke. In his first and most serious illness the President was totally removed from governmental affairs for only four days, after which he initialed papers. Sixteen weeks passed, however, before the President resumed his normal workload. Scarcely had he returned to full duty when the second illness crashed upon him. Both illnesses combined left the President partially disabled for twenty-two weeks.

Eisenhower's first illness raised a question that was settled then and for his subsequent lesser illnesses. During the President's disability, full or partial, who should discharge his duties? Although the Constitution pointed to the Vice President, Richard M. Nixon, the smooth-working team of White House staff and department heads posed an alternative. So freely had Eisenhower delegated duties and authority to his aides since the outset of his administration that they could function almost autonomously in his absence forced by illness. The "team's" director was Sherman Adams, "the assistant to the President," widely viewed as general manager of the executive branch. Another member of large importance was James Hagerty, the administration's chief public relations officer, the press secretary, who stood high in the President's esteem.

Two days after the President's heart seizure, Hagerty touched off the issue of who acts for an incapacitated President by disclosing that he had asked the Acting Attorney General, William F. Rogers, "for an opinion on any action that might be necessary at any time for delegation of powers." The next day Vice President Nixon told the press, "It is quite clear, of course, that the Attorney General must give an interpretation as to how some technical details can be handled during the time the President is away. There are many legal problems involved." The Nixon and Hagerty statements were interpreted as faintly auguring a Vice-Presidential takeover. Thereupon Sherman Adams arrived in Washington from a European sojourn and quickly dominated and recomposed the situation. He conferred with Nixon and Rogers. The discussion's outcome and Adams' mastery are disclosed in Rogers' statement to the press afterward that "it may not be necessary to make a formal delegation of powers." Thereafter Hagerty in press statements referred to Adams repeatedly as the President's "deputy" rather than the President's "assistant."[33] "The announcements served to emphasize," noted the New York *Times*, "that the powers of the President still rested with General Eisenhower and no one else [and] that in the exercise of these powers, Mr. Adams, and not the Vice President, was the chief assistant to the President."

Under the emerging formula Adams and the department heads handled the regular operations of the executive branch. Nixon took on certain established, more or less ceremonial capacities. He made public addresses and appearances and presided at meetings of the cabinet and the National Security Council, as he had done during past Presidential absences. Press conferences with Hagerty were supplemented by occasional Nixon press conferences where high-level comment was indispensable.

The executive functioning was far smoother during Eisenhower's illnesses than during those of his predecessors. His administrative machinery displayed an impressive capacity for self-direction, and thanks largely to Vice President Nixon's exemplary restraint there were no struggles for power. Conducting business from his own office on Capitol Hill or by visits to the departments, he shunned the White House. His comments to the press were scrupulously noncommittal. He turned aside admonitions like Styles Bridges' "You are the constitutional second-in-command and you ought to assume the leadership. Don't let the White House clique take command."[34]

Eisenhower's only incapacity of any duration, the heart attack, struck during a governmental lull. Congress was in recess, no international meetings or moves were afoot, public urgencies were few. In contrast, the third illness— the stroke—occurred during a critical period. The Russians had put their first Sputnik into orbit only a month before, and the prestige of America's military and technological might had become murkily suspect at home and abroad. A NATO meeting of heads of state was three weeks off. The early signs of the acute 1958 economic recession were visible. Executive-Congressional meetings to lay the coming year's legislative programs were scheduled for two weeks later. But the gathering crisis was confined by the President's quick recovery. The day following his stroke he met with aides, and on the second day he worked on executive business in his rooms. Two weeks later he was off to Paris for the NATO meetings.

Handling Disability: The Twenty-fifth Amendment

The nation's several encounters with Presidential illness and its attendant constitutional and administrative problems stirred wide and thoughtful concern, which finally led to some action in the 1950's and 1960's. The committee hearings of Congressman Emanuel Celler in 1956 and Senator Estes Kefauver in 1958 and 1963 and Senator Birch Bayh in 1964 tapped the thinking of public men and scholars, and Presidents Eisenhower, Kennedy, and Johnson were moved to institute special measures. The climax of this effort was the passage of the Twenty-fifth Amendment in 1967. The amendment, often known as the Bayh amendment after its chief Congressional manager, Senator Birch Bayh of Indiana, was carried by an irresistible momentum after President Kennedy's assassination. Former New York Senator Kenneth Keating reflected the mood of Congress when he declared that "as distasteful as it is to entertain the thought, a matter of inches spelled the difference between the painless death of John F. Kennedy and the possibility of his permanent incapacity to exercise the duties of the highest office of the land."[35] An awareness swept through Congress that careful action could no longer be postponed to protect the nation from the peril of a headless government in the nuclear age. However, discussion and action were complicated by the multitude of proposals advanced and by the dispersal of attention over several key questions.

1. What is disability? The Founding Fathers left the question unanswered in the Constitution, nor does the Twenty-fifth Amendment undertake to define it. Disability encompasses literally dozens of conditions that defy exhaustive cataloguing. Ruth Silva, the leading authority on the subject, concludes that the Constitution contemplates "any *de facto* inability, whatever the cause or the duration, if it occurs at a time when the urgency of public business requires executive action."[36]

Disability is clearly not limited to physical illness but extends to mental illness as well and covers periods when the President is missing or captured in military operations. In an era of intercontinental missiles, when decisions on which national survival may turn must be taken in minutes, any definition of inability must be made carefully to include all contingencies. "The ever-present possibility of an attack on the United States was always hanging over us," Richard Nixon wrote of the brief period of Eisenhower's unavailability following his heart attack, "Would the President be well enough to make a decision? If not, who had the authority to push the button?" Or again, Eisenhower's ileitis seizure necessitated an operation at Walter Reed Hospital where the President was under anesthesia for two hours. "The country," Eisenhower commented afterward to Nixon, "was without a Chief Executive, the armed forces without a Commander-in-Chief."[37]

2. Who determines disability? The question is specifically responded to by two actions resulting from the discussions of the 1950's and 1960's. President Eisenhower, after futilely recommending a disability amendment, concluded an "understanding," in writing, with Vice President Nixon, which was disclosed in outline on February 26, 1958 and five days later, under popular pressure, in detail. Under the Eisenhower plan, the President himself decides his disability and informs the Vice President. The manner of communication, whether oral or in writing, was not indicated.[38] The Eisenhower plan was perpetuated in the Kennedy administration by the announcement on August 11, 1961, of an identical agreement between the President and Vice President Johnson. Soon after his accession to the Presidency, Johnson

reportedly continued the agreement with Speaker John W. McCormack, then next in line in the Presidential succession. After the 1964 elections, President Johnson made a similar arrangement with Vice President Humphrey.

The Twenty-fifth Amendment, ratified February 10, 1967, also provides that the President determine his own disability but requires that he communicate his finding to the President pro tempore of the Senate and the Speaker of the House in writing.

But what if the President refuses to proclaim his disability or because of his physical and mental circumstances cannot? The Eisenhower plan stipulated that the Vice President would then decide the question of disability "after such consultation as seems to him appropriate under the circumstances." The Twenty-fifth Amendment provides that the Vice President, acting in concert with a majority of the cabinet, or of such "other body" as Congress may by law provide, could advise the President pro tempore of the Senate and the Speaker that the President was disabled. The "other body" was described in Congressional debate as a commission of private citizens, doctors, or psychiatrists, who might be summoned to pass judgment upon the President's competence.

Most discussions of the disability problem agreed that the Vice President should not have to bear sole responsibility for finding the President disabled but that he should have help, preferably from the cabinet. The cabinet, the argument goes, thanks to its daily contacts with the President, would be best informed of his plight. The department Secretaries' deepest inclination would be to act loyally and fairly to the President, since their job security depends upon him.

The cabinet's critics hold that it would be too blinded by self-interested loyalty ever to certify the President's disability. The possibility of retaliation by the President, when he recovered sufficiently, would encourage cabinet inaction. Wilson dismissed Lansing, and Harry S. Truman once declared in post-Presidential utterances that if his cabinet had ever declared him disabled while he was confined on the flat of his back, his first act upon rising would be to fire every culprit who had supported the finding.

The cabinet's limitations suggest the wisdom of the "other body," the alternative contained in the Twenty-fifth Amendment, whose members might include distinguished citizens and leading physicians and psychiatrists. Disability is most likely to be largely a medical question, for which authentic answers are best provided by qualified professionals. Disability is never only a medical question, however. It poses a tandem political question: Does the public interest at the time require the exercise of Presidential power? Doctors have no inherent superiority over other citizens in assessing "public interest." Even in medical questions genuine professional differences hold sway in diagnostic judgment.

There seems to be little prospect that justices of the United States Supreme Court will be available for duty on the "other body." Some years ago the Court bowed out from any connection with a special disability commission then under consideration. On January 20, 1958, Chief Justice Earl Warren wrote to a House Judiciary subcommittee in behalf of his fellow justices,

> It has been the belief of all of us that because of the separation of powers in our Government, the nature of the judicial process, the possibility of a controversy of this character coming to the Court, and the danger of disqualification which might result in lack of quorum, it would be inadvisable for any member of the Court to serve on such a Commission.[39]

3. If the President is disabled, to what does the Vice President succeed— to the "powers and duties" of the office, or to the office itself? Does he become Acting President, serving temporarily until the disabled President has recovered, or does he take over permanently for the remainder of the term? These troublesome questions can be blamed on the Constitution's ambiguity in Article II and on Vice President John Tyler's astute contrariness at his succession to the Presidency in 1841 upon William Henry Harrison's death. He was not merely "Acting" President, Tyler contended; he was succeeding to the Presidential office itself, and was President in the fullest sense of the word.

All six of the other Vice Presidents who have been elevated upon the President's death have clasped Tyler's precedent. Indeed Arthur and Marshall were deterred from taking over from their infirm Presidents by the wide opinion of their fellow public men that a disabled President once pushed aside could never return. The Constitution, they reasoned, did not allow for two Presidents to exist simultaneously, one acting and the other ailing.

The agreement between the last three Presidents and those next in line met the ambiguity head-on. Upon the President's disability, the Vice President "would serve as Acting President until the inability had ended." The Twenty-fifth Amendment should settle the whole problem once and for all. It declares that when the President is disabled, the Vice President shall assume "the powers and duties of the office as Acting President."

4. Who determines when the President's disability ends? Both the Twenty-fifth Amendment and the agreement adhered to by Eisenhower, Kennedy, and Johnson provide that the President shall decide. But what if the President wants to get back to work too soon, before he is sufficiently recovered from his disability? The amendment specifies that if the Vice President and a majority of the cabinet or of the "other body" did not agree that the President had recovered, then Congress would resolve the issue. It could, by two-thirds vote of each house, decide that the President was still unable to discharge his duties, whereupon the Vice President would continue as Acting President.

While under Congressional debate, the features of the Twenty-fifth Amendment permitting the Vice President and the "other body" to find the President disabled, as an alternative to a finding by the Vice President endorsed by the cabinet, were criticized. It was charged that such provisions would enable the Vice President to "shop around" for support of his view that the President was disabled. Senator Albert Gore warned that "this nation could undergo the potentially disastrous spectacle of competing claims to the power of the Presidency."[40] Senator Bayh contended that such a power scramble was unlikely, and the bulk of the testimony before his subcommittee contended that the amendment's disability provisions would be invoked only in the most extreme circumstances and that in the attending atmosphere of crisis executive officials and Congress could be expected to act responsibly. Witnesses paid no heed to the ghost of Andrew Johnson weeping at their folly. They were more impressed that in the nuclear age ambiguity was no longer tolerable and that it must be displaced with clearly defined rules and procedures. Committee witnesses, representatives of the legal profession, and citizen groups sounded a loud "amen" to Walter Lippmann's observation that the Twenty-fifth Amendment is "a great deal better than an endless search . . . for the absolutely perfect solution . . . which will never be found, and . . . is not necessary."[41]

Succession

The Founding Fathers, who were geniuses at spotting thorny problems and passing them on to hapless posterity to wrestle with, applied their sure touch to Presidential succession. The all-seeing Fathers anticipated the calamitous day when a double vacancy might befall the nation—when both President and Vice President might be unavailable because of death, resignation, impeachment, or disability. The Fathers, accordingly, posed no solution, but simply empowered Congress to enact a law "declaring what officer shall then act as President." Congress has thrice passed laws, the last in 1947, and each time its labors have provoked criticism and sent citizens scurrying for better remedies.

In its three laws, Congress vacillated between drawing upon its own leaders and the members of the cabinet in laying the lines of succession. Considerations of pure political science have seldom motivated Congress's actions. The first law of 1792 was no solution rooted in Olympian wisdom but a narrow partisan act. The law's object was to prevent the succession of Secretary of State Thomas Jefferson. The conservative leaders of Congress, who abhorred Jefferson, simply by-passed him and voted one of themselves into the succession. If the Presidency and the Vice-Presidency were vacant, the President pro tempore of the Senate, and after him the Speaker, would succeed. Neither officer was to become President upon the takeover, but only Acting President. If the double vacancy happened within the first two years and seven months of the Presidential term, Congress was required to call a special election "forthwith."

In 1886 Congress passed a new law, the pendulum now swinging to the cabinet. In a future double vacancy the succession would run from the Secretary of State to the Secretary of the Interior in the order in which the departments were established. No Secretary could be wafted by fate and the act into the Presidential chair if he could not satisfy the regular constitutional qualifications for the Presidency. The 1792 act's special election feature was dropped.

During Harry Truman's first weeks in the Presidency, into which he had been catapulted by Franklin Roosevelt's death, he perceived grievous limitations in the 1886 act. He incorporated his concern and recommendations for a new succession law in a special message to Congress on June 19, 1945. The 1886 act, placing the Secretary of State, an appointed and not an elected officer, next in line for the Presidency in effect permitted Truman to name his own successor. "I do not believe that in a democracy," the President declared, "this power should rest with the Chief Executive." In the new legislation he proposed Truman contended that after the President and Vice President in the succession line should come the Speaker of the House of Representatives, because he "is elected in his own district" and "is also elected to be the presiding officer of the House by a vote of all the representatives of all the people of the country." After the Speaker, in the Truman plan, would come the President pro tempore who is elected first by the people of his state and then by the whole Senate. Following the President pro tempore would be "the members of the Cabinet as provided now by law."[42]

Since Edward Stettinius, Jr., a career businessman, was Secretary of State at the time and Sam Rayburn, a career politician, the Speaker, the House of Representatives passed a bill reflecting Truman's views with vast cheers for Rayburn and a proud sense of doing something nice for one's own. When the bill reached the upper chamber, however, James F. Byrnes, a distinguished and popular former Senator and Congressman, had replaced Stettinius as Secretary of State. Congressional enthusiasm for the succession bill shriveled. It was nearly dead when the Republican triumph in the 1946 Congressional elections suddenly revived it. The bill passed in 1947, and Truman dutifully signed it, thereby establishing not a Democratic but a Republican Speaker, Joe Martin, as his successor. After the Speaker, under the 1947 act, come the President pro tempore of the Senate, the Secretaries of State, the Treasury, and Defense, the Attorney General, the Postmaster General, and the Secretaries of the Interior, Agriculture, Commerce, and Labor. The Secretaries of Health, Education and Welfare, Housing and Urban Development, and Transportation now also figure in the succession.

Like bygone succession laws, the 1947 act stirred more reproach than praise. It trampled upon the separation of powers principle by bringing two legislative officers into the Presidential line. Truman's estimable image of the Speakership as a popular "democratic" office is open to challenge. The Speaker's electorate is local rather than national, his district a patch of a few square miles on the face of a continental nation. His elevation to the Speakership reflects not simply the "popularity" Truman valued, but seniority, parliamentary skill, party fidelity, and finesse in personal politics. Even worse,

Speakers as a lot compare badly with Secretaries of State, the Treasury, or Defense as Presidential timber. As executive officers the Secretaries would afford better continuity in succeeding to the Presidency than an "outsider" like the Speaker. Ironically, the 1947 act revived the Ben Wade–Andrew Johnson "temptation" by creating for the Speaker and the President pro tempore a vested interest in the President's impeachment.

The 1947 act also stumbled upon the imperatives of the nuclear age. The act did not face up to the possibility that in a future nuclear war one tolerably aimed bomb could destroy Washington and with it the whole company of Presidential successors. Earlier succession laws would have done no better.

Criticism of the 1947 act became acute after John Kennedy's assassination and Johnson's assumption of the Presidency. Under the workings of the 1947 act, Speaker McCormack, one month short of seventy-two, became next in line, followed by the President pro tempore of the Senate, Carl Hayden, aged eighty-six. McCormack's advanced age and the manifestly greater relevance of his talents to the affairs of Congress than to those of the Presidency raised a considerable outcry either that McCormack remove himself from the succession or that the 1947 act be amended to eliminate him from it. But the agitations failed because of McCormack's popularity in Congress and his expressed view that the 1947 law was "preferable" to any alternatives yet advanced. The nation reverted to its "tendency," as James Reston put it, "to do nothing but pray for the President's health."

THE TWENTY-FIFTH AMENDMENT.   In 1967 the burden imposed upon the power of prayer was measurably reduced with the adoption of the Twenty-fifth Amendment. The amendment seeks to minimize the possibilities of a double vacancy occurring in the Presidency and Vice-Presidency. The amendment requires the President in the event that the office of Vice President is vacant to nominate a Vice President who will take office upon confirmation by a majority vote of both houses of Congress. This feature of the Twenty-fifth Amendment attracted the greatest unanimity in the Bayh subcommittee hearings. Lyndon Johnson's succession to the Presidency, which left the Vice-Presidency vacant for almost fourteen months, illuminated the wisdom of the provision.

The method of the Twenty-fifth Amendment, giving the President the power to nominate a Vice President, is consistent with the practice that permits the Presidential candidate to choose his running mate. In lieu of the people bestowing their approval, as they do in the national election, their representatives in Congress would act for them in filling a vacancy in the Vice-Presidency. The amendment provides the best possible assurance, of any arrangement conceivable, that the new Vice President would be compatible in views and temperament with the President.

Presidential Transitions

The environment of the modern Presidency makes imperative not only a rational method of succession but a smooth transition between the outgoing and the incoming Chief Executives. In an age when several foreign affairs crises are flaming simultaneously around the globe, when weapons systems consume an average of seven years in passing from drawing board to operation, when the economy grows ever more intricate and sensitive, a snarl or lapse in public policy invites disaster. Foreign leaders calculate their moves with an eye on the United States Presidential calendar. Several weeks after President Hoover's electoral defeat in 1932, Britain requested "adjustment" of her World War I debt and suspension of her payment due December 15. Other debtor European nations quickly made similar demands. The Europeans caught the United States during an interlude of governmental paralysis, with a President discredited by defeat, a Congress controlled by the opposition party, and the President-elect, Franklin Roosevelt, visibly and understandably reluctant to plunge onto a terrain full of economic and political booby traps, without the protection of official responsibility.

Succession presents a variety of problems: The President and the President-elect may be of the same party or of different parties; or the transition may be from Vice President to President, a reminder of the Vice President's function as the President's understudy. Of modern Presidents, Hoover was the first to seek consultations and joint policy-making with the President-elect. Both Franklin Roosevelt and Truman, when running for reelection, permitted aides to supply the opposing candidates with vital information on foreign affairs. President Truman, mindful of his own sudden and unbriefed trajectory into the Presidency, smoothed the transfer to the incoming Eisenhower administration, thus becoming the first outgoing Chief Executive to accept the responsibility squarely for orderly transition. President Eisenhower reciprocated by easing the Kennedy administration's advent in 1961.

Truman's and Eisenhower's transition arrangements covered two spans, one from the Presidential nominations to the November elections, the other from election to inauguration. In August 1952, just before the Stevenson and Eisenhower campaigns pulled into high gear, President Truman invited the candidates to come separately to the White House for a briefing on the world situation. Although Eisenhower declined, saying the lack of "grave emergency" made his attendance unnecessary, he accepted Truman's simultaneous offer of weekly Central Intelligence Agency reports, provided they would not "limit my freedom to discuss or analyze the foreign programs as my judgment indicates." As President, Eisenhower supplied intelligence briefings to the 1956 and 1960 Democratic candidates, Stevenson and Kennedy.[43]

For the interlude between election and inauguration, arrangements were more elaborate. In 1952, following his electoral victory, Eisenhower visited the White House in November when Truman wisely arranged a welcoming parade to sweeten an atmosphere heavily soured by campaign invective. President Truman and President-elect Eisenhower, tense and unsmiling at first, conferred privately and then were joined by Secretary of State Dean Acheson, Secretary of Defense Robert Lovett, Secretary of the Treasury John Snyder, and Mutual Security Director Averell Harriman of the administration; Joseph Dodge, the future Director of the Budget, and Henry Cabot Lodge, the future ambassador to the UN, accompanied Eisenhower. The topic discussed was foreign affairs, and it ranged over NATO and Korea, Iran, Indochina, and elsewhere. At the meeting's close Truman handed Eisenhower three large volumes prepared by the National Security Council that contained (1) a country by country summary of current United States policies, (2) an estimate of critical trouble spots, and (3) extraordinarily confidential plans for meeting an all-out Communist attack in Korea, Yugoslavia, or Iran. The White House session was followed by a briefing for Eisenhower and his aides at the Pentagon by General Omar Bradley and the Joint Chiefs of Staff.

In subsequent weeks Eisenhower's designated appointees, John Foster Dulles (State), George M. Humphrey (Treasury), Dodge, Lodge, and Sherman Adams (chief administrative assistant), conferred with their counterparts in the Truman administration. Future Director of the Budget Dodge was furiously busy since the budget is one of the knottier phases of transition, aggravated by the disharmonious scheduling of the Twentieth Amendment and the Budget and Accounting Act of 1921. The act requires that the budget be submitted fifteen days after Congress convenes. The new Congress was scheduled to meet on January 3, the budget's due date was January 18, or two days prior to the inauguration date of January 20 set in the Twentieth Amendment. Dodge, an efficient advance-runner, enabled the President-elect to acquire information that would facilitate changes in the budget after the new President took office.[44]

The mechanics of the Truman-Eisenhower transition were duplicated in the Eisenhower-Kennedy transfer. Kennedy was apparently satisfied, for he remarked just before his inauguration, "I don't think we have asked for anything that they haven't done." Eisenhower's assistant, General Wilton Persons, handled liaison arrangements for the outgoing administration and Clark Clifford for the incoming. Well before the election, the Bureau of the Budget and the executive departments prepared briefing memoranda for the President-elect and his aides. President-elect Kennedy set up twenty-nine expert task forces to study problems and formulate proposals for major policy areas. Use of the task forces also enabled Kennedy to appraise the suitability of their members for appointment in his administration, and those who were eventually chosen had a running start on their new assignment, thanks to the task force experience. Many task force proposals were taken up in President Kennedy's initial legislative programs.

Lyndon Johnson, thrust into the Presidency by Kennedy's assassination, was buoyed in the critical months of transition by Kennedy personnel on the White House staff, by institutional staff such as the Bureau of the Budget, and by the career services. In all, the 1963–64 transition produced few changes either in policies or personnel. The distinctive character and direction of the Johnson Presidency did not emerge until after the 1964 election.[45]

For all the surface appearance of cooperation and harmony, transitions are beset with the tensions and cross-purposes of the outgoing and incoming Presidents. The outgoing President, as Laurin Henry demonstrates in *Presidential Transitions*, prizes continuity and order, the preservation of his policies, and the maturing of his half-begun projects in the next administration. The President-elect is cautious and aloof, watchful of involving his freedom and the mandate and prestige of his electoral victory in policies of the incumbent administration over which he has no control. When in its closing days the Eisenhower administration decided to break diplomatic relations with Cuba, the incoming Kennedy administration was invited to associate itself with the move. The Kennedy camp, not surprisingly, declined. "In the absence of complete information on all the relevant factors," a Kennedy spokesman declared, the new administration could not participate.[46]

The new President's personal philosophy may be radically at odds with the incumbent President's, as Eisenhower's laissez-faire preferences were miles removed from the welfare-state commitment of Truman. The new and old Presidents may differ in their view of Presidential method: Harding's Whiggery was a long way from Wilson's dynamism. The transition may also be inhibited because the new or old President sees it as a manipulative opportunity for political gain. After Eisenhower's electoral victory, President Truman included in the customary congratulatory telegram an offer to put a military aircraft at the general's disposal "if you still intend to go to Korea," a promised venture that played no little part in the election's outcome. Eisenhower's response was coolly correct. Truman gibed again at a press conference when he announced to the nation that Eisenhower's Korean trip was nothing more than "a piece of demagoguery." Truman's comment, said an Eisenhower aide, meant "the finish of any informal across-the-desk meeting" between the two. If they conferred again prior to the inauguration, said the aide further, mindful of Eisenhower's deep displeasure, "it probably would be a cold affair."[47]

A blight on the President-elect's participation in the transition effort prior to his inauguration has been the cost involved. Kennedy's task forces, lacking government funds and office space, met in hotels, Washington law offices, and any other quarters that were proffered. The Democratic National Committee and the participants absorbed the considerable expenses. A welcome corrective has emerged in the Presidential Transition Act of 1963. Thanks to the act, the General Services Administrator will henceforth provide each President-elect and Vice President–elect with space, staff salaries, travel expenses, authority to employ consultants, and other necessities. Outgoing Presidents and Vice Presidents will also be helped in winding up their affairs.

The most pressing difficulties of Presidential transitions are constitutional rather than administrative. Although the Twentieth Amendment helpfully moved the Presidential inauguration from March to January, a yawning hiatus still stretches between the end of the old administration and the beginning of the new one. A lapse of eleven or twelve weeks between popular election and inauguration is absurd, given the gallop of today's affairs. The dates of the two events need to be juxtaposed within not more than four weeks of each other. Likewise, the interval between the national party conventions and the election, scheduled originally in horse-and-buggy days, has become thoroughly antiquated and ill serves the nation's interests. Following the conventions in July or August is a lull of four or five weeks of inactivity before the campaigns begin in earnest after Labor Day. Then come eight or more weeks of campaigning as compared with two weeks in Great Britain and Canada. The increasing efficiency of American campaign media could easily support a shorter campaign period. Our historical political calendar has plainly become outmoded. Wise compression could eliminate two months or more between the dwindling reign of a lame-duck President and his successor's arrival at the seat of power.

The Future Presidency

Thoughtful concern and discussion regarding disability, succession, and transition is apt to wax well into the future. Viewing the President, as we do, under the cruel pressures of the nuclear age, what seems best on each of these scores for keeping the Presidency continuously strong?

1. Although the Twenty-fifth Amendment is not flawless, it would probably be best to leave the subject of disability at rest and to anticipate, confidently and prayerfully, that its provisions could be applied in workable manner by responsible officials should the need arise.

2. There are several possible, although remote, contingencies of Presidential tenure that never troubled us in quieter bygone times. In the nuclear era, however, with its infinite perils and ever shrinking timetables, we should put our minds to them although the cloud they make on our political horizon is no larger than a man's fist.

(a) Suppose the Presidential or Vice-Presidential candidate should die or become disabled prior to the popular election in November. The situation is not covered by law. Both major parties have empowered their national committees to fill the vacancy, and the Republican committee has the further option of summoning a new convention. We would be on firmer legal ground if the procedure were incorporated into law.

(b) Suppose the Presidential or Vice-Presidential candidate should die after the November popular election but before the electors met in their respective state capitals in December to cast their votes. Under present law the electors could vote for anyone they pleased. Both major parties, however, have authorized their national committees to fill the vacancy, and the likelihood is that the electors would vote for the new nominee. If the Presidential nominee should die, the country would likely expect the Vice-Presidential nominee to fill the vacancy, and his place, in turn, to be filled by a new nominee. All this is a darkling plain, barren of precedent.

(c) Suppose that after the electors vote in their respective states and before January 6, when the electoral votes are opened, announced, and counted in Congress, the Presidential candidate should die. The possibilities are grisly. The candidate's death would raise the question whether votes for a dead man could be counted. If they could and if he were the winner, the election would be thrown into the House of Representatives. Some authorities argue that Congress could reconvene the electoral college to permit the electors to change their votes. Still others hold that Congress could make the Vice-Presidential winner the President-elect. Probably the easiest way out would be to declare the dead candidate, if he was the winner, the President-elect, and, under the Twentieth Amendment, the Vice President–elect would become President on Inauguration Day, January 20.

(d) Suppose no Presidential candidate receives a majority of the electoral votes, and the election is thrown into the House of Representatives, but before the House acts, one of the candidates eligible to be voted upon, dies? No procedure exists for filling the vacancy. The Twentieth Amendment, however, empowers Congress to resolve the situation. Conceivably, Congress could permit the national committee of the party affected by the death to propose a replacement.

Fortunately, the law of probabilities runs strongly against the occurrence of these several nightmares. But on the theory that the governmental structure must never falter in our troubled day, these are fit subjects for study by Congress and interested citizens.

3. For reasons we have explored, the 1947 Succession Act is a mistake, and it ought to be repealed. To replace it, the act of 1886 might be restored

with the line of succession proceeding through the cabinet, beginning with the Secretary of State. In addition, the line of succession might well be extended. Those now in the line pass most of their time in Washington, a circumstance that makes possible the extinction of the entire body of successors in a nuclear attack on the capital. Congress might well add to the succession persons distributed around the country. One possibility might be to include the governors ranked according to the population of their states in the last census.

4. In the interest of easing the transition between Presidencies, we might well cast a critical eye on our present scheduling of the national nominating convention, the duration of the postconvention electoral campaign, and the date of the inauguration. Each could be revised to shorten the transition. A three- or four-week electoral campaign should be altogether efficient and desirable. We could use a shortened campaign as a springboard for revising other parts of the Presidential calendar. We might redress the awkwardness of the Budget and Accounting Act of 1921, which requires a new President, days after his inauguration in January, to submit a budget that has been prepared largely by his predecessor. A rearranged Presidential calendar would give the new President more time to prepare a budget of his own for presentation in January or to amend the one inherited from his predecessor. On the basis of these necessities, one could project the following calendar, with approximately a four-week interval between most steps: August—the nominating conventions; September—the postconvention electoral campaign; October—the election; November—the inauguration; December—recruiting administration members and preparing initial policies; January—presentation of the new President's State of the Union and budget messages and the economic report.

5. Let every good friend of the strong Presidency pledge himself to work unstintingly for the repeal of the Twenty-second Amendment.

Party Chief   5

If there is an aspect of the Presidency that is hobbled by uncertainty and frailty it is the office's uncertain specifications for the role of party leader. The President is largely deprived of the advantage of strong party organization that the heads of other governments enjoy; the American national party organizations are strikingly weak. Parties are the best political invention yet struck by the mind of man to stabilize political influence and to transpose promises into policy. Yet little of the invention and less of its fruits have been made available to the President.

The major American party does well as a vehicle of power and badly as a vehicle of policy. The contemporary President needs both these means of political success in steady quantity. But while the party serves the President admirably as a campaign organ to bring himself and his party brethren into office and as a forum for broadcasting his platform to the people, it serves him ill in transposing his campaign promises into law. American parties, unlike those of any other major nation, fail to stabilize the Chief Executive's impact on policy-making. His party capacity endows him with only a fraction of the strength that the British Prime Minister has to transform campaign promises into established policy.

The lack of an effective national party institution forces the President into a heavy dependence upon his personal skills as party leader. His ability as a manipulator of party resources, such as funds and organization, and his exploitation of passing advantages produced by political events and circumstance are keys to his success as party leader. A few Presidents, notably endowed with party skills, or favored by exceptional circumstances, have reaped impressive political harvests as party leaders. They have dominated the governmental machinery and scored glittering legislative victories. But because success in party leadership depends so heavily upon personal skill, the role has never stabilized. One President who excels as party leader has never been followed by another who even approximates his predecessor's accomplishment.

The party role was plastered onto the Presidential office after the main structure was built. The Founding Fathers made no provision for parties in the Constitution, and their later emergence was attended with awkwardness. Although parties appeared in Washington's time, he abstained from functioning as party leader, deeming it incompatible with the nature of his office. For his successor, John Adams, the party was not an adjunct of the Presidential office but an instrument that his political enemies employed against him. Under Jefferson and Jackson and a sprinkling of their successors, party leadership flourished, but it has flourished even more in the states and localities, in the hands of governors, mayors, and local politicians.

The President's uneasy party role is aggravated by the continual tension between his responsibilities to his office and the claims of his party. His office, and therefore its duties and problems, presumably exceed any obligation the party can impose upon him. He is a politician who must also be a statesman. Yet the party often and insistently violates this assumption. Senate Republicans, blithely heedless of President Eisenhower's struggle with great and manifold problems of state, required him to work in harness with their chosen leader, William F. Knowland, who opposed most of his foreign and much of his domestic policy. President Kennedy was expected, at the first electoral opportunity, to stump against Senator Everett Dirksen, Republican leader, who had provided indispensable support for the test ban treaty and a string of other important measures.

The tension between office and party is heightened by the party's almost frivolous disregard of its obligations to the President. He may by splendid electoral triumph plant the party standard in the White House and carry many a legislative party colleague on his coattails across the victory line only to see his proposals spurned, sometimes seriatim, by a Congress whose two houses his party controls. President Truman, despite his spectacular electoral victory in 1948, which restored the Democrats to power in both Congressional houses, was able to obtain in the ensuing session the enactment of only several of a score of Fair Deal measures. President Kennedy, who summoned his fellow Democrats on Capitol Hill to rally behind an ambitious and popular program, did little better. He could well paraphrase for his own party role the memorable instruction of his inaugural address, "Ask not what your party can do for you; ask what you can do for your party."

President Eisenhower, just before his spectacular reelection victory in 1956, was questioned pointedly concerning the affinity of several old guard Republican Senators to his own Modern Republicanism. His perceptive response suggested several limits the President suffers as party chief. Eisenhower said,

> Now, let's remember there are no national parties in the United
> States. There are forty-eight state parties, then they are the ones that de-
> termine the people that belong to those parties. There is nothing I
> can do to say that [anyone] is not a Republican. The most I can
> say is that in many things they do not agree with me. . . . We have
> got to remember that these are state organizations, and there is
> nothing I can do to say so-and-so is a Republican and so-and-so is
> not a Republican.[1]

The President is an uncertain monarch of a loose and far-flung party
empire of several satrapies and dependencies and a host of self-governing
commonwealths. His sway is full over a few parts; over most it is little or non-
existent. He is a chief among chiefs. The local and state party organizations
are beyond his control and are subject, at most, to his influence. The major
parties function as viable national organizations only quadrennially when
their state and local parts more or less unite to win the Presidency and its stakes
of power. Thereafter the parts conduct themselves with jealously preserved
autonomy. The state and local organizations command a solid corps of workers
and followers, assert their own discipline, control the selection of Senatorial
and Congressional candidates, and possess financial resources of their own.
The Senate and House of Representatives maintain a quantity of party organizations: caucuses, steering committees, campaign committees, and policy
committees. Senators and Congressmen render their principal allegiance not
to the Chief Executive but to the state and local organizations to which they
owe their nomination and election. Legislators of the President's party both
help and hobble his program of legislation. The fact that an Eastland and a
Morse march under the Democratic banner and a Tower and a Javits under
the Republican demonstrates how undependable the party label is as a guide
to how legislators debate and vote. Nowhere in the vast party structure is
there a constant and effective source of power that the President can confidently turn to for support. The national committee, where his strength is
greatest and where the state and local organizations converge, is chiefly concerned with the choice and election of the Presidential candidate.

The unreliability of his party, the likelihood that numbers of its Congressional members may oppose him, must lead any President to ponder
privately just what good his party really is to him. Indeed, if he reads the texts
of Presidential history, he will discover that Presidents achieve many, if not
most, of their important policies and programs, whether in domestic or foreign
affairs, only with bipartisan support. The loyalty of his own party is never so
dependable that it can assure a succession of program victories. This unde-
pendability makes it necessary for the President to studiously cultivate support
in the opposition party. His own party's ambiguity of support promotes the
President's necessary ambiguity as party leader. For his program's sake, he
must not be so fiercely and devotedly the leader of his own party that he is
precluded from gaining support from the opposition.

The case for the President to treat his party role pragmatically and to conduct himself in a fashion that will pick up support beyond his party can be made in another way. The President, careful research demonstrates, is brought into office by a popular vote that is greater than his party vote. His electoral majority is a patchwork of voters from his own party, from the opposition party, and from the steadily growing body of "independents." He may have large support from big groups such as organized labor and national and racial groups. His own party may have chosen him as its standard-bearer principally because of his presumed ability to attract broad support. Ironically, the Republican party denied Robert A. Taft its nomination because he was too much a Republican ("Mr. Republican," in fact), and therefore thought unable to lure Democratic and independent voters into his column. Without substantial outside support, he could not possibly have become a winner.

The President and Vice President are the only officers of our government chosen by a national popular majority. In seeking to convert his promises to that majority into policy, the President is frustrated by the skillful arrangement of the governmental structure that permits what at most can be only limited majority rule. The system of checks and balances enables Congress, which is a series of disparate local majorities, to reject what the President, the voice of a national majority, proposes. The weakness of the parties assures that the principle of checks and balances, and therefore limited majority rule, will enjoy the full play the Founding Fathers intended. Congress's local constituencies in contrast to the President's national constituency and Congress's internal organization—its powerful committees with chairmen chosen by seniority—tend to produce a legislature and an executive of opposite policy outlooks, even when the same party controls both branches. In recent generations Congress has usually been the domain of conservatives of both parties and the Presidency the domain of progressives.

The President is forced by checks and balances and party weakness to scramble for support by a variety of expedients. He must court approval among progressives in both Congressional parties. He may endeavor as best he can to dominate portions of his own party by building alliances with state and local leaders and by discreetly influencing the choice of legislative candidates. He may rely heavily on his own personal organization—if he has one—to make his way in party affairs. He can move to change the popular base of his party by extending it to big pressure groups to whose interests his program is akin. Desperation is nowhere else so much the mother of invention as it is in the Chief Executive's party plight.

The Presidential Nominee

Even in its most serviceable roles—selecting the Presidential nominee and conducting the electoral campaign—the party's relation with its chosen candidate is uneasy and imperfect. The party provides no assurance that the platform he runs on accords with his wishes. His ability to make his preferences prevail depends upon a complex of factors—the power of his rivals, the nature of the issues, his own general political health. Franklin Roosevelt could confidently expect that the Democratic convention of 1936 would approve the platform prepared under his supervision. "I would like to have as short a platform as possible this year," he instructed his draftsmen, "and . . . I would like to have it based on the sentence of the Declaration of Independence, 'We hold these truths to be self-evident.' "[2] The convention approved the several parts of the Roosevelt-made platform with waves of ovations.

Grover Cleveland in 1888 had more difficulty. The tariff was the prickly issue of the day between radicals and conservatives, and the President's general political situation was not without weakness. Cleveland himself drafted the platform, carefully stating in moderate language the tariff question. For the sake of his own political necessities, Cleveland wished to provide the Republicans with no opportunity to charge the Democratic party with free-trade principles. At the St. Louis convention, unfortunately for Cleveland, the low tariff men unshackled their bonds. They and Cleveland's emissaries of moderation were about evenly divided on the platform subcommittee on the tariff. The subcommittee met at dusk in a steaming room of the Southern Hotel and fought over the issue all night. The free-trade men, led by Henry Watterson, the Kentucky editor, ultimately prevailed.[3] In the ensuing election, tariff reform became the leading issue, and, although the election did not turn on the issue, Benjamin Harrison, staunch defender of the tariff, defeated Cleveland.

Many a Presidential nominee views the available party organization as an enterprise of limited dependability and feels it the better part of wisdom to build a personal organization to conduct much of the postconvention campaign. John Kennedy relied upon an elaborate personal organization, consisting of his brothers, his brothers-in-law, a cadre of aides from his earliest political campaigns, and several members of the Harvard faculty, among others.

The Presidential nominee may be driven to build up a personal organization by the fickleness of state and local party organizations in providing support. Instead of devoting their resources in a substantial way to his race, they may concentrate upon local campaigns, especially in years when the Presidential nominee is deemed a likely loser. Adlai Stevenson, who campaigned under such circumstances, resorted to a trifurcated organization in 1956. In addition to the regular national party organization, a Stevenson-Kefauver Committee appeared in Washington, headed by James A. Finnegan Stevenson's campaign director, and housed across the street from Democratic headquarters. A third organization was Volunteers for Stevenson, whose province was the independent voter. The poverty of support that the regular party organization gave Stevenson made his decision in behalf of a personal organization eminently wise. The duplication of the Stevenson experience in other similar episodes raises a strong suspicion that a Presidential nominee cannot securely depend upon the regular organization unless his victory appears clear and imminent. In such a happy eventuality, when Senatorial and Congressional candidates eagerly press to ride his coattails, the Presidential nominee might be able to bar access to that privileged place to those whose known positions on policy promise to make them future saboteurs of his program. If the Presidential nominee distributed his support selectively at this juncture, he might gain more than by applying gentle pressures at the midterm elections when there are no Presidential coattails and his power is consequently very much reduced. Nowadays the legislative campaign committees of the President's party insist that he hit the campaign trail in Congressional elections. His cabinet Secretaries are expected to take their full turn, too.

But the President works with something less than total ease and comfort with the Congressional and Senatorial campaign committees of his party. The midterm election is often a season for exposing divergences in the policy views of the President and legislators of his party. The lengths to which the malaise may go was suggested in a remarkable statement by the Republican Congressional campaign committee chairman, Richard M. Simpson of Pennsylvania, in 1958. Republican candidates, Simpson counseled, should forget about Eisenhower's favor in the 1958 elections and "make known" to voters any "disagreement with the President's policies." Simpson, a conservative Republican, often opposed the President's Modern Republicanism.[4]

Despite the varying cordiality of the invitations he receives, the President has for many years now led the party in Congressional elections. The results, like the invitations, are mixed. Woodrow Wilson began the practice by appealing for a Democratic Congress in 1918, with a disheartening result. His party lost control of both houses. Franklin Roosevelt launched his purge in 1938, for which the electorate slapped him hard. Not only did the purge fail, but the Democrats lost the incredible total of seventy seats in the House and seven in the Senate. Roosevelt tried again in 1942 with results only slightly less bad. Truman fared no better, and in 1954 Eisenhower made a lavish effort, traveling more than ten thousand miles and making nearly forty speeches. His reward was the loss of eighteen Representatives, one Senator, and control of both houses. In 1958 Eisenhower turned over the campaigning to Vice President Nixon, who also was rebuffed. Kennedy, however, brightened the gloomy history of Presidential influence in the off-year 1962 elections by gaining supporters, although he lost a few Democrats, but he was aided no little by a useful coincidence—the Cuban quarantine crisis rallied the voters behind the incumbent Democratic party.

In the 1966 Congressional elections President Johnson apparently concluded that he could help the Democratic cause most by staying away from the campaign trail and attending to his official duties. Many of his party's candidates for state and national office concurred in his judgment. The President and his policies at the time were sagging in popularity. In the South

WINNING RENOMINATION   93

Johnson was a symbol of desegregation, which many local politicians in both major parties were profitably exploiting. His coming as a campaigner would only spur their attacks upon desegregation as a local political issue. Elsewhere he symbolized an unwanted war, mounting prices, and the bane of neglected farmers. Many a Congressional race seemed to turn on local issues and personality contests in which the President's influence was irrelevant.

On occasion the President undertakes a further function in Congressional elections. His encouragement may be vital to inducing able citizens to become their party's nominees for legislative office. The national Republican chairman, Leonard Hall, concluded in 1956 that John Sherman Cooper, then ambassador to India, was urgently needed to run for the Senate in Kentucky. Cooper had triumphed in the Senate race in 1952, but in 1956 he was unwilling to sacrifice contentment in India for the travail of a Senate race. Eisenhower, who thought it inappropriate for the President to persuade anyone to run for office, was pressed to take on Cooper by both Hall and Presidential Assistant Sherman Adams, who had tried and failed. Cooper was brought to Eisenhower's office, and the President, who never did ask him to run, spoke eloquently of the opportunity for service in the Senate. Cooper capitulated, ran, and won.[5]

Winning Renomination

The most important of a President's personal political objectives, needless to say, is securing renomination, and this can only be achieved with the help of the party organization. Normally, the party almost automatically grants this Presidential wish. Even the likelihood of defeat may not bar his renomination, as it did not for Hoover in 1932. Yet a few Presidents, such as Pierce, Buchanan, and Arthur, were denied renomination, and Benjamin Harrison achieved it only after a hard struggle.

Chester Arthur, who became President upon Garfield's assassination, failed to be renominated, although he approached the Chicago convention of 1884 with imposing credentials. Old-line political leaders, independents, and liberals all endorsed him. George William Curtis, distinguished reformer and old-time foe, wrote enthusiastically, "I say that a President whose accession by means of a most tragical event was generally regarded as a serious misfortune, if not calamity, has not only allayed all apprehension, but his pacific and temperate Administration has gained the general approval of the country." Henry Ward Beecher declared, "I can hardly imagine how he could have done better." And Mark Twain proclaimed, "It would be hard to better President Arthur's Administration."[6]

Arthur's defeat for renomination was the product of his alienation of key factions and bosses, his consequent weakness in key states, and poor convention strategy. A Stalwart, he acted moderately toward the Half-Breeds, the faction of James A. Garfield, his predecessor. Arthur's conciliation was resented by his own Stalwarts as ingratitude and weakness. Garfield men in Ohio, for all of Arthur's consideration, remained cool. Former governor Charles Foster bludgeoned the Arthur movement by declaring that Arthur would be "a very weak candidate in Ohio." In New York, Arthur's own state, Whitelaw Reid and Thomas C. Platt, ancient foes, united for a common cause against Arthur. Platt, having had small success with the Arthur administration in its dispensations of patronage, now believed that Arthur's rival, James G. Blaine's, "turn had come." The upshot was a badly divided New York delegation. Blaine went into the convention with a plurality, but not a majority, of the delegates. Arthur's convention campaign, which with modest skill might have weaved together a victory, was badly managed. The nominating speeches in his behalf were downright inferior. His managers were dull and laggard in fashioning deals with rival factions. "The management of Mr. Arthur's canvass here was a botch from beginning to end," an aide wrote.[7]

Both more difficult and more successful than Arthur's ordeal was Truman's quest for renomination in 1948, which he achieved in a steep uphill fight by a combination of pluck and luck. Before the convention, Truman's political stock was at rock bottom. The Republican Congressional victory in 1946 foreshadowed a Republican Presidential victory in 1948. Scandals had crashed upon the administration in waves. Henry A. Wallace had broken off from the Democratic party and announced his Presidential candidacy. Labor and New Deal liberals were restive, and Southern Democrats stood at the brink of revolt. Truman's popularity in the opinion polls had fallen dismally. To hold back the avalanche, Truman, in January of 1948, used his State of the Union message to project a platform for his party. The message recapitulated a quantity of Fair Deal proposals with a request for an improbable tax cut thrown in. Truman's choice of theme sought to hold together the crumbling Roosevelt Democratic coalition and to forestall liberals and independents from drifting to Wallace. In June Truman made a fiery whistle-stop tour through the Middle and Far West to show local Democratic leaders his strength with the crowds before the convention began.

But Truman's ability to be renominated depended not upon his own power and enterprise but upon the outcome of a caucus that gathered in Philadelphia, shortly before the convention, to arrange his overthrow. The caucus was called by Jacob M. Arvey, Chicago Democratic leader, James and Elliott Roosevelt, the late President's sons, and sixteen other party leaders. The active coalition against Truman was a cross section of the Democratic party and the old Roosevelt coalition. It included Mayor Hubert Humphrey of Minneapolis, Chester Bowles of Connecticut, Mayor William O'Dwyer of New York, and the Americans for Democratic Action. These Northern Democrats were joined by Southern Democrats such as Senator Lister Hill of Alabama, Governor Strom Thurmond of South Carolina, Governor Ben T. Lancy of Arkansas, Governor William M. Tuck of Virginia, and Senator Claude

Pepper of Florida. Harold Ickes and James F. Byrnes, Secretary of the Interior and War Mobilization Director, respectively, in the Roosevelt administration, both opposed Truman.

The Philadelphia caucus saw inevitable electoral defeat unless a substitute candidate for Truman could be found. Their acquisitive gaze fell upon General Dwight D. Eisenhower, then on the crest of his popularity from his European military triumphs. But Eisenhower dashed the hopes of his would-be benefactors by issuing a statement a week before the convention, saying, "I will not at this time identify myself with any political party and could not accept nomination for any political office." Leon Henderson, the ADA chairman, futilely urged the Democrats to ignore the Eisenhower statement and to go ahead with the general's nomination as "the best man the country can provide." The ADA next brought forward the name of Supreme Court Justice William O. Douglas, but many Democratic leaders balked, and Douglas issued a declining statement.

Truman was eventually renominated by default of the old coalition's failure to unite on an alternate candidate. The vote was not unanimous as befits a President seeking reelection but 947½ for Truman, 263 for Richard B. Russell of Georgia, and ½ for Paul V. McNutt of Indiana. The New York Post reflected the convention's mood when it wrote, "The Party might as well immediately concede the election to Dewey and save the wear and tear of campaigning." As everyone knows, Truman went on to win in one of the most dramatic election upsets in the country's history.[8]

But Truman in 1952 and Johnson in 1968, confronted with formidable competitors for the nomination and an unhappy trend in the primaries, withdrew early in the struggle.

The Congressional Party

But once nominated and elected, or reelected, a President is concerned with getting his program through Congress, a venture in which the party leadership and rank and file are as likely to fail him as to help him. Few Congressmen view their loyalties to their own careers, constituents, and party as related to their loyalty to their party's national standard-bearer and his program. Eisenhower's Senate leaders were successively Senator Taft, his chief rival for the Presidential nomination, and Senator Knowland, who opposed him on a wide range of policy. President Eisenhower steadily received more support from Democratic legislators than from Republicans. In Kennedy's time the House Democratic floor leader, and later Speaker, was John W. McCormack of Massachusetts, whose nephew contested with the President's brother Edward for the 1962 Democratic Massachusetts Senatorial nomination. Mike Mansfield, Senate Democratic leader and long-time ally of President Johnson, broke with the administration on the wisdom of the Vietnam war policy and registered his dissent publicly, pointedly, and repeatedly. In no other governmental system in the world are such oddities of party life to be found.

Creative and well-intended efforts to improve President-Congress relations in the party realm have gone awry. The Congressional reorganization legislation of 1946 founded what might fairly be called a noble experiment to build up Congressional party unity by establishing a policy committee for each party in the Senate. The House later also instituted such committees. The committees were conceived by their creators, Senators Robert La Follette, Jr., and Mike Monroney, as councils that would meet periodically with the President to improve interbranch understanding on questions of national policy. Like many other noble experiments, the policy committees have achieved only small success. President Truman met with the Democratic Senate Policy Committee of his day only once. In the Eisenhower administration's first days, the Senate Republican Policy Committee more or less accepted the President's program, although it quickly turned out that the legislative party for which it appeared to speak did not. There is no record of any Eisenhower meeting with the entire Senate Policy Committee. The committees have developed not as institutional organs, as their creators hoped, but largely as instruments by which Senate chieftains exerted their personal leadership. Lyndon Johnson and Robert Taft used the committees as vehicles for building up their personal influence. But most important of all, the committees have become effective not for policy-making but for service and research and legislative scheduling. They do not lead in drawing up a general legislative program, and rarely do they label their decisions party policies. The policy committees indeed may take stands decidedly hostile to the President. The House Republican Policy Committee called for "substantial" reductions of approximately three billion dollars in President Eisenhower's budget for fiscal 1958 and added pointedly that it expected all Republican Representatives to support its stand at the next party caucus.[9]

The President's party equips him with remarkably few pressures he can apply to Congress, and these are highly imperfect at best. His most ancient pressure is, of course, patronage. All Presidents are wholesale dispensers of offices, a part of their job that they dislike. In Lincoln's day job-seekers crammed the White House rooms, stairs, hallways, and even closets, prompting that noble spirit to cry out, "It is not the rebellion that is killing me, but the Pepperton post office."[10] The passage of the Civil Service Act of 1883, and its later extensions, protecting the tenure of designated employees, has gradually but sweepingly reduced the relative numbers of federal jobs tagged for patronage. In 1885 out of 126,000 federal employees some 110,000 were still political appointees.[11] A contemporary President's patronage appointments number a mere few thousand.

Patronage enables the President to strike at the legislator in his home district, to attract or alienate local groups on whose support he depends. For the favor of his juicy patronage plums, the Chief Executive can exact a *quid pro quo*. Many a President, before handing out jobs, first checks the voting record of the interested Congressman on the administration's legislative program. The search may bring down the heavens upon the errant. When Samuel J. Randall, Democratic high tariff advocate, fought Grover Cleveland's grand enterprise to lower the tariff, retribution was swift and severe. Word went forth from Washington that no Randall man need expect any patronage. At Randall's political base in Pennsylvania, reaction was quick. Two key Randall organizations, the Randall Club of Pittsburgh and the Eleventh Ward Democratic Association of Philadelphia, hastened to repudiate their leader and endorse Cleveland's tariff position. When the state Democratic committee met to elect a chairman and adopt resolutions, Randall's candidate lost to a low tariff man and the committee voted a hearty endorsement of Cleveland's tariff stand.[12] Yet, as Presidents well know, many legislators whom they might strike at by withholding patronage are by no means defenseless. "It was a smart practice in government," Roosevelt's party chairman, Jim Farley, once said, "to avoid antagonizing the men who vote the appropriations."[13] He could add, too, legislators of large influence on other key Congressional committees and those enjoying full sway over local party organizations.

The patronage weapon is not without flaw. Its worth rests upon the assumption that human gratitude is enduring, an assumption that sometimes falters in practice, especially in politics. Further, an appointment that recognizes a local political faction may antagonize competing factions. William Howard Taft, after a wealth of experience, concluded that every time he made a job appointment he created "nine enemies and one ingrate." Virtually anything the President does in the patronage field stirs bleats of disgruntlement. For all the attention of Franklin Roosevelt and Jim Farley, complaints poured in from state organizations that not enough Democrats were getting federal jobs. After several years of the New Deal, Arthur Mullen was contending that in Nebraska 60 per cent of the federal officeholders credited to his state were not Democrats at all.[14] President Cleveland, like many another Chief Executive doling out patronage, was caught in the crossfire of spoilsmen and reformers. The spoilsmen hungered infinitely for jobs; reformers such as Carl Schurz and the National Civil Service Reform Association proclaimed the necessity to hold the high ground of merit appointment. Seldom, when his job is done, does the President win the plaudits of either competing faction.

THE OPPOSITION PARTY.   The party, when it does not control the Presidency, may be expected, according to general political practice, to take on the function of responsible opposition. The recurrent failure to attain even a semblance of this expectation demonstrates the low capacity of the Congressional party organization to achieve party coherence. In 1950, as chairmen of the out-party, Republicans Hugh Scott, Jr., and his successor, Guy Gabrielson, urged some kind of national conference to develop a platform on which to base that year's Congressional campaign. House and Senate Republican leaders did not hide their displeasure at the suggestion, although Gabrielson managed to bring together an *ad hoc* committee to draft a widely publicized two-thousand-word statement on "liberty against socialism." Hereupon the Republican Senatorial and Congressional campaign committees reduced the statement to a ninety-word digest of their own. Senator Taft, chairman of the Senate Republican Policy Committee, quickly announced that the digest had "no official standing whatsoever."[15]

Soon after the 1956 election of Eisenhower, Senator Humphrey proposed that Congressional Democrats adopt their own legislative program, consisting of sixteen points, including civil rights, as a responsible opposition alternative to the President's program. "If you have a platform," Democratic Mayor David Lawrence of Pittsburgh commented to reporters, "you ought to follow it up with a legislative program, not just throw it out after you are defeated in an election." Senate Democratic floor leader Lyndon Johnson and Speaker Sam Rayburn declared their opposition to Humphrey's step and suggested that Congress wait and act upon the Eisenhower legislative program. When later Rayburn and Johnson proved fairly congenial to the Eisenhower program, Truman, Stevenson, Humphrey, and other Democratic leaders moved to form a Democratic Advisory Committee (or Council, as it came to be called) to keep alive the spirit of creative opposition. But the Speaker and majority leader agreed only to "consult" the committee, holding that they must retain their independence of action for their Congressional responsibilities. In such a tangled situation it is difficult if not impossible to find a meaningful national party leadership. Stevenson was discredited because of his two defeats for the Presidency, and Johnson's own party-mindedness, in light of his course, was a trifle obscure.[16]

The Jeffersonian Success Model

The President's success in party affairs is a mixture of many things: his own personality, his public popularity, his skill at maneuvering, his intuitive sense. It is a game played not with rules but with a master's instinct for the shifting sources of power. Some Presidents revel in their role as party commander. Jefferson, Franklin Roosevelt, and Kennedy, for example, enjoyed the game and usually played it with skill and finesse. John Quincy Adams and John Tyler, at the other extreme, were failures. And a President like Eisenhower accepted his party leadership reluctantly, holding that the White House should be above the party. It was as party leader that Lyndon Johnson accumulated considerably less success than he enjoyed in other branches of Presidential endeavor. Eminent among Presidents as a legislative leader, as party leader he secured for himself a quantity of black marks in the books of political professionals. The experience of each of these men is, in different ways, instructive.

Of all the Presidents, Thomas Jefferson is unsurpassed in the authority he asserted as party leader and in the fealty he commanded from state and local party organizations. He held sway with a thoroughly formulated theory of party principles and functions and a sure grasp of the means of party action. For Jefferson, the party was preeminently the instrument of majority rule. The party joined the executive and Congress into a majoritarian unit. The President and his department Secretaries provided the legislative agenda; the party members in Congress transmuted it into law.

The Presidential program was the party program, and fidelity to it in debate and vote was a principle to be jealously guarded and enforced. Jefferson wrote critically of his Congressional party brethren,

> Our friends have not yet learned to draw well together, and there has been some danger of a small section of them, aided by the feds [the Federalist party], carrying a question against the larger section. They have seen however that this practice would end in enabling the feds to carry every thing as they please, by joining whichever section of Republicans they chose; and they will avoid this rock.[17]

Jefferson could not abide Republican legislators who acted independently of their party. He called them "wayward freaks, which now and then disturb the operations."[18]

Jefferson worked through and dominated the Congressional party machinery. Caucuses of Congressional Republicans were summoned at his direction, and sometimes reportedly he presided. Secretary of the Treasury Albert Gallatin devoted no little time and skill to laying before the caucus the President's messages and requests. Jefferson, Gallatin, and other cabinet Secretaries watched over the progress of administration measures in Congress at all stages until their enactment. Jefferson and his aides invented the "floor leader," a legislator in each house who efficiently shepherded the administration's fondest projects over the craggy terrain of votes, committee hearings and reports, and parliamentary maneuver.

At the outset of a legislative session John Randolph, House floor leader and Ways and Means Committee chairman until he fell from Presidential grace, would dine with Jefferson to go over the administration's agenda. As the session proceeded, the Congressman was in almost daily touch with executive officials. Gallatin spoke of his "free communication of facts and opinions" to Randolph. Most of Gallatin's proposals were steered through the Ways and Means Committee and onto the House floor in the manner his fastidious tastes desired. Appropriations to purchase Florida, to establish a Mediterranean Fund, and to retire the debt moved steadily under Randolph's sure hand. As floor leader, he managed such major Presidential projects as the repeal of the Judiciary Act, the reduction of civil expenditures, and the bringing of charges of impeachment against Supreme Court Justice Samuel

Chase, a loud, violent Federalist who denounced Republicanism from the bench as a mash of anarchy, atheism, and the devil.

Jefferson viewed Congressional elections as a grand opportunity to eliminate obstructors and import supporters. Although James A. Bayard, Federalist Congressman of Delaware, had by his vote finally ensured Jefferson's triumph over Aaron Burr in their struggle for the Presidency, Bayard's subsequent leadership of the Congressional opposition alienated the Chief Executive. The President, as he was wont to do, searched for a candidate to beat Bayard at the polls. "For God's sake, run for Congress against him," he implored Caesar A. Rodney of Delaware. Bayard's "long speeches and wicked workings at this session have added at least 30 days to its length, cost us 30,000 D. and filled the union with falsehoods and misrepresentations." Rodney ran and was elected. The President's occasional manipulations had their costs. Major lieutenants like Joseph Nicholson and Nathaniel Macon were sometimes bedeviled with rumors that he was maneuvering to throw them over. To such men he wrote what became known as his "tares" letters: "Some enemy, whom we know not, is sowing tares among us. Between you and myself nothing but opportunities of explanation can be necessary to defeat these endeavors. . . . I must therefore ask a conversation with you."[19]

Jefferson employed patronage to induce legislators to cooperate and to assure executive loyalty to his policies. When things went awry in the party organization, he was quick with redress. Randolph was dropped from his two high posts soon after he erred. He had managed and botched the prosecution of Justice Chase and had demurred at the President's seeming tenderness to the culprits of the Yazoo land fraud and at the President's request for a secret appropriation of two million dollars to purchase Florida if circumstances warranted. Randolph announced his dissents with merciless invective on the House floor. The affronted Jefferson dropped word to Senator William Plumer that "Mr. Randolph's late conduct is very astonishing and has given me much uneasiness." Jefferson and his followers moved to depose Randolph as floor leader and to substitute Barnabas Bidwell of Massachusetts. This plan was foiled when Bidwell was defeated for reelection. Administration business that normally went to the Ways and Means Committee was routed elsewhere as long as Randolph remained chairman. In a speech on the House floor Congressman Thomas Mann Randolph, Jefferson's son-in-law, savagely attacked John Randolph as a betrayer of secrets and an inciter of clamor. From his constituency in southern Virginia, the embattled Randolph complained that "every engine has been set to work to undo me in the estimation of my constituents, and not without effect." The local press maintained a steady, hostile chant, and two prestigious Virginia politicians, William B. Giles and Wilson Cary Nicholas, campaigned mightily against him. Another Jefferson son-in-law, John W. Eppes, took up residence in Randolph's district, contested his House seat, and eventually won it in 1813, when Jefferson was long retired.[20]

Those Who Failed

If Jefferson achieved crowning success as party leader, John Quincy Adams and John Tyler floundered in the uttermost depths of failure. Adams won the disputed Presidential election of 1824 in the House of Representatives and then only, his enemies said, by a corrupt bargain with Henry Clay. In return for Clay-controlled House votes to assure Adams' election, Adams promised the Kentuckian the post of Secretary of State. Andrew Jackson, one of the vanquished candidates, termed Clay "the Judas of the West."

Adams was endowed neither by personality nor by circumstance to be a party leader. Austere and principled, he faced a wretched political situation. His cabinet contained no one who had openly supported him for President. Although his party controlled the House, the opposition ruled the Senate. Key Senate committees like the Foreign Relations Committee constantly opposed him. Adams' perilous situation in the upper chamber came into sharp relief when he requested authority to dispatch a mission to the Panama Congress of Latin-American states. The Foreign Relations Committee rejected his plan with a warning against entangling alliances, but somehow he managed to squeak through the Senate by a vote of twenty-four to twenty despite a punishing debate.

Randolph, who had returned to Congress in 1815, had a field day with the Panama Congress proposal. Charging that Clay had forged the invitations to the Congress, he resumed the attack upon the political partnership of the President and the Secretary of State. They were, he cried, "the coalition of Blifil and Black George . . . of the Puritan with the black leg."* For Adams, the worst aspect of this rowdy day in the Senate was not Randolph's crudity but the fact that the President's own party permitted it. Not a single Republican Senator called Randolph to order, and Vice President John Calhoun, in the chair, permitted the breach of privilege. Adams, furious at Calhoun's laxity, made a slashing attack upon the Vice President, writing under the name "Patrick Henry," in the press. Calhoun, who used "Onslow" as his pen name, reciprocated fully. The two party giants, the President and Vice President, demonstrated their rich talents for controversy in several exchanges.[21]

Adams' personal encounters were never softened by the favors at his command as party chieftain. He conceivably could heal wounds by applying the salve of patronage. But his principles stood in the way, taking precedence over the claims of party, as General James Tallmadge, lieutenant governor of New York and Tammany chieftain, sadly learned. Tallmadge had backed Adams unstintingly in his narrow victory. In a savage fight the lieutenant governor had stopped a move by Martin Van Buren's New York machine to break up

* A reference to two conspiratorial characters in Fielding's *Tom Jones*.

a joint session of the state legislature before the electors could be chosen. If Van Buren had succeeded, New York's electoral votes would have been wasted and Adams defeated. Van Buren and his ally, Governor De Witt Clinton, had their avenging knives poised. Tallmadge clearly needed to escape New York for a distant foreign mission if his political life was to be saved. Thurlow Weed, Tallmadge's emissary, laid the situation before the President. In a meeting that was "embarrassing and constrained," Adams quickly demonstrated his capacity to ignore political obligations. He could not appoint Tallmadge to any diplomatic post, he said, because another New Yorker, Rufus King, had just been named minister to Britain, and New York could not claim more than one overseas appointment. Weed sickened when he reflected that King had opposed Adams' election and Tallmadge had risked, perhaps given, his political life to assure it.[22]

John Tyler, like Adams, is at the bottom of the league of party chieftains, although for different reasons. A sure-footed politician, he was the victim of the relentless ambition of the leader of the Whig party in Congress, again Henry Clay. The New York *Herald* wrote of Clay,

> He predominates over the Whig party with despotic sway. Old Hickory himself never lorded it over his followers with an authority more undisputed, or more supreme. With the exception of some two or three in the Senate and fifteen or twenty in the House, Mr. Clay's wish is the paramount law to the whole party.[23]

Clay coupled with his great power a fierce drive to become President. A towering obstacle was the incumbent President Tyler and his likely desire to be reelected.

Not without reason, Clay scornfully spoke of Tyler as "a President without a party." Tyler's Whig following in Congress was so small that it was called, half-derisively, "the Corporal's Guard." In the Senate, only William C. Rives supported Tyler in the heavy fighting. The President's party weakness extended to his cabinet, which he had inherited from his late predecessor, William Henry Harrison. All the cabinet Secretaries except Secretary of State Daniel Webster and Postmaster General Francis Granger were allied with Clay. Even of Webster and Granger, Tyler could not be certain. The President's chief sustenance in his political weakness was his personality—"approachable, courteous, always willing to do a kindly action"—and his unlimited courage.[24]

Without a party Tyler could not well put his chief measures through Congress; with a party Clay had Congress in his hand and the President largely at his mercy. Time and again Congress rebuffed the President and the President vetoed Congress. Clay, pursuing his American system, a series of measures to promote the nation's economic development, put through a bill creating a new bank of the United States. Tyler, whose state rights disposition was offended, vetoed it, earning plaudits from Andrew Jackson. The Clay men drenched the President with invective. "The vocabulary of the language," a witness wrote, "seems to have been ransacked for words to express their angry denunciation."[25] A second bank bill passed, and Tyler vetoed it. At Clay's command, all his men in the cabinet resigned.

Tyler, bereft of party aid, saw many a favorite measure hacked to death in Congress. His proposed treaty with the German *Zollverein* was tabled in the Senate. His nominations to office habitually encountered rough handling in the same body. His fond project to annex Texas by treaty was lost, with every Whig but one voting against it. Eventually, almost miraculously, Tyler brought Texas into the Union by joint resolution.

Tyler's troubles lay not only in Congress. He was treated roughly in the organs of political communication, in the party press, and in the talk of the political professionals. Henry Clay was known to say that if it could have been foreseen at the Harrisburg convention, which created the Harrison-Tyler ticket, that Harrison would die after a month as President and that Tyler would veto the Whig's bank bill, either the convention would have ignored Tyler or he would not have received a single electoral vote in the subsequent election. The Clay press reechoed its leader's hostility. The Richmond *Whig* called Tyler "the accident of the accident," "a vast nightmare over the Republic." And when a dread influenza epidemic overtook the country, the Whig press was quick to name it "the Tyler Grippe."[26]

Franklin Roosevelt as Party Leader

Franklin Roosevelt, the most powerful of modern Presidents, was also the most assertive as party leader. Commanding unprecedented popular support, attested by his four-time election to the Presidency, he dared to attempt drastic renovations of his party: to expand its voting base by extending its commitment to programs and to displace the Democratic Congressional foes of the New Deal with those who promised to be its friends. Bold ventures almost inevitably involve a mixture of success and failure, and they did for Roosevelt.

Roosevelt's assertions were founded upon a close and constant mastery of those aspects of party functioning that fell most within his influence. Any President's authority is foremost in his party's national headquarters. He handpicks the chairman of the national committee and runs the national office as if it were his own organization. The President and possibly certain of his executive aides superintend the national chairman, but Roosevelt assumed more authority than most. James A. Farley, for example, in discharging the chairman's large responsibility for organizing and dispensing the patronage, was frequently overridden by Roosevelt and his aides. "While I transmitted a great many recommendations for appointment to the White House and to other Cabinet officials," Farley wrote, "only a small part of them actually were approved."[27] When Roosevelt and his secretary Steve Early grew displeased with Farley's preparations for Roosevelt's second term, the approaching 1936 campaign, they began to infiltrate their own people into the national committee. Roosevelt's first recruit was Edward L. Roddan, a newspaperman who had been covering the Presidency for the International News Service. He briefed Roddan personally on how he wanted things done. After Roddan took up his task, Roosevelt sent him a flurry of notes on campaign matters, not through Chairman Farley, but to Roddan directly. White House personnel were recruits for the national committee organization, too, among them Stanley High, a talented Presidential speech-writer, and Leon Henderson, a major administration economist.

Roosevelt's superintendency in the 1936 campaign dealt not only with personnel but with the full sweep of campaign strategy and detail. In a discussion of campaign methods with the National Emergency Council, a New Deal administrative agency, which often handled political assignments, he said, "Bring in as much as possible the simple illustrations that appeal to the average person back home. . . . Don't tell them in Georgia what is being done in Alabama; take the nearest project to where you are speaking in Georgia and tell them about that." Shortly before the 1936 national convention, he sent to Farley a memorandum reorganizing the national committee's activities. Let Charles Michelson oversee speech material, High the pamphlets, and so on, he instructed. He steadily pushed Farley to set up committees for independent voters, Republicans, businessmen, and other groups.[28]

Roosevelt's close attention to detail prompted him to pounce on lapses, large and small, in campaign management. When Jim Farley in a speech derided Alf Landon, the future Republican Presidential nominee, as the governor of "a typical prairie state," a huge uproar leapt from the Middle West. The resentment of this slight was compounded by the fact that its spokesman was the worst possible kind of Easterner, a New Yorker. Handbills soon flooded the West with pictures of Abraham Lincoln and the caption, "He, too, Came from 'a Typical Prairie State.'" The Presidential reprimand was quick. "I thought we had decided," Roosevelt wrote to Farley, "that any reference to Landon or any other Republican candidate was inadvisable." In the future, the President said, no state or section should be referred to except in laudatory terms. "If the sentence had read 'one of those splendid prairie states,' no one would have picked us up on it. . . ."[29]

A rare President may intervene not only in the elections themselves but also in his party's primaries for Congressional seats, seeking the nomination of candidates pledged to his support. Because of the grave hazards such an enterprise involves, most Chief Executives, such as President Eisenhower, stoutly refused to take sides in any primary of their party. Presidents who wisely keep aloof from local primaries know all too well that the local voters resent the intrusions of outsiders. Harry S. Truman abided by this rule except in his own Congressional district, where he publicly endorsed a friendly candidate. He followed the normal practice, however, in the 1950 North Carolina fight for the Democratic Senatorial nomination, when Truman's own personal friend,

Frank Graham, a leading Fair Dealer campaigning for "real Southern democracy," was defeated by Willis Smith. Truman was little more than a bystander while the defeat, a damaging one to his prestige in the party, was being fashioned.

Franklin Roosevelt mounted the heaviest Presidential assault yet upon the inviolability of the local primary in his attempted 1938 purge of a handful of Democratic Senators and Congressmen. If it had succeeded, it would have brought about a major revision of the Congressional Democratic party and the party's historic heterogeneity would have been displaced by loyalty to the New Deal program. The purge was sparked by the defeat of Roosevelt's Court-packing plan of 1937.* That defeat, the first major rebuff in five years of glittering victories, had rankled the President. Not a few Democrats who opposed the Court plan, he noted, had steadily voted against his New Deal measures. Roosevelt turned a receptive ear to his aides, Harold Ickes, Thomas G. Corcoran, and Harry Hopkins, who for months had talked of the desirability of a purge. On a hot June night he fired the opening salvo of the purge venture in a fireside chat. He declared,

> As the head of the Democratic party . . . charged with the responsibility of the definitely liberal declaration of principles set forth in the 1936 Democratic platform, I feel that I have every right to speak in those few instances where there may be a clear issue between candidates for a Democratic nomination involving these principles, or involving a clear misuse of my own name.[30]

The purge took on more definite form in Roosevelt's zigzag trip across the nation. He proceeded to distinguish between those who were with and those who were against him. In Texas he beamed on liberal Congressmen Lyndon Johnson and Maury Maverick and punished Senator Tom Connally, a Court bill foe, by announcing from the back platform of his train the appointment to a federal judgeship of a Texan whom Connally had not recommended. In Kentucky Roosevelt worked hard for Alben Barkley, his faithful Senate leader, embattled in a close race for his Senate seat with Governor Albert "Happy" Chandler, a strong campaigner with a potent machine. Roosevelt, upon reaching Kentucky, invited both Barkley and Chandler into his car for a drive to a huge political crowd at the Latonia racetrack. Roosevelt and Barkley were nettled when Chandler kept bowing to the right and left, acknowledging the great applause that presumably was directed chiefly to Roosevelt, and the President came roaring back with a speech heaping praise upon Bark-

---

* Faced with a Supreme Court that repeatedly declared his New Deal legislation unconstitutional, Roosevelt sought to "pack" the Court with new members who presumably would be more favorable to his purposes. He proposed to add one new justice, up to a maximum of six, for every justice of the Court who, having passed the age of seventy and serving for ten years, failed to retire.

ley and dismissing Chandler as a young man who required many years to match Barkley's knowledge and experience. In a later statement Roosevelt hinted that Chandler had approached the White House with a deal in judicial appointments in an effort to clinch his Senate seat.

Roosevelt had a fitting tactic for every situation. He crossed Nebraska without inviting Senator Edward R. Burke to join his party. In Wyoming Senator Joseph C. O'Mahoney was not invited but boarded the Presidential train at Cheyenne as a member of a citizens' welcoming committee. Roosevelt stuck out his hand; "Hello, Joe! Glad to see you," he said cheerily. At succeeding stops, he did not mention O'Mahoney, and when the Senator left the train at Casper, Roosevelt pointedly referred to politicians who paid lip service to the New Deal while frustrating its objectives. And in Colorado Senator Alva B. Adams, too, stood by uneasily while Roosevelt elaborately ignored him.[31]

The President was spurred on by the primary victory of Barkley and of another favorite, Senator Elmer Thomas of Oklahoma. He now concentrated his fire anew on several selected purgees. High on the list was Senator Walter F. George of Georgia. George's defeat, Roosevelt reasoned, would provide a lasting lesson to Southerners in Congress who had been opposing his social legislation. Other marked men in the Senate were Democrats Guy M. Gillette of Iowa, Bennett C. Clark of Missouri, Pat McCarran of Nevada, "Cotton Ed" Smith of South Carolina, Millard Tydings of Maryland, Frederick Van Nuys of Indiana, and Augustine Lonergan of Connecticut. In the House the men slated for defeat by the President were Howard W. Smith of Virginia, John J. O'Connor of New York, and E. E. Cox of Georgia, all determined foes of his New Deal program.

Roosevelt personally carried the fight against his principal purgees. En route for a vacation at Warm Springs, he stopped at Gainesville, Georgia, to dedicate a public square named in his honor. Senator George introduced the President, who proceeded to ignore the Senator and beam approval upon Governor E. D. Rivers, who he hoped would run against George. When Rivers declined, Roosevelt recruited Lawrence S. Camp, United States District Attorney at Atlanta. In another Georgia visit, this time at Barnesville, and with Camp and George on the platform, Roosevelt referred to the Senator as "my old friend" and proceeded to demonstrate his inadequacy by New Deal standards. The President described his test:

> First, has the record of the candidate shown, while differing perhaps in details, a constant active fighting attitude in favor of the broad objectives of the party and of the Government as they are constituted today; and secondly, does the candidate really, in his heart, deep down in his heart, believe in these objectives?[32]

The President proceeded to the excommunication. "I regret," he said, "that in the case of my friend, Senator George, I cannot answer either of these questions in the affirmative." Mixed boos and cheers rose from the crowd. Roosevelt shook hands with George who said, "Mr. President, I want you to know that I accept the challenge." "Let's always be friends," Roosevelt answered.

His strikes against "Cotton Ed" Smith were more subtle. Smith's rival, Governor Olin D. Johnston, opened his campaign in Washington after an interview with the President. In a speech in Greenville, South Carolina, Roosevelt observed, "I don't believe any family or man can live on fifty cents a day," a thrust at Cotton Ed who reportedly had said a South Carolinian could. Another chosen victim, Senator Tydings, took the heavy brunt of Presidential opposition. In a press conference, Roosevelt accused Tydings of running "with the Roosevelt prestige and the money of his conservative Republican friends both on his side." Roosevelt bolstered his Maryland favorite, David J. Lewis, with Maryland money and politicians and his own presence in two days of campaigning. Toward Tydings he was unsparing. At Denton, on the Maryland eastern shore, he spoke reproachfully of the Senator as one of "those in public life who quote the golden rule, but take no steps to bring it closer."[33]

The President was supplemented by a group of New Deal aides who had been in the thick of the latest legislative fights for the Court-packing and reorganization bills: Ickes, Hopkins, David K. Niles, Joseph B. Keenan, Corcoran, and James Roosevelt. Each, with varying degrees of subtlety, expressed the President's displeasure with legislators who had opposed him. Increasingly, members of this group took over the national party machinery, manipulating patronage and funds, and wrested quantities of authority from the national chairman, Farley, who opposed the purge.

For all of Roosevelt's effort, the purge ended a wretched failure. Although certain of his favorites triumphed, every Senator and Congressman he marked for defeat won except Congressman O'Connor of New York, and O'Connor's loss was attributed by New York Democratic professionals not to the President's intervention, but to O'Connor's own shortcomings—a poor campaign and a fat roster of enemies who joined together to take electoral revenge. In Georgia Roosevelt's candidate, Camp, ran a poor third; in Colorado Alva B. Adams was nominated without opposition; in Connecticut Augustine Lonergan prevailed in the Democratic state convention. "It's a bust," Jim Farley observed, as Roosevelt's political stock plummeted.

In the face of Franklin Roosevelt's grisly and unforgettable failure, no President has ventured onto the purge trail since his day. Of all post-Roosevelt Presidents, John Kennedy alone dared to veer, although only slightly, toward the 1938 tradition.

Yet despite Roosevelt's failure to transfer his own power and personal magnetism into victory against Congressmen who were entrenched in their local regions, he did shake his party at its roots and transform it through his own great political talent. The traditional Democratic party, on which he performed his drastic surgery, was a classical alliance of Northern city bosses and Southern and Western agrarians, bound together by state rights beliefs and federal patronage, and enlivened with intermittent bursts of progressivism. He replaced this old party order with a new Democratic coalition enduringly committed to positive government acting for national and group welfare. He had found the Democratic party a minority party. His graftings upon it of new group allegiances left it the instrument of the majority.

Roosevelt's vision of the new party was of one free from business domination and its debilitating effect upon political morality and public policy. He attracted into the party fold labor, farmers, racial and national groups, intellectuals, and women, all disadvantaged in the business culture. He brought in as well those businessmen who were restive under Wall Street and Eastern ascendance. Roosevelt established the new coalition by a lengthy, circuitous route. In staffing his administration after his 1932 victory, he drew talent not from the traditional Democratic organization but from the coalition. He brought Hugh Johnson, an independent, and Donald Richberg, a progressive, into NRA; Henry A. Wallace, a progressive, into agriculture; another progressive, Ickes, into public works. Hopkins, an independent, into relief administration; John Winant, a progressive, into social security; and Joseph P. Kennedy, a new entrepreneur, and James Landis, an independent, into securities regulation.

In Roosevelt's hands lawmaking was also an instrument of party reorganization. Major laws of his administration—the Social Security Act, the National Labor Relations Act, and the like—furnished the base of a new Democratic party, Northern and urban in orientation, attractive to city-centered groups, labor, Negroes, the new immigrants, women, and intellectuals. Policy and the unifying force of Roosevelt's personality, rather than pork barrel and patronage, cemented the new party. The breadth of his success was apparent as early as the 1934 Congressional elections. The Democratic returns showed an upsurge of labor and Negro votes, and of Northern Democrats in Congress with an ebbing of the relative strength of the South. Of 69 Democrats in the Senate, only 24 were Southern; of 322 Representatives, the South had 108.

The next major stroke in the Democratic party's transformation was the infiltration of New Dealers, or coalitionists, into the party's councils and operations. New Deal emissaries Edward Roddan, Stanley High, and Leon Henderson took up stations in the national committee. In electoral contests the party's chief campaigners were the New Deal coalitionists: Roosevelt himself, of course, and Ickes, Wallace, and Hugh Johnson. Administration policy was readily manipulated to feed the political necessities of the coalition. Roosevelt, mindful of the approaching 1936 elections, told Agriculture Secretary Wallace in February, "Henry, through July, August, September, October, and up to the fifth of November, I want cotton to sell at 12 cents. I do not care how you do it. That is your problem." When a WPA cutback in relief funds threatened the dismissal of many workers on October 1, Roosevelt instructed Secretary of the Treasury Henry Morgenthau, Jr., "You tell Corrington Gill that I don't give a god-dam where he gets the money from but not one person is to be laid off on the first of October."[34]

The courted urban groups provided not only votes but money, organizing energy, and publicity. In 1936 organized labor created Labor's Non-Partisan League, whose wealth and manpower were consecrated to Roosevelt's candidacy. Spurred and indefatigably aided by Eleanor Roosevelt, he won the enduring loyalty of Negroes to the New Deal. J. E. Spingarn, president of the National Association for the Advancement of Colored People, said of Roosevelt, "he has done more for the Negro than any Republican President since Lincoln."[35]

Roosevelt's experience showed that a powerful President can change the national image—and the reality behind the image—of his party. He succeeded by shrewd political finesse and also by promulgating a program with which many alienated groups could identify. And it was in defense of his new alliance, held together by a program—as well as in annoyance at the opposition—that he undertook the 1938 purge. The test of a party's success, he felt, was achievement of its program, and if a few entrenched party leaders had to go to achieve it, then this was a reasonable sacrifice. But he miscalculated local loyalties to long-time leaders and the refusal of local groups to think of the good of the party as a whole.

Eisenhower as a Bipartisan

Most Presidents climb to their exalted office by superior political skill and, upon arriving, eagerly take up their duties of party chief. But to a few Chief Executives, especially to hero-Presidents like Washington and Eisenhower, party activity is unwelcome, if not distasteful. Washington gladly delegated the partisan function to Alexander Hamilton, his Secretary of the Treasury, preferring to remain above the heat and dust of party battle himself. The new country, launched in perilous circumstances, required bipartisan unity in Washington's day. There was rather less compulsion for it in Eisenhower's. Nevertheless, during his two terms, Eisenhower resolutely, but not always successfully, shied away from partisan political duty. He immensely preferred nonpartisan and bipartisan politics to partisan. He could have been nominated for the Presidency by either party, and, indeed, a concerted effort for his Presidential services had been made by both parties. His most forceful lapses into partisanship occurred on the campaign trail, most notably his attacks upon the Truman administration in the 1952 electoral struggle. He supported almost any Republican who ran, and deleted from a speech in Wisconsin, in the interests of party harmony, a defense of General George C. Marshall, whose loyalty the local Republican Senator, Joseph R. Mc-

Carthy, had impugned. Eisenhower also permitted himself to be photographed with McCarthy. His foreign policy, which he largely entrusted to Secretary of State Dulles, was also hardly bipartisan.

Eisenhower's penchant for nonpartisan or bipartisan politics was a matter partly of temperament and partly of necessity. The strongest elements of his political faith were negative: return federal activities as far as possible to the states and to private responsibility, and balance the budget. His Modern Republicanism appeared to call for federal social measures, but these he chose not to push very hard. He eschewed partisan conflict, therefore, as something neither necessary nor relevant to his program, and avoided it if possible as activity that was troublesome and petty.

Eisenhower as President faced a Congress that had been dominated by the opposition party for a longer time and in greater numbers than any President since Zachary Taylor. Even in his first two years, when the Republicans controlled Congress, hard political reality necessitated cooperation with the Democrats. The Republicans' majority in the House was eleven, and in the Senate a mere one. Even more important was the inexperience of Republican legislators in cooperating with the Chief Executive. Not since 1931, nearly a quarter century before, had Republicans controlled the Presidency and both houses of Congress simultaneously. Not a single Republican Senator of the Eighty-third Congress, which began on January 3, 1953, had ever served with a President of his own party. Of the 221 House Republicans, only 15 had ever experienced a Republican President. The Republican habit of opposition did not cease with Eisenhower's advent. Indeed, it is not impossible to argue that Republicans gave Eisenhower a harder time than they ever gave Kennedy and Johnson. In the Senate Joseph McCarthy, William Jenner, Henry Dworshak, Herman Welker, Hugh Butler, and George Malone were relentless foes of the President's program in maneuver, speech, and vote. McCarthy, who was largely a gathering storm during the Truman administration, reached maximum fury during Eisenhower's first term. Most Presidents would have agreed with President Eisenhower, who decided, as he faced the Congressional session of 1953, that the coming effort of the administration and of legislative Republicans should be devoted to redeeming the 1952 party platform and his own campaign pledges. Eisenhower's State of the Union message of February 2, 1953, diligently mirrored these party pronouncements. But in the early Eisenhower Presidency, the Senate Republican leader was William F. Knowland of California, of whom Sherman Adams wrote, "It would have been difficult to find anybody more disposed to do battle with much of the President's program in Congress."[36] Franklin Roosevelt, in contrast, worked steadily—particularly in his first years—through a legislative party leadership that ran up a high batting average of support for his measures.

Although Presidents normally can assert a large and sometimes decisive influence in choosing their party's floor leaders, they differ in willingness to enter into the decision. When Robert A. Taft was driven from his Senate leadership by illness in 1953, Eisenhower could have replaced him with almost any Senator he chose. He scrupulously refrained, however, from influencing in the least way the selection of the new floor leader and even asked his administration colleagues not to express their preferences. Eisenhower felt that executive intrusion in this Senate affair was constitutionally inappropriate and might well be resented by Congressional Republicans. The President's staunch abstinence was ill rewarded. He got Senator Knowland. Eisenhower doubtless discovered that not to take a stand is, in fact, to take a stand. Two years later, in the struggle between the incumbent Joe Martin and his challenger Charles Halleck for the House floor leadership, Eisenhower took a wholly opposite stance. Martin had long displeased the administration by the mildness of his efforts in its behalf. Republican loss of House control in the 1954 elections made his continuance as floor leader highly doubtful. The administration did not hide its friendliness to Halleck's aspirations. When, after some struggle, Martin held onto the leadership and gave no place to Halleck in the leadership group, Eisenhower insisted that Halleck henceforth attend the legislative leaders' meetings at the White House. Eventually Halleck overthrew Martin as floor leader.[37]

On April 30, 1953, a historic explosion occurred when Eisenhower, meeting with Congressional leaders, broke the news that despite severe cutting he could not balance the new budget as Robert A. Taft and others who were present had hoped. The President and Defense Department officials explained that part of the difficulty was that certain revisions were necessary in the nation's defense program. Suddenly Taft erupted, losing control of himself, pounding his fist on the cabinet table, and shouting at the stunned President seated opposite him. "With a program like this, we'll never elect a Republican Congress in 1954," Taft cried, "You're taking us down the same road Truman traveled. It's a repudiation of everything we promised in the campaign!" Taft went on excitedly, and when he stopped, tension gripped the room. Fortunately, several of those present commenced an aimless conversation until Eisenhower, flushed and upset, recovered himself to state in measured tones the necessities of global strategy.[38]

Republican legislators were the most relentless foes of Eisenhower's mutual security program. Some Republicans wanted to reduce taxes at once regardless of the costs of the ongoing Korean War. Others wanted to scuttle the Reciprocal Trade Agreements Act and restore the high tariff Smoot-Hawley Act of the Hoover era. In jest and in no little truth, Harry S. Truman declared as the 1954 Congressional elections neared, "It seems to me that President Eisenhower should be secretly wishing for a Democratic Congress . . . and hope that we can save him from the misdeeds of his own party." Not surprisingly, Eisenhower sometimes speculated privately with his aides whether he really belonged "in this kind of Republican party."[39] He mused over the desirability of forming a new political party, internationalist, welfare-oriented, but conservative in spending and economic regulation.

Out of such experience, Eisenhower, understandably, never wore his hat as party chieftain gladly. To the Republican faithful, he denied even that he was a politician. "Everybody knew I wasn't a politician—and I'm not yet," he told a group of Republican workers on October 17, 1953. He clung to his chosen nonpartisan demeanor. He said at his news conference of February 10, 1954,

> I don't believe in bitter partisanship. I never believe that all wisdom is confined to one of the great parties, and I certainly have never in general terms criticized the other party, that is, to include its great membership. I believe there are good Americans in both parties, and I believe that the great mass of both parties is fundamentally and naturally sound.[40]

As the 1954 Congressional elections neared, he cautioned his cabinet against an overly partisan approach, adding that he must take care himself to remain nonpartisan in using the national radio and television networks except on programs paid for by the party. When Republicans everywhere, with the eagerness of those whose bread and butter was at stake, pressed Eisenhower to stump the country for the party tickets, he refused, acknowledging at a press conference, "I am deeply interested in what happens to the complexion of the Senate and the House of Representatives, but I do not intend to make of the Presidency an agency to use in partisan elections." His administration colleagues bolstered the President's view. Henry Cabot Lodge, Jr., ambassador to the United Nations, wrote to Eisenhower in July 1954, "The basic factor is and always will be the country's confidence in you. This confidence in you can be maintained and, with it, your immense influence for good, no matter what the election results may be." And yet as the 1954 elections came closer, and the party pressures mounted, Eisenhower finally yielded and took off for ten thousand miles of travel and forty speeches. His spreading involvement never overcame his distaste for campaigning. "By golly, sometimes you sure get tired of all this clackety-clack," he remarked to Jim Hagerty, his press secretary, on election eve.[41]

Soon after the Democrats captured Congress in 1954, Eisenhower informed his cabinet he did not see how there could be any question of the need for the White House to work with the Democratic leadership. He held bipartisan meetings with the legislative leaders and, when major happenings were afoot, diligently kept both sets of party leaders informed. Upon returning from his 1956 Bermuda meeting with Prime Minister Harold Macmillan, for instance, he invited spokesmen from both parties on the Hill to the White House for a report on the conference. In public pronouncement, as well as in private act, Eisenhower maintained a moderate demeanor toward the Democrats. "Whenever he thought any one of us became too harsh," Sherman Adams wrote, "he would remind us that we were not going to get anywhere in Congress without Democratic votes."[42]

Each President, as party leader, is expected to assist the campaigns of Congressional candidates indiscriminately, including the campaigns of those whose election would injure his program more than their opponents' victories would. Roosevelt's attempt to flaunt this tradition had ended in failure. In the 1954 Congressional elections President Eisenhower permitted himself to be photographed with a hundred or more Republican candidates, an imposing advantage in a local campaign. He also promised to make speeches delineating his program if he happened to be in the vicinity of a candidate who supported it and invited him to speak. Asked how he chose from among the Congressmen for bestowal of his photographic and rhetorical favors, he acknowledged that there was "a little bit of a check" on the legislators' voting record. In actuality, he was not known to withhold support in 1954 from any of the more recalcitrant legislators in his party who asked for it. For the President, loyalty to party generally transcended loyalty to program during campaigns.

Roosevelt and Kennedy took the position that support for their program *was* loyalty to the party. Perhaps a strong President inevitably assumes that he and his program and the party are synonymous. The party professional, however, makes no such assumption, except for pragmatic reasons in Presidential election years.

So Eisenhower, whose temperament was bipartisan, or perhaps more accurately apolitical, was forced by circumstances into assuming a highly partisan role in election years and a bipartisan role in between in his relations with a Democratic Congress. He was a man of uncomplicated loyalties and ideological simplicity, a man for whom conflict over program or over people was uncongenial. His election-year loyalty to his party, therefore, proved nearly absolute. Is it a political paradox that those Presidents who are less party-minded can be counted on to support the party most (but with least effect) and that those who are genuinely partisan—and strong—will defy the party when a few block the fulfillment of the party's promised program?

Kennedy and the Urban Era

President Kennedy had paid considerable heed to the lessons of both Roosevelt and Eisenhower. He was deeply concerned over the fact that a party's national program supported by its Presidential candidate may falter or fail at the hands of the party's own leaders in Congress. Was the answer not to wait for the election year to initiate a purge but to move upon the source of power ahead of time—in the state and local party organizations, where the seeds of trouble germinate?

The state party organizations are allegedly self-governing principalities, but Kennedy, who pursued his duties of party chief with zest, remorseless diligence, and ingenuity, moved upon them with aggressive enterprise. He acted principally through his personal organization—Lawrence F. O'Brien and Kenneth O'Donnell, his brother Robert and his brother-in-law Stephen E. Smith, and other associates, all of whom enjoyed close personal ties with state and local Democratic power centers in the big Northern industrial states on which Kennedy concentrated. His own organization in these states was in some ways more powerful than the regular Democratic organization. He maintained close ties with state leaders such as Jesse M. Unruh of California, city leaders such as Ray Miller of Cleveland, and local potentates such as Charles A. Buckley of the Bronx, dealing them considerable preferment. After the 1962 elections Smith, a man of quiet competence, served the Democratic National Committee as a trouble shooter in the key states of New York, Pennsylvania, Ohio, and Michigan, all of which had chosen Republican governors. Smith's chief responsibility in his uneasy capacity was to prevent fractious Democrats from feuding with one another. His early assignments included the laying of olive branches on such adversaries as "reform" Senator Joseph Clark of Pennsylvania and Philadelphia "machine" leader Congressman William Green, Jr. In Michigan Smith toiled to heal the rift between the United Auto Workers and Democratic regulars, and in New York to quell the party's long-standing strife and chaos.[43]

Kennedy did much "coordinating" himself. Soon after taking office, he worked mightily to revise the New York State Democratic leadership. He gave the cold shoulder to two top Democratic chieftains, Carmine De Sapio, New York County leader, and Michael Prendergast, state chairman. The more luscious patronage appointments credited to New York were awarded to members of a reform Democratic group dedicated to Prendergast's and De Sapio's ouster. The President appointed as ambassador to NATO Thomas K. Finletter, who with former Senator Herbert H. Lehman and Mrs. Franklin Roosevelt shared the top anti–De Sapio leadership in Manhattan. Lehman's grandnephew, Jonathan B. Bingham, was named United States representative to the United Nations Trusteeship Council. Francis T. P. Plimpton, appointed deputy representative to the United Nations, was a resident of Suffolk County, but no endorsement was sought from the Suffolk Democratic leader. John S. Stillman, Orange County Democratic chairman, who was named assistant to the Undersecretary of Commerce, was never regarded as an ally of Prendergast.

Kennedy's cold treatment of De Sapio and Prendergast had a social dimension. During his inauguration ceremonies, Kennedy had pointedly distinguished between New York Democrats in good and bad standing. Congressman Charles A. Buckley, the long-time Bronx Democratic leader, Joseph T. Sharkey, the Brooklyn leader, and Peter J. Crotty, the Erie County chairman, all enjoyed places in the Presidential box at the Inaugural Ball. Prendergast and De Sapio were among the fifteen thousand dancers who milled about on the floor. In a visit to New York City several weeks later, Kennedy rode with James A. Farley through the city streets, visited Lehman at his apartment, interviewed Sharkey, and talked with Buckley on the telephone. De Sapio was totally ignored and Prendergast heard only from a member of the Presidential staff.[44] By these and other means Kennedy implied he would never deal with Prendergast and De Sapio, and encouraged lesser New York Democrats to challenge their leadership.

Kennedy resorted to several expedients to advance the candidacies of legislative Democrats whom he viewed favorably. To further the cause of Wilkes T. Thrasher, Jr., an all-out New Frontiersman running in the Third Congressional District of Tennessee in 1962, he picked the candidate to represent him as a special ambassador at independence ceremonies in Trinidad. The scarcity of such plums underscored the importance of the President's action. As the 1962 elections neared, Kennedy seemed to take a giant step toward Roosevelt's method when he announced that he was "going to help elect Democrats" who supported his legislative program. The incumbent Representative Leonard Farbstein of Manhattan, who was running for reelection, faced a primary contest with Assemblyman Bentley Kassal, the reform Democratic candidate. In a letter to Farbstein, Kennedy praised his "clear judgment, wisdom, dedication and energy" and expressed "my personal appreciation for your sustained support of our legislative program." Farbstein made the letter public, terming it an endorsement.[45] His opponent, Kassal, contended that it was not, that he had been assured indeed that Kennedy would not take sides in the primary. The President said no more, and Farbstein swept on to victory. Reform groups are common casualties of Presidential party decisions, especially where the rival individual or group represents power the President cherishes or respects. Farbstein, as a member of the House Foreign Affairs Committee, had been an ardent advocate of bills favorable to Israel. In turn, the administration's attitude toward Israel was considered important by large numbers of Jewish voters in New York.

Kennedy, as other Presidents have done in by-year elections, viewed the 1962 electoral campaign not merely as an opportunity to elect Democratic legislators but to bring his goals and programs to the people. Two years of feet-dragging by a Democratic Congress added glow to the opportunity. But while the President serves his own purposes, at least partially, his presence is cherished by the Congressional candidates and the local party organizations. Kennedy's capacity to bring out the crowds gave tremendous publicity to the campaign and a great boost to campaign enthusiasm. Thanks to the perquisites of his office, the President also has campaigning facilities that no competitor can match. While out on the trail in 1962, Kennedy had an entourage of five press assistants, a reporting service that produced texts of his speeches within minutes of their delivery, and a busload of miscellaneous aides. The transportation of himself and his group was cared for by a fleet of White

House automobiles, two jet airliners, a DC-7 airliner, and four Army jet-powered helicopters. Everywhere he went he was followed by forty-four reporters, photographers, and television technicians traveling by chartered plane. His chief rival campaigner, former President Eisenhower, toured in an eight-passenger aircraft unaccompanied by press parties, mimeograph machines, or helicopters.

Like other Presidents before him, Kennedy in his attentions to the states was by no means always on the side of the reformers—if support for the regulars strengthened his own position. At a Democratic fund-raising dinner in New York City, he sent Charles A. Buckley a lavish verbal bouquet, described by a Kennedy staff member as "the most personal message I've ever known in all my twelve years' association with the President." The message, which was read at the dinner, was signed, significantly, by "Joe, Jack, Bobby and Teddy Kennedy." This fulsome tribute to one of the most encrusted and anachronistic of bosses brought the New York *Times* to protest the President's knowing recognition of a figure who needed to be "decried and deplored" rather than "promoted and protected."[46] Not the least importance of Buckley was that as chairman of the House Public Works Committee he was admirably situated to help the administration by influencing other House Democrats to vote for the President's bills. In the Pennsylvania struggle between Senator Joseph Clark, a liberal reformer, and Congressman William Green, an old-style political boss of Philadelphia whose habit was victory, Kennedy veered toward Green. The President needed the Congressman for the approaching 1964 election if the 1960 contest was a guide. In 1960 Kennedy had carried Philadelphia by a 337,000 vote majority, amply assisted by Green's machine. Yet he had carried the state of Pennsylvania by only 51.2 per cent of the vote. Green's obvious usefulness led Kennedy to shower him with attentions. The Congressman visited Kennedy in Florida, sat in his box at a football game, and accompanied him in his helicopter to the funeral of Senator Robert S. Kerr in Oklahoma. It was not that Kennedy was against party reform—though many party leaders thought so—but he believed that the only way to achieve it was to win over the power centers for himself first.

Publicity is another weapon a President can employ to promote his legislative party friends, and President Kennedy moved in 1963 to coordinate White House publicity with the needs of his Democratic supporters on Capitol Hill. The President brought Paul Southwick, an experienced newspaperman, into the White House from the Area Redevelopment Agency of the Commerce Department. Southwick, as part of the White House press office staff, forwarded useful news and information to the Democratic legislators with suggestions of how they might exploit the President's activities for their own publicity needs.

In another publicity gambit, Kennedy moved to wrest from the Republican party one of its proudest possessions, the observance of Abraham Lincoln's birthday. He celebrated that event in 1963, the centenary of the Emancipation Proclamation, with a White House reception for Negro and civil rights leaders and a host of Democrats, chiefly legislators who supported the Kennedy program. More than a thousand celebrants were on hand, including Negroes distinguished in endeavors ranging from law to jazz. The day was ripe with suggestion of the solid harmony between Lincoln's ideals and contemporary Democratic action. Prior to a buffet, Kennedy received at a ceremony in his office a report on civil rights progress in the hundred years since Lincoln's Emancipation Proclamation. The report noted that "as the century following emancipation draws to a close, more forces are working for the realization of civil rights for all Americans than ever before in history. Government is active in every branch and at every level, if not in every region." But it added, with a solid air of commitment, "The final chapter in the struggle for equality has yet to be written."[47]

Kennedy's death cut short the experiment that was to have been tested in the 1964 Presidential election and probably in the 1966 Congressional election. He died in the line of duty as party leader. The purpose of his visit to Texas, which ended in his assassination, was to reduce the widening cleavage between Texan Democratic factions identified with Senator Ralph W. Yarborough and the then Vice President Johnson. It is left for future Presidents to see whether the stalemate between the party's Presidential leadership and its Congressional leadership can ever be resolved in favor of the President and the majority of the nation who support him. The Kennedy formula looked for the eventual dominance of urban politics over Congressional politics. His legislative program was heavily directed toward the urban vote, and his personal political organization concentrated upon winning and holding the allegiance of the great Democratic organizations in the Northern urban states. The combination of a program geared to urban groups and a personal political organization that mobilized local party organization could conceivably have added up to a force that Democratic legislators would have found difficult to resist after 1964.

Johnson the Consensus Leader

Lyndon Johnson came into the Presidency with only a modest background in partisan leadership. The bulk of his political career was passed in a one-party setting in his home state of Texas, in an interval when only the Democratic organization could win at the polls. A one-party state, by definition, precludes indulgence in the arts of partisanship. As Senate Democratic leader he spent most of his tenure working in bipartisan cooperation with a Republican President. Neither were his initial years as President productive of emphasis on partisan leadership. The 1964 Presidential race was conducted under circumstances that made an "unpartisan" campaign Johnson's most logical choice. The identification of his opponent with an ultraconservative political philosophy that repelled the great body of the electorate inevitably prompted Johnson to soft-pedal Democratic partisanship and appeal to the broadest possible group of Republican and independent voters.

More important than the several circumstances of his career was Johnson's own philosophy of politics. As Senator and President his fundamental working principle was "consensus," a method that employs discussion, reason, compromise, and accommodation; that seeks to create the largest common denominator of agreement among the broadest combination of group and sectional interests. By its nature, consensus tends to eschew partisanship and takes the road of nonpartisan and bipartisan politics.

Against such a background of experience and philosophy, it is not surprising that Johnson as party leader did not compile a glittering record and sometimes even appeared to falter. A totaling up of errors and an articulating of grievances followed the 1966 elections that dealt the Democratic party substantial defeats across the nation. Among other things, the Republicans gained forty-seven seats in the national House of Representatives and eight governorships. In the aftermath Johnson assembled a quantity of Democratic governors at the LBJ ranch to hear their complaints and to formulate plans for 1968. Elsewhere other Democrats made known their unsolicited views. Criticism centered upon Johnson's chief resource as national party leader, the Great Society program, with its substantial expenditures for education, health, housing, poverty, and other political staples that bring advantage to vast reaches of the electorate. The dispensing of these program benefits presumably would be a great boon to the Democratic party, an expectation that the 1966 electoral results dashed.

The governors who assembled at the LBJ ranch complained that the administration of the Great Society programs was politically deleterious.[48] They were little consulted, or even informed, concerning the policies administered in their states. Governor Hulett C. Smith of West Virginia, a state that has a big stake in federal aid, complained of local dissatisfaction with penalties— such as reductions of grants-in-aid—that the federal government imposes for failure to meet its standards. The governors also contended that they were, in effect, called upon to campaign in 1966 in support of the national administration without having been consulted on national policy.

A second species of complaint sprang from the evident steep decline of the Democratic National Committee following the 1964 election. The committee, by tradition, is a Presidential adjunct, and the Chief Executive decides its policies and chooses its top personnel. Johnson ordered a cutback in services performed by the committee in an effort to retire the debt inherited from previous campaigns and increased in 1964. By dint of Johnson's economy measures, the committee liquidated its debts and even accumulated a reserve for the 1968 struggle. But the financial achievement was politically expensive. The committee was so weakened that it could not even mount a national registration drive in the 1966 campaign. There was also a curbing of the committee's influence. The White House regularly by-passed it on patronage. And, according to Governor John B. Connally, Jr., of Texas, the President's long-standing political friend, neither were the state Democratic leaders consulted.[49]

From other quarters came complaints that President Johnson's policies of financing had a weakening effect on state and local organizations. His principal fund-raising device, the President's Club, drained money out of the states and into the national party coffers. Democratic leaders in New York State, for instance, found it difficult to attract contributions for state party programs from many members of the President's Club. In 1966 almost seven hundred New Yorkers belonged to the club, a privilege that requires a contribution of at least one thousand dollars a year. The President thus siphoned off from New York a sum more than twice as large as the expenditure of the 1966 Democratic gubernatorial candidate, Frank O'Connor, whose Republican opponent, Nelson Rockefeller, ran a multimillion-dollar campaign. The outflow of funds also saps party strength at the grass-roots and hinders the normal development of young potential candidates and party leaders. Having limited resources, young aspirants encounter difficulty in attracting financial help from those already contributing substantially to the national party.

The feature of Johnson's conduct as party leader that rankled Democratic professionals most was his seeming aloofness from the 1966 elections. The campaign of that year was for him a noncampaign. Seldom did Democratic candidates receive less help from the White House. As the campaign moved into its climactic weeks, Johnson resorted not to the speaking stump, but journeyed to the Far East for consultations on international affairs. A decision to undergo surgery prompted the President to cancel a plan to venture onto the campaign trail after his return from the Pacific. Following his operation and convalescence, the President in a news conference, shortly before the election, failed to make a ringing endorsement of such embattled Democratic candidates as Pat Brown in California, Paul Douglas in Illinois, and Robert Duncan in Oregon. For that matter, although offered the opportunity by questions posed in his news conference, the President made no endorsement of any Democratic candidate. One disillusioned Democratic leader in California growled, "When it comes to working for Johnson in '68 he may find a loyalty gap here."

The President's behavior in 1966 was not a sudden lapse. It was characteristic of his behavior in other electoral situations. In 1965, for instance, a high point in the campaign of Abraham Beame, the Democratic nominee for mayor of New York, was a one hundred dollar-a-plate dinner with Vice President Humphrey as the featured speaker. The Vice President spoke glowingly of Beame, whose managers and followers eagerly awaited from Humphrey the disclosure of an appropriate endorsement from the President. At last the address of the evening reached that most welcome moment. President Johnson, the Vice President reported, conveyed "his warm regards, his hearty greeting and his good fellowship for this very happy evening." The address moved on to other matters. The absence of a direct Presidential endorsement for the Democratic candidate a week before the election in the nation's leading mayoralty contest was viewed as a major blow to Beame's campaign.

With a full backlog of resentments, and the 1968 elections on the horizon, Johnson in 1967 launched an intensive drive to improve his relations with Democratic governors and local party organizations. To smooth out administrative snags in federal programs, the President dispatched Farris Bryant, former Governor of Florida and Director of the Office of Emergency Planning, with a squad of experts from the federal departments to visit forty state capitals. In a further move, the President installed a plan by which each member of the cabinet is assigned four or five states as his personal responsibility, with instructions to facilitate personal contact between the governors and the White House. Late in 1967 and in 1968 each of the fifty states was scheduled for a "day" in Washington, when a planeload of its key officials was to be flown in for conferences with departmental officials, capped by a meeting of each governor with the President. In Washington state officials would sit across the conference table from their federal counterparts, and any important unresolved questions would be left to the governors to take up in their visit to the White House.[50]

In President Johnson's defense, it is clear that the protestation against his Great Society programs came chiefly from governors of the South and Southwest, whose states insisted upon more local autonomy and were habituated to standards of social and economic policy substantially lower than federal standards. The President was caught in a vise between his duty to upgrade the quality of the nation's life through federal programs and the pressures upon the state leaders of his party to maintain local autonomy, which resulted in lower standards. Johnson's noncampaigning in 1966 was encouraged by counselors impressed by the dominance of local issues and the President's dipping popularity at that moment at the polls. By disposition and philosophy, Johnson was a centralist, or one who tended to gather power into his own hands, and to distrust institutions whose autonomy and inclination might produce resistance to his purpose. His centralism was also encouraged by the strength of a competitor, Robert Kennedy, in state and local party organizations. With Kennedy men well stationed around the country, it was only natural for Johnson to use his most available resources of party leadership, the resources of centralism—federal programs, the national party structure, the Presidential office.

The Future Presidency

At most the President can be only a quasi–party leader. A variety of forces and pressures compel him to temper and contain his partisanship. He must at times give higher priority to his calling as leader of the nation, facing needs and goals greater than those of his party. He may face a Congress one or both of whose houses is dominated by the opposition party. The body of independent voters has increased to such a degree that in several Presidential elections they have held the key to the outcome. Thanks to weak party discipline, a President knows the difference between a "paper," or party, majority in Congress and a "working" majority. In many of his waking hours he is forced to be bipartisan or nonpartisan if he is to pick up needed legislative votes from the other party. Bipartisan leadership is exerted at a price. It rests upon consultation and compromise and necessarily reduces the forcefulness of policy and the President's program image.

Viewed another way, although the party system has enabled a national popular majority to choose a President, when he attempts to translate his electoral promises into policy, he finds himself in a government that permits only limited majority rule, thanks to separation of powers and checks and balances, among other things. Only a rare President, such as a Jefferson or a Franklin Roosevelt, succeeds in building a strength as party leader that enables him to extend substantially the principle of majority rule. Despite the limiting realities of the party and the governmental structure, what can be done to help the strong President also be a strong party leader?

1. The formula evident in John Kennedy's labor as party leader, one which his death prevented him from fulfilling, appears the most promising. Kennedy was bent upon subordinating party and Congressional politics to urban politics. He pitched his program to the great urban groups: economic, racial, and national. In light of his proven appeal to them, he could confidently cultivate state and local party leaders who determine the selection of and the support given to Congressional candidates. The Kennedy method, had he lived to follow it through, would have lighted hundreds of bonfires under Congressmen and Senators, fueled by an urban program and maintained by urban groups and local party chieftains. The movement of social forces strongly supports the Kennedy formula: the enormous growth of urban population; its interest, as Arthur N. Holcombe long ago reminded us, in class politics and therefore program politics;[51] and the growing sophistication of urban groups in political action—in organizing and defining their objectives on a national scale.

The urban-group formula admittedly carries weaknesses. The individual's identification is primarily with the group rather than with the party. A comparison of strong group identification with the Democratic party in the Franklin Roosevelt era and its weakening in the Truman-Stevenson era reveals its vulnerability to fluctuating events and shifts in group and Presidential personalities. The urban-group approach has limited relevance to Republican Presidential needs because of the growing tendency of the groups to identify with the Democratic party. The Republicans must resort to a diversified appeal to the urban and suburban voter, the independent, the detachable Democrat, and a broad range of other interests. The Kennedy recipe is good for Democrats but not Republicans.

2. Kennedy in his approach relied heavily upon a sizable personal Presidential organization to assist his party leadership by building contacts with state and local leaders. To "keep in touch" with fifty state organizations and hundreds of local organizations is a massive enterprise that a President must continuously conduct or oversee. Above all, he needs loyal and capable helpers who are best assured if he recruits them himself. In the manner of Jackson and Kennedy, a President is well advised to install in the executive branch a corps of aides for party affairs who can concentrate upon them as Amos Kendall and Frank Blair did in Jackson's day and Kenneth O'Donnell and Lawrence O'Brien did in Kennedy's.

3. Kennedy was building up a technique of the "soft purge," a useful device for future Presidents. Since Franklin D. Roosevelt's ill-fated experience, Presidents had backed away from the open, concentrated purge. Kennedy, in the tradition of Jefferson, quietly encouraged his favored candidates for Congressional office, without arousing local resentments over Presidential interference. Kennedy and his aides distributed pork barrels, publicity, campaign assistance, and Presidential blandishments in a fashion that heaped, within discreet limits, conspicuous attention upon proper voting legislators and pointedly reduced or withheld the several beneficences from offenders.

4. To strengthen the President as party leader, we might, not illogically, strengthen the parties themselves. The most comprehensive effort toward this end was proposed by a committee of the American Political Science Association in 1950, which after viewing British political parties admiringly recommended in a report, *Toward a More Responsible Two-Party System*, that several of their features be adapted for American use. The committee proposed that we revise the size and timing of our national conventions, create a national party council or cabinet, stimulate regional as opposed to state and local organizations, formulate more positive platforms, and encourage closed primaries.

Although the dream of this report has not come true, several trends are afoot agreeable to it. The Democratic Advisory Council, which has endeavored with mixed success to work out party positions on policy questions, is a substantial step toward the party council or cabinet proposed by the APSA report. The national party committee, which the APSA committee did not look upon favorably as a vehicle of policy influence, is nevertheless expanding its functions, particularly the Republican committee, in a manner potentially advantageous to the President's party influence. The national committee is the biggest collector, allocator, and spender of party money. It locates and channels patronage and is the party's dominant publicity agent in national elections. It focuses upon policy in its research, public relations, and speech-making activities. Often the committee is catalytic in policy matters. Both the Republican and Democratic National Committees are stressing ties with pressure groups. It would be foolhardy to expect any miraculous changes in national organization that somehow would suddenly and vastly improve the President's party position. Yet the national party organization will bear watching as a flexible and fluctuating phenomenon, particularly as its relationships to pressure groups extend and deepen.

5. The proposal of a tax credit for the federal income taxpayer who contributes to the party of his choice could be devised in a fashion that would broaden the base of contributors, make the parties less dependent upon the big donors, and strengthen the national party organization without weakening other available organizations—the state and local structures—and their vital contribution to American political life.

6. The gadgetry of Congressional party organization is least promising of all for future Presidential leadership. The main thrust in behalf of centralized party management is the policy committees that have proved a blunted sword. The committees' best uses are service and research, education, and legislative scheduling. Intermittently, however, they work out policy positions, significant not for their number but for the fact that they can and do materialize. The Senate Democratic Policy Committee, for example, in 1957 opposed sanctions against Israel upon her refusal to withdraw from the Gaza Strip. The Republican Policy Committee in 1953, with Secretary of State John Foster Dulles and Attorney General Herbert Brownell in attendance, prepared a compromise on the Bricker amendment that won support from two-thirds of the Republican Senators. In 1957 the Democratic Policy Committee forged a party position on the proposal to tie together measures for Alaskan and Hawaiian statehood.

The Congressional and Senatorial campaign committees are devoted chiefly to publicity, to doling out funds for campaigning, and to research on public reactions to issues. Thanks to the separation of powers and its psychological side effects, they are jealous of their autonomy and would spurn any plan to bring them into close conjunction with the Presidentially oriented national committees.

Legislative Leader 6

No function of the President is more beset with uncertainty, is more vulnerable to breakdowns, and is more readily the victim of the will and whim of men whose outlooks and responsibilities tend to be different from his own than his duty to lead in legislation. Nowhere else in the Presidential enterprise is there found a greater gap between what the Chief Executive wants to do, what he promises to the electorate in his contest for the office, and what he can do in bringing Congress to enact the laws that alone can give effect to the party program of the previous campaign. In no other major nation is the program of a head of government more susceptible to rebuff in the legislature, to unconscionable delay and crippling amendment, and to absolute, uncompromising rejection. The President runs an obstacle course on Capitol Hill that other heads of government would find strange and even incredible.

Congress's power to check and frustrate the Executive has been a matter of painful Presidential discovery from the very outset of constitutional experience. George Washington's election as President was delayed a month until the requisite number of legislators straggled into the capital to enable Congress to organize itself and witness the electoral count. After his inauguration Washington suffered more frustration. Congress dilly-dallied in providing the executive departments that the Constitution allowed for and without whose assistance the President could not function. Not until June 23, 1789, almost two months after the inauguration, did Congress provide the first department, a Department of Foreign Affairs.[1]

Even a President like Dwight Eisenhower, who generally viewed Congress with good will, was sometimes seized with sensations of futility. One of his severer attacks occurred in 1955, when the administration's highway program passed the Senate but was stopped in the House, and Congress adjourned. The country faced the unhappy prospect of falling further behind in its poor race to build roads for the swelling torrents of traffic. The lack of a highway construction program also hurt the general economy. Eisenhower's aides, with a sense of looming disaster, urged him to call Congress into special session to act on the vital highway program. "Well," the President said ruefully, "the special session might be necessary—but calling it could be at the cost of the sanity of one man named Eisenhower." There was no sense in spending money to call them back, he later added, "when I knew in advance that the result would be zero."[2]

Eisenhower long had known the unreliability of Congressmen in transmuting the national party platform and Presidential campaign pledges into legislation. In delineating his program at the outset of his initial term, he had taken pains to remind his cabinet and legislative leaders that the Republican platform of 1952 comprised "the minimum limits of achievement below which we must not fall." Eisenhower's dedication to the platform was received with open amusement by the legislative leaders. "To my astonishment," Eisenhower wrote, "I discovered that some of the men in the room could not seem to understand the seriousness with which I regarded our platform's provisions. . . . More than once I was to hear this view derided by 'practical politicians' who laughed off platforms as traps to catch voters."[3]

In his 1960 campaign John Kennedy spelled out a program by which alert and aggressive leadership might move the country forward again. He put forth several hundred specific proposals including parity for the farmer through a supply program, medical care for the aged under social security, full employment, equal rights for women, price stability, freer foreign trade, urban renewal, a new civil rights law, and the like. Most of Kennedy's campaign pledges required legislative fulfillment and therefore provided a ready foundation for his legislative program as President. But what came forth was a shrunken image of the earlier promises. Kennedy dropped permanent improvements in unemployment compensation and repeal of right-to-work laws, among other things; he trod softly on aid to education, oil depletion allowances, and medical care for the aged; and he postponed civil rights. There were no radical new ideas, no great transformations of policy like those implied in the rhetoric of the 1960 campaign. In the main his items were familiar holdovers from the Eisenhower era, items that might have been passed if Eisenhower had chosen to push them. Kennedy, in a sound appraisal of Congressional realities, chose to set his sights low.

The Good Legislative Years

Congress, the historical record discloses, consistently follows the Presidential lead only in three types of situations. One is crisis, when the survival of the nation or its social system may be at stake. In the gravity of the peril, national opinion demands action and the population looks to the President for initiative and brooks no denial. The crises of the two world wars and of the Great Depression created a popular opinion that demanded nothing less than Congress's full support of Presidential leadership.

The second situation in which Presidential leadership is assured is found in national security and foreign affairs since World War II. In these the President has enjoyed a high batting average of success. A Marshall Plan, a Truman Doctrine, a NATO, and wars in Korea and Vietnam are well supported, although the cement of union was provided not by Presidential skill or legislative charity, but by the doings of the Russians, the Red Chinese, the North Koreans, and the North Vietnamese.

The third situation of outstanding Presidential success is produced by rare occurrences of political abnormality under circumstances highly favorable to the Chief Executive. Theodore Roosevelt in intervals during his two terms, Woodrow Wilson in 1913 and again in 1916, and Lyndon Johnson in 1965 and to a lesser degree in 1966, enjoyed this special status. All three were uncommonly skilled at manipulation in legislative encounters and basked in the sunlight of exceptionally favorable political circumstances. Roosevelt and Wilson thrived upon the nation's expanding progressive sentiment. Johnson reigned at an interval when the explosive urgency of urban problems no longer permitted Congress to sleep upon the President's program.

Both Wilson and Johnson were favored with towering working majorities in the houses of Congress. In the Senate Wilson and his social program enjoyed the presence of progressives whose numbers comprised a majority in both parties. His Democratic majority in the House was large, and he was doubly blessed by the fact that 114 of 290 House Democrats had been elected for the first time. Eager to please, their future careers depending heavily upon executive patronage and the administration's general success, they were amenable to Presidential direction.

In 1965, Johnson, too, reaped rich legislative harvests with the aid of a substantial corps of freshmen Democratic Congressmen. Coming into office in an era when Presidents enjoyed strong success in the Senate only to meet steady rebuff in the House, Johnson derived from the 1964 elections a crop of seventy-one freshmen Democratic Congressmen. Sixty-seven of these voted for the top items on his agenda—the education bill and Medicare—and the entire body of them supported the President more than 80 per cent of the time on roll call votes. For most of 1965, House Democrats enjoyed a lopsided 152-vote margin over Republicans, which included a net gain of thirty-five seats from the 1964 elections. In certain instances, the President and his program twice profited when some conservative Democratic seats in the South were lost and some liberal Democratic votes in the North were added. A precious by-product of the top-heavy Democratic supremacy was the corresponding increase of Democratic party ratios on House committees. The Ways and Means Committee, a graveyard of key measures in the Kennedy years, was changed from a Democratic-Republican ratio of fifteen to ten to a ratio of seventeen to eight. The three Democratic vacancies on the committee were filled by staunch supporters of the President, and the committee proceeded to function in close harmony with the administration.[4]

With such imposing political resources at his command and with shrewd strategy and relentless drive, Johnson in 1965 presided over more legislative innovations on the home front than any other President in any other single session of Congress in the twentieth century. In scope as well as in number, the measures passed were impressive. These included medical care for the aged under social security, which had been on the Democratic agenda for twenty years; the first comprehensive aid to education legislation; a voting rights bill; immigration reform; a broad housing program that included rent subsidies to low income families; programs for highway beautification; programs for combatting heart disease and cancer and strokes and water and air pollution; and income guarantees for wheat-farmers. With ample reason, Johnson could call the Congress of 1965 the greatest Congress ever and "my Congress."

Following the 1966 elections and the upsurge in Republican strength, Johnson's fortunes on Capitol Hill veered toward the more usual pattern of inaction and rebuff for key items on the Presidential agenda. Prior to the elections, the administration lost its civil rights bill with its open housing provisions. It again sustained defeats on two major measures that it had lost in 1965: home rule for the District of Columbia and amendment of the Taft-Hartley Act to permit states to ban the union shop. The Great Society's major social programs subsisted on low appropriations. But Johnson's achievements constitute a vast improvement upon the dreary record of executive-legislative relations in the long interval from 1936 to 1963 when only two pieces of major domestic legislation were passed: the Fair Labor Standards Act of 1938 and the Taft-Hartley Act of 1947. The political landscape during those crucial years of national growth and adjustment is strewn with the wreckage of Presidential proposals.

Congress and the President: Basic Differences

Congress repeatedly checks and balances the President largely because it represents altogether contrasting constituencies. The President, chosen by the nation, is the natural instrument of majoritarian rule—is, as Max Lerner has written, "the greatest majority-weapon our democracy has thus far shaped."[5] It is, to be sure, a contrived majority, one normally more difficult to maintain than to create, an association of purposeful pressure groups and the great mass of little-organized citizenry, distributed across the several sections of the country, each with its distinctive social and cultural tradition and economic organization. Congress, in contrast, is the product of local constituencies: the Senate emerging from the substantial land mass of the states and the House, except for its members at large, from the smaller Congressional districts. The validity of both the national and the local viewpoints found in the executive and legislative constituencies is affirmed by the federal principle of government incorporated in the Constitution.

Congress's relationship to the "national majority" differs in other respects from the President's. The totality of the two-house Congress is never the product of any conceivable national majority, since only one-third of the Senate is chosen in any given election. The President's national majority and the Senate's and House's local majorities have varying periods of legitimacy expressed in the terms of office allotted to the candidates they elect: the Senators six years, the President four, the Congressmen two. The Senator or Congressman is identified with several kinds of majority: with the majority of his constituency, with the party majority in his house, and with the voting majority in his house. In carrying on the legislative process, the houses of Congress contain no continuing majority. A majority accumulates or emerges for limited purposes but never hardens into a durable entity. The legislative majority that passes a particular bill develops from a series of processes by which members are elected, the internal authority of the House and Senate are allocated, an agenda is selected, and procedures of debate and vote are followed. But once the bill is passed and others arise, new and almost invariably different majorities must be constructed. Congress is also the haven for the minority: the minority party, the maverick legislator. Congress speaks with many voices. The Chief Executive, with his concentration of authority and use of hierarchical organization, aims to speak with one. Congress represents the rich diversity of American life, the President its necessary unity.

Despite their imposing differences, no one branch, executive or legislative, can claim inherent superiority in articulating the national or public interest. A Washington and a Wilson are shining beacons of public interest, but who can say that in the quest for the common good President Harding was superior to Senator George Norris, or President Coolidge to Senator La Follette? During certain eras legislators sometimes speak with more initiative, force, and freedom on national issues than Presidents do. Webster and Clay are better remembered than most of their Presidential contemporaries. In the 1960's Senator Fulbright could undertake a candid and comprehensive review of the prevailing foreign policy in terms unthinkable, at least in public utterance, for the Chief Executive and his principal subordinates. Many of the nation's foremost economic and social policies were first championed by legislators well before Presidents were prepared to exert their influence. Thus the Federal Reserve System was preceded by the legislative spadework of Senator Carter Glass, the Tennessee Valley Authority by years of advocacy by Senator Norris, and key New Deal policies by the pioneering effort of Senator Robert F. Wagner. In 1965, when Johnson reigned so fully over legislative-executive relations, Congress passed a voting rights bill broader than the one he proposed, and the House Ways and Means Committee produced a major expansion of his Medicare bill. It would be folly, in light of the historical record, to view the executive branch as the seat of omniscience and Congress as merely negative and local. For Theodore Roosevelt a strong Presidency was premised upon a strong Congress.

But distinguished legislators are more common than strong Congresses. In brutal truth, Congress is far more often weak in accomplishment than strong. However memorable a La Follette or a Norris may be, the houses of Congress are more than assemblages of individuals; they are also corporate bodies with a hearty preference for inaction and conservative leadership. Compared with the judiciary and the Presidency, Congress has a special distinction. It is, as Senator Joseph Clark of Pennsylvania has put it, the one branch of our federal government where twentieth-century men are not in charge. In a series of speeches that he delivered in February 1963 Senator Clark candidly analyzed the Senate organization and found that body in the hands of a "dominant minority" rather than what he termed its "creative majority."[6] Both the House and the Senate work with a body of procedures that have an awesome capacity either for preventing Congress from acting at all or for ensuring that it will act only after unconscionable delay.

Inside Congress

Congress's internal organization and processes constitute a vast terrain of booby traps for the Presidential program. The standing committees and their chairmen, the negative power of the House Rules Committee, and the Senatorial filibuster are all potential occasions of disaster for the President. The regular center of the President's concerns is the standing Congressional committee, where party discipline is least potent.

Committees provide the money and authority indispensable to executive action. The committee chairman is a potentate presiding over a great satrapy, calling meetings when he chooses, setting the agenda, allocating time for testimony, and personally reporting the committee's measures to the floor. The sole principle by which he is chosen is seniority. He rises to his eminence not by proven excellence or loyalty to President or party but simply by being present year in and year out. Since seniority is most easily built by legislators from "safe districts," chairmen emerge most steadily from the Old South and Northern rural districts, and with such backgrounds they prove beyond doubt that a safe seat cultivates independence both from the national party and from the President. The geographic distortion of Senate committee chairmanships is evidenced by the fact that in 1968 nine of sixteen of these posts were occupied by Southerners. These included such crucial committees as Finance, Judiciary, Foreign Relations, Labor and Public Welfare, Government Operations, and Banking and Currency, where most of the legislation that was of major concern to the Johnson administration reposed.

Accordingly, any modern President, whether Republican or Democrat, faces an array of chairmen instinctively and philosophically hostile to his programs. In 1968, for example, major civil rights legislation was long delayed in the House Rules Committee, chaired by William M. Colmer, an anti-administration conservative Democrat from Mississippi. From 1967 onward, President Johnson was bedeviled by the opposition of Wilbur D. Mills, chairman of the House Ways and Means Committee, which enjoys jurisdiction over such vital subjects as taxes, social security, and tariffs. Mills kept bottled up Johnson's request for a tax increase and demanded deep cuts in federal expenditures before taking it up in his committee. In the Senate the chairman of the Judiciary Committee, a key committee where civil rights legislation is traditionally considered, was Democrat James O. Eastland, who on occasion has withheld his support of his party's Presidential ticket and platform.

Not only may the chairman of a standing committee be hostile to the President's program, but the committee's members may be as well. The appointment of committees is largely in the hands of what in actuality is the ruling oligarchy of each house. In the Senate, for example, the Steering Committee of the party in power, which serves as the party's Committee on Committees, exercises three vital functions affecting the standing committees. It gives Senators of their party their committee assignments, determines the committees' sizes, and establishes the ratio between parties in committee memberships. In discharging its duties, the Steering Committee can discriminate against Senators who strongly support the President's program. The 1958 elections, for example, brought fifteen new Democratic Senators into the Senate. They were chiefly from the urban and industrial North, Middle West, and West, and without exception supported a legislative program strongly directed toward those interests. At the time the Senate Democratic Steering Committee consisted of fourteen members, half of them from the South. While such a distribution was reasonably in line with the body of forty-nine Democratic Senators in the previous Senate, it was hardly representative of the new total of sixty-two Democratic Senators. Soon after the 1958 election, Senator Joseph S. Clark of Pennsylvania, whose outlook was that of the urban, industrialized North, urged the then majority leader, Lyndon Johnson, to alter the Steering Committee balance "so that it would reflect not only the party within the Senate, and the will of the people as expressed in the election, but also the coming-of-age of the Senate in the modern world." But to no avail. "The Majority Leader did not agree with me," Clark has written, "and he worked his will in the caucus."[7]

The dominance of the seniority principle—which is a custom, since it is not incorporated in any rule—is a standard but not an inexorable Senate procedure. In 1913, for instance, it was overthrown when Senate progressives of all parties united into a majority to displace senior committee chairmen with young men, some of whom had not served in the Senate for more than two years. Meeting privately, they laid plans that enabled them to take over the Senate, reconstitute the memberships of all committees, oust the committee chairmen, and replace them with men of their own. This enterprise was indispensable for the progress of the series of legislative enactments that soon became known as Wilson's New Freedom program.

The President also may be a reforming force in the committee power structure. President Kennedy set as his first order of legislative business an assault on the most powerful of committees, the House Rules Committee, which schedules or refuses to schedule the time and conditions under which important bills come before the House. Thanks to the exertions of Speaker Sam Rayburn, the Rules Committee was enlarged by three members, hopefully a safe voting margin for administration measures.[8] But thanks also to the behind-the-scenes bargaining over the new memberships, the administration emerged with only a precarious eight-to-seven vote advantage on liberal-conservative issues. The injection of religious, racial, or special economic factors, as events soon proved, was enough to capsize the administration's narrow majority. In 1963 the Rules Committee was permanently enlarged, an action Kennedy encouraged by declaring that if the committee were not continued in its expanded state, his program would be "emasculated."[9] Despite Democratic losses in the 1966 elections, Johnson retained a working majority on the Rules Committee, without which the administration's prospects would be grimmer than those of yesterday's newspaper.

There is no better proof that Congress is often more the instrument of minority than of majority than the Senate filibuster. It is an ancient and favorite weapon of obstructionists. President Johnson's severest legislative task in 1964 was to steer a meaningful civil rights bill past the shoals of a Southern filibuster. He prevailed, thanks to a rare imposition of closure, which brought debate to a close, and indispensable Republican support. But this sudden political bliss was short-lived. In 1966 filibuster killed two key Johnson measures, the civil rights bill and the bill to amend the Taft-Hartley Act.

Districting and Apportionment

The procedures by which Congress is weighted in favor of conservative interests are reinforced by distortions in the methods by which members of the House of Representatives are selected. The Constitution requires that seats in the House be apportioned among the states according to population determined by the census every ten years. After each census Congress allocates to each state the number of House seats to which it is entitled according to its population. The state legislature then determines the boundaries of each Congressional district and whether any of its House seats will be subject to election at large. This political enterprise often incurs several kinds of abuses. One is the "gerrymander," by which the state legislature will carve out boundaries of Congressional districts in a fashion that will assure optimum popular voting strength for the candidates of its own party. The result is frequently a district of bizarre artistry, resembling, perhaps, a shoestring, a saddlebag, a fish, a tomahawk, or other improbable objects. In addition, since one or both houses of the state legislature has historically been weighted in behalf of rural interests, Congressional districts, in their total view, over-represent the rural population and underrepresent urban and suburban dwellers. Rural-dominated legislatures are slow to adjust Congressional districts to shifts in population.

The United States Supreme Court has intervened with a two-pronged attack on the problem of unfair representation. In *Baker v. Carr* (369 U.S. 186, 1962) the Court ruled that the distribution of seats in state legislatures was reviewable in federal courts. In succeeding cases, federal courts have laid down standards of growing precision that will soon regularly provide fairer legislative representation within the states. A better state situation presumably will produce more equitable Congressional districts. The Supreme Court launched its second major attack in *Wesberry v. Sanders* (376 U.S. 1, 1964), when it ruled that the language of Article I, section 2, of the Constitution that stated "Representatives . . . shall be apportioned among the several states . . . according to their respective numbers" and that they shall be "chosen by the people of the several states" meant that "as nearly as is practicable one man's vote in a Congressional election is to be worth as much as another's." Congressional districts, accordingly, must reflect this principle. Acknowledging that Congressional districts cannot be drawn with mathematical precision, the Court nevertheless ruled that the Constitution's "plain objective" of making "equal representation for equal numbers of people" must no longer be ignored.

The *Wesberry* decision's largest significance was that it provided a legal formula to assure that the House of Representatives would reflect in its make-up the impact of population shifts, both past and future, from rural to urban and suburban areas. Since 1910 and especially during the two world wars and the 1950's, an enormous shift of population to the cities has occurred. The forecasts are that the long-building urban trend will quicken in coming decades. The course of this development will depend considerably upon the degree to which the migrating population concentrates in urban rather than suburban areas. An Eisenhower-type program might conceivably appeal most to the suburbanite whose environment is a conservative influence, and a Kennedy-type program to the urbanite whose need of governmental services is most acute.

A Johnson-type program, with its drive against poverty and emphasis on civil rights, may please the urban center; its strong stress on consumer protection—safer automobiles, cleaner air, more honest credit terms, and eradication of crime—may appeal to the suburban dweller. Johnson's Great Society program, in reality, sought to combine the people of the urban center, with their need for governmental services, and suburbanites, with their need for protection against society's sundry abuses, into a lasting political consensus. The Presidency will surely gain by future population shifts. The hard question is how much and how fast.

In its immediate consequences, the *Wesberry* ruling brought into question most seats in the House of Representatives. The American Political Science Association estimated that equalizing Congressional district populations "as nearly as practicable" should put them within about 15 per cent of the average district population in each state. Only ten states that elected Representatives from districts in 1962 met the 15 per cent standard.[10] The disposition of federal courts to apply high standards is evidenced by a ruling of March 27, 1964, holding Michigan's 1963 redistricting act unconstitutional. Districts in the Michigan plan ranged from 305,952 to 490,310. The Court did not specify a maximum allowable variance.[11]

Congressional Majorities

Congress and the President, for all their built-in antagonisms, must somehow work together. "I am part of the legislative process," Eisenhower rightfully said in 1955.[12] Article II, section 3, of the Constitution is the launching ground for Presidential leadership in legislation. The President is called upon to "give to the Congress information of the state of the Union, and recommend to their consideration such measures as he shall judge necessary and expedient." But what the President proposes Congress disposes, by approval, defeat, delay, or amendment. Congress, too, can initiate and the President dispose, by approval, or by veto that Congress, needing to muster a two-thirds vote of both its houses, can seldom override.

Although in the face of an overwhelming emergency Congress may cooperate with the President, it enhances its self-image when it rejects the President or compels him to compromise. Congress can be irresponsible in its dealings with the President because with two houses, hundreds of members, powerful committees, and dispersed leadership blame cannot be readily allocated. The Senator or Representative acquires and keeps his seat not by loyally serving the President but by maintaining the approval of groups and interests in his local constituency. A labor union, a Chamber of Commerce, or a citizens' group normally has greater impact upon a Senator's or Representative's future than all the will and might of the President of the United States.

The President may have a paper majority of his party in Congress but no working majority. Dwight Eisenhower, brought into the Presidency by the largest popular vote that had ever been cast and with his Republican party in control of both houses of Congress, quickly discovered the harsh realities of his new existence. A succession of hostile maneuvers were launched by his Republican colleagues on Capitol Hill, and all were directed at the White House. Not a few of the President's antagonists had been swept into office on his coattails, but neither sentiment nor gratitude dulled their purpose. Senator John Bricker of Ohio, a former Republican Vice-Presidential candidate, sponsored an amendment that would have emasculated the President's power to make executive agreements and convert the treaty power, already difficult in the constitutional arrangement, into the most cumbersome in the world. The amendment, in the full magnitude of its potential mischief, promised to do more to wreck the Union than the Confederacy ever dared to contemplate in the Civil War. Senator Joseph McCarthy was in open war with the executive branch. Daniel A. Reed, the octogenarian chairman of the House Ways and Means Committee, fought for an income tax cut that threatened to throw the budget into gross imbalance and wreck the President's program set out in his State of the Union message. Reed's obduracy made him known, not altogether affectionately, in administration circles as "the Syngman Rhee of Capitol Hill." The President's nomination of Charles Bohlen as ambassador to Russia was severely and protractedly challenged by Senator McCarthy and other formidable Republicans. Congressman John Taber, the economy-minded House Appropriations Committee chairman, slashed nearly one billion dollars from the President's mutual security request. The President was steadily harassed by riders contrived by Republican legislators. Small wonder that Eisenhower after six months of office was driven almost to despair of being able to succeed in the Presidency.[13]

The President's problem of getting voting majorities is twice compounded by the bicameral system, which provides for two legislative houses chosen by different constituencies for different terms. The Senate, the traditional "rich man's club" of the late nineteenth century, was the nemesis of Theodore Roosevelt and his Square Deal program; Franklin Roosevelt fared conspicuously better in the House than in the Senate. Eisenhower and Kennedy, in contrast, enjoyed strikingly greater success in the Senate than in the House. Measures approved by Kennedy and the Senate were rejected in the House or rewritten to its specifications. Johnson's program, too, proceeded with less assurance in the House.

Why did the Senate, historic slaughterhouse of Presidential designs, give John Kennedy and Lyndon Johnson almost everything they asked for, while the House dealt out struggle and defeat? A possible explanation may lie in the great population shifts to the cities since the 1940's. The Senator, answerable to a state-wide constituency, has become heavily dependent upon the great mass of urban voters for election. Kennedy's and Johnson's electoral campaigns and subsequent legislative programs were directed chiefly to the urban industrial United States. A basic and growing convergence of interest exists between Senate and President, extending across party lines. Representatives, in contrast, are answerable to a smaller, less complex constituency.

The vagaries of Congressional party loyalty compel the President, estimating his legislative prospects, to acknowledge two coalitions in which members of each major party are joined. One is a "conservative" coalition of Republicans and Southern Democrats who, voting together in Kennedy's first two years, comprised a majority in both chambers. This stark, imposing fact illuminated the necessity for the Kennedy administration to concentrate upon weaning away Republicans and Southerners from opposition to its bills. Notwithstanding the administration's acumen and zeal, the conservative coalition did heavy damage. In the Senate it defeated the proposals for an urban affairs department and medical care for the aged. In the House it likewise killed the urban affairs cabinet post and the college aid bill. When the conservative coalition lost, as it often did, it was because the administration won over sufficient numbers of Republicans or Southern Democrats to support the rival "liberal" coalition. This coalition consists of a majority of voting Northern Democrats and minorities of Republicans and Southern Democrats, mostly from urban and suburban constituencies. Many of Kennedy's victories were owed to liberal and moderate Republican support. In the House, Republicans provided the margin of victory in the fight to enlarge the Rules Committee and the passage of the emergency feed grains, depressed areas, and minimum wage bills. Similar victories were won in the Senate. A *de facto* coalition of Northern and Western Democrats and "Liberal Republicans" provided the Kennedy administration with most of its successes.

Johnson's extraordinary legislative successes in 1965 were built over the collapsed foundations of the old Southern Democrat–conservative Republican coalition. The 1964 elections decimated the coalition's rank and reduced it to a shadow of its former power. In 1961, a Kennedy year, for example, the coalition won 74 per cent of the roll calls for which it was present. In 1965, the big year for Johnson's Great Society program, the coalition's successes fell to a low of 33 per cent. But in the 1966 elections the coalition rose again and promptly took charge of the House of Representatives.[14] Revised committee ratios enabled the conservatives to dominate the House Appropriations, Ways and Means, and other key committees. Despite a renunciation by the House Republican leadership of any formal revival of a conservative coalition, its influence is felt simply by the tendency of its members to think and vote alike.

The President conducts many of his legislative enterprises through the floor leaders of each house. Floor leaders, with their split role as party leader and the President's legislative leader, vary widely in interpreting their total responsibility. Robert Taft and William F. Knowland in the Eisenhower administration cherished their independence and the long mile between the White House and the Hill. Taft, of course, was Eisenhower's chief competitor for the 1952 Republican Presidential nomination, and Knowland, when invited to switch California to Eisenhower to provide the general with a big victory, answered coldly, "We don't want any credit or any responsibility for *that* nomination."[15] In true Congressional paradox, Eisenhower's best leader was

Lyndon Johnson, the Democratic floor leader, whose entire distinguished service was spent under the Republican Eisenhower. Johnson consistently refused to turn Senate Democrats loose on Eisenhower at will but worked with the President with dispassionate professionalism, supporting or opposing as he believed he should. "We prod him," said Johnson of Eisenhower, "into doing everything we can get him to do, and when he does something good we give him a 21-gun salute."[16] In Johnson's own Presidency, Everett Dirksen, the Senate Republican leader since 1959, helped push administration measures through with such success that some of his party colleagues were dismayed, particularly as the 1968 elections approached.

Open and Closed Politics

The President advances his program in Congress by means which C. P. Snow, the British novelist and scientist, terms "open politics" and "closed politics," one visible and the other covert. In open politics the President sets forth his proposals for legislation, sends appointments and treaties to the Senate, brings Congress into extra session and puts an agenda before it, and makes public statements explaining and defending his legislative actions. His chief weapon in open politics is his messages—his State of the Union message rendered each January, followed since Woodrow Wilson's day by special messages that focus on single issues. These messages provide the record and delineate the scope of the administration's program.

Congress, too, invites messages, and therefore leadership, from the President. The Budget and Accounting Act of 1921 bids the President to submit an executive budget each January. This ponderous tome, equal in bulk to several metropolitan telephone directories, with its accompanying message is a detailed statement of policy objectives with means of achieving them for Congress's guidance. The Employment Act of 1946 calls for an Economic Report from the President that permits him to lay out policies fostering free competitive enterprise and maintaining employment, production, and purchasing power at maximum levels.

Theodore Roosevelt began the practice of supplementing his messages with actual drafts of bills. Although Roosevelt, mindful of the niceties of separation of powers, was a trifle sheepish and clandestine about it all, Wilson did it openly. Since then all Presidents, even Calvin Coolidge, despite his strict constitutionalism and tired blood, have drafted bills.

The Constitution endows the President with the veto, a most powerful weapon in the game of open politics. The veto's grave defect is that it is total and not partial. The President must accept or reject a bill as a whole; he cannot veto particular items and approve the rest. This permits Congress to engage with merry impunity in pork barrel legislation in appropriation bills and to attach riders like the one Senator Pat McCarran attached to the general appropriations bill for 1951, "That of this appropriation $100 million shall be used only for assistance to Spain." Nothing at the time was more alien to President Truman's foreign policy than to provide aid to Franco, the Spanish dictator. Early Presidents seldom used the veto and then chiefly to object on constitutional grounds. Andrew Jackson first employed the veto as a weapon of policy and of popular appeal in his war on the Second Bank of the United States. Franklin Roosevelt, who brandished the veto more than any other President, was known to say to his aides "Give me a bill that I can veto" to remind legislators that they had the President to reckon with. Harry Truman, taking his cue from Jackson, vetoed a string of measures of the Republican Eightieth Congress, peppering his sentences with vivid expletives like "dangerous," "clumsy," "arbitrary," "impossible," and "drastic," not so much for the legislators as for the public. Truman's vetoes were no small factor in his 1948 victory.[17]

The President plying the strong approach may, as another tactic of open politics, take his legislative program to the people. His unrivaled power to command the nation's attention and its disposition to side with him against all foes endow him with a capacity no legislator enjoys. By skillfully leading the public, Presidents have brought Congress around to actions from which, left to its own instinct, it would refrain. Theodore Roosevelt was the first of the modern Presidents to rely heavily upon appeals to the public. Gifted and joyous in public combat, Roosevelt, blocked in Congress, went to the people. Woodrow Wilson perfected what Theodore Roosevelt had begun. "He is the spokesman of the Nation in everything," Wilson said, describing the President's special capacity. A spellbinder in times when oratory was admired, Wilson's lean, gripping prose and romantic moralism stirred men's better senses.[18]

Wilson and other successful practitioners of the popular appeal follow several rules. Wilson went to the public sparingly and only when the need was strong. The issue chosen must be important to the people and one about which their feelings can be instantly rallied. There must be careful preparation; when issues are sprung, they fare badly. As Wilson well knew, the venture carries the high risk that the people will respond only fleetingly or not at all. The appealing President is laying both his own political reputation and the prestige of his great office on the line. Worst of all, the secluded executive session of a legislative committee and the artful parliamentary maneuver, where the controlling decisions on the President's program may be made, are not directly accessible to the legions of public opinion.[19]

The President in his relations with Congress also engages in the processes of closed politics. Relatively unpublicized, unseen, and unofficial, closed politics employs the personal contact, the patronage lever, the choice viands of the pork barrel, and sundry other exertions of power and influence. The negotiation in the White House office or Congressional cloakroom, the Presidential phone call to the legislator deciding how to vote, the accommodations and compromises necessary to patch together a legislative majority for an administration bill, are the warp and woof of closed politics. The resort to closed politics is a constant reminder of the weakness of open politics. Because the Founding Fathers made so little provision for Presidential leadership in legislation, the Chief Executive is driven to rely heavily upon the extraconstitutional resources of closed politics.

The President personally is, or should be, at the center of closed politics. There is no substitute for the force of his word and gesture. He therefore must explain and exhort to win backing for his program. His dealings and exertions cover the entire range from soft to hard sell. Kennedy, endowed with personal charm and a zest for closed politics sharpened in his legislative years, labored hard and sometimes fruitfully in this vineyard. He met weekly with the legislative leaders of his party and breakfasted or lunched with the Speaker of the House and the majority and assistant leader of the Senate. He also conferred systematically and individually with the chairmen of each of the standing committees of both houses, and sometimes with the entire committee when it was mulling over an item of the administration's program.

Kennedy was often found in the thick of battles on Capitol Hill. When a crucial vote approached, he not uncommonly put in long hours on the telephone, carrying his case to legislators who had not yet made up their minds or seeking to detach others from the opposition camp. Kennedy's attentions embraced Republicans as well as Democrats. Everett Dirksen was the object of various blandishments, including privileged rides in the President's helicopter. When the Democratic leader, Senator Mike Mansfield, hailed Dirksen as a "tower of strength" on foreign policy, Dirksen found it necessary to deny good-naturedly, for the partisan record, that he had "gone soft on Kennedyism."

Lyndon Johnson brought to the Presidency a high reputation and rich experience in the art of closed legislative politics, with service in both houses of Congress and a record as one of the most illustrious floor leaders in Senate history. He was master of two indispensable competences in closed politics. He was ingenious at discovering politically feasible compromises, and he commanded a relentless, overpowering persuasiveness at bringing those he confronted around to supporting them. His former occupancy of high Senate station provided him with an access to the centers of legislative power that Kennedy, whose Senate influence was considerably less, did not enjoy. Johnson as President seemed to range further and more insistently over legislative affairs than Kennedy ever did. "Kennedy came too late to many of his problems in Congress," said an official of both these Presidential administrations, learned in the fauna of Capitol Hill. "He would hold back, let things develop, come in at the top of the crisis. Johnson likes to stay ahead and anticipate what will happen and how to meet it."[20]

In dealing and bargaining with legislators, the President operates from an array of vantage points. He can dole out various degrees of help in the next

Congressional elections. He manipulates the several executive beneficences like pork barrel and defense contracts. The Kennedy administration, laboring mightily to induce Southern Democrats to vote for its measures, generated good feeling by increasing price supports for Southern cotton and awarding Southern plants big defense contracts, such as the million-dollar order allotted Lockheed Aircraft of Georgia. The depressed areas bill forged ahead when its rural aid outlays were doubled. A map demonstrating how nicely the gravy would flow to Dixie under the amended bill circulated on the floor.

Not the least of the President's loaves and fishes is federal patronage, the art of bestowing offices upon legislators' protégés—with votes, hopefully, the *quid pro quo*. Wilson sometimes disciplined legislators who persistently failed to support his policies by cutting off their patronage. "We not only ought to pay no attention to Senator Vardaman's recommendations for office," he wrote his Attorney General, "but we ought studiously to avoid nominating men whom he picks out."[21] Truman, exasperated in his futile efforts to force the repeal of the Taft-Hartley Act in the Eighty-first Congress, thundered that how Democrats voted on that matter would be weighed in handing out patronage. But patronage by Truman's day, thanks to the spreading coverage of the civil service merit laws, had been reduced to a light weapon. For all of Truman's ferocity, Taft-Hartley was intact when he left the Presidency.

Despite the weakness of his individual weapons, if the President chooses to direct his available means of both closed and open politics upon a selected objective, he can gather an imposing arsenal. An impression of the administration's diverse weaponry is provided by Congressman Otto E. Passman, chairman of the House Appropriations Subcommittee, charged with responsibility for foreign aid. A skillful, doughty foe of foreign aid, Passman offered this picture of the Kennedy administration's legislative technique in its first foreign aid fight. The administration, Passman noted, relied heavily upon the testimony of Treasury Secretary Douglas Dillon, a Republican, "with his usual smile and personality." Passman continued,

> Then Democratic National Chairman Bailey sends wires to Democratic officials all over the country, trying to get them to put the pressure on Congress. . . . Then there were letters from Dillon and Rusk. . . . The program was talked up at a State Department briefing for editors. . . . There was the Ayub [President of Pakistan] peptalk [urging foreign aid]. . . . The Citizens Committee for International Development was organized to exert more pressure. . . . McCormack [then House Democratic leader] sent letters to 2400 mayors across the United States including some in my own district. . . . Shriver [then Director of the Peace Corps and the President's brother-in-law] made a personal visit to every office on Capitol Hill. Although he came for the Peace Corps, foreign aid was mixed in. . . . The White House kept contacting business groups all over the country. . . . I jotted down some figures to show my thinking [i.e., of possible cuts in foreign aid spending]. A Republican subcommittee member

> leaked the figures to the President a few hours before the subcommittee was to act. . . . While I was presenting the subcommittee report in the full committee meeting, administration agents continued to place phone calls to committee members in the room. In the same meeting, letters from an Assistant Secretary of State to members of the committee, all calling for more funds, were actually slipped under the door.[22]

Yet for all the unstinting commitment of the President and his cohorts, Congressman Passman cut the foreign aid appropriation by 21 per cent, or $896 million. After the deed was done, Passman observed simply, "This is a great day for the taxpayers." President Kennedy and his aides were reported "stunned and angry."

Approaches to Legislative Leadership

A Chief Executive can choose between several possible approaches in setting the tone, pace, and pressure level of his legislative leadership. No President, to be sure, limits himself to any one approach. Like baseball pitchers, he prefers to mix his delivery, and the choice of an approach, like a pitch, depends upon how the game stands at the moment. The sheer number and variety of approaches are themselves witness to Presidential weakness in legislative leadership. The following are some of the possibilities from which the President may choose.

"FOX" VERSUS "LION."   All Presidents engage in periods of the foxlike or diplomatic approach. The Constitution's endowment of Congress with vital powers of legislation and the President's consequent necessity of inducing its cooperation force him to be diplomatic in method. The President's personality and political ideology may bring him to prefer it. So also may special circumstances.

Harry S. Truman, swept unprepared into the Presidency, where the late incumbent had already been encountering trouble on Capitol Hill, took a cautious diplomatic line in his first Presidential years. There was no "must" legislation in the manner of Franklin Roosevelt; Truman limited himself to making recommendations in general terms, leaving Congress to work out the specifics unguided by executive recommendation. Truman in the meantime exerted few personal pressures upon the legislators and rarely commented on a bill until it reached his desk. He used the veto power sparingly. He filled his administration's principal posts with members and former members of Congress: James F. Byrnes as Secretary of State, Clinton Anderson as Secretary of Agriculture, Lewis Schwellenbach as Secretary of Labor, and Fred M. Vinson as Secretary of the Treasury. His communications on legislative business were discreet and deferential. He made several surprise visits to the Senate, mingling nostalgically with his old colleagues and speaking modestly and hopefully of future executive-legislative cooperation.

In the foxlike approach the President fraternizes with legislators and plies them with blandishments. Franklin D. Roosevelt excelled at the art of Congressional gratification, at giving out the easy first name, the warm handshake, the contagious smile, the intimate joke, the air of concern, the quasiconfidential interview, the picture snapped at the White House desk, the headline in the hometown newspaper.

One Saturday afternoon in blossom time in 1961, when Senator Harry F. Byrd's friends and neighbors gathered in his Virginia apple orchard to commemorate his birthday and eat fried chicken, there suddenly burst from the azure skies President Kennedy's whirring helicopter. The President had taken time from his heavy duties to come personally to honor the Senator. The attention did not deter Senator Byrd, one year later, and in the same apple orchard, from publicly criticizing Kennedy for requiring an excessive number of airplanes, yachts, and limousines to move about, and from proposing that he "set an example by getting along with a little less."[23]

President Johnson labored tirelessly at the diplomatic or foxlike approach. He received Congressmen at the White House with unparalleled cordiality, danced with their wives, arranged briefings for them on world affairs by Defense Secretary Robert McNamara and Secretary of State Dean Rusk. He telephoned congratulations to Congressmen for documents they had inserted into the *Congressional Record*. As a standard tactic, he was prone to bring legislators to the White House in groups of thirty for idea-trading sessions on national and international problems.

The President who resorts to the direct or lionlike approach brandishes the veto power freely, turns on the pressures of patronage, pork barrel, and the ministrations of alert aides. He churns up public sentiment for his program to spur the legislators into support. The example supreme of the strong approach was Franklin Roosevelt in his first one hundred days, when in the depths of economic crisis Congress time and again put aside established procedures in the rush to do the President's bidding.

The President is apt to be lionlike in seasons when his political prestige is riding high. Truman, after his spectacular surprise reelection in 1948, was soon giving the pressure valves a full twist. He jarred the gaiety of a Jackson-Jefferson Day dinner of 1948 by threatening, in his address to the celebrating Democrats, to tour the country to force Congressional enactment of the party's platform pledges. Later he termed the vote on the Taft-Hartley Act's repeal a good test of party loyalty and uttered several strictures on the seniority principle and the inattention of Democratic legislators to their party's national platform.[24]

In fashioning his remarkable legislative successes in 1965, Lyndon Johnson, in many an interlude, moved about in his Congressional dealings as a menacing lion. Favored by extraordinary legislative majorities as a result of the 1964 elections, he acted quickly to reap a maximum yield on his wealth of political resources. He insisted that Congress begin work at once on two measures that had long eluded legislative action—education and medical care for the aged geared to the social security system. After impressive success with these, he pushed an avalanche of proposals upon Congress. In 1965 alone, in sixty-three separate documents, he requested a staggering variety of legislation and maintained a close personal watchfulness over its progress.

SYSTEMATIC VERSUS "BUCKSHOT." President Eisenhower applied to legislative affairs the high degree of system apparent in other phases of his Presidency. His legislative program was elaborately coordinated, setting forth the President's choices and priorities in every major area of federal action. The cycle began at midyear when the Bureau of the Budget called upon the executive agencies to submit by September 15 a statement including "*all* items of legislation (other than appropriations) which the agency contemplates proposing during the ensuing twelve months." A month after the Bureau's call in 1953, Eisenhower, looking toward the coming State of the Union message, asked each cabinet Secretary for substantive ideas based upon a "thorough rethinking of the mission of your department and the . . . means to achieve it." The response was a vast outpouring of measures, many long advocated by the career service. Sherman Adams, the President's chief assistant, and several aides spent two weeks with Bureau of the Budget help studying and sifting the proposals and checking with the President. Many complex and controversial measures of high policy and partisan significance —social security, taxation, agricultural assistance, and foreign aid—were tagged for presentation to the cabinet by the sponsoring department head. The White House staff previewed the presentations and gave advice. In November and December seven were presented to the full cabinet, with Eisenhower himself a leading participant, his questions and views sparking most of the changes made. In mid-December the President unveiled his program to Republican Congressional leaders in a series of carefully staged eight-hour sessions at the White House. The Vice President, the Speaker, the majority leaders, whips, most of the cabinet, and several White House aides were also present. Congressional committee chairmen participated when their subjects were discussed. When legislative leaders expressed concern over some item, the President was apt to modify it. The principal purpose of the sessions, however, was to inform the legislators, not to secure their approval or commitment.[25]

In the three weeks between the leaders' meetings and the presentation of the President's messages in January, the several messages—the State of the Union address (put together by the White House largely from agency submissions), the Budget Report (written largely by the Bureau of the Budget), and the Economic Report (largely the work of the chairman of the Council of Economic Advisers)—were coordinated for consistency and coverage by the

White House staff. Meanwhile, the departments concentrated on drafting special messages and detailed bills to follow promptly each proposal advanced in the more general messages. The State of the Union message of January 7, 1954, stated the President's program in general terms. Specifics were advanced in a series of seven special messages, delivered from January through March, on individual subjects such as social security, agriculture, Taft-Hartley, and foreign aid. An administration bill quickly followed each special message.

Eisenhower's successors have continued his emphasis on system, each with his own variation. President Johnson, in setting his goals for each session, made intensive searches for new legislative programs. He used study groups of private citizens, sent emissaries to university campuses to corral new ideas, and pressed an earnest search among departmental planners and thinkers for responses to national needs. In one ground-laying memorandum, he asked department heads to "insist that your staffs consider the issues objectively, free from what they think may be overriding political obstacles to constructive change. I want to pass judgment personally on such alleged political obstacles."[26] To weigh and choose from the ideas that flowed in, Johnson employed a study group pulled together from the Executive Office, which included his special assistant for legislation, and top personnel from the Bureau of the Budget, the Council of Economic Advisers, and the Office of Science and Technology. Johnson was also a busy and skilled employer of the special message and meetings with legislative leaders.

President Truman was addicted to the buckshot method of presenting a legislative program. His message of September 6, 1945, "one of the most important of my administration," projecting the nation's conversion from warmaking to peacemaking, contained nothing less than twenty-one points of domestic legislation, ranging from agriculture to Congressional salaries. Sixteen thousand words in all, the message was the longest since Theodore Roosevelt's marathon twenty thousand words in 1901.[27] Nor was this all. In subsequent weeks Truman sent up special messages with additional proposals. In his legislative presentation of 1962, President Kennedy followed a similar tactic by deluging Congress with requests for civil rights, special Presidential authority to cut taxes and start public works to avert a recession, medical care for the aged, higher education, foreign aid, urban affairs, an international communications satellite, permanent unemployment compensation, and other things. Judged by its fruits, the buckshot approach is unimpressive. Only a few of Truman's and Kennedy's requests ever became law. Both sets of defeats were easily predictable beforehand.

Why, then, do Presidents resort to buckshot? In both the Truman and Kennedy instances, the Presidents were faced with approaching elections—the national elections of 1948 and the Congressional elections of 1962. Both Presidents, firing a barrage of requests at Congress that were foredoomed to failure, aimed to exploit the Republican tendency to ride the brakes, to build a record for labeling it the "do-nothing" party in the electoral campaign. The buckshot approach is usually asserted in a cantankerous style. Truman blasphemed Congress, and Kennedy, who regularly employed a sober approach puffing Congressional dignity, picked a fight on selected issues, particularly the creation of a department of urban affairs, which cast him in the hero's mold with masses of metropolitan voters. In the buckshot approach, the President invests noticeably less effort in working out compromises and patching together majorities.

INVOLVED VERSUS ALOOF.   Far more than most Presidents, Woodrow Wilson was deeply involved personally in the legislative struggle. As a political scientist and an admirer of British public affairs, he had long been convinced that the President must be a kind of "prime minister, as much concerned with the guidance of legislation as with the just and orderly execution of law." Wilson oversaw the development of a body of legislation promoting economic and social justice, the "New Freedom." He believed that only the President could assure an integrated legislative program. Wilson, therefore, regularly planned it, shared in the toil and sweat of drafting bills, and oversaw their progress through Congress.

Preceding each Congressional session, Wilson drew up lists of measures to be pushed, discussed them with the cabinet, and then conferred personally with House and Senate leaders or sent his "political ambassador," Postmaster General Albert S. Burleson, in his stead. Carter Glass, chief legislative sponsor of the Federal Reserve Act, has written that Wilson "dominated" the act's preparation. Congressman E. Y. Webb maintained that Wilson personally drafted the Clayton Act's famous clause that says "the labor of human beings is not a commodity or article of commerce," that he pressed legislative committees to report his bills out, watched the Congressional calendars, and scrutinized amendments to forestall damaging changes. He also managed to keep in touch with conference committee deliberations, a traditional graveyard of progressive legislation.[28]

Wilson used his legislative influence selectively, pushing one measure at a time, but the key to his legislative approach was collaboration. The President, he said, in coming personally before Congress to promote his tariff legislation, should not be viewed as "a mere department of the Government hailing Congress from some isolated island of jealous power . . . he is a human being trying to cooperate with other human beings in a common service." Wilson put in a heavy schedule of hours on Capitol Hill. "Did you ever hear of a President occupying a room in the Capitol called 'the President's Room'? What would be thought of it," he asked the politically sophisticated Josephus Daniels, "if instead of asking Senators with whom I wished to consult to call at the White House, I should occupy that room for such conferences?" Daniels answered candidly that Senators would resent it. Wilson went ahead anyhow. When important bills were in the Congressional crucible, Wilson would see a score of legislators in his Capitol Room. At the White House he saw even more and installed a special telephone to reach Senators quickly from his office. If Congress balked, he went to the people.[29]

Presidential involvement in the contemporary era also includes a readiness to fight on issues that count, even where they concern Congress's internal organization. The big breakthrough, Lawrence F. O'Brien believes, came in the 1961 fight to enlarge the Rules Committee, which the Kennedy administration won by five votes.[30] Under Johnson, the White House involvement deepened. He reminded his cabinet members that "no persons in their respective departments could be more important than the heads of their Congressional relations activity."[31] The departments did not conduct their affairs on Capitol Hill independently but under the watchful eye of the White House. Each department or agency would give a weekly report to the office of the assistant for legislative affairs at the White House, covering its activity on Capitol Hill for the previous week and its forecast for the coming week. The White House assistant then reviewed the reports and prepared an analysis for the President plus an agenda for his weekly breakfast meeting with the Congressional leaders.

Johnson's interest in legislative relations covered the whole waterfront of executive concerns, large and small. "The President we have in the White House now," Representative Peter H. B. Frelinghuysen of New Jersey said, "follows with intense interest everything that affects his legislation. He apparently objects to any modification. He doesn't like a comma changed in anything he's proposed."[32]

In contrast to Wilson and Johnson, who were intensely involved, some Presidents have scrupulously held themselves aloof from the heat and dust of legislative combat. The progenitor of this approach was President Washington. The aloof style custom-fits the hero-President by removing him from the rough and tumble that might scratch the gilt of his flawless prestige. The aloof President addresses Congress in stately, general discourse and with a degree of deference. He avoids the specifics of issues, leaving them for Congress to determine, untutored by the Chief Executive. Washington's first annual message, eagerly awaited as a guide to major policy, was chiefly a general and thankful exposition of "the present favorable prospects of our public affairs." His recommendations were rendered up in broad, innocuous proposals such as "protecting the frontiers," "extension of the postal system," and "promotion of science and literature." The last proposal was delivered in a perfect straddle: "Whether this desirable object will be best promoted by affording aids to seminaries of learning already established, by the institution of a national university, or by any other expedients will be well worthy of a place in the deliberations of the Legislature." At every turn where controversy reared its ugly head Washington nimbly sidestepped.

A century and a half later another hero-President, Dwight D. Eisenhower, visualized his Presidential service as a kind of unifying and moderating influence above the struggle. He was the good man above politics who eschewed conflict, reconciled differences, and healed divisions. He avoided involvement in political controversy and expressed frank distaste for partisan politics. "In the general derogatory sense," he declared in a press conference, "you can say that, of course, I do not like politics."[33] In legislative affairs Eisenhower took on the pleasant missions and left to his colleagues, principally Vice President Nixon and chief Presidential assistant Sherman Adams, the tasks of conveying the harsh word and springing the fierce maneuver. Deeply respectful of the tripartite character of the government, Eisenhower was reluctant to assume executive leadership over a vast area that he viewed as legislative business.

BIPARTISAN VERSUS PARTISAN.   A modern President chooses between a partisan and a bipartisan approach to legislation. In certain areas of affairs, bipartisanship is preferable, even imperative. In crisis, in much of foreign policy, and in major social legislation political realities require the modern President to employ bipartisanship to build his legislative majorities. In the depths of economic crisis Franklin Roosevelt conducted a nonpartisan administration, drawing large support from both parties. After 1936, with the crisis subsiding and with huge Democratic legislative majorities created by the elections, his administration took on a more partisan attitude.

President Eisenhower depended heavily upon bipartisan support throughout his two terms. His dependence was not less in his first two years, when the Republicans possessed a legislative majority, than in the following six years, when the Democrats controlled both houses. Eisenhower, writing to the House majority leader, Charles Halleck, early in 1954, said,

> Because of the thin Republican margins in both Houses, both you and Knowland obviously require Democratic support in almost every tough vote. This being so, we must by all means quickly show our readiness to cooperate in every decent way, and particularly in those areas where bipartisan action is vital to the national interest.[34]

Eisenhower's conciliatory pitch was well rewarded. From Democratic leaders Johnson and Rayburn he received, according to Adams, "more sympathy" than from the Republican Senate leader, William F. Knowland, who plagued the President with his one-track mind on the menace of Red China, and Joe Martin, the House leader, whose support of the administration was spoken of in White House circles as "uninspired and lackadaisical."[35] Cooperation with the Democrats paid off at voting time. "Fifty-eight times," according to the *Congressional Quarterly Almanac* for 1953, the administration's worst legislative year, "Democrats saved the President . . . their votes providing the margin of victory when Republican defections or absences imperiled the happy glow." But Eisenhower paid a price for his collaboration. "This added more strain on his relationship with the right wing of his own party," Adams has written.[36]

Bipartisanship is attractive not merely to the President whose party lacks or barely enjoys a majority in Congress. It may appeal to a President such as Johnson, whose party, thanks to the 1964 elections, gained overwhelming majorities in both houses. In putting through his record-breaking program of legislation in the Eighty-ninth Congress, he steadily courted Republican support and abstained from partisan conduct likely to offend Republicans. He consulted with the Republican opposition constantly before settling on his budget or announcing his domestic legislative program. He relied on Senator Dirksen almost as if the Republican leader were the Democratic leader in the Senate. In assessing the output of the Eighty-ninth Congress he was always careful to recognize the Republican contribution. "I think the Congress has done a good job," he said on one occasion, "I am not just talking about Democrats. I am talking about Congress generally."[37] Or again, "Most of the key measures have received some support from progressive and moderate Republicans, and all Republicans in some instances."[38]

Some Presidents have traffic with bipartisanship only from sheer political necessity. Otherwise, by instinct and preference they take the partisan road. Left to his own devices, Kennedy preferred a partisan approach to legislation. "Legislative leadership," he said, "is not possible without party leadership." Wilson's Presidency was a telling application of this principle. In forwarding his New Freedom program, he acted true to his conceptions of the President as prime minister, party leader, and champion of a legislative program. Wilson advanced his legislative purposes through party means. He worked through Democratic legislative leaders and committee chairmen, cracked the patronage whip, and employed House and Senate caucuses in the English style. His tariff bill, for example, was taken up in the Democratic caucuses of each house at his insistence. The Senate occasion was termed "the first caucus of Democratic Senators that anyone can remember." Wilson triumphed in both forums. The House and Senate caucuses voted to support the tariff as a party measure. When the federal reserve bill was advancing, Wilson again resorted to caucus with happy result. The act was passed without any Democratic Senators opposing it; in the House only three Democrats dissented.

Wilson as legislative party leader traveled a rough road, given the divisiveness of parties and the localism of Congress. He had to cut through thickets of factional differences and convert the high tariff Senator F. M. Simmons, the Finance Committee chairman, to espouse the administration's tariff reductions. The House Democratic caucus on the tariff teetered upon collapse when seven Ohio Congressmen threatened to revolt against free wool and the Louisiana delegation fought to break the sugar schedule. But the skillful majority leader, Oscar Underwood, held his ranks, and only thirteen Democrats refused, because of pledges to their constituencies, to abide by the caucus's decision endorsing the tariff reform bill.[39]

INDEPENDENT.   President-Congress relations may deteriorate into such a state of futility that one or both branches may seek its purposes not through the usual channels of cooperation, but by independent action. The President, for his part, despairing at legislative obstruction, resorts to his prerogative. Franklin Roosevelt, administering price controls in World War II, concluded that his efforts to hold the lid on inflation were imperiled by several farm support provisions of the existing Emergency Price Control Act. In a message of September 7, 1942, he asked Congress to repeal the objectionable provisions by October 1. "In the event that the Congress shall fail to act, and act adequately," Roosevelt added, "I shall accept the responsibility, and I will act." How could the President legally carry out this threatened self-assertion? "The President has the powers, under the Constitution and under Congressional acts," said Roosevelt rather generally, "to take measures necessary to avert a disaster which would interfere with the winning of the war." Here in slightly different guise was the "stewardship theory" of Cousin Theodore.[40]

It is Abraham Lincoln who provides the most sweeping illustration of executive independence. At the outset of the Civil War he delayed calling Congress into session, judging presumably and altogether justifiably, in light of history, that the legislators might delay and obstruct while rebellion spread. Lincoln the Commander-in-Chief became for twelve crucial weeks the nation's lawmaker. The normal joint legislative-executive processes were suspended, and America had its first taste of dictatorship, fortunately a benevolent one.

Executive-legislative relations can also collapse into general debacle at Congress's instigation. In two of the worst crises the nation has known, Congress discarded every vestige of cooperation with the Chief Executive and pursued a bitter course of general sabotage. James Buchanan, who toiled hard and prayerfully to prevent the Civil War, and Andrew Johnson in the Reconstruction era were the victims of rampant Congressional hostility. In Buchanan's case Congress denied the President nothing less than the essentials of governance. As the South continued to mobilize in spite of his entreaties, Buchanan requested more military funds. Congress responded by cutting his estimates to a fraction of their original amount and restricting the service of any additional volunteers who might be raised to the Utah territory. Buchanan justifiably asserted that the last Congress he had the misfortune to experience had "throughout the entire session, refused to adopt any measures of compromise to prevent civil war, or to retain first the cotton or afterwards the border States within the Union." Congress was derelict in other vital duties. It failed to provide for any judicial process in South Carolina following the resignation of every federal court officer. Congress declined to provide the President with authority to call out the militia or volunteers to suppress the insurrection flaming in Charleston. Even after Buchanan's message of January 8, 1861, declaring the existence of revolution and reminding Congress that it alone could muster troops, three weeks passed before a bill was introduced, only to be immediately withdrawn. Not until two months after South Carolina seceded and ten days after the Confederacy was formed was another, more modest, militia bill proposed. The House killed it with a resolution to postpone.[41]

The Future Presidency

"There is nothing more important for the future of popular government in America," Charles A. Beard once wrote, "than an overhauling of congressional methods and the establishment of better relations with the Executive." The problems to which Beard pointed have over the decades stirred thought in political and academic circles and have evoked a quantity of proposals for reform. The more extreme of these have urged that separation of powers and checks and balances be rigorously altered and that some variant of the British parliamentary system be adopted. The seeds of this alternative have always fallen on barren soil since it is alien to the entire American tradition. A historically assertive Congress would never bear the subordination of the legislature to the degree implied in the British system. Any changes, if they are to occur, must be in accord with the spirit of an autonomous Congress endowed with considerable power.

We need a strong President and a strong Congress. The two are not incompatible but mutually reinforcing through their representation of valid constituencies—the President the nation, and the Congressional houses the locality, state, and region. Both the national and local sectors of political society must be rallied behind major policy. Accordingly, neither Congress nor the President can have a monopoly of wisdom and an exclusive claim to the exercise of leadership. What we seek is effective cooperation between the two branches, with each a positive, constructive participant. We need to avoid both Lincoln's tendency toward exclusive leadership and the executive-legislative deadlocks of the 1940's, 1950's, and 1960's.

In this present era of revolutionary social change, we can no longer afford a Congress that is nakedly negative, that rejects what the President proposes without substituting remedies of its own. A constructive Congress permits its majority to act and protects it from frustration by minority maneuver. A constructive Congress may go farther than the President wants, or not as far, so long as it goes somewhere. It is at its best when it uncovers flaws in the Executive's proposals that he has missed and represents opinion to which he is insensitive. With such purposes and within such limits, what can and ought to be done?

1. The President, the Senate, and the House should be simultaneously elected for a common term of four years. Historic data establishes that we could rightfully expect that an election so administered would produce a President and two houses of Congress better attuned in party and political outlook than their present staggered election permits. It is a rare Congressman, even from a Southern state, who will repudiate his party's platform in a Presidential year. Under existing practice, the Senate, with its six-year term, is never wholly elected during a President's four-year term, and it is not until he is at his own midterm that even a majority—two-thirds—of the Senators who will serve during the President's tenure has been chosen. Also, the House's two-year term, and consequent election at the President's midterm, subjects his administration to a severe test of its popularity at an interval that is unfair, coming when his administration has barely started. Defeat in the election can be damaging to the President's prestige in both foreign and domestic politics. All too often, either his party loses control of the House or Senate, or its majority is reduced.

2. The President should be empowered to veto individual items in appropriation bills, as Franklin Roosevelt, Eisenhower, and others have advocated. The absence of this power subjects the President unmercifully to legislative riders on tax and appropriation measures. The Interior Department appropriation bill of 1948, for example, contained a rider providing that the commissioner of the Reclamation Bureau and all its regional directors should have had at least ten years of engineering experience. Neither the incumbent commissioner, Michael W. Straus, nor the regional director in California was an engineer. "This rider is designed to effect the removal of two men," President Truman cried, "who have supported the public power policy of the government and the 160-acre law which assures that Western lands reclaimed at public expense shall be used for the development of family-size farms."[42] Truman nevertheless signed the appropriation bill. He had to. Congress had already adjourned, and a veto would have shut down the Interior Department.

The item veto would spare the President the curse of riders, it would regulate the pork barrel abuse, and it would promote the Executive's fiscal responsibility. Most important of all, it would endow the President with a powerful new bargaining strength to assert in the arena of closed politics. He could conceivably engage in his own kind of log-rolling, trading his acceptance of appropriations items for support of his own measures by legislators individually and in blocs. The item veto could well become the source of a new and commanding influence for the President in legislative affairs. It should preferably be adopted by amendment, although competent legal opinion holds that it might be created by a clause inserted into each appropriation bill, bestowing upon the President the power to strike out items. An item veto over state legislative appropriations has been given to a majority of governors.

3. The internal organization of the houses of Congress can be viewed as a maze of contrivances to assure inaction or minority rule. The majority is prevented from voting upon measures that by every indication it would approve, or it is able to act only after unconscionable delay. Often the thwarted majority opinion equals or approximates the President's view, and, consequently, a liberation of the legislative majority would frequently produce Congressional approval of key items in the President's program. The devices of minority rule are well known: the seniority principle in selecting committee chairmen, the method of assigning legislators to committees, the vast power of the House Rules Committee, and the Senate filibuster, to mention several of the most powerful. A concentrated attack needs to be launched upon them.

The seniority principle of choosing committee chairmen, which assures that the preponderance of these eminences will oppose much of the President's program, urgently needs to be modified. Legislators and thoughtful citizens have often advanced proposals to this end. In hearings held in 1965, the Monroney-Madden Committee on the reorganization of Congress heard testimony containing various proposals for substitutes for the seniority principle: election of the chairman by majority vote of the committee, rotation among senior members, election by the party caucus, removal of the chairman by majority vote of the committee after he has served a single term and reached age seventy, and the setting of meeting dates, agenda, and other procedures by majority vote in lieu of the chairman's decision. In urging the seventy-year age limit, Senator Joseph S. Clark has noted that it is the same limit that Congress itself has placed upon federal judges to induce their retirement. Under the Clark proposal, the overage chairman could still continue as a member of the committee.

The importance of the age limit was evident in the incoming Kennedy administration, where the President was forty-three years old upon his inauguration and had gathered around him leading policy figures most of whom were in their thirties and forties. The age picture in the Congressional committee chairmanships at the time was altogether opposite. In the House Howard Smith, the Rules Committee chairman, was seventy-six; Clarence Cannon, the Appropriations chairman, was eighty; Carl Vinson of Armed Services was seventy-six; Brent Spence of Banking and Currency was eighty-five. In the Senate Carl Hayden, the Appropriations chairman, was eighty-two; A. Willis Robertson of Banking and Currency was seventy-two; Harry F. Byrd of Finance was seventy-two; and James Murray of Interior and Insular Affairs was eighty-three. The relative youth of the Kennedy men was a handicap in their dealings with the senior Congressional leaders.

To assure that the President's program receives fair and prompt attention, several further adjustments might well be made in the standing committees. Because of their present size and memberships, many committees do not accurately reflect the majority opinion in each house, nor the strength of the apparent disposition of the houses' majorities toward the President's program. Accordingly, its items encounter delay, crippling amendment, or death in committee. Several remedies are possible. The majority party committee, which determines the ratios of majority and minority party memberships on the standing committees, might undergo a limited revision, and so might the committee of the opposition party responsible for distributing committee places to its members. Senator Clark, for instance, has fought to expand the Senate Democratic Steering Committee, which allots committee assignments. He has also proposed the expansion of several Senate standing committees, for example the Appropriations and Finance Committees. Presumably, the additional members would better represent the growing urban outlook of the Senate. The Kennedy administration and its House supporters responded to the problem of a recalcitrant Rules Committee by effecting a small increase in its size. A future Presidential administration will surely have on its agenda a further increase to reflect more accurately both the views of the House majority and the President's program. A mighty force in Johnson's extraordinary legislative successes in the Eighty-ninth Congress was the highly favorable readjustment in committee ratios wrought by the 1964 elections, which decimated Republican Congressional ranks. With Republican resurgence in the 1966 elections, committee ratios became less favorable to the Johnson administration and substantially curtailed its successes on Capitol Hill.

The Senate filibuster, historic obstacle to strong civil rights legislation and other Presidential legislative ventures, has focused attention on that chamber's rule 22, which requires a two-thirds vote for imposing closure upon debate. Several assaults were launched in the Kennedy era to liberalize the rule but without success. The Monroney-Madden Committee, in its 1965 hearings, received proposals to reduce the possibilities of filibuster, but the prospects for favorable action remain dim. This problem, too, remains upon the agenda of the future.

A variety of other Congressional reforms can be advanced to improve the ability of the legislative majority to act and the President's program to receive its just consideration: the conference committee, which often mutilates bills with arbitrary abandon, ought to include in the majority of its members from each house only those whose votes demonstrate their support of a bill that their house has passed and with which the other house disagrees. The President's program, which is often sabotaged by procedural delays, might also be helped if quorum calls, employed to bog down action, were eliminated. Electric voting machines, too, might step up the tempo of legislative processes. In addition, committees with an overburdening volume of business, such as House Ways and Means and Senate Finance, might have their excess redistributed to other committees, a step that might speed their work. "Super-committees," or coordinating committees, and a more extensive use of joint committees might be desirable to reduce the traditional tendency of standing committees to act independently; as Woodrow Wilson once put it, "They do not consult and concur in the adoption of homogeneous and mutually helpful measures; there is no thought of acting in concert."

4. Although legislators and private citizens have urged Congressional re-form for decades, little indeed has been accomplished. What are the pros-pects for the 1960's and 1970's and what are the most promising routes of action? There are several possible approaches to Congressional reform, and they can be employed individually or simultaneously.

If the American people continue to leave the farm for the city at the rate they did in the 1940's and 1950's—and by responsible forecasts they will —the urban vote will become more and more powerful. In *Wesberry v. Sanders* the United States Supreme Court provided an adequate legal doctrine for reflecting in the composition of the House of Representatives the grow-ing urban concentration of the American population. Urban voters require and expect more government services than their country cousins, so the growing urban pressure might bring Congress increasingly around to the President's program. The bulk of urban growth, however, is not at the city center, where the need for services is greatest, but in the suburbs whose outlook is more conservative. How different the attitude of the suburban voter will be from the conservative tendency of rural folk and whether the urban setting will foster a greater concern for education, health, transportation, and other services is yet to be clearly seen.

If, also, the big pressure groups, whether economic, racial, or national, can lift up their eyes to see beyond their immediate and obvious self-interest and to perceive that the highest public standards, whether in education, health, employment, civil rights, or other major social and economic policy, are good for the group as well as the nation, Presidents and legislators will both gain a far stronger support for programs that the general welfare plainly requires.

The President, too, can help in Congressional reform. Kennedy was moderately successful in tackling the Rules Committee, ancient citadel of minority obstruction to the President's program in the House of Representa-tives. He teetered on launching a fight on the Senate filibuster, but lacked the votes that a future President might some day possess.

Legislators themselves might take up the fight and win. Dominant Con-gressional groups and seemingly well established procedures can, as history teaches, be overthrown. "Uncle Joe" Cannon, Speaker and one of the most powerful of parliamentary tyrants, was overturned and his powers were sheered. Democratic and Republican progressives united in 1913 to scuttle the seniority system in the Senate and to install new committee chairmen devoted to a progressive program. Working harmoniously with President Wilson, they were able to enact an extraordinary list of major legislation.

Finally, the Monroney-Madden Committee, which reported in 1966 a quantity of proposals to enable Congress to formulate and express its majority will more quickly and efficiently, deserves support. It is the first committee of its kind since the La Follette–Monroney Committee, whose work led to the Legislative Reorganization Act of 1946. Although Congress investigates sternly any suspected inefficiency in the executive branch, it displays an almost pathological resistance to improving itself. Not since 1946 has Congress tidied its operations. The sound barrier has since been broken, the space age has arrived, but Congress limps onward with methods devised in the first days of the republic. The legislators on Capitol Hill have no monopoly over an interest in a better Congress. Senator Clifford Case of New Jersey, in urging extensive overhauling on Capitol Hill, once observed that the President of the United States is the man in Washington "who most needs Congressional reform."

Administrative Chief 7

I f there is one thing one would believe the title "Chief Executive" to convey, it is that its holder might expect the vast officialdom assembled in the executive branch to abide by his purposes and follow his directives. These are commonplace expectations in ordinary administrative situations in private life. For the President, however, even that modest standard is not within easy reach, if indeed it can be attained at all. The hard reality is that the nation's Chief Executive presides over the executive branch—the largest administrative enterprise in the western world, with its budget counted in tens of billions of dollars and employing 7 per cent of the nation's work force—with authority and a set of managerial tools that the head of a private corporate enterprise would deem laughably inadequate. Unlike the typical business chief, the President finds no designation in his fundamental charter, the Constitution, as administrative chief. Neither do its collective provisions confer any equivalent authority. The Constitution does grant him the "executive power," language the Supreme Court has sometimes interpreted to include certain powers normally associated with an administrative chief. He is charged to see that the laws are "faithfully executed," which suggests a general administrative responsibility, but duty is not power. He also enjoys express powers such as the power to make appointments. Still other authority is conferred by act of Congress and by weight of custom.

With this gift of imperfect authority, the President engages in varied administrative activities. He shapes and determines policy, from "grand policy" to clerical minutiae, from the Monroe Doctrine to the supervision of Washington's roads. James K. Polk was harassed by laborers responsible for the capital's streets who, as Congressman Samuel Vinton said, "were in the habit of running off to the President of the United States, besieging him day after day about the little affairs of the streets, grounds, and roads of this city."[1] In Eisenhower's day the White House staff was amused by the spectacle of scores of commissions for notaries public, spread out upon his office floor waiting for the ink of his signature to dry.

The President prepares for decisions by absorbing oral briefings and reading and pondering memoranda. Many a President would vouch for Truman's complaint that the reading is hard on the eyes and on the attention, for "nearly every memorandum had a catch in it."[2] The President supervises his executive subordinates with an attitude ranging from the tolerance of Harding, who approved everything his Secretary of State, Charles Evans Hughes, did, to the definitiveness of Polk, who required his Secretaries, seated before his desk, to read their reports aloud before forwarding them to Congress. The President has only limited power to recruit, train, and promote the personnel of the executive branch. Most of his key appointments require the advice and consent of the Senate, and even more are subject to vagaries of Senatorial courtesy. Since the first days of the republic he has shared general personnel powers with Congress, and since 1883, when the Civil Service Act (the Pendleton Act) became law, with a civil service commission.

His power to make removals, a subject on which the Constitution is silent, is likewise circumscribed by the civil service laws and by the courts. In *Myers v. United States* (272 U.S. 52, 1926) on President Wilson's removal of a postmaster, the Court seemed to find the President's removal authority unlimited. This sweeping ruling was trimmed back in *Humphrey's Executor v. United States* (295 U.S. 602, 1935). Humphrey, a Federal Trade Commissioner appointed by President Hoover, was removed by President Franklin Roosevelt not for causes cited in statute but, as Roosevelt candidly disclosed, because of policy differences between Humphrey and himself. The Court, finding for Humphrey, held that Congress can protect officials such as a Federal Trade Commissioner, who wield legislative or judicial power, against Presidential removal. An "executive officer," however, or one "restricted to the performance of executive functions," the Court took pains to declare, could not be similarly protected. The distinction between an "executive officer" and one exercising "legislative or judicial power" remains blurred, although in *A. E. Morgan v. TVA* (115 Fed. [2d] 990, 1940) the Circuit Court of Appeals viewed a member of TVA's board of directors as an "executive officer."

The President delegates functions and authority, and by grace of the Budget and Accounting Act of 1921, develops an executive budget—his budget—covering federal income and outgo. He coordinates the several agencies of the executive branch or, as Harry Truman put it, he makes a "mesh" of things.[3] Almost continuously since the Reorganization Act of 1939, a consequence of the famous Brownlow Committee, he has had a limited power to reorganize executive agencies by redistributing functions and overhauling structures.

Congress as Administrator

The executive branch has not one but two managers—the President and his rival, Congress. Nearly everything the President does Congress can do, sometimes with greater effect. The mission and structure of the departments are determined by act of Congress. Congress can give authority to subordinate officials to act independently of their department heads, prescribe specific and detailed administrative procedures, petrify the internal organization of an agency by statute, and require Senate confirmation for bureau chief appointments. Congress can establish independent regulatory commissions, like the Interstate Commerce Commission and the Federal Reserve Board, well removed from the President's direction and control. All executive agencies require annual appropriations which Congress provides as it chooses. The programs they administer Congress authorizes and amends. Congress can investigate departmental work in close detail, and its habit is not merely to query the leadership but to reach far down into the hierarchy. The stern fact of life for the department Secretary is that he must respond not merely to his official superior, the President, but to the standing committees and subcommittees of the House and Senate watching over his department, aided and abetted by the pressure groups whose needs it serves.

By tradition Congress is closely involved in personnel administration. In detailed laws, Congress sets down the elements of a classification structure, rates of pay, service ratings, retirement, and the like. Although Congress gives the President the power to develop an executive budget, legislative action on its parts may be so severe that much of the document's original validity may be lost. In 1957, for example, Congress sheered off nearly 25 per cent of the budgets of the Commerce Department and the United States Information Agency. Since the early days of the republic, Congress has made many of its appropriations in close detail, strait-jacketing administrative action. In many an appropriation subcommittee, the spirit of Representative John Sherman's nineteenth-century outcry still lingers:

> The theory of our government is that a specific sum shall be appropriated by a *law* originating in this House, for a specific purpose, and within a given fiscal year. It is the duty of the executive to use that sum, and no more, especially for that purpose, and no other, and within the time fixed.[4]

Some Presidents, accepting the realities, give the Congressional power centers a substantial part in the development of administrative decisions affecting program, budget, and personnel before consummating them and dispatching them to Capitol Hill. Lyndon Johnson was of this school. However important he considered the appointment of Thomas Mann to manage Latin-American affairs, Johnson checked first with influential Senators. His elaborate budget-cutting operation in his early weeks of office was a concession to the Congressional economizers. His appointment of a public commission to reconsider the entire foreign aid program served to diminish the rising Congressional outcry.

The Bureaucracy

Even more ominous for the President's quest for dominion over the executive branch is the giant bureaucracy itself, with its layers of specialists, its massive paper work and lumbering pace, its addiction to routine and stifling of creativity, its suspicion as a permanent power center committed to program and policy of a transitory, potentially disruptive Presidential administration. The single most powerful figure in the great pyramid is the bureau chief, who in many subtle ways can frustrate the President's purposes when they diverge from his own. He cultivates ties with the pressure groups whose interests his organization serves and the Congressional committees that provide him with money and authority. Congressional committees and subcommittees welcome his attentions. The subcommittee on veterans' affairs does not wish to permit any facet of veterans' services to fall into other hands. The bureau chief may enjoy impregnable prestige with the public. John Kennedy as President-elect engaged in a clear-headed political act when he announced at the time of his first appointments the retention of J. Edgar Hoover, a public hero, as Director of the FBI.

The remaining high-level departmental incumbents can be grouped, as Wallace Sayre has suggested, as: (1) career employees recruited under civil service regulations with permanent tenure, (2) patronage appointees chosen because of party identification, (3) Presidential appointees whose loyalties center upon the Chief Executive, and (4) program executives who are skillful in advancing programs that are congenial to the President's policies.[5] The latter three groups may enter government for a limited term of service. Beyond these is the vast body of civil servants of middle and lower ranks. Between the President and the massive departments are natural antagonisms of interest. The President wants to keep control, to receive early warning of items for his agenda before his options are foreclosed, to pick his issues and lift them out of normal channels, to obtain the bureaucracy's full support for his initiatives. The great departments represent a wholly different bundle of purposes and needs. They cling to orderly routines, mountainous paper work, and time-consuming clearance procedures. They tend toward caution, and to the departments the President may represent a temporary intruder who threatens established policy. Promising career men are driven by the stifling routine and the lure of higher salaries into private callings. Able individuals in business, universities, and the professions are deterred from entering government at middle and higher ranks for fear of losing promotions and other privileges in their private career base.

At times, Kennedy and his aides despaired more over their travail in winning cooperation from the departmental bureaucracy than over their deadlocks with Congress. After one heavy interval of bureaucratic obstruction, the administration in its private comment seemed to adopt the notion that the President must contend not merely with Congress but with a further branch, a fourth branch, the bureaucracy. There were distressing signs of the force of the bureaucracy's hostile impact. Kennedy despaired of the State Department's ability to manage foreign policy effectively. The military services teamed up with the Congressional committees against the President's military policies. Treasury careerists were decidedly not helpful in their testimony on Capitol Hill concerning the tax bill. The Bay of Pigs disaster taught Kennedy, according to his own avowal, the folly of relying completely on subordinates down the lines.

To assert his influence in his uphill struggle for dominion over the executive branch, the President resorts to his White House staff, the cabinet, and the cluster of agencies composing the Executive Office of the President. The White House staff consists of approximately a score of assistants who bear such diverse titles as press secretary, special counsel to the President, appointments secretary, and special assistant for national security, science and technology, or a miscellany of other affairs. The staff is the President's "lengthened shadow." They help prepare his messages, speeches, and correspondence; arrange his appointments; oversee the inflow and outflow of his communications; analyze and refine the problems confronting him; advance his purposes with legislators, departments, private groups, and party officialdom. Although White House aides cherish their anonymity, they cannot escape importance. Only a few cabinet Secretaries can rival leading White House staff members in influence and authority. Collectively, the staff tends to be more powerful than all other groups in the executive branch, including the cabinet and the National Security Council.

The White House staff harks back to President Washington's appointment of his nephew and of a former Revolutionary aide-de-camp as his secretaries. Until McKinley's time assistants were paid largely by the President out of his own pocket. Congress's parsimony in allowing the President assistance was purposeful: The President was not expected to play a creative role in the administrative system. Those Presidents whose pockets were not so well lined managed to carry their aides by allotting them a salaried sinecure in some department. Until the Franklin Roosevelt era, the chief White House aide was the secretary to the President, who handled a large miscellany of duties distributed nowadays among several White House staff members. Consider, for example, the regimen of James B. Henry, Buchanan's secretary and nephew. (Since the President was footing the secretarial bill, he tended to be nepotistic.) Henry attended the President in his office from 8 A.M. until 5 P.M., when Buchanan took a daily walk. Henry kept records of the receipt and disposition of correspondence. "Such letters as the President ought to see," Henry said, explaining his duties, "I folded and briefed and took them to him every morning at eight o'clock and received his instructions as to the answer I should make." Once a day he sent to each department a large envelope containing letters for its attention. In addition, Henry oversaw arrangements for state dinners, managed the library fund, paid the household staff, and kept the President's private accounts.[6]

The cabinet, founded by Washington early in his Presidency, has seldom been a source of advice upon which the President continuously relies. It exists by custom and functions by Presidential initiative and is therefore largely what the Chief Executive chooses to make of it. "It lives," Richard F. Fenno has written, "in a state of institutional dependency to promote the effective exercise of the President's authority and to help implement his ultimate responsibilities."[7] Wilson, Franklin Roosevelt, and John Kennedy used it little. Quick and hard-driving, they chafed under extended group discussion. Truman and Eisenhower resorted to it more but with uneven result. Johnson was more inclined than Kennedy to employ it, although often his purpose was not to secure counsel but to develop understanding and support in the cabinet "team" for a pending administration decision. But in no Presidential administration of the past three decades has the cabinet emerged to the forefront of influence in Presidential policy-making.

Unlike the British Prime Minister, who brings into office a team of ministers or department heads who have long been associated in common legislative and party enterprises with houses of Parliament, many of the President's department Secretaries come into office with no acquaintance with each other and indeed little with the President himself. The two principal appointees of the Kennedy administration, Secretary of State Dean Rusk and Secretary of Defense Robert McNamara, were both strangers to the President until the moment he interviewed them for their respective jobs. Historically, all sorts of considerations have governed the selection of department heads, including geography, to a degree: The Interior Secretary is ordinarily a Westerner, and the Secretary of Agriculture is hardly apt to hail from an Eastern metropolis but more likely from corn, wheat, or hog country. The Secretaries of Commerce and the Treasury will probably emerge from the business and financial worlds. Franklin Roosevelt's choice of Harry Hopkins, his relief administrator, as Secretary of Commerce and Harry Truman's choice of Henry A. Wallace, a liberal-minded farmer, for that post were hardly calculated to strike joy in the business community. The Secretary of Labor may be picked from the organized labor movement, as was the case with Martin Durkin in the Eisenhower administration and Arthur Goldberg in the Kennedy administration. Ordinarily the major party factions must be represented. Eisenhower dealt out recognition to protégés of Robert A. Taft, his rival for the Presidential nomination, by appointing George Humphrey and Ezra Taft Benson Secretaries of the Treasury and of Agriculture. For Johnson, the retention of cabinet Secretaries inherited from the Kennedy administration was useful as a bridge to the "Kennedy wing" of the Democratic party.

The Executive Office of the President includes the National Security Council, patterned after the British Committee of Imperial Defence and created by the National Security Act of 1947. It advises the President on national security objectives and commitments and the integration of national security policy. The NSC's top-level membership comprises the President, the Vice President, the Secretary of State, the Secretary of Defense, the director of the Office of Emergency Planning, and the statutory advisers—the chairman of the Joint Chiefs of Staff and the director of the Central Intelligence Agency. The President can invite such other officials as he chooses to attend NSC sessions. In the Truman and Eisenhower administrations the NSC included a substructure of several working levels that was dropped in the Kennedy administration. The Bureau of the Budget, whose director may be involved in a wide range of Presidential concerns, was created by the Budget and Accounting Act of 1921. In the President's behalf the Bureau prepares a single executive budget or consolidated financial program, although Congress has not committed itself to pass a consolidated appropriation bill. The bureau also clears and coordinates legislation for the President and promotes management improvement in the executive branch. The Council of Economic Advisers, a child of the Employment Act of 1946, thinks, plans, and reports on the maintenance of economic prosperity. The Office of Emergency Planning oversees the mobilization of civilian resources for national security.

The Executive Office also includes the Office of Science and Technology. This office was born in the Eisenhower administration when the Russians launched their Sputnik. The office has steadily grown in size and influence because of the emergence of science as a major claimant upon the President's attention. The office is a staff enterprise that sifts issues and opportunities in the fast-changing world of science. The office is a link between the President and the scientific community and is a modest symbol of science's new status and vast responsibilities in forming national policy. Yet because it is a staff activity, the office is largely unseen. Neither it nor any other office stands in open view for expressing the nation's goals for using its scientific resources. No single spokesman exists in the national government to articulate the synthesis of science and public policy, to explain and defend science to Congress and the public. Science's importance in national life makes wholly plausible the creation of a Council of Science Advisers of highest technical competence, paralleling the Council of Economic Advisers.

The Vice-Presidency, whose first incumbent, John Adams, termed it "the most insignificant office that ever the invention of man contrived or his imagination conceived,"[8] has, after dormancy through most of the nineteenth century, acquired a special usefulness in the twentieth. Vice Presidents of the past three decades have participated increasingly, although unevenly, in the President's administrative enterprises. Henry A. Wallace, as Vice President in the Franklin Roosevelt administration, took on important administrative duties during World War II. Alben Barkley in the Truman administration became a statutory member of the National Security Council. Richard Nixon in the Eisenhower administration presided over the cabinet and the National Security Council in the Chief Executive's absence, was chairman of the interdepartmental government contract committee, and undertook good-will missions abroad. He did not, however, discharge any important executive responsibilities. Vice President Johnson in the Kennedy administration continued in the Nixon pattern, with assignments overseas and chairmanships of several interdepartmental committees concerning space and government contracts important for civil rights policy. That Johnson also held a substantial place as a counselor in the Kennedy administration is suggested by his membership in the "Ex Com" of the National Security Council, an *ad hoc* group of a dozen top administration officials who aided the President in working out his responses to the 1962 Cuban crisis.

In the Johnson administration, Hubert Humphrey's most consequential toil was promoting the progress of Great Society legislation on Capitol Hill. Like his recent predecessors, he ventured to Europe, Asia, and Latin America to build acquaintance with foreign leaders, to lay the groundwork for new policy, and to serve as a prestigious official symbol of American concern for the countries visited. Humphrey was also charged to keep in touch with farm and urban affairs programs and was made White House liaison with the nation's mayors, governors, and major interest groups, such as the Leadership Conference on Civil Rights. In the earlier stages of his Vice-Presidential career, these duties seemed lacking in substance, but when the Johnson administration in its dealings with the liberal community subsequently passed through stormy seas churned up by the Vietnam war, the cutting back of poverty programs, and the candor and popularity of Senators Robert F. Kennedy and Eugene McCarthy, the President brought Vice President Humphrey into greater prominence. In effect, he exploited the Vice President's popularity in the liberal community and used him as a counterpoise to the Senators.

The Vice President has been chiefly useful to the President by relieving him of ceremonial duties and making good-will journeys abroad. A President prefers to have as his principal subordinates men of his own choosing, whom he can work with easily and discard if he wishes. The Constitution also makes the Vice President the presiding officer of the Senate, a duty which, although light, makes difficult his assumption of large and fixed executive responsibilities.

The acute question facing any President is how to best harness the administrative resources of the executive branch to his purposes—how can he transmute goal and plan into program and policy? How can he best awaken a sense of urgency in the bureaucracy, bestir its creativity, and command its loyalty against the blandishments of his Congressional and interest group competitors? Presumably his best ally in these causes is the Presidential staff, which after small and slow beginnings has since the New Deal era, and especially since World War II, burgeoned into a substantial bureaucracy itself, with more than one thousand employees occupying two buildings plus the east and west wings of the White House. Will the Presidential bureaucracy succumb to supreme irony and itself assume the very qualities of the greater bureaucracy it is designed to combat? The President must deploy his own aides and assistants in a fashion that will make his rule more effective and will avoid the pathologies of the greater bureaucracy. Each President responds to these challenges in his own way.

Roosevelt as Administrator

Franklin D. Roosevelt reigned as chief administrator by a highly unconventional system that gave the utmost play to his influence and enabled him to retain great power in his own hands. In pursuit of this supreme good he resorted to means that time and again violated the most sacred canons of efficient administration as taught with unflagging zeal in our schools of business and public administration. For Roosevelt, organization blueprints were often scraps of paper, and the rules by which good executives, according to the texts, delegate authority were honored by their breach.

The textbooks warn that duplication must above all else be avoided in administration. Roosevelt went out of his way to indulge in it. He instituted the New Deal and its revolutionary changes, notwithstanding the bureaucracy he inherited from the previous Republican era. Roosevelt triumphed over the established bureaucracy with its elephantine pace and resistance to change partly by ignoring it. He established his own bureaucracy to administer much of the New Deal. The job of regulating stock exchanges was given not to the Treasury or Commerce Departments but to the newborn Securities and Exchange Commission. The Wagner Act, enhancing labor's opportunity to organize and engage in collective bargaining, was consigned not to the Labor Department but the National Labor Relations Board. The bold new Tennessee River Valley project fell not to the Interior Department but to a special Tennessee Valley Authority. Before the normal pathologies of bureaucracy could mature, the New Deal was a going operation.

Roosevelt as administrator drew freely upon a large bag of tricks to get what he wanted done. He had little regard for the administrative niceties that are observed in most organizations. He was given, for example, to end-running his department heads and dealing directly with their subordinates. Frequently he would telephone J. Edgar Hoover at the FBI about something he wanted done quietly and in a hurry, and Hoover would promptly and wisely report the conversation to his superior, Attorney General Francis Biddle. Hoover knew of Roosevelt's habit of saying afterward, "By the way, Francis, not wishing to disturb you, I called Edgar Hoover the other day."[9] When department Secretaries, resentful of being undercut, sometimes protested, Roosevelt looked sheepish, apologized, and repeated the offense after a decent interval.

Roosevelt applied a competitive theory of administration, which kept his administrators unsure, off balance, confused, and even exasperated. With ambition pitted against ambition, the power of decision remained more securely in his own hands. Roosevelt at times deliberately kept the lines of authority blurred and jurisdictions overlapping. The administration of work relief thus was divided vaguely between Harry Hopkins, successively the Federal Emergency Relief Administrator and Works Progress Administrator, and Harold Ickes, the Public Works Administrator. Secretary of the Treasury Henry Morgenthau, Jr., was given, with Presidential approval, such large powers of interference in the expenditures of WPA that Hopkins nearly resigned. "There is something to be said," Roosevelt observed in behalf of his method of planned disorder, ". . . for having a little conflict between agencies. A little rivalry is stimulating, you know. It keeps everybody going to prove that he is a better fellow than the next man. It keeps them honest too."[10]

Roosevelt's devotion to the competitive principle and checks and balances led him often to prefer boards, commissions, and other variants of the plural executive to the single administrator. One of his more bizarre creations in World War II was the Office of Production Management, charged with administering much of the economy's mobilization. For this intricate and massive task, he resorted not to the leadership of a single administrator but to a biheaded authority consisting of William Knudsen of General Motors as Director General and Sidney Hillman of the CIO as Associate Director General. Although Knudsen's and Hillman's titles differed slightly, their authority, Roosevelt disclosed at a press conference, would be equal. But suppose, an incredulous reporter queried, Knudsen and Hillman disagreed, an altogether likely prospect given the conflicting premises of their respective worlds of management and labor. Might not the war effort be imperiled by dissension and impasse in OPM's biheadship? There would be no trouble whatever, Roosevelt answered confidently. If Knudsen and Hillman disagreed, he would simply lock them up in a room and not let them out until they could agree.[11]

In maintaining competition, Roosevelt was adept at cutting down or building up his aides as situations might require. He disciplined them by withholding honors and distinctions, by assigning new authority and programs to someone else. He rewarded administrators with his intimacies. Harold Ickes, a sore and troubled administrator, suffered his most distressful period when a year elapsed in which he never saw his chief alone. In Roosevelt's hand the simple small White House luncheon became a mighty sword of reward and fear. If Ickes or Wallace lunched with the President, every other member of the official family instantly knew of the event and speculated anxiously about what had been discussed and its consequences for their interests.[12]

Roosevelt sometimes had to knock an administrator down, but he was quick to help him up. If Ickes had been shorn of a coveted jurisdiction and Hull had lost an interdepartmental dispute, Roosevelt would favor the losers with attentions days later. The building-up might take the form of an elaborate compliment in cabinet for the way the vanquished Secretary had handled what was described as a difficult and sensitive matter. Another restorative was "hand-holding," as Roosevelt called it, a process of consolation at which his talent, in the discerning judgment of William Phillips, was "rare" and which took up, according to Grace Tully, the President's secretary, "hours and days" of his time.

Roosevelt, in the interest of competition, filled his administration with human opposites. His original Secretary of the Treasury, Will Woodin, was a conservative, respectable, trustworthy financier, and his first Director of the Budget, the economy-minded Lewis Douglas, viewed New Deal spending as "the end of Western civilization." Yet Roosevelt could also import a free-spender like Hopkins and legions of young lawyers schooled in the progressivism of Louis Brandeis and Felix Frankfurter. The philosophical pluralism of his administration enable Roosevelt to play off not merely men against men but dogma against dogma. It was a kind of double insurance for Roosevelt's own retention of the power of decision.

He loved to employ *enfants terribles* who would flay their fellow administrators and outsiders such as legislators and pressure group leaders who occasionally chose to interfere in the processes of the executive branch. General Hugh Johnson, the National Recovery Administrator, freely indulged his talent at brassy invective in violent denunciations of fellow administrators and the critical press. When told that Johnson had overstayed his usefulness, Roosevelt simply remarked that every administration had to have a Peck's Bad Boy.[13] The bellicose Ickes exchanged batterings with a similar breadth of foes, and Leon Henderson starred in the same capacity during World War II.

The crown of the formal organization, the department Secretaries, were individuals of initiative and drive, and deep in their commitment to program. Roosevelt permitted them great scope. Their collective organization, the cabinet, however, he restricted to a modest role. He did not value the cabinet as a source of collective wisdom, and its meetings were apt to be hollow affairs. The President began typically by engaging in a monologue of pleasantries, recounting stories and joshing selected Secretaries. He would then throw out a problem, usually one that he had been considering just prior to the meeting. Discussion rambled and was inconclusive. Roosevelt's next move was to turn to the Secretary of State and say, "Well, Cordell, what's on your mind today?" The same query continued around the table in order of the Secretaries' precedence. They responded usually with items of minor importance, preferring to take up larger matters privately with the President just before or after the meeting. Large matters, the Secretaries feared, might be excessively mauled or leaked to the Hill or to the gossip columnists.[14]

Roosevelt steadily employed a free-roving assistant who shepherded the President's fondest projects over the assorted hurdles in the executive branch and outside. The assistant, acting for the President ("This is the White House calling"), made short shrift of departmental hierarchy and red tape in expediting action. He was a major tool by which the President might prevail against the vast, sluggish executive branch. Originally, Louis Howe, shrewd and devoted, a soldier of Roosevelt's political fortunes for nearly a quarter century, seemed destined for the assignment of general assistant. But illness and then death intervened. Howe, while he still could work, brought the optimistic Roosevelt to see occasionally the darker side of issues and was his only aide whose candor stretched to the point where, confronted by a Presidential note, he could snort, "Tell the President to go to hell." Howe was followed by a series of general assistants, including Raymond Moley, Rexford Tugwell, Thomas Corcoran, and Harry Hopkins. Corcoran in his day was a stellar administration lobbyist on Capitol Hill, a Presidential speech-writer, a channel to Roosevelt for those with ideas, a trouble-shooter who would rush to New York City and rescue the PWA housing program bogged down in an internecine brawl, a hirer and firer of personnel, and doyen of a vast body of young lawyers catacombed in the departments—his "chicks" he called them— a government within a government whose hallmark was action.

In World War II Harry Hopkins was Roosevelt's number-one trouble-shooter. Known as "Generalissimo of the Needle Brigade," he prodded industry to speed war production, harassed laggard military administrators, and oversaw the distribution of supplies to the fighting fronts. Hopkins was Roosevelt's personal liaison with the war overseas. In conferences with Churchill and Stalin and military chieftains he did the legwork on which Roosevelt's central decisions were founded.

The Roosevelt method is the surest yet invented for maximizing the President's personal influence and for asserting his sway over the executive branch. It spurred the flow of information and ideas into his possession and magnified his impact on policy. It released the energies of men from confining bureaucratic routine. For the 1960's and beyond, however, the Roosevelt method has limited relevance. The new costliness of error in foreign affairs makes the Rooseveltian system of haphazard consultation, by which some departments may be left out, unthinkable. The internecine strife which marked the system is also barred by the necessity that the national executive appear before the world with the face of unity. Roosevelt enjoyed a luxury his successors are doomed never to know. He could create much of his own bureaucracy, first in the New Deal and then in the war. His successors must work with an inherited bureaucracy.

Eisenhower's Staff System

At a far opposite extreme from Franklin Roosevelt's highly personal managerial method was Dwight D. Eisenhower's preference for institutionalizing
Presidential relationships in the executive branch. The Eisenhower method was
a product of his military experience and several long-entertained convictions
concerning White House practice. "For years I had been in frequent contact
in the executive office of the White House," Eisenhower has written, "and I
had certain ideas about the system, or lack of system, under which it operated.
With my training in problems involving organization it was inconceivable to
me that the work of the White House could not be better systemized than
had been the case in the years I observed it."[15]

Eisenhower's key tactic was to delegate duties, tasks, and initiatives to
subordinates. After their study and formulation of decision, he as Chief Executive might ultimately accept or reject. "The marks of a good executive," he
advised his department heads, "are courage in delegating work to subordinates
and his own skill in coordinating and directing their effort." Eisenhower's
subsequent illnesses speeded his inclination to delegate.[16]

The vehicle of his delegations was the staff system. At its apex was the
assistant to the President, Sherman Adams, a former Congressman, governor
of New Hampshire, and early organizer of Eisenhower's Presidential candidacy. Eisenhower, Adams has written, "simply expected me to manage a staff
that would boil down, simplify and expedite the urgent business that had to
be brought to his personal attention and to keep as much work of secondary
importance as possible off his desk." Any issue, no matter how complex, Eisenhower believed, could be reduced to some bare essence. "If a proposition can't
be stated in one page," he declared, "it isn't worth saying." Impatient with
the torrential paper work of the Presidency and not one who took to reading
gladly, Eisenhower insisted that his subordinates digest lengthy, involved documents into one-page summaries, "which," said Adams, "was sometimes next
to impossible to do."[17]

Except in the singular case of Secretary of State John Foster Dulles, cabinet Secretaries approached the President through Adams. Policy proposals
were made in writing, the fruit of staff study and recommendation. Adams'
task was to see that every expert in the executive branch who could contribute
to a proposal had his opportunity to do so. Many final decisions were made not
by the President but by Adams. Eisenhower was brought in only if the matter
was very important or if the executive experts disagreed. The President was
not bothered very often, according to Adams, who has explained, "I always
tried to resolve specific differences on a variety of problems before the issue
had to be submitted to the President." He adds, "Sometimes several meetings
were necessary before an agreement was reached. But with a few exceptions I
was successful."[18]

Eisenhower kept the system on its toes by his own close knowledge of governmental detail mastered in a long military career and a capacity to put sharp, piercing questions that could reduce premises and argument to a shambles. He could not bear flawed performance, a sentiment conveyed at times by fierce outbursts of the Presidential temper.

Adams was an ubiquitous influence. When a caller or official sprang a new proposal, Eisenhower was prone to say, "Take it up with Sherman." If a paper came to the President, he would run his eye over it for the familiar notation, "O.K., S. A." If it was missing, Eisenhower was sure to ask, "Has Governor Adams approved this?" Although each cabinet Secretary had an ivory telephone connecting directly with the President's line, the connection—except for that of Secretary Dulles, who consulted Eisenhower constantly on foreign policy—was seldom used. Cabinet Secretaries found it wise to call Adams instead. For the several specialists constituting the White House staff—the press secretary, the appointments secretary, the staff secretary, and the cabinet secretary—Adams was a coordinator. Though all these colleagues enjoyed direct access to the President, only Adams by dint of the breadth of his responsibilities could speak with the President on broad, general affairs. Adams dealt with policy in sweep, his colleagues in chunks. The major staff positions interlocked smoothly with Adams' undertakings; his controls extended over the communications system running to and from the President. The appointments secretary, for instance, in setting up the President's daily list of visitors, routinely checked with Adams, enabling him to veto prospective callers or fit others in. Adams also could arrange his own schedule in order to be on hand, if necessary, when Eisenhower met with visitors. The staff secretary, who presided over a system installed under Eisenhower's supervision, was a great boon to Adams. He kept records on hundreds of papers, many of high import and secrecy, dealing with national security and domestic affairs. Within minutes, Adams, thanks to the staff secretariat, could track down the location and status of reports, memoranda, and letters that had come into the White House or gone out for clearances in the far reaches of the executive branch. He could tell who had prepared a given document, the concurrences received and objections encountered, who was dragging his feet, and other essential facts of paper-work life. Adams was no mere merchant of dry-as-dust routine. He uplifted some of the administration's finest achievements in their wobbliest beginnings—the Atoms for Peace plan, the civil rights program, and the Refugee Relief Act.

The ancient institution of the cabinet also felt Eisenhower's reforming hand. Shocked that the department Secretaries, the government's principal executives, should gather without any preconception of the business to be considered, Eisenhower created the post of cabinet secretary. This new official arranged an agenda for cabinet meetings, circulated it beforehand among the members, oversaw the preparation of "cabinet papers" presenting proposals for the President's action, and recorded the results of cabinet discussion.

Keenly aware of the gap between Presidential decision and departmental reliability in carrying it out, Eisenhower had his cabinet secretary meet after a session of the cabinet with "cabinet assistants," a group of assistant secretaries and departmental executive assistants with responsibilities for implementation. Every several months a cabinet meeting was converted into "Judgment Day" on the "Action Status Report," in which each department head revealed how much (or little) he had honored his obligations to take actions called for by the President's decisions in cabinet.

In adapting the military staff system to the Presidency, Eisenhower viewed his cabinet Secretaries essentially as theater commanders. Like field generals, the Secretaries were invested with broad initiative and responsibility for their allotted sectors of operation. In the wake of unsettling exposures by the McClellan Committee on Improper Activities in the Labor Management Field, for example, Eisenhower was asked whether he considered new legislation necessary to cope with the problems typified by Dave Beck, James Hoffa, and the Teamsters' Union. "Well," the President answered in a press conference, "I have merely been told by the Labor Secretary they are watching this very closely [to] see whether we have any responsibility or anything we could do reasonably."[19] In the Eisenhower administration the cabinet Secretary typically chose his own assistants. There was no Raymond Moley or Sumner Welles, who in secondary positions in the departments in Roosevelt's day trafficked directly with the President over the head of the Secretary. Eisenhower backed up his department Secretaries even in the face of heavy political cannonade. When a score of Middle Western Republican Congressmen, with elections in prospect, grew restive over Agriculture Secretary Benson's hard line on farm price supports and suggested it would help politically if he would resign, Eisenhower, controlling his fury, answered at a press conference that "for any group of congressmen, either informally or formally, to raise a question concerning my appointment to the Cabinet would not seem to be in order."[20]

One of the more complex and important elements of Eisenhower's institutionalized Presidency was the National Security Council. Eisenhower, who utilized the NSC heavily, often met with it two or more times a month, with an agenda of intelligence reports, policies to be innovated or revised, and reports on progress in fulfilling established policies. Backstopping the council proper in the Eisenhower administration was the Planning Board, considered the most influential part of the NSC system and consisting of representatives and observers from member agencies, usually at the assistant secretary level. The Planning Board provided an unremitting flood of documents with each drop painstakingly considered. "The Planning Board normally does not send a paper forward without meeting three or four times on it," said Gordon Gray, Eisenhower's National Security Affairs assistant. Planning Board members, according to report, debated not merely high policy but the subtleties of idiom and terminology. Hours of anxious effort were invested in clearance procedures, with intensive review and interdepartmental negotiation of words and phrases. Critics hold that papers worked out in such proceedings were highly watered down, lowest-common-denominator-of-agreement affairs, and there were snide remarks about this being "the century of the comma man." Defenders of the stress on paper work hold that such exercises foster exactitude in an area of utmost sensitivity and complexity.

Another NSC offshoot was the Operations Coordinating Board, created by the Eisenhower administration, which was made up of deputy-level officials who tackled the job of getting things done, of devising ways to put into operation, at home and overseas, NSC policies ranging from psychological and economic warfare to international cooperation in science. Like the Planning Board, the OCB reveled in paper work and meticulously negotiated detail.

Eisenhower, anxious to avoid the noisy administrative altercations of the Roosevelt era, relied upon several expedients. Sherman Adams was a one-man peace-keeping constabulary, practicing his coordinating arts with rugged firmness. Eisenhower himself preached the gospel of teamwork and the Secretaries responded, aided by their general lack of profound convictions about public affairs. The several who entertained strong beliefs either fought for them only sporadically or lacked talent to make them persuasive. Political ambition, a disturbing force in Franklin Roosevelt's cabinet, was slight in Eisenhower's. Most of his Secretaries were businessmen, eager to return to lucrative careers.

The attraction of the Eisenhower system is the assurance it promises that the President will have the benefit of coordinated counsel in an age when major problems require the best expertise of several or more departments. Adams' operation strove systematically to include every relevant department. The omission of skill and information, given the world's dangers, could be severely costly.

The Eisenhower system can be viewed as purporting to provide a security that is unattainable, given the vastness of the executive branch, the interminable Niagara of executive transactions, and the severely limited timetable imposed by events. The Eisenhower experience indeed bears instances of human and organizational failure in spite of all the elaborate safeguards. As the Dixon-Yates contract episode,* a major political disaster, was building, Republican Senator John Sherman Cooper of Kentucky, whom Eisenhower highly esteemed, called at the White House to lay before the President his several objections to carrying the project forward. Adams refused to grant the Senator an appointment. When the Bureau of the Budget and the Atomic Energy Commission prepared chronologies of the principal facts of Dixon-Yates for the President's use and for distribution to the press, an essential de-

---

* The Atomic Energy Commission's increasing demands upon the TVA for power, coupled with Eisenhower's reluctance to expand TVA, resulted in the so-called Dixon-Yates contract with a combination of private utilities that were to supply the necessary power to TVA. Disclosures of irregularities in the negotiation of the contract led the Eisenhower administration to cancel it.

tail was omitted: that Adolphe Wenzell, a Bureau of the Budget consultant for the contract, was simultaneously an official of the First Boston Corporation, which was financing the Dixon-Yates group. Eisenhower's staff left him helpless and exposed while the administration's foes leaped with full cry upon the error.[21]

The Eisenhower system appears to afford the President both too little initiative and too little total impact upon policy. He depends overmuch upon others to discover and assess the magnitude of problems. He enters into policy-making only in the final stage of decision, when his area of choice is small and his dependence upon his staff great. To the ailing Eisenhower, the staff was at times a kind of tranquilizer, comforting the Chief Executive with a therapeutic but unwarranted calm and optimism. The President was apparently allowed to assume that the 1957–58 recession was less serious in its early stages than it really was. Remedial public measures were delayed and the recession deepened, to the harm of the administration politically and the country economically.

Kennedy's Personal Management

John F. Kennedy's administrative method veered decidedly toward Roosevelt's. Like Roosevelt, Kennedy aimed to carve out a maximum personal role in the conduct of the Presidency but without some of the more jagged methods and much of the turmoil of the Rooseveltian model. Kennedy clearly visualized his Presidential role when he declared in his 1960 campaign that as President he would want to be "in the thick of things."[22] Kennedy the President was true to the promise of Kennedy the candidate. He put in abundant hours at deskside conferences and on the telephone, pursuing details well down the line of departmental hierarchy, and took a constant hand in coordination, its weight laid not merely upon top-level endeavor but upon minor affairs as well.

Kennedy's intensive involvement was more than an applied philosophy of the Presidency. It was a reflection of his personality, aptitude, and body chemistry. Kennedy personally comprised a bundle of restless curiosity, a high quotient of vigor, and an extraordinary spongelike capacity to absorb the daily torrent of governmental data.

To carry forward his administrative view of the Presidency, Kennedy relied upon several operating principles and expedients. Unlike Eisenhower, who stressed institutional structure, Kennedy placed great store in personal relationships. The person—his talent, perception, and reliability—counted more than his organization. Kennedy's person-centered approach reflected his pre-Presidential career, passed chiefly in legislative politics and in political campaigning, in both of which working relationships are highly personal. Accordingly, in dealing with department Secretaries and White House staff members Kennedy insisted upon direct relationships, unhampered by organization and hierarchy. He, for his part, remained highly accessible to a large circle of colleagues.

Kennedy, dealing with the departments, did not stop with the department head but reached down the hierarchy to lesser levels. A loud, clear hint of this practice was sounded in the preinaugural period in the manner of the President-elect's selection of his foreign policy aides. He designated an Assistant Secretary and an Undersecretary of State and the ambassador to the United Nations before selecting his Secretary of State. To underscore the principle implied in the sequence of these appointments, of direct Presidential superintendency of foreign affairs, Kennedy for his first three foreign affairs nominees, and for others after them, accompanied the public announcement of their selection with a phrase hailing the "post" as "second to none in importance."[23] The President-elect's pointed tribute signified his intention to deal directly with second- and third-echelon subordinates. Kennedy's own assessment of his experience in the Presidency affirmed the wisdom of this tactic. In a year-end television interview in 1962, he was asked, "Is it true that during your first year, sir, you would get on the phone personally to the State Department and try to get a response to some inquiry that had been made?" "Yes," Kennedy replied, "I still do that when I can, because I think there is a great tendency in government to have papers stay on desks too long. . . . After all, the President can't administer a department, but at least he can be a stimulant."[24]

Kennedy injected himself at any point along the decision-making spectrum from problem-selection to final judgment. Whereas Eisenhower wanted decisions brought to him for approval, Kennedy wanted problems brought to him for decision. Eisenhower preferred a consensus to be laid before him, stated briefly and in general terms. Kennedy eschewed consensus; he wanted to know a problem's facets and alternative answers, keeping decision for himself in consultation or "dialogue," as the administration called it, with advisers. Kennedy's keen nose for detail took him far into the interior of problems. Although interested in general principles, he was essentially a pragmatist and had, as a colleague said, "a highly operational mind." Policy separated from operations, in his view, was meaningless. His desk, not surprisingly, was piled high with reports and memoranda which he read closely. Conferring with an official, he would reach into the pile, pull out a memorandum, and resort instantaneously to a paragraph to make a point or raise a question. "President Kennedy," a colleague said, "is a desk officer at the highest level."[25]

Kennedy entertained well-defined views of the proper role of the individual department. His tactic was to devolve upon individual department heads and on identified subordinates the responsibility for recommending policy initiatives and overseeing the execution of decisions. He took a stern view of a luxuriant bureaucratic phenomenon, the interdepartmental committee, beholding it as an intruder upon departmental responsibility and therefore something inherently bad, to be extirpated if at all possible. After several months in office he abolished a lengthy list of interdepartmental committees and reassigned many of their functions to department Secretaries and other officials. Committees, being hardy administrative plants because they serve vital purposes, cannot be eliminated by mere Presidential prescription. They are an inevitable bureaucratic routine for establishing interdepartmental collaboration at the working levels. Seldom do problems of any significance appear that are not interdepartmental in their contours. The committees that Kennedy killed, not surprisingly, did not stay dead. Many on his list resumed a more or less surreptitious existence after a decent interval.

In lieu of committees the Kennedy administration resorted to "task forces," a name appropriately suggestive of vigor and purpose. Task forces, which consisted of departmental representatives and usually one or more White House staffers, were not merely committees by another name. "They operate with a consciousness of having a mandate, often from the President himself," a participant explained. Task forces carried a sense of the importance of getting things done, which often stirred bureaucracy to faster, more constructive effort. The attendant White House staff member was a powerful reminder of the Chief Executive's need and interest, a bearer of his influence upon decision, not merely in the moment of final choice but along much of the journey of its formation. Departmental participants in the task forces were not altogether enthusiastic about the contribution of their White House colleagues. "When the President's man says something, you don't know whether he is speaking for himself or for his boss," a department man exclaimed, "The effect can be, and often is, to cut off discussion too soon."[26]

Kennedy, like Roosevelt, viewed the White House staff as a personal rather than an institutional staff, a vehicle for maximizing his influence rather than its influence throughout the executive branch. Impressed that the larger a staff is the more apt it is to become institutional, Kennedy tried heroically to cut back the sizable staff he had inherited from the Eisenhower administration, but with small success. In meting out staff assignments, Kennedy put his staff on action-forcing rather than program tasks and gave it a mixture of fixed and general-purpose responsibilities. These expedients likewise were intended to reduce the advance of institutionalization and to keep the staff personal.

Kennedy's White House staff, unlike Eisenhower's, was not organized by hierarchy or pyramid but like a wheel whose hub was the President and whose spokes connected him with individual aides. Five aides occupied major functional posts. The staff assistant to the President, Kenneth O'Donnell, handled appointments and Presidential travels and was an omnibus "chief White House official for party politics," in touch with the Democratic National Committee and local party figures. The special counsel, Theodore C. Sorensen of Nebraska, whose association harked back to Kennedy's Senate days in 1953, had responsibilities running across the board. His office, comprising two assistants, focused Presidential objectives, planned programs, broke impasses, and passed judgment on timing. Sorensen drafted Presidential messages and speeches with high artistry and a capacity that Richard Nixon once hailed as "the rare gift of being an intellectual who can completely sublimate his style to another intellectual."[27] Sorensen sat with department Secretaries formulating their budget and legislative programs and attended the President's meetings with legislative leaders and prepress conference briefings. Sorensen had an acquisitive, cosmopolitan intelligence, which, as a colleague put it, "can understand anything from sugar subsidies to bomb shelters."[28]

McGeorge Bundy, a former Harvard graduate dean, was special assistant for national security affairs. Bundy, aided by a small band of assistants ("the Bundy group"), kept watch for weakness and trouble in defense and foreign policy administration and saw to remedies and repairs. In the President's behalf he occupied a central place in the stream of intelligence. He received copies of virtually all the incoming cables to the Secretaries of State and Defense and the Director of the CIA. He sorted these out and put the most important before the President. Other key aides were the assistant for Congressional relations, Lawrence F. O'Brien, and the press secretary, Pierre Salinger.

There were other important aides not so involved in the major daily tasks of the President. Ralph Dungan, who was responsible for personnel, or "headhunting," as he put it, maintained a permanent list of talent available for government posts, checked job recommendations from legislators, the Democratic National Committee, and the departments. Beyond this, Dungan took on roving assignments—he was Presidential overseer of foreign aid and of African and Latin-American policy. The assignments of Arthur M. Schlesinger, Jr., the historian, were even more diverse—he acted as a liaison between the President and United Nations Ambassador Adlai Stevenson and between the White House and the State Department on Latin-American policy, and he occasionally gave assistance with Presidential speeches.

The White House staff reaped a steady harvest of influence from Kennedy's habit of entrusting important responsibilities to individuals in whom he had confidence. Staff members, therefore, oftentimes performed functions traditionally handled by departments and diplomatic representatives. Schlesinger—not high-level State Department officials—traveled through Latin America to survey the area's requirements, gathering data and impressions that became the basis of the future aid program. Press Secretary Salinger —not the State Department or the United States Information Agency—negotiated in Moscow an agreement for the exchange of information. The attendant publicity of such assignments stripped many of the White House staff posts of their traditional anonymity.

Kennedy deployed his White House staff as critics of departmental performance and as emergency repair crews when departmental undertakings went awry. He restored direct work-flows between departments and himself and made his staff responsible for "monitoring," but not "obstructing," departmental access to him personally. A key function of the White House staff was to spot political and policy weaknesses in departmental proposals. Staff members played a decisive part in heading off a tax increase that may have made sense economically but not politically during the Berlin crisis of July 1961; they delighted liberals by implanting several public-ownership features into the communications satellite bill; they knocked down a State Department proposal that action on the trade bill be postponed for more than a year, until 1963. There was wide agreement that a large advantage of the Sorensen-Bundy service was penetrating analysis. "When Sorensen gets into something," a Bureau of the Budget career man said, "it gets a thorough scrubbing." It was also the lack of such a scrubbing that plunged the staff to the far depths of its worst failure, the abortive Cuban invasion in the young administration's fourth month. The staff was admittedly timid about raising questions that should have been asked. "At that point," a White House aide confessed, "we just didn't have the confidence to tell the veterans of the bureaucracy, 'Look, you're crazy.' "[29]

In another blow at the institutionalized Presidency, Kennedy performed drastic surgery on the most advanced expression of that phenomenon, the National Security Council. He abolished the NSC's nerve- and work-center, the Planning Board, and its organ for implementing decision, the Operations Coordinating Board. Most important of all, he shunned the NSC by seldom bringing it into session. He sought counsel for major crises like Berlin of 1961 and Cuba of 1962 by bringing together an *ad hoc* group of advisers in whom he had special confidence. In lieu of the Planning Board and the OCB was the Bundy office, which greatly scaled down the former mountainous paper work.

Kennedy also largely dispensed with cabinet meetings, holding that the entire body of Secretaries should be assembled only for matters of full breadth and significance. He saw no reason for the entire cabinet to ponder matters affecting only three or four departments. The cabinet, consequently, met infrequently. In the summer of 1962 various department heads, then occupied with the political campaign, happened to converge upon Chicago. There they laughingly acknowledged that what had not transpired in Washington for some months was at last happening in the Middle West, a cabinet "meeting"!

The Kennedy technique clearly maximized the President's involvement and imprint upon policy, breathed vitality into sluggish bureaucracy, and extended the reach of a highly knowledgeable President and his staff into the departments. Yet there were also disadvantages. There was feeling that Kennedy was too accessible to operating personnel, too much "in the thick of things," overimmersed in minor policy and small detail, with too little time for major business. Or again, that Kennedy's emphasis on swiftness—terse statement, quick strides from one problem to the next—resulted at times in inadequate consideration of alternatives. Much public business, like reducing the arms race or overhauling the tax system, does not permit quick, concise expression. "The system now," a frequent participant said, "favors people who know exactly what they want to do. It is tough on people who have dim misgivings—even if those misgivings happen to be very important."[30]

One strength of the Kennedy system may also have been a weakness. His method rested upon the realistic view that the executive branch, lacking the apparatus of collective responsibility found in Great Britain, depended heavily, for action and decision, upon the President's judgment. Yet what ordinarily was plausibly realistic may have caused at times an overdependence upon the time, energy, and talent of the President. The great risk of the Kennedy method is that no single mind, even a Presidential mind, can absorb the information or muster the wisdom necessary for sound judgment of many intricate issues pouring upon the President.

The problems with which American statesmanship must deal have acquired a complexity that renders them no longer fit for individual insight and judgment, no matter how perceptive. To be dealt with adequately, they must at some stage be subjected to collective study involving diverse technical skills, specialized knowledge, and organizational viewpoints. Decision without collective study is apt to be founded on inadequate information and to lack roundness of judgment.

Johnson and His Staff

President Lyndon Johnson's method blended elements of the Franklin Roosevelt–Kennedy, President-centered style, on the one hand, and the Eisenhower tendency to system and institutionalization on the other. Like Roosevelt he tried to maximize his personal influence in the executive branch, and he deployed and used his staff with similar unorthodox managerial methods. Like Roosevelt he often sought counsel outside the government. He frequently consulted Dean Acheson, once Secretary of State in the Truman administration, and old New Dealers Benjamin Cohen, Thomas Corcoran, and James Rowe. Abe Fortas numbered in this group until his appointment to the Supreme Court somewhat curtailed his availability, and Clark Clifford until he took over as Secretary of Defense.

Johnson also had a sturdy streak of administrative orthodoxy. He placed greater reliance upon the departments than Kennedy or Roosevelt did. Promptly after coming into office, Johnson accorded new recognition to the departmental Secretaries. Secretary of Defense McNamara quickly achieved an influence surpassing his considerable status under President Kennedy. When Dean Rusk faced heavy cannonades of criticism over Vietnam on Capitol Hill and from public quarters, Johnson expressed openly his admiration for his Secretary of State. Johnson also made greater use than Kennedy did of the cabinet and the National Security Council. For the cabinet, Johnson adopted the Eisenhower practice of a formal agenda and assignment of a special assistant to act as cabinet secretary.

The way Johnson used his staff was shaped essentially by his own political goals, prior career, and work habits. His chosen, often proclaimed purpose was to bring the executive branch to work within a consensus that the President discovers or constructs. His working method resembled the Congressional leader's, a role he occupied for much of his own career. As a broker in political consensus, he would withhold his own commitment until the commitments of other men were reconciled, or, in effect, until a majority was built.

From his White House staff Johnson expected help in defining issues, in articulating his views, and in protecting his freedom of movement. In calculating and constructing his position, Johnson preferred to be in touch himself with labor, business, local leaders, Congressmen, the press, and chieftains of the executive bureaucracy. Sometimes he acted as his own press secretary, Congressional liaison officer, and speech-writer. His staff constantly experienced the phenomenon of their leader both delegating power to them and taking it away. Johnson needed a staff that could move rapidly without getting in his way and without attracting attention or committing his position prematurely. No one on Johnson's staff approached the influence of Harry Hopkins or Samuel Rosenman under Roosevelt, Clark Clifford under Truman, or Theodore Sorensen under Kennedy. Bill D. Moyers, a young, bright, articulate fellow Texan, enjoyed impressive influence before departing for private employment. As assistant to the President, he oversaw departmental preparations of the vast legislative program of 1965, supervised the drafting of Presidential messages, was in constant touch with Johnson, and reviewed the whole Great Society program with the President just before its launching in the State of the Union message. Unlike the top aides of past Presidents, Moyers shared his duties with other White House staff men. Douglass Cater, a former editor, handled matters concerning health and education. Richard Goodwin, originally of the Kennedy staff, dealt with anything in the spheres of urban affairs, conservation, and the arts. Economic matters fell to Horace Busby, a long-time Johnson aide. Civil rights matters were handled by the legal counsel, Lee White, another Kennedy holdover.

The fluidity of the Johnson staff was reinforced by the background and personality of its members. Heavily represented in its ranks were writers and others with public relations experience, a breed of men of high adaptability. They were not especially identified with any policy area, and if they shared a personality characteristic, it was that they were self-effacing. Thus they were able to adjust to the President's moods and demands and to refrain from attracting attention to themselves in the press and from building ties with special interest groups—tendencies that might have impaired their ability to move on to other assignments.

For expertise and sophistication in developing policy, Johnson turned less to his White House personal staff and more to his institutional staff. Under Johnson the Bureau of the Budget, oldest and largest of the institutional staffs, reached new peaks of influence. Its key officials were at the center of the development of the President's domestic program. The administration's 1965 farm program, for instance, was evolved and even presented publicly not by the Agriculture Department but by the Director of the Budget. The Bureau's influence also climbed following its assumption of a new duty—the application to major nondefense projects of the techniques of cost effectiveness analysis that Secretary McNamara introduced in the Defense Department.

Johnson also leaned heavily upon two new institutions that emerged within the White House staff in the Kennedy era. Where once Colonel Edward M. House and Harry Hopkins were personal advisers to Presidents Wilson and Franklin Roosevelt on national security matters, McGeorge Bundy in the Kennedy and Johnson years handled the duty more systematically. He and his successor, Walt W. Rostow, made the White House staff a regular and substantial participant in foreign policy. Bundy installed and Rostow continued to use a handful of assistants specializing in Africa, Europe, Latin America, Southeast Asia, international economics, and science and defense. Rostow, like Bundy, participated regularly in the President's meetings with his Secretaries of State and Defense. Similarly, the President's dealings with Congress were institutionalized during the Kennedy-Johnson era by Lawrence O'Brien. He, too, expanded his office, developed a staff and secretariat, and was a regular participant in the President's meetings with Congressional leaders. The Congressional relations and national security offices have been converted into separate institutions, connected with, but not a part of, the White House staff.

The transformation of the White House staff, begun under Kennedy and rounded out under Johnson, affords the President an adjustable blend of personal and institutional aides. Closest to him is his personal staff, which provides devotion and relaxation and facilitates and expedites the development of his decisions. Next in proximity is the institutional staff that offers information, professional analysis, and orderly procedure. Johnson's personal staff had less influence on policy than those of his recent predecessors. Most of the struggle in policy development took place in the institutions. Being several steps removed from the President, the institutions may weaken the President's impress on policy. They are prone to compromise differences rather than bother the President. The spreading out of work in the bureaus of the institutions sometimes gives a fuzziness to the end-product and its reflection of the President's style. These are but minor reservations against a background of generally successful performance. The output of the Johnson staff was remarkably high, as the 1965 legislative program proves. The staff arrangement also nicely satisfied Johnson's own preferences to hold decision in his own hands, to enjoy maximum freedom of movement, and to keep a veil around his operations.

A safety valve against the danger of undue dependence on the institutional staff was Johnson's personal method as an operating administrator. He approached policy issues with strong convictions rooted in his New Deal beginnings. His favorite tactic with those whose advice he sought was, "I want to do this. You tell me why I shouldn't." Above all, Johnson's own cyclonic activity in eighteen-hour workdays, his talent at forcing the pace in meetings and in scores of phone calls a day, and his overwhelming persuasiveness were a mighty energizing influence on the institutional staff agencies.[31]

The Future Presidency

The activist President, bent upon extracting as much mileage as possible from his resources as general manager, must plainly commit great quantities of his own personal energy and talent fully to the task. The Presidency is no place for semiretirement. The President does best with a small cadre of assistants, with flexible assignments and responsibilities of both action-forcing and program-building nature. Yet he must be watchful that his immediate staff does not, intentionally or no, exercise its enlarging authority for its own purposes rather than his. The competitive principle of advice and action has been successfully used by activist Presidents since the days of Washington. It is the surest means yet devised for extending their influence and control.

But no contemporary President can live by personal assistants alone. He must make large use of the Presidency's institutions such as the Bureau of the Budget, the NSC, the CEA. Given the enormousness of his problems and the dangers of the times, he can no longer reign with the informal splendor of a Franklin Roosevelt of the 1930's. The institutionalized Presidency is the best available guarantee that the multiple specializations a major problem requires will be addressed to that problem.

In actuality, the contemporary President requires a dual organization. One is institutional, which is largely inherited and is a major link for the President with the operating departments. If its leadership is closely attuned to its purposes, it can be a mighty host for producing departmental action responsive to his needs. The other organization is a personal staff, flexible, versatile, and fast-moving, competent to exploit departmental resources and hammer out policy as the President finds it necessary. In a word, the President must have a formal structure capable of handling the great stream of business and a modifying, informal mechanism capable of intervening in and adjusting executive processes responsively to his purposes.

Four distinguished study groups, the Brownlow Committee (1937), the first and second Hoover Commissions (1949 and 1955), and the current Subcommittee on National Policy Machinery, headed by Senator Henry Jackson, provide in their reports a mine of recommendations for strengthening the President's position as general manager. Some of them have been acted upon, and others would be immensely helpful if they were. Taking the recommendations of these several groups together, they urge that the Civil Service Commission, which is largely independent of the President, be abolished and replaced by a civil service administrator appointed by and responsible to the President. The recommendation assumes that personnel policy ought to be centered in the Chief Executive, in preference to its present diffusion between the President and the commission. The commission, as the traditional watchdog of the vast merit system, has been primarily a regulatory body alert to shut out spoils, a mission that also fosters red tape, routine, and impersonality. Also recommended is a "positive" personnel policy, one that would promote a working environment and career development opportunities to attract and keep the best available younger talent. The federal service suffers a heavy loss of such talent after some years of training have been invested, owing to the superior attractions of private employment.

The President's natural interest, it is assumed, would be to develop the strongest possible personnel system, both for his own operating convenience and for his administration's public image. Toward this end a strong mobile career corps, a "senior civil service," was recommended to be chosen from upper-level civil service employees on the basis of leadership, judgment, adaptability, and promise for assignments in the highest civil service grades. In addition, the adoption of an array of measures was proposed, for both government and private employers, to ease the transfer of top talent in business, the universities, and the professions for limited-period service in government at middle- and high-level positions. The Washington bureaucracy could thus be regularly infused, more than it is now, with new blood, new ideas, and zest for accomplishment.

An array of proposals was designed to strengthen also the position of the Chief Executive. Congress was urged not to delegate authority directly to bureau chiefs since that breaks the President's line of command. Congress's habit of requiring Senatorial confirmation of designated bureau chiefs was criticized in the same vein. Proposed, too, was consolidation of the outrageous number of agencies the President is called upon to supervise—some two score and ten—to a number that a mortal can reasonably be expected to manage. The redistribution of all independent commissions and government corporations to the existing departments was recommended. Consolidation is desirable only if the departments can be made responsive to the President, despite group interest and bureaucratic restraints. Furthermore, departmental Undersecretaries and Assistant Secretaries might be arranged in a fashion that would strengthen departmental leadership vis-à-vis the bureau chief and orient departmental policy-making more directly to the needs of the President. Another recommendation was a top command of management and policy-making aides, coupled with a blend of political, career, and program appointees whose breadth of view and combined skills might be an effective counterpoise to the bureaus.

The United States Supreme Court, which in rulings on civil rights and Congressional districting has befriended Presidential power, may well come in some future day to strengthen his power as administrative chief. The necessary judicial ingredients are at hand in the sweeping "executive power" clause. A friendly Court ruling might reduce Congress's administrative scope and invest the President with authority that he sorely lacks and that every good business executive fully enjoys. He would then have a clear, legal warrant for becoming the boss of the executive branch, the administrative chief that the nation so badly needs.

Public Leader 8

The hours when the American Presidency has enjoyed its most brilliant effectiveness are those when the Chief Executive rallies public sentiment behind his policies. Theodore Roosevelt moving against the abuses of giant railroads, Woodrow Wilson advancing his New Freedom program of social justice, Franklin Roosevelt combating the Great Depression and reforming the economy were achievements of leadership that stirred the understanding and support of the generality of the people.[1]

Given the realities of the political system in which he works, it is well that the President enjoys impressive resources for reaching the public and rallying public opinion. The built-in conflict between the President and Congress assured by checks and balances, the ease with which Congress can rebuff him, leaves the President dependent upon his ability to summon broad public support as his most substantial means of bringing Congress around to an accommodation productive of policy and action.

But the President's relation with public opinion, for all its importance and potential for good, has a darker side. It is also difficult and uncertain, something that he must deem at times, in his private thoughts, an onerous liability. Some of the most tragic moments in Presidential history have been those when the public has spurned proposals the Chief Executive has advanced in the careful and honest conviction that the nation's interest, and even mankind's, required them. Woodrow Wilson, despite valiant effort, could not get enough public support to win Senate approval of the Versailles treaty and American entrance into the League of Nations.

The President's most agonizing encounters are those where public opinion holds tenaciously to views that he, by his own best information, knows are wrong and contrary to the nation's interest. It was public opinion that forced the President to engage in a rapid and sweeping demobilization of our armed forces promptly after World War II to the resulting advantage of the Soviet Union, which quickly launched a campaign of expansion. Although the President and his counselors well knew the folly of "bringing the boys back home" so quickly and in such large numbers, they bowed to public opinion. A rare President may choose to defy it.

George Washington is one who did, in the war revolutionary France levied against Britain in 1793. Citizen Edmond Charles Genêt was dispatched as France's minister to the United States, and his eloquence and the ideological sympathies of the American people developed an overwhelming demand for an immediate declaration of war upon the British and George III. Washington, in a shining hour of greatness, rejected the popular will and issued his memorable proclamation of neutrality. His reward for maintaining his view that the nation must not squander its precious strength in war was unmerciful vilification in the press and in public meetings. Even his safety was in jeopardy. "Ten thousand people in the streets of Philadelphia," John Adams reported, "day after day threatened to drag Washington out of his house, and effect a revolution in the Government, or compel it to declare war in favor of the French revolution and against England."[2]

Few Presidents can resist public opinion in the manner of Washington, whose prestige enabled him to withstand majority public sentiment. The real choice that most Presidents since his time have faced is whether to convince the public or to drift with its poorly informed will.

Constituencies

The President of today has many publics or constituencies whose wills hold the key to his policies' success and his political future. His most vital public is, of course, his bread-and-butter constituency, the national electorate, upon whose favor his reelection depends. Because of this incomparable gift, the electorate is exceeded by no other in its importance to the President. He deals daily with lesser but powerful publics—the pressure groups—that characteristically are informed, articulate, and efficient. The contemporary President's increasing projection onto the international plane brings within his concern a series of publics situated behind the foreign leaders with whom he deals. These further publics range from the general population to specialized groupings, just as his several American publics do. Prime Minister Harold Macmillan absorbed an object lesson in the President's relationship with the British public in his 1962 Bermuda conference with President Kennedy, who induced the Prime Minister to accept the submarine missile Polaris in lieu of the missile-bearing aircraft Skybolt. The agreement evoked such general disapproval among the British public that the Conservative government's chances were gravely weakened for the coming national elections.

On occasion Presidents, particularly twentieth-century Presidents, have heeded world opinion. In his address of January 25, 1919, to the Paris peace conference, Woodrow Wilson declared, "We are assembled under very peculiar conditions of world opinion . . . we are not representatives of governments, but representatives of peoples. It will not suffice to satisfy governmental circles anywhere. It is necessary that we should satisfy the opinion of mankind."[3] During the 1962 Cuban crisis, the Kennedy administration responded to the force that Wilson invoked in 1919. In deciding to refrain from invading Cuba, the administration was moved in no small way by fear of adverse world opinion, although an even greater factor was the risk of war with Russia.

The President's deepest and most continuous relation is with the American people, who not merely award the prize of his election but are at once the source and affirmation of his policies and program. When the people are behind him, he can prevail against any of the lesser publics—the pressure groups with their lobbyists and their Congressional spokesmen who dare oppose him. Woodrow Wilson called the President's mammoth capacity the "Voice of the People" when he wrote,

> His is the only national voice in affairs. Let him once win the admiration and confidence of the country, and no other single force can withstand him, no combination of forces will easily overpower him. His position takes the imagination of the country. He is the representative of no constituency, but of the whole people. When he speaks in his true character, he speaks for no special interest. If he rightly interpret the national thought and boldly insist upon it, he is irresistible; and the country never feels the zest for action so much as when its President is of such insight and caliber.[4]

In bidding for general public favor, the President can choose among several leadership roles. One leadership role that all Presidents play is that of "conservator." In this role the President is guardian of the existing order, of its social, economic, and political parts. He maintains programs and policies founded by his predecessors or at most extends them, but in a fashion consistent with hallowed patterns of the past. He reveres precedent and established procedure.[5] Presidents who stress this role have administrations characterized by little controversy and are popular and even beloved figures. Their popularity, however, remains a largely unused resource; they treat the day's problems cautiously and neglect ones likely to be significant in the future.

A second Presidential leadership role is "protective." The Chief Executive provides security against external danger to society's survival and well-being and protects its members from bodily harm and physical destruction.

He familiarizes the people with their peril and maintains their confidence in his measures. If their confidence is shaken, as it was when Kennedy attacked the Eisenhower administration's military stewardship in the 1960 Presidential campaign, the administration's candidate suffers losses of popular votes.

A third leadership role is "innovative," stressing that the Presidency abides in a world of change, whether in the stirrings for popular rights and social justice, in the economy's transition from an agricultural to an industrial base, or in the emerging need for the creation of an international community. A President who responds to the forces of change undertakes novel action and revises the existing economic, political, or social order by enacting new laws and establishing new accords and arrangements among nations. To make innovations he must sustain controversy and even risk political defeat. Although the innovative President, like any other President, prizes popularity, he will occasionally give higher priority to securing objectives.

All three types of leadership may not always be applicable simultaneously. Each will, if successfully applied, evoke ultimate approval, for as Thomas Hobbes long ago noted, mankind will respond to anything that promises to secure him his basic human wants. Men want the comfort of an established order, they want security against violence and death, and they have a creative urge to conquer new worlds.

Discovering Public Opinion

The President invests quantities of time and ingenuity discovering and estimating the opinions of his publics. He needs to know what his publics want, how his program is being received, what the folks are saying at the grass-roots. Because of the amorphous, fragmented character of opinion, the task of discovery is not simple, particularly when it is conducted largely in the peculiar isolation of Washington. Difficulty, however formidable, does not deter most Presidents from working hard at the job. President Franklin Roosevelt, for example, developed such expertise that he amazed his associates with his "complete and precise knowledge" of opinion.[6]

In flushing out public opinion, Presidents rely heavily on "scouts," literally packs of them, who traverse numerous parts of the political landscape. William McKinley extracted invaluable intelligence from his cabinet members traveling about the country, from legislators of both parties returning after visits with their constituents, and from leading citizens, chiefly businessmen, in widely scattered communities. Franklin Roosevelt profited enormously from the extensive and observant traveling of Mrs. Roosevelt. Harry Hopkins, his administrator of public works, had informative subadministrators posted across the land who reported local sentiment. Once when knowledge of Middle Western agricultural opinion was most vital, Harry Truman dispatched his trusted and perspicacious friend Leslie Biffle, the secretary of the Senate, to the region, where, disguised as a farmer, he learned the authentic opinion of the wheat and corn country.

Most Presidents read the newspapers closely to learn what is being said both for and against their administrations. McKinley regularly put in two hours after breakfast scanning the papers. From his hometown paper, the Canton, Ohio, *Repository*, he proceeded to "five or six New York dailies, the Washington evening and morning papers, one or two from Chicago, and perhaps a half dozen others from large cities." When Franklin Roosevelt entered the White House, his secretary, Louis Howe, compiled a daily digest of editorial opinion from 750 newspapers representing every city of more than 25,000 population. Thanks to the press, Roosevelt reputedly was convinced that he possessed an infallible method of knowing whether he was right or wrong on an issue. If certain newspapers opposed him, he felt that he must be generally correct. If they were with him, he became suspicious.[7]

Presidents since Franklin Roosevelt's day can keep their eyes on the public opinion polls, those conducted both by private sources and by governmental departments. Presidents also look to their mail and to visitors for soundings of opinion. In Harding's time letters numbered about four hundred a day; in Franklin Roosevelt's they soared to an average of four thousand. The mail of Roosevelt's successors is similarly heavy, requiring a considerable staff to answer, digest, abstract, file, and index it. Roosevelt, it appears, seldom read the general mail but watched the abstracts. Visitors, as Truman has said, are "valuable to the President, for they help him keep in touch with the cross section of American interests and opinion."[8] Truman's predecessor, Franklin Roosevelt, regularly saw a diversity of people from many sections of the country, from whom he skillfully extracted information, often without their knowing it. Truman, for his part, closely systematized the considerable time he devoted to visitors. By setting aside an average of four hours each work day, he could take on ninety-five appointments a week, in the course of which he might see 250 persons.

Acting on Public Opinion

Presidents with knowledge or even a bare inkling of public opinion may choose to act. Their aides set to work to amass ideas for new policy. They may appoint study commissions of experienced and esteemed citizens to investigate a chosen problem. They may direct the great departments to act. If it is a matter of significance, the President personally may speak on it in his press conference, in a special White House statement, in any or all of his messages to Congress, and, if it is worthy of a grand effort, in an address by television and radio to the nation. A President may choose to champion not one or several proposals of policy, but a quantity, linked more or less into a program. Such were Lyndon Johnson's Great Society, Franklin Roosevelt's New Deal, and Woodrow Wilson's New Freedom, essentially collections of proposed legislation to which the President's leadership was committed.

Presidential success in popular leadership rests upon a dual foundation of opportunity and personality. If the country is floundering in economic depression or gripped in war or the threat of it, Presidential leadership will not only be welcomed, but it will be demanded. There is, happily, a lesser range of problems and situations upon which innovative Presidential leadership can be bestowed, as the Theodore Roosevelt administration attests in its economic and social policies. The second major underpinning of Presidential leadership, the human personality, although infinitely varied, must have certain traits if it is to be successful. Three of the most preeminently successful practitioners of popular leadership from the high place of the Presidency have been Theodore Roosevelt, Woodrow Wilson, and Franklin Roosevelt.

Each was a man of courage, firmness, and hope. Each was blessed with gifts of charismatic power, radiating a dynamism that stirred hearts and inspired minds. All three were forceful moral teachers who exposed social and economic evil and pointed the way to constructive reform. They had the demagogue's ability to simplify the complex world for their fellow man and to convince him of their fervent concern for his problems and their high resolve to do something about them. All three Presidents, whether by word or by gesture, were superbly articulate. Wilson was the most moving and exact in his use of words, the master of a lean and forceful style. Each was adept in providing the memorable phrase. T. R.'s "malefactors of great wealth," Wilson's castigation of "a little group of willful men," and F. D. R.'s "We have nothing to fear but fear itself" live in memory. All were "characters" in the best sense of the word, adept at focusing attention upon themselves and at converting the Presidency into a kind of venture in dramaturgy. T. R., whose talent in this regard is unrivaled, was aptly conveyed in the cartoons of the day depicting him as a huge creature with enormous clenched teeth, a thick spiked club, and a belt full of pistols, all adding up to a blustering, roaring, swashbuckling ruffian who wowed the electorate.

As part of his showmanship, the popular leader communicates a sense of mastery and confidence, even when the situation confronting the nation little warrants it. F. D. R.'s ringing avowal of faith in the future was hardly justified in his 1933 inaugural, in the face of the soaring unemployment rate, the failing banks, and the swaths of mortgage foreclosures. One shudders at what a more literal interpretation of the facts would have done to the status of the new administration in the national psychology.

Great popular Presidents such as Wilson and the Roosevelts excel at manipulation; they are flexible and even opportunistic. One of the most intriguing, as well as fruitless, pastimes is to speculate on the individual political alchemies of these Presidents, on how much of their official conduct represented an idealistic concern to improve the lot of their fellow humanity, and how much of it a desire to pick up large blocs of votes among the discontented. Franklin Roosevelt's admonition to one of his subordinates, a chafing reformer, that an administration must take care in "picking its fights," suggests that not blind idealism, but a concentration upon the attainable is an inevitable preoccupation of the President when he makes strategical and tactical choices.

The Grand Tour

Most Presidents reach their publics by engaging in "grand tours," a tradition that George Washington founded in a two-month journey through the South in 1791. Then, as now, the peregrinating President ordinarily has a dual purpose: to discover popular sentiment and, by his presence and word, to rally support for his administration. Washington's original precedent-setting journey involved two thousand miles of travel in a new light chariot, in the company of his secretary and a servant. In planning his trip, the President wisely allowed eight days for "casualties." Of these, the worst occurred in the crossing of the Occoquan, when a horse fully harnessed to the chariot fell into the stream and created such general excitement that the entire team followed him. Only the quick and expert work of all hands, especially the President's, prevented a fearful loss.[9]

Washington's itinerary was crowded with ceremony and business. His two-day stop at Richmond included a parade, a civic dinner, an illumination, an address and answer, and a formal leave-taking. He briefed himself on local sentiment in a lengthy conversation with Colonel Edward Carrington, his appointed United States marshal for the district of Virginia. His further stops included Tarboro, a hamlet where, he noted, "We were received . . . by as good a salute as could be given by one piece of artillery." The ceremonial climax of the journey, which wound through North and South Carolina, occurred at Charleston, where Washington in a week's stay survived tests of gastronomic and physical endurance that no future President has exceeded. He weathered three receptions, two breakfasts, and seven sumptuous formal dinners, listened and replied to four addresses, was the honored figure at two assemblies and a concert, rode through the city, went twice to church, observed a display of fireworks, visited the scenes of military operations, and drank sixty toasts.

For all its rigors, Washington considered the trip enormously rewarding. He was impressed with the improved state of trade and industry and was surprised and gratified to find his government as popular in the South as in Federalist New England. "I am much pleased that I have taken this journey," Washington wrote to David Humphreys, friend and aide-de-camp, "as it has enabled me to see with my own eyes the situation of the country thro' which we traveled and to learn more accurately the disposition of the people than I could have done by any information."[10]

The contemporary President must not only pass before the view of his American public; he must also appear periodically before foreign publics whose approval his administration values. Although various Presidents have traveled abroad, Dwight D. Eisenhower was the first Chief Executive to do so on a large scale to reach his multiple publics. In 1959 Eisenhower made a journey of 22,370 miles to visit eleven nations from Italy to India, conferring with his fellow chief executives and shaking the hands of thousands of people.

But Presidential travel is costly. Although Eisenhower's 1959 journey was heroic in the face of his illnesses, perhaps he might better have employed his time and strength for the sake of world peace by remaining in Washington to grapple with knotty foreign policy problems, instead of placing himself before the clamoring multitudes. In leaving Washington, the traveling President removes himself from vital tasks that only he can do and that may be crucial to the success of his policy projects. At a crucial juncture when the House Rules Committee was deliberating on his school aid proposal in 1961, John Kennedy, who might have slowed or stayed a rapidly deteriorating situation if he had conversed with several committee members, was in Paris conferring with President de Gaulle.

In taking up travel, the President may have more momentous purposes than consultation with his fellow executives and bringing himself before the people. He may take to the road, in full armor, to do battle for his basic policies. Confronting obstruction from Congress and group interests to legislation incorporating his program, the President may choose to "go to the people." By adroit and moving appeal, he aims to stir the masses into a state of such general and intense approval that the opposition will crumble and his measures will prevail. Although certain Chief Executives have moved mountains in such undertakings, the loud clear warning of history is that going to the people is a perilous venture that can succeed only in an exceptional combination of circumstances.

Franklin Roosevelt, the Presidency's foremost master of the art of popular appeal, made his way thanks to the happy coincidence that the nature of the times called for the play of his formidable political talents. His principal achievements of popular leadership occurred in the first hundred days of his administration while in the pit of the depression. Goaded by chaos and despair, the people demanded action, and Roosevelt provided it. By skillfully maintaining public opinion in a state of general approbation, he could indulge in the political luxury of making short shrift of Congress. He relied chiefly upon his twice-a-week press conferences, supplemented by his inimitable "fireside chats," speeches over the radio by which he projected into millions of homes his intimate, informative reports on his stewardship. The

President's oratorical skill and the prevailing public mood made his demands upon Congress irresistible. The President's least intimation that Congressmen were balking would unloose a torrent of mail upon the legislators insisting that they do whatever the President wanted.

For all his success, Roosevelt was keenly aware that the tactic of public appeals was not without weakness. He knew it could easily be overdone; the public's attention and enthusiasm were limited. Even in his balmiest political season, the first hundred days, he presented only four fireside chats. The following year he offered two, and only one in each of the next two years. Roosevelt himself once explained his rigorous selectivity. He wrote,

> The public psychology and, for that matter, individual psychology cannot, because of human weakness, be attuned for long periods of time to a constant repetition of the highest note in the scale . . . people tire of seeing the same name, day after day, in the important headlines of the papers and the same voice, night after night, over the radio.[11]

Presidential appeals have also known disastrous and humiliating failure. Andrew Johnson's "swing around the country" in 1866 to bring off the election of a Congress favorably disposed toward his policies and Woodrow Wilson's 1919 Western tour to evoke popular support for the peace treaty he had negotiated and United States membership in the League of Nations are monumental reminders to Presidents that to entrust their political fortunes to the turning wheel of public opinion is to engage in a highly uncertain gamble.

Long before he became President, Wilson had entertained a high, almost romanticized regard for the constructive potentialities of public opinion in governmental affairs. In 1908 he wrote in *Constitutional Government,* "Opinion is the great, indeed the only, coordinating force in our system." The President, of all the officers of government, was the people's chosen instrument, owing to "his close and special relation to opinion the nation over."[12] Wilson's twenty-two-day trip in September of 1919 was not born of the aggressive optimism of his earlier writing. It was an act of desperation. The Republican majority of the Senate Foreign Relations Committee was pressing ahead with plans to amend the peace treaty drastically. Such Republican personages as William Howard Taft and Elihu Root, who had once supported the League, now failed to come forward in its behalf. Worst of all, there were ominous indications of betrayal by Wilson's own Senatorial followers. "I ask nothing better," he declared in the face of rising obstacles, "than to lay my case before the American people." He hoped that an aroused people would bring the Senate into step with the President. The state of public opinion, or what was known of it, made Wilson's course seem altogether plausible. Every available gauge of public opinion—polls, resolutions of state legislatures, mass meetings, speeches, editorials, and letters to the press—revealed that the mass of people demanded some kind of league to forestall the horror of war again.[13]

His fighting blood in a high boil, Wilson mapped out a plan of speech-making rigorous enough to stagger an athlete. Approximately forty formal speeches were arranged for the tour, plus innumerable unscheduled appearances on the rear platform of the Presidential train. The formal speeches delivered—in stadiums, opera houses, tabernacles, and tents—were a great strain in an era that did not know the microphone, particularly upon a man of Wilson's declining health. Obviously ill before the trip began, his twitching facial muscles and gray color worried his friends. Although by sheer heroism Wilson completed twenty-two days of his planned twenty-five-day journey, he ultimately collapsed in Pueblo, Colorado, the victim of a stroke. To compound the tragedy, there was not even a flicker of compensating political gain from this noble effort. The hard truth was that the large and sympathetic audiences that came to see and cheer him never felt committed to follow him through fire and water. Far from welling up in a great directing shout upon the Senate, they returned quietly to their daily concerns. "We are so busy making money that we haven't time to worry about the Peace Treaty," confessed a leading Omaha businessman who, like so many of his fellow citizens, came to see Wilson merely out of curiosity.[14]

Even if Wilson's trip had rallied opinion to a pitch that exceeded his highest expectations, it is impossible to see how he could have forced the Senate into speedy and unreserved approval of the peace treaty. The majority of Senators had no reason to be fearful of aroused opinion. The next Senatorial elections were far distant—fifteen months away—and even then only one-third of the Senate would face reelection. The remoteness of the next election, the lengthy Senatorial term of six years, the public's short memory, the likelihood that new issues would arise and distract in the meantime, and the prospect that if a Senator was "right" on local issues he would not have to fear the remote League drained all force from Wilson's impact. As Thomas A. Bailey has suggested, it would be difficult to prove that a single Senatorial vote was changed by Wilson's unstinting journey. Its enormous personal cost encourages the speculation that Wilson might have done far better to remain in Washington where he could have guarded his health and perhaps converted the reservations that would inevitably be made to the treaty into acceptable compromises.

The Mass Media

The President commands the nation's attention as no one else can. Whatever he says, does, or thinks is big news. The front page, the television screen, and the magazine cover are his for the taking. The Kennedy administration plainly surpassed all others in the attention it was allotted in the mass media. Consider, for example, the communications scene of the first days of May 1962. The President himself dominated the political news on television and in the press. Simultaneously, he and his wife were featured in two big circulation magazines, *McCall's* and the *Saturday Evening Post*. Meanwhile, in personal appearances at the University of California and in New Orleans, the President reached vast audiences. These were followed by a nationally televised address at Atlantic City, a Presidential press conference, and a gigantic Presidential rally in Madison Square Garden in New York City with a generous assortment of stars from Hollywood and Broadway in the supporting cast. Kennedy's cumulative publicity well exceeded that of the most skillful of his predecessors in public relations—Franklin Roosevelt, who lacked the advantage of television, and Theodore Roosevelt, who never knew the intriguing possibility of instant communication with an entire continent. The President's powers of publicity are impressive compared with those of his fellow chief executives of the western world. His coverage well exceeds the French President's and is even more than that of the Prime Minister and Queen of England combined.

The formidable public relations position of President Kennedy was by no means representative of Presidential history. In seasons past, when the fortunes of the office were comparatively parlous, the Chief Executive was sometimes overshadowed by his powerful competitors for public attention. Tyler and Taylor were Presidents, to be sure, but they are little remembered. The historical period they straddled is symbolized by the towering personages of Daniel Webster and Henry Clay. The leading figure in the Presidential years of Franklin Pierce was not the rather hapless Chief Executive but the shrewd and competent Senator Stephen A. Douglas. Similarly, the worthy Rutherford B. Hayes was overshadowed by the far less worthy but more spectacular Roscoe Conkling and James G. Blaine. Even modern Presidents may be hard pushed by competitors of formidable talent. In 1916 Woodrow Wilson could view from the White House the spectacle of Theodore Roosevelt in the East calling upon the nation to intervene in the current world war, and William Jennings Bryan in the West, thrice a Presidential nominee, pleading for peace.

To communicate with his publics abroad, the present-day Chief Executive profits from the spreading international dimension of the communications media. His global projection has been speeded by the growing number of American periodicals, led by *Time* and *Reader's Digest*, which developed foreign editions as early as the 1940's.[15] The inexpensive, popular transistor radio is rapidly expanding the foreign audiences that the President reaches over the Voice of America's facilities. The launching of the communications satellite Telstar in 1962 gives the President access to a world-wide television audience.

In his first year of office President Kennedy engaged in a wide-ranging review of American policy on a taped British television interview program with the editor of *Izvestia*, Alexei Adzhubei, Khrushchev's son-in-law. The Voice of America beamed the President's words to vast audiences on several continents. In the 1962 Cuban crisis President Kennedy's address on the evening of October 22 was relayed around the world in English and thirty-seven other languages. As the President spoke, 102 United States Information Agency posts overseas were receiving the full text by radio teletype and quickly translating and reproducing his remarks for delivery to local government officials and newspaper editors.[16] President Johnson enjoyed equal coverage in his 1967 Glassboro conference with Soviet Premier Kosygin, and, in addition, was represented in various shadings in the media of the communist nations.

Communications Experts

Although the President is normally his own best publicity agent, he is assisted by a large and growing staff of communications experts. Presidents got along with a press secretary and a speech-writer or two earlier in this century, but it is possible for a present-day Chief Executive to become an enclave surrounded by communications specialists.

Dwight D. Eisenhower knew something of this experience as President. His press secretary, James Hagerty, was a former reporter and press secretary for Governor Thomas E. Dewey. A Presidential administrative assistant, Emmet Hughes, on leave from *Life* magazine, was a leading speech-writer. The President's economics assistant, Gabriel Hauge, was a former editor of *Business Week* and member of the executive committee of the McGraw-Hill publishing company. Hauge was a ghost-writer in Dewey's 1948 and in Eisenhower's 1952 Presidential campaigns. In the early Eisenhower years C. D. Jackson of *Fortune* doubled as a speech-writer and research director. The associate press secretary, Anne Wheaton, had previously been assistant publicity director for the Republican National Committee. Elsewhere in the Presidential staff, Frederic Morrow, administrative officer for "Special Projects," was a former field secretary for the National Association for the Advancement of Colored People and public relations officer of the Columbia Broadcasting System. Howard Pyle, deputy assistant for "Intergovernmental Relations," had public relations experience as announcer, writer, and program director and numbered among his professional achievements the production of the Grand Canyon Sunrise Easter Service. Robert Cutler, the assistant for national security affairs, was a distinguished fund-raiser for the Community Chest and other projects in his home city of Boston. The President's "television coach," Robert Montgomery, was a Hollywood star and producer.[17]

Although public relations is not a new profession, only recently have its practitioners come into high estate in both politics and private affairs. They have climbed from secondary status as technicians to participation in top policy councils. Where once they were fund-raisers, publicity men, and press secretaries, now they are often dignified by the designations "social engineers" and "practicing social scientists." The public relations man's ascent in politics is a by-product of the burgeoning mass communications technology and the steady enhancement of the "power of public opinion" in democratic society: the universalization of suffrage, the advent of mass education, and the galloping rate of population growth. The vast electorate can be reached efficiently and economically only by the mass media. The technician who can conceptualize policy problems so that they can be presented on television, on the radio, in the press, and in specialized publications becomes indispensable. In the stress he places by professional necessity upon unity of image, the public relations man is a potent centralizing force in administration and politics. He deplores dissent and irregularity because they blunt his impact. Like other professional people, he serves, and therefore tends to identify with, the established interests rather than with new ideas and less privileged groups that also have social importance.

The public relations man uses the communications apparatus not merely to distribute information, but to exert social control. As Edward L. Bernays, the public relations pioneer, has written, "He helps to mould the action of his client as well as to mould public opinion."[18] In politics the public relations expert strives to "market" his client in a favorable image, and, in the case of the Chief Executive, to establish and maintain him as a figure beloved, and perhaps idolized, by the masses. Policy, as it is formed and asserted, is subordinated to the necessities of image. Controversy and risk are avoided, and the taint of failure shunned. Actions attributed to the Chief Executive are selected and staged to reinforce his image of virtue and infallibility in the popular mind. Thus President Eisenhower was marketed as the war hero, the beloved nonpartisan, noncontroversial figure who stood above the political battle. When, therefore, in certain seasons, the Democrats had to be lashed, the task fell not to Eisenhower but to subordinates such as Richard Nixon and Sherman Adams. When the civil rights issue gathered in the ugly clouds of the Little Rock crisis, Eisenhower's involvement was carefully minimized.[19]

A prime illustration of the career possibilities of the public relations expert in the contemporary Presidency is provided by the press secretary of the Eisenhower administration, James Hagerty. Like other press secretaries before him, Hagerty handed out news releases, answered reporters' questions, excelled as an advance man on the President's trips, and was in general a buffer between the President and the public. But Hagerty was more than the efficient press secretaries preceding him. He was the President's confidant and enjoyed full status in top-level policy discussions and personal political decisions. The press secretary was among the dozen friends who gathered with the President at a White House dinner on a January evening in 1956 to consider the advisability of his candidacy for a second term. Of all the members of the White House staff, he had the warmest personal relations with Eisenhower, regularly accompanied him on trips, and shared in his golf, bridge, and fishing.

Hagerty regularly attended cabinet meetings and the President's weekly sessions with Congressional leaders and is reputed to have spoken forcibly. "Probably more than anybody in the President's official family," Sherman Adams once said during his term as Presidential assistant, "he relies on Jim for the testing of the new idea. He looks to him as the man to mirror the public reaction and in a large majority of cases would dispose of the matter then and there and on the basis of Jim's judgment."[20] Hagerty reached the pinnacle of his importance in the crises of Eisenhower's illnesses. In the face of the most trying circumstances, the press secretary mastered the situation and presented the country and the world with a reassuring image of confidence and calm.

More than any press secretary in the past, Hagerty was the authentic voice of the White House. In intervals between the President's speeches and press conferences, during his vacations and illnesses, Hagerty was the daily source of Presidential pronouncement. The press secretary excelled at rendering up the minutiae of administration happenings of interest to most newspapers, in lieu of concentrating on policy. When the President in extemporaneous statements floundered in error, it would be Hagerty who picked up the pieces by issuing statements "clarifying" the President's meaning. If Hagerty provided most of what the world learned about the President, he was also the source of most of what the President learned about the world. Since Eisenhower was not given to reading the newspapers, Hagerty kept up with an array of publications, culling from them the information which, he believed, warranted the President's attention.[21]

In an administration that prized harmony and teamwork, Hagerty was a public relations chieftain of great power. His controls over news and statements emanating from the departments were unprecedented. He met regularly with departmental press officers, scanned departmental news bulletins prior to their release, and ably rescued departmental Secretaries whose loose talk plunged them into the briny depths of trouble. Cabinet members learned the value of checking their speeches beforehand with Hagerty, and the Republican national chairman, Leonard Hall, found it advantageous to consult with him on many matters.

The Hagerty pattern raises several kinds of criticism. His concentration on the operational convenience and necessity of the newsmen and the incidental minutiae of the Presidency tended to diminish his attention to interpretations of the administration's purposes. His close rein on departmental sources prevented reporters from getting fuller expositions of policy and perhaps contrasting views directly from department spokesmen. The number of informal background briefings by leading administration officials declined substantially. They began to feel a widespread distrust of reporters and left the field to Hagerty. On occasion, the President seemed inadequately informed of the activities of his administration. In press conferences his comments upon such critical and controversial episodes as the Dixon-Yates contract and the inflamed situation at Little Rock betrayed an astonishing ignorance of basic fact. How much of this is attributable to Eisenhower's personal disinclination to become entangled in administrative detail and how much to Hagerty's overefficiency in shielding the Chief Executive from official problems remains a mystery.

The Hagerty instance invites the question of whether the public relations function was excessively important to the inner councils of the Eisenhower administration, whether its centralized controls over the departments and its dominance in the President's illnesses constitute a reach of power that is altogether harmonious with democratic processes.

The Press Conference

To reach their publics, most contemporary Presidents rely upon the press conference, an institution that harks back only to the administration of Woodrow Wilson. Soon after his inauguration, reporters gathered by general invitation in his office for a question-and-answer exchange on the administration's business. The reporters assembled with lofty expectations encouraged by Wilson's solemn invocation of "pitiless publicity" for public business in his pre-Presidential writing on political science. The new practice of the press conference replaced the old arrangement by which Presidents had granted interviews only to selected reporters, a tactic permitting favoritism and penalization. In the press conference, reporters enjoy equal footing.

Unfortunately, the sessions under Wilson and his early successors fell far short of the initial optimism. Wilson's glacial reserve inhibited interchange. He was often irritated by the reporters' habit of speculating about the news and of persisting with questions before he was prepared to release information. He considered the reporters' cross-examining a reflection upon his honesty. Wilson's successor, Warren G. Harding, a trusting, genial, former newspaperman, took the press freely into his confidence until a Presidential misstatement during the negotiation of the Four Power Treaty brought such painful diplomatic repercussions that henceforth reporters had to submit all questions beforehand in writing. Calvin Coolidge continued the practice of written questions, and by drastically sifting them and selecting only a few to answer with laconic, noncommittal remarks, he quickly reduced the press conference to a drab and fruitless exercise. Under Hoover the press conference continued to be a stilted, meager source of news.[22]

The advent of Franklin Roosevelt finally brought the little-tried institution into its own. Roosevelt set up two press conferences a week, canceled the requirement of written questions, and with his facile charm turned the sessions into lively occasions on which he provided the public with a running account of what he was doing and what he proposed to do and why.[23] Truman's sessions, although numerous, were briefer, less sprightly, and more staccato. On several occasions he made statements that constitute a monumental lesson on how easily and how thoroughly a President can put his foot into his mouth. Once when asked if the atomic bomb was under active consideration for possible use against Red China in the Korean War, he replied that use of the bomb was always under active consideration. This seemingly ominous announcement stirred a flurry of anxious protests in Congress and the press until the White House issued a clarifying statement.

Eisenhower's penchant for a balanced statement that permitted him to avoid taking a position reduced the newsworthiness of his conferences. His further habit of freely delegating tasks and decisions to subordinates sometimes left him shy of details when facing queries. Eisenhower permitted the innovation of televising his press conferences and presenting them, with minor editing, to the public. With John Kennedy there was no editing; the televised presentation was made exactly as his encounters with the reporters occurred. Kennedy's press conferences were highly effective, his responses to questions revealing an almost photographic memory for detail and a gift for keeping abreast of policy development from incubation to implementation. His brisk assurance and his opening statements charged with newsworthy content lent zest and excitement to his administration. Despite his success, he used the news conferences erratically. Three and four weeks would pass without meetings with the press. The longest lapses occurred in the Berlin and Cuban crises, when the President apparently concluded that a public discussion would not be helpful and that some chance and unstudied remarks might be greatly harmful.

Kennedy's news conferences took place in the vast State Department auditorium, with about three hundred newsmen on hand. Millions of citizens later took in the half-hour's proceedings on television and radio. Although superficially the press conference appeared informal and off-the-cuff, Kennedy, like his predecessors, did considerable preparing beforehand. He and his aides engaged in intensive pondering to anticipate the questions. His wide reading of newspapers and magazines and his listening to broadcasts apprised him of the mental stirrings of the journalists and therefore of what they were apt to ask. On the afternoon before the conference, the President's press secretary, Pierre Salinger, summoned the information chiefs of the executive departments to his White House office to share their experiences of the past week with press inquiries. On the day of the news conference Salinger, with his sundry notes, breakfasted with the President. Also partaking of the meal were Secretary of State Dean Rusk; Walter Heller, chairman of the Council of Economic Advisers; Theodore Sorensen, the President's counsel; McGeorge Bundy, assistant for national security affairs; and

Myer Feldman, deputy counsel. The breakfast group canvassed the news questions that occurred to them and supplied Kennedy with data for answers.[24]

President Johnson, who excelled more in conversation and in encounters with small groups than in large, formal presentations, was always seeking for the most suitable forum for his news conferences. He tried such places as the vast, windowless, international conference room of the State Department, the New York World's Fair, a two-mile walk, his own office, the office of the White House press secretary, the cabinet room, the LBJ ranch, and the East Room, the White House's largest and most formal room, where reporters sat on gilt chairs in a semicircle around the President, who stood in front of a golden drapery flanked by huge portraits of George and Martha Washington. A talker rather than a performer, Johnson fared best in a setting where he was most natural.

Like Eisenhower, Johnson preferred the cautious statement, seldom responded directly to questions, and in his answers rarely surprised or startled. A wise and guarded politician, he avoided sudden commitment and fighting words.[25] He did not employ humor and was given to lengthy opening statements and full-blown answers that devour news conference time. Like many of his Presidential predecessors, Johnson was sensitive to criticism, especially when it was personal.[26] Toward criticism of his policies his equanimity was greater. Once when pelted with a deluge of criticism of his course in Vietnam, he remarked philosophically, "I'm just like a jackass in a hailstorm. You just hunker up and take it."[27] Before withdrawing from the 1968 contest, Johnson radically altered his pose and took on a "give 'em hell" stance reminiscent of Truman in the 1948 campaign, accompanied with shafts of humor and ridicule.

For all its slow start, the Presidential press conference occupies a vital place in American political life. It is the only regular occasion on which the nation can view the Chief Executive in an active interchange with people outside his administration and without the props of speech-writers and idea men. Notwithstanding the President's preparations, there is still much spontaneity, owing to the unpredictable twists reporters often give their questions. The sessions are also invaluable opportunities for the President to present his opinions and raise trial balloons. He can be sure that what he wants to say gets said by having it arranged beforehand for a reporter to ask a convenient question—a planted question—an old, productive device.

Nevertheless, press conferences can also be unproductive. The President can easily dodge and parry questions; no mere reporter can nail an incumbent of the awesome office to the wall. Many of the questions are not keen. The prolixity with which they are sometimes put may produce a question substantially longer than the President's answer. Some queries have no other merit than to gratify the urge of reporters to appear on television. Since the advent of television, reporters have asked more and more questions of a regional or minor character that titillate the folks back home but lack the national quality the press conference deserves.

The Art of News Management

In the estimation of Arthur Krock, the political analyst, the Kennedy administration practiced the art of news management "boldly," "cynically," and "with the utmost subtlety and imagination." The reward of this effort, Krock contended, was a portrayal of the administration in the press with a radiant aura of approval that neither its achievement nor the country's circumstances warranted. In the Kennedy era as in other eras, many critics voiced concern for the continued integrity of Thomas Jefferson's dictum that the people have a right to "full information of their affairs thro' the channel of the public papers."[28]

News management, which is a craft of many tricks, can cultivate the image of the President as infallible even in the face of flagrant error. If things go wrong, blame is placed upon others, usually his subordinates. A major tool of news management is the use of selective personal patronage, whereby those reporters who "behave," or write favorably of the administration, are granted privileges unavailable to their fellows. Thus Stewart Alsop and Charles Bartlett, co-authors of a widely noticed magazine article on the 1962 Cuban crisis, which could not have been undertaken without the unparalleled privilege of access to National Security Council proceedings, were candidly referred to by the President in a news conference as "old friends." Another plum was a 1962 year-end informal televised interview of the President by three cooperative reporters covering an extraordinary range of subjects and witnessed by a vast audience. A contrasting and less selective Kennedy tactic was the use of "social flattery," by which a succession of groups of editors and publishers were feted at the White House. In May 1961, for example, the President had to luncheon eight editors from Florida; in October a throng of New Jersey publishers followed by twenty-four publishers and news executives from the state of Washington; and in December twenty-five Minnesota news executives. The pattern was used even more extensively in 1962 and 1963. Kennedy reached reporters and editors on a large scale in occasional intimate, far-ranging background briefings. The press participants emerged, Krock observed, "in a state of protracted enchantment evoked by the President's charm and the awesome aura of his office." The mood carried over into the news columns and editorials.[29]

The Kennedy administration's news policy had a reverse side, a regulatory aspect that did not gain favor with the press. In the 1962 Cuban crisis Assistant Secretary of Defense Arthur Sylvester declared, in a moment of mismanaged candor, that the administration's management of the news was "part of the weaponry" of government in the cold war, and that "the results justify the methods we use."[30] Presumably, concealment and distortion were permissible when necessity required. The perils of official fabrication were glaringly revealed some weeks later when Senate Republican leader Everett Dirksen of Illinois revealed that four Americans had been killed in the 1961 Bay of Pigs invasion. The disclosure was especially upsetting because two months earlier Attorney General Robert F. Kennedy had denied emphatically that any Americans had been killed at the Bay of Pigs. The Attorney General's statement reinforced a pledge by the President, uttered just five days before the invasion, "to make sure that there are no Americans involved in any actions inside Cuba."[31]

News management was not a creation of the Kennedy administration, however. It is an ancient and common practice of the Presidency. Management assumes a variety of forms, from the complex to the simple little expedient Chester A. Arthur employed to present to his critics the appearance of being busy. Having a large reputation for indolence, Arthur maintained a "property basket" filled with official-looking documents that a secretary would carry into the President's office when he was with visitors to create the impression of industry.[32]

Earlier Presidents, indeed, applied managerial strokes that no contemporary Chief Executive would dare consider. At the height of his battle to secure legislation to establish a Bureau of Corporations, for example, Theodore Roosevelt, knowing all too well that John D. Rockefeller's Standard Oil empire was massively pressing legislators to vote against the measure, resorted to a desperate move. The company was sending quantities of unsigned telegrams to numerous members of Congress bearing the terse and imperious message, "We are opposed to any anti-trust legislation—it must be stopped." Looking for advantage in the grim struggle, Roosevelt declared in a public statement that the author of the reprehensible message was no one less than Rockefeller, reigning monarch of the Standard empire. Roosevelt's enemies gleefully spread out for public view incontrovertible evidence that the author was in fact John Archbold, Standard Oil president. Totally bereft of rebuttal, Roosevelt subsided, for once, into silence. "The last thing in the world that John D. Rockefeller would have done," wrote Ida M. Tarbell, biographer of Standard Oil, with headshaking resignation, "was to send such a telegram to anybody."[33]

Flattery and favors are also old Presidential tactics. John Tyler treated the New York *Herald*'s Washington correspondent, Parmly, as a confidant. A rival and less fortunate journal observed that Parmly enjoyed

> the run of the presidential kitchen, and is favored with copies of his messages and other public acts before they have been submitted to his cabinet ministers. For these high privileges and distinguished favors, he, of course, evinces his gratitude, and does his share of the dirty jobs about the palace, by abusing in the most gross and vulgar language, the members of the late cabinet. . . .[34]

Some Presidents also bestow disfavor upon certain papers and their Washington reporters. Theodore Roosevelt was a busy feuder whose worst war was with the New York *World*. The conflict reached a point where the paper solemnly informed its readers that the President was a madman soon destined for an asylum. Roosevelt's several countermoves included a large attempt to put Joseph Pulitzer, the *World*'s publisher, behind bars.[35]

Occasionally, Presidents have distributed a considerable largess to awaiting journalistic hands. In the republic's early decades the piecework and job-printing of the executive departments were awarded to struggling journals that trumpeted the administration's accomplishments with loud adulation. Abraham Lincoln, who greatly respected the power of the press, appointed several influential journalists to responsible posts in his administration. Gideon Welles, the Secretary of the Navy, was a former editor of the Hartford *Times*, and the Assistant Secretary of War was Charles A. Dana of the New York *Tribune* and later of the *Sun*. William Dean Howells, the Ohio newspaperman and author of a Lincoln campaign biography, became consul at Venice, John Bigelow of the *Evening Post* minister to France, and James Watson Webb of the New York *Courier and Enquirer* minister to Brazil. At least a half-dozen other major appointees were journalists, and in the early weeks of the administration no fewer than four employees of the New York *Tribune* were named to posts abroad. This prompted the rival *Herald* to notice acidly, "It is evident that Mr. Lincoln has determined upon an evacuation of the New York *Tribune* office, if he has not decided about Fort Sumter." The transplanted journalists were normally expected to continue writing in their own papers and to cultivate those of the country in which they were residing, with a view to influencing public opinion.[36]

JOHNSON AS NEWS MANAGER. True to Presidential tradition, Lyndon Johnson too was a news manager. The Johnson years are marked by a ceaseless churning out of activity, pronouncements, speeches, messages, and trips. As in other branches of his Presidency, Johnson wielded increasingly centralized control over departmental public relations officers. "We want first refusal on anything that should appropriately come from here," the departments were informed.[37] Not surprisingly, there have been intervals of overexposure, when the President accumulated enormous footages on the television screen, much of it on subjects that earlier Chief Executives left to subordinates or mimeographed releases.

Although Johnson did not set any records in the quantity of his formal advance-notice news conferences, he surpassed his predecessors in terms of time spent talking to reporters, editors, and commentators. He preferred to see them individually and in lengthy interviews. It was not unusual for the President to sit in his rocking chair and talk with a reporter for several hours, a duration that overwhelmed some Presidential visitors with a guilty suspicion that they were keeping the Chief Executive from other more important business. Johnson in these interviews would review his hard problems and narrow choices, and he sometimes put to the visitor the self-involving question, "What would you do in my place?" Whether the President intended it or not, his interview procedure was a subtle form of news management. The private interview is a confidential, personal relationship that may confine a reporter more than it frees him to do his job.[38]

It was part of Johnson's method to control both what was disclosed about his administration and when it was disclosed.[39] If a reporter revealed that the President on a given date was to do a certain thing, Johnson would regard this as an impertinence and punish it by changing his plans. One reporter who saw the draft of a speech Johnson was to make at the twentieth anniversary celebration of the United Nations published the President's views on how to solve a financial crisis that the UN was suffering. Johnson was distressed to the point of ordering the speech rewritten to eliminate the views attributed to him.[40]

Critics of Johnson hold that he was pushed into such activity by an inordinate love of secrecy. But his former press secretary, Bill Moyers, once explained Johnson's thinking: "It is very important for a President to maintain up until the moment of decision his options, and for someone to speculate days or weeks in advance that he's going to do thus and thus is to deny to the President the latitude he needs in order to make, in the light of existing circumstances, the best possible decision."[41]

President Johnson was known to employ the same secrecy in dealing with his own staff as he did with reporters. He employed a series of press secretaries—Pierre Salinger, George Reedy, Bill Moyers, and George Christian—which in itself suggests that the function was handled uneasily. Because of his desire to preserve his options, to act only when, politically, he was ready to act, he was largely his own press secretary. The post of press secretary, ordinarily a top position on the White House staff, suffered something of a decline, owing to Johnson's working methods. Pierre Salinger, who stayed on with Johnson after service with Kennedy, discovered that he no longer enjoyed the privilege of walking into the President's office at any time to be filled in on matters for the press. His successor, George Reedy, also suffered the uncomfortable experience of working for a chief who did not supply him with the information necessary for his job. It was not until Bill Moyers, Johnson's former chief assistant, took on the added duty of press secretary that the post was finally upgraded.

Johnson's critics hold that his most heinous offense in managing the news was his several species of conduct that served to produce the "credibility gap"—the contrast between what is happening and what the administration says is or is not happening. Those who envision such a gap hold that the President consistently tried to make the news sound or seem better than it was. The lengthy, escalating war in Vietnam was a major contributor to the gap. A committee of the American Society of Newspaper Editors voiced the sentiment of many critics when it said, "The war has escalated to the accompaniment of an almost unbroken succession of pronouncements that it was going in the opposite direction, or at least that something else was happening." The committee lamented the damage Johnson's course did to "his image and his credibility."[42]

In part, the credibility gap was a by-product of a Presidential administration that was so pervasively political that it thoroughly subordinated its public relations and news policy to political necessity. For example, to prevent an aluminum price increase in 1965, Johnson moved strongly by releasing aluminum from government stockpiles. Despite the highly strained situation, the administration denied that an announcement about forthcoming releases from government stockpiles had anything to do with the price increase, which it patently did.

THE PEOPLE'S RIGHT TO KNOW.   The sorties of various Presidents into the fine art of news management raises difficult but basic questions involving democratic values and practices. In deciding what to tell the nation, the President must strike a balance between the people's right to know what their government is doing and planning, the nation's safety and welfare, which may not always be served by disclosure, and his own political interests. Disclosures to the public might embarrass our relations with a friendly nation. But secrecy also may do nothing more than enable him to make gross errors in solitude. The opinion has been expressed, and President Kennedy agreed with it, that less official secrecy and more publicity before the invasion of Cuba at the Bay of Pigs might have saved the nation from that debacle.[43]

No neat formula for resolving the dilemma of secrecy versus disclosure can be constructed that would be meaningful or useful. The choices must be worked out in specific instances, with sensitivity for democratic necessities. Fortunately, the President has no monopoly of power or influence on this difficult terrain and can be buffeted toward a different course by those who raise their voices in criticism: legislators, group interest leaders, prestigious private individuals, and the press. In confronting the ways and wiles of the Chief Executive in managing the news, the press is not without defenses. If the press is alert and professionally responsible, it should be able to cope with the President's slickest manipulations. The newspapers can, with ingenuity and enterprise, do their share of "managing" as well. They can, if they choose, put before the public an impression of the Chief Executive that is utterly contrary to reality. They converted the dour, colorless, withdrawn, futile Calvin Coolidge into a forceful, red-blooded, two-fisted, strong, silent "sage of Vermont," a man who never was. They can oppose and harass the President with little regard for truth and overlook every shred of merit his administration possesses. Many of the most powerful press organs of Lincoln's day, for example, fought his administration without letup. The New

York *World,* the New York *Daily News,* the Chicago *Times,* the Baltimore *Exchange,* and the Columbus *Crisis* all contended against him. Among the heaviest crosses Lincoln had to bear was James Gordon Bennett, Sr., of the New York *Herald,* a fast-growing, widely influential paper. Toward Lincoln, the *Herald* vacillated between the far extremes of praise and condemnation. In certain seasons the President was "a sorry joke," "a standing joke," "a broad joke," "a solemn joke"; other times he was "master of the situation." The *Herald's* mercurial tendencies seemed to depend upon the administration's willingness to award Bennett the high office and social recognition he wanted. He was given invitations to the White House for himself and his wife and son, and then he was appointed minister to France, whereupon the *Herald* finally settled down. "Mr. Lincoln deemed it more important to secure the *Herald's* support than to obtain a victory in the field," explained Thurlow Weed, the administration's principal intermediary with the newspaper.[44]

The President as Consensus Leader

The President, in his cumulative roles of chieftain of public opinion, party, Congress, and administration, tends to conform to two general patterns of leadership: leadership by consensus and majoritarian leadership. A given President may first veer toward one pattern and then toward the other.

The most common form of Presidential leadership is rooted in the politics of consensus. According to Lyndon Johnson, one of its most thoroughgoing practitioners, there is for every national problem a national answer that reasonable men can construct through discussion and accommodation. The national answer is not simply what the majority wants. Majorities are transitory and ought not dominate the minority whose thought and action too might contribute valuably to consensus.

To produce consensus and action rather than disagreement and inaction, the President is at the center of the effort, possessing political means capable of invoking a fundamental unity of interest, purpose, and belief in all the nation. As a consensus leader, the President formulates goals having the broadest possible appeal and charts the route to them by offering the specifics of immediate action. The President tends to undertake what Johnson liked to call the "do-able"—or that for which there are enough votes or support, a consensus. The President extends the scope of consensus by discovering and developing common denominators of agreement. Prior to the Education Act of 1965, bills providing general aid to education were steadily wrecked on the issue of public aid to church-supported schools. Through discussions with the National Education Association and the National Catholic Welfare Council, the Johnson administration developed a formula acceptable to both groups: to aid not schools as such but their children, whether in public or private schools, and especially in poor areas. With the two major education lobbies brought into a consensus, the administration incorporated the new-found formula into its education bill with an eye to securing maximum votes in Congress. The bill passed without major amendment and a political dead-lock that had endured for decades was finally overcome.

The President who is a consensus leader uses his powers with restraint and prefers bipartisan support to partisan strife. For the legislative achieve-ments of his Presidency, including its remarkable record in the Eighty-ninth Congress, Johnson was careful to give credit to the minority Republi-can party and to praise Congress. The consensus President also seeks to broaden the base of his party by making it a party "which serves all our people."[45]

The consensus approach is apt to thrive most in the initial years of a Presidential administration, the "honeymoon period," when sentiments of hope and good will and a sportsmanlike desire to give the new incumbent a fair chance prevail. Consensus may rise in time of war and economic crisis, and it may flourish in eras of moderation like the Era of Good Feeling that Monroe briefly enjoyed.

But the consensus approach, even in the hands of its most devoted Presi-dential practitioners, carries certain weaknesses. When the hard business of constructing policy reaches the phase of choosing between competing in-terests, men divide, partisanship rises, and agreement is lost to conflict. John-son was bedeviled by breakdowns or the sheer unavailability of consensus, in the perversity of Ho Chi Minh in the Vietnam war, in the rioting in American cities, in the unwillingness of Congress to flesh out the Great Society programs with substantial appropriations.

The Majoritarian President

Instead of pursuing the consensus method, a President may act as a majori-tarian leader who is prepared to take up, if necessary, the politics of combat. He puts himself at the head of a program behind which he rallies majority support and moves toward his goal by persuasion, manipulation, and con-flict. His program is more definite and stable than the offerings of the con-sensus President, and his administration has more of an ideological coloring or emphasis. Andrew Jackson constructed a majority following and, among other things, engaged in a full struggle with the Second Bank of the United States, an agency largely of private economic power and regional rule.

The President who chooses the majoritarian path and the politics of com-bat uses different methods and resources than the consensus President and applies different values. The program or purpose of the majoritarian Presi-dent takes precedence over the claims of his individual supporters. If a partic-ular supporting group rejects portions of his program, he will hold to it and push it through, while, hopefully, his remaining supporters still add up to a majority. He will take up causes, in the full anticipation that in doing so the wrath of powerful groups will tumble down upon his head. Harry Truman pursued a strong response to the Soviet Union in the general deterioration of U.S.-U.S.S.R. relations following World War II, even though it meant the alienation of Henry A. Wallace and other influential New Dealers and the loss of a substantial heritage of political support left by his predecessor, Franklin Roosevelt. Truman offered a national health program even though he knew he would earn the unflagging opposition of the American Medical Association.

The majoritarian President who takes up the politics of combat tends to use certain resources of his office more than others. He is apt to "go to the people," to "educate" them on the issues, and, hopefully, to rally them to his side in the strife. He uses the veto power more, not simply to resist and reject, but as a dramatic weapon that serves well to identify him with his cause. His discourse carries a strong vocabulary and he is prone to be mercilessly specific in identifying his enemies. Harry Truman startled his whistle-stop audiences in the 1948 campaign by attacking the "bloodsuckers of Wall Street." An even more useful "enemy" in that election was the Republican Eightieth Congress, labeled the "Do-Nothing Congress."

The majoritarian President is willing to lose battles in order eventually to win wars, even those where, in the final moment of victory, he may no longer be in office, and another may bask in the success that rose from his efforts. He takes a broad view of success and is willing to sustain defeat as the price for changing, or setting into motion the forces that may change, the country's prevailing opinion. He appeals to emotion as much as to rationality and is apt to view Presidential politics as not simply a continuing dialogue, seeking adjustments and accommodations, but as an enterprise analogous to a military campaign, with strategies and maneuvers, and fierce clashes of men with opposing interests.

The Future Presidency

The strong President has the gift of rallying public opinion, of bringing it to perceive the nation's problems and interest and the rightness of his measures. But public opinion, speaking through public and private leaders, through the communications media, and through the electorate, can also reach the President. In its ultimate severity, an electorate, can drive the President from office. To avoid that possibility, the President, faced with increasingly hostile opinion, might choose to alter his policy before the elections transpire. Public discussion and debate may develop alternatives to prevailing policy that the President may deem wise to adopt.

Just as public opinion can deal positively and constructively with the

President, so he can with it. In the world of great change that the 1960's and 1970's and beyond promise to be, his gift becomes ever more valuable. The President's task is made all the more difficult by the tendency of public opinion to lag behind change. The American public mind in the 1960's appears overcommitted to long-established conceptions in domestic and foreign affairs. In foreign affairs the public holds views acquired in the Roosevelt and Truman eras that are unsuited to changes that have since transpired in the world. The initial blandness of the public response to the far-reaching recommendations of the President's Commission on Civil Disorders in 1968 was widely attributed to lack of public understanding and concern. How are future Presidents to be strong in their high task of educating and rallying the public?

1. Future Presidents might restore the fireside chat of Franklin Roosevelt, or some adaptation of it, which would enable them or their aides to inform the people periodically on major problems. The most preeminent problem will continue to be the urban crisis, with its subproblems of education, health, housing, civil rights, unemployment, and the like. These are matters the President in years ahead might well take up with his domestic public. Like certain of Roosevelt's fireside chats, these might be background presentations, without specific requests for public support. The public would simply be "educated." For such a leadership venture, it is worth noting, President Johnson's speaking style was especially well suited. For example, in his televised address to the nation amid an upsurge of urban rioting in the summer of 1967, the President was very effective in delivering the calm, philosophical talk exploring the implications of an urgent national problem.

2. In addition to informative presentations, Presidents can "go to the people" to solicit their support on a specific issue, admittedly a hazardous enterprise. But as both Roosevelts demonstrated, it can be a formidable weapon if used with careful timing and in reasonably promising situations. Going to the people must be done sparingly, on issues which interest the public and in circumstances where the tide of events will command general attention for them.

3. If the President wants to communicate effectively, he will need speechwriters and other aides of whom at least some are not public relations professionals. The professional's attachment to the *status quo* and his tendency to subordinate policy to image mean that the President will need a representation of communications people of altogether different backgrounds—men like Samuel Rosenman, a lawyer of wide public experience who was a draftsman for Franklin Roosevelt; Malcolm Moos of the academic community who served Eisenhower; or Theodore Sorensen, Kennedy's draftsman, whose background combined law and politics.

4. To maintain his far-flung foreign constituencies, the President requires several kinds of staff assistance. As Nixon and Johnson proved in the Eisenhower and Kennedy administrations, the Vice President is an invaluable emissary in representing the President before his foreign publics. As the number-two executive leader, the Vice President is well fitted by the prestige of his rank to relieve the President from large and strenuous duties. Above all, the President needs aides whose gifts with ideas and words will infuse his public statements with intellectual and moral vigor and with phrases that are memorable.

5. In the contemporary age the Presidency can operate with maximum effect in a pluralistic society that is strong in all its parts. This is to say that the better informed the public is, the more alert and interested it is in the agenda of public affairs, and the better organized the sources of private opinion and expression, the stronger will the Presidency be. With an interested public the President can tackle more problems and venture bolder solutions than if the country is ignorant or indifferent.

The road to the political paradise of an understanding people cannot be built by the President alone. The chief executive in a pluralistic society has a right to expect creative thought and effort addressed to educating the public by private leaders and spokesmen. Leaders of religious, business and labor organizations, racial and national groups, and the artistic and academic worlds must become better social critics than they have been. They must show stronger awareness that in a fast-changing world a narrow view of self-interest is one of the surest ways to decline and extinction. They have a common cause with the President to help lead the nation into a better society.

Chief Diplomat 9

"I make American foreign policy," said Harry S. Truman, discoursing on his office one day in 1948 to a visiting body of Jewish War Veterans.[1] Truman's candid dictum finds support in the pronouncement of another Chief Executive, Thomas Jefferson, who once termed the conduct of foreign affairs "executive altogether."[2] In the late 1950's, when the President was struggling with great difficulty under the confines of our political system to develop an imaginative and vigorous foreign policy that world circumstances seemed desperately to require, Senator J. W. Fulbright was moved to observe that "for the existing requirements of American foreign policy we have hobbled the President by too niggardly a grant of power."[3] The contemporary President was viewed as performing his mammoth diplomatic toil with powers laid in the eighteenth century by men who assumed that the nation's external affairs would be few and insignificant.[4]

The Two Presidencies

In reality, as these testimonials suggest, there are two Presidencies in foreign affairs, and both have been constructed and shaped by the Founding Fathers, by the adaptation of the office to changes in the world with which it deals, and by its own peculiar suitability for the management of foreign affairs.

The two Presidencies have parallel powers and functions, and yet they are radically opposite in nature. One possesses a maximum autonomy, in which the President in relative privacy can make decisions that choose between war and peace, that commit treasure and lives, and that may determine the nation's foremost priorities for years to come. The President may take these decisions in secrecy and freedom, beyond the reach and even the knowledge of Congress and the people. Or, if Congress or the people are related to the decision, they can act only marginally. They have no real choice but to ratify what the President has done or will do. It is this Presidency that has grown by leaps and bounds in the nuclear age. It is this Presidency in which the largest decisions in foreign affairs repose and that invites one to coin the maxim that the larger the issue the more freedom the President has to act upon it. This is the Presidency that allowed Truman to order the use of the atomic bomb against Japan and to make his choice risking only the private criticism of a limited circle of counselors. This is the Presidency that can act on an instant's notice in defense of the nation, that can respond to the outbreak in Korea in 1950, that can launch an indirect invasion of Cuba in 1961, and that can send an ever-increasing force to Vietnam.

In no small degree the "independent" Presidency is the adjustment the office has made to the communist presence. Able to move swiftly and to act subtly, the communists have made short shrift of such traditional diplomatic acts as the declaration of war and its termination by peace treaties. The two major wars the United States has fought since 1945 have been "Presidential wars," or conflicts in which Congress has not exercised its constitutional power to declare war—partly because a declaration imposes rigidities that make the restoration of peace difficult; partly because a declaration takes time, and in a quickly deteriorating international situation time may be in short supply; partly because the United States had not granted diplomatic recognition to its opponents in either war—North Korea and North Vietnam.

The other Presidency in foreign affairs is marked by its dependence upon Congress and upon public opinion. Instead of operating with autonomy, its method and emphasis are cooperation and accommodation. It fits the democratic image of the powerful, responsible executive whose decisions are open to external view and debate. In a bygone day, this Presidency embraced the largest questions of foreign policy: McKinley and Congress reaching a consensus on whether to go to war with Spain; Wilson trying and failing to secure the Senate's approval for the nation's entry into the League of Nations. But in the nuclear age the activity of this Presidency falls to a secondary level of importance.

To a remarkable degree, each Presidency can, action for action, discover constitutional powers and institutional resources that are counterparts of the other's. The independent Presidency employs the executive agreement to commit the United States in its relations with others, freely uses special agents or personnel to carry forward the President's missions and purposes, and utilizes the Commander-in-Chief power to conduct the enterprise that might well be called Presidential warmaking. The "dependent," or cooperative, Presidency has legal powers and institutional resources that include the treaty power, which involves Senate participation, and the executive agreement when money or other Congressional support is required for its effectiveness; the appointment of ambassadors, ministers, and other officers of foreign affairs with the advice and consent of the Senate; and the concrete provision of the Constitution by which war is declared by Congress. To understand the nature of the two Presidencies in foreign affairs, we need to look more closely at their several kinds of resources.

Constitutional Limitations

The Constitution in Article II, section 2, provides that the President "shall have power, by and with the advice and consent of the Senate, to make treaties, provided two-thirds of the Senators present concur." Significantly, this language associates the President with the Senate throughout the course of treaty-making. President Washington, interpreting the Constitution literally, understandably felt obligated to secure the advice of the Senate on certain questions arising in the course of treaty negotiations with the Southern Indian tribes. But the Senate chose to respond churlishly, resolving to consider the questions privately, without the Chief Executive present. Washington, incensed by this treatment, withdrew, according to Senator William Maclay, "with sullen dignity."[5] This little set-to finished Washington, and for that matter all future Presidents, on consultations with the full Senate. Not, however, with individual Senators. Although the Executive negotiates treaties, he has deemed it wise on occasion to involve key Senators in the enterprise. Senators Tom Connally and Arthur Vandenberg were members of the United States delegation to San Francisco to construct the United Nations Charter. Negotiations of the 1963 test ban treaty were conducted in the presence of a panel of Senators. Some historians blame Wilson's League of Nations defeat on his failure to include Senators in the United States delegation to the Paris peace conference.

In practice, the Senate can approve or reject a treaty outright or impose conditions or reservations that may or may not be acceptable to the President. When the test ban treaty was in the Senate's hands, President Kennedy, at the urging of Senator Everett Dirksen, the Republican minority leader and a supporter of the treaty, sent a letter to the Senate carrying "unqualified and unequivocal assurances" that the treaty would not deter him from maintaining a vigorous weapons program. Kennedy gave other explicit assurances, including one that the treaty would never be amended by Executive action but only by treaty procedure.[6] The President's action headed off possible Senatorial reservations.

The constitutional requirement that two-thirds of the Senate give its advice and consent establishes for the President the unavoidable and sometimes difficult test of winning support from the opposition party. Wilson's failure to attract sufficient Republican backing wrecked United States membership in the League of Nations. Franklin Roosevelt, anxious to avoid the Wilsonian disaster in his quest for a United Nations organization, took elaborate precautions to win both Republican and Democratic cooperation. While the European war was yet proceeding, a Joint Advisory Committee on Postwar Foreign Policy was established, chaired by Secretary of State Cordell Hull and comprising various executive officials and leading legislators of both parties. The principles on which the future world organization might be constructed and the nature of the United States affiliation were thoroughly canvassed. Hull was often in touch privately with key Senators such as Connally, Walter George, and Vandenberg. Connally, Fulbright, and others sponsored resolutions approving United States participation in an international peace organization. Not merely Republican Senators, but the national Republican party organization voiced its support.[7] The Republican Mackinac Island declaration of 1943 endorsed the tenor of the legislative resolutions, as did the 1944 Republican and Democratic platforms and Presidential campaigns. Finally, Senators of both parties were members of the United States delegation to negotiate the United Nations Charter. Again, the 1963 test ban treaty could never have passed without Republican votes in the Senate and the skillful cooperation of Senator Dirksen. Johnson's success in 1967 in steering the consular treaty with the Soviet Union through the Senate depended upon Republican support, and the unanimity of both major parties brought the treaty of the same year barring weapons of mass destruction from outer space through the Senate without a dissenting vote.

The President may choose to disregard the treaty procedure and resort to "executive agreements." These entail no Senatorial review, and may stem from several types of independent Presidential authority—the executive power clause or his power as Commander-in-Chief—and from statute or treaty. These agreements are not mentioned specifically in the Constitution. The exchange of United States destroyers for British bases in World War II was founded upon the Commander-in-Chief power and executive power clauses and a statute permitting the transfer of "obsolescent" military materiel. Presidents have used executive agreements for nearly every conceivable diplomatic subject: fishing rights, boundary disputes, the annexation of territory, and so on. In *United States v. Curtiss-Wright Corp.* (299 U.S. 304, 1936) the Supreme Court seemed to contemplate an almost limitless variety of matters for executive agreements. Yet what the President can do in law he may be unable to do in politics. Most executive agreements depend for their effectiveness upon support from Congress. The legislators are not loath to exploit their leverage. When Congress in 1951 put up money for President Truman's emergency agricultural aid to Yugoslavia, several strings were attached. Aid, for example, was to be distributed "without discrimination as to race or political or religious belief." Legislators critical of Yugoslavia's penchant for collective farms required that nation to pledge itself "to take all appropriate economic measures to reduce its relief needs, to encourage increased production and distribution of food stuffs. . . ."[8] In a word, Congress was instructing the President's negotiators to require the Yugoslavs upon entering an executive agreement to partake of its benefits not by their accustomed dictatorial but by democratic means; not by communist economics but by free enterprise.

The President, the Constitution says, "shall nominate, and by and with the advice and consent of the Senate, shall appoint ambassadors, other public ministers and consuls. . . ." Ordinarily, the Senate raises no objections to the President's nominees for diplomatic posts, but trouble is by no means unknown, and President Eisenhower drew a full draught of it early in his term when he nominated Charles E. Bohlen as ambassador to the U.S.S.R. A leading expert on the Soviet Union, Bohlen numbered among his experiences service as Franklin Roosevelt's Russian language interpreter and adviser on Russian affairs at the Yalta conference. Bohlen's presence there made him a renegade in the eyes of many Republican Senators. His prospects did not improve when he testified to the Senate Foreign Relations Committee that he saw nothing wrong with the Yalta agreements. Senators Joseph McCarthy and Pat McCarran questioned Bohlen's loyalty, compelling Eisenhower to come out strongly for Bohlen in a press conference. Senator Robert A. Taft, the Republican leader, backed up the President and the Bohlen nomination finally prevailed. Mopping his brow, Taft got word to Eisenhower that he did not want to carry any more Bohlens through the Senate.[9]

The Constitution empowers the President to receive the diplomatic representatives of other nations. The power to receive or exchange ambassadors enables the President to recognize new governments without consulting Congress. Congress, however, can pass resolutions expressing its wishes and intent. The President indeed may welcome the step. After France fell in World War II, the Senate and House passed companion resolutions reaffirming a policy to which the United States had been committed at the earlier Havana Consultative Meeting of pan-American foreign ministers agreeing not to permit the transfer of sovereignty of any European possession in the Western Hemisphere to another non-American power. Congress's action signified the unity of the two political branches in policy. By implication, the President's power to receive diplomatic representatives also enables him to demand their recall. Washington began the latter practice when he could bear no more the extravagantly undiplomatic deportment of Citizen Genêt, representative of the new France of the Revolution.

Although the Constitution vests in Congress the power to declare war, the United States has declared war in only five of its eleven major conflicts with other countries. In each of the five instances, Congress declared war only in response to the President's acts or recommendations.[10] The five declared wars were the War of 1812, the Mexican War, the Spanish-American War, and the two world wars. A declaration of war was neither made by

Congress nor requested by the President in the naval war with France (1798–1800), the first Barbary War (1801–05), the second Barbary War (1815), the Mexican-American clashes (1914–17), and the Korean and Vietnam conflicts. Presidents, evidently, have tended to apply to the fullest limits the view of Alexander Hamilton that the Constitution intends "that it is the peculiar and exclusive province of Congress, when the nation is at peace, to change that state into a state of war;" but "when a foreign nation declares or openly and avowedly makes war upon the United States, they are then by the very fact already at war and any declaration on the part of Congress is nugatory; it is at least unnecessary."[11]

The President finds authority for involvement in violence or potential violence as Commander-in-Chief, as custodian of the executive power, and on certain occasions since World War II under Article XLIII of the United Nations Charter. Congress does not ordinarily begrudge the President the use of his initiative. If anything, one or both of the legislative houses may fret because the President seems to be moving too slowly. Within a space of two weeks in 1962, for instance, the House of Representatives adopted resolutions expressing determination to use all means, including force, to defend United States rights in Berlin, about which a crisis was stirring, although the wall went up some months before, and a similar resolution was adopted for the Cuban missile crisis.

But Presidential military initiatives can be hazardous politically. Dwight Eisenhower, who well appreciated this fact of Presidential life, in order not to use his rightful power to the full, evolved an ingenious tactic to couple Congress with his Chinese policy. In 1955, in the face of Red China's menacing activity in the area of Formosa, Eisenhower dispatched a draft resolution to Congress authorizing the use of armed forces to protect Formosa and the Pescadores Islands against invasion.[12] As enacted by Congress, the resolution "authorized" the President "to employ the Armed Forces of the United States as he deems necessary for the specific purpose of securing and protecting Formosa and the Pescadores against armed attack." In his request, Eisenhower was careful to say that "the authority for some of the actions which might be required would be inherent in the authority of the Commander-in-Chief."[13] His purpose, of course, was to stifle any inference that he was yielding to Congress his constitutional power to employ force upon his own responsibility. In seeking the resolution, Eisenhower had two discernible motivations. He believed that by associating Congress with his effort, his declaration of his readiness to fight for Formosa would have greater impact on Peiping. Equally, Eisenhower did not want to repeat what he considered Truman's mistake in sending air and naval forces into Korea in 1950, and later the army, without consulting Congress. When, eventually, the Korean conflict became politically unpopular, President Truman took the brunt. Eisenhower invited Congress to share any similar liability in a drawn-out Formosan struggle. The technique of the Formosa resolution, known as the Eisenhower Doctrine, was renewed in the 1956 Middle Eastern crisis. With communist maneuvers stirring, Eisenhower again brought Congress to authorize the President to resist "overt armed aggression" by "any nation controlled by international Communism" in the "general area" of the Middle East.[14]

A similar resolution, which subsequently became the subject of bitter controversy in hearings of the Senate Foreign Relations Committee in 1967 and 1968, was adopted in 1964 following an attack on two United States destroyers by North Vietnamese PT boats in the Gulf of Tonkin. The resolution, which passed in 1964 with only two dissenting votes, was couched in sweeping language. It authorized the President to take "all necessary measures" to "repel any armed attack" against United States forces and "to prevent further aggression." As the Vietnam war escalated not a few of its critics, including members of the Senate Foreign Relations Committee, contended that the President had exceeded the intent of the resolution. In 1967 hearings, committee members charged that the President had used the resolution to dispatch ground forces to Vietnam and to order bombing attacks upon North Vietnam, including territory close to the border of Communist China, actions that were uncontemplated when the resolution was passed. Defenders of the President contended—and altogether correctly—that he did not depend upon the resolution for legal authority as he already enjoyed that authority under the Constitution. Just as Jefferson sent naval frigates to fight the Barbary pirates, as McKinley dispatched troops to China to subdue the Boxer Rebellion, as Kennedy flung a naval blockade around Cuba, and as Johnson sent marines to the Dominican Republic, Johnson as Commander-in-Chief could wage war in Vietnam.

What courses of action lay open to those legislators who were disenchanted with the independent Presidency, or, in effect, with the Vietnam war? They could have, as President Johnson himself suggested, repealed the Tonkin resolution. But it is unlikely that a majority of Congress would be willing to pay the price involved—of facing a great war with the two political branches of the government divided. The houses of Congress could pass further resolutions indicative of their latest intent, as the Senate did on March 1, 1967, pledging support for the efforts of the President and "other men of good will" to prevent the expansion of the Vietnam war and to reach "a negotiated peace."[15] But a difficulty with this tactic is its inherent ambiguity; some legislators thought the resolution simply affirmed what the President was already doing; others that it deemphasized the war and therefore comforted the enemy. Although frustrated in attacking Vietnam policy, the President's opponents could make their force felt by other means. When the Johnson administration in July 1967 dispatched three transport aircraft to the Congo to help quell a threatened outbreak, a Congressional protest, apparently in fear that the move might roll on into a larger commitment, brought the administration to withdraw the aircraft. Drastic cuts in the administration's foreign aid program for fiscal 1968 and delaying approval of the President's request for a 10 per cent tax surcharge to help finance the war were other opportunities for assertion available to legislators opposed to the Vietnam policy.

Beyond Congress, the President is vulnerable to public opinion. There is little doubt that President Johnson felt sustained in the belief that a majority of the people supported his course in Vietnam, and he kept close watch on the state of public opinion as it is reflected in the widely published polls and in private surveys that the White House initiated.[16] In 1968 the Presidential election loomed as an inevitable testing of the Vietnam policy.

Cooperation with Congress

When the President needs money or new authority—and for an abundance of his policies he needs one or the other—he must forsake the independent Presidency and enter into the cooperative phase of his office.

President Johnson, aiming in 1967 to launch a major foreign policy initiative by promoting "peaceful engagement" with the communist bloc, had no choice but to travel to Capitol Hill to seek approval of five pieces of legislation: a treaty with the Soviet Union barring nuclear weapons in outer space; a consular convention, also with the Soviet Union; an East-West trade bill, authorizing the President to extend "most favored nation" tariff treatment to the Soviets and communist countries in eastern Europe; removal of restrictions to the Food-for-Freedom program; and a ban of food shipments to any nation trading with North Vietnam or Cuba. Congress of course can, if it chooses, amend or thwart the President's proposals. Kennedy in 1962, for example, proposed that Congress adopt legislation permitting the President to grant to Yugoslavia and Poland the most favored nation treatment given noncommunist trade partners. Congress rejected the request, urgently recommended by the United States ambassador to Yugoslavia, George F. Kennan, who remonstrated that "without the support of Congress it was impossible to carry out an effective policy there."[17]

By his own acts the President may stiffen the opposition to what he wants to do. Johnson, to the extent that he created an indispensable public and Congressional support for his prosecution of the Vietnam war, had also created a body of opinion unfriendly to his policy of "building bridges" to the communist world. His staunchest Congressional supporters for the war became the most resolute opponents of his bridge-building. Since legislation in foreign affairs is less apt to enjoy the group interest support prevalent in domestic legislation, the President's foreign projects were more susceptible to the several species of mishap lurking in legislative processes. Parliamentary delays, crippling amendments, and headline-capturing investigations can erupt from many places.

To avoid potentially hostile opinion in Congress, John Kennedy held something of a record for the lengths he went to in order to create a bipartisan administration in foreign affairs. He handed over much, if not most, of foreign affairs administration to Republican appointees, presumably to stifle Congressional criticism. One of his first acts was to announce the retention of a Republican, Allen Dulles, as director of the Central Intelligence Agency. When Dulles resigned after the Cuban invasion debacle, he was replaced by another Republican, John A. McCone, who in the Eisenhower administration had been chairman of the Atomic Energy Commission. Two members of Kennedy's cabinet were Republican, and both were in major posts: Douglas Dillon, Secretary of the Treasury, and Robert McNamara, Secretary of Defense. McGeorge Bundy, another Republican, was special assistant for national security affairs. A Republican, John J. McCloy, was the President's first disarmament chief, and McCloy's successor was another Republican, William C. Foster.[18] These Republicans—and there were others—were responsible for certain of the most important foreign policy areas: defense, intelligence, finance, and disarmament. Each area, at one time or another in the decade before Kennedy's advent, had been a source of political controversy, a focal point of legislative investigation and discussion. They represented some of the most fruitful areas of Kennedy's own attack on the Republican record in the electoral campaign of 1960. Yet, upon coming into office, Kennedy proceeded to appoint Republicans to administer these very areas. In return, legislative discussion regarding them was less hostile than it often is.

The Foreign Aid Program

Power is widely scattered among autonomous legislative committees run by chairmen with little, if any, political attachment to the President, and they can act with minimum detection and maximum effect. The foreign aid program of military and economic assistance, a keystone of United States foreign policy involving billions of dollars of annual expenditure, demonstrates the lengths and hazards of Congressional policy-making. The program runs the gauntlet of six committees: the foreign affairs, armed services, and appropriations committees of each house. It presents an annual suspense drama, in which the President's proposals are subject to drastic cuts, partial restorations, and great delays, and the eventual result is usually well below his original request.

Foreign aid's worst troubles have been suffered at the hands of hostile Congressmen such as Otto E. Passman, Democrat of Louisiana, chairman of the Subcommittee on Foreign Aid Operations of the House Appropriations Committee. Passman, who delights in referring to himself as a "country boy," though he is modestly wealthy and indulges a fondness for snow-white

silk suits, applies his "countryman's axe" to the President's foreign aid requests. Although there is some redress elsewhere in the legislative review,
the net damage is severe. In 1963 one of Passman's more effective years, a
Presidential request for a $4.9 billion foreign aid appropriation was chopped
to $3.9 billion. President Johnson, however, having just succeeded President
Kennedy, repulsed Passman's attack.

To counter his legislative hazards, the President resorts to two major
strategies. He resists chiefly by mobilizing bipartisan support for the aid program. He goes along by deferring to Congress, indulging in expedients that
silence or win over the legislative critics. In his bipartisan campaign for his
1961 foreign aid request, President Kennedy was backed by the nation's two
leading Republicans, Eisenhower and Nixon. When Passman, in a single
flourish of his axe, severed 21 per cent of the administration's request,
Eisenhower from his Gettysburg farm cried out that "these slashes are in-
comprehensible to me, especially in light of present world tensions." Later,
both Eisenhower and Nixon issued statements in behalf of foreign aid, and
an amendment by Congressman Gerald R. Ford, Jr., Republican of Michigan, restored half of Passman's cut. More restorations were made by a Democratic-Republican coalition in the Senate Appropriations Committee. These
were accomplished with help from further prestigious sources. Governor Nelson Rockefeller sent telegrams to each Republican of the House. A citizens'
committee, composed largely of leading international-minded businessmen,
contacted legislators and poured out publicity. The legislative representatives
of the White House, the State Department, and the AFL-CIO descended
on Capitol Hill. President Ayub Khan of Pakistan, who was in town, was
hustled over to a joint sitting of Congress for "a pep talk," as Passman
called it, on the urgency of foreign aid.[19]

In his acts of deference toward Congress, in the hope of winning votes
and silencing critics, the President may subject his aid program to the hard
scrutiny of people whose word presumably carries weight with Congress.
Eisenhower, soon after coming to office, dispatched teams of businessmen to
observe foreign aid operations abroad and make recommendations.

The President is also given to a drastic reshuffling of foreign aid administration, a hopeful by-product of which is a resurgence of Congressional
confidence and support. He may, as Kennedy attempted, turn to the business
community for his foreign aid administrator. Upon the establishment of his
new Agency for International Development, Kennedy moved to bring to its
head George D. Woods, chairman of the First Boston Corporation, a leading
financial enterprise. But the connection between First Boston and the Dixon-
Yates contract episode of the Eisenhower administration throttled the appointment. Kennedy next reached into another hopper of respectability by nominating Fowler Hamilton of a large, distinguished Manhattan law firm.

Choosing foreign aid administrators is a busy task for any contemporary
President. Since Paul G. Hoffman took over direction of the Marshall Plan

in 1948, ten different administrators with an average tenure of eighteen months have guided the aid program. Eisenhower had four aid administrators, Kennedy three. Each new administrator is accompanied by a busy reshuffling of functions, promises of saner working principles, and even a change in the agency's name. While these deeds are committed to build Congressional confidence, they also have certain costs: a slowdown of effectiveness as the program adjusts to the new structure, an erosion of employee morale, and an impairment of public, if not Congressional, confidence in the validity of foreign aid.

The Secretary of State

Given the high moment of foreign policy to their administrations' success, many Presidents have become, as the cliché goes, "their own Secretaries of State." The Roosevelts, Woodrow Wilson, and John Kennedy are rightly remembered as such. A President—Secretary of State closely involves himself in major problems, sets high policy, intrudes upon routine, and engages heavily in diplomatic negotiation. He is both general commander and front-line soldier. But an activist President by no means requires a passive Secretary of State. The dynamic Theodore Roosevelt successively retained two eminent Secretaries, John Hay and Elihu Root, whose distinction increased with their tenure.

At another extreme are the Presidents who delegate freely to their Secretaries of State, as Harding did to Charles E. Hughes and Eisenhower to John Foster Dulles. Dulles enjoyed an unparalleled authority as policy formulator, negotiator, and chief spokesman in foreign affairs. Indeed Dulles' sweeping power brought Senator Fulbright to protest that "Secretary Dulles seemed at times to be exercising those 'delicate, plenary, and exclusive powers' which are supposed to be vested in the President."[20] A hazard whenever the Secretary of State assumes a large role is that he will pursue policies reflecting his own well-considered convictions rather than the President's. The Dulles-Eisenhower enterprise, however, was conducted within certain ground rules. Dulles abided by Eisenhower's rejection of a "Go It Alone" philosophy pressed by isolationist Republicans. Eisenhower himself contended that Dulles never made a major decision without Presidential knowledge and approval. In the judgment of Sherman Adams, "Far from relieving Eisenhower of the burden of foreign problems, this unique partnership required him to spend more time in consultation with Dulles than he did with other department heads."[21] Dulles, according to Adams, had from six to ten hours a week of private conversation with Eisenhower. The Secretary reported faithfully as situations and policies were developing and relied heavily upon the President's estimates of consequences. They worked by little notes, telephone calls, and late evening conversations, sometimes held in the White House Trophy Room. Eisenhower was well impressed with the Secretary's knowledge and skill in world affairs, hailing him as the best Secretary of State since Thomas Jefferson.

Eisenhower, as Adams has written, "delegated to Dulles the responsibility of developing specific policy, including the decision as to where the administration would stand and what course of action it would follow in each international crisis."[22] Dulles ranged far and wide over the foreign affairs spectrum. He was a familiar on-the-scenes figure at the world's trouble spots. When trouble boiled at the Suez in 1953, Dulles journeyed there, spent five hours in anxious conference with the Egyptian leader, General Mohammed Naguib, and visited eleven other Middle Eastern countries concerned with the gathering crisis. When Suez affairs reached the United Nations, it was not the resident United States ambassador but Secretary Dulles who presented the nation's case. Or again, when the European Defense Community faltered in attracting national support in 1953, Dulles executed a trouble-shooting itinerary through seven capitals: Rome, Paris, London, Bonn, The Hague, Brussels, and Luxembourg. In all, Dulles traveled farther, visited more countries, and personally got to know more statesmen than any other diplomat before his time. His Secretarial career is a monument of dedication to his country and his President.[23]

Those Presidents who have suffered most from their Secretaries of State suffered almost invariably if the latter were major political figures. A Chief Executive who imports eminent politicians to find favor in Congress or in party quarters sometimes does so to his grief. The least promising appointee is one who believes the higher office should have been his. Lincoln's Secretary of State, William H. Seward, had expected to win the 1860 Republican nomination and regarded the victorious Lincoln as an upstart. Ability was now serving mediocrity. Seward in his rationalizations began thinking of the President as monarch and the Secretary of State as Prime Minister, and the train of these quaint ideas led to a memorandum entitled "Thoughts for the President's Consideration," probably the most extraordinary document ever presented to a Chief Executive by a subordinate. "We are at the end of a month's administration," it read, "and yet without a policy, domestic or foreign." Further delay will "bring scandal on the administration and danger upon the country." Seward generously offered to take on the great task of policy-building himself. Lincoln's reply, fortunately, was an unsparing squelch. "If this must be done," he said, "I must do it."[24]

Later Presidents who have brought in erstwhile political rivals as Secretaries of State have fared no better. Wilson chose for his Secretary the perennial Democratic Presidential nominee, William Jennings Bryan. His stubborn pacifism and neutrality eventually collided with Wilson's drift toward involvement and its risk of war, and the nation was rocked by the Secretary's resignation.[25] Harry S. Truman appointed as his Secretary of State

James F. Byrnes, his rival for the 1944 Vice-Presidential nomination, the route to the Presidency upon Roosevelt's death. Truman indeed had nominated Byrnes for the Vice-Presidency. After the convention chose, Truman wrote that "Byrnes, undoubtedly, was deeply disappointed and hurt. I thought that my calling on him at this time might help balance things up."[26] Again the relationship did not work.

The President's Staff

Power for the President reflects, among other things, the quality and usefulness of his staff. Upon them he depends for the funneling of information and problems to himself and the communication and interpretation of his directives to those sectors of the huge, sprawling executive branch that administer the diplomatic, economic, military, scientific, intelligence, and psychological phases of foreign policy. Whether the executive agencies are alert and effective, whether they can perceive his own interests and necessities, instead of representing merely their own preferences, may have much to do with how well or ill the President fares in foreign policy.

When a President chooses to assert himself in foreign affairs, as when Eisenhower on occasion chose to circumvent Dulles, he turns to the White House staff. Time and again, Eisenhower used his staff to generate creative spark and produce bold ideas for hard problems. The important Atoms-for-Peace proposal was handed over to a White House special assistant, C. D. Jackson, an executive on leave from Time-Life. Jackson prepared it and single-handedly pushed it through the Atomic Energy Commission, State and Defense Departments and elsewhere, against objections, evasions, and indifference. The Open Skies proposal was the province of another White House assistant, Nelson Rockefeller, and a special group, and disarmament was the bailiwick of still another assistant, Harold Stassen. Of both enterprises, Secretary Dulles was suspicious and skeptical.

A regularly potent force, too, in foreign affairs is the President's speech-writers. Dean Acheson, while Secretary of State, felt behooved to join White House speech-writing groups as often as he could, however odd such activity seemed for an already overburdened Secretary of State. "But this is often where policy is made," Acheson wrote, "regardless of where it is supposed to be made."[27]

John Kennedy regularly used the White House staff to maximize his own involvement in foreign affairs. He relied heavily upon his national security assistant, McGeorge Bundy, and a small band of aides to monitor foreign policy and national security problems and the progress of decisions throughout the executive branch. Kennedy turned over great chunks of Latin-American policy to members of his White House staff—Adolf A. Berle, Jr., a special Presidential coordinator of Latin-American affairs; Arthur M. Schlesinger, Jr., a special assistant to the President; and Richard Goodwin, assistant special counsel to the President.

President Johnson continued to employ McGeorge Bundy as national security assistant at a level of influence equal to that under President Kennedy. In the Washington community, Bundy in both Presidential administrations was widely regarded as the virtual equal of Secretary of State Dean Rusk and Secretary of Defense Robert McNamara. However, unlike the Secretaries, who were subject to the constant scrutiny of legislative committees, Bundy conducted his duties in well-protected privacy. His status as Presidential assistant made him privileged against Congressional inquiry, while allowing him to function as a leading adviser on policy. His views are believed to have been effective in the development of American involvement in Vietnam, in the diplomacy following American intervention in the Dominican Republic, in several confrontations with the Soviet Union, and in efforts to reduce conflicts within the Atlantic Alliance.

As the Johnson administration wore on, the Bundy post, like other White House staff positions, became captive to Johnson's preference for checks and balances within the White House staff. Prone to keep his staff aides cut down to size, the President did not exempt the Bundy function. Relying as he usually did on the self-regulating effect produced by giving two or more aides overlapping assignments, Johnson in 1965 brought in Joseph A. Califano, Jr., as a special assistant with free-ranging duties. Califano came from service as a top assistant to Secretary McNamara, and the Defense Department was not long in shortcircuiting the Bundy operation and dealing with its former colleague. After Bundy's departure for a private career, his title and most of his functions passed to his former deputy, Walt W. Rostow. A leading influence in foreign policy-making, Rostow nevertheless was a step removed from the pinnacle of influence enjoyed by Bundy.

In general, Johnson, unlike Eisenhower and Kennedy, was not prone to include on his White House roster many assistants with major influence in foreign affairs. A notable though brief exception was Robert W. Komer, who served as special assistant to the President for peaceful reconstruction in Vietnam. In 1967, Komer was transferred to Saigon on the theory that he might make better progress there with his assignment.[28]

Other institutions that the President may turn to include the Central Intelligence Agency, the cabinet, the National Security Council, and the Joint Chiefs of Staff. The cabinet originated in the diplomatic crisis of 1793, when it charted United States neutrality in the Franco–British war. The cabinet's role has been erratic. It reached the height of its influence in fashioning the Monroe Doctrine; in the two world wars its activity was slight. The fortunes of the National Security Council, which has largely displaced the cabinet in foreign affairs, have also wavered. Truman and Eisenhower resorted regularly to the NSC, but Kennedy used it infrequently, preferring instead meetings with administrators individually and in small groups. Modern Presidents throw together *ad hoc* groups to provide counsel in diplomatic crises. To weigh the American response when Israel invaded Egypt in 1956, Eisenhower summoned to the White House Secretary of State Dulles, Admiral Arthur Radford, chairman of the Joint Chiefs of Staff, Secretary of Defense Wilson, CIA Director Allen Dulles, and Sherman Adams.[29] Eleven years later, when Israel scored its lightning military success against Arab arms, President Johnson sought to prepare policies for the "new peace." For this purpose he drew together a group that would function as a subcommittee of the National Security Council. He brought back McGeorge Bundy, on leave from the presidency of the Ford Foundation, to serve as executive secretary, and appointed a committee consisting of Secretary of State Rusk as chairman; Secretary of the Treasury Henry Fowler; General Earle G. Wheeler, chairman of the Joint Chiefs of Staff; Richard Helms, director of the Central Intelligence Agency; Clark Clifford, then a part-time chairman of the Foreign Intelligence Advisory Board and subsequently Johnson's Secretary of Defense; and Walt W. Rostow.

For counsel and action the President turns also to the Department of State, home of a vast assemblage of specialists, and to the United States Foreign Service, a distinguished career organization. Many activist Presidents have become disenchanted with the State Department and the Foreign Service, however. Woodrow Wilson and Franklin Roosevelt, for example, held them in low esteem. Forewarned by Adlai Stevenson that he would find the State Department a "tremendous institutional inertial force," John Kennedy soon spoke of the department as "a bowl of jelly" and complained bitterly, "They never have any ideas over there: never come up with anything new."[30] Kennedy's feelings about the department did not, of course, extend to his Secretary of State, Dean Rusk. Lyndon Johnson, in contrast, displayed no similar distrust of the department. His feelings for the department were buoyed by his affection for Secretary Rusk. Time and again Johnson expressed preference for dealing with his cabinet Secretaries directly, viewing them as the primary experts in their assigned fields. Johnson did not fail to show his warm approval of Secretary Rusk publicly, hailing him as "the best foreign minister in the world," and in 1966 issued a far-reaching order designating Rusk, supported by his department, as "director of foreign policy" with jurisdiction over any civilian agency involved in foreign affairs, and in effect constituting the department as the chief forum of foreign policy debate.[31]

Presidents enjoy almost limitless freedom to employ special agents on high missions abroad if for any reason they prefer not to use the regular ambassadors. Unlike ambassadors and ministers, special agents are appointed solely by the President, without referral to the Senate; they are not mentioned specifically in the Constitution, although their employ is implied by the treaty power and the all-purpose "executive power" clause. George Washington dispatched John Jay to England to negotiate the treaty bearing his name, Thomas Jefferson sent James Monroe to the court of Napoleon to help Robert Livingston arrange the Louisiana Purchase, and Lyndon Johnson had Attorney General Robert F. Kennedy go to Sukarno to induce the Indonesian President not to fulfill his threat to crush the new country of Malaysia.

Special agents command the President's confidence and trust, which is not always the case with ambassadors. Special agents know better than anyone else the latest intentions and objectives of their Chief Executives. They radiate prestige because they come directly from the White House, and at their approach the gates of foreign ministries open wide. But special agents are at best a mixed blessing. They undercut the resident ambassador, whether intentionally or not, and often they lack relevant diplomatic training or experience.

They are most often employed by strong Presidents and achieve their fullest potential in time of war. In World War I Colonel Edward M. House and in World War II Harry Hopkins, as special agents, conducted major negotiations of United States foreign policy. Indeed, so momentous were their activities that the United States, in those intervals, had in reality two foreign offices: the State Department, which concentrated on voluminous lesser policy, and the special agents, who concentrated on making and implementing top-level policy.

Hopkins, a former social worker and New Deal administrator, was Franklin Roosevelt's chief liaison with foreign affairs and the war overseas. "His was a soul that flamed out of a frail and fading body," Winston Churchill said of Hopkins, who was often ill. "He was a crumbling lighthouse from which there shone the beams that led great fleets to harbor." Hopkins negotiated with Churchill and Joseph Stalin their needs in armaments and munitions that the United States might supply. He sat in on White House sessions of the Joint Chiefs of Staff and on meetings in London and Washington of the Anglo-American Combined Chiefs of Staff. He was in the thick of sessions, thrashing out the decisions and details of the North African and Normandy invasions and the alternative Mediterranean campaigns.

As chairman of the Munitions Assignment Board, he allocated materiel to American forces, to the Allies, and to all the theaters of war. His protégés occupied the principal production and diplomatic posts. Donald Nelson as chairman of the War Production Board and Edward Stettinius, Jr., first a lend lease administrator and subsequently Secretary of State, owed their appointments chiefly to Hopkins. Stettinius got word of his lend lease position not from the President but from Hopkins. "Does the President want to talk it over with me first?" Stettinius asked, incredulous that Roosevelt should not personally confer the seals of an office so vital to the war. Hopkins assured him that this was not necessary. Several days later Stettinius received a letter from the President. "Harry Hopkins," it blandly read, "is, of course, familiar with the administration of Lend Lease, and I hope you will consult with him and with me where matters of major policy arise." Stettinius maintained the same consultations with Hopkins in his tenure as Secretary of State.[32]

Foreign Leaders

For the President, power in foreign affairs lies in the ability to persuade foreign leaders, whether friend or foe or neutral, to back or accept his policies. Our leadership of the western alliance, our infinite cornucopia of foreign aid, and our military might have made rapport with the American President an important concern of other national executives. His chief policy objectives—keeping nations out of the communist orbit and controlling situations in order to avoid a nuclear confrontation with the Soviet Union—have led him to pursue these contacts diligently with meetings and correspondence.

The Johnson era witnessed a steady trek by heads of other governments to the White House. To the President these occasions are valuable not so much for the specific agreements they produce, which are few, but for several intangibles. The meetings may clear away suspicions, cement personal relations, and lead to broad understandings of positions.

The abundance of personal letters that Kennedy dispatched to a wide circle of foreign leaders were no mere puffs of good will but dealt with major problems. At the height of the 1962 Cuban crisis, the Kennedy-Khrushchev exchanges opened up an understanding that averted general war. An essential feature of the arrangement was the secrecy both countries threw about the exchange. Personal communication permitted greater privacy and was less susceptible to leaks than regular channels, and, unlike formal diplomatic notes, custom does not require its publication. The Soviet news media did not mention the exchange at all. The White House kept secret the number of letters involved, the content of most of them, and the channels used. Top-level communication was also nicely attuned to Khrushchev's preference for personal diplomacy and to that of his Foreign Minister, Andrei Gromyko, who functioned as a technician rather than a policy-maker. Nevertheless, the Kennedy-Khrushchev notes were not a substitute for normal diplomatic endeavor but a supplement, resorted to when the diplomats were unable to agree or when the problem exceeded the bounds of the forum in which they were negotiating.

To help in keeping up contacts in his global constituency, the President may send forth his own special emissaries. Soon after taking office, Kennedy snatched Dean Acheson from private life and sent him off to see Chancellor Konrad Adenauer to review the future of NATO. West Germans had become increasingly uneasy over the thought that the new administration would withdraw Eisenhower's offer to equip NATO forces with atomic missiles. Vice President Johnson was a busy emissary for President Kennedy, dispensing assurances on all the continents. In effect, he had to convince his foreign hosts that United States foreign policy did not mean altogether what it seemed. To Iran, Greece, and Turkey, all economically troubled allies on the Soviet-bloc periphery, he stressed in 1962 that the United States would continue its full-scale support despite its shift to a self-help policy for foreign aid recipients. When the Berlin wall was thrown up, he journeyed to the scene for the not very easy task of giving assurances that despite the absence of major action, the United States was staunch behind that beleaguered city.

A President's relationship with world leaders may be harassed by the vagaries of American domestic politics. Nehru was moved to withdraw his request for United States assistance to help India build a state-owned steel plant at Bokaro after the House of Representatives, objecting to the project because it would use large United States loans to spread socialism in India, prohibited the administration from proceeding with the venture. Nehru's offer to withdraw his request for American aid was accepted by Kennedy, however reluctantly, and administration officials gave a collective sigh of relief to be rid of a grave political embarrassment.[33]

The domestic politics of foreign countries too may be a jarring influence. At times the President has to shore up other chief executives whose perpetuation in office suits his purposes. When the 1953 West German elections left Adenauer's Christian Democratic Union party badly weakened in the Bundestag and dependent upon votes of several smaller parties, cries went up for the Chancellor to step down as Foreign Minister, the first presumably in a series of steps to curb his large powers. Faced with this serious political crisis, Adenauer badly needed a success in foreign affairs to bolster his imperiled fortunes. President Eisenhower, who viewed the Chancellor with great favor, moved to provide it by personally superintending the admission of Germany into the NATO alliance. Adenauer's long campaign for a rearmed German Federal Republic was now realized, and his political stock for a time resurged. Then his political strength again declined, placing the American President, particularly Kennedy, in a full predicament. The official leadership of West Germany was on the way out, and the identity of the future leadership was not yet clear. Kennedy played both sides of the street. He fortified Adenauer and widened his contacts with the rising German leaders. His visitors included Erich Mende, leader of the Free Democratic party of West Germany, which from 1962 onward controlled the balance of power in the Bundestag; Gerhard Schröder, also of that party, Foreign Minister and possible successor to Adenauer; Willy Brandt, then mayor of West Berlin and leader of the Socialist opposition, another possible successor; and Ludwig Erhard, who eventually prevailed. Each, as well as Adenauer, trekked to Washington in an effort to create in the West German public mind his image as the best guarantor of good relations with the White House.[34]

Fortunately, the President's foreign visitors can redound to his political profit too. In his early Presidential weeks, Johnson displayed Erhard to the

German-American voters of Texas and entertained then President Antonio Segni of Italy with an imposing Italian-American night at the White House. Later, Pope Paul, when in New York to address the United Nations, met with Johnson, an occurrence that was not lacking in political profit for the President.

In pursuing a major foreign policy, the President may face an array of nations, each with its purposes and needs, and its leaders with their domestic political necessities and career ambitions, all of which he must venture to put together as a kind of grand jigsaw puzzle of nations and men, whose many pieces must somehow fall into place if he is to succeed. Consider, for example, the full scene that confronted President Johnson in Spring 1967 in the Middle East: the mounting crisis, the eruption into a flashing war, Israel's extraordinary victory, and the aftermath when a new peace had to be constructed.

Johnson's own overriding purpose was to avoid a swelling of the crisis to the point of a U.S.-U.S.S.R. confrontation. To resolve the crisis, he sought to enlist other maritime nations, some of them America's staunchest allies, in a test of the Egyptian blockade of the Gulf of Aqaba, but these nations proved reluctant to risk a clash with the Arab nations. He then endeavored to induce Premier Levi Eshkol of Israel to put off military action. But as time melted away, and Johnson through diplomacy could not loosen the Egyptian grip, the domestic pressures upon Eshkol to resort to military action mounted severely. Eventually these pressures prevailed.

To contain the perilous unsettlement in the Middle East, Johnson met at Glassboro, New Jersey, later in June, with Soviet Premier Kosygin, during the latter's visit to the United Nations. In seeking accommodation with Kosygin, Johnson could take heart from the advice of his Soviet specialists that the Premier was the leader of the Moscow "doves" and his path to power was as a leader of Soviet consumer goods production, which reinforced his image as a man of reason and peace. But when Kosygin conferred at Glassboro, he was obviously a prisoner of the Moscow line, uttering only rigid stereotyped demands. The Premier had also to protect his own and his country's image in the communist world. Amid his talks with Johnson he was reminded of this necessity by Premier Chou En-lai from far-off Peking, who declared unmincingly that Johnson and Kosygin "are engaging in a dirty bargain."

Eventually, Johnson prevailed in his original purpose, but not via the route he intended. He did avoid the confrontation with the Soviets, but the allied nations did not come to his aid as he had requested, and Israel had already ignored his counsel not to fight. His loneliness and embarrassment were short lived, thanks to the triumph of Israeli arms. "Many of us," observed Premier Eshkol afterward, "thought we would perform a good deed for him [Johnson] if we acted."

Presidents must be struck at times with the resemblances between their dealings with foreign chief executives and their encounters with Congressional committee chairmen. Both foreign executives and committee chairmen respond to local interests and constituencies, face the test of periodic election, and enjoy resources to act, if they choose, with independence, indeed defiance. They test hard the President's means of persuasion and often prove them wanting.

Syngman Rhee, President of South Korea, ardent patriot and anticommunist dedicated to the cause of reunifying his country, opposed President Eisenhower and Secretary Dulles, who sought to conclude a truce with the communists to end the Korean War. Rhee refused to negotiate because he deemed it tantamount to betraying his country. As Rhee's aloofness persisted, resentment ran so high in American councils that Eisenhower had to remind Republican legislative leaders at one juncture that the enemy in Korea was still the communists and not Rhee. The Korean President meanwhile was professing his intention to continue the fight even without American or United Nations help. The United States, Rhee was told repeatedly, could not risk world war for a reunified Korea. "I can't remember," Eisenhower said of his unavailing encounters, "when there was ever a forty-eight hours when I felt more in need of help from someone more intelligent than I am."[35]

Midway in the truce negotiations, Rhee precipitated a grave crisis by releasing thousands of anticommunist North Korean prisoners in his charge well before he was authorized to do so. Fearful of further excesses, Eisenhower wrote a personal letter to Rhee but to no avail. In cabinet one day Eisenhower cried out in his perplexity, "If anybody has any ideas, for God's sake, don't hold them back."[36] Rhee was finally corralled when Eisenhower dispatched Walter S. Robertson, Assistant Secretary of State for Far Eastern Affairs, to talk with him. The quiet, soft-spoken Robertson brought Rhee around by sitting in a room with him for several days and listening patiently to his complaints and then leading him shrewdly to accept the United States position.

If American Presidents from Franklin Roosevelt onward were asked to name the most difficult allied chief executive to work with, there is little doubt that Charles de Gaulle would be at or near the top of every list. Harry S. Truman was not long in office when the French at De Gaulle's decision, taken unilaterally, occupied parts of the Aosta Valley in northwest Italy. Despite all entreaties, De Gaulle would not withdraw until Truman threatened to stop United States supplies. Truman soon was finding that "my own feelings about General De Gaulle were less and less friendly," and he breathed a loud amen to the judgment Winston Churchill cabled, calling De Gaulle "one of the greatest dangers to European peace."[37] Kennedy crossed swords with De Gaulle on major issues, including the general's thesis that in crisis the United States might not risk nuclear war to save Europe.

John Kennedy's most dedicated antagonist, however, was not in France but in Canada, whose friendly relations with the United States are a matter of mutual pride. In his 1961 visit to Ottawa, Kennedy, apparently through inadvertence, left behind a "working paper" intended for Presidential eyes only for guidance in discussions with Canadian Prime Minister John Diefenbaker.

The working paper suggested that Canada be pushed to join the Organization of American States and step up her aid to embattled India. The paper came into the hands of Diefenbaker, who held onto it, personally and politically incensed. Another unsettling episode occurred at a 1962 White House dinner for Nobel Peace Prize winners that included Lester B. Pearson, Diefenbaker's rival and eventual successor as Prime Minister. Before dinner, Kennedy had a private chat with Pearson, which the latter referred to as "casual and innocuous."[38] Coincidentally, Diefenbaker was opening his 1962 electoral campaign and, upon learning of the Kennedy-Pearson conversation, was enraged at the President's act of singling out his opponent and, in effect, intervening in the Canadian election. Diefenbaker threatened to expose the 1961 working paper, adding that it contained an insulting reference to himself in the President's handwriting. The threat fortunately did not materialize; Diefenbaker built his campaign on a strong anti-American theme, but the strategy failed and Pearson was elected. Kennedy, in a sense, had won the elections, and Canadian-American relations were quickly restored to a smooth-running track.

Summit Conferences

The President as chief diplomat often engages in diplomatic ventures himself, notably the summit conference. From Franklin D. Roosevelt onward, the summit, a rare experience prior to World War II, has become standard Presidential fare: Roosevelt at Yalta, Truman at Potsdam, Eisenhower at Paris, Kennedy at Vienna, and Johnson at Glassboro.

Presidents have, in general, displayed no great enthusiasm for summitry. Roosevelt journeyed to Yalta reluctantly to meet with Churchill and Stalin. Reports that the area was unhealthy and unsanitary troubled the President, and its far removal from Washington, exceeding the capabilities of direct mail communication, threatened harm to public business. Truman did not go to Potsdam gladly, holding that the State, War, and Navy Departments should negotiate with their foreign counterparts instead. Kennedy early in his administration pointedly expressed appreciation for the quiet, normal diplomatic channels. President Johnson, soon after taking office, uttered the friendliest Presidential statement extant for summitry when he declared his readiness to meet with any world leader, including Premier Nikita Khrushchev, should such a meeting contribute to his loftiest goal, achieving "peace and prosperity." But in actuality, Johnson, with the exception of the one with Kosygin at Glassboro, did not indulge in meetings of the kind contemplated by his statement.

Pressures for summit meetings beat most insistently upon the President in time of great crisis. Indeed an almost invariable Soviet tactic in such moments is to propose a chief executives' meeting. Khrushchev did so in the 1962 Cuban crisis and at several junctures when Berlin issues were at their crest. For the Soviets, the move is a fruitful propaganda stroke and a brake on the momentum of the President's moves. Presidents, for their part, have found that summits work best when dealing with questions well prepared at lower diplomatic levels. Sometimes they unfreeze disagreements that regular diplomacy cannot resolve. Kennedy, meeting Khrushchev in Vienna, was eager to size up the Soviet leader. Although De Gaulle, Adenauer, and Macmillan had briefed him on the subject, he thought he had better see for himself in the interest of informed decisions. Even more, Kennedy said afterwards, "The direct give and take was of immeasurable value in making clear and precise what we consider vital." But the sizing up of Khrushchev was also a grim experience, as Kennedy made clear in reporting to the nation. The U.S.-U.S.S.R. quarrel over Laos, then at high flame, was "not materially reduced," and his hopes for a nuclear test ban agreement had received "a serious blow." Johnson's meeting with Kosygin at Glassboro was valuable in underscoring the interest of both powers in avoiding situations threatening nuclear war, in permitting first-hand exchanges of views, and in establishing a potentially useful personal acquaintance.

Summit meetings generally score low on policy achievement and high on general failure. They force the President to negotiate issues that deserve to be mastered well beyond the point where the Chief Executive merely reads papers that aides put before him. Not surprisingly, no President has brought off at the summit a negotiation comparable to Philip Jessup's handling of the first Berlin blockade, Dulles' Japanese peace treaty, and Llewellyn Thompson's Austrian settlement. Summits can create moods of optimism that the realities of policy hardly warrant. Eisenhower could note "the new spirit of friendliness" that the 1955 Geneva meeting seemed to burst upon the world. Yet a scant three months later the high hopes of Geneva were punctured by the Soviet-Czechoslovak-Egyptian arms deal. The 1959 Eisenhower-Khrushchev meeting produced "the spirit of Camp David," again a benevolent mood without tangible policy. Within months, the Paris meeting of the two leaders exploded into an international disaster. Although Kennedy hailed his Vienna encounter with Khrushchev for "making clear and precise what we consider vital" and for diminishing "the chances of a dangerous misjudgment," two months after Vienna the Berlin wall went up, and in the following year the Soviet Union was not deterred from installing missiles and manpower in Cuba. For all of the cordiality at Glassboro, the Johnson-Kosygin meetings yielded no substantive agreements and provided no clue concerning a key question of the moment: Did the Soviet Union propose to continue arms shipments to the Arab nations of the Middle East, and, in actuality, did the Soviet Union intend to make that region a place of future East-West confrontation?

Harry S. Truman, as a new President only briefly in office, put in a month at Potsdam, wrenched away from duties that had been suddenly thrust upon him and that he was only beginning to master. Understandably, in the final stages of the Potsdam conference, as Truman wrote later, he got "tired of sitting and listening to endless debate on matters that could not be settled at this conference yet took up precious time. . . . I was becoming very impatient, and on a number of occasions I felt like blowing the roof off the palace."[39] High-level meetings also can severely tax the strength of a President. At the Yalta conference, Franklin Roosevelt, fatigued and engrossed in running the war, "had made little preparation," his aide James F. Byrnes observed.[40] Further, summit meetings, rather than facilitating communication, may actually muddy it. At Vienna Kennedy greeted Khrushchev warmly but with deference, a gesture that in some Soviet quarters was misunderstood as personal awe rather than as a young President's courtesy toward an older man.

COMMUNIST DIPLOMACY.   The contemporary President faces the jarring idiosyncrasies of communist diplomacy, involving strains and stresses that his nineteenth-century predecessors never knew. They lived in the era of the "old diplomacy," whose marks were gentility and serenity and whose pride was quiet, professional negotiation. The communist method often reduces diplomacy to a branch of propaganda and employs a variety of rough expedients, not the least of which, from the President's standpoint, is its resort to calculated rudeness. Franklin Roosevelt, who labored valiantly for constructive U.S.-U.S.S.R. relations, received shortly before his death a message from Stalin so offensive that he laid it aside in order to cool off sufficiently before answering. At Paris in 1960 Khrushchev toppled the summit conference into crashing ruins by heaping upon Eisenhower a barrage of abuse over the Gary Powers U-2 incident. President Eisenhower heroically rose to the test and made an even, effective reply. Defense Secretary Thomas S. Gates, Jr., who sat next to the President, characterized his deportment as "the most remarkable performance of strength of character and dignity of any man I have ever seen."[41] Even Jefferson, Lincoln, and Cleveland knew no test such as this.

The President's agenda for foreign affairs depends as much upon communist initiatives as upon his own. Moscow loves to alternate between threats and acts portending doom and destruction and pleas for sweet reason and peace. By manipulating crisis and its eventual resolution, communism supplies the President with his chief diplomatic diet. As every postwar President knows, the communists tend to keep agreements as long as it is to their interest. To a professional politician like Harry Truman, steeped in the mores of his craft of honoring one's word, this was the worst of faults. "No contract should be entered into lightly," he commented on the Soviet habit, "I don't give my word lightly. When I say I'm going to do something, I do it, or bust my insides trying to do it."[42] Communist officialdom is apt to view the United States through the unflattering lenses of Marxist ideology. They see a nation of capitalists and imperialists, a nation doomed to collapse by impending economic disintegration. They take fixed positions that the most compelling presentations of reason and fact cannot budge. Yet the President and his aides, in the face of the ominous hazard of general war in a nuclear age, must toil away at unpromising negotiation which their nineteenth-century forebears, in their simpler times, would have soon abandoned.

Alliances

The President's need to establish and manage a series of alliances has soared since World War II. Alliances or understandings exist with individual countries and with regional groupings around the globe: Europe (NATO), Southeast Asia (SEATO), Australia and New Zealand (ANZUS), the Middle East (CENTO), Latin America (OAS), and Central America (OACS). When NATO was forming, Truman promised "the support which the situation requires," backed the bipartisan Vandenberg resolution endorsing the United States' association with NATO, featured the treaty in his 1949 inaugural address, urged upon Congress a vast program of military aid to the NATO countries, and assured its passage by announcing the first atomic explosion in the Soviet Union. Presidents have led in NATO's sharper turns of direction, too. Truman pushed West Germany's rearmament and inclusion in the western European defense system. Eisenhower promoted the European Defense Community treaty to merge the armed forces of six western European nations into a "hard and dependable core" for NATO. Kennedy advocated a NATO missile fleet of surface ships manned by crews of mixed nationality. Johnson led in the adjustment of NATO following De Gaulle's assault upon its military structure in requiring the removal from France of all military units or bases not under complete French control.

The President does much of his alliance toil in "working meetings," abroad or in Washington, to transact quantities of operational business or to thrash out issues at the topmost level. A model of such enterprise was Churchill's visit to the White House shortly after Pearl Harbor. In a fourteen-day stay, Churchill and his aides staked out with their American counterparts the political-military-economic lines of cooperative war effort. The Chief Executive is never loath to bid such foreign allies to join his battles on Capitol Hill. Churchill addressed several joint sessions of Congress, and he and his Foreign Secretary, Anthony Eden, appeared before the Senate Foreign Relations Committee. When Senators Joseph Ball, Harold Burton, Carl Hatch, and Lister Hill introduced a resolution in 1943, committing the United States to stipulated peace objectives and calling upon the President to summon an immediate international conference, the Britishers' remarks before the Foreign Relations Committee gladdened the Roosevelt administration, which feared the resolution's disruptive effects. Churchill and Eden usefully warned the committee against prematurely specifying peace objectives in the absence of soundings and probable agreement among the major allies.

Presidents can reverse the trend and visit allied chieftains abroad, as Kennedy did in his 1963 tour of Germany, Italy, England, and Ireland, involving public appearances and intensive private consultations. The depth of the latter is suggested by his entourage, which included Secretary of State Rusk, Special Assistant for National Security Affairs Bundy, Special Counsel Sorensen, and a quantity of other White House and State Department aides. At stops in each country Kennedy took up major business. Thus in Britain it was the test ban treaty, the NATO nuclear force, international trade, and British-American aid to India invaded by Red China. No shiny new diplomatic agreements emerged, but advances were made. Probably the main achievement was Kennedy's projection of himself and his purposes before several national European publics. In speeches before great multitudes and to national audiences by television he put his plea for an integrated Europe, attacked De Gaulle's nationalistic course, and affirmed the United States' resolve to defend Europe.

But Kennedy's 1963 "swing around" the NATO alliance also had its debit side. It removed him from Washington at a crucial juncture in the civil rights crisis, with street demonstrations nearing their peak. The President was investing great quantities of hours in negotiating with lame duck European statesmen, a chronic, unavoidable species in democratic politics. Adenauer's remaining days in office were numbered; the Macmillan government was not expected to survive beyond a few months. In Italy a scrambled political situation had produced a caretaker government little inclined to discuss major new commitments. The extravagant, intoxicating acclaim of his enormous audiences brought Kennedy to say things in speeches that were at variance with his previous policy positions. In Berlin, where a million inhabitants hailed him with wild acclaim, the President declared, "And there are some who say in Europe and elsewhere, 'We can work with the Communists.' Let them come to Berlin."[43] This was hardly in accord with his speech at American University some two weeks before, proposing new negotiations with the U.S.S.R. to end the cold war.

Alliances can be hobbled to the point of crisis when their members engage in hot pursuit of national interest. A case in point is the Suez crisis, which burst upon the Eisenhower administration in 1953 from the determination of the Egyptian government of General Mohammed Naguib to throw out the British from their vast base along the Suez Canal. The British Foreign Secretary endeavored to bring President Eisenhower into the dispute as a kind of mediator, but Eisenhower declined to undertake the task without encouragement from Naguib, which was not forthcoming. Eisenhower nevertheless dispatched emissaries Dulles and Stassen with a gift to Naguib, a handsome Colt revolver. The gift's symbolic import—a vast future flow of American firearms for the Egyptians—consternated the British, and Eisenhower was constrained to provide reassurances.[44]

Dulles consulted with the Egyptians in May 1953 but with no satisfactory developments. The situation continued to deteriorate. In 1956 Israel moved into Egyptian territory on the Sinai Peninsula, and British bombers from Cyprus attacked Egyptian airfields. The move, according to Sherman

Adams, "caught the President completely by surprise and the suddenness of it shocked him. He had received no previous warning from the British or the French. . . ."[45] Eisenhower called off an electoral campaign trip, explained the crisis in a nation-wide television address, and asserted the principle that "we do not accept the use of force as a wise and proper instrument for the settlement of international disputes."[46] Eisenhower ordered the dispute taken to the United Nations, a step that produced a strange array of bedfellows—the U.S. and the U.S.S.R. joined against France, Britain, and Israel. The Anglo-American alliance was at rock bottom.

Almost as disturbing was a dispute emerging from John Kennedy's efforts to rearrange the structure of political influence of one of his allies. With the war going badly in South Vietnam, and therefore constituting a threat to his own domestic political welfare, President Kennedy sought to force the removal of Ngo Dinh Nhu, whose influence over his brother, President Ngo Dinh Diem, was apparently great and the cause of several unfortunate turns of policy. In a televised interview President Kennedy criticized the Vietnamese regime for losing touch with the people whose support against the communists was essential in the local war. The President attributed much of the declining popularity to repressions against the Buddhists, which culminated in attacks by secret police on their pagodas. Popular support, Kennedy suggested pointedly, could be regained only by "changes in policy and perhaps with personnel."[47] As Kennedy spoke, a Vietnamese newspaper accused the United States Central Intelligence Agency of planning a coup d'état against President Diem's government. The United States ambassador Henry Cabot Lodge, Jr., was soon advising President Diem that the United States regarded the removal of Ngo Dinh Nhu as vital and that unless the regime could solve its problems mounting Congressional pressure might force the Kennedy administration to cut economic and military aid to South Vietnam. The Vietnamese regime continued intact, and Mme. Ngo Dinh Nhu, President Diem's sister-in-law, journeyed to the United States in a highly publicized transcontinental tour, launching counterblasts against the Kennedy policy. Midway in her campaign, President Diem's regime was overthrown, he and his brother were murdered, and the "changes" of "personnel" proceeded.

The United Nations

In setting his foreign policy, the modern President must reckon, of course, with the United Nations. President Kennedy, striving to alter the tone of U.S.-U.S.S.R. relations, found the UN General Assembly a useful forum in which to urge that in the future the two nations compete in "leadership and responsibility" instead of competing in a search for better methods of destruction.[48] In Kennedy's 1962 confrontation with the U.S.S.R. over Cuba, the UN served its classic functions as a forum in which the American complaint could be ventilated and world opinion marshaled, and where machinery could be found for negotiation and conciliation. But for the President the UN may also be a hazard. Kennedy, in the agony of a Berlin crisis, was urged by certain of his counselors to lay the problem before the UN General Assembly. Charge Khrushchev, they said, with threatening the peace over Berlin and call for economic sanctions if he fails to accept the UN verdict. Kennedy quickly spurned this advice, pointing out that a UN verdict might favor Khrushchev and that the neutralist nations might be persuaded to accept his suggestions for a free city.

For the President faced with situations where military forces must be utilized, the United Nations will often provide a better alternative than the direct engagement of American power. Bringing to bear the UN's international policing apparatus has entailed less expense, misunderstanding, and abuse than the direct involvements that Presidents have chosen to make in Korea and Vietnam. UN policing in the Congo, Cyprus, and at the Gaza Strip plainly displayed the several attractions of international action. UN procedures are also valuable as a face-saving or cooling-off device, as the *Pueblo* crisis of 1968 demonstrates. The President, faced with a grave affront to the United States, was able, by resorting to the UN, to provide a semblance of action rather than undertake a more direct and dangerous response.

The Future Presidency

The realities of the nuclear age and the practices of communist nations require a Presidency of great strength and tending toward autonomy in basic decisions of foreign policy. The nice question of our time is how can such an independent Presidency be held sufficiently accountable to enable it to reflect the popular will, the nation's historic purposes and values, and how can it be linked to institutions and practices upon which democracy depends?

It is clear enough that when the President makes his great decisions— whether to use the atomic bomb against Japan, whether to blockade Cuba, whether to escalate in Vietnam—both he and the nation are dependent upon the quality of the counsel he receives from his administration. Truman did not make his atomic bomb decision in privacy but in consultation with his Joint Chiefs, a scientific advisory committee, and a polling of the nation's leading scientists. His decision emerged only after a careful quest for viable alternative decisions, none of which attracted any substantial support from his advisers. Both the President personally and the nation itself with its stake in the quality of his decisions are best served by a pluralistic administration, in which counselors of varied backgrounds—scientists, military men, business and academic representatives present in his administration—can bring to bear diverse experience, outlooks, and values that will guide and temper the President in his momentous choices.

A "great decision" is seldom a "final decision" but part of a continuum in which other great decisions may follow. Thus American Presidents from Eisenhower to Johnson each have made a series of momentous choices in Vietnam. The critical discussion in Congress or the public reaction to an earlier decision may affect a later decision.

The quality of the President's decisions and the genuineness of his responsibility depend then also upon the effectiveness of the organs of debate and criticism: the press, private leaders and groups, and committee discussions and floor debate in Congress. Consideration might well be given to the establishment of an annual Presidential report on foreign policy in the manner of the annual Economic Report that the President makes under the Employment Act of 1946. Such a report could incorporate the proposal of Senator Charles H. Percy of Illinois that the President present to Congress each year a list of "our national commitments as he sees them, detailing the nature of each commitment, its limitations and the justification for it in terms of national interest."[49]

What the President does in his "great decisions" is subject to the grand review of the electoral process. A national election is an occasion when the quality and consequences of the President's great decisions can be debated and where alternative policies for the future can be presented. Thus, in 1968 Presidential hopefuls of both parties were facing the challenge of "selling" a majority of the people on a new approach to Vietnam so that they could drive the President from office and start implementing a new policy.

For the dependent President, the one that shares the foreign affairs function with the legislature, several steps might well be taken to improve his situation.

1. The proposals of Chapter 6 to improve the President's position as legislative leader are fully applicable to his duties in foreign affairs. What he can do in world affairs depends increasingly upon what he is doing or has done in domestic affairs, and Congress applies to foreign affairs legislation many restrictions that it imposes upon domestic. Detail in legislation handicaps the President in dealing flexibly with communist satellite nations. Appropriation subcommittees employ their discretion roughly against the administration. These and other jarring tendencies make it all the more urgent to strengthen the President's leadership position in Congress. He therefore needs the item veto, stronger party leadership in Congress, and a revision of committee chairmen's method of selection and powers. He badly needs appropriations for substantial periods of three, five, or ten years so that the highly *ad hoc* management of foreign aid can be replaced with the advantages of integrated planning.

2. The treaty power should be revised by constitutional amendment to replace the required two-thirds approval of the Senate with one of a simple

majority. If in future decades the United States is to enter into international arrangements to solidify the world community and strengthen its powers at the sacrifice of national sovereignty, the practicality of the treaty power will become crucial. The present two-thirds majority requirement imposes upon the President the necessity to secure heavy bipartisan support, in which lurks the peril of easy defeat, of which the League of Nations fight is the classic example. The two-thirds requirement also slows down the American government's capacity to act while the huge Senatorial majority is painstakingly compiled.

3. The Presidency, whether the dependent or independent model, must heed the forewarnings that in the 1970's and beyond, the nation's attitudes toward its sovereignty and toward its relations with the individual nations of the communist bloc must be revised. It must in all likelihood extend its affinities with the regional alliances to which it belongs and speed their development as organs of political and economic union. These future tasks were heralded in Kennedy's "Strategy of Peace" speech at the American University on June 10, 1963, in Fulbright's Senate address of March 25, 1964, and are represented by President Johnson's program of "building bridges" to the communist world in 1967. Perhaps the most difficult part of this enterprise for the future President is the necessity of interpreting persuasively to the public the urgencies of the times and his prescriptions for them. He will need to wrestle with the truth, as Fulbright suggested, that "a creative foreign policy . . . is not necessarily one which wins immediate general approval."

4. However substantial may be the limitations the President suffers in dealing with Congress and public opinion, they must not be used as whipping boys to expiate the executive branch's own shortcomings. The President and his executive aides are far better situated than anyone else to provide creativity in foreign affairs, despite the limitations of their power. They, more than any other groups, determine the balance between principle and expediency, between clarity and contradiction in the nation's foreign policy. Thus when President Kennedy said in his June 1963 visit to Europe that United States forces would remain there as long as they were "required and desired," and Deputy Secretary of Defense Roswell Gilpatric declared four months later that an eventual reduction was planned in American forces overseas, the resulting bewilderment and outcry in western European capitals can be laid to but one source—not to Congress or public opinion, but to the United States executive branch.

5. Making and conducting foreign policy has become a vast enough task to absorb the simultaneous efforts of a strong President and a strong Secretary of State. Historical experience with special agents and White House aides does not refute the wisdom of making the Secretary of State the President's chief

deputy in foreign affairs. The Secretary of State, more than any other executive aide, is entrusted with the responsibility for formulating all aspects of national policy bearing upon the national interest and security. He can best take the lead in integrating the political, military, economic, and cultural efforts of the executive branch into coherent foreign policy. To succeed he needs a high order of personal talent and sophistication in foreign affairs, the President's backing, and the ability to prove himself constantly in his daily battle with shifting world problems to win and retain the confidence of his chief and his executive colleagues. He needs help in the struggle from high caliber top officials in his department and a strong career service.

In the absence of internal reform of Congress, the President will continue to rely heavily upon the Secretary of State and his aides to win the understanding and support of Congressional committees. In the absence of reform, only executive candor and a willingness to discuss difficulties and problems, as well as accomplishments, are apt to produce Congressional support for the mountainous problems awaiting the nation in foreign affairs.

Commander-in-Chief 10

For all the seeming power that should logically derive from his position as manager of the mightiest military enterprise the world has known, the President—the Commander-in-Chief—is by no means a complete and undoubted master. He enjoys no monopoly of direction over American military power but shares it with others who may withhold what he needs, challenge or even veto what he does, or commit acts that leave him no choice but to respond within channels that they, rather than he, establish. Congress, of course, has a substantial military power. The professional military, some steps removed from an image of absolute obedience, may resist, delay, and amend. The courts may upset what he does in their duty to protect the rights and liberties guaranteed by the Constitution. And in wartime the electorate may weigh the quality of his military stewardship and decide whether to keep him in office or fire him. What he does with his vast military power may also be determined by what opposing nations do. When the Russians, for example, throw an elaborate antimissile defense around their country, the President faces the unpleasant prospect of reshuffling the priorities of his military program—and of his social program as well—to provide a similar defense. There are times when he may well wonder whether in truth he is the "chief," given the powers and opportunities of the other members of his military world, and whether his function is indeed to "command."

The Defense Department

The President's main reliance and help in his duty as Commander-in-Chief is the Defense Department, which shelters most of the military endeavor.

The department was created in 1947 with strong leadership and support from President Harry Truman. Certain of his proposals were not adopted, signifying the capacity of the individual services to resist the President with backing from friendly legislators, and from Truman onward the President has engaged in periodic struggles with the military services. The President habitually presses for "unification" and "economy" and makes hard choices between competing proposals to develop weapons systems pressed by the individual services. They, in turn, are jealous of their traditional autonomy and vested functional interest, and are driven by professional commitment and responsibility to accord military security a higher priority than fiscal "soundness."

The President's chief deputy, the civilian officer who most approximates his alter ego as Commander-in-Chief, is the Secretary of Defense. There is also the National Security Council, which, although uneven in effectiveness, has endeavored to approximate Truman's view of it as "the place in the government where military, diplomatic, and resources problems could be studied and continually appraised. This new organization is available to give the President a running balance and a perpetual inventory of where we stood and where we were going on all strategic questions affecting national security." The national security sector's representative on the White House Staff is the special assistant for national security affairs.

The President's principal professional military advisers are the Joint Chiefs of Staff, created by President Roosevelt shortly after Pearl Harbor. The Chiefs existed wholly by Presidential fiat until 1947, when the National Security Act inspirited them with the firmer breath of statutory life. Relations between the President and the Joint Chiefs since the Roosevelt years have been troubled and sometimes stormy. The severest encounters occurred under Eisenhower, whose incomparable professional prestige lent enormous weight to his evaluation of military issues. In addition, he brought into the Presidency a skill for dealing with his military colleagues that makes other Chief Executives gape with amazement. Although his professional military chieftains strove to resist his policy, Eisenhower expertly overcame their dissent. Soon after taking office, Eisenhower announced that his administration would instill a "New Look" into military policy. The New Look relied heavily upon the new weapons of mass destruction to deter aggression, large or small, and permit reductions of conventional military forces. Since nuclear weapons were less expensive than a conventional military establishment, the New Look permitted budgetary cuts cherished by the Eisenhower administration. "More bang for the buck!" was the watchword.

Eisenhower's reverence for economy was shared, perhaps with even greater fervor, by two men of big business who towered in his military decisions: Secretary of Defense Charles E. Wilson of General Motors and Secretary of the Treasury George M. Humphrey of the M. A. Hanna Company of Cleveland. The President, by several simple administrative expedients, placed the economy-minded businessmen in firm ascendance over the professional military. Reorganization Plan Number Six of April 30, 1953, was issued, expanding the powers of the Defense Secretary over budget, weapons, and strategic planning. The Secretary of the Treasury and the Director of the Budget, who was also economy-minded, were brought into the center of the National Security Council's work, where the military budget was scrutinized.

With the launching of his new doctrine Eisenhower simultaneously recruited a wholly new Joint Chiefs of Staff. His views of the Chiefs' functioning quickly emerged. They were members of the administration "team" (a favorite Eisenhower word), working for its objectives under civilian guidance. In formulating military advice, the Chiefs should appreciatively weigh their superiors' views and avoid submitting contentious recommendations. They must accept public responsibility for the administration's military policy, regardless of their personal views.

The President and his aides manipulated sanctions to nurture the team spirit. The new Chiefs were appointed for no specified term, and each appointment, it was disclosed, would be reviewed after two years. "Again and again . . ." General Matthew B. Ridgway, then Army Chief of Staff, has written, "pressure was brought on me, in the name of economy, to keep the semblance, but not the reality, of a fighting force overseas."[1] Secretary of Defense Wilson pressed continually for economy. "Why don't you reduce the strength of your combat divisions?"[2] he would ask Ridgway in a budgetary conference, clearly implying that the President was interested in reductions of unit strength. Ridgway bridled at directives slashing the uniformed forces from 1,500,000 to 1,000,000 and Army expenditures from $16.2 billion to $8.9 billion. The Army, he argued, would be so weakened that it could no longer perform its missions. Although Ridgway persisted in his dissent, it was to no avail. His distress was compounded when he came upon the following in the President's State of the Union message for 1954: "The defense program recommended for 1955 . . . is based on a new military program *unanimously recommended* [italics supplied] by the Joint Chiefs of Staff."[3] The general's resulting state of shock was worse, he said, than he had hitherto suffered from ambush, aerial bombardment, or any other unsettling experience in his professional career. Ridgway was not long in retiring as Army Chief of Staff. General Maxwell Taylor, too, fell out with the Eisenhower administration on budgetary issues.

Although John Kennedy's advent to the Presidency was a great day for the advocates of conventional weapons, relations between the Joint Chiefs and the Chief Executive lost none of their turbulence. The debacle of the attempted invasion of Cuba in 1961 brought the Chiefs into the ill graces of the new President. According to the view widely held in the administration, the President suffered this supreme disaster mainly because of the faulty counsel of his principal military advisers. In the months following the debacle, Kennedy and his high aides criticized the Chiefs, sometimes caustically and by name. The Chiefs' chairman, General Lyman Lemnitzer, was shifted to Europe as commander of United States forces and was replaced by General Taylor, whose return from retirement into private life reflected badly upon the military. Trouble again fell upon the Chiefs when certain of the incoming Taylor's views proved sharply at odds with those of Admiral George W. Anderson, Chief of Naval Operations, and General Curtis E. Le May, Air Force Chief of Staff. Not the least of these differences were Taylor's proposals for an expanded Army and the abolition of the Joint Chiefs and their replacement by a single chief.[4]

In less than a year the forces of conflict were resolved thanks to forceful Presidential intervention. President Kennedy failed to reappoint Admiral Anderson as Chief of Naval Operations and hence to the Joint Chiefs. General Le May was not reappointed for the standard two-year term but only for one year. The drastic maneuver against Anderson shocked the naval officered community where both his reappointment and his eventual rise to chairmanship of the Chiefs were generally expected. Anderson had earned himself black marks by semiprivately criticizing a reorganization of the Navy's command structure that the President was to recommend to Congress, limiting the province of the Chief of Naval Operations. The admiral had publicly opposed the administration's position on key issues. General Le May had also been critical, but less pointedly. Both officers were widely influential on Capitol Hill, able to summon with their own dissents a sizable chorus of legislative opposition to administration policies. Ultimately, President Kennedy removed Admiral Anderson some distance from Capitol Hill by appointing him ambassador to Portugal. Anderson's successor as Chief of Naval Operations, Admiral David L. McDonald, was little known in Congressional circles.[5]

For his part, President Lyndon Johnson had to apply a goodly measure of his persuasive talents to his military commanders who sought more troops for Vietnam, while he gave them less than what they asked for as he juggled their requests against the political and economic demands of civilian society.

The President and the Generals

As Commander-in-Chief the President appoints and removes his field generals. In wartime the responsibility is especially important because of the consequences of the President's choice for the nation's survival and his own political future. Several Presidents have faced major crises either in bringing their field generals to engage in battle or in keeping them within bounds, not simply on the battlefield but within the framework of constitutional government. General George B. McClellan, the most lagging of field generals, was a great trial to Abraham Lincoln. Bold in his strategic conceptions,

McClellan nevertheless dreaded execution. His standard tactic was to demand more reinforcements after overestimating the enemy's strength and deprecating his own. He was a wonderfully imaginative procrastinator. If he had Lee at a disadvantage, he almost invariably failed to exploit it. He must wait, McClellan would report to his impatient superiors at Washington, until the Potomac rose to be sure that Lee would not recross it; he must finish drilling new recruits, reorganize his forces, and procure more shoes, uniforms, blankets, and camp equipment. McClellan also passed some of his battle-idle time pouring his innate arrogance into a letter of July 7, 1862, to Lincoln, pointing out that it was high time the government established a civil and military policy to cover the full canvass of the nation's troubles. The general generously offered to inform the President of what it should be.

The McClellan question became critical with his failure to exploit his victory at Antietam by pursuing Lee's fleeing army. Lincoln worked mightily, as his secretary John Nicolay put it, at "poking sharp sticks into Little Mac's ribs." When the general included among his ingenious excuses one that an epidemic had afflicted his army's horses with sore mouths and weary backs, Lincoln was goaded into a sharp reply. "I have just read your dispatch about sore tongues and fatigued horses," he telegraphed. "Will you pardon me for asking what the horses of your army have done since the battle of Antietam that fatigues anything?"[6]

Lincoln and his administration were now at a critical juncture. Winter was approaching and would assure that except for Antietam the long record of Eastern defeat and stalemate would remain intact. Congress, restive with this state of affairs, was soon to convene. Governors were nervous, the cabinet was divided, and the extreme-war men and advocates of immediate peace were thundering against the President. Nor was Lincoln unmindful of McClellan's personal softness toward the South and the presence on his staff of some who advocated a waiting game to prolong the war until both sides were exhausted and the Union might be preserved with slavery intact. Replace McClellan? The available generals were a sorrowfully undistinguished lot, many already well scarred with failure, and others abysmally inexperienced.

After heavy deliberation, Lincoln cast aside the adverse factors and on November 5, 1862, relieved McClellan and appointed General Ambrose E. Burnside in his place. Upon reading the President's order, McClellan exclaimed, "Alas for my poor country!"[7] Certain of his officers urged him to disobey. He later wrote that he might have marched his troops into Washington and taken possession of the government. Instead, he handed over his command of 120,000 men in an elaborate ceremony. But this was by no means the last encounter between McClellan and Lincoln. In 1864, two years after his removal, McClellan met Lincoln on a new terrain—as the Democratic nominee for the Presidency.

In another day, President Truman experienced a confrontation with a field general prone to do too much rather than too little. General Douglas MacArthur, commander of the United Nations forces in Korea, possessed a military career of rare distinction: peerless hero of the Pacific theater in World War II, successful viceroy of postwar Japan, and a widely mentioned potential Republican Presidential nominee. His handsome, erect presence and majestic eloquence were marks of an imperious figure.

Truman's difficulties began when the general, midway in the Korean War, visited Chiang Kai-shek at Formosa. After their meeting, Chiang declared, "The foundation for Sino-American military cooperation has been laid."[8] Since these words were both obscure and potentially expansive, and the administration was anxious to keep Formosa neutralized, Truman dispatched Averell Harriman to review with MacArthur the entire Far Eastern political situation. Harriman's apparent success was shattered when MacArthur released a statement to the commander of the Veterans of Foreign Wars urging a more dynamic United States–Formosa partnership. The President himself now went forth to see MacArthur in a hastily cleared-out Quonset hut on Wake Island. According to information released to a subsequent Senatorial investigation, the whole Eastern policy was broadly and congenially discussed. The part of Truman's visit that the public saw seemed entirely happy. The President pinned the Distinguished Service Medal on the general and presented a five-pound box of candied plums to Mrs. MacArthur. The general reciprocated by declaring, through the President's press secretary, "No commander in the history of war has had more complete and admirable support from the agencies in Washington than I have during the Korean operation."[9]

MacArthur pressed the war forward, routed the North Koreans, and received approval from the United Nations General Assembly to pursue the fleeing foe across the thirty-eighth parallel, the division between the two Koreas. Hereupon Communist China entered the war. The struggle proceeded to seesaw between MacArthur's forces and the enlarged enemy. On March 17, 1951, in a public statement issued from his United Nations headquarters, MacArthur lamented the "abnormal military inhibitions" upon his command and pointed to the necessity for "vital decisions—yet to be made." These presumably were to incorporate his proposals to the Joint Chiefs for broadened military action against Red China, including a blockade, air bombardment, and ultimately invasion. MacArthur's public statement was issued simultaneously with efforts of the President and the State Department to end the Korean conflict by reopening diplomatic negotiations.[10]

MacArthur made other public statements, not the least of which was a reply to Joseph W. Martin, the House minority leader, who had asked the general for his views on the use of Chinese Nationalist troops. MacArthur indeed believed they should be employed, and added, in words implying that it was necessary to vastly expand the Korean conflict, "Here we fight Europe's war with arms while the diplomats there still fight it with words

. . . if we lose the war to Communism in Asia the fall of Europe is inevitable." Congressman Martin read MacArthur's letter on the House floor.[11]

Anxiety flowed like wine in foreign capitals. Kenneth Younger, British Minister of State, typified the mood of America's allies in lamenting "irresponsible statements . . . from highly placed quarters, without the authority of the United Nations, or indeed of any member government." President Truman now concluded that decisive action was unavoidable if Presidential authority, civil supremacy, and established policy were to be preserved. He wrote to a friend, "I reached a decision yesterday morning after much consideration and consultation on the Commanding General in the Pacific. It will undoubtedly create a great furor but under the circumstances I could do nothing else and still be President of the United States." On April 11 the President announced MacArthur's removal from his command.[12]

Truman explained his decision in an address to the nation. MacArthur, returning to the United States, addressed Congress and advanced his policy tenets with superb oratorical skill. Several legislators moved to impeach Truman, and the Senate Armed Services and Foreign Relations Committees commenced a joint investigation. The top military unqualifiedly supported the President.

Presidential power was eventually vindicated by Truman, as it had been earlier by Lincoln. In both episodes, civil supremacy had been maintained over the professional military, a cardinal arrangement of the democratic state. Both Presidents in their self-assertion faced grave political risks: the possibility that the successors of the deposed generals would compile a less favorable military record, that public opinion would feel affronted, and that legislators would exploit the situation for personal political gain. But both Presidents clung to duty and brushed aside political expediency and the temptation not to act. The military rallied around them, the public understood, and ultimately the Chief Executive, as Commander-in-Chief, was reaffirmed, but he trod no unperiled, primrose path.

Sources of Authority

The President, functioning as he does in a democratic state, requires legal authority to pursue his military purposes. In wartime, of course, the need and the quest become most compelling. The pursuit of it may send the President to the Constitution to contemplate how much authority its lean language really provides, or to Congress for new laws. And in what he does he must reckon with the courts, guardians of the fundamental law and private right against governmental, and therefore Presidential, encroachment.

Presidents in the nation's major wars have invoked two contrasting patterns of legal justification for their acts. One, the Lincolnian, asserts an expansive view of the President's independent authority based on the Commander-in-Chief clause in Article II, section 2, of the Constitution and on the duty "to take care that the laws be faithfully executed" expressed in section 3. In the twelve weeks between the outbreak at Fort Sumter and the convening of Congress in special session on July 4, 1861, Lincoln employed these two clauses to sanction measures whose magnitude suggests dictatorship.

In the twelve-week interval, Lincoln added 23,000 men to the Regular Army and 18,000 to the Navy, called 40,000 volunteers for three years' service, summoned the state militias into a ninety-day volunteer force, paid $2 million from the Treasury's unappropriated funds for purposes unauthorized by Congress, closed the Post Office to "treasonable correspondence," imposed a blockade on Southern ports, suspended the writ of habeas corpus, which protects the citizen against arbitrary arrest, in certain parts of the country, and caused the arrest and military detention of persons "who were represented to him" as engaging in or contemplating "treasonable practices." He later instituted a militia draft when voluntary recruiting broke down and extended the suspension of the habeas corpus privilege to a nation-wide basis for persons "guilty of any disloyal practice." His first Emancipation Proclamation freed the slaves in states in rebellion against the United States and pledged "the Executive Government of the United States, including the military and naval authority thereof," to protect the freedom conferred. Lincoln invited Congress to "ratify" his enlargement of the armed forces, which it did, and it sanctioned his handling of the writ of habeas corpus. Altogether, Lincoln's actions, as Edward S. Corwin has written, "assert for the President, for the first time in our history, an initiative of indefinite scope and legislative in effect in meeting the domestic aspects of a war emergency."[13]

The world war Presidencies of Woodrow Wilson and Franklin Roosevelt afford a contrasting pattern. The spreading character of war, its encroachment upon the economy, the involvement of growing numbers of people, and the resort to propaganda have fostered an executive-legislative partnership in war leadership. In both world wars statutes were passed delegating broad powers to the Chief Executive. Selective service laws in both wars enabled the President to administer a vast manpower draft. The Lever Act of 1917 empowered the Executive to license the mining, importation, manufacture, storage, and distribution of necessities; it authorized the seizure of factories, pipelines, mines, and the like; and it fixed the prices of wheat, coal, and other basic commodities. In World War II the Lend Lease Act permitted the President and his deputies to transfer "defense articles," meaning anything from bacon to battleships, to the "government of any country whose defense the President judged vital to the defense of the United States," on any terms he "deems satisfactory."

By gift of legislation, Roosevelt managed much of the domestic economy in World War II. Through deputies he allocated "materials," fixed prices, controlled rents, settled labor disputes, and seized strikebound plants. Like Wilson, Roosevelt as Commander-in-Chief created "executive agencies," such as the Office of Price Administration and the National War Labor Board, to administer delegated legislative power.

The President needs not only laws from Congress but a variety of other cooperative deeds to assure effective military policy and administration. By grace of the Constitution, with its mechanisms of checks and balances, the Chief Executive shares a wide range of military powers with Congress. Congress raises the armed forces, provides for their regulation, and investigates the military enterprise; the Senate gives its advice and consent to military nominations; Congress passes laws governing military organization, appropriates vast funds for equipment and materiel, and declares war. Its powers, Presidents would gladly testify, enable it to act forcefully in military affairs. The results are not always positive and cooperative. Checks and balances, bolstered by rivalries between the armed services, sometimes bring the President and Congress into incipient or actual conflict.

In 1962 President Kennedy faced a gathering crisis that threatened to become a head-on clash not simply over the merits of a military artifact, but between Congress's and the President's respective military powers. The subject of controversy was the RS-70 bomber, then in its final stages of development. Air Force leaders strongly backed the RS-70, stressing the necessity of a manned bomber program to avoid excessive reliance upon missiles. Substantial Soviet bomber advances were cited. Army and Navy leaders, and President Kennedy, like President Eisenhower earlier, opposed the RS-70, holding that great numbers of long-range missiles would be available before the new bomber could be produced in sufficient quantity. When the Kennedy administration requested $180 million in 1962 to continue the RS-70 development program, the House Armed Services Committee lavishly authorized $491 million. The committee's bill "directed" that the funds it authorized be spent.

The choice of this particular word signified the beginning of a possible massive constitutional confrontation between Congress and the President for dominion over military policy. The House committee based its wording "direct" upon Article I, section 8, of the Constitution, which vests in Congress the responsibility for raising and maintaining the military forces. In choosing its ground, the committee likened the President, or Commander-in-Chief, to a field general who can direct and order his forces but must use the weapons furnished by Congress. Representative Carl Vinson of Georgia, chairman of the Armed Services Committee, a patriarchal influence in military policy, candidly admitted that his committee's maneuver was intended to force the Pentagon to respect Congressional insistence that continued manned bomber development was essential to maintaining "an adequate military establishment."

President Kennedy refrained from picking up the gauntlet of the constitutional issue thrown down by Vinson. Instead he took the "Swamp Fox of Georgia," as Vinson was otherwise known, for a stroll one sunny March afternoon in the White House rose garden. The President and the Congressman fortunately arranged an honorable, peacemaking compromise by which the administration agreed to spend more than was originally budgeted for the RS-70 if a new review and technological developments warranted an increase.[14]

Presidents must also reckon with a favorite preoccupation of Congress in the military realm—investigation. Truman's Senate Committee to Investigate the Defense Program was a model of searching, but constructive, criticism that produced fruitful change in the administration of World War II. Success as a wartime investigator established Truman's chief claim upon his subsequent Vice-Presidential nomination. A contrasting view of the investigatory power is provided by a great cross Lincoln had to bear in the Civil War, the Joint Committee on the Conduct of the War. Spotty and arbitrary, the committee concentrated upon the Army of the Potomac and selected generals—McClellan, Charles P. Stone, Fitz-John Porter, and William B. Franklin—to investigate. John C. Frémont and Benjamin Franklin Butler were its favorites and could do no wrong. The committee investigated its selected victims with preconceived notions of guilt, employed wild rumor and irresponsible publicity, and became the factional instrument of the radicals. Its busiest members were staunch anti-Lincoln men such as Zachariah Chandler, Benjamin Franklin Wade, and George Washington Julian; Chandler, in a typically unflattering estimate of the administration, wrote, "Folly, folly, folly reigns supreme. The President is a weak man." Lincoln reciprocated in his judgment of the committee. He said,

> I have never faltered in my faith of being ultimately able to suppress this rebellion and of reuniting this divided country; but this improvised vigilant committee to watch my movements and keep me straight, appointed by Congress and called the "committee on the conduct of the war," is a marplot, and its greatest purpose seems to be to hamper my action and obstruct the military operations.[15]

The Courts

As Commander-in-Chief the President also faces tensions with the remaining governmental branch concerned with military affairs—the federal courts— with its high duty in a democratic state to protect the Constitution and the laws against encroachment. The most perplexing and consequential issues between the Executive and the courts may arise during actual war, when the President is driven to curtail, or even to suppress, key liberties sanctioned in the Bill of Rights. To further the progress of war, to safeguard the nation's imperiled safety, the President has set aside political and economic liberties that in peacetime are inviolable.

The Civil War, fought within the nation's borders and jeopardizing its capital, was resented and resisted in many sectors of the North sympathetic to the Confederacy, to the point that President Lincoln promulgated several orders and proclamations restricting individual liberty. The most important of these was his suspension of the constitutional privilege of the writ of habeas corpus. Lincoln's first habeas corpus proclamation, issued in the war's early weeks, was triggered by events in Maryland. Underground resistance and open defiance were rampant in that state. Federal troops were attacked by mobs in Baltimore, communications to the capital were severed, and the mayor and police chief were unabashedly pro-Confederate and anti-Lincoln. Bridges were destroyed to hamper the passage of Union troops, and newspapers hostile to the administration fanned disunion sentiment. The state legislature was soon to convene, and a formidable bloc of its members aimed to have the state secede from the Union.

Union generals moved to nip the growing conspiracy by arresting the mayor of Baltimore, the chief of police, and several police commissioners. Even more sensational was the arrest of members of the Maryland legislature. To forestall the passage of an act of secession, Union General Nathaniel P. Banks barred the legislature from meeting and arrested nine of its members and the chief clerk of the senate. Still other Marylanders were arrested, including one John Merryman "charged with various acts of treason." Merryman was languishing in Fort McHenry when the Chief Justice of the United States, Roger B. Taney, on circuit duty, ordered "the body of John Merryman [produced] and . . . the day and cause of [his] capture and detention" made known. A head-on clash between the President and the Court, between the war and the Constitution, was in the making. Taney, to the administration's great relief, confined himself to declaring that the power to suspend the writ, which should be exercised only with "extreme caution," belonged to Congress, and not to the President (17 Fed. Cas. 144). Taney's opinion, nevertheless, put the administration under the cloud of the likelihood of a hostile Supreme Court decision, an event the Attorney General, Edward Bates, said would "do more to paralyze the Executive . . . than the worst defeat our armies have yet sustained."[16]

The administration's position was strengthened when Congress, after much struggle, passed the Habeas Corpus Act of 1863, affirming the President's power to suspend the writ. Despite several procedural devices incorporated to placate the courts, the act left to the Executive the setting of policy concerning arrests and imprisonments. Prisoners were tried, as before, by military tribunal and punished or released under authority of the War Department. Arrests continued apace. Clement L. Vallandigham, fiery Copperhead, after his arrest, trial, and sentencing by a military commission, appealed to the United States Supreme Court to lift his case into civil court. But

the Supreme Court ruled that it had no jurisdiction, since a military commission was not a "court," to which the federal judiciary was limited under
existing law (*Ex parte Vallandigham*, 68 U.S. 243, 1864).

Although Vallandigham never lived to see it, his legal position was ultimately vindicated in the celebrated case of *Ex parte Milligan* (4 Wallace 2,
1866). Milligan too was a Copperhead, tried by a military commission for
"treasonable" speeches. Condemned to hang, he invoked the habeas corpus
writ. But the war was now over, and the Court was prepared to act boldly. It
ruled that Indiana, where Milligan resided and spoke, was not part of the
"theater of war" and that the civil courts there were "open" and therefore
available to conduct his trial. Under such a combination of circumstances,
the writ could not be constitutionally suspended. The *Milligan* case, needless to say, has become the source of permanent consternation to the friends
of Presidential power. It establishes the principle that the courts shall determine, even to the point of overriding the Executive, what is the area of
war and public danger, a principle that could well work havoc with Presidential effectiveness in actual emergency.

Despite the hazards of the *Milligan* doctrine, the Court proved tolerant
of Presidential power in the two world wars. In *Ex parte Quirin* (317 U.S. 1,
1942) the Court broadly construed the Commander-in-Chief's capacity as
executor of the Articles of War, enacted by Congress to further the United
States' obligations under the laws of war, a branch of international law. The
Articles of War provide for their enforcement through courts-martial and
military commissions. *Ex parte Quirin* concerned eight saboteurs, seven Germans and one American, who were trained in a Berlin espionage school
and deposited on Long Island and the Florida coast by German submarines
in 1942. They doffed their German military uniforms for civilian attire, and
with their tools of sabotage set out for New York City, Jacksonville, and
other points to practice their art on American war industries. Arrested by the
FBI before they could get down to work, they were turned over to the
provost marshal of the District of Columbia. As Commander-in-Chief, President Franklin D. Roosevelt appointed a military commission to try the would-
be saboteurs for violating the laws of war by not wearing fixed emblems revealing their combatant status. Midway in the trial the defendants petitioned
the United States Supreme Court and the District Court for the District of
Columbia for leave to bring habeas corpus proceedings.

The defendants argued that the offense charged against them was not
known to the laws of the United States and was not one "arising in the
land and naval forces," as described by the Fifth Amendment of the Constitution. Nor was the military tribunal that was trying them, they said, constituted in keeping with the Articles of War. The Court struck down the
latter contention by declining to distinguish between the powers of the
President as Commander-in-Chief and of Congress to create a military commission. The Court rejected the other arguments, holding that cases involv-

ing enemy personnel had never been deemed to fall under the constitutional guarantees of the Fifth and Sixth Amendments. The Court also cited the long-standing practice represented by an act of 1806 that imposed the death penalty on alien spies "according to the law and usage of nations, by sentence of general court martial." The saboteurs, accordingly, were tried and sentenced by military commission.

The most extreme application of the Commander-in-Chief's power to designate the theater of military operations was President Roosevelt's executive order of February 19, 1942, directed at the presumed danger of Japanese sabotage on the West Coast. In the high excitement over the Japanese bombing of Pearl Harbor, Roosevelt was pressed by the military, Congress, West Coast groups, and the newspapers to remove persons of Japanese ancestry from that area farther into the mainland. By Executive Order No. 9066 Roosevelt empowered the Secretary of War to establish "military areas" from which "any or all persons" might be excluded to prevent espionage and sabotage, and he designated military commanders to police these areas. The Secretary of War was directed to provide food, shelter, and transportation for persons evacuated. Soon the three westernmost states and a part of Arizona were declared "military areas 1 and 2" by Lieutenant General J. L. DeWitt. In a brief resolution of March 21, 1942, Congress endorsed the Presidential action by making it a misdemeanor "to knowingly enter, remain in, or leave prescribed military areas" of the Secretary of War or of the commanding officer. A War Relocation Authority was established to care for persons cleared out of the military areas. In all, some 112,000 persons were removed from the West Coast, of whom the vast majority—70,000—were United States citizens. Both the transplanted United States citizens and the aliens were eventually placed in ten "relocation centers" in California, Arizona, Idaho, Utah, Colorado, Wyoming, and Arkansas.

The relocation enterprise was challenged several times, but never effectively. In *Hirabayashi v. United States* (320 U.S. 81, 1943) the Court, by the drastic surgery of legal technicalities, reduced the issue to the right of the West Coast commander to subject citizens of Japanese ancestry to a special curfew order. The Court stressed the nation's plight and the state of the war in reaching its decision. Japan was achieving striking victories in 1943, the West Coast lay exposed, defense plants were heavily concentrated there, and, in the eyes of the Court, the ethnic affiliation of Japanese-Americans with the enemy posed a danger unknown from those of other ancestry. The Court deemed relocation within the powers of the President and Congress "acting in cooperation." In *Korematsu v. United States* (323 U.S. 214, 1944) a United States citizen, a Japanese-American, was convicted in district court for remaining in his California home. The Supreme Court again severely narrowed its decision and reasserted the reasoning of earlier relocation cases, though Japan was now in full retreat throughout the Pacific.

The most general abrogation of civil liberties in World War II occurred in the territory of Hawaii. Soon after the Japanese bombed Pearl Harbor, Governor J. B. Poindexter of Hawaii invoked section 67 of the Hawaiian Organic Act of April 30, 1900, proclaimed martial law throughout the territory, and turned over to the commanding general of the Hawaiian Department the exercise of all normal gubernatorial powers "during the present emergency and until the danger of invasion is removed." President Roosevelt approved Poindexter's decision, and a regime of martial law commenced that remained in force until October 24, 1944, when a Presidential proclamation terminated it. Habeas corpus was suspended and the civil courts were supplanted by military tribunals in which civilians were tried for crimes by summary procedures.

The Hawaiian arrangement was challenged in 1943, when District Judge Delbert E. Metzger issued a writ of habeas corpus in behalf of two naturalized Germans interned by the Army. The Hawaiian commander, Lieutenant General Robert C. Richardson, countered by forbidding writs of habeas corpus, including those of Judge Metzger. The issue was soon settled administratively.

Finally, the Court in *Duncan v. Kahanamoku, Sheriff* (327 U.S. 304, 1946) cited section 5 of the Hawaiian Organic Act, which declares that the Constitution of the United States has "the same effect within said Territory as elsewhere in the United States." The war was now well past, and the Court declared that the suspension of normal judicial processes had been unlawful. The Organic Act of 1900, it found, did not authorize the supplanting of civil courts by military tribunals.

In addition to seizing persons, the President as Commander-in-Chief has also seized property. Six months before Pearl Harbor, while the nation was still officially at peace, President Roosevelt, citing his earlier proclamation of an "unlimited national emergency," seized the strikebound North American Aviation plant at Inglewood, California. Roosevelt's claim of authority was sweeping and somewhat imprecise—"the duty constitutionally and inherently resting upon the President to exert his civil and military as well as his moral authority to keep the defense efforts of the United States a going concern," and "to obtain supplies for which Congress has appropriated money, and which it has directed the President to obtain." Both before and after the United States became a belligerent, Roosevelt seized other aircraft plants, shipyards, and a railroad.

The most serious legal challenge of the President's authority was levied by Montgomery Ward and Company, the giant mail-order house, with three factories, seventy thousand employees, and seventy million customers, who purchased everything from auto parts to boots and shoes. Montgomery Ward was racked with waves of labor troubles and work stoppages until the entire enterprise was seized by Presidential order. The resulting litigation had enormous implications. Montgomery Ward was not a war industry in the manner of the shipyards and aircraft plants previously seized. It was consumer-oriented; if the President could seize it, he could conceivably take over much of the economy.

The principal judicial pronouncement in the Ward situation occurred in the Federal Circuit Court of Appeals (*United States v. Montgomery Ward and Co.*, 150 Fed. [2nd] 369, C.C.A., 7th, 1945). The United States held that both as Commander-in-Chief and as executor of the War Labor Disputes Act, the President could make the seizure. Montgomery Ward argued that the Commander-in-Chief clause was strictly a military power and that the War Labor Disputes Act was not intended to authorize the seizure of plants like its own. The circuit court concluded that the act was applicable and did not choose to consider whether the President acting solely as Commander-in-Chief could make the seizure. A rapprochement between the government and Montgomery Ward precluded a definitive finding by the Supreme Court.

In the Korean conflict President Truman brought down the Supreme Court upon his head when he ordered the seizure of most of the nation's steel mills in the face of a threatened strike, citing "the authority vested in me by the Constitution and laws of the United States." The President ignored the Taft-Hartley Act, which established special procedures for national labor emergencies but did not give him the power of seizure. The Supreme Court in *Youngstown Sheet and Tube Co. v. Sawyer* (343 U.S. 579, 1952) ordered the President and his executive colleagues to stay out of the steel mills, holding that in seizing them he had seized legislative power. Only Congress could have ordered the mills seized; the President lacked power to seize them without its authorization. Like the *Milligan* case, this hastily improvised opinion throws a lasting shadow of doubt over the President's independent seizure power.

Labor too has felt the pressure of the Commander-in-Chief power. In World War II the President by executive order created a War Manpower Commission to manage the mobilization of manpower for employment in the war production industries. Later Roosevelt added to the commission's province the administration of the Selective Service System. The WMC was not long in issuing a "work or fight" order requiring all workers designated as "nondeferable," or those engaged in "nonessential" enterprise, to choose between induction into the armed services and transfer to war production jobs. Draft requirements were simultaneously lowered, and the nation's workers faced a categorical choice: work in a war plant or be drafted into the armed forces.

Communist Warmaking

What the President does as Commander-in-Chief, how he uses his power, is not the simple choice of a self-willed Chief Executive. Far more it is shaped and directed by the environment or the world in which he toils. He is the prisoner of its demands and its possibilities. He has had to adjust his office to the rigors of the nuclear age that have increased his responsibilities to global and interplanetary dimensions. Faced with the dread possibility of nuclear confrontation, he has had to exercise, in his simplest acts in international affairs, a care and caution his predecessors were never burdened to observe.

In the protracted war in Vietnam, with the risky politics and diplomacy that attends it, President Johnson exercised personal command and control over the United States military, distant almost halfway around the world. Johnson visited Vietnam to see the troops and inspect installations. With computerized electronic gear, the President and his aides could talk by telephone with the headquarters of the Pacific command, with planes in flight, and with ships at sea. He could also keep in touch with the front via the Syncom 2 satellite. Spurred by opportunity and necessity, President Johnson and his aides specified targets in North Vietnam, and the numbers of planes and ships and types of weapons to be used in particular raids.[17]

Not the least of the novelties the President has had to cope with are the several species of warfare that the communist powers choose to wage and with which the United States has had little, if any, experience. These are the techniques of guerrilla warfare, infiltration and takeover waged by communist operatives. Contemporary Presidents have faced large-scale "police action," or undeclared war, in Korea, civil war in Greece, guerrilla war in South Vietnam, insurrection in the Canal Zone, a communist revolution in Cuba, and communist infiltration and threatened takeover in other lands. Presidents have committed American forces to combat, as in Korea and Vietnam, and to watch over a change of government in the Dominican Republic. The President oversees vast programs of military and economic aid to nations around the globe, particularly on the communist periphery. He engages in a range of other acts of fluctuating subtlety and success through the CIA.

Something of the strains upon Presidential method caused by communist assertion is conveyed by President Eisenhower's moves to foil a takeover in Guatemala in 1954. In that brief drama's early stage, a ship from the Skoda arms factory in Czechoslovakia bearing two thousand tons of small arms, ammunition, and light artillery pieces, a quantity far beyond Guatemala's normal military requirements, was bound for that country. Nicaragua, alarmed at communist infiltration from neighboring Guatemala, broke off relations. Guatemala's procommunist government suspended constitutional rights, made mass arrests, and executed the leaders of the political opposition. To offset the incoming Czech weaponry, the Eisenhower administration flew arms into Honduras and Nicaragua, threw up a naval quarantine around the beleaguered countries, and detained in the port of Hamburg, Germany, still another shipment of arms destined for Guatemala. Anticommunist forces led by Carlos Castillo Armas, a former Guatemalan colonel, crossed from Honduras into his country and made good progress until they lost two of their three bombers. President Eisenhower, mindful of Latin-American sensitivities and taking anxious counsel, decided to replace the planes. The existing procommunist government was soon deposed, and a new anticommunist ruling junta was established under the watchful eyes of United States Ambassador John Peurifoy, with Colonel Armas at its head.[18]

John Kennedy gave some novel twists to the craft of revolutionary overthrow in the abortive invasion of Cuba in 1961. What distinguished the Cuban enterprise was that its base was on American soil and that the United States government was intimately, although indirectly, involved in its decisions. The initial preparation of the invading force of a thousand and more exiled Cubans was undertaken by the Eisenhower administration in its twilight days. The invaders were trained under United States auspices in Guatemala, and they used staging bases in Nicaragua. They were outfitted with United States aerial bombs, rockets, ammunition, and firearms. Their transports were equipped with guns and radar in New Orleans. The invasion plan was prepared by United States military experts; D-day was known in advance and approved by President Kennedy. He delimited the United States' relation to the project when he declared in a public statement, "There will not be, under any conditions, an intervention in Cuba by United States armed forces." When the invasion, in its desperate hour, faced collapse without United States cover and logistical support, help was not forthcoming. The President held to his word, and the ill-conceived venture failed.[19]

Alliances

In another major response to the division between the western and communist worlds, the contemporary President is heavily engaged as a builder and custodian of alliances, a responsibility his forebears never had to face. He and his deputies have constructed bilateral alliances with nations around the world, committing money, technicians, armaments, and even American soldiers. He has played a leading role in the founding of such multilateral alliances as NATO, SEATO, CENTO, and OAS. He participates in top-level annual NATO conferences. He buoys up the alliances when their inspiration lags in seasons of communist quiet and enheartens them when disaster threatens. He views alliances at times as a step toward a world community, a vehicle for advancing objectives urgent for all mankind. He and his fellow chief executives are restrained and goaded in the common task by the pressures of their inescapable domestic political necessities. The promise and frustration alliances hold for American Chief Executives are illustrated by several encounters John Kennedy experienced with allies.

Kennedy included among his objectives the adoption by the United

States and its allies of efficient and economical American-built weapons systems. He also worked mightily to forestall individual European nations from building their own nuclear weapons, but proposed that their development and use be integrated into the NATO alliance. Kennedy, whose keen sense of political realism extended to the international plane, took up his task conscious that "you can't possibly carry out any policy without causing major frictions."

Kennedy and his principles were severely tested in his confrontation with British Prime Minister Macmillan at their meeting in the Bahamas in December 1962. The subject of discussion was Skybolt, a thousand-mile nuclear-tipped missile launched from high-speed bombers. In a conference with President Eisenhower at Camp David in 1959, Macmillan had arranged for the purchase of one hundred Skybolts at a relatively low price for delivery in 1964. The United States Air Force's candidate for the top weapons vehicle of the next generation, Skybolt was being developed in competition with Polaris and Minuteman. Relying upon Skybolt, the British abandoned their own Blue Streak, a land-based missile, in 1960. The Kennedy administration, faced with climbing weapons costs, decided to abandon Skybolt and concentrate upon other weapons systems. The land-based Minuteman, tests proved, could reach any Skybolt target from underground launching silos in the United States. The administration felt that Minuteman plus Polaris, a submarine-launched missile, would satisfy both American and allied needs for long-range weapons. Abandoning Skybolt would slow the big weapons drain on the United States budget, and, if the British could be induced to accept Polaris, Kennedy could advance another valued objective —the vesting of nuclear weapons not in individual nations but in the trust of alliances to which the United States belonged.

At Nassau, Kennedy gave Macmillan the tidings that Skybolt would be no more and proposed instead that Britian adopt Polaris within a framework of NATO control. Macmillan apparently had little forewarning of the proposal, the President and his aides having just emerged from the engrossing Cuban missile crisis. The Skybolt cancellation was a hard blow to the Royal Air Force and its manned bomber. It was bad budget news for Macmillan because Skybolt, coupled with existing British bombers, was the cheapest possible way of maintaining an independent British deterrent. The cancellation also had implications for British domestic politics. Several days before venturing to Nassau, Macmillan had been a supplicant at the court of Charles de Gaulle, seeking entry to the European Common Market. The Prime Minister suffered the political ignominy of rebuff. At Nassau, with Kennedy's sudden confrontation, he was threatened with a second major political defeat. His party's fortunes were already badly in eclipse at home and an election was impending. Looming political disaster brought Macmillan to drop his accustomed Edwardian gentility and roar back at his Presidential antagonist. But Kennedy held fast and offered Polaris to the British at the lowest possible price, with the proviso that although the missiles would operate under NATO, they would pass under British command in "supreme national" emergency. Macmillan ultimately acquiesced, enabling Kennedy to improve his budgetary position and advance his purpose of international-izing nuclear weapons.[20]

Kennedy's policy of nuclear interdependence fared less well with another traditional American ally, France. His careful and reasoned arguments were repulsed by the imperial personality of President de Gaulle. Bent upon re-storing French grandeur and perhaps upon asserting his own, De Gaulle was not one to work easily in alliance. Kennedy meanwhile pushed his policy to the point of withholding American aid for French nuclear ambitions. But the Kennedy policy was not all of one piece. His administration delivered to the French an atomic-powered submarine, promised by the Eisenhower ad-ministration, and a dozen aerial tankers of the KC-130 type, capable of refueling French bombers that could be armed with nuclear weapons. The Kennedy administration termed these concessions "peripheral" (its standard term for retreats from major objectives) and a sensible recognition of France's commitment to an independent nuclear policy.[21]

As leader of alliances, the President has the unhappy task of prodding laggard member nations to honor their obligations. President Kennedy had several sharp encounters with the Diefenbaker government of Canada over its failure to act upon commitments under the American-Canadian military alliance. Canada had never fulfilled a 1958 agreement with the United States to install nuclear warheads on Bomarc missiles at two sites on Cana-dian soil. Canada likewise had not acted upon her NATO obligation to equip her interceptor squadrons in Europe with nuclear weapons. Canada's lapses brought Kennedy to permit hostile expressions from his own State De-partment and the NATO commander, General Lauris Norstad.[22]

But if the President gives criticism, he is also the object of it and the suspicions and resentments of his country's allies. West Germany, fearful of any weakening of western military defenses in Berlin, was privately dis-tressed and required considerable reassurance in mid-1963 after the United States removed six hundred troops from its West Berlin garrison.[23] The United States' Asiatic allies were often critical that the United States over-concentrated upon Europe to the neglect of the East, at least prior to the Vietnam war. Pakistan openly charged in 1963 that the United States was indifferent to CENTO, in contrast to NATO, upon which it seemed to shower its treasure and concern.[24]

Nuclear Weaponry

The President bears the awesome responsibility to our allies, to his own peo-ple, indeed to all mankind, of deciding when if ever to use the vast arsenal of American nuclear weaponry. Under law only he, the Commander-in-Chief, can give the order. He has done so on but one occasion—near the end of World War II, when Truman ordered atomic bombs to be dropped on Hiroshima and Nagasaki in 1945. Later Presidents have threatened to use nuclear weapons. In 1953 President Eisenhower threatened Communist China with nuclear attack unless it supported a truce in Korea.[25] In his 1962 confrontation with the Soviets over their emplacement of offensive missiles in Cuba, President Kennedy put the Strategic Air Command and Air Force missile crews on maximum alert. One hundred fifty-six intercontinental ballistic missiles, based in the western part of the nation and with flight ranges of at least 6,300 miles, were readied and pointed presumably at the Soviet Union, if the President's speech to the nation on October 22 is a guide. Kennedy then warned, "It shall be the policy of this nation to regard any nuclear missile launched from Cuba against any nation in the Western Hemisphere as an attack on the United States requiring a full retaliatory response upon the Soviet Union."[26]

In facing his responsibility for nuclear weapons, the Chief Executive has been absorbed in two concerns. One is keeping the ultimate decision in his own hands. "I don't want some young Colonel to decide when to drop an atomic bomb," President Truman was known to say. The other is the avoidance of the dread possibility of an "accidental" nuclear war. Both problems thrust the President well into a complex of mechanisms and procedures regulating the release of nuclear weapons.[27]

The complex begins at the Ballistic Missile Early Warning System (BMEWS) in Thule, Greenland, where radar screens are poised to pick up Soviet missiles, if they are ever launched against the United States. BMEWS intelligence is simultaneously flashed to the North American Air Defense Command (NORAD) in Colorado Springs, Colorado, for interpretation; to the Strategic Air Command (SAC) control post near Omaha, Nebraska; to the Joint War Room of the Joint Chiefs of Staff in the Pentagon; and to the President. Several kinds of radio systems, telephones, teletypes, and television link these points. Multiple routings, frequencies, and circuits; alternate locations; verifications by senders and recipients that the messages actually come from their presumed source; procedures to challenge and counterchallenge the verifications; hundreds of men to pass the word to the button-pushers, who also number in the hundreds, all contribute to the vast effort to find safety.

The policy-makers, generals, psychologists, sociologists, and physicists charged with tightening the safety factor must deal with several types of possible human failure. Elaborate testing and "redundancy" procedures help thwart the kind of situation that arose in 1958 when a berserk sergeant threatened to fire a pistol at a nuclear bomb but was fortunately talked out of it by a supervisor. Suppose the President of the United States "goes ape," as the military say? Or suppose he singlehandedly decides to reverse national policy and launch a preventive war? The President too is subject to checks. Even he cannot simply pick up his telephone and order "go," nor does he know the one signal for a nuclear strike—the "go code." In an emergency he would receive intelligence via the "gold phone circuit" that connects him with the offices, action stations, and homes of the Secretary of Defense, the Joint Chiefs of Staff, the SAC commander, and others, all of whom could assist in his decision. An agenda with key questions concerning the probable emergency has been prepared, which could be administered quickly and in code. Time is a slight safety factor. In the existing state of weapons systems, the President has a possible thirty minutes after the report of launched enemy ICBM's to consult and await further information before unleashing a full, irrevocable "go" order.

Suppose the President is out of reach, dead, or believed dead? In his book *The Death of a President,* William Manchester contends that the assassination of President Kennedy caught Lyndon Johnson so poorly briefed on his responsibilities as Commander-in-Chief that if a Soviet nuclear attack had been launched that afternoon, it could have crippled the American power to retaliate. But security officials who were on duty at the time immediately challenged this view and contended that Johnson had been coached thoroughly on the procedures to be followed in case of a nuclear attack. President Kennedy, the officials said, had insisted that the Vice President be fully informed.[28]

Chief Executives have been concerned with several species of non-Presidential safety factors. President Kennedy asked for more funds from Congress to speed movements across the whole gamut of warning systems. He pushed construction of the Polaris and hardened Minutemen capable of withstanding surprise attack, thus reducing the need for a hair-trigger response to enemy actions. Kennedy arranged the "hot line" to Moscow to deal with breakdowns and miscalculations of the kind featured in the novel *Fail-Safe.*[29] The Kennedy administration also instituted a new lock system for the nation's huge and far-flung nuclear weapons arsenal. Through remote-control devices comparable to those used on ordinary television sets, officials at central locations can control the many thousands of United States nuclear warheads around the world that are in stockpiles or attached to weapons maintained in a continuing alert status. In his further notable efforts to reduce the risks of nuclear war, Kennedy consummated the 1963 test ban treaty with the Soviet Union and labored tirelessly, although unsuccessfully, to dissuade the French from building their own nuclear forces.

President Johnson promoted the treaty prohibiting states from placing nuclear arms or other weapons of mass destruction in orbit around the earth. The treaty also bars the installing of those weapons on the moon or on other celestial bodies.[30] In 1968 Johnson could hail the adoption of a treaty to prevent the spread of nuclear weapons by barring the five nuclear powers from transferring nuclear weapons to nations that do not have them.

The Scientific Community

A major by-product of the President's preoccupation with nuclear weapons is his deepening relationships with the scientific community. The capability of his military establishment depends increasingly upon the efficiency of their research; in hard decisions he looks for their counsel. Scientists were consulted when President Truman weighed how he would use the newly developed atomic bomb. Then, as they often have been in facing momentous Presidential issues, the scientists were divided. Some advocated a purely technical demonstration, others a military application best designed to induce Japanese surrender.

Scientists, like the President they serve, have lived in the coils of a continuing predicament. They spend their lives improving the United States' weapon capability, but they feel conscience-bound to reduce the possibilities that the terrible weapons will ever be used. Scientists counseled the President when he took his first steps toward committing the United States to the international control of atomic weapons. The result was the Truman-Atlee-King declaration of November 15, 1945, which called upon the United Nations to establish a commission to develop proposals to promote peaceful uses of atomic energy, eliminate nuclear weapons, and foster an open world. The declaration was prepared by Vannevar Bush, director of the Office of Scientific Research and Development, with the help of Niels Bohr, Leo Szilard, and other scientists.

The Soviet Union's development of an atomic bomb in 1949 hurtled the scientists and the President into a formidable new issue. Should the United States, in the face of the Soviet achievement, forge ahead in the race by developing a hydrogen bomb? The President again received divided scientific counsel. One sector of scientific opinion deemed the bomb both feasible and necessary to the nation's security. Another sector urged the President "to tell the American public and the world that we think [it] wrong on fundamental ethical principles to initiate the development of such a weapon." America's abstention, these scientists also argued, would set an example that might limit the extent of war and raise the hope of mankind. President Truman ultimately ordered the development of the hydrogen bomb.

The Russians' atomic achievements also thrust the President into a difficult and at times agonizing new relationship with scientists. He had to determine at times whether particular scientists were "security risks" and therefore should be barred from access to classified government information. After 1949 the suspicions of legislators and administrators of the loyalty of scientists rose markedly. Late in 1953 William L. Borden, a former executive staff director of the Congressional Joint Committee on Atomic Energy, wrote to FBI Director J. Edgar Hoover that it was his "own exhaustively considered opinion, based upon years of study, of the available classified evidence, that more probably than not J. Robert Oppenheimer is an agent of the Soviet Union." An FBI report on Oppenheimer was prepared and ultimately forwarded to President Eisenhower. "This report," he has written, "jolted me."[31] The President, after consultations, directed that sensitive agencies were to erect at once a "blank wall" between Oppenheimer and classified information. With the President's approval, a three-man board headed by Gordon Gray, president of the University of North Carolina, was appointed to conduct a hearing. The hearing drew upon forty witnesses and produced three thousand pages of testimony. By a vote of two to one the Gray board found Oppenheimer a security risk, although a loyal citizen. The Atomic Energy Commission (AEC), Oppenheimer's employer, approved the Gray board's finding by a vote of four to one. President Eisenhower concurred in the finding and Oppenheimer's clearance was not reinstated.

But the President not only taketh away, he also giveth. Shortly before his death President Kennedy concluded plans for a White House ceremony for the presentation of the Enrico Fermi award to Oppenheimer for his "outstanding contributions to theoretical physics and his scientific and administrative leadership." When Kennedy's assassination intervened, President Johnson made the presentation in an early act of office-holding, to the satisfaction of many in the scientific community, who had long been seeking a symbolic clearance of Oppenheimer's name.[32]

Before the Soviet Union's launching of Sputnik, in October 1957, the President, for all of the importance of science in national life, had no regular, full-time scientific staff in his White House organization. In the wake of Sputnik the post of special assistant to the President for science and technology was created, with James Killian, president of the Massachusetts Institute of Technology, as the first incumbent. The existing Science Advisory Committee was brought to the White House level. President Eisenhower was soon turning to his scientific associates for alternative advice to the views of the Pentagon and Atomic Energy Commission. In Eisenhower's closing Presidential years, his scientific counselors debated intensively the scientific feasibility and the political desirability of a nuclear test ban. Ultimately Eisenhower, spurred by certain scientific advisers and Secretary of State Dulles, embarked upon negotiations for a nuclear test ban agreement, a major reversal in American nuclear policy that was finally consummated in the test ban treaty of President Kennedy.

In the test ban venture scientists served Presidents Eisenhower and Kennedy as both negotiators and counselors.[33] Eisenhower dispatched a scientific delegation to Geneva in mid-1958 to meet with their British and Russian counterparts and consider methods for policing a nuclear test ban. Out of their work emerged Eisenhower's proposal on August 22, 1958, that the three nuclear powers negotiate a treaty for the permanent suspension of nuclear weapon testing. To provide himself with continual advice on test ban problems, Eisenhower appointed a Committee of Principals—outside the

National Security Council, interestingly—whose membership included the special assistant for science and technology plus the heads of the State and Defense Departments, the CIA, and the AEC.

Although the Eisenhower disarmament effort ended in an impasse, President Kennedy, upon entering office, resolved to try again and convened a panel of scientists under James Fisk, president of Bell Laboratories, to evaluate the American position and recommend modifications. Out of Fisk's panel and the work of the President's disarmament adviser, John J. McCloy, came a draft treaty. The awakening hopes were crushed when the Soviet resumed its testing program and soon, at Kennedy's order, the United States did likewise. For this new situation the President again needed scientific counsel. Had the self-imposed moratorium on American testing enabled the Russians to overcome the American lead in nuclear weapons? The finding that the American lead was intact although reduced encouraged Kennedy to pursue the test ban treaty. As the negotiations advanced, Kennedy like Eisenhower was faced with absolute cleavage within the scientific community on the technical feasibility of a control system to monitor a nuclear test ban. Ultimately, Kennedy drove himself to choose between the conflicting schools. Presidents, with their ample experiences of the 1950's and 1960's, would readily concur with C. P. Snow that the task of decision-making in the modern scientific world is "one of the most intractable that organized society has thrown up."[34] Although scientists have not provided neat, reassuring guideposts in Presidential policy-making in the field of nuclear weapons, they have achieved a full partnership with political administrators and the military.

The Future Presidency

It is debatable whether the contemporary President, for all of his riches in terrible weapons, has more self-determining military power than such predecessors of his as Theodore Roosevelt and James K. Polk. The contemporary President suffers limitations of power unknown to nineteenth- and early twentieth-century incumbents. He must work with allies whose good will must be courted and whose favor fluctuates. His acts are challengeable in an ongoing world organization, the United Nations. Earlier Presidents suffered neither of these fetters. Because of the sheer horror of nuclear weapons, the contemporary President is conscience- and duty-bound to leave nothing undone to avoid general war. This solemn obligation requires him to protect national security by toiling diligently even at unpromising negotiations and to resort to force only in the most extreme urgency. He lives with the haunting realization that the merest local incidents can escalate into situations of world-wide importance. His predecessors worried little over such subtleties. When, in the early nineteenth century, the Tripolitan powers dared seize a

United States frigate, the President dispatched a force to punish them and Congress showed its enthusiasm by declaring war. But in 1968, when North Korea seized the *Pueblo*, President Johnson was a model of restraint, limiting himself to diplomatic moves, in which the general opinion of Congress heartily concurred.

As Commanders-in-Chief, future Presidents will face the test of the adequacy of their powers and their adaptability to fast-changing world realities as never before.

1. The Commander-in-Chief must now and hereafter be both strong and restrained. His most solemn duty is to maintain his nuclear power and the general military establishment in a state of strength that will effectively deter the rival camp. Not only must he possess this strength, but he must communicate its true degree intelligibly and convincingly at home and abroad. But his companion duty is to keep his nuclear power in check, to avoid the appearance of bomb-rattling, and to press simultaneously for the settlement of international differences through diplomatic negotiation.

2. The President will face the continuing question of "How much is enough?" in developing the nation's armed strength. His answers to this question involve him with Congress, the allied powers, and his own scientific and military communities. It is the weightiest question our political system imposes upon the fragile structure of President-Congress relations. The question admits of no single answer but evokes many responses. At one extreme is the tendency of Presidents of the nuclear age to appreciate that missile production, too, has diminishing returns; President Johnson expressed the view that nuclear defense expenditures can never be justified as a grand relief project for the economies of local communities and the states. At an opposite extreme is former Secretary of Defense McNamara's 1964 testimony to the House Foreign Affairs Committee that Congress had jeopardized the nation's security in cutting the foreign aid program of the year before by 30 per cent.[35] Both Democratic and Republican committee members were understandably stung by the Secretary's implication that Congress had acted irresponsibly and could not be relied on to provide an adequate military program.

3. It has never been more urgent for the President to demonstrate to our allies and competitors that the President is truly the Commander-in-Chief, supported by the vast Department of Defense, by highly competent Joint Chiefs of Staff, and by the houses of Congress. Only a strong President can rise to and hold such dominance. To be strong he clearly requires a strong Secretary of Defense, his chief deputy, whose powers have steadily increased since the office began in 1947. The JCS have seen a limited increase in the powers of their chairman, though their relations with the President have been uneven. Any tendency toward a still more powerful chairman, even

perhaps a single chief of staff, would sizably strengthen the President's position as organizer and director of the armed forces.

4. The limitation of the arms race through international agreement will remain a large preoccupation of the President. Only a strong Chief Executive can press the case upon Congress and the people that a spiraling arms race is a threat to the nation's security. The individual services and the Congressional committees to which they are allied will provide a fierce resistance that only the Chief Executive can overcome. He alone can keep alive useful proposals that at first are rejected and assure that new possibilities are considered. The Commander-in-Chief does not simply conduct war or stay prepared for the threat of it. He has a further mission upon which the nation's and the world's future depends—the Commander-in-Chief also keeps the peace.

The Economy 11

In his economic duties the Chief Executive is caught in a power gap. He functions in the one major nation of the world whose economic order and tradition are founded on private enterprise. He presides over a pluralistic economy in which private enterprise makes the key decisions of what and how much to produce, when and at what price, and how profits shall be used. The extent of private decision is evidenced by the gap that may exist between what the President tries to do and what he accomplishes. The President can toil, plan, and hope for prosperity, but there may be only depression. He can thunder against the trusts, but big enterprise may grow apace. He can come into office pledged to get the country "moving again," but for all his exertion the economy may only lag.

The several administrative agencies of the executive branch dealing with the economy differ widely in their responsiveness to the President. The Bureau of the Budget and the Council of Economic Advisers are *his* agencies and behave accordingly. The great operating departments—Treasury, Commerce, Labor, and Agriculture—are part of his cabinet family and partners to large and intimate decisions of his administration. An array of independent regulatory commissions—the Federal Reserve Board, the Securities and Exchange Commission, the Interstate Commerce Commission, and the like— make basic decisions in vital economic areas such as banking and credit, the sale of securities, the conduct of the stock exchanges, transportation, and communications. The independent commissions are carefully removed from the President's line of command. He has influence but lacks authority over them.

The limitations of his economic powers enthrone the President on the jagged prongs of a predicament. His authority over the economy does not equal his responsibility for its condition. Legally and administratively, he has important but severely limited means to influence its health and growth. As Martin Van Buren and Herbert Hoover would gladly have testified on the election nights of 1840 and 1932, the voters hold the Chief Executives responsible for the plight of their jobs and their pocketbooks above all else.

Yet for all of the limitations he suffers in his authority, the President has more impact upon the economy than any single source or possible combination of private power.The substantial authority and influence he possesses make him the head of the economic administration of the country. He applies quantities of laws promoting, regulating, and planning economic affairs. The Employment Act of 1946, a grand codification of his responsibilities, broadly charges him to lay before Congress each January an economic report on levels and trends of production, employment, and purchasing power, and to recommend ways to stimulate them. He collects taxes to provide roads, airports, research, and other services vital to industry. Thanks to its military needs, the executive branch, which the President manages, is the nation's largest purchaser. The aircraft and shipping industries would indeed be in a perilous state were not the United States government their best customer. Through loans and guarantees administered by the Commodity Credit Corporation, the Federal Housing Authority, the Federal Deposit Insurance Corporation, and other vast agencies the President reduces or erases the risk to private enterprise. As administrator of the social security programs, he softens the cruelties of unemployment, illness, and old age. In the nearly two centuries of his office's existence, the Chief Executive has in fact presided over a variety of economies, including simple agricultural, industrial, financial, and state capitalism. He has lived through the scientific and technological revolution of the mid-twentieth century, and its crowning feature, automation, may well require him to face basic changes in social attitudes toward work and leisure. In that great and difficult event, the President will rightly be expected to provide leadership.

The President as Friend of Business

Living as they do in an economic world where decisions of private industry have much to do with economic health, Presidents as a lot assume that harmony and confidence between government and business are profitable to both. This benign assumption burns weakest in economic depression and brightest in war, when the nation's survival depends upon coordinated public and private economic effort. Presidents, for all their good intentions, differ widely in their individual dispositions toward business. Calvin Coolidge's worshipful dictum "The business of America is business" bespeaks his administration's total dedication to helping business. No President can be said to be antibusiness. Franklin D. Roosevelt, who waged fierce struggles to reform the worst business malpractices and said harsh things about "economic royalists" and "unscrupulous money-changers," accepted the basic structure and premises of the business community. "I am certain," his Secretary of Labor, Frances Perkins, well observed, "that he had no dream of great changes in the economic or political patterns of our life."[1] Roosevelt limited his rejection of private enterprise to TVA and several sister projects in the belief that popular and business power needs could not be adequately supplied by private means. He apparently never wished government to take over the railroads, the coal mines, or any other basic industry. He considered government ownership both clumsy and unnecessary.

Republican Presidents view business fondly, and their modern Democratic brethren tend to be critical, although Lyndon Johnson's position was somewhere in between. He treated business as a most favored constituency against a background of pulsating prosperity and record profits, conditions of well-being that he never tired reminding his business audiences of. Johnson won business support for his 1964 program of tax cuts by promising to hold down government spending and by blotting out tax reforms that Kennedy had asked for earlier. As well, Johnson let it be known that business was not to be harassed, a sentiment that quickly prompted federal regulatory agencies to curb any aggressive tendencies that might have been budding. Johnson put through a relaxation of tax rules on depreciation, affording hundreds of millions of dollars in bonuses to corporations. He promised to sell off government enterprises competing with private business and pushed through a big reduction in excise taxes long clamored for by manufacturers. Although he nurtured radical social programs, he held them to moderate size by feeding them modest budgets and developed an image of fiscal respectability that delighted the business community. On the several occasions when he went to the mat with giants of the business world, Johnson avoided head-on conflicts and preserved a framework of ever-renewable relations. He acted as though consensus politics is the key to economic prosperity. The economy does best when confidence surges between business and government, and consensus politics is the wand that weaves the magic spell.

The President's relations with the components of the business community may differ widely at any one time. The community is not a monolith but a sprawling, continental, indeed intercontinental, pluralism whose members' interests differ markedly by region (Wall Street and the East versus the West), by size (big, intermediate, and small business), and by function (manufacture, wholesale, and retail). A single industry may contain both "liberal" enterprises that are public-minded and public-relations conscious and "conservative" enterprises whose self-interest blinds them to national necessity and who habitually fight governmental regulation in Congress and the courts. Presidents are wily enough to exploit business differences. The easiest and most commonly employed tactic is to pursue policies that appeal to the many and offend the few in the business community. In launching his famous antitrust suit against the Northern Securities Company, a giant consolidation of the James J. Hill, J. P. Morgan, and E. H. Harriman railways, which embraced nothing less than the Northern Pacific, the Great Northern, and the Chicago, Burlington, and Quincy systems, Theodore Roosevelt scored a ten-strike in the esteem of the majority of the business world. They hailed Roosevelt's crusade joyfully because the Northern Securities Company was the outcome of a massive struggle between Morgan and Harriman on which most businessmen blamed the panic of 1901.

By word and deed the business community bestows its approval or disfavor upon the Presidents. The United States Steel Corporation abstained from raising its prices in the eight Presidential years of Dwight Eisenhower but boosted them twice during the three years of John Kennedy. The New Deal's cleansing and chastising of business created a lasting embitterment. No President has been more widely hated in the upper economic stratum than Franklin Roosevelt was. Visitors to J. P. Morgan in New Deal days were forewarned against mentioning the Roosevelt name lest it launch the mighty financier into apoplectic rage.[2]

Winning Business Confidence

Presidents hankering to rouse business confidence in their administrations apply a variety of old and proven nostrums. A standard remedy is the appointment of businessmen to responsible administration posts. Even Presidents like the Roosevelts, with large reputations for ferocity toward business, carefully provided "balance" in their administrations by including prestigious businessmen in them. Franklin Roosevelt counted heavily upon Jesse H. Jones, chairman of the Reconstruction Finance Corporation, to maintain an image of respectability in the eyes of the business community. A wealthy, monumental Texan who had built a fortune in the grand manner in banking, real estate, and newspapers, Jones was a paragon of success by business standards. The price of his services came high, but Roosevelt cheerfully paid it. "Whenever we did anything of importance, that was on the borderline of our authority," Jones said once in explaining the ground rules at RFC, "I would try at first opportunity to tell the President about it, but after the fact. He was always interested, and he never criticized." Roosevelt, in turn, never failed to appreciate the usefulness of Jones's gilt-edged prestige with business and Congress. "Your conservatism is a good thing for us in this Administration," the President would reassure the great Texan.[3] In the Kennedy and Johnson years, the Treasury and Commerce posts were reserved for appointees who stood high in the confidence and regard of the business community.

In cultivating business confidence, Presidents work hard at tilling an image of fiscal responsibility. When national circumstances force the budget into imbalance, Presidents, with the aid of wizard-technicians of the fiscal arts, resort to elaborate hocus-pocus to maintain at least the window-dressing of fiscal respectability. For example, in his early Presidential years Franklin Roosevelt could face the nation with a balanced budget by the simple expedient of putting his costly recovery programs into a separate account. Even Democratic Presidents with solid reputations as big spenders put in hours of anxious cogitation in choosing between launching a costly program and suppressing it in the interest of fiscal soundness. The President's attention to economy may be as much a reflection of personal conviction as it is of deliberate public relations. Franklin Roosevelt was viewed by several of his colleagues as perpetually torn between two contending forces in his Presidential psyche. His natural instinct tended to fiscal tidiness and a balanced budget; he wished also, during the depression's depths, to do right by the unemployed. As plans were laid for work relief and social security, the question he was most apt to ask with unfeigned anxiety was, "Will it ruin us financially?" Invariably he included among his counselors those whose lives represented an unbroken consecration to conventional fiscal policy. Lewis Douglas, Director of the Budget, chanted the virtues of the balanced budget and a Hoover-like program of subsistence relief, with wages, hours, and prices shaped by natural economic forces. When Douglas eventually departed, Henry Morgenthau, Jr., as Secretary of the Treasury, made temperate public spending his special cause.

A President may keep business confidence at high flame by fraternizing with leading businessmen conspicuously more than with any other species of citizenry. The guests most frequently invited to President Eisenhower's stag dinners, social functions with incidental discussions of the administration's purposes, were businessmen. In his hours on the golf course Eisenhower's favorite companions were George E. Allen, a puckish corporation director; William E. Robinson, president of Coca-Cola; and Clifford G. Roberts, a New York banker. A President and his aides may seek to rally the business community behind their cause by wooing it with speeches. During his first year in office Kennedy waged a campaign of proportions unequaled in Presidential history to induce industry's cooperation in his efforts to maintain stable prices, without which he could not hope to secure labor's vital support in paring down its wage and fringe demands. Business could swallow the bitter price medicine more easily if it were sweetened with evidences of the administration's general concern for its interests. Administration officials plied business with sympathetic speeches and promised a balanced budget, better depreciation allowances, and other policies that business cherished.

A President may cultivate business by consulting it on problems and policies of mutual concern. In 1962, following his head-on collision with the United States Steel Corporation over its rising prices, which had resulted in part at least from a failure in business-government communications, Kennedy moved to avoid any similar lapses in the future by establishing the Business Council. The President took up with the council, composed of the presidents and chairmen of large corporations, such knotty problems as the balance of payments and the outflow of gold. One year after the steel price encounter, at the council's meetings at Hot Springs, West Virginia, Kennedy could listen with high satisfaction to the testimony of corporate executives that they were less nervous about business-government relations than they had been at any time since his inauguration.

Much of the President's economic policy may advance both the President's and business's purposes. The income tax, established by constitutional amendment in 1913, is not merely an enormous producer of revenue but a reflector of an administration's underlying economic philosophy and a means of slowing or quickening general economic activity. Presidents Harding, Coolidge, and Hoover were more or less the spokesmen for the view of their Secretary of the Treasury, Andrew Mellon, that "the prosperity of the middle and lower classes depended upon the good fortunes and light taxes of the rich." Taxes that were too high, Mellon believed, would prevent the rich from saving and would make them reluctant to invest. If they failed to save and invest, the economy would ultimately falter. When Mellon took office in 1921, the income tax's top rate was 73 per cent; in 1925, thanks to Mellon's pressure, it was down to 25 per cent. A broader distribution of stimulants was arranged by the Kennedy-Johnson tax-reduction bill enacted in 1964. It was expected by both its Presidential sponsors to stimulate consumer demand and business investment, which in turn would promote increased employment and production, sustain the growth of the economy, and hopefully avert recessions.

The most pervasive of all taxes—the tariff—can also advance or obstruct a broad sweep of the President's economic policies. When in 1921 the Republican Congress pushed through an emergency tariff bill raising the rates to protect the United States against the produce of depressed European labor, President Wilson declared in a veto, "If there ever was a time when America had anything to fear from foreign competition, that time has passed. If we wish to have Europe settle her debts, governmental or commercial, we must be prepared to buy from her."[4] But Wilson's wish was in vain and the Fordney-McCumber Tariff Act of 1922 boosted rates to new highs. And Presidents Harding and Coolidge, employing their discretionary authority under the act to adjust rates, tended to raise them even further. The Fordney-McCumber Act and its administration fostered the concentration of domestic economic power, prevented Europe from paying her obligations to the United States in the form of goods, and brought reprisals from foreign countries.

But discretionary Presidential authority to adjust rates may also promote trade, as demonstrated by the Reciprocal Trade Agreements Act of 1934, which authorized the President to negotiate with various countries trade agreements altering United States tariffs by not more than 50 per cent. The Trade Expansion Act of 1962 goes even further. It authorizes the President to cut tariffs in general as much as 50 per cent, to eliminate tariffs on goods of which the United States and the European Common Market account for 80 per cent of the free world trade, and to cancel tariffs on tropical products on which the tariff is no more than 5 per cent of the value. Never before has the President possessed so much power over foreign trade. The act was designed to help the balance of payments problem and to open up the Common Market and other countries to American goods, especially farm products.

Frictions

The President's dialogue with business takes on a tougher weave when he endeavors to persuade the business community to come around to some action that although vital to national welfare does not altogether square with business's self-interest. One of the more emphatic passages of Presidential discord with private enterprise occurred in 1916, when a major railroad strike confronted the nation. President Wilson summoned the railroad owners to the White House and eloquently appealed to them to accept a compromise he had devised to resolve the dispute. Wilson's formula called for an eight-hour day, no raises, and time and a half for overtime. For all Wilson's exhortation that his plan was fair and that the national interest required its acceptance, the railroad owners were negative and adamant. The President was butting his head against the rock of Gibraltar. Upon reaching this conclusion, Wilson, not a man of any great patience, rose from the conference table. His face twisted with anger, he exclaimed, "I pray to God to forgive you; I never can," and left the room.[5]

A President may also negotiate with individual titans of industry with great consequence to the economy. The most fabulous of these negotiations took place in 1905 between Theodore Roosevelt and the unsurpassed presence, J. Pierpont Morgan. Morgan was building his empire with no-holds-barred fury; the administration had mounted its trust-busting policy; a head-on collision was a matter of time. Morgan decided to talk to Roosevelt. In the lengthy interview Theodore Roosevelt was bemused by the mighty Morgan's notions of the character and status of the United States Presidency. "Mr. Morgan," Roosevelt noted afterward, "could not help regarding me as a big rival operator, who either intended to ruin all his interests, or else could be induced to come to an agreement to ruin none."

The Morgan way of dealing with the United States Presidency came into full play on a January day in 1905 when an official of the Bureau of Corporations of the Department of Commerce and Labor appeared in the offices of Elbert Gary, board chairman of the United States Steel Corporation, a Morgan enterprise, to discuss the bureau's impending investigation of the company. With Morgan's encouragement, the astute Gary, a suave erstwhile judge, arranged a meeting at the White House with Secretary of Commerce and Labor Victor H. Metcalf, Commissioner of Corporations James R. Garfield, and Theodore Roosevelt. Gary opened the session by amiably declaring that he would not challenge the constitutionality of the Commerce and Labor Department's request that U.S. Steel open its books and records. In return for this benevolence, Gary tactfully invited the administration to pledge that any information gleaned from U.S. Steel's files would be used not by subordinate government officials but "by the President alone for his guidance in making such suggestions to Congress concerning legislation as might be proper, expedient, and for the actual benefit of the general public." If questions should arise over the use of material that Gary deemed confidential, he, Garfield, and Metcalf would seek agreement, and that failing, the President would decide. A memorandum of the conference was prepared to Theodore Roosevelt's satisfaction.

The Gary-Roosevelt concordat was put to a test one year later when the administration brought International Harvester, another Morgan company, under scrutiny. Would International Harvester be satisfied with whatever the Commerce and Labor Department's findings were, Theodore Roosevelt teasingly asked George W. Perkins, the Morgan representative. Perkins responded uninhibitedly. The company expected, he said, "the Department frankly [to] come to us and point out any mistakes or technical violations of any law; then give us a chance to correct them, if we could or would, and . . . if we did, then we would expect the Attorney General not to bring proceedings."[6] Although Roosevelt, in ensuing brass-tacks discussions, was somewhat more demanding than Perkins anticipated, International Harvester pretty well passed muster at the White House.

In making secret deals with Morgan and his men, Roosevelt risked raising the hackles of progressives who surely would interpret his behavior as a betrayal of the people. But Roosevelt was not merely doling out approval to the Morgan interests. The President was playing a game, too. In arranging secret pacts, Roosevelt was achieving a cherished peace with Wall Street at a juncture when its aid was critical to the advance through Congress of the topmost item of his economic program, the Hepburn railroad bill. Roosevelt also aimed to achieve in the Morgan consultations new and mutually more rewarding government-business dealings than the barren negativism of the Sherman Act had thus far permitted.

How Presidents Fight Business

When business fails to cooperate or openly fights the President, he may resort to an armory of diverse and potent weapons. A most important one is the whiplash of adverse publicity. When Standard Oil was charged with secretly eliciting lower shipping rates from the railroads to the utter grief of its competitors, Theodore Roosevelt accompanied the ponderous government report in which the finding was made with a lusty personal blast at Standard Oil. The President's remarks took on an extra surge of vehemence from his discovery that a glaring national disclosure of Standard's sins would greatly enhance his chances for securing his precious Hepburn railroad bill. President John Archbold of Standard Oil, after several applications of the shrillest Presidential criticism, concluded that "darkest Abyssinia never saw anything like the course of treatment which we experienced at the hands of the Administration."[7]

At his beck and call the President has scores of statutes enacted over the decades by which he can prod business toward behaving as he wants. One of the President's favorite weapons in moving upon recalcitrant industry is the antitrust laws, beginning with the Sherman Act of 1890. John Kennedy, for example, busily used these laws to hold back prices in his fight against inflation. His administration brought case after case against the price-fixing of bakery products, milk, moving vans, building materials, and the like.

The President can also regulate business by drawing upon his "prerogative," or power directly granted him by the Constitution. The most enriching provisions for the prerogative-minded President are the opening clause of Article II ("The Executive power shall be vested in a President of the United States of America") and his designation as "Commander-in-Chief." Prerogative is usually exerted in crisis, in war or economic decline, and it is often buttressed by statutes delegating broad powers to the President. From World War I on, industry's growing involvement in warmaking has made it the frequent object of Presidential prerogative. Before the Pearl Harbor attack, for example, Franklin Roosevelt, citing his earlier proclamation of "unlimited national emergency," seized an aviation plant and pointed to the "duty constitutionally and inherently resting upon the President to exert his civil and military as well as his moral authority to keep the defensive efforts of the United States a going concern" and "to obtain supplies for which Congress has appropriated money, and which it has directed the President to obtain."[8]

The employ of Presidential prerogative in labor-management disputes was set back badly in the Supreme Court's review of President Truman's seizure of the steel industry midway in the Korean "police action." In *Youngstown Sheet and Tube Co. v. Sawyer* (343 U.S. 579, 1952) the Court struck down the President's action as unconstitutional. The President, in moving upon the steel strike, had relied upon prerogative and ignored the Taft-Hartley Act passed by a Republican-controlled Congress in 1947, subjecting Presidential intervention in labor-management disputes to a specified procedure. Truman had vetoed the bill, holding partly that his prerogative was sufficient for labor-management crises. Congress, in turn, overrode his veto and Truman solemnly avowed he would observe the new law. When a steel strike loomed in April 1952, however, the President ignored the Taft-Hartley Act and its eighty-day no-strike provision and, brandishing his prerogative, seized the steel mills. Pointing to the mountainous military requirements of the nation and its allies, he invoked "the authority vested in me by the Constitution and laws of the United States."

The central proposition of the Court's opinion was that since Congress could have ordered seizure of the steel mills, the President lacked the power of seizure without specific legislative authorization. This altogether novel doctrine was unsupported by reference to previous decision or practice. The Court also blithely overlooked innumerable historical instances of Presidential pioneering in territory eventually occupied by Congress, in the manner of President Washington's issuance of the first neutrality proclamation in 1793 and Congress's enactment, a year later, of the first neutrality statute.

In addition to statutes and prerogative, the President can summon a variety of "pressures" to encourage industry's "cooperation." Glimpses into the character of these pressures are provided by John Kennedy's sharp encounter with U.S. Steel in 1962.[9] Eager to hold the steel price line against inflation, the Kennedy administration, by energetic persuasion, had brought the steel union to curb its wage and fringe demands and agree to a two-year compact with the United States Steel Corporation. The administration emerged with the blissful expectation that the steel industry in reciprocal sensitivity to the nation's welfare would make no price increases. Suddenly U.S. Steel raised its prices, and other big steel companies quickly followed its lead.

Kennedy and his aides, deeming the steel companies' action nothing less than a double-cross, unloosed a barrage of pressures. Hopefully, the few steel companies that had not raised their prices could be induced to refrain from doing so. Several administration aides even dared to surmise that if only a few companies held out, market forces would induce the giants to drop their price increases. The administration gave the pressure faucets a quick full turn. In a nationally televised news conference, the President questioned the patriotism of the "tiny handful of steel executives—whose pursuit of power and profit exceeds their sense of public responsibility." The President asked Senator Estes Kefauver, Democrat of Tennessee and chairman of the Senate Antitrust subcommittee, to express publicly his "dismay" over the price rise and consider an investigation. These the Senator gladly did. The Justice Department and the Federal Trade Commission announced that the price action would be closely scrutinized for possible violations of the antitrust laws. The President, Secretary of Defense McNamara, and leading officials of the Treasury and Commerce Departments and the Council of Economic Advisers put in friendly low-key telephone calls to contacts in the steel companies that had not raised prices, gently suggesting the wisdom of continued abstinence.

At Democratic national headquarters calls were made to Democratic governors across the nation inviting them to make public statements supporting the President and encouraging local steelmakers to hold the price line. When it appeared that the proceedings of a stockholders' meeting of Bethlehem Steel Corporation, held shortly before the price rise, might be relevant in possible antitrust prosecutions, the Justice Department moved to secure the potential evidence. In the middle of the night overzealous FBI agents routed out for questioning three newspaper reporters who had covered the Bethlehem meetings. In testimony on Capitol Hill administration officials unloosed alarming analyses of the impact of the steel price rise upon military and economic foreign aid and the nation's relationship to the Common Market. In the Defense Department, Secretary McNamara ordered military agencies to shift their buying to the few steel companies that had not raised their prices. The Kennedy administration's "divide-and-conquer" strategy ultimately paid off when the several hold-out companies announced they would not raise prices. Fearful of a disastrous loss of sales, U.S. Steel and all other companies that had followed its lead quickly canceled their rises. But U.S. Steel and other companies bounced back, nearly a year later, by raising prices, this time without administration opposition.

President Johnson who regarded Kennedy's open assault upon U.S. Steel as a mistake and who bent every effort, as a steadfast consensus politician, to keep his fences with the business community well mended, nevertheless sustained several confrontations with industrial giants. He struggled manfully, in an era of high prosperity, against the heavy demands of the Vietnam war and in the absence of price control legislation, to keep inflation from breaking into a gallop. His chief strategy was to deter price increases in key industries— aluminum, steel, copper, for example—whose products affect the prices of a great web of other products.

One of Johnson's favorite economic weapons was the manipulation of government stockpiles of critical and strategic materials. The United States government has stockpiles of about one hundred strategic materials, from asbestos to zirconium, in more than two hundred storage sites throughout the country. Congress established the stockpiling program under the Strategic and Critical Stockpile Act of 1946 for materials difficult to obtain in wartime. Later in the Defense Production Act of 1950, Congress specifically provided that stockpiled commodities might be sold publicly in a manner that would not disturb the commercial market. The use of stockpiles for price regulation in the civil economy is patently beyond the statutory intent of Congress. But Johnson was not deterred from manipulating the stockpiles to advance his war against inflation by a process that is well suited to the spirit and method of consensus politics.

Johnson's employ of commodity stockpiles is well illustrated by his success in bringing the Aluminum Company of America (Alcoa), the nation's largest producer, to roll back a schedule of price increases. When Alcoa first announced the increases, Johnson refrained from comment, and when the press reported he was "sputtering mad," the White House took pains to deny it. But while Johnson carefully maintained a tight verbal silence, he launched two attacks. Gardener Ackley, chairman of the Council of Economic Advisers, released detailed figures on aluminum profits, wages, and productivity, and concluded that Alcoa's price rise, compared with government guidelines, was "inflationary." Simultaneously, Secretary of Defense McNamara announced that 200,000 tons of aluminum would be released from the federal stockpile.

Both the quantity and the price of the stockpile releases was expected to "relieve price pressures." Unlike Kennedy in his encounter with steel, Johnson remained personally silent and made no demand that Alcoa rescind its price increase. Administration officials took pains to stress that the stockpile move was unconnected with the price problem. Within days, Alcoa and other aluminum companies that had followed its action, announced that the price increases were rescinded. McNamara at once declared that the government would immediately confer with industry for "orderly disposal" of the stockpile releases, and the government's threat to alter the market price by pouring in aluminum from its stockpile was removed. Johnson for the first time publically entered the situation when Secretary McNamara quoted him as hailing Alcoa's decision as "an act of industrial statesmanship."[10] The consensus structure was a trifle battered but still very much intact. There was no crisis of confidence such as had followed Kennedy's assault on U.S. Steel, manifest in a drastic decline in the stock market.

The "New Economics"

The Kennedy-Johnson era marked the advent of the "New Economics," by which government is becoming a manager of prosperity, in addition to its long-standing role of savior in the depths of a depression or recession. The President is coming into his new prosperity role not by legislative mandate, judicial decision, group consultation, or public discussion but largely by autonomous executive decision. One example of the President's new role is his use of "guidelines," which he can apply to labor-management wage negotiations and to industry's price policies. The guidelines provide a formula for testing whether particular wage or price increases are inflationary; that is, whether they exceed the nation's average annual gain in productivity, or output per man-hour, over the last five years. The generally prevailing gain in the Kennedy and Johnson years was 3.2 per cent. If, in a given industry, the productivity gain equals the national average, the wage increases can be absorbed by the gain without necessitating a price increase. The Council of Economic Advisers provide the guidelines, with the aim not of preventing all price or wage changes but of preserving overall economic stability.

A difficulty that constantly bedevils the guidelines is that they are enforced more effectively against prices than wages. Industry leaders show more sensitivity to Presidential pressures than labor leaders. Although industry dislikes the guidelines, it dislikes even more the publicity and other costs of embroilment with government. Union leaders, in contrast, are apt to feel that to accept a governmental decision that determines labor's slice of the economic cake is to abdicate their responsibilities. A 1967 air mechanics strike won a settlement that exceeded the guidelines despite the President's personal intervention. In many important industries bargaining is local and remote from

Presidential influence, and in a situation such as the 1965 New York City transit strike, government must either countenance a violation of the guidelines or suffer a lengthy shutdown of vital services.

Paradoxically, although industry is held more closely to account for its prices, its profit levels have well outdistanced wage gains. From 1960 to 1965, profits after taxes rose 67 per cent, while the weekly take-home pay of factory workers climbed 21 per cent.[11] Guidelines are applied only to so-called basic industries and not to hundreds of other industries affecting the cost of living, such as food, clothing, and housing. Under labor's pressure to regain lost ground in the economic race, President Johnson decreed in 1966 that the guidelines should be more "flexible," that their limits should be breakable to enable labor to catch up with rising living costs. And despite their loud complaints, both labor and industry prefer the flexible guidelines to the more drastic and rigid remedies of wage and price control legislation or compulsory arbitration. They find more freedom and gain under Presidential policy than if Congress were to take over the problem.

A second bastion of the President's New Economics is his manipulation of tax policy to restrain a business boom. In 1966, for example, Johnson recommended to Congress the temporary repeal of incentives for business investment. Earlier that year, he asked Congress to restore previously reduced excise taxes on automobiles and telephone service to help avoid an overheated economy. Likewise, the President's 1967 proposal of a special surcharge on the income tax was intended not only to raise needed revenue but to check the economy's high tempo.

Business's Weapons

Business, too, has an abundance of sinew that it can flourish in encounters with the Presidency. Not the least element in business's potency is money, which takes on an added allure when elections are approaching. The iron baron and political boss Mark Hanna dexterously intertwined the national Republican organization and a coterie of top-level businessmen into a working alliance. By assessing the magnates shrewdly, Hanna assured a perpetually well-stocked campaign fund and, to gladden his generous donors, a respectably conservative program. Hanna's crowning success was handpicking William McKinley for the Presidency and installing him.

Theodore Roosevelt's campaign manager, George B. Cortelyou, gave the Hanna technique an added twist by employing methods approaching blackmail in enlisting contributions from the large industrial trusts. When Alton Parker, the Democratic Presidential nominee, began charging that the trusts were underwriting the Republican campaign, Roosevelt was put upon to denounce the accusations as "unqualifiedly and atrociously false."[12]

Businessmen or their proven servants may fill strategic elective and appointive offices of government whence they can exert a channeling influence upon the President. For example, Theodore Roosevelt, bent upon a progressive program, was faced by the "Big Four" Republican leaders in the Senate: Nelson W. Aldrich of Rhode Island, John C. Spooner of Wisconsin, Orville H. Platt of Connecticut, and William B. Allison of Iowa. Time and again Theodore Roosevelt, in inescapable reckonings with these hard-line conservative leaders, had to trim his progressive measures. In the executive branch, businessmen may dominate the cabinet Secretaryships, lesser departmental posts, and the independent regulatory commissions. President Eisenhower's original cabinet, for example, was described, not without exaggeration, as a "millionaires' corporation." So captive were the millionaires to their traditional economic doctrines that Eisenhower had the steady chore of lecturing to his cabinet on the importance of avoiding actions lending credence to critics' epithets that his was a "business administration." The administration, Eisenhower would say, must never fail to demonstrate its concern for the little man.[13]

Business's political attention is constantly focused on the independent regulatory commission: the Federal Trade Commission, the Securities and Exchange Commission, the Federal Reserve Board, and the like. These are the principal regulators of the economy, and their policies can do much to curb the practices and profits of business. The best insurance against inconvenient regulation, business has found, is to fill the commissions' positions with its own men. Undoubtedly, the most complete takeover of the commissions was engineered by the Harding-Coolidge appointments to those bodies. John J. Esch, a Harding nominee to the Interstate Commerce Commission, had long and amply proven his deep love for the railroads as a former member of the House Commerce Committee. The Esch appointment, Senator Robert La Follette thundered, was "a travesty on justice." President Coolidge's nomination to the Federal Trade Commission of William E. Humphrey, an efficient, dedicated counsel to great corporations, goaded Senator George Norris into branding the nominee "a fearless advocate of big business in all lines." Coolidge's naming of T. O. Marvin, secretary of the Home Market Club of Boston and editor of the *Protectionist*, to the U.S. Tariff Commission drove Norris to exclaim, "It seems to be the idea of those in control that the Tariff Commission should be composed of men whose whole lives disclose the fact that they have always advocated an exorbitantly high tariff."[14]

Presidents who champion progressive social programs are both sensitive and vulnerable to economic pressures from the business community. Theodore Roosevelt was visited with two economic "panics," as they were known, each a large threat to his political fortunes. In the late spring of 1903, when his nomination and election appeared certain, economic panic suddenly struck. The stock market fell into deep decline, wiping out $2 billion in security values; credit tightened and business failures soared. The high priests of finance, in their analytic incantations, attributed the disaster to a single and simple cause—Roosevelt's harassment of business. Only a few business spokesmen mentioned the contributing factors of an inflexible monetary structure and the overcapitalization of trusts like U.S. Steel. Roosevelt's own analysis of the ominous events, confided to his Secretary of State, Elihu Root, was that "certain of the big men" in Wall Street were not reluctant to see the panic get worse to discredit the administration and "to force the Republican party back into the path of conservatism." Mark Hanna, waiting in the wings, was a tailor-made conservative candidate, in fact. Root, for his part, brought the President corroborative intelligence that a pro-Hanna, anti-Roosevelt campaign among "the substantial men" of New York was blooming in the Union League Club of which Root was president. When the further bludgeon of the 1907 panic smote his fortunes, Theodore Roosevelt made no bones about articulating his suspicions in a public statement charging that "certain malefactors of great wealth" had combined to intensify the panic "in order to discredit the policy of the government."[15]

Labor Leaders and the President

The second member of the great economic tandem, labor, like other groups, attracted significant attention from the President of the United States only after it attained major political strength. Samuel Gompers, president of the American Federation of Labor, was not given the privilege of visits with Presidents until the late nineteenth century, and even then the occasions were few and brief. Gompers first extracted sustained Presidential interest from Theodore Roosevelt. Roosevelt invited the labor leader to the White House socially, consulted him on a wide range of subjects, and meted out honorific recognitions. Upon receiving the Nobel prize, for example, the President set up an industrial peace foundation and named Gompers to its board of directors.

Of all Presidents, Franklin Roosevelt maintained the most extensive relations with labor leaders. With labor he employed the same technique he applied to other private organizations. Viewing the nation's politics as essentially group politics, Franklin Roosevelt was wont to approach groups whose support he cherished through their leaders. Roosevelt's dealings with labor leaders ran the gamut from intimacy to mortal enmity. Dan Tobin of the Teamsters' Union was such an exalted favorite that Roosevelt made his "labor speech" of the 1944 campaign at a Teamsters' dinner, after rejecting entreaties of a dozen other unions for his presence.

Roosevelt's most intimate and profitable rapport was with Sidney Hillman, president of the Amalgamated Clothing Workers and vice president of the CIO, a Lithuanian émigré whose sensitivity and appreciation of social workers, intellectuals, and others outside the labor movement set him apart from rougher-hewn colleagues. Hillman served in responsible government posts in the New Deal and World War II, on NRA's Labor Advisory Board, on the National Defense Advisory Council, and as Associate Director of the Office of Production Management. To Roosevelt, Hillman was one of "the longest-headed individuals I have ever met." A constant visitor at the White House, Hillman enjoyed the rare privilege of a right-of-way by telephone to the Chief Executive. By the mid-1930's, a CIO official could plausibly assert that "a whisper from Sidney Hillman of the Amalgamated is louder than the loudest shout of almost anyone in the national Cabinet." And CIO president John L. Lewis, even when he was beholding the CIO vice president with a critical eye, declared, "Sidney Hillman was after all the driving force behind many of the measures attributed to the New Deal. If it had not been for him there would probably have been no Fair Labor Standards Act."[16] Probably Hillman's thorniest assignment in the mid-1930's was smoothing the troubled waters that kept churning up between his superior, John L. Lewis, and Franklin D. Roosevelt. Hillman's busy diplomacy was made doubly difficult by Lewis' resentment of his aide's privileged closeness to Roosevelt. The ordeal ended when Lewis finally broke with Roosevelt in 1940.

The Hillman-Roosevelt nexus, although resting upon a sturdy underpinning of personal regard, was mutually advantageous. For Hillman an unrivaled access to the White House meant speedy advancement in his labor career. For Roosevelt Hillman was a constant friend in the court of labor who could cushion the blows of unwelcome policy decisions like the administration's proposed labor draft in World War II. In the New Deal and the early war years Hillman was a kind of auxiliary Secretary of Labor at the White House's beck and call on myriad problems. Indeed, Roosevelt seems to have seriously considered making Hillman his Labor Secretary at several junctures, but was dissuaded by Mrs. Roosevelt, who did not like having her old friend, Secretary Frances Perkins, the only woman in the cabinet, superseded.[17]

With John L. Lewis, the leonine, bushy-browed master of ornate rhetoric, Franklin Roosevelt's relations were unceasingly tempestuous. Lewis, like Roosevelt, loved power and position; when they met, giants clashed. A stickler for the amenities for himself and his office, Roosevelt was offended by Lewis' spiny arrogance. The President, who had a large talent for noncommittal generalities, would be brought up short when Lewis would stop him in mid-sentence to ask, "Well, will it be yes or no?" Roosevelt was also distressed by Lewis' occasional crudity in exploiting his White House access. Soon after Section 7a of the National Industrial Recovery Act went into effect, for example, a provision designed to encourage union organization, Lewis' United Mine Workers organizers raced through the coal fields shouting, "The President wants you to join the Union." This unseemly and wholly unauthorized use of the Presidential office put Roosevelt squarely on the spot. Politically, he could not disavow the organizers' activity but could only writhe in private anguish. By 1936 Lewis was referring to Roosevelt as "my man." Roosevelt conveyed his own estimate of the labor leader in an interview with Max Lerner. "You know, Max," said the President, "this is really a great country. The framework of democracy is so strong and so elastic that it can get along and absorb both a Huey Long and a John L. Lewis." Lewis, when he heard the remark, growled, "The statement is incomplete. It should also include 'and Franklin Delano Roosevelt.' "[18]

In 1940 the fragile Roosevelt-Lewis connection was snapped asunder by the coming of the war and Roosevelt's third-term candidacy. During a White House visit in January 1940, according to Frances Perkins, whose report of the interview was corroborated by Philip Murray, a later CIO president, and denied by Lewis, the United Mine Workers chief made a startling proposal. He suggested to the President that he, Lewis, should run for Vice President of the United States on the third-term ticket. A strong labor man, Lewis argued, would ensure full labor support plus the support of all the liberals who, he added pointedly, would be a little troubled by the constitutional irregularity of a third term.[19]

The rebuff of Lewis' Vice-Presidential aspirations launched a train of bizarre events that widened the chasm between himself and the President from miles to oceans. After weeks of intensive wooing by the camp of Wendell Willkie, the Republican Presidential candidate, Lewis abandoned Roosevelt. "He is not an aristocrat," Lewis said, endorsing Willkie in a labor-oriented statement, "He has the common touch. He was born to the friar and not to the purple. He has worked with his hands, and has known the pangs of hunger." In a radio address Lewis urged the workers of America to vote against Roosevelt. In a flourish that left his fellow labor leaders gasping with disbelief, Lewis declared he would consider Roosevelt's reelection a vote of no confidence in himself and would thereupon resign from his CIO presidency. The labor rank and file, forced to choose between Roosevelt, beloved as their President, and Lewis, their adulated leader, chose Roosevelt at the polls. Honoring his threat, Lewis resigned from the CIO leadership.[20]

Differences cropping up between John Kennedy and the unions were handled with scrupulously quiet decorum. When the AFL-CIO politely criticized the Kennedy antirecession program in 1961 for not going far enough in the face of burgeoning unemployment, the President's reply took no specific note of the criticism but resorted to a high incontrovertible ground of noble sentiment. All groups, he wrote to the union leadership, should concentrate upon finding points of unity instead of "belaboring those problems which divide us."[21] The unions, too, employed the soft manner. When the AFL-CIO executive council concluded in 1963 that the President was not doing enough to stimulate the economy, it voiced its criticism on so vital a matter not in hostile resolution or public outcry. It authorized its leaders, George Meany and Walter Reuther, to bring its views quietly and privately to the President. Labor's absolute commitment to Democratic Presidents wellnigh mutes, for the duration of their administrations, public discussion of labor problems in an era of cataclysmic economic change.

Like other Democratic Presidents, Johnson in his relations with organized labor faced a conflict between personal political necessity and the requirements of national economic policy. In the 1964 Presidential race, Johnson received invaluable help from labor. In the great Northern industrial states, where Johnson's party ties were weakest, union officials pitched in to get out the electorate, both for registration and for the election. Later in the din of criticism of his policies in the Vietnam war, Johnson enjoyed the comfort of publicly spoken approval by George Meany, president of the AFL-CIO, and by David Dubinsky, who declared that the President "deserves the support of the American people and of liberty-loving people everywhere for his vision, determination and vigor in such a crucial period."[22] On occasion, Johnson called upon labor to support the administration's key projects on Capitol Hill, such as his 1967 effort for a 20 per cent overall increase in social security benefits. The President's plea was conveyed in a filmed message to thousands attending social security rallies sponsored by the AFL-CIO in major cities.

Like every President since World War II, Johnson worked mightily to check inflation by bringing labor to hold down its wage demands. In his effort he suffered quick rebuff by Walter Reuther, president of the United Automobile Workers, who served notice in 1964 that he, for one, did not intend to be bound by the President's limitations in that year's negotiations with the automobile industry.[23] Passing time did not improve labor's hospitality to Johnson's pleas for moderation in formulating wage demands. In 1967 the AFL-CIO executive council, finding that prices were rising faster than wages, issued a call for "substantial increases in the buying power of wages and fringe benefits," a sentiment that augured labor's disinclination to comply with the President's appeal for "wage restraint."[24]

Doing Things for Labor

Twentieth-century Presidents, particularly those of Democratic vintage, perform various functions to further labor's interests. Annually on Labor Day the President of the United States, be he Republican or Democrat, will make a speech, preferably in Detroit, full of praise for labor's contribution to the republic. At other times in messages, press statements, and letters he will approve of labor's goals and sterling achievement. Since 1933 all Presidents, Republican and Democratic alike, have promoted new legislation beneficial to labor. The removal of obstacles to the effective exertion of labor's economic power, the increase of labor's legal rights, and the enlargement of the government's welfare services are areas of legislation that vitally interest labor. Since labor legislation ordinarily is not passed without a long and impassioned struggle, a President proposing it sets the agenda not merely of his own administration, but often of future administrations. In 1905 Theodore Roosevelt proposed that Congress "regulate" the "procedure" for granting labor injunctions. Not until twenty-seven years after his initiative, in the Norris–La Guardia Act of 1932, did Congress finally do it.

Although most of the laws promoting labor's fundamental interests were enacted in Franklin Roosevelt's administration, and he of all Presidents is the most revered in the labor community, the truth of the matter is that Roosevelt was not an eager champion of labor's causes, but a reluctant hero. In the enactment of each of the three basic labor laws of his administration—section 7a of the National Industrial Recovery Act, the Wagner Act of 1935, and the Fair Labor Standards Act of 1938—his participation was cautious and halfhearted. Section 7a was included in the National Industrial Recovery Act not because Roosevelt rushed to put it in but because John L. Lewis insisted on it. Roosevelt's principal involvement in the NIRA's preparation was to order the industrialists and labor leaders who drafted individual bills to "get into a room and weave it all together." In the ensuing Congressional phase of the NIRA, Lewis was fearful that 7a, blessed with little Presidential support, might be dropped, so he entered into an intrigue with a labor-minded White House assistant. Lewis would write to the President, and the compliant assistant, who drafted Franklin Roosevelt's reply, would slip in a dash of exhortation for 7a. The tampering, according to Lewis, passed unnoticed. With the letter in hand, the labor leader spread the word among fence-sitting legislators that Roosevelt really wanted 7a.[25]

Roosevelt's commitment to the Wagner or national labor relations bill, which enhanced labor's right to organize and obliged employers to engage in collective bargaining, was also mild. In 1934, indeed, a Presidential decision had sidetracked the Wagner bill. Senator Robert Wagner was encouraged to reintroduce his measure the following year not by the President but by the labor movement. Franklin Roosevelt, to Wagner's dismay, despite expressions of mild approval the year before, now took a hands-off attitude. Even in the bill's late stages, Secretary of Commerce Daniel Roper was predicting a Presidential veto. After the bill had passed the House, and just before the Senate's final action, Roosevelt convened a White House conference where Senator Wagner and Donald R. Richberg, the administration's labor adviser who opposed the bill, debated its merits at the President's invitation. Midway in the discussion, Roosevelt, whose position still was unknown, finally made clear that he wanted the bill. On the fair labor standards bill of 1938, Franklin Roosevelt likewise engaged in belated, feet-dragging decision. It was not the President or his administration, but Sidney Hillman, the CIO vice president, who rallied the labor bloc of legislators and worked out the minimum wage of twenty-five cents an hour in a hard-wrought compromise with the Southern Democrats. Roosevelt, ever skeptical of the bill's chances, gave help only when its success was assured and political prudence required that he quickly identify himself with it.[26]

Why was Roosevelt so chronically reserved and reluctant? For one thing, born into comfortable gentility, he had no first-hand understanding of labor problems. Instinctively and intellectually he sympathized with labor's objectives, but he had little grasp of its needs and feelings. On setting the priorities of his administration, he gave labor's objectives a secondary place. In the depression years of 1934 and 1935 and in the recession of 1938 his primary interest was economic recovery. Time and again he seems to have been impressed by the argument that production might climb faster in the depression-bound economy if labor decisions could be postponed until business was on its feet again. Labor's most drastic weapon, the strike, sometimes annoyed him, especially when it obstructed his own political and economic purposes. In the main, he envisioned himself not as labor's champion but as a balancer and adjuster between labor and management in which he approached both sides with a good measure of judicious detachment.

In the post–Franklin D. Roosevelt era the fate and substance of labor legislation have varied strikingly between the Republican Eisenhower Presidency and the Democratic Presidencies of Harry Truman, John Kennedy, and Lyndon Johnson. Eisenhower's personal preference for state rather than federal action and his apparent lack of philosophical sympathy with labor's aims wrought results considerably below labor's aspirations. Twice Eisenhower vetoed legislation providing federal aid to depressed areas with severe unemployment. When the AFL-CIO proposed amendments to the Fair Labor Standards Act, raising the minimum wage from $1.00 to $1.25 an hour and adding some 5 million employees not covered by the act (chiefly in retail trades), the President recommended an increase of 10 to 15 cents an hour and the extension of coverage to some 3.2 million employees. Consistent with Eisenhower's avowed preference for state action, his administration achieved a major extension of the state-oriented Social Security Act, the largest in the act's history.

Kennedy, in contrast, stressed national action in labor matters. Kennedy pushed through legislation for depressed areas, which Eisenhower had vetoed, and the $1.25 minimum wage, which Eisenhower had resisted. Kennedy also won liberalizing amendments to the Social Security Act that increased minimum benefits and lowered the eligibility age. He won legislation extending unemployment compensation for up to thirteen additional weeks and giving special benefits to the children of the unemployed.

Since the days of Franklin D. Roosevelt, labor has expected Presidents, particularly Democratic Presidents, to resist legislation hostile to its interests. The noisiest and most politically profitable instance of Presidential jousting in labor's behalf was Harry S. Truman's veto of the Taft-Hartley bill of 1947. An omnibus measure that was passed in the wake of a large upsurge in strikes, Taft-Hartley aimed to equalize employer-employee responsibilities by regulating union organization and practices. After polling the Democratic National Committee and the state Democratic chairmen and vice chairmen for advice, Truman delivered a fiery veto which was overridden by the Republican-controlled Congress. For Truman the defeat was merely the beginning of a long, implacable, politically rewarding crusade. In the 1948 Presidential campaign and after, he lost no opportunity to identify the legislation with Republican conservatism, though a majority of the Democrats in both houses had voted for it.

From Truman's day on, Democratic Presidents have been expected to put their shoulder to the wheel to bring about the repeal of the most objectionable features of the Taft-Hartley Act. Faithful to this political custom, Lyndon Johnson, following the 1964 election, urged Congress to repeal Section 14b of the act, which allows states to pass laws banning the union shop. Johnson was able to compress his enthusiasm to the point that his recommendation required merely a single sentence in a lengthy message touching on many subjects. In taking this step, Johnson paid his principal political debt to organized labor for its considerable help in his 1964 campaign. Johnson's recommendation, however, proved fruitless; repeal of Section 14b was killed by a Senate filibuster in 1965, a year when the President was fashioning brilliant successes on Capitol Hill. The contrast between the President's general success and his failure to bring off labor's most cherished purpose prompted some union leaders to grumble that repeal could have been obtained if the President and Senate Democratic leaders had worked a little harder.[27]

The President may bring labor into his official family by appointing as his Secretary of Labor a figure from the organized labor movement. Woodrow Wilson inaugurated the practice when he made William B. Wilson of the United Mine Workers his Secretary of Labor in 1913. The precedent was renewed not by his Democratic successors Roosevelt and Truman but by the Republican Eisenhower, who named Martin Durkin, president of the plumbers' union, Secretary of Labor. The appointment proved ill-fated; after eight months Durkin resigned, vexed because the White House rejected his views on amending the Taft-Hartley Act. Kennedy's first Secretary of Labor, Arthur Goldberg, general counsel to the United Steel Workers' Union, did not, like Durkin, hail from the workers' ranks, but from labor's growing professional wing. In appointing a nonlabor man as Labor Secretary, a contemporary President will make a selection that is inoffensive to the labor movement.

Since the 1930's the great bulk of organized labor has made a clear and absolute choice in Presidential politics, in casting its lot with Democratic candidates and opposing the Republicans. When a Republican occupies the White House, labor constitutes a major opposition force second only to the Democratic party. If the Democratic party is divided and dominated by moderates and conservatives, as it was in Eisenhower's first term, organized labor "plays a role of *the* major loyal opposition within American politics," as James Tracy Crown has put it.[28]

For the Democratic Chief Executive, labor is the major interest group in the American polity supporting his domestic program, and, to a large but lesser degree, his foreign policy. In seasons when his foreign aid legislation encountered rough sledding in Congress, President Kennedy could count on help from a squad of expert and experienced lobbyists of the AFL-CIO and its constituent unions who descended upon Capitol Hill. Before he launched his foreign trade bill, Kennedy emphatically invited labor's support in an address to the 1961 AFL-CIO convention. "Don't worry about us," George Meany replied. "We will cooperate 1,000 per cent."[29] When labor's co-operation slackened to unsatisfactory percentages, Kennedy did not hesitate to call the union chiefs to account. In 1961 he let the word go forth that he was disappointed and displeased at some unions' failure to lobby more strenuously for his minimum wage bill in the House of Representatives.

From Franklin D. Roosevelt onward labor has played a central part in selecting Democratic candidates for the Presidency. Indeed no Democratic candidate during that time has been named without its approval. There was truth in Kennedy's jest when he acknowledged in a speech to the 1961 AFL-CIO convention that he was "one whose work and continuity of employment has depended in part upon the union movement."

Labor has displayed an almost equal interest in the selection of Democratic Vice-Presidential candidates. In the fateful selection of Harry S. Truman for the Vice-Presidency in 1944, labor had at least as great a part as the incumbent President, Franklin Roosevelt. The latter's frail health, a fact well known to the labor leaders, lent urgency to their task. Roosevelt himself contributed only confusion by recommending no less than four candidates for the Vice-Presidency. Robert E. Hannegan, Franklin Roosevelt's representative embarking for the Chicago convention, beseeched his chief for instructions on the Vice-Presidential question. Before making a final selection, Roosevelt was heard to say Hannegan and his aides must first "clear it with Sidney" (Sidney Hillman), the CIO vice president. The union leaders, after rejecting James M. Byrnes and expressing indifference toward Henry Wallace, the incumbent Vice President, settled upon Truman. "Clear it with Sidney" quickly took its place in the national lexicon and raised a drumfire of conservative indignation. Cried Westbrook Pegler, "How came this nontoiling sedentary conspirator who never held American office or worked in the Democratic organization to give orders to the Democrats of the United States!"[30]

Also since Franklin Roosevelt's day, Democratic Presidential campaigns have counted heavily upon labor's contributions of treasure and legwork. "The election of John F. Kennedy is Labor's number one job," proclaimed George Meany in 1960.[31] Union halls across the nation were turned into Kennedy campaign centers, and union registration drives in the cities were indispensable to his success. Franklin D. Roosevelt cemented labor and the Democratic Presidency into close bond in the embittered election of 1936, when he courted the aid of AFL and CIO leaders. They responded lavishly in the conviction that for labor's fortunes and future everything turned on

Roosevelt's reelection. Lewis' United Mine Workers made cash contributions and loans by its own count of $486,288.55 to the Democratic party and a nearly equal sum to the Nonpartisan League, labor's own campaign organization zealously devoted to Roosevelt's cause. Hillman's Amalgamated Clothing Workers added $100,000 to the Roosevelt coffers and a further $400,000 to the League's. In all, labor committed a full $1 million to Roosevelt's reelection.

Sidney Hillman made it plain that labor expected something of a *quid pro quo* in a telegram to Franklin Roosevelt after Amalgamated pledged its treasure. "Labor anticipates your support," Hillman wired bluntly, "for decent labor legislation . . . the guarantee of the right to organize and the enactment of minimum labor standards." Roosevelt in a telegram to Amalgamated and a letter to "Dear Sidney" expressed gratitude and blithely ignored the suggestion of a bargain, saying merely that Amalgamated's action had given him "new strength and courage." Following the electoral victory, when Lewis began growling that Roosevelt had better start reciprocating, the labor leader expressed impatience with those who were shocked by his temerity in demanding a dividend on labor's $1 million investment. "Is anyone fool enough to believe, for one instant," asked Lewis, "that we gave this money to Roosevelt because we were spellbound by his voice?"[32]

The Lewis-Hillman technique of direct financial contributions was banned by law in 1943 and again by the Taft-Hartley Act in 1947, which also prohibits direct union expenditures for candidates for public office. Similar restrictions apply to business corporations. Both unions and corporations freely circumvent the laws, however, with Congressional and Presidential acquiescence.

Labor-Management Disputes

Twentieth-century Presidents have regularly become entangled in labor-management disputes over union recognition, collective bargaining, and bread-and-butter issues of wages, hours, and general working conditions. The President's participation ranges from leadership in labor-management negotiations—personally or through deputies—to the seizure of struck properties and the use of the military to maintain law and order. In his earliest interventions in labor-management disputes, the President used military force under acts of Congress of 1792, 1795, and 1807 to enforce national laws in local disorders and to guard the states against domestic violence as guaranteed in Article IV, section 4, of the Constitution. In the 1877 railroad strike in ten states, Rutherford B. Hayes furnished state authorities with arms from national arsenals and, as Commander-in-Chief, transferred troops from remote posts to the scenes of trouble. In the Pullman strike of 1894, President Cleveland, against Governor Altgeld's strenuous protests, dispatched troops to Chicago to protect United States property and "to remove obstructions to the

United States mails." The Supreme Court upheld Cleveland in *In re Debs* (158 U.S. 564).

Theodore Roosevelt reversed the Presidency's promanagement tendencies in resolving the anthracite coal strike in 1902, the largest work stoppage up to that time. The severity of approaching winter, the popularity of the miners' cause, and the anthracite industry's membership in a close-knit trust drew Roosevelt actively into the crisis. He ordered his commissioner of labor to investigate the strike and make recommendations, which furnished the basis of a compromise solution that Roosevelt proposed to the operators and miners. When the operators rejected it, Secretary of War Elihu Root rushed to New York to confer with J. P. Morgan, and together they drafted an agreement to submit the dispute to an arbitration commission. The imperious Morgan pressed the agreement upon George Baer, president of the Reading Railroad Company and the operators' chief negotiator. Morgan's achievement approaches the awesome, for Baer had sprouted a bad case of self-righteous intransigence. "The rights and interests of the laboring man," he maintained, "will be protected and cared for not by the labor agitators, but by the Christian men to whom God in his infinite wisdom has given the control of the property interests of the country, and upon the successful management of which so much depends."[33]

Acting on the Root-Morgan agreement, Roosevelt appointed an arbitration commission. To assure that the award would not go too decidedly against the miners, Roosevelt took pains to include a cleric and a union official, the latter filling the place designated for an "eminent sociologist." The commission's findings were made and accepted by both sides, and the strike ended. It remains a landmark of Presidential innovation in labor policy. For the first time in a labor dispute, representatives of both capital and labor were called to the White House, where Presidential influence induced a negotiated settlement. For the first time, both sides promised to accept the decision of a Presidentially appointed arbitration board. If the board had failed, Roosevelt in an equally innovative step, was prepared to "put in" the army to "dispossess the operators and run the mines as a receiver."

Succeeding Democratic Presidents have elaborated on the patterns originated by the Republican Roosevelt. In the Colorado coal strike of 1913–14, Woodrow Wilson employed federal troops not to protect strikebreakers, but to protect the property and safety of both labor and management while they negotiated a settlement. The theme of equality persisted in legislation that was passed in the Wilsonian era establishing the Department of Labor, with a Division of Conciliation in which the bargaining parties, labor and management, enjoyed identical status.

Franklin D. Roosevelt clung to his preference for keeping out of specific labor-management disputes even in the most ruinous confrontation of his time, the sit-down strikes of 1936. Both the sprawling General Motors organization, the focus of the strikes, and the CIO pressured Roosevelt to intervene.

His personal political interest was to end the conflict quickly without becoming involved in the specifics of its settlement—a purpose calling for fine maneuver. At one juncture Roosevelt called the CIO leaders to the White House and asked them bluntly to "get the men out of the G.M. plants." John L. Lewis would only promise that the men would leave "when the company begins to bargain with them or even with me, in good faith." To balance the scales, Franklin Roosevelt publicly spanked Alfred Sloan, the General Motors president, for breaking off negotiations. In a characteristic tactic, Roosevelt forced negotiations to proceed at lesser levels of authority—between the disputants themselves and through the good offices of the Conciliation Service and Governor Frank Murphy of Michigan, where the strikes were heaviest. Roosevelt viewed the Presidency as a supreme arbiter, to be held jealously in reserve and used only as a last resort. Ultimately, Roosevelt brought General Motors to begin what it had never done before—negotiation with union representatives and the CIO to end the strikes.[34]

In World War II strikes were few, thanks largely to Roosevelt's and Truman's insistence that labor-management disputes must not hamper war production. When strikes erupted in vital war industries, both Presidents seized and operated the struck industries. In the Truman era of postwar reconversion, with labor meaning to hold its wartime gains, strikes soared. A corporation-wide General Motors strike, national steel and railroad stoppages, the CIO Electrical Workers strikes against General Electric, General Motors, and Westinghouse, and several coal strikes hobbled the economy and blanketed the nation's cities with "dim-outs" and "brown-outs."

The embattled Truman resorted to fact-finding boards, and his principal assistant, John R. Steelman, was not for nothing plucked from the directorship of the U.S. Conciliation Service. Much of Steelman's time was devoted to White House conferences with the disputants in key labor-management impasses. In addition, Truman instituted a general labor-management conference in Washington in 1945, and when restrictive labor bills began stirring on Capitol Hill, he rushed to beat Congress to the punch by advancing labor-management legislation of his own. For his provident action Truman was accused by Philip Murray, the CIO president, of yielding "in abject cowardice" to Congressional pressure. Eventually Truman's proposal was submerged by the harsher Taft-Hartley Act.

Dwight Eisenhower and John Kennedy both avoided Truman's personal involvement in labor-management disputes. Truman's successors have benefited from increasing labor-management stability and by labor's marked shift in tactical emphasis from the strike to the bargaining table. In contrast to Truman, Eisenhower and Kennedy had no Steelmans but kept labor-management issues largely locked up in the Labor Department. James P. Mitchell, Eisenhower's Labor Secretary, and Arthur Goldberg and Willard Wirtz, Kennedy's Labor Secretaries, were the chief engineers of administration labor policy. Kennedy, although personally more involved than Eisenhower, worked chiefly behind the scenes. When he did act publicly, Kennedy preferred a moderate decorum.

Kennedy employed standard Presidential discourse in his invocations of a labor-management duty to heed national interest, but his own conduct was not always free from the taint of expediency. Indeed a double track was sometimes discernible in the Kennedy administration's approach to labor-management relations. Two labor disputes of 1962 illuminate the contrast. In the first, strikes loomed at North American, Ryan, General Dynamics, and Lockheed, manufacturers of missiles and aircraft. A special Presidential board recommended union-shop elections to resolve the dispute. The two powerful unions involved—the United Automobile Workers and the International Association of Machinists—welcomed the board's recommendation, but the employers cold-shouldered it. Kennedy backed up his board in a strong statement holding that if the employers rejected the peace plan, the country should blame them for the ensuing trouble.[35]

In a second dispute, where labor, rather than management, rejected a Presidential board's findings, Kennedy's course was altogether different. A strike of the Chicago and North Western Railway that inflicted severe economic injury upon nine Middle Western states, began when the Order of Railroad Telegraphers rejected a Presidential board's recommendation that the union abandon its demand for a veto over job reductions caused by new technology and other factors. The Presidential board proposed a formula to cushion lay-offs through liberalized unemployment, retraining, and severance benefits. Kennedy, departing from his accustomed procedure, pronounced no words of personal endorsement of the board's report nor censure for the union. Wholly ignoring the railroad's readiness to negotiate a contract reflecting the board's proposals, the President entreated "both sides" to make "sufficient concessions" to find accord.[36]

Like Kennedy, Lyndon Johnson's heart was where the votes were, and he too discriminated between business and labor. While dealing roughly with price increases pressed by the aluminum and steel industries, he maintained a discreet silence when Michael J. Quill in the same interval was exacting wage increases for New York City's Transport Workers Union well beyond the administration's guidelines.

Under pressure of the Vietnam war, President Johnson moved strongly to avert strikes in vital industries. He invoked the emergency provisions of the Taft-Hartley Act, which establish an eighty-day "cooling off" period for strikes affecting the national interest. He brought Congress to pass special legislation to prevent a national railroad strike in 1967. He also masterminded and participated in the negotiation of contracts between management and labor in vital industries. In 1965 Johnson, with the scrupulous attention he would give to a foreign policy crisis, watched over contract negotiations between the steel industry and the steelworkers union. After special mediators failed to resolve the parties' differences, the President summoned the negotiators to Washington and in the cabinet room quietly exhorted them on the necessity of avoiding a strike for the sake of the national interest; he pointed out that a strike would harm troop morale in Vietnam and comfort the nation's enemies. He asked that negotiations continue in the executive office building next door. Johnson kept in close touch with their progress, and after several days of futile meetings, stepped up the pressure. Joining the negotiators, he thanked them for their efforts, but added that "this is not a ladies' game you're playing over here and I think the time has come to do more." Acknowledging that each negotiator had a constituency to keep faith with, the President added, "Mine, I think, is a little larger— 190 million people." He asked both the industry negotiator and the union negotiator "to go 51 per cent of the way" to "wrap this up." As days passed without agreement, Johnson told his aides that the late Sam Rayburn had once told him that the most important thing in politics, as in poker, was knowing when to "put the stack in." Convinced that such a time was at hand, Johnson instructed his aides to give the negotiators specific suggestions for resolving the remaining issues. The aides feared that both sides might be hostile, but Johnson's instinct proved sound, and an agreement soon emerged.

As a negotiator, Johnson correctly assumed that administration suggestions that split the labor-management differences nearly down the middle would be acceptable because they enabled both sides to back off gracefully from firm bargaining positions. The President also calculated that the union negotiator, I. W. Abel, had to take a tough stance since he had recently ousted the incumbent union president in an election campaign that promised more militant bargaining.

Despite Johnson's sparkling success, the President's personal intervention in labor-management disputes has certain drawbacks. The knowledge that the President is available through ultimate appeal may prompt the parties, particularly labor, to treat less seriously the earlier stages of negotiations. The President, in intervening, also takes substantial risks. If the parties do not agree, after his best efforts, his prestige and influence suffer damage, which can wilt his effectiveness in other interventions. He cannot intervene too much, or his efforts shrink in value. He can intervene successfully only if he can exert sufficient pressures, and these in turn depend upon the presence of a genuine national danger if a work stoppage occurs in the industry involved.

The Future Presidency

The gap between the President's formal legal authority and his economic responsibilities steadily widens. In his most vital activity as economic regulator—holding down inflation and preserving labor-management peace—his available statutory authority is far exceeded by his dependence upon a combination of personal influence, threats, and pressures. It is an interesting political phenomenon that all the interests concerned want it this way: The President, Congress, business, and labor prefer the vague and therefore flexible present power of the Chief Executive to a price and wage control statute or compulsory arbitration.

The President's ability to influence, direct, or control the economy is addressed to several kinds of ends that today are receiving increasing emphasis. There is widening recognition that ours is an "affluent society" and an "age of high mass consumption," and those whose social conscience is pricked are questioning whether more of the new-made wealth ought not be used for constructive public ends—rather than for personal material gratification—such as schools, hospitals, and recreation facilities. The President is looked to for leadership: to stir the country's conscience, to rally Congress, to structure his fiscal policy and executive programs in behalf of the public sector.

The President is also increasingly becoming the shepherd of the "other economy," the economy that is not affluent, and the participants of which have won no place on society's gravy train. They are the millions of citizens who are consigned to a life of poverty: the aged, increasing numbers of youth, a large proportion of Negro citizens, and the chronically unemployed. The President champions measures to improve their employability and their environment and to reduce the cruelties that the "other economy" inflicts upon them.

For the future—the 1970's and beyond—the President will rightly be expected to cushion the effects upon society of possible revolutionary changes in the economy.

One effect may be caused by the cybernetics revolution that promises to increase unemployment to such a degree that the traditional link between jobs and income will be badly broken. The electronic computer and the automated, self-regulating machine may largely invalidate the general mechanism that undergirds people's rights as consumers. The day may not be far when the President will have to urge upon Congress legislation guaranteeing every American an adequate income as a matter of right. Both the President and the economy will have to cope with that great cauldron of trouble that boils ever-higher—the urban problem, with the shortages of jobs, and the inadequacies of housing, health, and educational resources that afflict our cities. What is the President, whose economic responsibilities far exceed his economic authority, to do in light of these gathering demands for policy?

1. He must, of course, seek new statutory authority. He must resume the fight that Kennedy began, to gain the power to raise and lower income taxes within limits, in response to general economic conditions. He will need massive appropriations to extend the fight against poverty begun by President Johnson and to strengthen the economic opportunities of Negroes, nearly 45

per cent of whom have yearly incomes of less than two thousand dollars.

2. The President can ask for new statutory authority, but whether he will get it, given separation of powers, checks and balances, and weak parties, is problematic. It is on economic questions that the President's weakness as legislative and party leader is most frustrating. The 1950's and 1960's have been especially barren of major domestic economic legislation, producing nothing comparable in importance to the Taft-Hartley Act and the Employment Act of the 1940's. As the New Deal of the 1930's demonstrated, the President fares best in securing economic legislation during severe and dramatically evident crises. But the economic crisis of the 1960's and 1970's is apt to be a quiet one—an undramatic, although steady and substantial increase in unemployment—a crisis unlikely to stir Congress and the nation the way the depression did.

3. The President's most promising recourse in the face of a balky Congress and a quiescent public opinion is to urban groups—to organized labor and to racial and national minorities lacking access to ordinary economic privileges. The Kennedy formula of linking program and urban groups to influence Congress will face its hardest test and, if it succeeds, will gain its finest achievements on economic issues.

4. Presidential politics based upon group politics will be complicated by drastic alterations in the nature of the groups wrought by economic change. Unlike Franklin Roosevelt, who thrived upon a growing organized labor movement, future Presidents face a declining movement, both in memberships and political influence. For all Johnson's strength in securing Great Society legislation in 1965, organized labor failed to secure the enactment of a single bread-and-butter measure in the Eighty-ninth Congress. Structural changes in the economy, the shift in the national job pattern toward more white-collar workers, and the absence of the organized spirit of the 1930's and 1940's all contribute to union decline. The weakening of organized labor may require the President to rely more heavily upon racial and national groups and to direct his appeal more pointedly to consumer interest.

5. The President's role in emergency labor-management disputes will doubtless increase as the public becomes less tolerant of work stoppages, a mood evident in the late 1960's, and as the economic demands of war, whether in Vietnam or elsewhere, militate against prolonged production breakdowns. As long as the vital processes of collective bargaining are adequately safeguarded, the President might be given increased, although carefully limited, authority to intervene in disputes that might create a na-

tional emergency. The President might be provided more possibilities of action than he now enjoys under the Taft-Hartley and Railway Labor Acts. If the President's alternatives are increased, both labor and management will be uncertain that he will intervene at all, and if he does, what he will do. Presidential intervention will be taken less for granted than it is now. If Presidential authority were used sparingly, it would hold to a minimum strikes that are deemed emergency-creating, and genuine collective bargaining would be best preserved.

6. In the absence of adequate statutory authority, the President will need to rely all the more upon executive means to forward his economic policies. He and his aides can use the conference method more widely to spread information and to help form opinion as, for example, among industry and union leaders on issues of price and wage stability. Power can be more safely entrusted to the President if interested groups are consulted and participate in policy development. President Johnson moved in this direction in 1966 when he tossed into the laps of his Advisory Committee on Labor and Management the assignment to develop something better than the guidelines. The President might do even better if he would add to that group representatives for that long-suffering forgotten man of the American economy, the consumer.

Social Justice 12

Presidents face a struggle that they can neither direct nor control—a struggle that goes on in our society, as in any other society, between those who have wealth and power and are loath to share them and those who do not have wealth and power and seek to get them. The advantaged want to hold to their privileged position and the disadvantaged to improve their condition. A dynamic democracy makes no lasting arbitration between the contestants, and their conflict is an enduring feature of politics. The President, as the principal elective officer of American democratic society, has made no enduring and unqualified commitment to either the advantaged or the disadvantaged. Particular Chief Executives have been heavily committed to one of the sides; others have remained largely indifferent or have been distracted by other problems of their administration. Nineteenth-century Presidents were uneven and chiefly negative in their attention to social justice; in the twentieth century unevenness still prevails, but positive actions have become far more numerous and more forceful. Yet if one thing is clear, it is that the President can effect no lasting accommodation that will bring the struggle for wealth and power to a close. Its endurance and the likelihood that it will move on to new phases and intensities provide some of the more formidable facts of the President's political life.

Social justice has a dimension beyond social rights and social welfare. It includes the civil liberties of the individual and their protection against encroachments by government. In this sense government is conceived of not simply as the promoter of social justice but as the perpetrator of social or individual injustice. Government and the individual are linked in a basic tension that Lincoln expressed in his message to Congress about the newborn

Civil War on July 4, 1861: "Must a government of necessity be too *strong* for the liberties of its own people, or too *weak* to maintain its own existence?" In the deepest sense, Lincoln was expressing a fundamental problem of democratic society—finding the proper balance between the individual's liberty to live his life as he will and government's authority to protect and enhance the welfare of its people.

A Historical View

Although Thomas Jefferson is rightly placed at the forefront of our Chief Executives who have championed human justice, his finest achievements occurred rather less in his Presidency than in other offices. As Chief Executive his concerns centered largely upon foreign affairs and partisan politics: the Louisiana Purchase, the embargo, war on the Barbary pirates, the impeachment of Federalist judges, and the repeal of the Federalists' Judiciary Act. His inaugural address viewed government as essentially negative: Let it keep men from injuring their fellows; otherwise leave them to regulate their own concerns. He spoke against special privilege and rejected the Hamiltonian view that government should encourage manufacture but instead conceived of agriculture and commerce "as its handmaid." An exponent of state rights, he circumscribed a limited role for the federal government, chiefly in foreign affairs, and proposed to leave local affairs to the states. But Jefferson demonstrated the capacity of the President and government to promote individual liberty. Capsizing the previous Federalist administration's Alien and Sedition laws of 1798, which granted the Chief Executive summary power to deport any alien "deemed dangerous to the public peace or safety" and made it a crime to publish false, scandalous, or defamatory writings with intent to discredit the government, Jefferson pardoned all persons imprisoned under the legislation, and Congress, following his cue, ultimately ordered all fines returned.

Andrew Jackson, despite his military affinities and contrasting intellectual endowment, was an extension and adaptation of his great Republican-Democratic forebear, Jefferson. Jackson, too, indulged a large, although somewhat erratic, devotion to state rights. His position on two major issues of his administration—his opposition to federally developed internal improvements and his war upon the Second Bank of the United States—reflected a strong surge of state rights sentiments. His war upon the Bank, which he did not begin, was the product of many forces, including the anti-Bank persuasions of his advisers, Amos Kendall and Martin Van Buren, and the Bank's own ill-advised, heavy-handed tactics that encouraged Jackson's view of it as a monster of concentrated economic power and potential tyranny. But most of all, whether he altogether deserved to be or not, Jackson was a rallying point for the common man.

Yet the chief curative for those who were restive under the heel of privilege was not governmental reform but the opening of new territories, the push of human settlement westward. If one became dissatisfied with his lot in society—his income, his rights, his prospects—he could journey westward to the new country, start over again, and hope to do better. The frontier was America's magic medicine for social injustice until it too eventually failed as a healer of the most divisive issue in society—slavery—and the Civil War erupted. To wage it, Lincoln, relying upon Presidential authority, imposed drastic restrictions upon civil liberty: without legislative authorization he suspended the privilege of habeas corpus and subjected those who discouraged enlistments, resisted the draft, or engaged in other disloyal practice to martial law and trial by military commissions. Newspapers were suppressed by military order. To some, although not to most, the Civil War was a fight for social justice. The war produced the foremost blow yet struck by a President in behalf of any massive class cursed with injustice. The Emancipation Proclamation was indeed limited in scope. But Lincoln's document was only a beginning, and the progress of its ideals, entrusted to other hands and eras, has been an enduring issue, sometimes relegated to the background of national affairs, other times to their forefront.

Lincoln's successor, Andrew Johnson, a Southerner and proclaimer of state rights, assumed a contrary position toward the Negro cause that was aggravated by his titanic struggle with Congress leading to his impeachment trial. He vetoed the extension of the Freedmen's Bureau and the Civil Rights Act designed to guarantee to freedmen, through federal courts, certain rights from infringement by state law. He vetoed the Reconstruction Act, which, among other things, required individual Southern states to accept Negro suffrage and to ratify the Fourteenth Amendment before they might again secure representation in Congress. The act was passed anyway. But there was another side to Johnson. Because of his conviction that well-to-do Southerners had led the humbler classes of the South into secession, in his special procedure for alloting pardons he required those whose estimated value of taxable property exceeded twenty thousand dollars to subject themselves to a more rigorous review than their brethren in lesser circumstances.

The remainder of the nineteenth century is a glorious saga of national growth, although it is not an era of notable advance for social justice. The Presidency became the preserve of the Republican party, save for the two intrusions of Grover Cleveland. Republicans could claim that their party had saved the Union, and Democrats were tainted with the odium of secession. With but one exception every Republican Presidential candidate between 1868 and 1900 had been an officer in the Union army. A country engrossed in flinging railroads across mountain barriers, felling forests, ravishing the earth of its riches, enlarging its cities beyond count, and bestowing mansions upon the rich whose ornate display verged upon vulgarity had neither time nor inclination to erase social evil.

Wealth dominated commonwealth. The President was little more than titular leader. Hayes, Garfield, Arthur, and Harrison made no enduring contributions to social policy or for that matter to public policy. Hayes, to be sure, made limited motions in behalf of reform. He included the egregious political reformer, Carl Schurz, in his cabinet, and vetoed a popular Chinese exclusion bill—on legal rather than social grounds.

Politics was an annex of business. Politicians like James G. Blaine and Nelson W. Aldrich were deputies of such masters of capital as J. P. Morgan and Jay Gould and such captains of industry as Andrew Carnegie and John D. Rockefeller. The ethics of business was the ethics of politics. The major political parties seldom divided along economic lines and straddled important issues. Railroad and trust regulation was ostensibly favored by both parties, but neither lent it meaningful support. Labor was anything but a courted political object. Hayes in the railroad riots of 1877 and Cleveland in the Pullman strike of 1894 countenanced the use of the injunction and sent federal troops to protect business interests. Notwithstanding the eloquence of party platforms, Presidential pronouncement, and sharp legislative conflict, the land laws, tariff reform, and the money question, each bearing powerful social implications, produced results little distinguishable from one Presidential administration to the next.

If the history of social justice possesses turning points, one indeed is the ascent of Theodore Roosevelt to the Presidency. The talents and instincts of that extraordinary man and the climactic momentum of forces that had gathered great speed in the final decades of the nineteenth century combined to produce an epoch of Presidential social achievement. The forces were many and diverse. The two great groups most injured by big industrialism—agriculture and labor—were well astir.

Theodore Roosevelt's assumption of the Presidency was prophetically acknowledged by a plunge in the stock market. The first President to wage large-scale war upon economic abuse, he viewed his office as a "bully pulpit." Endowed with moral fervor and oratorical gifts, he awakened Congress and the people to the urgency of reform. The curbing of railroad rate discriminations, the pure food and meat inspection laws, the brassy warfare upon the trusts, and the federal employers' liability act typify his trail-blazing achievements. Certain of his proposals were so far-reaching that they were not adopted until the distant day of the New Deal.

Theodore Roosevelt was spurred by his own large capacity for social initiative and moral fervor and the play of forces about him. Progressive sentiment was at a crest. If social reform tends to come when economic power becomes too concentrated too fast, when disparities between wealth and poverty become too glaring, the times indeed were right. Huge corporate profits and the lack of graduated income or inheritance taxes had created at the economy's apex a set of fabulously wealthy people.

Theodore Roosevelt was also goaded by the two great evangelists of progressivism, of whom he was ever wary, the Democrat William Jennings Bryan and the Republican Robert La Follette. To counteract the Bryan–La Follette preachings that the size of the trusts should be rigorously curbed, Roosevelt trundled out a competing doctrine that size in itself was not evil and that the trusts consequently should not be broken up. Roosevelt proposed that the trusts be regulated by making their operations public and outlawing dishonesty.

Although he profited greatly from the Muckrakers' skilled endeavors, Roosevelt knew interludes of moderation in which he by no means altogether welcomed their contribution. It was he indeed who coined the name "Muckrakers" as a term of disrepute. Fearful that the Muckrakers were driving the American people into socialism and stirring revolution abroad, Roosevelt in a violent speech once lowered the boom on the valiant writers. They dwelt only upon the "vile and debasing," he cried, like the man with the muck rake in Bunyan's *Pilgrim's Progress*, who with his eyes on the ground raked incessantly "the straws, the small sticks, and dust of the floor." Conservatives joyfully took up the Presidential epithet.

In his later Presidential years, Roosevelt veered sharply to the left, fearful of Democratic liberalism and the opposition of union labor in the approaching Congressional elections of 1906. Roosevelt's leftward swing was evident in his special attentions to eminent Senatorial progressives—La Follette, Jonathan Dolliver, and Albert Beveridge. These men he favored with general notes and summonses to the White House for chatty visits. The conservative Senate leaders, once an object of Presidential solicitude, were doused with Presidential criticism; playing the bull in the conservative china shop, Roosevelt moved on to harsh words about "plutocracy" and stepped up his requests for reform legislation. A powerful, perhaps indispensable, force to keep the Chief Executive moving down the road of social justice is the pressure of political rivals. His competitors for the Presidency in his own and the opposition parties and legislators, especially Senators, who command national publicity and large followings can jog the President onward.

Woodrow Wilson could hardly have gained his New Freedom's social and economic reforms without the thunderous schooling of the Democratic party in progressivism by William Jennings Bryan in his three races for the Presidency. Wilson also prospered from the progressive's infiltration of Middle Western Republicanism. A majority of both Democratic and Republican opinion demanded tariff, tax, and currency reforms; increased federal aid to farmers, workers, and other disadvantaged groups; and national controls over banking and industry. Wilson did not have to create a progressive public outlook in 1913; it was already there. He came to power at a time when social reform was in its ascendancy and the elections of 1912, with their overwhelming progressive sentiment, produced a President's dream of opportunity. With good working majorities in both houses of Congress, Wilson swept through a bulging social program.

The closer the United States drew to involvement in World War I, the more strenuously Wilson campaigned to ease tensions between government and business. He cut back his antitrust prosecutions as a first step and petted the business community with soothing deeds and honeyed words of confidence. War or threat of it smothers the ardor for reform. War again was damaging to the civil liberties, the chief offender this time being Congress, whose laws on espionage and sedition seriously curtailed freedom of speech and press and other liberties. "Once lead this people into war," Wilson predicted, "and they'll forget there ever was such a thing as tolerance." His Attorney General, A. Mitchell Palmer, proved the force of these words when he employed private spies, made lawless raids on private homes and labor headquarters, rounded up several thousand aliens, held them incommunicado, and subjected them to drumhead trials. Eventually a few hundred were deported.

Wilson's trio of Republican successors—Harding, Coolidge, and Hoover —were as solidly aligned with the interests of business as any nineteenth-century President of their party, not excepting Benjamin Harrison and William McKinley. Coolidge clung to the *status quo*, admired business, and distrusted progressivism. His principal policies were high tariffs, tax reduction, and government support to industry. The reward for his steadfast partiality to business was the nation's soaring prosperity. Although Hoover preached doctrines of economic self-government, his administration, prodded by the Great Depression, undertook positive measures to bestir business activity.

Franklin Roosevelt, more than any other Democratic President, identified his party with social and economic reform and with the desires of major disadvantaged groups, such as labor and the Negroes, to better their position. The New Deal, like the "deals" of other reforming Presidents, implied that in the game of life a beneficent superintending government can deal out a better playing hand to the great mass than can the unregulated market place of society. In the breadth and number of its innovations, the New Deal stands at the head of the list. Relief for the jobless, insurance against unemployment, pensions for the aged, help for labor to organize, aid to the farmer, protection for the Negro against discrimination in employment, regulation of securities and the stock exchanges, the Tennessee Valley Authority—the list is lengthy. The depths of the Great Depression provided Roosevelt with a magnificent opportunity to act. Social justice, paradoxically, advances most in times of misery.

Like other reform Presidents before him, Roosevelt had his most productive period in the first half of his first term, marked by the election of a new President and Congress, both Democratic. With the coming of World War II his revelation that old "Dr. New Deal" was henceforth superseded by new "Dr. Win-the-War" signaled the primacy of military victory and a shutdown on social legislation for the duration. Restraints upon civil liberties again took over, although on the whole the Justice Department functioned with commendable moderation. The wartime administration's worst offense to civil liberty was the relocation of the persons of Japanese descent residing in West Coast areas at the war's outset. The Smith Act, or Alien Registration Act, outlawed various activities knowingly designed to foster the government's violent overthrow.

The post-Roosevelt administrations have undertaken, in varying degree, extensions and adaptations of the New Deal. Truman's Fair Deal ventured further into civil rights, championed a vast program of national health measures, and gave social justice an international dimension through his Point Four program by making "the benefits of our . . . industrial progress" available to "underdeveloped areas." The Truman era also witnessed the maturing of international communism into a major challenge and the initial American restrictions upon domestic civil liberties. Congress passed over Presidential veto the Internal Security or McCarran Act, requiring "communist-action" organizations and their members and "communist-front" organizations to register with the federal government. Previous laws on espionage, sabotage, and assassination remained in force. Federal employees were tested for their loyalty.

Eisenhower shifted the emphasis of the employee test from "loyalty" to "security," thus reaching an employee who might be loyal but nevertheless a security risk because, for example, of his indulgence in personal indiscretions that might invite blackmail from enemy agents. The Eisenhower administration made several restrained assertions in the social field. It brought off the largest extension of social security coverage since the law was first established. Eisenhower trod cautiously on civil rights, preferring to leave responsibility for that troubled field to the states and the private citizen. Yet his administration also witnessed the passage of the first civil rights laws since the post-Civil War era. The Eisenhower administration exhibited at least a limited recognition that the general disposition of the Coolidge-Harding-Hoover era opposing federal assertion in behalf of the disadvantaged had become obsolete in the practice of the Presidency. It alienates too many voters.

John Kennedy's New Frontier program in the 1960 campaign was a large-scale program of social services and reforms pointedly addressed to the great urban groups. Kennedy's narrow popular victory, however, and his lack of a "working majority" in Congress led him to lower his sights. His major social proposals were a rise in the minimum wage, medical care for the aged, the liberalization of social security benefits, aid to education, aid to depressed areas, and an omnibus housing bill. Some of these were familiar holdovers from the Eisenhower era that might have been passed in some form if Eisenhower had chosen to push them. Civil rights, a large subject in the 1960 campaign, was treated vigorously and imaginatively by the Executive. Kennedy made striking use of his inherent executive authority and his powers under existing statutes. Meanwhile, he held back his civil rights legislation because of his wobbly Congressional strength until the civil rights demonstrators pried it loose in the summer of 1963. Many of Kennedy's advisers and supporters were waiting for the 1964 elections to provide a firmer platform of popular and legislative votes on which to launch the far-reaching social program heralded in his 1960 campaign.

Lyndon Johnson's Great Society program would have made William Jennings Bryan, the Roosevelts, and other stalwarts of social justice beam with pride as he succeeded in putting on the statute books measures long struggled for in American political life and as he took on new goals that earlier Presidents would never have dared to entertain. The Great Society program aimed to erase poverty and the inequities that afflict the underprivileged. Johnson sought to make Negro citizens equal partners with whites in American society. In its further dimensions, the Great Society program offered something to everybody, privileged and underprivileged, by waging intensive drives against disease, crime, and ugliness. The beautification of the nation through the development of national park areas, the elimination of billboards and junkyards from highways, the reduction of pollution in air and water, and the encouragement of the arts and humanities promised a better life for all and testified to a basic working principle of the Great Society that maintained that social justice is indeed for everyone. In the same vein, Johnson took up causes beneficial to the consumer—and everyone is a consumer—by promoting higher safety standards in automobile production, the control of pesticides, truth in lending, and the like. A host of evils that Americans have endured beyond memory were marked for extinction in the Great Society. But the drain of the Vietnam war and conservative appropriations relegated the Great Society program more to the realm of promise than to here-and-now fulfillment.

The President as Social Critic

Social reform depends upon more than a set of special circumstances; it also requires the vital ingredient of the man—the President. Without his talent and involvement, circumstances, however favorable, will be wasted. If circumstances are not advantageous, we may well wonder whether a President endowed with conviction and creative gifts can bring off major achievement in the face of limited opportunity. Those Presidents who have wrought the greatest social achievements—the two Roosevelts and Woodrow Wilson—were all endowed with certain personal qualities. However much they differed otherwise, each possessed a strong sense of right, a confident faith in man's capacity for progress, and an aristocratic heritage of *noblesse oblige*. Wilson, the Calvinist, *knew* what was right and faced public questions with bristling faith in his predestined ability to find righteous solutions with God's help. "Talking to Wilson," Clemenceau once remarked, "is like talking to Jesus Christ."[1] Theodore Roosevelt, morally, was rather different. He had a strict sense of personal morality that he followed impeccably in private life and held others to in public life. In pursuing public or political ends, however, Theodore

Roosevelt often forgot his moral code in choosing means. Gifford Pinchot once told Roosevelt that he had to be either a great politician or a great moral teacher; he couldn't be both. But as the historian John M. Blum has pointed out, Theodore Roosevelt had to be, and he was, both.[2]

The Roosevelts and Wilson were all, in their way, aristocrats—Wilson by dint of his Calvinistic faith; the Roosevelts by birth and fortune. They were men apart from the usual run of aristocrats who evidence no particular sense of responsibility for others. The Roosevelts each bore a hard vein of benevolent paternalism; Theodore Roosevelt often articulated his conviction that superior station meant superior responsibilities to the less fortunate and to the state. Wilson was inspired by the ideal of service as man's highest endeavor. By grace of their aristocratic condition, all three Presidents enjoyed detachment from the existing economic order. Neither their material sustenance nor their moral tenets depended upon it. They were free to be its critics. Franklin Roosevelt's limited experience in business—he dabbled briefly in law and insurance—his lack of understanding of the importance of making a profit, Frances Perkins, his Secretary of Labor, deemed all to the good. "It gave him freedom to think," she was convinced, "in fields in which common people need their leaders to think."[3]

All three Presidents were cosmopolitan, endowed with a sturdy intelligence and curiosity to seek out new and provocative ideas. They were not rigid and inflexible in their sympathies and associations, as aristocrats tend to be, but were eager to know the world about them and excelled as assimilators of ideas. They represented, in a word, the aristocratic tradition at its best. No modern President has brought to the office a more enterprising or cosmopolitan intelligence than did Theodore Roosevelt. At the age of forty-three, when he assumed the Presidency, his far-ranging interests had established him as a naturalist, a discoverer of rivers, and a prolific author. Scientists, labor leaders, corporation executives, and religious chieftains numbered among his friends, and for them, as indeed for anyone of distinction, the welcome mat was always out. The White House calling lists in Theodore Roosevelt's day read like an occupational encyclopedia.

Woodrow Wilson began his gubernatorial candidacy as a spokesman of Democratic conservatism, which was the viewpoint of his sponsor, boss James Smith, Jr. Quickly learning the issues that were agitating the people, Wilson displayed his capacity for assimilation by cutting loose from the Smith machine and supporting the reforms that progressives of both parties had been pressing for a decade.

Franklin D. Roosevelt was also a great assimilator. "He was easy of access to many types of mind," Frances Perkins noted. The roots of his social philosophy, nourished by many sources, reached far back into his life. "One who is trying to discover the economic origins of New Deal," Rexford G. Tugwell has written, "cannot ignore the Harvard class of 1903."[4] There Franklin Roosevelt took in W. Z. Ripley's strictures on corporate finance and the lectures of O. M. W. Sprague, a future New Deal adviser, on the merits of central banking and credit control as devices for economic stability. Certainly one of his foremost teachers in the elements of social justice was Eleanor Roosevelt. Observant and reportorial, especially after his illness, Mrs. Roosevelt excelled at bringing to her husband persons expert and stimulating in social subjects. Among Mrs. Roosevelt's importations were Rose Schneiderman and Maude Schwartz of the Women's Trade Union League, who subtly tutored Roosevelt in the mission of trade unionism. He habitually preferred to assimilate background from conversations rather than from books. "I doubt," acknowledged Frances Perkins, "that he had ever read any of the standard works on trade unionism." It was during his Albany days that Roosevelt, with the encouragement and guidance of his counsel, Samuel I. Rosenman, founded his brain trust of Raymond Moley, Tugwell, Adolf Berle, and other Columbia professors. In gubernatorial seminars with his university friends, Roosevelt, as Tugwell put it, was brought "to grapple with the complex realities of industrial life, and to move beyond his oversimple reactions which were insufficient as guides to policy."[5]

Wilson and the Roosevelts all had a faith in man's capacity for progress and in government's ability to help achieve it. All had a vision of Presidential leadership that was positive and assertive. They discovered what the people wanted or needed and rallied them with great gifts of oratory. Social justice requires in large degree the passage of legislation, and all three possessed a dynamic philosophy of the Presidential role as legislative leader and a sturdy knack of success. Indeed, they exploited the full legal and political potentialities of the Presidential keyboard. "I believe in a strong executive," Theodore Roosevelt exclaimed, "I believe in power."[6] To this Wilson and Franklin Roosevelt would add a firm amen.

The Limitations of Politics

The President's political necessities take priority over ventures in social justice. No matter how lofty the cause or how intense the Chief Executive's dedication, he obeys a higher law of political survival. He must win the next election and carry on his coattails his fellow party candidates on national and local tickets. One day Franklin Roosevelt, pressed by the impatient idealism of several youthful aides, discoursed on the realities of the political world in which he and they worked. Roosevelt began,

> You know, the first thing a President has to do in order to put through good legislation? He has to get elected! If I were now back on the porch at Hyde Park as a private citizen, there is very little I could do about any of the things that I have worked on. So don't throw away votes by rushing the gun—unless there is some good sound reason. You have to get the votes first—then you can do the good work.[7]

The subordination of ideology to politics means that even those Presidents whose achievements of social justice are monumental often make their way by a course that is bafflingly erratic. Their social undertakings evolve according to no master plan but piecemeal, with quick, and not too costly, visible results preferred. The President's course is full of half-steps, forward and backward, covered with smoke clouds of obfuscation.

Theodore Roosevelt's State of the Union message of 1902 demonstrates how a President of strong political and social instincts can mix his gestures to produce a common bewilderment. The message, a thirty-thousand-word affair, was widely hailed as "safe," a result he doubtless hoped for. For assassins and anarchists Roosevelt had harsh words, which surely pleased the general citizenry. He titillated a broad swath of the more privileged population by advocating economic and educational tests for future immigrants. He said the things that the business community liked most to hear: that big corporations were "natural," that foreign trade should be expanded, and that the merchant marine should be subsidized. Camouflaged in profuse and cautious verbiage were three references of large importance for Theodore Roosevelt's future Presidency: a request for national conservation of natural resources, reciprocal tariff treaties, and national supervision of corporations. If the message's real intent was obscure, its underlying political necessities were not. Theodore Roosevelt had read several handwritings on the wall. Unless he cooperated with the conservative Republicans of the Senate, led by Nelson W. Aldrich, he could expect precious little legislation. His most sacred political objective, his renomination in 1904, required protection. Not surprisingly, he invited the men who he felt had the greatest influence upon his renomination, Senators Aldrich, John C. Spooner, William B. Allison, Orville H. Platt, and Mark Hanna—the Senate Republican leaders, all conservatives—to go over his message in draft before he sent it to Congress.

Like any other political leader, the President can at most push his ideas only a little beyond the tolerance of his constituents. As Tugwell has written, he must balance "the risk of alienating support against his conviction about what must be done and his desire to put it into practice."[8] Franklin Roosevelt thus had to find a broad base of support and gain the specific consent of powerful groups he had to work with: labor, national and racial groups, and the like. He had to impress upon them that no matter what happened, he cherished their interests at heart. Yet he also had to carry a Congressional majority. He could not alienate articulate groups such as business, the press, the lobbyists, or vote-rich groups like the several immigrant bodies and the Catholic Church. Or, more precisely, he could not alienate enough of them at once to bring real trouble.

No President of the United States has been or is ever likely to be a social zealot. The political system which selects him for the great office precludes it. To win election, he must cast the net of his promises wide; the more he can offer to more people of diverse economic interests, geographic sections, and national and racial groups, the more likely he is to triumph. The balancing effect of promise upon promise keeps the President from extremes. Indeed, the political system sifts so finely that it has invariably produced Presidents who are "safe" not merely in public utterance but in personal conviction. Franklin Roosevelt was altogether accurate in speaking of himself as "a little left of center," despite his opponents' fierce characterizations of him as a "socialist" and a "Bolshevik." Woodrow Wilson, architect of the New Freedom, bore the stamp of a Southern upbringing. He remained at heart a state rights Democrat who conceived that federal power should sweep away special privilege and other restrictions on individual energies. In his view, tariff legislation should be sheared, credit liberated from Wall Street, and the antitrust laws invigorated to restore competition. In turn, he opposed direct federal aid to depressed groups and would not fortify the natural economic power of workers and farmers. This too was special privilege.

Theodore Roosevelt likewise was a safe man. He is well described by George E. Mowry as an orthodox heretic, a respectable agitator, an intellectual Philistine, and a conservative revolutionist.[9] "At times I feel an almost Greek horror of extremes," Theodore Roosevelt once said. He abhorred "the dull, purblind folly of the very rich men, their greed and arrogance." At the other extreme, he possessed an almost morbid fear of socialists and social violence. To Theodore Roosevelt, the Populist William Jennings Bryan and the Socialist Eugene Debs were the monstrous American replicas of Marat and Robespierre.[10] His own high and solemn function, as Roosevelt saw it, was to bring balance between the greedy rich and the violent poor.

The President Keeps the Balance

In working for social justice, the President must strike a balance between that element least interested in its promotion—usually business—and those elements most devoted—once known as "progressives" and now as "liberals." He must shun extremists on both sides.

Despite the caution and balance of Presidents, their administrations tend to show a predominant concern either for the advantaged or for the disadvantaged. Since the Civil War Republican Presidents have been largely disposed to favor business and Democratic Presidents labor and Negroes. The Republican party of Coolidge is the party of business; the Democratic party of Franklin Roosevelt is the party of the disadvantaged groups. Roosevelt remains enshrined in business's embittered memory. He and his two Democratic successors—Harry Truman and John Kennedy—were involved in severe altercations with business. Kennedy's outcry upon discovering the steel price rise of 1962, "My father always told me that all [steel] businessmen were sons of bitches," is memorable not only for its unbridled candor but as a display of viscera not uncommon among Democratic Presidents.

Yet there is substantial evidence that since the Eisenhower era our political parties and Presidential administrations have reached a point where they can no longer be overwhelmingly disposed either toward the advantaged or toward the disadvantaged. Neither party, this is to say, can any longer afford to be labeled probusiness or antibusiness. Each must have general appeal. The pressures producing this circumstance are a blend of economics and politics. For any Presidential administration, prosperity is good politics. Prosperity turns on business confidence in the existing Presidential administration. If Kennedy lost his temper over steel prices, he quickly recovered it and in his subsequent deeds and words sought to mollify the business community. Lyndon Johnson tirelessly endeavored to convince business of his good will and his commitment to governmental economy and fiscal sanity.

A historic distinction of the Eisenhower Presidency is its break with the Republican tradition of overriding favoritism for business as exemplified by Coolidge, McKinley, and Benjamin Harrison. Eisenhower's Modern Republicanism called for a retention and in some instances an extension of the major social programs of the New Deal, including improvements in the social security system. How else could the Presidency be won and kept? But social changes were not made simply to win votes. As many of Eisenhower's counselors appreciated, they were also the key to general economic well-being. What is good for the country as a whole—to borrow and adjust Charles E. Wilson's famous adage—is ultimately good for business.

The President ordinarily is regarded with suspicion and even with disapproval by the progressives or liberals whose reform convictions are more advanced than his. Tension regularly prevailed between Wilson and the advanced reformers. To them he loomed as a slippery rhetorician whose heart belonged to small businessmen and manufacturers. Advanced progressives gagged over his devotion to state rights and his simple faith that regulated competition could solve the big business evil and bring to pass a fairer distribution of wealth. Inevitably, Wilson was compared to his disadvantage with such urban-Democratic reform mayors as Tom L. Johnson of Cleveland, an apostle of Henry George, and John Purroy Mitchel of New York City, who cleansed city hall of corrupting business influence, combatted urban squalor with enlightened social services, and brought mass transportation under public ownership. The cautious Wilson seemed oceans removed from the mayors' tradition when he vetoed legislation prohibiting child labor and easing farm mortgages. Franklin Roosevelt, in his day, was widely regarded by progressives as a chameleon who spurned progressivism in 1934 and embraced it in 1935. Roosevelt, who cherished acceptance by the progressives, courted their favor with mixed success. John Kennedy, in his turn, experienced a frequent questioning of his social course by a major political organization to the left of him, the Americans for Democratic Action. Lyndon Johnson, in the eyes of his social critics, readily escalated the war in Vietnam instead of escalating the war on the urban front.

The reform President also views uneasily the rare elements of the extremists who achieve major political strength. Franklin Roosevelt's adoption of a program of old age assistance was encouraged by the rise of the Townsend movement, named for Francis Everett Townsend, an unemployed physician who, looking out his bathroom window while shaving one morning, saw in an alley below, cluttered with rubbish barrels and garbage cans, "three haggard, very old women, stooped with great age, bending over the barrels, clawing into the contents." Angered by this indignity to his generation, Townsend launched a plan for old age pensions calling for two hundred dollars a month for everyone over sixty, a sum that in those deflated days seemed outrageous. Eventually other economic lures were embroidered onto the movement. By 1935 its membership and impact had mounted so that Raymond Moley was calling it "easily the outstanding political sensation as this year ends," and Edwin Witte was writing, "The battle against the Townsend Plan has been lost, I think, in pretty nearly every state west of the Mississippi, and the entire Middle Western area is likewise badly infected."[11] With the Townsend fever burning high, Franklin Roosevelt, moving with a decisiveness he never showed for unemployment compensation, directed that an old age insurance plan be incorporated into the social security bill.

Reform as Legislation

When the President's reform proposals require legislation, they must traverse a labyrinthian course filled with obstructions and quicksands. They must run the gauntlet of committee hearings and floor debates, parliamentary motions and conference committees, where a reversal at any time may be fatal. A common ordeal for Theodore Roosevelt was the predisposed negativism of both houses. In the Senate the "Big Four" Republican leaders, all intractable conservatives, ruled with a firm hand and a granitic hostility to change. In the House a tyrannical Speaker, "Uncle Joe" Cannon, held sway. Cannon controlled committee appointments and rules of procedure and acted as a crusty, unsleeping, self-appointed watchdog over the federal treasury. He greeted every proposal of social reform with the cry, "This country is a hell of a success." Cannon and the Big Four stacked the key committees with members whose conservative instincts, they knew, would prompt them to nip Theodore Roosevelt's measures in the bud.

SUPPORTIVE LEGISLATORS.   By uncommon good fortune, a President may discover a legislator whose prestige, committee assignments, parliamentary skill, and ideological convictions all harmonize with executive necessities. By these criteria, Senator George Norris' service in the cause of Franklin Roosevelt's fond dream of a Tennessee Valley Authority was almost idyllic. Prestigious progressive and chairman of the Senate Agriculture Committee, Norris for years had pushed for public power development in the Tennessee region. In 1933 Franklin Roosevelt and Norris drove through the shabby, eroded countryside along the Tennessee River in the President's open touring car, happily devising plans for a millennium of cheap electric power, flood control, soil conservation, afforestation, diversified industry, retirement of marginal farm land, and general developmental planning. Norris hailed Roosevelt's message to Congress broadly delineating the bold new idea of TVA as "the most wonderful and far-reaching humanitarian document that has ever come from the White House."[12]

APPROPRIATION PROCESS.   One of the more formidable hazards a social measure must survive is the appropriation process, easily manipulated by the foes of reform. After the Social Security Act was passed, when its advocates were rejoicing in the afterglow of victory, the wily Huey Long launched into a Senate filibuster to forestall any appropriation for the new program. Coming near the close of the legislative session, the filibuster was successful. The President had a new program but no money to administer it. The chagrined devotees of social security implored Roosevelt to foil Huey Long by summoning Congress into special session. "We shall have a riot on our hands if we call them back for an appropriation," laughed Roosevelt. Then, goaded by the spectacle of his crestfallen colleagues, he put to work his genius for improvisation that saved many a social measure in its evil hours. His colleagues watched entranced as he spun out a solution to unbind their new program. "Well, the N.R.A. is being liquidated," he mused. "There has been an appropriation from Congress to enable them to liquidate. You can take the people laid off there." There was, at least for a brief time, money to administer the program. In another Roosevelt-contrived gambit, the Labor Department asked the WPA to start a "research project" on the ways and means of administering social security. The WPA in actuality supplied personnel to operate the program. "The President was always willing to try even a risky technique to accomplish things," Frances Perkins noted appreciatively.[13]

OPPOSITION IN THE HOUSE.   John Kennedy, in his key social proposals, was bedeviled by the delaying tactics of hostile legislative committees. His plan for medical care for the aged, presented within a month after his assumption of office, was bottled up in the House Ways and Means Committee for the duration of his Presidency. Although the Committee heard a long parade of witnesses on both sides of the issue in 1961, it failed to report out the bill and chalked up a major defeat for the administration. In 1962 and 1963 the committee placed the bill behind the President's tax proposals. Since the latter received interminable review, the bill for the aged remained immobile and, like many other languishing bills, magnificently reinforced the reputation of the committee chairman, Wilbur Mills, for cautious and unhurried deliberation.

President Johnson's smashing electoral victory of 1964 was accompanied by a gain in the House of Representatives of thirty-eight more Democratic members and a more liberal outlook, which was promptly reflected in the Ways and Means Committee. When the committee was reconstituted in 1965, with more seats allotted to the Democrats because of their increased strength and with its defeated and retired members replaced, a majority of the committee supported Medicare. Chairman Wilbur Mills dropped his opposition to the bill and became its leading supporter, producing a bill more far-reaching than the administration called for, swinging other Democrats into line, and expertly managing the bill on the floor. Mills's conversion from opposition to support is not attributed to an ideological awakening but to alterations in basic political mathematics. Had he supported Medicare prior to 1965, he would have been defeated both in his committee and in the House, a disastrous blow to prestige that few committee chairman are willing to suffer. By waiting until 1965, Mills became the field marshal of a historic victory.

A second major New Frontier project, a vast proposal of aid to education, encountered fatal opposition in committee and from the House leadership. The battle was touched off by John Kennedy's unequivocal opposition to federal aid to parochial elementary and secondary schools. The principal strategist for the concerned Catholic interests was Democratic Majority Leader John McCormack of Massachusetts, the evident chieftain of a large bloc of Catholic-oriented Representatives. In the school aid fight, McCormack unofficially stepped out of his role as majority leader to operate independently of the regular Democratic organization headed by Speaker Rayburn. The fatal blow to Kennedy's 1961 education proposal occurred in the House Rules Committee, which by a vote of nine to six decided not to clear the administration's education bills until it had in hand a bill to aid private and parochial schools. Rayburn informed the President, with accurate prophecy, that the public school bill was "as dead as slavery." Four years later in 1965, on the crest of his overwhelming Presidential victory and with the substantial new liberal strength in the House, Johnson was able to push through Congress the first comprehensive education legislation in the nation's history. This time, with a dominant membership friendly to the President's social program, the Rules Committee was not a stumbling block but a compliant ally.

SUCCESS IN THE SENATE.   The Senate, which earlier in the twentieth century was known as a citadel of hostility to social legislation, has undergone something of a transformation well evident in John Kennedy's and Lyndon Johnson's experiences. Kennedy enjoyed conspicuously greater success in the Senate than in the House, where measures approved by the Senate were rejected or drastically revised. Kennedy's 1961 education program was approved in the Senate only to be rejected in the House. The Senate passed his depressed areas and minimum wage bills; the House severely amended them. Johnson, to whom appropriations were vital for the progress of his Great Society program, sustained in the House drastic cuts on nearly all his requests for funds for urban measures. In the more favorable climate of the Senate, he had to push for substantially larger appropriations to strengthen his hand in the later House-Senate conference negotiations that would settle upon a final amount.

Kennedy's and Johnson's greater successes in the upper chamber than in the House are largely explained by the mounting population shifts to the cities in recent decades. The Senator, answerable to a state-wide constituency, depends increasingly upon the great mass of urban voters for election, a happy coincidence for Kennedy's and Johnson's legislative programs, which were heavily directed to the cities. The Representative, in contrast, responds to a smaller, less complex constituency. Rural voters, who tend to look askance at social legislation, possess a powerful voice in the House, owing to the lag in the redistricting of House seats to reflect the swelling population shifts from rural to urban and suburban areas. The Supreme Court's 1964 decision in *Wesberry v. Sanders*, requiring that as nearly as possible one man's vote in a Congressional election shall be worth as much as another's, promises to compel a more equitable districting for the underrepresented areas. Likewise, if population shifts to those areas live up to predictions for future decades, the Court's decision may provide the basis for an improved capacity of the federal government to enact social legislation. Much will depend upon the suburban voter's attitudes, on whether he will be more tolerant of federal social action.

COALITIONS.   Social legislation in the contemporary era faces a hostile coalition that reaches back to the Franklin Roosevelt administration. In the Eisenhower administration Southern Democrats and conservative Republicans repeatedly played a decisive part in defeating or modifying social legislation for civil rights and medical care for the aged. The same coalition flourished in Kennedy's time. (As defined by the *Congressional Quarterly Weekly Report*, the coalition exists in a house when a majority of the voting Southern Democrats and a majority of the voting Republicans oppose the position of a majority of the Northern Democrats.) In what Kennedy styled as his "Big Five" programs of 1961—medical care for the aged, aid to education, aid for housing, a higher minimum wage, and aid to depressed areas—the only item on which the coalition did not operate in the House of Representatives was housing. The coalition's single absolute victory was on federal aid to education; the medical care bill, bottled in committee, did not come to a vote. In the Senate the coalition appeared in the voting on four bills: depressed areas, minimum wage, housing, and school aid. On none of these was the coalition victorious. Despite the coalition's eclipsed influence, Kennedy was consistently wary. He withheld civil rights legislation until late in his term, anxious not to alienate Southern Democrats either simply on civil rights or on other social proposals. For the cause of social justice, the real significance of the 1964 election was that it smashed the conservative coalition. Johnson responded swiftly by moving onto the statute books the three major measures long blocked by the coalition: civil rights, education, and Medicare. When the 1966 Congressional elections restored the conservative coalition to dominance in the House, Johnson responded to the change in political atmosphere by scaling down his requests for new social legislation.

Kennedy's successes against the conservative coalition and Johnson's achievements after 1966 were vitally assisted by an offsetting bipartisan liberal coalition. Most of Kennedy's victories where opposition was strong were indebted to liberal Democratic and Republican support. In the House liberal Republicans provided the votes for the victories of the depressed areas bill and the minimum wage bill and the battle to enlarge the Rules Committee in the hope of brightening prospects for social measures. The conference report on the depressed areas bill, which prevailed by thirty votes, was supported by thirty-one Republicans. In the Senate Republican help enabled the administration to push through the temporary extension of unemployment benefits, the minimum wage bill, the school aid bill, and housing. Time and again the practical problem facing Kennedy and his strategists was putting together a bipartisan liberal coalition to defeat the conservative coalition.

In the Senate the liberal Republican bloc in the Kennedy era consisted of eight to thirteen members and in the House about twice that number. Republican bloc members of both houses tended to come from urban industrial states and explained their frequent siding with administration positions on the ground that Kennedy had preempted the middle of the road and left them no alternative but to go along or yield the center and with it their grip on their constituencies. The result was a *de facto* coalition of Northern and Western Democrats and "liberal Republicans," the source of most of Kennedy's victories on social issues. After 1966, with reduced Democratic majorities, a similar coalition helped Johnson secure the enactment of stricter meat inspection laws, expansion of federal air pollution programs, extension of the Appalachian Regional Development program, and reorganization of District of Columbia government, among other measures.

The Executive Branch

The executive branch, with its abundance of talent, data, and organizations, provides the President with vital resources of social reform. His success in social enterprises depends in no small way upon his skill in exploiting these resources, particularly his cache of human talent. Within the executive branch are various specialists whose common effort is required to transmute the President's reform agenda into reality.

ADVISERS. To make social innovations, the President requires advisers with ideas and access to his attention. Advisers may do their most fruitful toil well before their chief takes office. Woodrow Wilson, facing his 1912 Presidential campaign and looking about for a vivid and solid issue, conferred hopefully with Louis Brandeis, then a distinguished private lawyer with defined views on policy. The Wilson-Brandeis meeting of August 28, 1912, was fraught with consequence for the subsequent New Freedom program. A champion of regulated competition, unhampered enterprise, and economic freedom for the small businessman, Brandeis guided Wilson into the conception that the worthiest issue his future administration might take up was the preservation of economic freedom in the United States. Business, by grace of government action, was to be freed from the shackles of monopoly and privilege. The Brandeis proposal fitted very precisely the necessities of the campaign. Its approach to the trust problem differed markedly from that of Theodore Roosevelt, Wilson's chief rival in the 1912 race. Roosevelt would legalize "good" monopolies; Wilson, taking his cue from Brandeis, argued, in contrast, that competition should be regulated and safeguarded so that all monopoly and its potential for evil would eventually be destroyed.[14]

Some Presidents resort not merely to solitary advisers but to whole teams of them like Franklin Roosevelt's brain trust. John Kennedy preparing for the Presidency, recruited task forces to study and report on foreign and domestic problems. Lyndon Johnson, faced with the rising urgency of urban problems, appointed in 1967 several commissions to develop recommendations in specific areas of federal concern. One commission, headed by the industrialist Edgar Kaiser, was assigned to prepare a plan to lower the cost of housing for the poor through less expensive and more efficient methods of construction and financing. Another commission, led by former Senator Paul Douglas, examined local zoning laws and building codes to see how they might be altered to speed construction of low-cost housing.

Presidential advisers hail from all sorts of nooks and crannies of the executive branch and of society at large. Andrew Jackson's principal counselor in his war upon the Bank of the United States was Amos Kendall, fourth auditor of the Treasury. The President's adviser may be a general counselor whose attention to a social justice project is but one of a host of assignments. Edward House, whose main beat was foreign policy, worked mightily in the service of Woodrow Wilson to bring about the Federal Reserve System. House harried the nation's professors of economics for the cream of their theory and data and conferred with bankers of varying viewpoints on the issue. Or again, the President's chief adviser may be, as plain logic suggests, the cabinet Secretary whose department bears most closely upon the social reform at stake. Frances Perkins, Franklin Roosevelt's Secretary of Labor, for example, made the social security program her special cause. A social worker and New York Industrial Commissioner during Roosevelt's governorship, Miss Perkins, before accepting appointment to the national cabinet, had laid out a program, including unemployment and old age assistance, that she would insist upon if she came to Washington. Franklin Roosevelt promptly invited her to come along.

EXPERTS.   Since projects of social justice are founded upon the conceptualizations and data of social science's several branches, experts and technicians play leading roles in Presidential ventures. The chief expert toiling for the creation of the Social Security Act in 1935 was Edwin E. Witte, executive director of the Cabinet Committee on Economic Security. With this lordly bureaucratic title, Witte oversaw quantities of outside experts, a technical board of government experts, an advisory council, and a national conference. Prior to these responsibilities, Witte had served as secretary to progressive Congressman John M. Nelson, statistician and secretary to the Wisconsin Industrial Commission, and chief of the Wisconsin Legislative Reference Library. In the last capacity he drafted pioneering social legislation for which Wisconsin is distinguished. He taught at the state's university, served as acting director of the Wisconsin unemployment compensation law and studied social insurance methods in Europe.[15]

To launch his new Washington job, Witte made a month's grand tour of the American social security world, conferring with knowledgeable Washington officialdom, professors, mayors, state legislators, business executives, and social workers. "Very contradictory advice was given me by the people consulted," he noted, "but I still regard these conferences as having been distinctly worthwhile, as they served to rapidly acquaint me with the widely varying views entertained within the Administration circle and the difficulties to be overcome."[16] At the behest of Raymond Moley, then a leading Presidential adviser, Witte prepared a lengthy statement on the problems of economic security for inclusion in Franklin Roosevelt's scheduled speech at Green Bay, Wisconsin. Although only two of Witte's sentences were eventually used, their effect was electric. The stock market dropped five points. Appalled high Treasury Department officials sprang forth to demand that social security be soft-pedaled at once. In his lesser concerns, Witte oversaw the handling of the voluminous mail on social security pouring upon the President, the executive committee, and its members. Much of the mail, which climbed to fifteen hundred letters a day, concerned not the administration's social security project but the wild and booming Townsend plan.

Witte's most trying task was to find and hire social security experts willing to subordinate their professional predilections to the necessities of the executive committee and the President. Working under severe time limitations set down by Roosevelt, Witte had to badger the specialists into putting aside their accustomed standards of perfection so their reports would be finished on schedule. Witte had to shepherd the executive committee's report, which emerged from the specialists' reports, through agonizing rounds of negotiations. Several committee members refused to sign the report without having every word in it and the accompanying draft legislation scrutinized by subordinates in whom they had absolute confidence. Witte's worst hours were spent in the Treasury where two groups opposed social security, one conservative, bent upon holding down expenditures and avoiding any stir that might alarm business, the other radical, which felt that given the deep economic morass in which the country was wallowing the proposals had little value. Witte's ordeal was topped off with four days of testimony on the technical phases of social security before the House Ways and Means Committee and three days before the Senate Finance Committee. His experience illuminates a common fate of Presidential experts. Their talents are useful at both ends of Pennsylvania Avenue.

PROMOTERS.   Social justice measures, taking the form of legislation, have touched off the most violent battles that Congress has witnessed. Among the most inflamed of these scenes was the Franklin Roosevelt administration's public utility bill, with its "death sentence" provision, designed to outlaw some of the grosser abuses of the holding companies of gas and electric utilities. To guide his cherished legislation through the pending strife, the President turned to a lieutenant with proven talent for the rough and tumble of legislative politics, Thomas G. Corcoran, a youthful, cherub-faced protégé of Felix Frankfurter and former law clerk of Oliver Wendell Holmes.[17]

Nominally a counsel of the Reconstruction Finance Corporation, Corcoran with his partner in several New Deal enterprises Benjamin V. Cohen, the counsel of the Power Policy Committee, had drafted the utilities bill they were now promoting. To touch off his campaign, Corcoran prepared a Presidential letter of fitting exhortation to accompany the bill to Capitol Hill. He provided full-time, all-around assistance to the bill's sponsors, Senator Burton K. Wheeler of Montana and Congressman Sam Rayburn of Texas. Corcoran and Cohen coached the sponsors and a parade of government witnesses on the bill's many intricacies. For Senators and Congressmen friendly to the bill, they ghostwrote letters addressed to legislative colleagues and influential constituents, entreating their support. Corcoran negotiated compromises on hostile amendments and frantically lobbied in cloakrooms and hallways, lining up votes. The juggernaut of influence that the utilities were wheeling through Congress lifted his effort to a high and steady pitch.

The President's youthful promoter was faring tolerably well until an explosion of ominous publicity was touched off by Congressman Ralph O. Brewster of Maine. At the height of battle, Brewster rose in the House to declare,

> During the consideration of the "death sentence" clause in the Holding Company bill, Thomas G. Corcoran, Esquire . . . came to me in the lobby of the Capitol and stated to me with what he termed "brutal frankness" that, if I should vote against the death sentence

for public utility companies he would find it necessary to stop construction on the Passamaquoddy dam in my district.*

Promptly after Brewster's disclosure, Corcoran was faced with two inquiries.
One, a cryptic request from Franklin Roosevelt, read "Please send me as
promptly as possible a complete statement of all your dealings on governmental matters" with Congressman Brewster.[18] The second was a House committee investigation of the incident. Corcoran passed both tests with flying
colors. In putting his case before the House committee, he had the advantage
of a witness, a fellow official of the executive branch, while Brewster was
handicapped by having no corroborator. Meantime the utility bill was passed.

ADMINISTRATORS.   A victory won in social legislation can be lost in the
selection of the administrative agency to carry it out. Since the President
initiates the selection of the agency's leadership, he is sometimes the perpetrator of defeat. In reality, he may yield to conservative pressures. To the newly
established Federal Reserve Board, Wilson appointed an array of leading
bankers and businessmen, a stroke that put the progressive community into a
state of shock. "Why, it looks as if Mr. Vanderlip [president of the National
City Bank of New York] has selected them," sputtered one dazed progressive.
When Wilson, in a similar tactic, loaded the Interstate Commerce Commission
with devoted friends of American railroads, Senator Robert La Follette exclaimed, "What an inspiring spectacle to the millions who voted for Wilson as
a true Progressive." The newly created Federal Trade Commission was not
long at work when Louis Brandeis, who had envisioned it as a dynamic force
to relieve the economy of strangulating monopoly and to restore competition,
was driven to dank despair. Wilson, he said, had ruined the FTC by his choice
of commissioners. A typical Wilsonian choice was Edward Hurley, a Chicago
industrialist and an ardent disciple of business-government cooperation.[19]

The cabinet of Franklin Roosevelt was, in its majority sentiment, at least
middle-of-the-road and even conservative toward social questions. The state
of the cabinet partly reflects the mixed sentiment of the body politic itself
regarding social reform and partly the unsettled attitude of the President.
Roosevelt's original Budget director, Lewis Douglas, and his Secretary of
State, Cordell Hull, were devoted to sound money, fiscal orthodoxy, and tariff
reduction. Old-line progressivism was embodied in Harold Ickes, a Bull
Mooser, and the preferability of government-business collaboration in Raymond Moley on the right and Rexford Tugwell, Assistant Secretary of Agriculture, on the left. These and other philosophical schools scored successes,
although the predominant image that emerged was of social reform.

It was part of Franklin Roosevelt's administrative genius that he encour-

* The dam was a huge work relief project established primarily to develop public
power. "Quoddy," situated across from Campobello, Franklin Roosevelt's summer
home, was a pet enterprise of the President.

aged his diverse administrators to ride and expand their own programs vigorously and never think of sparing him. "Thus a very energetic set of people were stimulated by their leader to develop programs of reform and action," Frances Perkins noted.[20] The pressures unloosed upon the President were often exerted in collusion by his several administrators. In the early New Deal, for example, those who wanted a gigantic public works program to relieve the misery of the unemployed and to bestir general economic activity continuously pressed the Chief Executive. Secretary Perkins would bring up the matter at one session of the cabinet; Jim Farley, the Postmaster General, at the next; and then Ickes at the one after that. The object of this unceasing harassment was to keep the subject stirring in the President's mind. The allied Secretaries had a sense of special urgency because Douglas, the chief opponent of large-scale public works, managed through his skillful argument at cabinet meetings to raise doubts in Roosevelt's mind and forestall him from acting at once. Eventually, however, Roosevelt chose to establish a mammoth public works program.

Early Efforts for Civil Rights

Of all social justice fields, civil rights for the Negro has evoked the most various and sometimes the most enterprising executive responses. It has also been frequently ignored by Presidents.

Despite the beacon light of Lincoln's Emancipation Proclamation, Presidents have dealt gingerly with Negro civil rights since his time. After Lincoln, Theodore Roosevelt was the first President to act assertively, at least by the standards of his day. He was attentive to Booker T. Washington, the eminent Negro educator. Early in his administration, Roosevelt appointed William Crum as customs collector in Charleston and Minnie Cox as postmistress in Indianola, Alabama. Both were Negroes. Although Roosevelt's moves seemingly championed the Negro cause, they were not unalloyed. His eye was fixed upon the 1904 Presidential nomination and his considerable rival, Mark Hanna. The latter's awesome strength at past Presidential nominating conventions was founded no little upon unswerving Southern delegations of "lily-white" Republicans. To counterweigh Hanna, Roosevelt had to enlist the "black and tan" Republicans, and for this high enterprise Booker T. Washington was his staff and reed.

Roosevelt's good progress was suddenly jeopardized by the Brownsville affair, when Negro soldiers, angered at their treatment by the local folk of Brownsville, Texas, made a shooting sortie into the town, killing a citizen. Efforts to lay responsibility for the slaying failed; the soldiers would not talk. Roosevelt, the Commander-in-Chief, conscious of his duty to maintain discipline, meted out punishment by discharging "without honor" every man of three Negro companies. Republican politicians, mindful of the traditional

Negro vote for their party, grew fearful, and Roosevelt redoubled his attentions.

Although Woodrow Wilson appealed openly for Negro support in the 1912 elections, once in office he and his principal administrators quickly exhibited the predominant Southern background of his Presidency. Civil service workers were rigidly segregated in offices, shops, restrooms, and lunchrooms. Negro political appointees, including those with civil service status, were widely dismissed. Herbert Hoover, despite his Quaker roots, evidenced little interest in the Negro's plight. He made, said W. E. B. Du Bois, "fewer first-class appointments of Negroes to office than any President since Andrew Jackson."[21] Franklin Roosevelt accomplished the awesome feat of transferring the Negroes' traditional loyalty to the Republican party, which had been cemented by Lincoln, from that party to the Democrats. The New Deal was, by contrast to the barren Democratic past, rich in its dispensations to the Negro. The National Industrial Recovery Act set a single standard for Negro and white wage earners in the South. Relief funds, housing projects in the wake of slum clearance, rural resettlement, land-utilization schemes providing parks, picnic grounds, and beaches for the Negro, and growing federal attention to education and health were a great boon to that race, which suffered more than any other part of the population in the depression. Harry Truman created a Commission on Civil Rights whose distinguished report, *To Secure These Rights,* charted a wide ground for future action. He accepted the 1948 Presidential nomination with a fiery speech, broadcasting his future call of Congress into special session to act on civil rights. Truman tarnished his promising record by never mentioning civil rights again in his ensuing campaign until a wind-up speech in New York's Harlem. Otherwise Truman moved to establish a permanent Fair Employment Practices Commission, fought the Senate filibuster by prodding Democratic leaders to bring about an amendment of the Senate rules, attacked racial discrimination, and backed the United Nations' Declaration of Human Rights. His strong stand on civil rights was diminished by the occasional fluctuating character of his support for legislative and administrative action and by off-the-record comments that he made on several occasions after his Presidency that were hardly in keeping with his administration's record.

Negro civil rights first assumed crisis proportions, in the Presidential view, in the 1957 Little Rock school episode of the Eisenhower era and boiled over into the multiple crises of the Kennedy administration. The two Presidents differed radically in their views on civil rights, particularly on public school segregation. The several Supreme Court rulings of 1954 striking down segregated public schools as a violation of the Fourteenth Amendment's requirement of equal protection of the laws were followed by widespread resistance by state and local government to the point where activity in the South toward integration came almost to a halt. President Eisenhower made little effort through federal policy to support the Supreme Court holdings, leaving the question of compliance to voluntary action and local lawsuits. He intervened personally only after Governor Orval Faubus of Arkansas defied a federal court order and employed the National Guard to prevent Negro school children from attending the Little Rock Central High School. In addition, after withdrawing the guard, the governor failed to prevent a mob from blocking the Negro children's entry to the school. Eisenhower, stung by the governor's defiance, federalized the Arkansas National Guard and called out Regular Army units to enforce the court order and protect the Negro children. Eisenhower, nevertheless, refused to declare that he personally favored elimination of segregation from public schools, holding that policy on the question was the province of the Supreme Court and not the President. He sometimes remarked that race relations could not be effectively regulated by law but depended upon voluntary action.

John Kennedy and Civil Rights

John Kennedy, in contrast, became the first Chief Executive to place himself at the head of the Negro civil rights movement. He publicly asserted his support of the Supreme Court's rulings in the school segregation cases; enforced the enrollment of James Meredith at the University of Mississippi and of Vivian Malone and James Hood at the University of Alabama; quelled the raging strife in Birmingham, Albany, Jackson, and other cities, North and South; and quietly encouraged or at least failed to discourage the 1963 march on Washington. Kennedy was faced with social revolution and had to act. That it was congenial to his own nature to act made his stand more consistent and more forceful. In meeting the civil rights issue, whether in its more subdued stage earlier in his administration or in its later critical phase, Kennedy and his aides wielded, with skill and enterprise, a variety of executive tools.

LITIGATION.   The 1957 Civil Rights Act authorizes the Justice Department to sue in federal courts or to seek injunctive relief where the right to vote is denied or threatened. In its first year, the Kennedy administration initiated twice as many cases as the Eisenhower administration did in three years. Although the latter administration commenced the first exploratory cases under the Civil Rights Acts of 1957 and 1960, the Kennedy administration displayed greater litigious vigor and resourcefulness. Kennedy's Justice Department stepped up the tempo of school segregation cases and forged a major innovation by casting itself as plaintiff in the Prince Edward County, Virginia, case. The Kennedy administration's law arm also struck in other urgent civil rights situations. When the city of Albany, Georgia, sought an injunction banning further Negro protest demonstrations in that city, the Justice Department filed a friend-of-the-court brief in opposition. Likewise, when Governor Ross Barnett of Mississippi interposed obstructions to the enrollment of James Meredith at the University of Mississippi, the Justice Department petitioned the Fifth Circuit Court of Appeals to levy a fine of $100,000 upon the governor.

THE PRESIDENTIAL CONSTABULARY.   The United States Code authorizes the President to suppress domestic violence stemming from unlawful assembly or a state's inability or unwillingness to protect a constitutional right. To keep order, the President is assisted by a tripartite constabulary: the Regular Army, the federalized National Guard, and the United States marshals. In the severe rioting in Birmingham, Alabama, in May 1963, Kennedy vowed before the nation, "This Government will do whatever must be done to preserve order, to protect the lives of its citizens and to uphold the law of the land." Even as the President spoke, units of the armed forces specially trained in riot control moved into military bases near Birmingham. The President simultaneously ordered the taking of all "necessary preliminary steps" to call the Alabama National Guard into federal service. James Meredith's presence and safety at the University of Mississippi depended, at least in its early season, upon units of the Regular Army and the federalized Mississippi National Guard. The busiest unit of the President's constabulary was the United States marshals, called upon to protect variously the freedom riders and demonstrators in Albany, Georgia. When a mob took over the bus station in Montgomery, Alabama, six hundred marshals moved in to fill the law enforcement vacuum.

THE GOVERNMENT CONTRACT.   Presidents since Franklin Roosevelt have employed the government contract as a weapon to clear pathways for civil rights progress. The one hundred largest defense contractors and their subcontractors employ approximately ten million persons. Countless other workers are employed under federal contracts or aid. From Franklin Roosevelt onward, interdepartmental committees composed of the departments contracting most heavily have existed to overcome job discrimination by private employers performing government contracts. Congress's disinclination to establish a fair employment practices commission has made reliance upon the interdepartmental committees all the heavier. Through the committees, Presidents have insisted upon antidiscrimination provisos in government contracts, heeding their implied duty as executors of the Constitution, with its affirmation of equal rights, to see that federal money is not tainted with racial prejudice.

THE CIVIL SERVICE.   The United States government, as the nation's largest employer, has its own house to put in order. Legal authority to do so is abundant. The 1883 Civil Service Act established merit as the primary test for federal employment, and from 1940 onward various statutes prohibit discrimination "on account of race, creed, or color." The President's official oath and responsibility as chief administrator impart further authority. The Kennedy administration's personnel policies put new stress upon the appointment and upgrading of qualified Negroes. Complaint procedures concerning discrimination were liberalized and the Committee on Equal Employment Opportunity investigated agency compliance.

The Kennedy administration's emphasis upon Negro recruitment was reinforced symbolically by Kennedy's exercise of the Presidential appointment power. The selection of Robert Weaver as head of the Housing and Home Finance Agency, of Andrew Hatcher as White House associate press secretary and of Carl Rowan as Assistant Secretary of State for Public Affairs and later as ambassador to Finland were indicative of the administration's commitment.

ADMINISTRATIVE REGULATION.   The freedom riders' visitations in Southern territory spurred the Kennedy administration to petition the Interstate Commerce Commission to desegregate facilities in terminals providing interstate bus travel. After months of delay and insistent Justice Department pressure, the desegregation order was issued. The administration lacked power to move similarly upon airports under the Civil Aeronautics Act. To foster desegregation in various Southern airport facilities, the Justice Department relied upon court action and private persuasion.

FEDERAL FUNDS.   The expenditure of federal funds is a Presidential weapon of vast potency in the civil rights struggle. Few aspects of American life are untouched by the incessant outpouring of federal money. In many states and localities the federal wherewithal has, in actuality, supported rather than checked racial discrimination. Housing, education, job training, the National Guard, recreation facilities, hospitals, libraries, university research, agrricultural extension, state employment services, vocational rehabilitation, school lunches, and highway and airport construction are objects of federal largess and occasional sources of racial discrimination.

In his 1960 campaign Kennedy flayed the Eisenhower administration for not blotting out racial discrimination in federally supported housing, holding it could be achieved merely by "a stroke of the pen." After long delay and much pressure by racial groups, the President finally issued an executive order on November 21, 1962, barring discrimination in the sale or rental of housing financed through federal assistance. The executive order's seeming breadth was badly sheared by administrative interpretation. "Conventional" or private financing, houses "already built," houses that were not in commercially developed neighborhoods, and FHA-insured loans for home improvements were ruled to be not covered.

President Kennedy was insistently pressed to issue a blanket order prohibiting discrimination in all federal programs. Indeed in Kennedy's encounters with Governor Barnett to enroll James Meredith in the state university, the Civil Rights Commission urged that Mississippi be barred from all federal funds. "I don't have the power to cut off the aid in a general way as was proposed by the Civil Rights Commission," Kennedy responded, adding that "I think it would probably be unwise" to grant the President that power.[22]

PUBLIC APPEALS.   In the major civil rights crises, Kennedy as a regular tactic made radio and television addresses, pleading and lecturing to the nation, stressing the moral aspects and local responsibilities. In the University of Alabama episode of 1963, Governor George C. Wallace stood in the doorway of a university building to prevent the registration of two Negro students, Vivian Malone and James Hood. The governor, in his chosen stance, was both fulfilling a campaign pledge and violating a court order rendered to assure the students' registration at the university. Kennedy's public expressions included an appeal to Wallace to stay away from the university campus. The governor's plan, the President said in a published telegram, was "the only announced threat to orderly compliance with the law." The students eventually embarked upon their studies with the help of the National Guard. In his television address on the Alabama episode, Kennedy termed the rising tide of Negro discontent "a moral crisis," which "faces us all in every city of the North as well as the South." The problem of the Negro's place in American life, the President declared, "must be solved in the homes of every American across the country."[23] In an address to the 1963 National Conference of Mayors, he urged increased local responsibility in coping with disturbances in Northern and Southern cities, the establishment of local biracial human relations committees to spot developing tensions and push for the revision of local segregation laws, and the adoption of equal opportunity ordinances for housing, public accommodations, and employment.

Kennedy's public appeals were also put to specific local communities and their key citizens. His most eloquent appeal in behalf of civil rights was his televised address to the nation in the crisis of James Meredith's enrollment. Kennedy appealed to the students and people of Mississippi to comply with court rulings and therefore with federal law to bring the crisis to an end. "The eyes of the nation and all the world are upon you and upon all of us," he said, "and the honor of your university and state are in the balance."[24] As rioting spread and Negro houses were bombed in Birmingham in 1963, the President implored that community to restore peace. The burning of Negro churches near Albany, Georgia, in September 1963, he termed "cowardly as well as outrageous." When a general civil rights impasse seized that unhappy city, Kennedy declared in a news conference that he could not see why city officials could not sit down with Negro citizens to work out racial problems.

In the New Orleans school integration crisis, he reminded segregationists that the Supreme Court's school desegregation decision was both constitutionally and morally unassailable.

PRIVATE PERSUASION.   To head off brewing civil rights crises or to steady them at a low boiling point, President Kennedy, Attorney General Robert Kennedy, and their aides counted heavily upon the arts of private persuasion. President Kennedy met at the White House with whole delegations of Southern businessmen, theater owners, and newspaper editors to present the case for voluntary desegregation and warn of the danger that Negro extremists might gain power should the moderates fail. Cabinet Secretaries sometimes joined the effort. Secretary of Commerce Luther Hodges, a North Carolinian, wrote letters of encouragement to fellow Southerners; the Attorney General telephoned friendly and unfriendly local officials, encouraging, persuading, or scolding, as required. The Justice Department in private, unpublicized talks helped some Southern communities desegregate their schools without incident. That department also quieted several violent intervals in Birmingham by negotiating agreements between the contending groups; as tensions mounted in Jackson, Mississippi, in June 1963, a peace-building meeting took place in the local Masonic Lodge between John Doar, Assistant Attorney General for Civil Rights, and Negro representatives. In its discussions with white Southern leaders, the administration stiffened its language with appeals to party loyalty and used higher and lower forms of political inducement. The administration also engaged in dialogue with Negro civil rights leaders, including an intensive discussion in New York at the peak of the 1963 crisis when Robert Kennedy reviewed with the leaders both what they were seeking and what the administration could do.

In addition, President Kennedy and his aides invested many hours in White House discussions with Negro leaders to plumb their views and to convey the administration's intentions and a sense of the political realities it faced. Soon after taking office, Kennedy invited the emissaries of several Negro groups to outline what they would consider a good administration civil rights program. A sixty-one-page memorandum resulted, and, midway in discussing it with Roy Wilkins and Arnold Aronson, chairman and secretary, respectively, of the Leadership Conference on Civil Rights, Theodore Sorensen, the President's special counsel, let out the bitter news that the administration would not push civil rights legislation, at least in its first year. This disclosure bathed the 1961 conference of the National Civil Liberties Clearing House in Washington in gloomy lamentation.

Like other Presidents who, because of political restraints, could give social groups only a part of what they wanted, Kennedy sustained public criticism from Negro civil rights leaders. In the administration's first years, when it held back civil rights legislation and shunned a futile fight to throttle the Senate filibuster, NAACP secretary Roy Wilkins sadly declared that an "atmosphere of super-caution" had "pervaded" all civil rights discussions with Kennedy and his staff since Election Day. In a television interview in June 1963, amid the demonstrations crisis, the Reverend Martin Luther King, viewing the cheerless scene, conceded that President Kennedy "may have done a little more" than President Eisenhower, "but the plight of the vast majority of Negroes remains the same." In the spirit of constructive criticism, Dr. King urged the President to forego a trip to Europe scheduled later in the month, and remain, instead, in Washington to push his civil rights program. Kennedy, however, disregarded this counsel and embarked for Europe.

Lyndon Johnson and Civil Rights

Like John Kennedy, Lyndon Johnson employed the substantial armory of his executive powers to advance civil rights, including public appeals, the manipulation of federal funds, and litigation. He broke precedent by bringing distinguished Negro citizens onto the Supreme Court and into the cabinet by his appointments of Thurgood Marshall as a justice and of Robert Weaver as Secretary of Housing and Urban Development. Johnson also appointed Carl Rowan as director of the United States Information Agency. It was in the Johnson era that civil rights legislation pressed by Kennedy before his death became law in 1964, followed by the Voting Rights Act of 1965. In 1966 Johnson labored to bring Congress to enact open housing legislation, the first civil rights bill to affect the North. But the slipping popularity of the civil rights movement and widespread white Northern hostility assured the legislation's defeat. The more conservative make-up of Congress following the 1966 elections imperiled any major legislation. Johnson, nevertheless, managed to steer through Congress the modest Civil Rights Act of 1967, making it a federal crime for anyone to interfere with another's civil rights. And finally, in 1968, following the assassination of Dr. King, President Johnson secured passage of the long-awaited open housing bill.

The several civil rights laws more or less close the chapter of the Kennedy-Johnson struggle for legal freedom and equality for the Negro. In a 1965 address at Howard University, President Johnson exhorted the nation to take up a new and loftier civil rights goal, "to give twenty million Negroes the same chance as every other American to learn and grow, to work and share in society, to develop their abilities—physical, mental and spiritual—and to pursue their individual happiness."[25] The President in effect was saying that the major strides in civil rights assured the Negro only the "legal right" to vote, get a job, go to unsegregated schools, and enjoy due process of law, and provided him with only "separate but equal" citizenship. Yet these legal rights, however important, are little availing if the great body of Negro citizens are poorly educated, confined to ghettos, and condemned to a life of poverty. The President pleaded that the Negro be accepted as an equal. It is, he said, "not enough to open the gates of opportunity. All our citizens must have the ability to walk through the gates."

Limitations of Power

The Negro civil rights revolution throws a sharp, unflattering glare upon the limitations of Presidential power as an instrument of social change. Johnson, in posing his new and higher goal, could envision government programs providing schools, homes, even jobs, but these, he candidly confessed, were but "part of the answer." "An understanding heart by all Americans," he added, "is also part of the answer." Absolute equality for the Negro depends not upon federal laws, troops, and money, but upon how individual citizens behave toward one another in endless transactions that the government cannot regulate. The President can influence the human heart, but he cannot control it.

The limitations of Presidential power are sadly evident when the plight of the Negro prior to the civil rights movement is compared with his condition after the movement matured. In the late 1960's a greater proportion of Negroes are unemployed than in 1954, the year of the first judicial decisions on civil rights. More Negroes are concentrated in unskilled employment where the highest displacement occurs from new automatic machinery. Negro slums grow apace. The President, as head of the civil rights movement, in stressing legal rights and remedies, has raised Negro economic expectations that neither government nor private industry up to now have been able to satisfy.

To tackle the economic crisis of the Negro, qualified testimony holds, would require outlays on the scale of a major war. The 1968 report of the President's Commission on Civil Disorders made recommendations on a scale whose costs it did not dare to estimate. Bayard Rustin, a leader of the civil rights movement, speaks of replacing the slums of New York City with public housing worth seventeen billion dollars. After the Detroit riots in the summer of 1967, Vice President Humphrey urged that a "Marshall Plan" be developed to eradicate slum area. Humphrey contemplated a massive, long-term public-supported commitment of several billion dollars.[26]

Despite riot and insurrection in cities across the land and sweeping proposals provided by the Commission on Civil Disorders, not the least sign of any massive response to the Negro question appears on the political scene. The cost of the Vietnam war has taken money from urgent domestic programs, and Congressional conservatives dealt harshly with appropriations for President Johnson's domestic programs. In 1966–67 the House of Representatives systematically cut every request for urban expenditure. For example, for his model cities program, an imaginative comprehensive attack on Negro urban problems, the President asked for $662 million for the fiscal year 1968, but the House granted only $237 million. For another key measure of 1967, the rent supplement program, the President requested $40 million, but the House refused to appropriate a cent. At a high point in the 1967 rioting, Sargent Shriver, director of the Office of Economic Opportunity, which administers much of the poverty program, acknowledged that a $2.06 billion appropriation requested by the administration was not enough for immediate needs. He was fearful, he said, that Congress would not grant even that amount. If the President asked for a really huge increase in anti-poverty funds, he added, "we might get nothing, because many people in Congress would consider that irresponsible, even though the need might be there."[27]

The effectiveness of Presidential power depends heavily upon the support of administration, which reposes in the hands of the federal departments. It is one thing for the President to issue executive orders and proclaim high policy; it is quite another to transmute policy into action and orders into compliance. In the acid test of performance, the President depends upon a vast federal bureaucracy and far-flung field organizations staffed heavily with local personnel. John Kennedy's housing order, for example, however bold and well-intentioned on its face, was softened by administrative interpretation —the sweeping exemptions and the stress upon "persuasion" rather than enforcement. The unacknowledged motivation behind such choices is the fear that vigorous executive action will alienate Southern legislators situated on strategic committees. In the Johnson era, when the Department of Health, Education and Welfare stepped up its program to desegregate Southern schools, the outcry on Capitol Hill from legislators of that region brought a quick administrative retrenchment. In another quarter, the U.S. Commission on Civil Rights found widespread discrimination in 1967 against Southern Negro farmers in the administration of government farm programs, extending from education to land conservation.[28]

Since the Negro question appears in essentially an urban context, the President must work within the confines of the federal system. His programs combatting poverty, creating "model cities," spurring urban redevelopment, and the like depend upon the quality of local administration in the cities. The urban picture, unfortunately, presents no bright landscape of efficient government. The nineteenth-century traditions of neglect and incompetence in local government still hang over us. To depend upon the cities to administer his programs, the President all too often must witness their strangulation in red tape, municipal ignorance, and the competitive chaos that occurs when one city moves to solve problems in ways that hurt its neighbors. The civil rights revolution has brought the President into new and delicate political relations with mayors and governors. The new relationship presents to local officials the temptation to brush off on the President local problems and inadequacies—an easier, politically safer course than facing up to them locally. In a Presidential election year, bearing the blame for local chaos could do the Chief Executive incalculable damage, for it is in the cities that Presidential elections are won.

An Overview

Social justice brings the President, Congress, the parties, and the nation to grips with the most urgent and difficult choices in public affairs. It is a continuous testing of the capacity of men and institutions to adjust to change. It provokes struggle between those, on the one hand, whose self-interest weds them to the *status quo* or fills them with nostalgia for the past, and those, on the other hand, who are disadvantaged in present society or are troubled in conscience by the severe inequities dealt by economic and social forces to their fellow men. The exponents of social justice are not only alive in conscience; they believe progress is possible and look confidently to the future.

To compound the difficulties, social justice is itself wrapped at times in obscurity, its substance and meaning anything but clear. When does government welfare stray into paternalism; when does public authority unjustifiably intrude upon private initiative and private right? Since social justice is a human enterprise, those it involves can err. It is dispensed by no omniscient, infallible source, and the men, groups, and sections of the nation associated with it have no monopoly on wisdom and rectitude. A Theodore Roosevelt fights splendidly for conservation of natural resources but acts with questionable judgment and severity against the Negro regiments in the Brownsville episode. Franklin Roosevelt champions the New Deal, a vast mission of mercy for the downtrodden, but countenances the uprooting of Japanese-Americans in World War II, one of the most flagrant mass injustices in the nation's history. The South, although the stronghold of racial injustice, produces for the United States Senate a Lister Hill or Claude Pepper, whose political toil played no little part in identifying the New Deal with the Negro's cause. In one of those strange ironies of history, it is the South or Southwest that produced the President who moved to the most advanced ground on Negro civil rights, Lyndon Johnson. The East is the stronghold of traditional business resistance to social change; yet it also produced three Presidents—the Roosevelts and Kennedy—who perceived the character of social change most acutely and acted on what they saw. The Middle West can look askance at "do-good" internationalism but it still produced Bryan and La Follette, whose influence upon the Presidency's commitment to social reform was enormous.

The strong Presidency of the future will need to be continuously and deeply involved in furthering social justice. The ambitions and resentments of disadvantaged peoples at home and abroad have long passed the point where Presidential attention to social justice can be a part-time concern, or predominantly the pursuit of one major political party rather than the other.

The Eisenhower Presidency, representing as it does a limited break with the Republican Harding, Coolidge, and Hoover tradition of identification with the advantaged, must be carried forward and enlarged by any future Republican President in his attentions to the disadvantaged. The Democratic President has the easier, but no less vital, task of building upon an impressive heritage. By now it is clear beyond doubt that the time is fast fading when the President dispenses social justice because it wins votes or bespeaks conscience. Without justice the nation cannot be true to its traditions and historic values; society cannot hold together.

Political Personality 13

To win and keep his office, to maximize his exploitation of its opportunities and its resources, the President functions as a political personality. "Personality" is useful as an integrative concept, a kind of union of his needs, values, and traits or style in the context of his office.[1] Far more than most offices, the Presidency is plastic and responsive to variations in the political personalities of its incumbents, a circumstance that mirrors the commonplace observation that what the Presidency is at any moment in history depends supremely upon who is occupying the office. Lesser offices can be regulated, institutionalized, and bureaucratized, but the Presidency has eluded the rigidity and servitude of impersonality.

Like other human beings, the President is apt to have certain needs that find gratification in political endeavor. As a political personality, the President may have needs that earlier office-holding has responded to and that find even more fulfillment in the larger dimensions of the post of Chief Executive. The needs a President seeks to satisfy in his office can be inferred from conduct, and they sometimes are articulated. For example, an examination of Theodore Roosevelt's political career from its state and local beginnings to the Presidential and post-Presidential phases reveals a hunger for popularity and a dread that the public might reject him. Almost invariably, he was convinced that he would lose the election for which he was campaigning. Between elections, he was certain that his support was shrinking, and even in political triumph, he remained pessimistic. After important successes in the New York legislature, he wrote, "I realize very thoroughly the absolutely ephemeral nature of the hold I have upon the people."[2]

Roosevelt used public office with enormous imagination and success to win and maintain popularity. He was blessed with a powerful personal magnetism and was astute in projecting it by exploiting the resources and opportunities of office-holding. Time and again, his specific conduct reflected his need. His craving for popularity drove him to a kind of perpetual political exhibitionism. One evidence of this phenomenon was his love of costumes. For years he struck his favorite photographic pose in his Rough Rider uniform and in his cowboy clothes, complete with pistol and rifle. Attired in a favorite cowboy suit, "I feel able to face anything," he once claimed. As New York police commissioner, he made headlines, checking up on his underlings by prowling about the streets at night in evening clothes.

The President is driven by the need to maintain his self-esteem. Woodrow Wilson, one of the more hard-driven of Presidents in this need, was goaded by Calvinistic upbringing and faith to prove to himself regularly that he was an adequate and virtuous human being. He struggled with this aspect of his ego on the ample proving grounds of the Presidency. The opportunities for assertion in the Presidency helped compensate for the damaged self-esteem of his youth sustained from an exacting father. Yet the adult Woodrow Wilson's brittle self-esteem also crippled his capacity to react objectively to the issues of his administration, a failing that reached disastrous proportions in the League of Nations fight. He needed to dominate others, such as his formidable antagonist in the League of Nations struggle, Henry Cabot Lodge, and to achieve his political objectives in order to bolster his self-esteem. Another criterion of his continuous self-evaluation was provided by his religion that stressed "good works"—the League—for which he strove and fought even to the point of his own physical collapse.[3] For Wilson, the League of Nations represented a value to which he committed his energies and his reputation unstintingly.

Values

Values, as Gordon W. Allport has suggested, are usually social in nature and are objects of common regard by socialized men.[4] Values may silence the President in controversy or send him roaring into the front line of combat. They may bring him eagerly to shoulder a task as altogether worthy of his administration or cause him to turn it aside.

Values have enormous variety. A President has personal values that govern his deportment toward problems, colleagues, and adversaries. Loyalty, for example, is a personal value that may control Presidential conduct. Presidents rightly prize and insist upon loyalty to themselves and their administrations, but they are as a lot somewhat spotty in the loyalty they, in turn, accord to aides and supporters. To be let down and let out is not an uncommon experience of good and faithful servants of Presidents throughout the office's history. Yet the record also carries not a few sagas of Chief Executives who were loyal to their friends well after these friends had abused their trust. Harry S. Truman's abiding loyalty to aides who were also his friends and cronies survived the severest tests. Roy Roberts of the Kansas City *Star*, who knew Truman well, catalogued his several qualities in 1945, at the outset of his sudden Presidency.[5] Near the top of Roberts' list was "loyalty, perhaps excessive loyalty that sometimes gets high officials into trouble . . . ," a prophesy that unfortunately came true when old friends among his White House aides were lured by the bait of mink coats and deep freezes into indiscretions of office. In the din of criticism that followed, Truman stood firmly behind these aides, well beyond the obligations of friendship.

The President as a rule is endowed with a hierarchy of values that is highly relevant to questions that the office churns up for him to decide. In the value scheme that President Grant applied to his decisions, education ranked high and religion low in his estimation. Education, he felt, was a boon to the republic and merited unstinting emphasis in public policy. "We are a republic," he declared, "whereof one man is as good as another before the law. . . . Hence the education of the masses becomes the first necessity for the preservation of our institutions." Grant's conviction led him to propose a constitutional amendment requiring each state to "establish and forever maintain free public schools" for all children irrespective of "sex, color, birthplace, or religion." Toward churches, however, Grant displayed a hostility as ardent as his devotion to education. He seldom let pass an opportunity to strike at churches or put them in their place. Impressed, for example, that one billion dollars worth of church property was tax free, Grant contended in a message to Congress that "so vast a sum . . . will not be looked upon acquiescently by those who have to pay the taxes." In an extraordinary step for a President, he bluntly proposed that church property be taxed.[6]

Most Presidents have a hierarchy of values that is seldom articulated but is discernible in their actions. Many a President has by his actions identified the nation's survival as the supreme value. Abraham Lincoln acknowledged that he knowingly violated provisions of the Constitution in order to assure the nation's survival. Survival, not the Constitution, was the fundamental law. In the absence of the critical national plight that Lincoln grappled with, Presidents have attached the highest value to preserving the Constitution and the integrity of their office. As Andrew Johnson's troubles boiled up furiously in Congress—to reduce the President to a figurehead, Congress had virtually deprived him of control of the army and denied him the right to remove all civil officials, including cabinet members, without consent of the Senate—he perceived his duty to be one of upholding his office and the Constitution. The means he must use for this highest of purposes, he reasoned, must also be constitutional. For all the severe unconstitutional treatment he sustained from Congress, he held himself closely to the path of legality and rejected the counsel of well-intentioned friends that he employ the Army to reorganize the legislators plus and array of less drastic, but clearly unconstitutional acts. Nor would he, to save his own job, submit to the Congressional radicals, who, to destroy him, were bent upon running a steamroller over the Constitution. If the Constitution went down, he would go down with it.[7]

The jeopardy of a superior value may bring a President to act when a lesser value cannot. President Eisenhower long maintained the detachment of himself and his office from a most dynamic issue of his time—civil rights. When asked whether he endorsed the epochal ruling of the Supreme Court in *Brown v. Board of Education of Topeka*, which held that separate schools for Negroes, although equal in quality to white schools, violated the Constitution, or whether he merely accepted it, as the Republican platform did, he replied, "I think it makes no difference whether or not I endorse it . . . The Constitution is as the Supreme Court interprets it. . . ."[8] In other expressions on civil rights, Eisenhower similarly abstained from committing himself on Presidential power. He observed several times that laws could not change morality or that "laws could not change men's hearts." In a news conference he declared, "I can't imagine any set of circumstances that would ever induce me to send federal troops . . . into any area to enforce the orders of a federal court, because I believe that the common sense of America will never require it . . . I would never believe that it would be a wise thing to do."[9] These several utterances constituted in a sense Eisenhower's own private dissent from the Supreme Court's decision.

Eisenhower's expressions of Presidential self-abnegation spurred Governor Orval Faubus of Arkansas to order his state troops to defy the Supreme Court's desegregation decision by blocking the entry of Negro children to the Little Rock high school. Faubus' defiance was, in the constitutional sense, a challenge to Presidential power and to federal authority. Quite possibly it was also founded upon a misapprehension of Eisenhower's value system. Eisenhower hesitated, then negotiated with Faubus, but in vain, and finally asserted federal authority by issuing a statement warning that he would "use the full power of the United States, including whatever force may be necessary." The Arkansas National Guard was federalized, and troops from the U.S. 101st Airborne Division were ordered to Little Rock to join in patrolling the high school. For Eisenhower, to see a cherished lesser value pushed aside by the dictates of the higher value of constitutional and Presidential authority created a bitter choice. Sending the paratroopers into Little Rock, his assistant Sherman Adams observed, was the performance by the President of "a Constitutional duty which was the most repugnant to him of all his acts in his eight years at the White House."[10]

The President may attach a higher value to a role or function in which he is skilled or experienced and a lesser value to sectors of his office with which he is little familiar. Eisenhower, for example, was more intellectually at home and more committed by personal taste to meetings of the National

Security Council than to meetings of the Republican National Committee. The higher value he attached to foreign affairs, in which he was deeply experienced, was also reflected in his greater receptivity to decisions in that sphere in contrast to the more restricted record of his Presidency in domestic affairs, with which previously he had little encounter. Lyndon Johnson, in contrast, experienced and masterful in legislative affairs, preferred to work in that arena rather than in foreign affairs, which seemed strange, remote, and elusive. He succeeded most in the work he loved most—legislative affairs—and he suffered the most trouble and vexation in the work he probably loved least—foreign affairs.

The arrangement of a President's hierarchy of values is determined no little by his attitudes toward morality and power. His emphasis of one over the other will produce a strikingly different roster of values than if his choice were reversed. He may stress morality and neglect power. Andrew Johnson, conceiving of what he thought was right, pursued it with little attention to power—to the winning of allies in Congress and the parties, to the construction of compromises that might assure that at least part of what he deemed right would prevail while lesser parts might be sacrificed. Johnson's predecessor, Lincoln, viewed morality and power as complementary. He rose to the heights of moral splendor in his Gettysburg and second inaugural addresses and yet perceived that what he proposed to achieve required a bold, resourceful assertion of all available—and sometimes unavailable—power of the Constitution.

In matters of importance or controversy, most Presidents take pains to clothe their actions in rectitude. They prefer to act or prefer to appear to act, not upon grounds of expediency, as they may seem to, but upon grounds of what is "right." Wilson liked to visualize his work as a kind of "service," an ennobling moral framework in which he fitted a remarkable variety of deeds. Andrew Johnson, faced with a decision whether to approve or veto the Freedmen's Bureau bill, which created an agency to relieve white and Negro suffering in the postwar South, was buffeted by ponderous forces, some eager to punish the South, others aiming to heal the wounds of war quickly and restore the Union. If he withheld his veto, he was promised, Senators and Representatives from his own state of Tennessee would be admitted to Congress and he could enjoy their voting support, which he badly needed. Leading members of his cabinet, Edwin M. Stanton, James Harlan, and James Speed urged him not to veto. But Johnson was unyielding to bribes or intimidation. "He could do no wrong," he told the cabinet, "to assure right."[11]

Some values that shape a President's decisions are highly idiosyncratic. Other values, equally important, may have a common incidence among Presidents. Andrew Jackson, moved perhaps by not inconsiderable personal experience, had a horror of debt, public and private, to a degree rare among Presidents. Soon after taking office, he discovered that many executive officials were deeply in debt or even insolvent. His profound sense of personal and economic integrity was revolted and he directed that the debt-ridden members of the executive branch be dismissed at once. To flush out these undesirables, he ordered a search of jail records that exposed a multitude of delinquents, who were quickly banished from the departments. Jackson's abhorrence of debt did much to fashion his position on the Maysville bill, which would commit the national government to an elaborate road- and canal-building program and to a huge public debt that such undertakings represented. Jackson chose to veto the bill, thereby leaving the lion's share of public works construction to the states. His veto message depicted a future marked by "a scramble for appropriations." He preferred instead that federal funds be employed to extinguish the national debt, an act that would enhance the national character and present to the world the hardy image of a nation that had passed through two great wars, united, prosperous, and debt-free.[12]

The President's values can be viewed in their relationships to the world in which they are applied. They may possess a definite, even a controlling, attribute of time. Presidents like Woodrow Wilson, Franklin Roosevelt, and Lyndon Johnson, staunch believers in progress, in man's capacity for improvement, entertained values that were oriented toward the future, toward "the better society of tomorrow." Dwight Eisenhower, in contrast, was heavily oriented to the past on a broad sweep of economic and political questions. From the eminence of the Presidency he longed to apply to his administration's tasks a simple faith in an earlier America that had all but vanished in the innundation of technological revolution, the social and economic upheavals of the Great Depression, and the burgeoning of government and giant industry. Viewing the hard plight of agriculture, he declared that his administration would improve it "in ways that minimize governmental interference in the farmers' affairs . . . and that encourage the farmers themselves to use initiative in meeting changing economic conditions."[13] He condemned TVA as "creeping socialism" and declared his opposition to "the socialization of medicine." The great need for hospital and medical services, he contended, "can best be met by the initiative of private plans." Early in his term, he revealed that his new administration was "finding things it can stop doing rather than new things for it to do." When government had to act, Eisenhower preferred the state and local governments to take over. "I suppose," he said, "if you were going to class me as anything else, you would class me as a States' Righter."[14]

Goals

The President acts not only in response to values. He also chooses goals for himself and his administration. His commitment to goals tells much of the maturity and sophistication of his Presidency and of the degree of his involvement in the tasks of the nation and the opportunities of his office. In choosing goals, he sets the tone and character of his administration, the level of its striving, and the missions to which his aides and supporters may subscribe their energy, skill, and loyalty.

Goals come in assorted shapes and sizes. They may be finely precise or general to the point of vagueness. Presidents may establish goals in several or more of the multiple roles of their office. President Eisenhower, for example, seemingly took on a major goal as party leader in his announced intention to convert his party to the principles of Modern Republicanism. Eisenhower's most notable proclamation of this goal occurred at the 1956 convention at the Cow Palace in San Francisco in his acceptance speech, when he sought to chart a course between the New Deal and the Republican right wing.

Some goals that a President chooses to support have the attraction of guaranteeing almost universal approbation and support. Only a rare and contrary-minded member of society could reject the ringing commitment some Presidents have offered to "a better life for all" or—and sometimes almost in the same breath—to reduce taxes. Presidential roles permit the selection of goals that create an instantaneous impression of absolute high-mindedness. Time and again the President as administrative chief has proclaimed his devotion to the administrative reform of the executive branch for the sake of efficiency and economy, a goal that carries an unfailing aura of moral nobility and excites well-nigh universal support, at least so long as it stands as a broadly stated proposition. Grover Cleveland reaped a good political harvest from this kind of goal when, in the altogether proper supposition that a decade of one-party rule had produced lethargy and decay, he set as his first task the reform of the executive departments. Cleveland launched his goal by devoting his first cabinet meeting exclusively to departmental reform and the next half-dozen dealt almost exclusively with it. By late summer, the New York *World* could hail the administration for destroying "the nests of corruption in the Navy Department, the Treasury, the Indian Bureau, the Land Office, the Coast Survey, and the War Department."[15] Cleveland clinched for himself a glittering reputation for honesty and efficiency in government that he never lost.

The President may sometimes manipulate goals in one area of national interest to deflect attention from public tensions and animosities raging in another area. James Buchanan so related himself to domestic and foreign affairs. Beset by the crashing tempest of "bleeding" Kansas where the winds of Northern and Southern sectionalism converged, he chose, in composing his second annual message to Congress in December 1858, to turn the nation's attention to foreign affairs. Buchanan posed a series of goals for foreign policy worthy of the nation's united effort for years to come. He aimed to enable the United States to "attract to itself much of the trade and travel of all nations passing between Europe and Asia" and to become thereby the wealthiest nation on the globe. He proposed a string of measures that would make large claims upon the nation's resources of men and money: the purchase of Cuba to assure the United States' dominance in the Caribbean; the increase of the navy to enlarge and protect transportation routes through Panama, Nicaragua, and Mexico; the conclusion of commercial treaties with China, Japan, and other countries of the Far East; the revision of the tariff to increase revenues; the construction of a Pacific railroad. How much better, Buchanan left little doubt, for the nation to pursue these acts of self-aggrandizement than to dissipate its strength in internal strife.[16]

The President entertains personal goals, the more common of which are his reelection, a vote of confidence in a Congressional election, and the prevailing of his choice of a successor. He may aim to provide the deeds and words for the use of future historians in inscribing an admiring account of the wonders of his administration. His several goals, whether in foreign affairs, social justice, or whatever, may well reflect his underlying philosophy of life, which in actuality is his supreme personal goal. "What is your philosophy?" a young man once asked Franklin Roosevelt. "Philosophy?" Roosevelt answered, "Philosophy? I am a Christian and a Democrat—that's all."[17] Church and party implied for Roosevelt a series of commitments: respect for fellow man, nature, and freedom, or what was the very essence of his New Deal and wartime administrations.

Goals, like values, are not coins of common worth but exist in relationship to each other. There are the greater and the lesser. The greatest is a Presidential administration's central purpose, vision, or grand design. Terms like the "New Deal" or the "New Freedom" conjure up a vision of the central purposes of Franklin Roosevelt and Woodrow Wilson. A President's foreign and domestic politics may join harmoniously in support of his grand design. President Kennedy well discerned the central purpose in the administrations of several of his Democratic forebears when he declared in Ann Arbor, Michigan, in October 1960 that "because it fitted in exactly with what they were trying to do here in the United States, the Fourteen Points were the international counterpart of the New Freedom; the Four Freedoms of Franklin Roosevelt were directly tied to the aspirations of the New Deal; and the Marshall Plan, NATO, the Truman Doctrine, and Point Four were directly tied to the kind of America that President Truman was trying to build."[18]

Below the generalized grand design may stretch a great array of lesser goals that both individually and collectively may constitute the distinguishing mark of the Presidential administration. Some may be vaguely and others precisely defined. Grover Cleveland, choosing to embark on the settlement of the long simmering dispute between Britain and Venezuela over the latter's boundary with British Guiana, confided to a friend that his aim was to bring, at one sharp stroke, the whole matter into his own control, push Britain into arbitration, and put Congress in a position where it could not interfere. "My action, you see," the President said, "has been in the interests of peace—permanent peace."[19] The President sometimes makes considerable effort to assure that some goals are, and remain, subordinate and contributory to others. The distinguished reformer, Carl Schurz, wished to make the casting out of the spoilsmen and the establishment of civil service reform the immediate goal of the Cleveland administration. Cleveland, however, chose to give priority to his larger aim of general reform in the executive departments. "To me," the President said, "the importance of general administrative reform has appeared to be superior to the incidental matter of civil service reform. Good government is the main thing to be aimed at. Civil service reform is but a means to that end."[20]

Goals set the level of aspiration of an administration. John Kennedy contended, altogether plausibly, that goals should be inspiring, no matter how great the difficulties and delays in their realization.[21] Goal-setting reflects the President's instinct for the future, his understanding of the past, and his mastery of the present. It must capture the nation's needs and yearnings, perceive the potential of its resources, and grasp the directions in which the world is moving. "The President's got to set the sights,"[22] Truman once said.

However, the President, if the record of his administration is to be impressive, must be able to formulate solid, possible goals. Wilson had a special knack for selecting as his political goals projects that were ripe for realization and excelled at carrying them out with shrewd political maneuver. The goal-setting President must think in terms of trends, of locating his administration and its times in the stream of events; he must be capable of developmental thinking, of conjuring up pictures of the future, of perceiving alternatives to achieve his goals, and of choosing wisely between them.[23] He must also excel in configurative thinking, visualizing each available power, tool, and project as part of the total process and keeping them in balance.[24]

Style

The President develops in the eyes of those who view his conduct over time the appearance, or impression, of a "style." The raw material, or input, of style embraces the President's gestures and flairs, his communicative acts oral and written, his enthusiasms, prejudices, and interests. Style, as an output, is a cumulative, more or less representative impression inferred from all of these elements of conduct.

Style as the product of gesture, speech, mood, and manner may tell much or little of the President's controlling impulses, attitudes, and approach to duty and decision. The cliché that appearances are misleading has special point in estimates of Presidents. Senator Robert M. La Follette, a shrewd judge of men, witnessing the passing of the Presidency from Chester Arthur to Grover Cleveland, was moved to compare the new President with the old. La Follette noted, "The contrast with Arthur, who was a fine handsome figure, was very striking. Cleveland's coarse face, his heavy inert body, his great shapeless hands, confirmed in my mind the attacks made upon him during the campaign." Before many days of the new President, however, La Follette revised his initial estimate and came "to admire the courage and conscientiousness of his character."[25]

Cleveland illustrates how style reflects the impact of mind and character upon the Presidency. By every appearance, Cleveland was a man of plain mind and simple talents. He was singularly lacking in imagination, unpracticed in abstract thinking, and habitually captive to preconceived notions. Yet, in the fair estimate of his biographer, Allan Nevins, Cleveland "imposed himself upon his time in a way that no mediocre man could for a moment have done."[26] The major element in Cleveland's achievement seems to have been his massive strength of character. He was committed to the homely virtues of honesty, economy, and efficiency in public service. A model of industry, he tirelessly pursued the facts of problems, chose his course with full conscience, and once reaching a decision, he held to it against every force. After making his decision, Cleveland, unlike many another President, was not racked with doubts. He was a President who in the midst of national financial crisis stood for sound money and who resisted the snowballing demands for inflation, when few spoke in his defense. Against the merciless pressure, he could smite his desk with his fist and cry, "Never, never." He fully lived up to those words.[27]

Style also springs from the vast, diverse realm of temperament. Cleveland was at times impulsive, as in sending in troops in the Pullman strike without awaiting a request from Governor Altgeld of Illinois; Wilson was at times compulsive, rigid in dealings with others. A President's temperament, as it is manifested in private, may be wholly different from its public display. James Buchanan was known to the nation and the world as an exemplar of the quiet, flexible negotiator and compromiser. His private demeanor, according to testimony of aides, was altogether different from his public reputation. Attorney General Jeremiah S. Black voiced the general opinion of his cabinet colleagues when he said of Buchanan, "He is a stubborn old gentleman—very fond of having his own way. . . ." John B. Floyd, Buchanan's Secretary of War who also knew Andrew Jackson well, observed, "Mr. Buchanan was different from Genl. Jackson; . . . Genl. Jackson could be *coaxed* from his purpose, but . . . Mr. B. could neither be coaxed nor driven."[28]

A President's private stylistic traits can serve to evoke the confidence and loyalty of his associates and to extend his influence in the executive branch. Franklin Roosevelt provided a model of such artistry. "It was part of his conception of his role," his Undersecretary of Agriculture and intimate counselor, Rexford G. Tugwell has written, "that he should never show exhaustion, boredom, or irritation." His patience, grasp of detail, his composure as emergencies fell upon him, his timing, evasiveness, and humor, his reserve, his occasional severity, his sense of office and history numbered among the rewarding stylistic administrative traits by which he held sway in the executive branch.[29]

John Kennedy often left associates and others who watched him at work in a state of awe at his capacity to see and weigh all sides of an issue or decision. The most remarkable aspect of this capacity was his ability to judge himself—his needs, aptitudes, shortcomings—with unflagging objectivity. For all of the might and majesty of the Presidency, he had a gift for self-deprecation. Master of an irony that could be gentle or keen, he directed it at himself as often as at others. When the first volume of Eisenhower's Presidential memoirs appeared, Kennedy remarked to an aide, "Apparently Ike never did anything wrong. . . . When we come to writing the memoirs of this administration, we'll do it differently."[30] Detachment helped Kennedy to maintain an extraordinary composure in crisis, to keep his assessments of people and problems in balance, to emancipate himself from the stereotyped responses of the past. More than anything else, the New Frontier was the product of Kennedy's gift of detachment: It was a state of mind, a spirit, a capacity for objective self-criticism that might free the American character from the self-satisfied society in which it was captive in the 1950's.

Another style, by no means uncommon among Presidents, is that of the compromiser. "I am a compromiser and a manipulator," Lyndon Johnson said. His critics spoke of him, less flatteringly, as a "wheeler-dealer" type. But regardless of the name of the game, Johnson played it from his earliest political days in Texas to his ascendance to national leadership, first on Capitol Hill and then in the White House.

As manipulator and compromiser, Johnson prided himself in being, as Mrs. Johnson noted, a "can-do President." As such, Johnson acted to satisfy forces far to the right and left of center, distributing his effectiveness in behalf of both and leaving everyone concerned in doubt of where he really stood. Mixed with Johnson's pragmatism was a strain of populism that beheld America as "the big barbecue," where abundance is available for all. The Chief Executive, in Johnson's view, dispenses the good things of life to every class and group. Service in Congress developed and refined Johnson's skills of political maneuver and cultivated a preference for manipulated results over oratorical main force. His perceptions of the nature of power moved him more to the backstage than to frontstage in the political drama. "In every town," he said, "there's some guy on top of the hill in a big white house who can get things done. I want to get that man on my side."[31] Johnson, then, was prone to think and act not in terms of "the people" but to carry the play to the legislative committee, the leaders of the big interest groups, and other power centers whose favor or decision could provide what he believed the country needed.

The manipulator-compromiser style carried a built-in cautionary device. By the very nature of the style, nothing is ever final; everything is susceptible to accommodation and adjustment. Or, at least, the President will exercise his "options" to perpetuate as long as he can his freedom to act in a given situation. Thus, if a vacancy was to be filled, Johnson sometimes took months in examining and evaluating candidates before committing his trust. If the administration was to prepare a legislative proposal, Johnson followed an elaborate course to avoid booby traps. He consulted beyond his staff with departmental officers, private counselors, key legislators, random visitors, and labor and business leaders. The elaborate procedure often created lengthy delays, reversals of decisions, the impression of tentativeness, of lack of conviction and confidence.

Some expressions of style may be little more than minor excrescences of personality; others may be purposefully indulged in to facilitate the Presidential task. Franklin Roosevelt and Andrew Jackson were masters of delay, a pose they found highly valuable in politics. Thanks to delay, tumultous political forces had more time to settle or grow distinct; the President could better weigh factors and consequences before choosing his course. Jackson also, to a degree rare among Presidents, employed the terrible rage as a standard administrative weapon. Time and again, he would break up meetings and conferences with rousing demonstrations that were shrewdly calculated and rendered so convincingly that visitors retreated in utter confusion, forgetting what they had come for. Jackson steadily preferred this volcanic method to time-consuming and perhaps inconclusive argument. Martin Van Buren, Jackson's discerning associate, perceived that the President's view of his general political strength was also an element in shaping his conduct. "The conciliation of individuals," Van Buren said of Jackson, "formed the smallest, perhaps too small a part of his policy. His strength lay with the masses, and he knew it."[32]

Presidents have stylistic traits that may become the mark of their reign and an element of their memorability in history. Benjamin Harrison is accurately remembered as frigid and intellectual. President Grant's administration was handicapped by an abysmal lack of political facility. Grant had launched his administration on a high note in an inaugural address that the New York *Tribune* hailed as "the utterance of a man of the best intentions profoundly desirous to govern wisely and justly. . . ." But the *Tribune* also sensed from the address what was to become the underlying cause of the egregious failure of the future Grant administration. Grant, the *Tribune* noted, was "profoundly ignorant of the means by which good government is secured." In a day when waves of corruption beat upon his administration, a bold statement from the President conveying his own high purpose and moral rigor would have served himself and the country well, but Grant, who was endowed with an inarticulateness that amounted to a kind of verbal lockjaw, responded feebly.[33]

Lyndon Johnson's reign was marked by a patriarchal concept of politics, which controlled his style. This concept holds that politics and its storm and stress are the preserve of the President, and from them the private citizen is spared. Except when the election campaigns of 1964 and 1966 were in progress, Johnson in public discourse tended toward a pose of serenity that exhorted good men to do good deeds, dispensed praise, and gave scant acknowledgment to problems. Doubt, defeat, and strife are repressed from view in a haze of serenity, according to the patriarchal theory. Policy must appear to evolve smoothly: It does not shift suddenly.[34] If the roof falls in, it is the sunlight that is seen. Enemies may be acknowledged, but they are not scolded. Under the patriarchal concept of the Presidency, the people are not privy to the President's current concerns and feelings. The concept worked both favorably and adversely in the Johnson era. In the upheaval of John Kennedy's assassination, Johnson gratified and reassured the nation by a masterful display of composure while he quickly and privately restored to normal working order the Presidential machinery. The patriarchal concept served him less well in the lengthy, tortuous, shifting war in Vietnam, with whose pressures he struggled largely in private. His course probably helped maintain an uneasy domestic tranquility, but it did little to promote the understanding and support of the nation. He became exposed, too, to the attacks of critics who charged that despite his election by the largest majority in history and possession of the most elaborate trappings of power yet known, he did not often inspire the nation.

The chief occasion on which Johnson abandoned the patriarchal pattern occurred in his extraordinary address to the nation on March 31, 1968, announcing a new policy of deescalation in Vietnam and his decision not to accept another term of office. In effect, Johnson drew back the curtain only at the point when he chose to disclose the inadequacy of his Vietnam policy and the termination of his stewardship. These courageous and selfless acts, in their immediate effect, electrified the nation. Johnson, now in direct and candid communication with the public, had, in the words of his critics, inspired and moved the people.

Presidents appear divided into two schools on the question of choice of external stylistic traits. One school tends toward the model of George Washington, fitting their conduct to the intrinsic dignity of the office. In modern day, Franklin Roosevelt and Dwight Eisenhower wrapped themselves in the mantle of dignity in public appearance. Eisenhower's manly candor inspired confidence. John Kennedy veered to this school, although he tempered his proper decorum with an apposite sense of humor. At the other extreme is the warm, little inhibited manner of Andrew Johnson, or in later day, Harry Truman and Lyndon Johnson. President Truman, soon after taking office, conveyed the flavor of his style in a visit to the Pemiscot County Fair at

Carhuthersville, Missouri. The new President mingled with the crowd on a "Harry" basis and discussed local problems with farmers wearing overalls. When a doddering American Legion locomotive came by, he ran into the street to toot its whistle. He played piano for the Methodist Church ladies, winking broadly as he said, "When I played this, Stalin signed the Potsdam Agreement."[35] Lyndon Johnson's tendency toward old-style oratory, his reputation for manipulation and compromise, his air of Southwestern Populism did not wear well with academic audiences and with many Easterners. Regardless of the school he follows, the President must indulge in traits that develop general confidence and affection, transmutable into support for his policies and votes at the polls.

Views of the Presidency

What the President does and how he behaves depend much upon his own view of the Presidency. His view is not an unsegmented monolith but a mosaic of many pieces of different hues and sizes.

A view of the Presidency embraces the attitudes of the incumbent toward the problems presented by the outside world with which he might conceivably deal. President Eisenhower began with the uncontrovertible proposition that the American people should not look to the Chief Executive to solve all their problems. This general view was supported by a more specific philosophy according to which President Eisenhower, by personal preference, chose to eliminate large sectors of problems from the purview and therefore the action of his Presidency. His expressed fear of "the menace of bankrupting waste inherent in a centralized bureaucracy . . ." lent force to his ambition to return various federal functions to the states or to private activity. For example, his views on electric-power development, the "partnership" principle, as it was known, called for a larger role for state and local government and for privately owned utilities than was known in previous Presidential administrations. Or again, when pressures developed in his administration for substantial national programs to improve schools, hospitals, and other welfare services, Eisenhower stressed the responsibilities of local governments and citizens, declaring, "Here we rely not primarily upon government grant or political panacea but upon our own wisdom and industry to bring us the good and comforting things of life."[36]

A view of the Presidency includes a view of legal authority, especially the basic law of the Constitution, and of relationships with the two other branches—the legislature and the judiciary. Presidents' views of Congress, their great political competitor, range from Lincoln's, which regarded the legislature as a nuisance to be avoided if at all possible, to Buchanan's, which was deferential almost to the point of abjectness. Andrew Johnson, on the brink of launching his Reconstruction policy, took an expansive legal view of his office and, as events proved, a disastrously simplistic view of its politics. Johnson reasoned that if Lincoln inaugurated the war by deeming that the states were in rebellion and, in effect, declared war, then his successor in the Presidency had the corresponding power to say when the states were no longer in rebellion and when each was fit to return to its place in the Union. As Lincoln had, Johnson relied on the Commander-in-Chief power, his duty to take care that laws are faithfully executed, his oath of office, and the constitutional guarantee of a republican form of government to each state.[37] The boldness of this legal doctrine, Johnson's rugged tenacity, and his utter lack of political sense provided the ingredients for a struggle that came to threaten, as none ever had, the Presidency's very existence.

Above all, the President's view of his office depends upon his view of politics. To achieve policy, to use the enormous potentialities of his office, he must act by political means. The Presidents who have extracted major successes from the office—Jefferson, Jackson, Wilson, and the Roosevelts—all were eminent Presidential politicians. Politics have been notably eschewed by some Presidents, a Washington or an Eisenhower, whose extraordinary ability to symbolize the nation's intrinsic unity was little tarnished by personal political involvement. Some Presidents notably prefer certain forms of political activity to others. John Kennedy loved the arts of political management but was chary of taking his programs to the public in a nationally televised appeal. Lyndon Johnson displayed a prowess in many branches of politics that compared with the ablest political figures of any age. Yet in this strength there also lay weakness. He was so adept at politics that his mastery of that suspect art became legendary and hampered his ability, as President, to command national popular confidence. If there be a first commandment in Presidential politics, it must be this: Let the President excel at politics, but let him not be obvious about it.

An Overview

The President as a political personality, we have seen, combines, in that concept, the man, his needs, and the office. He may have personal needs that find satisfaction in political office-holding and, above all, in the Presidency. The President is a broker in values that shape his decisions and policies. He chooses between values, gives higher priority to some than others, and may over time shift his support of them. He may formulate and subscribe to goals that set the achievement levels of his administration. Above all, as a political personality, he can be seen as possessing a bundle of traits, which both separately and in combination constitute that elusive, mysterious element called "style."

The relation of the President, or the man, to the office is dynamic to the extent that an incumbent may come into office not particularly admired, as was the case with Lincoln and Truman, and develop and display a combination of values and traits that arouses widespread public approval and even admiration. A reverse tendency also may take place. Lyndon Johnson, confident, assertive and self-reliant, gratified the nation with the skill of his takeover in the turmoil of the Kennedy assassination. But these very qualities seemed to weaken his popular standing in the context of the Vietnam war.

On occasion it has appeared that how the President does things is more important than what he does. A President who does less may be better appreciated than one who does more. An underachiever who is blessed with a collection of traits or style that delights the public and even the historians may fare better in the public opinion of his day or in his country's annals than the overachiever whose major sin may be that he does not possess a comparably pleasing style.

The President lives in a culture in which the profession of politician has uncertain status. The values of his society emphasize private endeavor and private success. Politics is tainted as a calling less worthy than most private pursuits. To succeed in the Presidency in the largest sense, the incumbent must be a master politician. But society and the culture are reluctant that he be so. Not the least restraint upon the strong President is the distaste society is apt to have for the strong politician.

Decision-Making 14

Decision-making is an area where the strong Presidency depends most upon the strong President—upon the caliber of the man, his talents, prudence, and resolution. His choices point up the issues of the Presidency, give substance to its policies and effect to its purposes. Decision-making is a continuous process of the President's existence, his choices tend to be difficult, and the end-products often have great consequences. "There are no easy matters that will come to you as President," Eisenhower counseled the incoming President Kennedy. "If they are easy, they will be settled at a lower level."[1]

Varieties of Decision

Actually, the President makes all kinds of decisions: routine or programmed decisions (which focus upon tasks rather than problems); adaptive decisions (the adjustment of existing policy to new circumstances); and innovative decisions (major departures from established policy). Some Chief Executives may choose to devote themselves to one kind at the expense of the others.

A President who chooses to concentrate upon routine or adaptive decisions sacrifices the opportunity to make major or innovative decisions. Franklin Pierce, in his first Presidential years, sat two hours each day with his assembled cabinet engaged in the hard business of dispensing patronage. Together they read recommendations, weighed qualifications, and estimated political consequences. He proclaimed lofty standards to guide the task: "If a man who has attained [this] high office, cannot free himself from cliques and act independently, our Constitution is valueless." But a President like Pierce who concentrates so heavily upon such choices neglects the big decisions. Pierce loved detail and injected himself into an ever-shifting miscellany of petty problems. He visited the departments regularly, heeded minor matters, encouraged his Secretaries to bring him a full store of middling business; tracked down all manner of complaints pouring in from his mail; and kept his door open to the public. A disgruntled humanity, bearing paltry complaints, streamed in. The incessant puttering with trivia was, in actuality, Pierce's kind of compensation for his inability to handle major policy. The larger problems slid by little touched by Presidential power: trouble in Cuba, Mexico, and Central America; ailing relations with England; Kansas torn and bleeding.[2]

Programed decisions, repetitive and routine, following established rules, precedents, and strategies, are part of any Chief Executive's day: the hour when he starts work, his choice of tasks, the distribution of his time, what he reads or ignores. But some Presidents are controlled by routine. Calvin Coolidge is the supreme example of Presidential subordination to programed decision. His inviolate schedule was breakfast at eight, to work at nine, lunch at twelve-thirty, back at his desk at three, and at four he called it a day. This admittedly mild routine, contrasting shockingly with the hours of the average factory worker, he clocked from minute to minute. So, in fact, did he regulate the time of his retirement at night. William Allen White, the journalist, made this discovery during a festive outing aboard the Presidential yacht, the *Mayflower*. The conversation was gay and voluble, with everyone joining in but the Chief Executive, who was proving his large reputation for silence. "Literally," noted White, "we forgot him." At the stroke of ten Coolidge rose, walked across the room to his wife, and stood in silence. Mocking his Yankee accent, she laughed, "Time tur go tew bed!"[3]

Some of the President's most important decisions are really nondecisions or decisions to do nothing. A President's nondecisions may be as exacting as his decisions. John Kennedy, faced with Castro's refusal to permit on-the-spot inspection for the presence of missiles and launching sites in Cuba, made several protests, and then apparently relegated the thorny matter to the limbo of nondecision. But some Presidents specialize in nondecisions; Warren Harding smiled and maneuvered his way out of difficulty until his whole kingdom of neglect tumbled down upon him.

Some of the President's decisions come in response to emergencies, but more are called for automatically at established intervals by a network of fixed deadlines that he does not set and cannot change. He faces the catalysis of the electoral calendar—the next Congressional or national election. His State of the Union message, his Economic Report, his budget, which together are a massive compilation of decisions embracing the full sweep of policy, are all rendered up to Congress in January. Each of these documents has an extended subcalendar for its preparation. Budget ceilings are set in April;

departments prepare their estimates in the summer; the Bureau of the Budget reviews them in the fall. His fixed schedule heightens the tyranny of events. In Monroe's day, the surge of revolutions in Latin America and the opportunistic stirrings of the imperial European powers lent special force to the President's oncoming State of the Union message. Since it would have been unthinkable for the President not to discuss in its paragraphs relations between the hemispheres, his Union message posed, in actuality, a deadline by which he was forced to formulate his historic doctrine.

Decisions vary in the risks they hold for the President's prestige and political fortunes and the nation's welfare and safety. In putting forward his Supreme Court packing plan in 1937, Franklin Roosevelt risked the prestige of his smashing electoral victory the year before that had lifted him to the crest of his influence.* In arranging the sale of wheat to the U.S.S.R. in 1963, John Kennedy risked offending sectors of American opinion and probably losing votes. His stand on civil rights appeared to alienate millions of white voters; yet to have refused to take it would have alienated millions of Negroes and damaged his country in the eyes of the world.

Since Dwight Eisenhower's second term, Presidential risks have acquired a new and forbidding dimension. Eisenhower became the first President to live with the Soviet Union's possession of a substantial nuclear delivery capability. The mutual nuclear capacities of the United States and the U.S.S.R. give the decisions of their chief executives the quality of "irreversibility." Decisions based upon miscalculation cannot be called back nor can actions once taken be revised. Nothing that the erring chief executive might do subsequently could compensate for the costs levied upon mankind.

Sometimes a President has time to study and consider his decisions; sometimes he must act immediately. President Monroe acted on a tight time-budget at a dinner he tendered one night for the resident diplomats. Charles Vaughan, the British minister, was seated opposite Count de Serurier, the French representative, and, as always in that era, relations between their countries were edgy. So indeed was the deportment of these diplomats.

---

* In 1935 and 1936 the Supreme Court worked havoc upon Roosevelt's New Deal legislative program by declaring one measure after another unconstitutional. Roosevelt interpreted his imposing reelection victory in 1936 as a popular endorsement of his program and decided to move against the Court. In a message of February 5, 1937, he asked Congress for legislation that would add "younger blood" to the Court. A justice, upon reaching age seventy, under the President's proposal, could resign at full pay. If he did not resign, an additional judge would be appointed. The plan aroused a political furor. Roosevelt was accused of seeking to "pack" the Court, lusting for power, and undermining the sacred principle of separation of powers. Conservative and progressive legislators alike, most of the press, and distinguished lawyers, among others, rallied against the President, who had few defenders. Debate raged in Congress through the spring and summer of 1937. The bill was eventually defeated, not so much by popular opinion as by the Court's turnabout, by which it now proceeded to find New Deal legislation constitutional.

Vaughan in time noticed, to his great annoyance, that whenever the French minister spoke, he bit his thumb. Finally, unable to contain his irritation any longer, Vaughan inquired, "Do you bite your thumb at me, Sir?" "I do," replied the count. Both instantly left the table, withdrew into an adjoining hall, and unsheathed their swords. Monroe, who had followed them, made a split-second decision that conceivably saved two nations from war and his own from possible involvement. With expert flourish, he forced up the ministers' crossed swords with his own, called his servants, sent the battling ministers to separate rooms, and ordered their carriages.[4]

Time is a boon when it is available. After the 1962 Cuban crisis President Kennedy expressed his thankfulness for the length of time—some fourteen days—that the situation permitted him to take to determine the nation's response. "If we had had to act in the first twenty-four hours," Kennedy observed, "I don't think . . . we would have chosen as prudently as we finally did."[5] When the *Maine* blew up and a great outcry for war, fanned by the yellow press, swept the country, McKinley declared to his young friend, Senator Charles W. Fairbanks of Indiana, "I don't propose to be swept off my feet by the catastrophe. My duty is plain. We must learn the truth and endeavor, if possible, to fix responsibility. The country can afford to withhold its judgment and not strike an avenging blow until the truth is known."[6] But McKinley used his gift of time less competently than Kennedy, and the country was pushed into war.

The Environment

The President is driven to make decisions by the vast, dynamic environment in which he works. The environment is laden with situations and events pressing for attention; with ideas and movements; with the interests and ambitions of men and nations; with political friends and foes; with previous decisions that have failed and succeeded. The environment is the first of several elements that comprise the process of decision-making. The President maintains surveillance over the environment for developments on which to act.

The President cannot act without situations, which may develop spontaneously or which he may manage somehow to contrive. But there are limits to his inventions. If fate had wafted Franklin Roosevelt into the Presidential chair in 1880, the serenity of that age would have presented only a miniature opportunity for decision-making compared with the broad canvass of trouble on which he could splash his imprint a half-century later.

Situations may develop into events that are more focused and visible. Abraham Lincoln, considering the realities that would make the issuance of his Emancipation Proclamation a plausible act, gave great weight to a victory on the battlefield. Abolitionists and others had long urged Lincoln to deliver his proclamation and criticized his delay. He held back, fearful that border states would join the Confederacy if it were issued. He believed that without a victory the proclamation would be a hollow gesture. Finally, the battle of Antietam came, and though the Union's claim of victory was disputed, Lee had been checked. This was enough for Lincoln, and he hurried off to the quiet of the Soldiers' Home to put the finishing touches on his Emancipation Proclamation.[7] Issued September 22, 1862, the proclamation declared that slaves who were in rebellion on New Year's Day, 1863, would henceforth be free.

But events can also be unanticipated. In the balmy June days of 1950 Harry S. Truman and his most sapient military and diplomatic aides basked in the assumption that the tiny republic of Korea, which was little on their minds, stood in no danger of aggression from the communist North Korean People's Democratic Republic. Indeed, on June 24, 1950, President Truman, dedicating a new international airport near Baltimore and exuding the then existing global serenity, voiced "his faith in a peaceful future" and flew away to Independence, Missouri, to visit his mother and brother. His sojourn was suddenly collapsed by a telephone call from his Secretary of State, Dean Acheson. A telegram, Acheson reported, had just been received from American Ambassador John J. Muccio at Seoul, the South Korean capital. "North Korean forces," Acheson read, "have invaded the Republic of Korea. . . ." The force of this sudden intelligence rushed Truman back to Washington and for weeks the events it heralded took a full toll of his effort.[8]

Situations and events are not simply physical and material things; they encompass the world of the mind. Ideas, assumptions, motives, and values abound in the President's environment. Many great Presidential decisions borrow heavily from the previous formulations of other politicians and associates. Elements of the Monroe Doctrine, for example, were provided some years prior to its appearance by the utterances of Henry Clay and Thomas Jefferson.* Of the incipient Latin-American revolts, a key event in the doctrine's development, Jefferson said in 1808, "We consider their interests the same as ours, and the object of both must be to exclude all European influence in this hemisphere." The roots of the great doctrine reached back before Jefferson and Clay to the formative years of the republic and the pronouncements of Washington, particularly his Farewell Address. In an important sense Monroe's decision had been made for him.[9]

The President, of course, can turn anywhere for ideas: to Congress, the universities, friends, his wife, old classmates, anyone. The operative ideas of

---

* Monroe proclaimed his doctrine in a message to Congress, December 2, 1823, of which Secretary of State John Quincy Adams was principal draftsman. The message was evoked by the revolt of the Latin-American colonies from Spain about 1815, the creation of new republics in Latin America, and the gestures of several European nations toward intervention. Monroe, in effect, threatened war against European powers that attempted to "extend their system to any portion of this hemisphere."

many a great Presidential decision may emerge from the researches and findings of the bureaucracy. The idea of how to pack the Court seems to have
come from Roosevelt's Justice Department. The Attorney General, Homer
S. Cummings, a lanky, elderly politician, had been given an important secret
assignment by Roosevelt. His task was nothing less than to contrive a plan
that would thwart the Court's tendency to rule unconstitutional many of the
most sacred laws of the New Deal. As he mused over this delicate assignment in his lavish office, pince-nez in hand, Cummings was picking aim-
lessly through a pile of books one day when he came upon a volume,
Federal Justice, that had been written by Carl McFarland, a departmental
aide. The book, a study of the ills of the lower federal courts, posed a most
intriguing solution. Let "worn-out" judges be retired on respectable pensions, the author argued. If after a reasonable interval an eligible federal
judge did not retire, let the President add a judge to the court. McFarland's
prescriptions for lower federal courts were joyfully taken up by Cummings
for the Supreme Court. When the Attorney General spread his handiwork
before the President, Roosevelt was enormously pleased. Here in essence
was what quickly became the Court-packing plan.[10]

The Presidential environment is strewn with assumptions that he and
his aides fashion and entertain. Assumptions preclude certain decisions and
shape and control others. Assumptions are also fragile things, easily crushed
by the rude impact of events. The unanticipated war in Korea smashed an
assumption generally embraced by top American military authorities and
sanctioned by Presidents Franklin Roosevelt and Truman: United States
ground forces, the view went, should never be engaged on the Asian mainland lest they be needed elsewhere. Least of all should they be committed to
an area like Korea, slight in military value and difficult to defend. This assumption was an early casualty of the Korean War; its violation intensified
as the conflict dragged on, until eventually 250,000 American troops were
dispatched to that unhappy land.

The President beholds his environment through political lenses. He
knows that much of what he does faces the hostile scrutiny of the opposition
party bent upon dragging him from office at the next election. Unfriendly
factions in his own party may manipulate against him. In his 1803 move to
purchase Louisiana, Jefferson knew full well that he was supplying the rival
Federalist party with invaluable political capital.* The Federalists, who had
been shouting for a war of conquest, greeted his decision with the cry that he
was bankrupting the Treasury to buy a desert. But in Jefferson's own party

---

* Jefferson moved to purchase the vast tract known as Louisiana when Napoleon
forced a weakened Spain to cede him the entire territory. War with England soon
dissolved Napoleon's dream of a vast overseas empire. He suddenly decided to sell
the territory to the United States for an estimated fifteen million dollars, and a
treaty was signed April 30, 1803. Jefferson thus chose to add territory to the United
States by purchase rather than by conquest.

the purchase was a huge political success. The Republican factions scrambled madly to claim credit for it. Northern Republicans, sniffing hungrily for a strong candidate to rid them once and for all of the "Virginia succession" to the Presidency, aimed to establish one of their own as the hero of the Louisiana conquest, and a lavish campaign was launched to prove that Robert Livingston of New York, who with James Monroe negotiated the purchase, deserved entire credit for its success.[11]

In choosing what to decide, the President acts as a kind of filter between his office and its environment. The state of his political fortunes, his interpretation of them, his miscalculations, and how he hopes the record of his administration will be engraved on the pages of history all may influence his choices. President Johnson's decisions, announced on March 31, 1968, to deescalate the Vietnam war and not to seek another term of office, served almost to quiet the severe attacks upon him from domestic quarters and to stake out a firm and advantageous ground upon which his eventual reputation in history might be established.

The Alternatives

Having chosen an event or situation as the occasion for a decision, the President and his aides canvass the alternative courses of action. These must be formulated and analyzed, pursuits that Herbert Simon calls "design activity." Before the alternative courses can be plotted, the raw information amassed from the environment must be studied for meaning, particularly as it foreshadows the future.

Interpretation, at its best, is a frail and inexact enterprise. At the level of the Presidency, a seemingly simple act can mean many things. When North Korean troops marched across the thirty-eighth parallel into South Korea in 1950, President Truman and his counselors started with the plausible assumption that the heavy hand of the Soviet Union was behind the venture and faced the question of the Kremlin's motive and purpose. General Omar Bradley, chairman of the Joint Chiefs of Staff, contended that the North Korean attack was a diversionary gambit preparatory to a major Soviet blow, possibly against Iran, and urged that few American troops, therefore, be committed to Korea, since they would be needed elsewhere. George Kennan, a premier authority on Soviet behavior, argued that the communists were engaging in "soft-spot probing" and advised that "situations of strength" be created wherever the Soviet thrust came, even in Korea. Others believed that the Soviets were testing the will of anticommunist nations to resist open aggression, as Hitler did when he reoccupied the Rhineland. Still other counselors advanced a "demonstration" theory stating that the U.S.S.R. expected to make Korea a show of their strength and of allied impotence, with worldwide repercussions. Finally, there was the view that the Soviet

Union was promoting a general "Far Eastern strategy."[12] For example, John Foster Dulles, then negotiating the Japanese peace treaty, saw the Korean attack as a Soviet thrust to block American efforts to bring Japan into its alliances.

Once having interpreted the environment, the President and his aides advance to the next hurdle—developing alternative responses. Not infrequently, this step may be dispensed with in the face of what seems to the President a clear, convincing solution. Harry Truman, boarding his plane after violence in Korea had rudely terminated his weekend back home, came quickly and solitarily to a fundamental decision: North Korea's aggression across the thirty-eighth parallel must be countered by force. The communists had launched a challenge that could not be sidestepped: "An outlaw was terrorizing the world community"; to ignore him meant risking "a third world war." At a meeting with his military and diplomatic aides at Blair House that evening for dinner and discussion, Truman apparently did not even consider the possibility of a nonviolent response.[13] An implicit decision that American armed forces must be committed provided the operating premise. From it other necessary decisions and their alternatives would follow; what kind of force, how many men, and within what territorial confines should the Americans fight?

Alternatives may be developed by random steps over a period of time by the President and others commanding his attention. Franklin Roosevelt, vexed by the Supreme Court's mounting tendency to strike down New Deal laws as unconstitutional, developed a variety of alternatives during the exasperating months of rebuff. An earlier forceful Chief Executive, who also suffered from the judiciary, was instructively recalled. Andrew Jackson, for the moment, became Roosevelt's inspiration. When the Court weighed one important case, Roosevelt, anticipating a hostile decision, prepared an address, which borrowed Jackson's famous defiance of the Court, "You have made your law, now enforce it." But the Court's deciding in the government's favor made the address unnecessary. When, subsequently, the justices struck down the New York minimum wage law, boding ill for a great amount of national and state labor legislation, the eminent progressive, Senator George Norris, urged Roosevelt to center his approaching 1936 electoral campaign upon the Court. Of these alternatives, electoral campaigning versus packing, Roosevelt eventually chose the latter.

Alternatives are manufactured by scores of aides in the executive branch who earn their daily bread by anticipating situations and events well before they occur and preparing possible responses when they do. Some of this preparation is "contingency planning"—preparation for emergencies that might happen—a process applied since World War II to the world's most likely trouble spots, especially, in the Eisenhower, Kennedy, and Johnson periods, to Berlin. The planners have built up crowded files of events likely to take place in Berlin and the appropriate responses. Ironically, none of these plans anticipated the wall the East Germans threw up in 1961.

More than any other contemporary President, Eisenhower relied upon subordinates to define situations and present alternative approaches to them. The President's own contribution was largely one of choosing between alternatives in whose formulation he had had little part and with whose substance he may have been unfamiliar. The Eisenhower method placed a premium on "presentations" and "briefings," on charts and one-page summaries. Eisenhower also made heavy use of committees of Presidential aides drawn from departments and the White House staff. Such committees selected problems for study, developed alternative solutions, and chose between them, leaving the President the simple task of ratification. Critics of the committee system contend that it rewards the wrong qualities by stressing fluency and "averageness," promoting agreement but discouraging creativity. They contend that Eisenhower was often kept ignorant of alternatives that his subordinates rejected and therefore never laid before him. Eisenhower's defenders point to a considerable body of "split decisions," or alternatives that his subordinates could not decide between themselves and did lay before the President for his choice.

John Kennedy, eschewing the Eisenhower method and vowing to put himself into "the thick of things," expended great quantities of energy and time spreading himself all across the decisional spectrum. The President, he thought, should hover constantly over the quest for alternatives, and if he does not, he is a prisoner of the choices that his aides finally put before him. Kennedy consulted with many advisers both outside the executive branch and inside, at various ranks in the hierarchy, at deskside conferences and over the telephone. Hans J. Morgenthau argued that the Kennedy method exposed him to too much advice, steeping him with all shades of opinion, engendering a state of mind that makes timely and forceful decision difficult. He cited the Cuban invasion fiasco of 1961 and the delayed response to the rise of the Berlin wall as case studies of Presidential irresolution. Kennedy's reaction when the Russians built the Berlin wall in 1961 was characterized, Morgenthau noted, by a duality. Kennedy responded with a "hard" line in what he said and how he said it. His style was truly Churchillian. But what he did was something else. He acted "flexibly," or, less euphemistically, he did little, and he did it late. His deeds were reminiscent not of Churchill but of Chamberlain. The contradiction, this analysis concluded, confused the American public, the nation's allies, and probably the U.S.S.R.[14] Yet Morgenthau's critique came in 1961, after Kennedy had been in office only a few months. Later Kennedy achieved widely hailed results by using the broad consultation method: in the Cuban crisis of 1962, the controversy over the admission of James Meredith to the University of Mississippi, and U.S. Steel's price rise.

The gathering and weighing of alternatives may be more than a private act, reflecting the President's own necessities. The act may also bear dimensions in public relations. In 1965, Lyndon Johnson, before deciding to increase the American commitment in the Vietnam war, weighed his alternatives in a fashion evidently intended to refute critics who charged that he was given to impulsiveness in conducting foreign affairs. In preparation for the President's decision, Defense Secretary McNamara made a five-day tour of battle areas and consulted with United States and Vietnamese leaders. Upon McNamara's return, Johnson began a series of conferences with his principal advisers: McNamara, Secretary of State Dean Rusk, Undersecretary George Ball, Presidential Assistant McGeorge Bundy, CIA Chief William Raborn, Joint Chiefs of Staff Chairman Earle G. Wheeler, the newly appointed ambassador to South Vietnam, Henry Cabot Lodge, and other officials. At the end of the second day's meeting, Bill Moyers, the President's assistant, disclosed to the press, "I think it is safe to say that a lot of the deliberation is behind the group now, and the next stage involves what to do about these recommendations and deliberations." But the discussions still continued for days and were joined by two leading Republicans experienced in foreign affairs, Arthur H. Dean and John J. McCloy. Johnson also consulted former President Eisenhower by telephone. After these discussions, Johnson ordered further special studies on "the additional strength that each military service may need in South Vietnam." These several procedures served to suggest that Johnson's decisions for Vietnam would be methodical and controlled.[15]

Choice-Making

The climactic stage of decision-making is the President's "choice activity"—selecting a particular course of action from the alternatives available. Of the several steps of decision-making, choice is the only one the President is least able to escape. He can delegate the tasks of watching the environment, selecting problems for action, fashioning alternatives, and even making some choices or decisions. Yet he is expected to make the important choices or decisions as the unavoidable price of his incumbency.

Despite their monopoly of responsibility for hard choices, some Presidents excel in bringing others to make them. As revelations of the Teapot Dome corruptions of the previous Harding administration unfolded in his own young Presidency, Coolidge resisted counsel, urgently pouring upon him, that he fire his Attorney General, Harry Daugherty. Even when the prestigious progressive leader, Senator William E. Borah of Idaho, proposed the step, Coolidge demurred. "I am here to carry out the Harding policies," he said. "I am here as a Republican President. Daugherty was Harding's friend. He stands high with the Republican organization. I do not see well how I can do it." The importunities from many sides to dump Daugherty continued, but the President would not act.

At last, when a Senate resolution was introduced calling upon the President to dismiss Daugherty, Coolidge summoned Borah to the White House one night for "urgent business." After several minutes of Presidential silence, Borah was still puzzled about what the urgent business was when Daugherty came up the grand stairway to Coolidge's study, "his jaw set," according to a White House secretary, "and his eyes like flint." Coolidge tersely introduced his visitors, adding, "Well, don't let my presence embarrass you!" This instruction was superfluous. Borah and Daugherty went at it for an hour of shrill debate. Coolidge sat by, slumped in his chair smoking. In the din of the exchange, Borah exclaimed that it was not for him to tell the Attorney General to resign; it was the President's duty. Coolidge said not a word. When at last the antagonists finished, the little President, standing to hurry his parting guests, quacked, "Senator, I reckon you're right!" Daugherty, "white with rage," according to the secretary, who witnessed the encounter, stomped "angrily down the stairs and out of the White House."[16] He soon resigned. Coolidge had put upon Borah the burden of confronting Daugherty, thus forcing the decision.

The President determines what choices or decisions are possible. His choices are influenced not only by his personal ideals but by his knowledge of what has worked in the past, his estimate of the response of his adversaries, his judgment of what his publics at home and abroad will bear, of whether the bureaucracy will comply, and whether his party will go along. No one else in American government or society has a sweep of duties, and therefore of decisions, like his.

Each President has his own preferred manner of choice. Eisenhower preferred to be calm and composed. "Boy, there's just one thing I really *know*," he once said, "You *can't* decide things in a *panic*. Any decision you make when you are panicked, you can be sure of only one thing. It will be a bad one."[17]

Franklin Roosevelt's method of making choices was, as Arthur M. Schlesinger, Jr., has described it, "involved and inscrutable." Roosevelt weighed a basket of factors in a typical major decision: political timing, consequences to his personal public fortunes, interest group reactions, partisan advantage, impact on Congress and the public.[18] He permitted situations to develop and crystallize, he let competing forces pull in conflict, and then through some system of "unconscious calculation," as Rexford Tugwell termed it, the decision finally emerged. Roosevelt's method, Tugwell observed, made it seem that "no choosing had taken place" and forestalled discovery of his "governing principle."[19] Decision and policy were not thought out; rather, the President's intuitions seemed to coalesce and initiate a result. That his decisions were sometimes untidy never troubled the President. Clear-cut administrative decisions, he felt, worked only if they reflected clear-cut political realities.

If they did not, the decisions would prove hollow and weak. He was devoted to final objectives and flexible means. Roosevelt, like many another President, valued procrastination. Wait long enough for clamoring forces to settle, for the momentum of events to slacken, and the imperatives of today will be gone tomorrow. Time he considered a great corrective, one that spares the President many hard choices. He loved to make minor choices in a dramatic way that shocked and surprised the public. "I'm going to spring a bombshell," he delighted to announce, and then stunned his gaping audience with a novel proposal such as changing the date of Thanksgiving or imposing national daylight-saving time the year around to aid the war effort. "He delights in surprises—clever, cunning and quick," Hugh Johnson observed, "He likes to shock friends as well as enemies with something they never expected."[20]

Some Presidents when they decide are disinclined to make certain choices, either by personal preference or force of circumstance. President Eisenhower eschewed personal criticism of others and the entire terrain of political counterattack. Tormentors could loose their salvos; Senator Joseph McCarthy could apply the torch of insinuation and unsupportable charge with full confidence that Eisenhower would not retaliate. The President said to aides who urged sterner measures, "I simply do not believe it does a damn bit of good wasting time answering the other fellow. All you do is double the audience he had the first time when he proclaimed whatever it is you are trying to answer." Or again, when President Truman launched his "give 'em hell, Harry!" attacks upon the Republican ticket in the 1952 campaign, Eisenhower brushed aside all suggestions that he counterattack. "I'm sure they would like me to get down to *their* level," he declared. "Well, that's *one* satisfaction they will *never* have."[21]

The President, if he wants to, can elaborate upon and qualify his choice at some length. At a news conference on July 3, 1957, President Eisenhower spoke candidly of the administration's civil rights bill then afoot in Congress in words that revealed his feelings better than a previous terse official statement accompanying the bill did. "I was reading part of that bill this morning," he told the newsmen, "and I—there were certain phrases I didn't completely understand. . . . I would want to talk to the Attorney General. . . . Naturally, I am not a lawyer." In three sentences the President had punctured the status of a bill drafted in his Justice Department and offered to Congress as a major part of "the President's program."[22] The bill's champions on Capitol Hill were further disheartened several days later when the President, again in a press conference, applied more cold water. "If you try to go too far too fast," he reminded the nation, ". . . you are making a mistake."[23]

Viewed collectively over time, Presidential choices appear wavering and inconsistent. They seldom approximate neat consistent patterns like soldiers on parade. Shifting events, the alchemy of competing pressures, the President's own political sensitivities bring disarray. Franklin Roosevelt, therefore, almost alternatingly advanced upon and backed away from a progressive line. He began with an isolationist economic policy and shifted to an internationalist trade policy. He turned from cooperation with business to regulation. In reality, he was responding to changing events and situations, to the necessity of winning and holding a broad base of support.

In making choices, the President must be heedful not to commit more resources than he needs to secure his objectives. His resources—whether popularity, legislative favor, military weapons, or whatever—are all limited and must be used prudently and with maximum effect. John Kennedy, faced with a string of Soviet provocations in Berlin in 1961, warned his aides of the danger of the "false climax"—of going all out for a Soviet-contrived challenge that would not finally materialize. It was important, Kennedy stressed, not to commit everything you had at once but to keep something in reserve. His subsequent choices illustrated his point. In January 1961 he ordered an increase of airlift capacity, thereby enhancing the mobility of American forces; his March defense message to Congress outlined steps to be taken to prepare for conventional war. In May he appeared before Congress offering five recommendations to strengthen conventional forces. In late summer he called up reserves to expand the base of the enlarged conventional army.[24]

Making the Decision Known

The President, having made his choice or decision, next makes it known. The means of promulgation are usefully varied. The President can convey his choice by simple statement or artful inference, by silence or gesture, by proclamation signed and sealed. How he communicates may be idiosyncratic. Presidents, for example, are wont to incorporate important decisions about their administrations in carefully prepared inaugural addresses. Not Franklin Pierce; despite the significant policy it had to convey, his inaugural was unwritten and extemporized without a note. Most Presidential decisions are not deliberately and systematically promulgated. As Chester Barnard observes, "most executive decisions produce no direct evidence of themselves and . . . knowledge of them can only be derived from the cumulation of indirect evidence."

Presidential decisions, when they become known, produce sensations of pleasure and pain. Some Chief Executives limit as far as possible their own acts of promulgating to the announcements of pleasurable decisions. They leave the dispensing of the hard negative to subordinates. Harry Hopkins in his day securely established himself in the craw of many a defeated decision-seeker as Franklin Roosevelt's abominable no-man. Sherman Adams excelled in his day in the same role for Dwight Eisenhower. Indeed Adams' eventual departure from the Presidential scene was hastened by the large and ever-growing body of the disgruntled created by his capacity to say no. Some decisions, regardless of their effect, can be communicated only by the President. It is inconceivable that President Johnson's decision not to seek reelection, which produced pain for his friends and pleasure for his foes, could have been disclosed by anyone but himself.

A President's own mood and gesture can enhance the force of his decision, just as diffidence can drain a strong decision. Lincoln added immeasurably to the force of the Emancipation Proclamation when he declared, upon signing it, "I never, in my life, felt more certain that I was doing right than I do in signing this paper."[25] Johnson's decision to halt the bombing of North Vietnam was given special force when he coupled it with his disclosure that he would not accept another term of office.

Promulgation involves timing. The decision must be revealed neither too late nor too soon. Not surprisingly, Presidents withhold their decision until the time is ripe. Lincoln had composed and firmly decided upon his Emancipation Proclamation some weeks before he finally issued it. He bided his time, waiting for a Union victory on the battlefield to enhance the historic document's importance and reception. Union victories were not easily come by at this stage in the war, and weeks passed. While he waited, one of his most formidable critics, Horace Greeley, editor of the New York *Tribune*, took him to task in a moving, widely read editorial, "The Prayer of Twenty Millions." The President's followers, Greeley charged, were "deeply pained by the policy you seem to be pursuing with regard to the slaves of rebels. . . . We think you are strangely and disastrously remiss in the discharge of your official and imperative duty with regard to the emancipating provisions of the new Confiscation Act."[26]

Some Presidents precede a statement of their choices with a subtle ritual. Franklin Roosevelt, fresh from his decision to launch the Court-packing plan, tendered the annual Presidential dinner for the judiciary. All the high court justices appeared at the White House except the aged Louis Brandeis, who never ventured out in the evening, and Harlan F. Stone, who was ill. Approximately eighty notables gathered, and those seated at the President's table presented a spectacle tinged with an irony that Roosevelt relished. At his table were all but two of the justices he was about to subjugate, and at the table also were Attorney General Cummings and several other faithful helpers who had prepared the artifacts for the subjugation. When the packing plan would be sprung, the justices would recall, and presumably with not a little awe, the President's droll finesse.[27]

The act of promulgation may require several ancillary decisions. Priority was vital to Roosevelt's Court-packing strategy, and so he directed his legislative leaders to place his judiciary bill ahead of the farm bill, the wages and hours bill, and the "little TVA" bill on the Congressional calendar. The precedence of the bill would communicate to farm and labor leaders and to liberals the loud, clear message that the quickest way to secure their cherished legislation was to put their shoulders behind the President's bill. The faster it was passed, the faster would their measures advance.

Consequences

Decisions are applied and implemented, and, like all acts, have consequences. For the President decisions represent successes and losses, costs and gains. A Presidential decision of magnitude may lead to bitterness or it may touch off national exultation and create a mood rich with political promise. When a horseman rode into Washington from New Orleans on January 15, 1804, with the news that Louisiana had been peaceably delivered to the United States three weeks before, the nation rejoiced. Congress gave a great dinner, with the President and the cabinet as the honored guests, to celebrate the gain of a new empire. French representative Louis Pichon, informing his government of the jubilation, well observed that "the acquisition of Louisiana and the peaceful manner of possession have raised Jefferson and his friends to a high point of popularity and regard. His re-election must be considered as assured."[28]

In great decisions it is ordinarily not the President's fate to receive the lavish approval that befell Jefferson but mixed praise and censure. The Emancipation Proclamation evoked large doses of both. Governor David Tod of Ohio endorsed "every word and syllable of it." Charles Sumner of Massachusetts exulted, "The skies are brighter and the air is purer now that slavery has been handed over to judgment." Frederick Douglass was "greatly encouraged." The New York *Times* declared, "No more important and far-reaching document ever issued since the foundation of this Government." But doubt was expressed in much of the press that any real good would come from the proclamation. Lincoln acknowledged that his expectations were

> not as sanguine as . . . those of some friends. . . . While commendation in newspapers and by distinguished individuals is all a vain man could wish, the stocks have declined, and troops come forward more slowly than ever. . . . The North responds to the Proclamation sufficiently in breath; but breath alone kills no rebels.[29]

Consequences are almost endless in variety. Some Presidents are compelled to make choices that change the entire direction of their administration or indeed of the country itself—Jefferson's decision on the Louisiana Purchase, for example.

Jefferson's political career had long been given to cultivating amity with France. He had served with distinction in its court and had been its unstinting friend in his years as Washington's Secretary of State. His party was traditionally attached to France. Still, as President he deemed it necessary to sacrifice his attachment in the face of the new and ominous situation.

France, led by Napoleon, that incomparable maker of empires, had recently acquired the vast province of Louisiana and loomed threateningly at the United States border, superseding Spain in North America. Jefferson deemed it "impossible that France and the U.S. [could] continue long friends when they meet in so irritable a position." The Jefferson administration stressed that it was in the interests of inland communication for the United States to possess New Orleans and the Spanish Floridas. "The United States," said Secretary of State James Madison, in explaining his government's point of view to Pichon, "had no interest in seeing circumstances rise which should eventually lead [the United States'] population to extend itself on the right bank of the Mississippi." The extensions, said Madison, could not but "weaken the state" and perhaps lead to dangerous separatist movements.[30]

Decisions have consequences that cannot be immediately, if ever, perceived. A weapons system requiring seven years in passage from drawing board to operations plainly forestalls any prompt revelation of the consequences of the decisions it represents. Consequences may not be perceived because the President is blinded by prejudices and ambitions. Weeks passed in the Court-packing fight before Roosevelt regarded as credible the grim daily reports his lieutenants brought him of voting prospects on Capitol Hill. He was unaccustomed to the possibility of defeat. When his Court fight wallowed inconclusively for weeks in Congress, Thomas Corcoran and Secretary of the Interior Harold Ickes noticed a marked shrinkage in their chief's aggressive leadership. The President, Ickes noted in his diary, "has acted to me like a beaten man."[31]

An Overview

The President's method in decision-making has something of the quality of fire. It can serve for good or ill; it can be a virtue or a vice; at one time it can succeed, at another it leads to abysmal failure. There is no available body of absolute directives like the Ten Commandments to assure correct decision-making. "Don't put off unto tomorrow what can be done today," the adage says. But, according to another, "Sufficient unto the day is the evil thereof." A Franklin Roosevelt can long postpone a key decision, and, endowed with a kind of charmed political life, manage to get away with it. William McKinley on the eve of war with Spain, a peace-minded man eager to avoid conflict, delayed so in his bewilderment at events that war-minded legislators and the yellow press grabbed the initiative and with it the issue of war or peace.

The President does well to consult, but he does ill to consult too much. Truman and the Democratic party paid dearly for his failure to involve Congress substantially in his early Korean decisions. Later, when the Korean War became unpopular, he could not share the resulting political liabilities with a Congress shut out from his original decisions. But consultations also can be too wide, productive of such contradictory counsel and excessive information that decision is delayed and weakened. Decision is a blend of fact, thought, incisiveness, and vigor; to stress one ingredient is to diminish others.

When the occasion requires a decision, the President must communicate his will clearly and not create havoc, as Wilson did in proclaiming, "We are too proud to fight," a well-intentioned moral standard for the nation, which the Allies understandably misinterpreted as an evidence of cooling ardor toward their cause. Yet the President will also need an instinct for ambiguity in his daily grapple with petitioners and their pressures for his favor. For others to know his will too clearly and too soon may bring him political trouble and grief.

There are discernible in the world of the President several principles that seem far more often right than wrong. Above all, the President must keep the initiative in decisions that are his, and not permit it to be grabbed by Congress or private groups. He should not decide in anger, or grief, or other high emotion but only in composure. Presidents by this standard have been remarkably successful. As a lot they have not been hotheads or desk-pounders. The magnitude of the Chief Executive's power and responsibility and his need to maintain to the outside world an image of self-confidence require that he appear to be "in charge," that he speak and act with assurance, hold his subordinates in rein, and comprehend the problems they are struggling with. Decision is more than the creation of policy. It reveals the President as a person.

Crisis   15

Sometime in the first hundred days of the New Deal, Norman Davis, a distinguished roving ambassador of that era, encountered Raymond Fosdick outside the White House. "Ray," said Davis, "that fellow in there is not the fellow we used to know. There's been a miracle here."[1] Wrote editor Oswald Villard of the *Nation* during the same period, "Many of us who have known him long and well ask ourselves if this is the same man."[2] Crisis had thrust the man, Franklin D. Roosevelt, as it has other Presidents, up to a level of effectiveness that he had never before achieved. But crisis can also be the severest of all the limitations that the Chief Executive works under; it can reduce him to the depths of ineffectiveness, in which, despite his best efforts, he flounders helplessly against overwhelming forces.

Crisis is a crucible in which a President and his administration are tested as nowhere else. No other condition tries so rigorously the capacity of the President for decision, perceptiveness, physical endurance, self-confidence, and prudence. Crisis is a cruel master that forces the Chief Executive to rearrange his priorities and recast his plans. If it brings him to wage war, he will do less in social policy, no matter how high his aspirations are for that endeavor, no matter how solemnly he laid his plans before the electorate and how enthusiastically they were approved. At no other time are the stakes so high as in crisis. The consequences of his actions are enormously magnified; he may find new strengths; and his weaknesses may be glaringly exposed. His decisions may determine nothing less than national survival and the preservation of the existing social order. What he does in crisis will be more remembered in history than anything else he does. If he fails, his short-

coming will be recalled, when a thousand successes he may have won in quieter times are long forgotten.

Most great Presidents have been crisis Presidents. Lincoln brought the
nation through the holocaust of civil war, Wilson through World War I, and
Franklin Roosevelt through the depression and toward victory in World War
II. But the brilliant success of Presidents in crisis cannot blind us to the debit
side of the balance sheet, to the substantial failures. James Madison, administrator of the War of 1812, suffered defeats and retreats and the ignominy of
having the White House burned from under him. Lincoln was preceded by
Buchanan's administration, which failed to stay the onrush of civil war. Under
Hoover the nation sustained almost four years of Jobean torment from soaring
unemployment and unrelieved despair.

Contemporary Presidents are surfeited with opportunities for greatness,
facing as they do crises of a scale unknown to their predecessors. Since the end
of the American nuclear monopoly, the Presidency has existed in a state of
perpetual crisis in its enforced vigil to prevent some incident or issue from
escalating into general war. Presidents since World War II have chronically
been caught up in multiple crises, thanks to the capacity of communist nations to strike on many fronts and our domestic society's capacity to churn up
big trouble. For Kennedy 1962 was a year of crisis. The Soviets emplaced
missiles in Cuba. Civil rights crises exploded in Mississippi and Alabama, and
a price rise in steel threatened to smother the administration's foremost economic goals: curbing inflation, bettering the balance of payments, speeding
economic growth, and relieving unemployment. Lyndon Johnson, in his first
hundred days as President, faced violence in Panama, upheaval in Zanzibar,
civil war in Cyprus, threatened war over Malaysia, a coup in Vietnam, and
churning trouble in Laos, among other worries.

No nation can endure to live in a state of maximum commitment in crisis
after crisis, and so a President must assign priorities even to crises. In 1968
President Johnson, heavily committed in the Vietnam war, deemed it necessary to limit himself to nonviolent responses when North Korea seized the
Pueblo, a United States intelligence vessel. Presidents may be betrayed by
subsequent events into a posture of overreacting to a situation seemingly bearing all the marks of crisis. In Johnson's first months in office, Cuba suddenly
launched a radio campaign for the "return" of the Guantánamo base, and her
fishing boats began intruding into United States waters. The boats were seized,
whereupon Castro shut off the Guantánamo water supply. The United States,
sensing crisis and mindful of the 1962 confrontation with the U.S.S.R. over
Cuba, announced that most of the several thousand Cubans commuting
daily to the base would be dismissed unless they spent their earnings there.
Just after this stern measure was announced, Castro pulled his reverse lever
and poured out conciliatory words. The President was left with a strong public
stand but no crisis.[3]

Crisis distorts relations between the branches of government. It may drive Congress and the President far apart, as Buchanan and Hoover learned, and shut out even the most elementary cooperation. Or it may be an overriding force for unity as the normal divisions and rivalries between the legislative and executive branches are abandoned and partisan skirmishing is put aside. Congress, which ordinarily does not delegate the President authority gladly, may do so with a lavish hand. In the hundred days after his inauguration in 1933, Franklin Roosevelt was showered with matchless gifts of statutory authority. "Since March 4, 1933," Lindsay Rogers wrote in those incredible days, "Presidential government has been stronger than at any previous time— even during the War. The powers granted to President Roosevelt are considerably in excess of those which Congress allowed President Wilson to exercise and the popular support at present manifest is immeasurably greater."[4]

Crisis spotlights the inadequacies of the existing order and opens wide the opportunities for creating sweeping new policy. The exigencies of World War II brought the first large modern strides for Negro civil rights in permitting the federal Fair Employment Practice Committee to administer new public standards in human relations. Civil rights crises in 1965 provided further underscoring; the rioting in the Watts section of Los Angeles illuminated the dreadful circumstances of Negroes in American cities. The grave economic crisis of 1933 invited the government to stimulate and control a vast economic revolution. The central question fiercely debated in New Deal councils was: How big a revolution should it be? To some, the changes accomplished were awesome. "Never was there such a change in the transfer of government," Supreme Court Justice Harlan Stone wrote to Herbert Hoover after two months of the Roosevelt administration. "To judge by the rapidity of changing events, as many decades might have passed."[5] But there was also disappointment that the President did not exploit his opportunity more fully, that he had not attacked unemployment with more basic solutions, that he had not reconstituted the entire banking system rather than merely saving the banks. "I think back to the events of March 4, 1933, with a sick heart," Senator Bronson Cutting later wrote. "For then . . . the nationalization of banks by President Roosevelt could have been accomplished without a word of protest."[6]

Four Presidents in historic situations provide a panorama of crisis: Herbert Hoover and the Great Depression, Franklin Roosevelt during his first hundred days, James Buchanan and his handling of events preceding the Civil War, and John Kennedy and the Cuban crisis of 1962. Some of these Presidents succeeded and others failed. All were caught in the worst hazard of their office, the merciless vise of crisis from which there is no full escape, unless, if the President is lucky, it is a kind that can be solved.

Two Presidents—Herbert Hoover and Franklin Roosevelt—faced the Great Depression of the 1930's, the worst economic crisis the nation has ever experienced. The effectiveness of these two Presidents in dealing with their common problem was as different as night is from day.

Herbert Hoover and the Great Depression

It was Herbert Hoover's lot to confront the Great Depression when it commenced with the great stock market crash seven months after his inauguration. The whole economy was clawed and gouged; no worker, farmer, or lofty business executive escaped the infinite, invisible adversary.

In October and November 1929 stocks listed on the New York Stock Exchange fell over 40 per cent in value, a loss of twenty-six billion dollars. Although President Hoover bravely announced, "The fundamental business of the country, that is, production and distribution of commodities, is on a sound and prosperous basis," events soon slashed the President's optimism.[7] Commodity prices, freight-car loadings, pig iron and steel production, coal output, and automobile production, the crucial economic indicators, fell sharply. But the most fearsome aspect of the collapse was the soaring unemployment that at its peak numbered one-fourth of the labor force. Men eager to work found factory gates shut, so they sat home, their spirits rusting. In those times the unemployed were maintained by private and local public resources, and support was scanty. In Allegheny County, Pennsylvania, according to Benjamin C. Marsh, executive secretary of the people's lobby, "There are families who have not even salt in their homes. It is a matter of beans, week after week."[8] Waves of foreclosures of farms and workingmen's homes swept the country.

The creaky, jerry-built banking system passed through a vale of utter darkness. Bank failures, which had been building up in the twenties, rocketed at the spark of the depression. In all, 5,102 banks went under from 1929 through 1932. Depositors marched on banks and thousands of veterans of World War I with their wives and children marched on Washington to press Congress to award immediately a bonus for World War I veterans not due until 1945. Commander Walter W. Waters of the marching veterans spoke of them as the vanguard of a general revolt of the unemployed. Men in high places did strange things and appeared in odd lights. Samuel Insull, emperor of a vast public utilities network, resigned his eighty-five directorships, sixty-five chairmanships, and eleven presidencies and abruptly departed for Europe. J. P. Morgan, it was later revealed, did not pay one cent of federal income tax in 1930, 1931, or 1932, nor, in the last two years, did any of his partners. The Great Depression had an international dimension. The failure of Austria's largest bank, the Credit-Anstalt, precipitated a general panic in central Europe that swept rapidly westward.[9]

The general economic ruin fell upon Herbert Hoover, a solemn and wealthy engineer. He had become a household symbol of merciful efficiency as relief administrator in World War I, and then as Secretary of Commerce and strong man of Harding's cabinet. Because of confusion over his party affiliation, important Democrats had boomed him for the Presidency in 1920.

"He is certainly a wonder," Franklin Roosevelt had said, "and I wish we could make him President of the United States."[10]

On March 4, 1929, Hoover took the Presidential oath. The new Bible used for the ceremony was then turned back to Proverbs 29:18, which read, "Where there is no vision, the people perish; but he that keepeth the law, happy is he."[11] Seven months later, however, the stock market crashed and the holocaust of the Great Depression, which had long been gathering in the Harding and Coolidge administrations, struck with total fury. In responding to the disaster, Hoover was controlled by a personal philosophy that he believed had forged the nation's past extraordinary economic growth while simultaneously preserving the basic liberties.

"It is not the function of the [federal] government," he said later on August 11, 1932, in accepting renomination for the Presidency, "to relieve individuals of their responsibilities to their neighbors, or to relieve private institutions of their responsibilities to the public, or of local government to the States, or of State governments to the Federal Government." At most, the federal government might employ "reserve powers" in behalf of citizens and communities, but only after insisting that "all of them assert their responsibilities in full." Man's responsibility to his neighbor was "God-imposed," he declared in his inaugural address of March 4, 1929, and the cooperation of man with his fellows and of private organizations with one another was "an advance toward the highest conception of self-government." The choice between local and federal activity was a choice between liberty and tyranny. And in 1931 in a radio address he told the nation:

> Where people divest themselves of local government responsibilities they at once lay the foundation for destruction of their liberties. . . . At once when the government is centralized there arises a limitation upon the liberty of the individual, and restriction of individual opportunity . . . can lead but to the superstate where every man becomes the servant of the State and real liberty is lost.[12]

The depression's root cause, in Hoover's view, was not material or political, but psychological—the erosion of confidence and the spread of fear. "The courage and enterprise of the people still exist," he wrote to Senator Simeon D. Fess, "and only await release from fears and apprehension." The federal government could best restore confidence by balancing its budget. "The government no more than individual families can continue to expend more than it receives without inviting serious consequences. . . ." A balanced budget meant less spending and lower taxes. "It is the relief of taxes from the backs of men which liberates their powers."[13]

Hoover, true to his doctrines, stressed public works by states and municipalities for the unemployed. He stepped up federal construction and halted immigration, but would go no further. When Senator Robert F. Wagner introduced legislation calling for advance public works planning by a Federal

Employment Stabilization Board, a strengthened employment service, and improved statistical data on the unemployed, Hoover supported only the last proposal. Unemployment relief belonged to the states, local charitable organizations, and the employer. Federal action would open the way to evil "politics," and the time required to train a suitable bureaucracy could not be spared.

In Hoover's view the federal government might "indirectly" help the unemployed, the farmer, the bank depositor, by aiding employers and banks. Rising production and cheaper credit would diminish the misery of the hard-hit groups. As bank failures soared, Hoover proposed that the leading banks pool their funds to provide a credit reserve for their weaker fellows. When this proved to no avail, he proposed to Congress on December 8, 1931, the creation of the Reconstruction Finance Corporation to make loans to shore up credit, check inflation, expand employment, and bolster the badly wobbling banks and railroads. He modeled the RFC after the War Finance Corporation of World War I and believed it would accomplish its mission within two years. But as the depression worsened, the RFC, his principal contribution to recovery, continued to be needed. By March 31, 1933, the RFC had lent $1,785,315,120 to 7,411 institutions, principally banks and railroads. Eventually the RFC provided loans for unemployment relief. Belatedly and grudgingly, Hoover took this long step away from his philosophical hostility to federal action. With equal tardiness and reluctance, he tried to improve the credit facilities of the farmer and the home owner. As the international economic picture deteriorated, Hoover, pushed inexorably by events, proposed a moratorium on intergovernmental debts.[14]

Hoover was chronically opposed to increases in Presidential power to cope with the emergency. When revival of the wartime Council of National Defense was proposed to widen the attack upon the depression demon, he scotched the idea, holding that it was more important to balance the budget. When the Democratic-controlled Congress, in the face of the deepening misery, moved to empower the RFC to make loans "for any conceivable purpose on any conceivable security to anybody who wants money," he vetoed the legislation.[15]

Few, if any, Presidents have worked as hard on the job as Hoover. "Work is life," was his motto. Up at six and at his desk by eight-thirty, he drove his staff ragged by relentless application. His own life was incessantly preoccupied with the crisis. "A repairman behind a dyke," he described himself. "No sooner is one leak plugged up than it is necessary to dash over and stop another that has broken out. There is no end to it." His mastery of the situation's facts was dazzling. "He has the greatest capacity for assimilating and organizing information of any man I ever knew," said his Secretary of State, Henry L. Stimson. "To Hoover's brain facts are water to a sponge," noted Bernard Baruch, "They are absorbed into every tiny interstice." But Secretary Stimson lamented the President's habit of "seeing the dark side first" and likened their conferences to "sitting in a bath of ink."[16] Although Hoover fought hard, his darkling views drained his zest.

However much Hoover valued public confidence, his administration was a monumental failure in public relations. Shy and sensitive, he considered political polemics alien to the dignity of his office. "This is not a showman's job," he would say, "I will not step out of character."[17] When on occasion he resorted to the radio, he read from a manuscript in a dull monotone that quickly lost his audience.

The Hoover era was more than a failure of the uses of Presidential initiative and power; it was, of course, a failure also of society to use its own alternative sources of leadership. The businessman who in 1925 had been rightly characterized as "the most influential person in the nation" lay prostrate in failure. The imperious J. P. Morgan might take to the radio in 1932, but the heavens opened not a crack. The grand academic economists, Taussig, Ely, Commons, Mitchell, and Seligman, were almost totally unprepared for the collapse. Organized labor was in the hands of little men. Except for the thirty-hour week, their pronouncements were barren of concrete proposals. Congress, which passed into Democratic control with the 1930 elections, tended to reject the President's proposals. Democratic measures, in turn, calling for more vigorous action than Hoover's ideology could bear, were vetoed time and again. And the President-elect, Franklin Roosevelt, chosen by the people in a massive rejection of the Hoover leadership, treated gingerly Hoover's invitation to a kind of joint leadership in the four-month lame-duck interlude between the election and the inauguration. With only a few minor exceptions, Roosevelt chose not to act until his formal investiture in the Presidential office.[18]

Franklin Roosevelt's Hundred Days

On March 4, 1933, Franklin D. Roosevelt was sworn into the Presidency before a hundred thousand spectators crammed upon forty acres of lawn and pavement before the east front of the Capitol, while millions more gathered at their radios. The nation was gripped in tension. For weeks devastating runs on savings banks had continued unslackened. When Roosevelt took the oath, every bank in the nation had locked its doors.

Roosevelt's inaugural pronouncements set the themes of his approach to the crisis and his operation of the Presidency. "This nation asks for action, and action now," he declared. "This great nation will endure as it has endured, will revive and will prosper." He quickly provided action. He called Congress into special session and proclaimed a national banking holiday from March 6 to March 9. In that interval his administration worked out plans to revive the banks. The convening of Congress on March 9 signaled the beginning of the "one hundred days," in which the President literally engulfed the legislature with proposals for economic recovery and reform. At the top of the list was legislation to regulate the resumption of banking. "I cannot too strongly urge upon the Congress the clear necessity for immediate action," read the President's message. Congress needed no urging. In less than forty minutes the House of Representatives passed unanimously the administration's bill, which few of its members had seen. It swept through the Senate and reached the President for signature less than eight hours after its introduction.[19]

The next day Roosevelt sent over his message on economy in government, curiously reminiscent of Hoover's strictures on the subject. On March 16 the President asked for agricultural legislation, the first of a series of proposals to reorganize the nation's economic processes. The central feature of the administration's agricultural bill was the provision of a price subsidy to the farmer who pledged to limit his output. It was hoped that these procedures would help restore the farmer's badly eroded purchasing power. The administration's bill eased the farm mortgage crisis and increased the value of farm loans. On March 21 the President tackled the problem of unemployment by asking for federal grants to the states for direct unemployment relief, a step the Hoover administration had grudgingly begun in its twilight days. He next called for a civilian conservation corps, consisting eventually of a quarter million of the youthful unemployed, who built dams, planted trees, improved streams, fought forest fires and diseases, and cleared beaches and camping sites. On March 29, spurred by the revelations of abuses in the stock markets, he asked for supervision of the sale of investment securities in interstate commerce. On April 10 came the New Deal's most monumental achievement, the plan for a Tennessee Valley Authority with responsibilities for planning the "proper use, conservation and development of the natural resources of the Tennessee River drainage basin and adjoining territory." Power development, flood control, soil erosion, reforestation, the retirement of marginal lands, industrial development, indeed planning for the entire watershed were on the TVA agenda. On April 13 the President urged legislation to save small home mortgages from foreclosures that were averaging a thousand a day. On May 4 came emergency legislation to improve the ailing railroads and on May 17 a national industrial recovery bill to foster "a great cooperative movement throughout all industry in order to obtain wide reemployment, to shorten the working week, to pay a decent wage for the shorter week and to prevent unfair competition and disastrous overproduction." The President also requested a vast three billion dollar program of public construction to spur employment.[20]

In these hundred days Roosevelt sent fifteen messages to Congress and shepherded fifteen laws through to enactment. He made ten major addresses, held press conferences and cabinet meetings twice a week, received innumerable visitors and delegations, conferred with the heads of other nations, and made all the important executive decisions. In the months after the one hundred days Roosevelt's further policies unraveled in an atmosphere of urgency. In 1934 the stock exchanges were regulated, a new labor policy was inaugurated facilitating union organization and imposing upon employers a duty to engage in serious collective bargaining. A social security system was installed to cushion the hardships of old age and unemployment. To push the economy, Roosevelt engaged in "pump-priming," chiefly through an elaborate program of public works. He dabbled briefly in the intricacies of a commodity dollar, contrived to raise the price level, and went off the gold standard. Periodically, he stoked business confidence by retrenching public spending and balancing the budget. The New Deal's frantic activity succeeded. The banks reopened, their health vastly improved, the United States government guaranteed their deposits, and the rain of failures ceased. Employment rose, the farmer kept his home and bettered his land, business failures dropped; the sun shone again.[21]

How had Roosevelt reversed the plunge of crisis into enheartening upturn? His administration indeed was, as his inaugural promised, action-oriented. Crisis, in his view, could not be coped with merely by hopeful public pronouncement and private hand-wringing, or by defensive response to the depression's newest attack. The hundred days and after witnessed a grand offensive. Roosevelt made his way by taking a sweeping view of his powers and of Presidential leadership. In his inaugural address he asserted a well-nigh limitless vision of Presidential authority. "Our Constitution," he declared, "is so simple and practical that it is possible always to meet extraordinary needs by changes in emphasis and arrangement without loss of essential form." He went on to reveal that if the nation's worsening plight or a laggard tendency of Congress required it, "I shall ask the Congress for the one remaining instrument to meet the crisis—broad Executive power to wage a war against the emergency, as great as the power that would be given to me if we were in fact invaded by a foreign foe." As his administration proceeded, Roosevelt commanded his legal counselors to tell him not what he could not do, but what he could do.[22]

His conception of Presidential leadership was formed by the models of Woodrow Wilson and Theodore Roosevelt, which teach that the people respond to vision and moral purpose. For Franklin Roosevelt, the models illuminated weakness as well as strength. Theodore Roosevelt, he discerned, lacked Wilson's "appeal to the fundamental" and capacity to stir "the truly profound moral and social convictions." Wilson, in contrast, failed to raise "people to enthusiasm over specific individual events," as Theodore Roosevelt did. Franklin Roosevelt, setting his own performance in the economic crisis, endeavored to combine the best of Wilson and Theodore Roosevelt by appealing to underlying convictions, by stirring the nation over specific events, and by making government the positive instrument of the people.[23]

The New Deal, he said, "implied a new order of things designed to benefit the great mass of our farmers, workers, and businessmen would replace the old order of special privilege. . . ." In countless ways he expressed his administration's commitment to the welfare of all the people. When the banking community lay sprawled in utter helplessness, Roosevelt noticed, not without amusement, how bankers who once had objected so high-mindedly to federal assistance for farmers and the unemployed now cried for it themselves. It was more important to save the people, Roosevelt said, although he cast many a lifeline to bankers, too. He measured his administration's progress in terms of improvements in the people's condition. Mrs. Roosevelt, whose far travels and keen eye made her the President's star reporter, would depart with his instructions, "Watch the people's faces. Look at the condition of their clothes on the wash line. You can tell a lot from that." He greeted her return with a barrage of questions on what people whom she visited had to eat, how they lived, and what their homes and farms and educational facilities were like.[24]

The hundred days and beyond was an interlude crammed with improvisation and experimentation such as the nation had never seen. Unlike Hoover, who was ruled by dogma, Roosevelt had few preconceptions and no panaceas. The New Deal was a coat of many colors, of centralization in the manner of NRA, of decentralization in the states' large role in the workings of the unemployment compensation system, in the nationalism of the United States at the London Economic Conference, and the internationalism of reciprocal trade agreements. Those mindful of the wide chasm between Theodore Roosevelt's New Nationalism, with its stress upon planning and government operation, and Wilson's New Freedom, with its devotion to regulation and the retention of private ownership, rubbed their eyes in disbelief in beholding elements of both in the hundred days. TVA was a monument to planning; regulating securities was in the Wilsonian tradition. To assure this rich diversity, Roosevelt skillfully kept about himself a circle of administrators and advisers of clashing views and backgrounds.[25]

As befits an administration pledged to action, the qualities Roosevelt valued most in his subordinates were initiative, vitality, and vision. Most major posts of the New Deal were occupied by men with ideas and drive—chiefly lawyers, professors, economists, and social workers who were at home in the world of ideas and its workaday procedures of analysis and dialectic. The administrators were not simply specialists but generalists confident of their capacity to illuminate any social problem with positive rationality. Yet Roosevelt retained his own grip on decision sufficiently to recapture jurisdictions whenever an administrator faltered. To assure that programs would be carried out with maximum action, he entrusted their administration not to the old-line departments, as a rule, but to newly created agencies. The old departments, he noted, were wedded to bureaucratic routine and the policies of bygone Republican administrations. The new agencies offered the energy and enthusiasm of their youthfulness and commitment to New Deal policy.

Roosevelt's success in pushing an unprecedented quantity of major laws through Congress had something of a pattern. He outlined his proposals in brief, general messages, and followed them with bills or detailed memoranda prepared by his executive aides and introduced by friendly Congressmen. In the follow-up, Roosevelt excelled at face-to-face persuasion with legislative leaders and at coordinating them and his administrative aides in common cause. The stock exchanges law, for instance, was the joint product of James M. Landis, Benjamin Cohen, and Thomas Corcoran of the executive branch, who coached witnesses and prepared data for the legislative committees; Congressman Sam Rayburn and Senator Duncan Fletcher of the legislature; and Ferdinand Pecora, who brilliantly investigated the malfeasance of bankers and brokers.

Roosevelt's progress was speeded by his tactic of bipartisan or nonpartisan appeals, which won strong Republican support. "The house is burning down, and the President of the United States says this is the way to put out the fire," the House Republican whip, Bertrand Snell, cried when the emergency banking bill came up for debate. Roosevelt, enheartened by the constancy of Republican support, held rigorously to a nonpartisan approach throughout his administration's first year. When an exuberant Democratic organization man invited the President to the party's celebration of the birthday of its founder, Thomas Jefferson, Roosevelt indignantly refused. "Our strongest plea to the country in this particular year of grace," he replied, "is that the recovery and reconstruction program is being accomplished by men and women of all parties—that I have repeatedly appealed to Republicans as much as to Democrats to do their part."[26]

Roosevelt's approach to the crisis was a massive venture in public relations. Like Hoover, interestingly, Roosevelt considered the root cause of the depression to be psychological, but where Hoover crumpled in ineptitude in his public relations, Roosevelt gloriously mastered them. "The only thing we have to fear is fear itself," he said memorably in his inaugural. He perfected two techniques to bathe the country regularly in the ointments of hope and optimism—the press conference and the fireside chat. He transformed the press conference from an interlude of dour secretiveness, which it was under Hoover, into a vehicle of lively and informative interchange between the President and the press. After a week in office, on Sunday evening, March 12, Roosevelt gave his first fireside chat, a radio address to the nation on the banking situation. The President, said Will Rogers, the humorist, made banking clear to everybody, even the bankers.[27]

To associates and to the country at large, Roosevelt shone with confidence. His flashing smile, his cigarette holder set at a jaunty angle, his ready humor and booming laugh were the trademarks of his self-possession against the pressures of crisis. A brief exposure to Roosevelt was enough to repair the panicky, quiet the agitated, and inspirit the downhearted. No adversity could quash the President's eversoaring mood. To Anne O'Hare McCormick of the New York *Times* he was "apparently the least worried man in the country." Said his aide Rexford Tugwell, "Roosevelt was a man with fewer doubts than anyone I had ever known." Various explanations have been offered of the President's impregnable serenity. "F.D.R. was very tough," said his Attorney

General, Francis Biddle, "He had got on top of life. Nothing could touch him." Tugwell put it more strongly: "He had a source of detached exaltation which could not be touched by the outcome."[28]

James Buchanan: Peace-Keeper

The contrast in method and skill between two Presidents who faced the threat of war—Buchanan before the Civil War and Kennedy in the 1962 Cuban missile crisis—reveals how much individual talent and personal judgment determine a President's style and effectiveness in crisis and his standing in history.

"Blessed are the peacemakers," say the Scriptures, but politics takes a different view of this quiet breed. Often the search for peace seems like appeasement, and "appeasement" has become a term of scathing political reproach. James Buchanan, the President who more than any other in American history practiced conciliation and moderation—appeasement—against tremendous odds, is remembered with derision and falls well toward the bottom of the list in ranking of Chief Executives by their success and failure. Buchanan, ironically, has been dealt this ignominy even though he prevented war from breaking out between the North and South in his Presidential term. Five weeks after he left office, the fratricidal explosion occurred. (Lincoln, who carried the nation into war, is remembered as one of the greatest Presidents.) Ironically, too, Buchanan's peace policy seems to have been supported by the public opinion of the day. The country, North and South, wanted caution and delay, and Buchanan strove as hard as he could to provide them.

Buchanan worked for peace against crushing obstacles. Nowhere was the brewing holocaust more evident than in the unbridgeable divisions of his cabinet. Three of his Secretaries, Cobb, Thompson, and Floyd, defiantly espoused the right of secession, and three, Cass, Holt, and Black, denied it. Congress was also hopelessly divided. The Senate was Democratic and the House Republican, and each house split into numerous factions on questions of secession, compromise, and force. Worst of all, Buchanan eventually became a repudiated President. In April 1860 he was denied renomination by his party and was reduced to the position of titular head of an organization that the Republican Lincoln defeated in his race for the Presidency. In Northern political circles, Democratic and Republican alike, Buchanan was an outcast, the suspected ally of the secessionists, a potential betrayer of the Union to the promoters of rebellion.[29]

Not the least of Buchanan's handicaps were his own personal limitations. True, he came into the Presidency with gilt-edged training and experience. Congressman, minister to Russia, Senator, Secretary of State, minister to England, Buchanan was a rarity with three decades of service in the nation's most responsible posts. But he came into the Presidency at a ripe age and in ill health, despite the contrary impression created by his tall figure and his ruddy face crowned by a pile of gleaming white hair. In 1859–60, when the slavery crisis came to a head, he was seventy years old, afflicted with heart trouble, a glandular difficulty in his neck, polypous growth in his nasal passages, myopic vision that induced a squint, and general infirmity which prevented him at times from moving outside his upstairs rooms. His head was tilted and drawn askew by scars from an operation, and he tried to cover these blemishes with a large collar and an expansive neck cloth, which gave him the appearance of being perpetually dressed for cold weather. In addition to his physical torments, Buchanan suffered from psychological stresses. A broken romance of his youth still burned in his bachelor's memory. Religion tormented him. Seeking anxiously the "experience of salvation," he engaged in intensive private devotion and constant church attendance. In 1859, a year of grave national crisis, he pursued a series of discussions with the Reverend William M. Paxton of the First Presbyterian Church of New York City on the intricacies of regeneration, atonement, repentance, and faith.[30]

Buchanan's political style was diplomatic rather than combative. His forte was not the hustings and debate but conference and negotiation. Patient and meticulous in procedure, he shunned irretrievable commitment and was infinitely willing to yield matters of minor advantage. He bore his terrible burdens by clasping and repeating such maxims as "Sufficient unto the day is the evil thereof" and "It is better to bear the ills we have than to fly to others we know not of." By converting these maxims into a kind of political rosary, he resigned himself to bad situations, dodged decision, and surmounted failure. The brilliant stroke, the gamble, the sudden move were not for him. He considered political discussions of moral principles and abstractions futile and dangerous. "The Bible for Heaven, the Constitution for earth," he would say. "You cannot legislate morality." Mutual accommodation, the avoidance of extremes, and the majority's forbearance toward the minority were the cement of lasting union in his eyes.[31]

Buchanan's Presidency was strongly Southern in coloration. Indeed he sided with the radical slavery men on every issue except the revival of the slave trade. He opposed any bar against slavery in the territories, against expansion of slavery in Cuba and Mexico, against new slave states. Slavery, he believed, should be treated not in moral terms, but as a question of constitutional law. He was closely tied to the Southern Democratic wing and permitted Howell Cobb of Georgia, Jefferson Davis of Mississippi, John Slidell of Louisiana, and Henry A. Wise of Virginia to dominate his administration. At heart he considered Southern grievances valid and Republicans guilty of sectional excess.

Late in 1859, the final year of Buchanan's Presidency, the long-gathering crisis broke. In October John Brown raided the federal arsenal at Harpers Ferry, turning the slavery issue into a soaring flame and pulling the Democratic party hopelessly asunder. In November 1860 Lincoln was elected President, although with only 39.8 per cent of the popular votes cast. In South

Carolina, which long had threatened to secede if Lincoln were elected, the wheels of disunion began to turn. The federal grand jury at Charleston and the federal district court resigned. No one could henceforth be charged with breaking federal law, since no federal courts existed to try offenders. South Carolina's Governor William H. Gist asked his compatriot, Assistant Secretary of State William H. Trescot, to ascertain Buchanan's intentions concerning the four federal forts at Charleston: Forts Sumter, Moultrie, Johnson, and Castle Pinckney. The President, in fact, pacing in his library and passing sleepless nights, was quite baffled. The forts were hopelessly weak, only a sergeant at Pinckney, seventy-five officers and men at Moultrie, and a handful at Sumter, which was still under construction. The cabinet, debating the wisdom of reinforcements, was hopelessly divided. By late November the federal commander at Charleston, Major Robert Anderson, was calling urgently for reinforcements. South Carolina would soon leave the Union and seize Fort Moultrie, he reported, and nothing could better prevent bloodshed than to strengthen the forts to the point "that it would be folly and madness to attack us."[32]

Buchanan had little hope of deterring South Carolina from her expected next step, adopting a secession ordinance. Rather, he aimed to dissuade other Southern states from joining her. This happy result might be best achieved if the federal government demonstrated, by scrupulous behavior, how little cause any state had to secede. Then, if South Carolina took the step, it would appear in its solitude foolish and precipitate. The President, accordingly, must avoid any menacing posture or unconstitutional action which might provoke or justify secession.

While mulling over his position, Buchanan received a lengthy statement from his general-in-chief, Winfield Scott, aged seventy-four and in ill health. Scott's "Views" largely ignored the Charleston forts, conceded a right of secession to the states, detailed the probable horrors of civil war, and beheld as "a smaller evil" the Union's dissolution into several confederacies. Buchanan dismissed the "Views" as imbecilic and improper.[33]

Scott's weakness seemed to goad the President into action. He instructed Secretary of War John B. Floyd to supply the forts with all necessary men, arms, and provisions. He next took up with his cabinet a plan he was evolving to preserve peace and union. Buchanan envisioned a convention of the states, authorized in Article V of the Constitution, to devise some plan of adjustment. A constitutional convention, he believed, would congeal and express popular sentiment, override a hopelessly divided Congress, and avert disunion. The cabinet split on the proposal.

The President received more helpful counsel in calling upon his Attorney General, Jeremiah S. Black, for a statement of available legal powers in several possible contingencies of the crisis. Federal law, the Attorney General wrote, required the President to collect import duties and protect federal property. An act of 1795 empowered the President to enforce United States laws when opposed "by any State, by combinations too powerful to be suppressed by the ordinary course of judicial proceedings." But the 1795 act contained a flaw. The President was duty-bound to employ it not merely against South Carolina, but against various Northern states as well whose Personal Liberty Laws had undermined enforcement of the federal Fugitive Slave Act. The Northern states had committed overt acts of defiance; South Carolina as yet had only talked. The President could not march against a state that merely threatened while ignoring others that had long and actively opposed federal law. Black regretfully rejected the supposed precedents of the Whiskey Rebellion and the 1832 nullification crisis, in which federal forces moved to local trouble spots at the President's command. In contrast to the earlier instances, Black pointed out, no state or federal officer in the present crisis had asked for help or complained that a law had been violated.[34]

On December 3 Buchanan dispatched his anxiously awaited State of the Union message to Congress. The document reflected his aspiration to stand between the quarreling sections as a moderator "with my hand on the head of each, counseling peace." The message, aimed to pacify everyone, pleased no one. It irritated the South, incensed the Radical Republicans, and frustrated the Douglas Democrats. Secession, Buchanan said, was unconstitutional, but Congress and the President were without power to compel a state to remain in the Union. Turning to the North, he blamed its antislavery agitation as primarily responsible for the crisis. Turning to South Carolina, Buchanan said that although the President was duty-bound to enforce the laws, he really could not do so because no machinery now existed in South Carolina to administer the laws. No statute empowered the President to use force against South Carolina. He followed this confession of executive helplessness with a specific proposal. Let Congress call a constitutional convention to add an explanatory amendment to the Constitution affirming the right of property in slaves in states and territories where it now existed or might in the future exist. Let the title of masters to fugitive slaves be reaffirmed and all contravening state laws be declared null and void. Hopeful that his message would arrest the secession movement, he dispatched an advance copy to Governor William Gist of South Carolina.

But there was only disappointment. South Carolina elected delegates to its secession convention, and the state's legislators in Washington called on Buchanan seeking understandings to avoid future bloodshed. The President upbraided his visitors for their state's "ingratitude" and precipitation in leaving the Union before suffering any injury. He would collect the revenues "at all hazards," he said. The vigor of this statement was diluted minutes later when he was asked whether he would use force to execute the laws. "I will obey the laws," he answered. "I am no warrior—I am a man of peace—but I will obey the laws."[35]

Troubles now fell upon Buchanan in whole battalions. Secretary of the Treasury Howell Cobb resigned, signifying Georgia's impending swing into the secession movement. The South Carolina delegation brought Buchanan, reeling under Georgia's blow, to declare that it was not his policy to reinforce the Charleston forts. The President's shift prompted his Secretary of State, Lewis Cass, to resign in protest. The radical Northern press interpreted the step as the refusal of a patriotic statesman to remain any longer in the house of a President flirting with treason. Buchanan reconstituted his cabinet by shifting Attorney Black to the State Department and preserved the ideological balance by appointing Philip F. Thomas of Maryland and of Southern sympathies to the Treasury. The new Attorney General was Edwin M. Stanton of Ohio, a hard-core Unionist.

Ugly rumors and reports concerning the President were circulating widely. "Buchanan is today as truly a traitor as was Benedict Arnold," Lincoln was warned. Horace Greeley's New York *Tribune* declared that the President was insane; other reports said he was a coward, sick with terror, and alternated between praying and crying. Anti-Buchanan conspiracies were stirring. Senator Louis T. Wigfall approached Secretary of War Floyd with a plan to kidnap Buchanan and install Vice President Breckinridge in the Presidency. Floyd, to his credit, angrily rejected the scheme.[36]

The crisis climbed to new intensity when Major Anderson, taking the initiative into his own hands, brilliantly maneuvered his forces from Fort Moultrie to the more defensible Fort Sumter. A Southern delegation carried the first news of the development and their protests to the White House. "My God," cried the President, standing at the mantelpiece of his bedroom and crushing a cigar in his hand, "are misfortunes never to come singly? I call God to witness, *you*, gentlemen, better than anybody, *know* that this is not only without, but against my orders. It is against my policy." Yet when his Southern visitors pressed Buchanan to repudiate Anderson and restore the *status quo*, the President refused to act until he consulted the cabinet and had Anderson's report. Ultimately, Anderson held fast. Secretary Floyd, now under the clouds of gross scandals in the War Department, used Anderson's move as the pretext for an honorable resignation. South Carolina, for its part, countered by seizing Fort Moultrie, Fort Castle Pinckney, and the U.S. custom house. Adversity leaped from still another quarter. Buchanan's intermediaries who journeyed to Springfield, Illinois, to induce Lincoln to back up the proposed constitutional convention were flatly rebuffed.[37]

As the new year 1861 dawned, Buchanan still wrestled with the question of reinforcements to Major Anderson. South Carolina lent urgency to the Presidential deliberations by seizing the lighthouse in Charleston harbor, by blocking mail service to Fort Sumter, and by announcing that all United States ships were henceforth to be excluded from Charleston's vicinity. Buchanan, after much anguished temporizing, decided to reinforce Anderson by dispatching the U.S.S. *Brooklyn*. General Scott, fearful that a heavy vessel might ground upon a bar near the fort, insisted upon chartering the *Star of the West*, a side-wheel merchant steamer. On January 5, the *Star* quietly sailed from New York, loaded with foodstuffs and troops below deck. Two cabinet Secretaries who were Southern in their sympathies and who had not been informed of the maneuver resigned. The *Star of the West*, alas, was driven off by shore batteries as it entered Charleston harbor. New denunciations of Buchanan rang to the heavens from both sides of the Mason-Dixon line. During the din, Buchanan again realigned his cabinet by appointing John A. Dix of New York as Secretary of the Treasury and Moses Kelly, chief clerk of the Interior Department, to the Secretaryship. The cabinet was now entirely Northern and in general harmony with the President's outlook.[38]

On January 8 Buchanan sent Congress a special message on South Carolinian affairs. "The prospect of a bloodless settlement fades away," he warned. He intended "to collect the public revenues and to protect the public property" to the point that existing laws permitted. His province was "to execute" the laws and not "to make them." Congress alone could authorize the use of troops, declare war, or legislate the removal of grievances. He again appealed for a constitutional convention. "In Heaven's name," he pleaded, "let the trial be made before we plunge into armed conflict upon the mere assumption that there is no other alternative." But Congress did nothing. The Senate refused to confirm his nomination of a revenue collector at Charleston and thereby deprived him of his only means under existing legislation of calling up the militia. (Only if a collector had appealed for aid could the President act, Buchanan felt, without special law.) Senate Republicans buried his constitutional convention proposal in committee.[39]

The deterioration rushed on. Georgia elected a prosecession convention and seized Fort Pulaski at Savannah. Florida and Alabama occupied federal properties, and in Washington Southern Senators charted the creation of a confederacy. At no point in the spreading debacle did Congress gird the President with new authority to call out the militia or raise volunteers to suppress insurrection. Why did he not act boldly on his own, without waiting for Congress, Buchanan was asked. To do so, he replied, would be to make war not only upon South Carolina but upon Congress, which was resolved to do nothing until Lincoln's advent. On March 4, 1861, the scepter finally passed. "My dear sir," Buchanan greeted Lincoln, "if you are as happy in entering the White House as I shall feel on returning to Wheatland, you are a happy man indeed."[40]

John Kennedy and the Cuban Missile Crisis

Kennedy's style in handling the threat of nuclear war with the Soviet Union was altogether different, though it too was based upon a desire for peace. The Cuban crisis of 1962 began in the whirring camera of an Air Force U-2 reconnaissance plane high over San Cristobal on October 14. Analysis of the developed films the next day struck the Kennedy administration with massive impact. Soviet medium-range missiles, a mobile type used by the Red Army, were in place near San Cristobal, one hundred miles west of Havana. Every American city was potentially only a few minutes away from them. The revelation set off fourteen days of diplomatic maneuver and military buildup which brought the United States to the threshold of nuclear war.

The U-2's October discovery was the climax of a Soviet buildup commencing in July. Soviet technicians and instructors, surface-to-air missiles, patrol boats with missiles, and MIG-2 fighters, according to U.S. intelligence sources, were pouring into Cuba. The executive branch was not alone in its watch. Republican and Democratic legislators alike followed and exclaimed upon the ominous developments.[41]

A frequent Republican critic of Kennedy's Cuban course was Senator Kenneth B. Keating of New York. On September 2 he urged that an Organization of American States mission investigate reports of Cuban missile bases. If the OAS failed to act, the United States should blockade Western Hemispheric waters against vessels carrying armed forces personnel or materiel.[42] In early September, at the instigation of Democratic Senator Richard B. Russell of Georgia, chairman of the Armed Services Committee, Congress passed a resolution invoking the Monroe Doctrine against foreign intervention in the Western Hemisphere and the 1947 Rio pact for joint Western Hemispheric defense. The United States, the resolution declared, was determined to prevent, by "use of arms" if necessary, any Cuban military buildup threatening American security. The resolution's backers, who hailed from both parties, had a double purpose: to warn Khrushchev and Castro, and to invigorate certain administration policy-makers who seemed to them to be taking too detached a view of the Cuban developments.[43]

The administration appeared to accept Khrushchev's characterization of the weapons imported into Cuba as "defensive," although the President stated publicly on September 4 that "were it otherwise the gravest issues would arise." The close surveillance the United States intelligence community was simultaneously maintaining upon Cuba was spurred by reports from Cuban refugees in Florida that surface-to-surface missiles with nuclear warheads, capable of reaching American cities, were on the island. In a speech at Albuquerque, New Mexico, on October 6, Vice President Johnson brushed aside the critics' proposal of a blockade by declaring that "the stopping of a Russian ship is an act of war." Answering a call by Senator Homer Capehart, Republican of Indiana, for more action on Cuba, President Kennedy in a campaign speech at Louisville, on October 13, hit at those "self-appointed generals and admirals who want to send someone else's sons to war."

The momentous news of the U-2 discovery was conveyed to the President at 8:45 A.M. October 16 by his special assistant for national security affairs, McGeorge Bundy, who had learned of it the night before. Bundy later explained, when Kennedy himself inquired, that nothing could have been done that night and that to call advisers in from dinners about town would have touched off alarmed public speculation. The possibility remains, however, that the President could have been informed personally, without disturbance of his aides at their dinners. The question lingers whether Bundy had such a right of choice, and whether in making it he was not, in a limited way, superseding the President. Kennedy was immediately aware of the atomic danger, and was outraged at Khrushchev's barefaced duplicity. The President ticked off to Bundy a list of officials he wished to see. These included his brother, Attorney General Robert Kennedy, and Treasury Secretary C. Douglas Dillon, upon whose judgment he often relied.[44]

The implications of the Soviet move were clear enough. By placing medium- and intermediate-range missiles in Cuba, Russia was narrowing its gap with the United States. Missiles of such range in Cuba would provide the Russians with immediate power without the long wait necessary for equivalent increases in her intercontinental missiles arsenal. A missile fired from Cuba promised far more accuracy than an ICBM from Russia. Cuba-based missiles would reduce the United States' attack-warning time to virtually seconds. The Strategic Air Command would have to be dispersed on a more or less permanent basis.

At 11:45 A.M. on October 16 Kennedy met with a group later known as the Executive Committee (Ex Com) of the National Security Council. The President presided, and his fellow conferees included Vice President Johnson, Secretary of State Rusk, Secretary of Defense McNamara, Dillon, Robert Kennedy, Undersecretary of State George Ball, Deputy Secretary of Defense Gilpatric, CIA Deputy Director Carter (CIA Director McCone was away from Washington in the crisis's first days), Assistant Secretary of State for Inter-American Affairs Martin, General Maxwell Taylor (chairman of the Joint Chiefs of Staff), and Theodore Sorensen, Presidential counsel and principal speech-writer.

The atmosphere of crisis clung thickly over the group as they canvassed the possible responses to the Soviet thrust. If the United States did nothing, it would have to live with communist missiles at its doorstep, its prestige would tumble, and the credibility of its pledges would be destroyed. Latin America might fall into the Soviet basket. If, as a second possibility, the United States bombed or invaded Cuba, its moral position would be tainted, its alliances would be disarrayed, the neutral nations would burst into great cry, and the Russians might make a countermove in Berlin or elsewhere. A third possibility was a blockade, but it too might stir a Soviet response and offend our allies, particularly the maritime powers. The meeting produced two immediate decisions. One was that air surveillance over Cuba should be intensified and the other that any action the United States took should as nearly as possible coincide with United States' public disclosure of the Russian bases.[45]

The vast departmental machinery began to turn. The Defense Department estimated the kinds of units, numbers of men, and time factors necessary for various military actions. The State Department explored the possibilities of Latin-American and European support, and its most sophisticated analysts of Soviet behavior began mulling over the probable effects of various actions on the Russians. United Nations Ambassador Adlai Stevenson was brought into the discussions.

The President had other commitments in addition to the crisis. The Congressional electoral campaign was in full swing, and Kennedy set out for Connecticut to honor long-established speaking dates. The discussions on Cuba were to be kept secret—Khrushchev did not know that Kennedy knew about the offensive missiles, and the secret could best be kept by maintaining a normal Presidential schedule. During his absence, the Ex Com met day and night in Undersecretary of State Ball's conference room, or "think tank" as it was dubbed, a windowless chamber furnished with a long table, pumpkin leather chairs, prosaic water decanters, and Dixie cups. The meetings were informal, the participants wandering in and out to keep up simultaneously with their regular duties. Further incoming U-2 reports of new discoveries of medium- and intermediate-range missile sites compounded the situation's urgency. Former Secretary of State Dean Acheson was brought into the meetings.[46]

Upon returning to Washington from the Connecticut hustings, the President took up a varied schedule of regular business, ceremonial duties, and crisis management. He met often with the Ex Com, brought former Defense Secretary Robert Lovett into the discussions, and deliberately absented himself to encourage his aides to express their views uninhibitedly. In moments away from the Ex Com, Kennedy received the Crown Prince of Libya, conferred with a former Finance Minister of Japan, discussed a new threat to Berlin with the West German Foreign Minister, lunched at the Libyan embassy, vetoed a Tariff Commission recommendation to raise duties of self-closing coin purses, and rejected a proposal for the exclusion of foreign-made nails. Although poised on the knife's edge of incipient decision that could long determine the fate of the nation, the West, the world, and mankind, Kennedy bore up with his accustomed composure even in his severest test, a White House meeting with Andrei A. Gromyko. The visit of the Soviet Foreign Minister had been arranged prior to the crisis. In his two hours and fifteen minutes with Kennedy, Gromyko reaffirmed previous assurances that Soviet activity in Cuba was defensive only. Kennedy repeated to Gromyko his belief that the Soviet effort in Cuba was defensive and his warning that any change in this estimate would have grave consequences. The President refrained from confronting Gromyko with the damning truth because the administration had not yet decided what action to take, and the Russians, faced with exposure, might resort to an evasive counterthrust to blunt the eventual decision.

Gromyko dined that evening with Secretary of State Rusk and other officials on the eighth floor of the department. On the floor below, in the "think tank," the planning group continued its crisis discussions. In midevening they piled into a single limousine, sacrificing comfort for security, and journeyed to the White House. In this meeting the President seemed to be moving toward a blockade. Ambassador-at-large Llewellyn Thompson, Jr., stressed the need for the solid legality of any action taken. The Russians, he said, had a feeling for "legality," and well-grounded legal action would impress world opinion. The State and Justice Departments began work on the legal justification for a blockade.

On October 19 Kennedy resumed his political campaigning, partly to quiet press suspicions that great happenings were afoot, with stops at Cleveland, Chicago, and at Springfield to lay flowers on Lincoln's tomb. Before departing, he expressed approval to the Ex Com of the trend of decision toward a blockade. In the continuing Ex Com discussions, advocates of an offensive air attack vigorously pressed their case, but the blockade attracted the dominant support, even with its admitted danger that, in Vice President Johnson's words, "stopping a Russian ship is an act of war." Staff work proceeded on each alternative to preserve the President's choices to the very moment of decision.

The next day a telephone call from Robert Kennedy brought the President back from Chicago to Washington. Time was running out and secrecy was crumbling, said the Attorney General. The White House informed the press that the President was forced to return by a slight infection of the upper respiratory tract, with one degree of fever. In actuality, the President's cold, which was mild, did not require his return, but it was necessary to mislead the reporters by some contrivance in the interest of security. Kennedy, arriving at 1:37 P.M., went over a speech Sorensen had prepared upon the assumption that a blockade would be imposed. The final speech emerged after five drafts. The President all but clinched the decision for blockade and directed the relevant operations to proceed, subject only to his final word the next day. The State and Defense Departments drafted a blockade proclamation, the chief of Naval Operations made the plans necessary to enforce it, the State Department laid out an approach to the Organization of American States, Acheson prepared to embark for Paris to confer with De Gaulle and the NATO council, and Alexis Johnson, Deputy Undersecretary of State for Political Affairs, worked up a "master scenario" depicting every necessary preparation prior to the President's speech; briefings, orders to embassies, ship movements, and the like. A military helicopter picked up former President Eisenhower at his Gettysburg farm and flew him to Washington for a briefing by the CIA. Vice President Johnson dropped his election campaigning in Hawaii and flew back to Washington.

The next day, October 21, the scenario was converted into action. Kennedy, after conferring again with numerous key officials, definitely decided upon the blockade. In the afternoon he met with the statutory National Security Council. The State Department drafted forty-three Presidential letters to the heads of government of all the alliances and to Willy Brandt, mayor of West Berlin. A Kennedy-to-Khrushchev letter was prepared to accompany a copy of the TV speech announcing the blockade. Instructions were readied for distributing the speech to sixty embassies. On October 22 Lawrence O'Brien, the President's Congressional liaison assistant, telephoned twenty Congressional leaders of both parties for a meeting with Kennedy. The Soviet ambassador to Washington, Anatoly Dobrynin, was called to the State Department. General Lauris Norstad, the NATO commander, was alerted. In the meeting with Congressional leaders, Senator Russell, supported by Senator Fulbright, the Foreign Relations Committee chairman, who interestingly enough had opposed the Bay of Pigs attack, bluntly asserted that a blockade was too slow and therefore involved great risk, but the President was not to be dissuaded.[47] At the State Department, Undersecretary Ball and Intelligence and Research Director Roger Hilsman briefed forty-six allied ambassadors in the State Department's International Conference Room.

At 7 P.M. in a calm but intense and blunt eighteen-minute television report, the President delivered his speech alerting the public for the first time. He blamed not Cuba but the Soviet Union for the crisis, which, he said, had violated its leaders' most solemn assurances that only defensive weapons were going to Cuba. The President said he had ordered a "quarantine"—a word he had substituted for "blockade"—on all offensive weapons for Cuba. Ships carrying them would be turned back. Furthermore, he said, the preparation of the missile sites must cease, and if it did not, "further action" would be taken. He was ordering the surveillance continued, and he called upon Khrushchev to withdraw "all offensive weapons" from Cuba.[48]

While the President was speaking, his vast administrative machinery was in full motion. At the State Department the forty-six allied ambassadors watched the speech on a large screen, Assistant Secretary Martin gave a further private briefing to Latin-American ambassadors, Secretary Rusk and Director Hilsman briefed the neutral nations, including Yugoslavia, Undersecretary Ball briefed the diplomatic correspondents, and Defense Secretary McNamara the military correspondents. "Whatever force is required"—even striking—said McNamara, would be employed to enforce the blockade. At the United Nations, Ambassador Adlai Stevenson requested a special meeting of the Security Council.

Thirteen hours after Kennedy's speech came the Soviet's first reaction, a long, rambling, published statement of accusations and warnings of thermonuclear war, plus a letter from Khrushchev to Kennedy. These the administration interpreted as betraying that the Kremlin was caught off guard and playing for time to think out its moves. Developments elsewhere were encouraging despite protest marches in various world capitals. In Paris marchers carried placards reading "Kennedy the Assassin" and "Peace in Cuba," and in London two thousand demonstrators screamed "Long Live Castro" and "Down with Kennedy." British Prime Minister Harold Macmillan telephoned his full support. In a meeting with Acheson West German Chancellor Konrad Adenauer was equally positive. At the United Nations the NATO countries supported a United States resolution calling upon the Soviet Union to withdraw the missiles and dismantle the sites under United Nations verification, after which the United States would end the quarantine. Citing the Rio pact of 1947, Secretary Rusk offered the Organization of American States a resolution authorizing the use of force, individually or collectively, to enforce the blockade. The OAS Council adopted the resolution nineteen to zero. The NATO and OAS unanimity surprised both the United States and the Soviet Union and apparently added to the latter's confusion.

There were less gratifying developments, however. U Thant, Acting Secretary General of the United Nations, urged several weeks' suspension of the blockade and arms shipments to Cuba while negotiations were held. Khrushchev accepted with alacrity, but Kennedy, anticipating the disarming of his powerful diplomatic and military initiative and doubting that they could ever regain momentum if negotiations failed, as they were expected to, turned down Thant's request. "The existing threat," the President replied, "was created by the secret introduction of offensive weapons into Cuba, and the answer lies in the removal of such weapons."[49]

A nearly two-day lapse between the announcement of the blockade and its imposition permitted the Soviets to redirect any ships headed for Cuba. On October 25, twenty hours after the blockade began, the United States Navy made its first interception, stopping a Soviet tanker, the *Bucharest*. It was allowed to proceed without search because the Navy was satisfied it carried only petroleum. Two days later the Lebanese freighter *Marucia* was stopped, boarded, and searched by a five-man party from the destroyers *Joseph P. Kennedy, Jr.*, and *John R. Pierce*. The *Marucia* also was allowed to proceed after it was ascertained that she carried nothing but peaceful cargo.

On October 26 and 27 Khrushchev dispatched two letters to Kennedy. Embedded in the first, although not explicitly stated, was an offer to withdraw the offensive weapons under United Nations supervision if the United States would lift the blockade and promise not to invade the island. The President heard the transcription of this letter with great relief. Then a second Khrushchev letter came clattering over the wires bearing another catch. The Soviet Union would trade its bases in Cuba for the NATO missile base in Turkey. In a National Broadcasting Company telecast of February 9, 1964, McGeorge Bundy stated that the Soviet offer also proposed that the United States pull its missiles out of Greece as well. As Kennedy and his aides pondered a reply, incoming intelligence reports disclosed that Soviet technicians were building away furiously at the Cuban sites. It was estimated that the sites would be ready for missile launchings within a mere five days. Kennedy decided to write again to Khrushchev, saying that if he understood the Premier correctly—that the offensive weapons would be removed in return for an end of the blockade and a promise of no American invasion of Cuba—then it was a deal. It could now go "either way," the President remarked grimly to his aides.[50]

If it should go the bad way, the United States armed forces were ready. The Tactical Air Command's 19th Air Force had moved into the sprawling base outside of Homestead, Florida. By October 23 nearly one thousand attack-fighter and fighter-bomber aircraft were poised in Florida, with a conventional airborne firepower rivaling that of the Allied forces in England prior to the Normandy invasion in 1944. Army divisions from Fort Bragg, North Carolina; Fort Campbell, Kentucky; Fort Riley, Kansas; and Fort Benning, Georgia, were on full alert. These divisions plus marines at sea, in Florida, and at Guantánamo, formed a one hundred thousand-man force the United States stood ready to hurl into Cuba. Drop-zones in the Cuban interior had been carefully designated for paratroopers of the 82nd and 101st Airborne Divisions. Globemaster transports poured into the Key West naval base with soldiers, sailors, marines, mobile radar units, photographic gear, trucks and jeeps, and weapons of all types. The Association of American Railroads was alerted, and 2,418 flatcars and 299 equipment cars from as far distant as Denver and Minneapolis began rolling to Fort Hood, Texas, to take on Honest John Rockets and rocket-launcher vehicles, Patton tanks, self-propelled howitzers, and other cargo. Bases at Miami, Canaveral, Orlando, and Homestead were mushrooming with fighter and fighter-bomber aircraft.

The United States military preparations indeed were proceeding on a global scale. U.S. Navy ships and submarines in the European Atlantic, Pacific, and Mediterranean were hurrying out to sea. Three Polaris-firing submarines scurried to sea from their berths at Holy Loch, Scotland. The Strategic Air Command was on Defcon 2, or full war footing, from which it needed but one signal to go to Defcon 1, which puts it at war. For the first time in history, SAC's medium-range bomber force of B-47's were ordered to disperse. ICBM firing crews, spread in complexes throughout the United States, were brought to full alert and missiles were raised. The Navy's Fleet Ballistic Missile submarines were on station, carrying 128 Polaris missiles, within range of major Soviet targets. The United States had made full preparations to lay the explosive equivalent of more than thirty billion tons of TNT upon the Soviet Union.

The United States was also maintaining close air surveillance over Cuba. On October 27 Major Rudolf Anderson, Jr., one of two U-2 pilots whose photographs touched off the crisis, was shot down over Cuba.[51] In cryptic comment during a speech at Columbia, South Carolina, on April 25, 1963, six months after the crisis, Attorney General Robert Kennedy said that Major Anderson's death "led the President to notify Mr. Khrushchev that strong and overwhelming retaliatory action would have been taken unless he received immediate notice that the missiles would be withdrawn." United States officials connected with the crisis believe that this Presidential message, the text of which was not revealed, coupled with the open movement of American military power were the factors that really brought Khrushchev around to his ultimate decision in the immediate crisis. "What got the message through to Khrushchev was action," one official said. "The message was clear that something was going to happen and happen soon."[52]

October 28 brought Khrushchev's answer, the fifth Premier-President exchange in seven days. Khrushchev said that he had ordered work on the bases stopped and the missiles crated and returned to the Soviet Union. Representatives of the United Nations, he promised, would "verify the dismantling." In return, the President's no-invasion pledge would be trusted. After hurried consultations with his aides, the President issued a statement welcoming Khrushchev's "statesmanlike decision," and the blockade was lifted.[53]

In the months following the crisis, the United States and the Soviet Union handled the Cuban question with high caution, neither side appearing to contemplate any drastic action so long as the other kept the October "gentlemen's agreement." Senator Keating remained attentive to Cuba, declaring on the Senate floor on January 31, 1963, that "there is continuing, absolutely confirmed and undeniable evidence that the Soviets are maintaining the medium-range sites they had previously constructed in Cuba. . . . Without on-site inspection, it is hard to see how we will ever know for sure the true missile situation in Cuba." In a press interview, Keating said he would be glad to disclose his information, but not his sources, to the President.[54] Senator Strom Thurmond, Democrat of South Carolina, made similar charges. But intelligence estimates one year after the crisis disclosed that the Soviet force in Cuba was down to ten thousand from twenty-two thousand at the peak of the crisis. The remaining personnel were believed to be devoted to training the Cuban armed forces.

In a 1966 interview Premier Castro, asked if he could "state unequivocally" that there were no offensive ground-to-air nuclear missiles in Cuba, replied that he had "no objection to declaring that those weapons do not exist in Cuba" and added that "unfortunately, there are none." In the same interview, Castro also remarked, mysteriously and without elaboration, that "one day, perhaps, it will be known that the United States made some other concessions in relation to the October crisis besides those that were made public."[55]

The Art of Crisis Management

The Cuban crisis was the first confrontation of its kind since the onset of the age in which the two great nuclear powers possessed the capacity to destroy each other and much of the world. The decisions that Kennedy was called upon to make were therefore the most delicate and the most perilous that any President has ever faced. Not only the welfare of the American public, but the fate of peoples everywhere who had no voice in his selection, of unborn generations, of western civilization itself depended upon his choices.

The stressful decision-making of the Cuban crisis—the pattern of action by which the President mastered the tangled skein of intense events—was a nightmarish experience. The President is often spoken of, to the point of cliché, as a lonely figure. He has never appeared more solitary than in nuclear confrontation. Surrounded though he is by aides and data and counsel, he must decide alone. His choice cannot be delegated. It is a cruel test of self-confidence that has undeniably removed the Presidency for all time as a refuge for the fainthearted.

Kennedy followed several elementary procedures in facing the nuclear showdown. He rightly insisted that before publicly according the Cuban events the status of crisis, he needed "hard intelligence" and could not act simply upon rumor and report. He held to his course despite the revelations and criticisms of legislators of both his own and the opposition party and despite the hostile Congressional resolutions. To be careful and responsible, as Kennedy had to be, is neither easy nor popular. Political outcry was perhaps not the worst of the afflictions he had to bear. The atmosphere in which the President acted was charged with danger and uncertainty, with inexorable climax and with scores of opportunities for surprise. For all their knowledge of the Soviet Union, American officials could not predict what the Soviet leader would decide to do—especially since he delighted in surprise as a source of strength in foreign affairs. The Russians took advantage of seasonal fluctuations in our political system, launching their gambit during an election campaign. They expected that the President would be eager to postpone the prickly Cuban issue until after the election, and by that time it would be too late.

In the Cuban crisis the President sought always to leave Khrushchev with an option or choice. Above all, the aim of Kennedy and his advisers was to avoid backing him into a corner, where his only recourse would be military. A military attack of any kind upon Cuba, a communist power, would have posed to the Soviet Union the necessity of either a military response or a humiliating surrender, badly damaging to their prestige around the world. The blockade afforded the advantage of giving Khrushchev a choice. He did not need to have his ships approach the blockade and be stopped and searched but could divert them, as he did. The blockade, therefore, left an acceptable way out for the Soviet Union, a cardinal principle of decision-making in the nuclear confrontation. Equally important, Kennedy carefully preserved the United States' own options; that is, he did not rely wholly upon the blockade but simultaneously speeded the full-scale alert of American forces, a procedure which Robert Kennedy and others felt did more than anything else to bring Khrushchev to agree to remove the missiles from Cuba.[56]

Another cardinal principle was evident in the effort of the President and his aides to slow down the escalation of the crisis to permit Khrushchev time to consider his next moves. Deliberation, it was hoped, might produce a more measured and less drastic response than fast-moving exchanges. Hence the value of notes and ambassadorial visits and the preferability of a blockade, a relatively gradual procedure compared with the precipitous engagement of an invasion or an air strike.

Kennedy took the fullest precautions to keep the decisions in his own hands, both the initial decision settling upon the blockade and the further critical decisions required to implement it. When a United States Navy reconnaissance plane spotted the *Marucia* headed for Cuba, the information was sped to the President, and it was he who gave the order to board and search it. Other procedures assured that control of the blockade operation remained in his hands. Kennedy was resolved that the issue of peace or war should not turn upon the decision of a local commander.

In making his choices, the President must be mindful of several constituencies but still keep decision in his grasp. He must be willing to act, as Kennedy was, notwithstanding the express disapproval of certain of these constituents. Kennedy accordingly convened members of his legislative constituency, leaders of both parties. Paradoxically, his party's leading legislators in the fields of foreign affairs and national security held that his decision was inadequate for the situation and urged him to do more. The House Republican leader, however, Congressman Halleck, declared, "I'm standing with the President." The dissent of several of his own party leaders did not deter the President. He won the approval of another great constituency: the leaders of the nation's great allies—Macmillan, De Gaulle, and Adenauer—and the member countries of major alliances, NATO and the OAS. Kennedy was fortunate enough to win an approval from his foreign constituency extending well beyond his expectations. But it is also clear that he was prepared, as a President in a nuclear confrontation may need to be, to carry forward his decision even without allied endorsement. In choosing his course, the President must weigh and balance factors that no ally can know or perceive, owing to the simple circumstance that only he occupies his Presidential place, and only he, therefore, holds the responsibility.

Nuclear crisis is more than an intensive exercise in decision-making. Equally, if not more important, it is an enterprise in communication. The evidence is impressive that a major cause of the crisis was a misreading by Khrushchev and his colleagues of the Kennedy administration's attitude and intentions. In their June 1961 Vienna meeting, Khrushchev reportedly found Kennedy somewhat deferential, which the Soviet leader apparently interpreted as weakness. The fiasco of the Bay of Pigs and Kennedy's restrained response to the Berlin wall may well have encouraged a Soviet impression of American softness. The strength of this impression was conveyed in Khrushchev's remark to Robert Frost that the United States was "too liberal to fight."

A nuclear confrontation involves a desperate resort to various communications channels and an intensive scrutiny of the opponent's act and word for clues of his intent and meaning. Kennedy and his counselors were heavily occupied in the dangerous and difficult task of estimating the probable Soviet reaction to possible United States moves. Equally to be anticipated was the effect upon our allies, upon trouble spots around the world, whether Berlin or Turkey, which held our bases that the Soviet Union was discussing, or the Formosa straits, where the Chinese were preparing for belligerent action. Likewise the effect upon Latin America: If the United States responded strongly, would the Latin countries become alarmed? Would they be even more alarmed if we did too little? For Kennedy and his aides, the crisis was a rigorous introspective experience in determining American purposes, in anticipating what our reaction might be to the Soviet reaction, and so on, until each possible course that might be chosen was followed to its ultimate conclusion.

The Cuban crisis is a good model for any future nuclear confrontation because of the administration's recourse to almost every conceivable channel of communication between the opposing powers: the letters between Kennedy and Khrushchev, the proper reliance upon the American and Soviet ambassadors, the visit to Moscow of the American businessman William Knox, chairman of Westinghouse Electric International, to whom Khrushchev conveyed the dire warning that if the United States Navy stopped and searched Soviet vessels on the high seas, it would be piracy, and that after several such incidents, Soviet submarines would be ordered to sink American vessels.[57] But according to available evidence, the most effective channel for communicating American intentions was the open, full-scale mobilization of our armed might.

An Overview

The four Presidents in the four crises described above were not free agents, let alone "dictators," as demagogic critics sometimes portray them. The President in crisis is bound by a web of restraints, institutional, social, and personal. In a government of laws he must act within the Constitution and other statutes; in foreign relations he must act in accordance with his country's commitment to international law. But in a crisis law is not merely confining; it is also a means of conciliation and conflict resolution. Buchanan, in setting his course, chose to walk a legalistic tightrope to convince the South of national good will and thereby weaken the case for secession. Kennedy's counselors valued legality for itself and as a means of impressing the Russians and world opinion.

The President must reckon with the nation's past commitment to principle and his own and his predecessors' pronouncements and decisions. Significantly, at the outset of the Cuban crisis Kennedy sent for copies of all his earlier statements on the situation. He and his aides were driven to reject an air strike on military installations in Cuba in large part because the United States had taken a strong stand against invasion of a sovereign country, however serious the provocation of self-defense. An attack on Cuba could be regarded as Pearl Harbor in reverse. Franklin Roosevelt's memorable label of that 1941 event as a "day that will live in infamy" was an invisible barrier—moral and pragmatic—between hard-pressed Kennedy officials and the choice of a surprise offensive.

In facing a crisis, the President can be either helped or hampered by his personal ideology and opinions. Hoover was a prisoner of ideology; it narrowly channeled his conduct for three long years while the nation sank ever deeper into economic despair. He fought the economic enemy with clichés about "rugged American individualism" and the nobilities of localism and private charity, which proved to be paper weapons. What the President does in crisis is also governed by his view of his office. Franklin Roosevelt was instructed by the models of Theodore Roosevelt and Woodrow Wilson, impressed by the Presidency's resources for moral leadership and its potential for making government the instrument of the people. He viewed the Constitution as a simple, adjustable document which vested in the President the equivalent of a wartime power to combat the economic depression.

Much of a President's effectiveness in crisis depends upon his image of himself. Nearly as important as his policy is the self-confidence he projects to the country. If Franklin Roosevelt displayed political genius in 1933, it was not in offering solutions to the economic puzzle, for he had none, but in projecting confidence that the nation soon would be restored. The ringing voice, the flashing smile, and the cigarette holder set at a jaunty angle portrayed an impressive confidence that obscured the slender reed of reality on which it perched. In contrast to Franklin Roosevelt, handsomely at terms with himself, is the unfortunate Buchanan, indecisive, troubled in spirit, the object of bizarre tales and hostile rumor.

If the past be our guide, Americans prefer that in crisis their Presidents be men of action, calm but confident. Hoover, putting his store in private resources, vetoing acts of Congress that would have broadened his powers, taking the defensive rather than the offensive, was overwhelmingly voted out of office at the first opportunity. Activist Presidents who slay the dragons of crisis are the nation's folk heroes: Jackson, Lincoln, the Roosevelts, and Woodrow Wilson. They attack problems frontally and aggressively, interpret their powers expansively, and radiate confidence. In contrast to the activist or "doer" President is the negotiator or "talker" who relies primarily not upon deed but upon discussion. He seeks to talk out with his adversary the issues threatening terrible conflict. He values procrastination to cool off issues and allow events to settle into a less perilous state. He holds closely to the law. Buchanan, a negotiator, was forever consulting his Attorney General, and his basic solution for the slavery crisis was legal, his constitutional amendment from which he expected so much. At most, the doers and the talkers, as we are using the terms, are mere types. No President is wholly one or the other.

In crisis, Congress may prod the Chief Executive, preferring to move at a faster pace than he deems wise. In the New Deal individual legislators time and again championed social and economic measures toward which the President was unenthusiastic or downright opposed. Roosevelt showed little ardor for the proposed Federal Deposit Insurance Corporation pushed by Arthur H. Vandenberg and other legislators. Or again, when Senator Robert F. Wagner led the way for the legislation bearing his name, enhancing labor's opportunities for organizing and engaging in collective bargaining, Roosevelt regarded Wagner's whole enterprise with doubt and suspicion. Senators of both parties demanded action on Cuba more than a month before Kennedy acted. "A member of Congress or the press," his aide Theodore Sorensen has written, "can achieve some measure of fame by reporting rumors or stating problems or raising questions. But that is not enough for a President."[58]

Crisis exacts its own distinctive patterns of decision-making and administrative organization. Crisis heightens the President's dependence upon his staff, yet it is more vital than ever that he keep the reins of decision in his own hands. As long as he can, he must make decisions in a manner that will permit him to make further decisions. Kennedy, mindful of the enormous hazards in confronting the Soviets over Cuba, made certain that his early moves did not close out all his options or all of theirs. Franklin Roosevelt, Frances Perkins noticed in the early New Deal, "rarely got himself sewed tight to a program from which there was no turning back."[59] A President can more easily control decision by keeping in his fund of counselors representatives of the principal alternative responses to the crisis. Buchanan had in his cabinet Southerners and New Englanders, or human replicas of the views dividing American society and his own deliberations. In the Cuban crisis Kennedy maintained conflicting groups of counselors, some advocating an air strike, others a blockade. He did not fear controversy, rather he welcomed it as a corrective to impulse.

Although John Kennedy and Franklin Roosevelt were men of action, and therefore a breed of President that is most admired, they were not, in any degree, creatures of impulse. The latter type, installed in the contemporary Presidency, would be disastrous for the nation and mankind. An activist President triggered by emotion, who neither consulted advisers nor pondered consequences, would be both decisive and wrong-headed, a type who would keep the nation, so long as it survived, quaking in high alarm. Kennedy and like Chief Executives root their actions in thought and validated evidence. They are decisive and forceful only in response to reason tested by qualified opinion.

The Presidency Compared 16

Comparisons, we are often warned, are odious. But comparisons have a special usefulness in the study of political institutions. We can better estimate the value of one political institution if we measure its performance against other institutions. We can better perceive what the American Presidency has been and what it might become if we compare it with other relevant institutions of our and other political societies. The comparisons may illuminate those aspects of the Presidency that reflect our deepest traditions and most tightly held values and those aspects, as well, that represent large and clear exceptions to the established ways of our political community.

The American President invites comparison with the other members of the nation's family of political executives: the state governor and the local chief executive. As with most families, the several executives bear certain resemblances to each other, and any one of them has influenced the development of all. They have imitated and inspired one another and have felt the brunt of common historical forces. The governor and the mayor can rightfully be viewed as Presidential-type executives, having the contours and much of the power and function of the national executive.

The Governor

In shaping the Presidency, the Founding Fathers were influenced to a large degree by the New York governorship; weaknesses in other governorships warned them of mistakes to avoid. The state governorship was influenced by experience with the colonial governorship, which was commonly viewed as the agency of monarchic tyranny. Thus, state constitution-makers in the Revolutionary era tended to look askance at the strong executive, and they chose to concentrate power in the state legislatures, which during the colonial crisis acquired a reputation as defenders of the popular interest. But the abuses that state legislatures made of their powers caused the Founding Fathers to resolve to create a Presidency of substantial strength.

Although the Presidency and the governorship have swelled in influence and power since the eighteenth century, the latter has always been the substantially weaker of the two executive offices. The change was slow-building for the governor. In the early state constitutions, legislative supremacy was firmly established. According to many constitutions, the legislature appointed the governor, and the governor lacked a veto power over legislation. Leadership in public policy reposed with the legislature. Unlike the President, whose power derived from general constitutional provisions permitting generous interpretation and enlargement, the governor had to struggle for the increase of power through the rewriting of state constitutions and by wringing out concessions of power from the legislature. The Jacksonian era caused more governors and their fellow executive officials (including, sometimes, even prison superintendents) to be popularly elected and entrusted more power to their care, but all through the nineteenth century, while Jackson, Lincoln, and Cleveland demonstrated the primacy of the Presidency, the legislature endured as the dominant instrument of state policy-making.

It is in the twentieth century that the governor comes into his own, through forces in that era that served to enlarge the President's influence and power. The increase of government's social and economic tasks, especially from World War I onward, and the ever-broadening base of democratic government profited both the governor and the President. In addition, the governor gained from new constitutions and executive reorganizations that imitated the Presidential model. As well, the clear inadequacy of the state legislature in an era of positive government contributed to the governor's growth in function and power. Yet there remains an ambiguity about the role of the states, and therefore of the governor, in public affairs. The states fall somewhere between local government, with its natural responsibility for urban or local problems, and the national government, which most naturally deals with foreign affairs and problems incident to a grand-scale economy. The states lack any comparable natural jurisdictions enjoyed by the other governments.

If a typical early governor were compared with a typical contemporary governor, the influence of the Presidency upon gubernatorial change would become evident. Most contemporary governors enjoy a four-year term rather than the one- or two-year span of their predecessors. A little more than half the governors can be reelected to the office indefinitely, while in earlier times a one-term limitation was commonplace. Early governors shared the exercise of their veto power with a council, on which legislators might be represented, yet the present-day governor enjoys a veto power over his legislature fully equal to the President's. Indeed four-fifths of the governors enjoy an advantage that the President lacks—an item veto over individual appropriations in general revenue bills. The governor's power to appoint his administrative colleagues, long a source of weakness because these key figures might be popularly elected or chosen by the legislature, has improved to the point where more than half the governors can appoint, with or without the consent of their senates, the heads of the chief departments and the budget and tax officers. A major source of the President's power in the executive branch is his strong appointing power. Although the governor is some distance removed from the President's handsome salary of $100,000 a year plus allowances, the governors have gained from a general toning up of the public executives' money market. Ten governors receive more than $25,000, with the New York governor at $50,000 and California's at $40,000 enjoying the most princely stipends. Ten governors, however, receive less than $10,000 in salary.

In the general layout of his functions and powers, in the relationship of the incumbent's personality to the office, the governor resembles the President, although with important variations springing from differences between the nation and the states and the imprint of historic forces and tradition. Like the Presidency, the governorship provides a spacious arena for the play of personality. Just as the Presidency has developed under the touch of creative incumbents, the governorship developed strength and resilience in the tenures of Robert M. La Follette in Wisconsin, Hiram Johnson and Earl Warren in California, Charles Evans Hughes and Alfred E. Smith in New York, Gifford Pinchot in Pennsylvania, to mention a few. Some governors, such as Woodrow Wilson of New Jersey and Franklin Roosevelt of New York, displayed skills and indulged in techniques of leadership that they later applied with marked success in the Presidency.

Just as the President tends to be the outstanding political leader in the nation, the governor enjoys the same distinction in the smaller domain of the state. The governor, more than other political personalities in the state, is identified with the "general public good." Whatever he does makes news in the local press. Radio and television can command him a state-wide audience; he travels frequently about the state, makes numerous personal appearances, handles a high volume of correspondence and telephone calls, and receives large quantities of visitors. Many governors keep their doors open to one and all who wish to interview them. Coleman B. Ransone, Jr., in his study of the governorship, concluded that public relations is the most time-consuming role of the state executive.[1] As with the President, much of the governor's success turns upon his skill as a party and legislative leader. His party role most resembles the President's in states that are populous and where a genuine two-party system flourishes. The interparty competition fosters a discipline that the governor can exploit as party leader. In many states, particularly in the South and Middle West, there is a steady one-party dominance that casts the governor in a role as the leader of a party faction or a coalition of factions whose support he manages to attract. In the factional structure, state politics may become highly responsive to the governor's personality. Georgia, therefore, in the era of its colorful Governor Gene "Red Suspenders" Talmadge, was dominated by Talmadge and anti-Talmadge factions, and Louisiana, in the heyday of Huey Long, by Long and anti-Long factions. A governor is less apt than the President to be the acknowledged leader of his party because he may have rivals for the role in one or both of the United States Senators of his state. Thus in 1968 Governor John B. Connally of Texas and Senator Ralph Yarborough were the leaders respectively of the moderate and liberal factions of the Texas Democratic party. There was no single, generally acknowledged leader of the state party. Unlike the President, the governor does not enjoy uniqueness as the only elected official of his constituency.

The governor, like the President, is heavily judged by his success as legislative leader. Increasingly most of the important policies that the legislature considers come from the governor or the executive departments. As legislative leader, the governor enjoys political means that are fully comparable to the President's. He reports to the legislature on the conditions of the state and recommends legislation. Much turns upon his ability to persuade legislators of both major parties to support his proposals. He has the inducements of patronage and public works construction—nothing can be more eloquent than building a new highway in a legislator's district; he can speak in support of a legislator's candidacy; or he can grant a pardon to one of his constituents. The governor's power is also buttressed by substantial formal authority. He gains leverage from budget-making powers if he has them, which enables him to include or omit the favorite projects of legislators.

Most governors can also gain leverage with the item veto. Legislators, however, may blunt the effect of the item veto by combining objectionable and unobjectionable items in the same clause. The item veto also invites buckpassing, by which legislators vote appropriations with the expectation that the governor will bear the political blame for disallowing them.[2] In four states—Alabama, Massachusetts, New Jersey, and Virginia—the governor has an "amendatory" veto. He can return a bill without his signature to the house where it originated, with suggestions for change that would make it acceptable to him. The legislature first considers the question of accepting the changes before deciding whether to pass the bill over his veto or return it to him for final consideration. The device has strengthened the governor's hand in shaping legislation. Like the President, the governor can call the legislature into special session, and, unlike the President, he can, in about half the states, specify the matters to be considered, thus increasing executive authority over the legislative agenda.

But even more than the President, the governor faces a formidable legislative power-structure. In most state legislatures, the speaker of the house, the presiding officer of the senate, and the chairmen of the leading standing committees, enjoy authority and influence that overshadows the substantial power of their counterparts in Congress. In the states, the rules of seniority, geographical distribution, and party representation are often far less well established than in Congress, thus enhancing the leaders' influence. The leaders, that is, can be more arbitrary in the selecting of committee slates and committee chairmen. Further, the general body of legislators are more dependent upon the personal favor of the legislative leaders and more pressed to win and keep their approval than in the national Congress where these matters are more regularized. The actions of state legislative leaders are, in addition, less covered by official written records and the press. The resulting obscurity increases the power of legislative leaders to manipulate against the governor.

The governor is also an administrative chief whose powers are more qualified than the President's. In nearly four-fifths of the states, he shares administrative power with other elected executives: the secretary of state, the attorney general, the treasurer, the controller, and others who already are or will be his political competitors. A heavy trend in the states toward the creation of independent agencies, authorities, and commissions, endowed with their own fiscal powers, represents incursions into the governor's administrative primacy on a scale well exceeding the President's difficulties with the independent commissions. Frequently the governor lacks power to appoint or remove a department head, and many departments may not be subject to the executive budget and other fiscal controls. Not surprisingly, governors tend to feel that administration should receive no heavy portion of their time and that success in that endeavor contributes little to their reelection.

For the rest, the governorship reflects the Presidential system, although on a smaller scale and with milder strength. The governor is commander-in-chief of the state military forces, a capacity of special importance in the Revolutionary era, when not a few governors commanded in the field. The governor may enter into industrial and civil rights disputes, under his duty to assist local officials in maintaining public order. The governor conducts various external relationships that more or less parallel the President's activity in foreign affairs. He is the official organ of communications between his state and other states and with the national government. He certifies election results in his state for national officers; the state's participation in federal-state cooperative programs may turn upon his approval; he may make "good will" visits abroad.

The Mayor

Of the several types of local executives, the one most deeply rooted in the American tradition—the mayor—also fits most securely into the Presidential pattern. Two other forms of the local executive that first appeared in the twentieth century—the city manager, who is a professional and appointed executive, and the commission, in reality a plural executive—constitute sharp departures from the Presidential format and therefore will not concern us here.

Like the governor, the mayor has long been engaged in a struggle to convert insubstantial powers into strength. Of the two general types of mayor plans, the older is the "weak mayor," widely prevalent in the nineteenth century and still the predominant plan in middle-size and smaller cities. Under that plan, various executive and administrative officers are either popularly elected or are appointed by the city council or legislature. Budget-making powers and powers of administrative supervision are reserved to the council. Los Angeles and Atlanta are the principal cities employing the "weak mayor" plan.

In the twentieth century the nation's largest cities have been veering sharply to the second type of mayor plan—the "strong mayor"—which bears greater resemblances to the Presidential model. In theory, at least, the plan seeks to establish the mayor as the chief executive with the fullest possible control over departments and agencies; it empowers him to prepare a comprehensive executive budget and to propose legislation. He possesses a strong veto power and enjoys broad powers of appointment and removal. Practice is some steps removed from theory. Of the largest cities, only Boston and Cleveland make the mayor the sole elected incumbent of the principal executive offices; in New York, Chicago, and Detroit, the mayor shares budget and administrative powers with other governmental organs that he does not direct or control. In Chicago, for example, a council committee prepares the budget.

It is useful for students of the Presidency to examine the strong, big city mayor type because it illuminates dependence and weakness at the local level of government that could conceivably appear in a later day at the Presidential level. The big city mayor is the front-line soldier who deals with the most urgent problems of American domestic politics located as they are in the urban sector. The problems of health, education, civil rights, housing, and the others that stand high on the President's agenda are the daily grist of the big city mayor. The mayor meets close up, and in the most concentrated form, problems from which the President enjoys a greater distance and whose priority he can balance and juggle with his nonurban concerns, especially those in foreign affairs. Despite the resemblances of his formal powers to the President's, the mayor's actual power to deal with the problems is only a fraction of the national executive's substantial capacity to act.

The gap between what the mayor can do and what the President can do is all the more striking since both officers have been buffeted by common historic social forces. Both the President and the mayor are affected by the radical change in the urban environment of late decades. The massive increase in urban population, the radical alteration of its composition, the ever-enlarging bureaucratization of government, and the almost infinite appetite for government services are the common lot of mayors and Presidents. Faced with these common pressures, the President, on the whole, has been able to respond with greater initiative and force than the mayor. The explanation does not lie wholly in the superiority of federal resources. Especially important are essential differences in the political environments of the mayor and the President.

The mayors of our great cities, as Scott Greer has suggested, reign but do not rule.[3] Big city mayors often assume heroic or Presidential poses and work hard at constructing images of vigorous creative leadership that are some distance removed from the record of actual achievement. The watchword with big city mayors is caution. They preside over routine, caretaker governments and struggle with the most urgent and complex problems on the domestic scene without the capacity to mount major offensives or launch bold initiatives. Meanwhile the problems and the forces producing them work their havoc. Industry continues its move to the suburbs; the differentiation between the central city and the suburban populations becomes ever sharper; the predominance of city groups who suffer most from economic depression grows apace. The strong mayor must endure several handicaps from his political environment. His governmental jurisdiction, although large, is not large enough. His city is one among a number of governmental divisions of a metropolis, which consists of numerous municipalities, counties, and special districts, each empowered to do certain tasks and to withhold cooperation from other local governments.

Big city government is largely one-party government, or in reality nonpartisan government. The big city mayor tends to be the dominant political personality in the metropolitan area. Yet for all of his prominence, his ability to achieve political results is modest. One-party government frees the mayor from many pressures, but the freedom he enjoys is negative rather than positive. He is free from partisan limitations, but not free to make new and radical departures. With the evaporation of the threat of electoral defeat that the one-party system affords, the party structure loses its discipline, on which the mayor, or any executive, depends to push his program through the legislature. In the one-party arrangement, the central city electorate becomes a captive electorate of the Democratic party, which dominates the big cities, much as the Southern voter too has been its captive since the Civil War. There is no effective alternative party to turn to, and the electorate tends toward passivity. The mayor must cope with factional leaders who have substantial personal and political power, wielded in the legislature and in appointed and elected executive posts.

The big city mayor must also cope with a bureaucracy that easily eludes his control. New York City, for example, has an educational bureaucracy of 50,000, a police force of 26,000, and 13,000 firemen. Here and elsewhere, the bureaucracy may cling to established ways and resist innovation, which is viewed as a threat to the existing distribution of power and privilege. In the cities, the indulgence in independent agencies and authorities is even greater than in the states, which further bolsters the autonomy of municipal bureaucracies.

Above all, the big city is hobbled by political segregation, by the separation of numbers and wealth, by the concentration of population in the central city and resources in the suburbs, by the separation of need from means. In effect, government is segregated by social class, with the middle class on the one hand, and the working class on the other, each having its own local government. Relations between the central city and the suburb are ruled by mutual suspicion, an attitude that can be profitably exaggerated by candidates for office.

Foreign Executives: Selection and Tenure

The strengths and weaknesses of the American Presidency also may be better perceived if we examine the chief executives of other major nations. We may find in the experience of others clues for eliminating flaws from our own system and for keeping up better in the race every nation is running against the forces of change. Possibly, too, we may take some small comfort if we find that weaknesses that afflict own own Chief Executive are also bedeviling other nations.

No major nation can boast a method of selecting its chief executive that assures a choice from among the proverbial "best men available" by means that are assuredly democratic. Because of the enormous stakes, the contest is almost universally a great scramble to which the arts of pressure and maneuver are fully committed. It is an enterprise in which democratic values and procedures are vulnerable. The United States prefers its Presidents from large states and therefore arbitrarily excludes worthy contenders from the small. It requires long primary campaigns, thus loading the dice for the candidate with money. The creaky electoral college machinery is a standing invitation to disaster in opening wide the gates of chance that a Presidential candidate with a minority of popular votes may be elected.

In Great Britain the selection of the Prime Minister after a national election follows a well-regulated routine. The voters elect a new House of Commons, and the leader of the majority party is automatically made the new Prime Minister. Following the election, the Queen requests the leader of the winning party to form a government, in effect ratifying the electorate's choice. But the selection of the party leader in the first place, prior to his appearance before the electorate, is largely a matter of intraparty maneuver. The magic key is the building of support among the factions. Harold Wilson bested George Brown in their contest for the Labor leadership in 1963 as a kind of middle-of-the-roader who had least offended the factions whose support was vital. When Labor won the national elections the following year, it was only a formality for the Queen to summon Wilson to form a new government.

The American President, once elected, enjoys relative stability of tenure, rather greater than the British Prime Minister's and rather less than that of the President of the French Fifth Republic and the established Soviet leaders. The sole legitimate means of removing the American President—impeachment—is constructed to operate only in the utmost extremity. A Buchanan or a Hoover persists in office until the next inauguration even though the majority of public opinion is set against them. To be sure, the Twenty-second, or two-term, Amendment is a severe hobbling of Presidential power. This enactment not only imposes an absolute deadline on Presidential tenure but cuts deeply into his effectiveness in his second term. President De Gaulle, in contrast, who came into power in 1958 as the last Prime Minister of the Fourth Republic, renewed his mandate in January 1966 in the run-off of a national election and won the prize of another seven-year term. De Gaulle enjoys both a long term and indefinite reeligibility.

Although the British Prime Minister enjoys a term of five years, his retention of power over that span is less assured than the American President's is during his established four-year term. In his five-year interval, the Prime Minister can be toppled if he loses the support of his majority in the House of Commons. In actuality, however, the historical record shows that the twentieth-century Prime Minister is no longer in any real danger of losing the majority support of his highly disciplined party colleagues.

The fact that the possibility exists that a Prime Minister can be pulled down by fiat of his party in the House of Commons makes him vulnerable to plots against his political security, particularly in seasons when policy may go awry and the country's fortunes dip, common occurrences in the present stage of Britain's historical experience. Nineteen forty-seven was just such a bad year for the Prime Minister. A general economic decline was aggravated by the ill luck of a terrible winter, the worst since 1880, which touched off a fuel crisis and temporarily brought all industry to a stop. Stafford Cripps, a member of the cabinet, let it become known that in the sudden crisis the country required greater inspiration than the mild-mannered Prime Minister Clement Attlee could possibly provide. Cripps proposed that Attlee step down and permit the Prime Ministership to be handed over to Ernest Bevin, whose toughness he admired. Attlee, Cripps generously suggested, could take over the Foreign Office in place of Bevin. Alternatively, if Bevin did not want to leave foreign affairs, to which he was extremely devoted, Attlee could go to the Treasury while Cripps himself took over the Prime Ministership. Newspapers to which the plan was carefully leaked and right-wing Labor M.P.'s, who opposed Attlee's left-wing faction, rallied behind Cripps's plan. Attlee nevertheless held fast by several adroit maneuvers, including a sudden reshuffling of his cabinet, not the least part of which was the installation of Cripps in the new post of Minister of Economic Affairs with more extensive powers over the economy than any minister in peacetime had ever before possessed.[4]

The tenure of Soviet leadership is vulnerable to palace revolution. Premier Nikita Khrushchev was challenged in two known and severe tests, one of which he narrowly survived; the other he failed, and was quickly swept into the limbo of political disgrace. In his first crisis of June 1957, Khrushchev seemed doomed when the majority of the party Presidium called an extraordinary session and by a vote of seven to four elected to remove him from his party post as First Secretary. The anti-Khrushchev majority comprised the older members and former associates of Stalin: Voroshilov, Molotov, Kaganovich, Bulganin, and Malenkov; and, from the newer generation of leadership, Pervuklin and Saburov. The hazardous maneuver was apparently born of fear of Khrushchev's ambition and growing doubts of his capacity to rule. But the power of the rebelling group was limited. Khrushchev controlled the parent body of the Presidium, the Central Committee. He dominated the vast party apparatus across the Soviet Union, and his impregnable influence blocked his foes' access to the means of physical force—the political police and the armed forces. Backed by such enormous strength, Khrushchev could counter with swift and bold measures. He quickly mobilized the Central Committee members who were then in Moscow, summoning them into a meeting where they reversed the Presidium's decision and expelled the anti-Khrushchev factions from both the Presidium and the Central Committee.

Seven years later in 1964, Russia experienced another October revolution, this time a palace revolution resulting in Khrushchev's overthrow. Where before his friends of the Central Committee had saved him, they now forsook him. The committee replaced Khrushchev as First Secretary of the party with his own protégé of many years, Leonid Brezhnev, and delivered the crowning blow of disgrace by taking away Khrushchev's seat on the party Presidium. He next was stripped of his governmental position as Premier, and that post was handed to his successor, Alexei Kosygin.[5]

Succession Compared

When the Vice-Presidency is filled, the American Presidency clearly holds the advantage over other chief executives in handling the problem of succession. John Kennedy's assassination, for all its rending tragedy, was also the occasion of a remarkable demonstration of the velocity and assurance with which executive power can be transferred in the American system. Less than two hours after Kennedy's death the Presidential oath was administered to Vice President Johnson, with Mrs. Kennedy by his side, herself a brave witness to the continuity of the American system. No other major government affords such quick and automatic transfer.

Nearly a month before the catastrophe in Texas, a succession occurred in the British Prime Ministership. The procedure of deciding who the new Prime Minister should be took all of eleven days to consummate, with lengthy passages of farce and satire. Through much of this anguished interlude, the effort to find a successor to the ill and hospitalized Prime Minister Harold Macmillan foundered upon the deadlock of two intractable and opposed groups in the Conservative party. To the left were the liberal revisionists, headed by R. A. Butler, Deputy Prime Minister in the Macmillan cabinet and the man who, according to party and public opinion polls, enjoyed the greatest backing. Prime Minister Macmillan reportedly wished above all else to bar Butler's succession. A second major contender was Viscount Hailsham of the Conservative right wing. Several lesser contenders made up the field. Early in his quest for an heir, Macmillan pressed Alec Douglas-Home, the Foreign Secretary, to enter the lists, but Home declined.

A polling that Macmillan ordered taken of the cabinet revealed that Home was running strong as a second and third choice. Soundings were likewise made among the 50 junior ministers, the 350 M.P.'s, and the active Conservative peers. The party whips were instructed to gather answers to three questions: 1. Whom would you like to see in office? 2. Do you want to choose *possible* runners-up? 3. Is there anybody you would rather *not* see in office? Home emerged with a slight majority of first preferences and a clear margin of second choices, but the column most in his favor was "against"; few opposed him. Martin Redmayne, chief whip and poll supervisor, also weighted the votes according to each M.P.'s status in the party, a process that Home's opponents later disputed. A Butler man said, "Redmayne could have weighted Home's votes and tied little balloons to Rab's."

Buttonholing and telephoning proceeded intensively. Hailsham's candidacy began to sag with Home's advance, although Butler's held strong. Meanwhile Home, notwithstanding heavy pressure from Macmillan, would not declare his candidacy. With more time, he told Macmillan, either Butler, Hailsham, or a third candidate, Reginald Maudling, might come through.

Maudling, who might have thrown in with Butler, thereby establishing a majority for the latter, made no move. Macmillan, bound to his sickbed, dreaded a deadlock that would entitle the monarch to send for Harold Wilson, leader of the opposition Labor Party, who would have then formed a government, dissolved Parliament, and called an election. Macmillan again appealed to Home, who now acquiesced. The Prime Minister called the polltakers to his bedside to arrange an updated tabulation of Conservative Parliamentary opinion. Butler was now revealed to have gained strength, although he was outnumbered by combined Hailsham and Home first preferences. The black-ball again provided the clearest impression. So many interviewees opposed Butler and Hailsham that the double negative in a sense produced Home as a positive. Macmillan wrote out a lengthy, complex assessment of the balance of opinion.

Hours before Macmillan resigned and presented Home's name to the Queen, an emergency cabal led by Iain Macleod, co-chairman of the Conservative party and leader of the House of Commons, and Enoch Powell, Minister of Health, met with Redmayne, who was requested to inform Macmillan that both Hailsham and Maudling were prepared to support Butler. Michael Adeane, the Queen's link with the party, was telephoned and told that, irrespective of what Macmillan might say, Butler could now form a government. Butler telephoned Macmillan at King Edward VII's Hospital, but the call was not accepted. Macmillan resigned, presented his written estimate to the Queen, with supplementary oral comment. The Queen sent for the Earl of Home. In the aftermath, critics assailed Home's elevation "on the heap of blackballs cast against his three rivals" and the "tricky maneuverings" of Macmillan and Redmayne and called for "modernization" of the selection procedure.[6]

Succession goes little better in other lands. Chancellor Adenauer marred an otherwise luminous career with the ungainly procedures by which he eventually yielded power to the successor he did not want, Ludwig Erhard. De Gaulle's spacious rule has not made any provision for a possible successor. Soviet Russia, like all dictatorships, cannot solve the problem of succession. The transfer of power, for which the Soviet constitution makes no provision, can be the occasion of numbing uncertainty, subterfuge, terror, and violence. One or more of those elements attended the successions to Lenin, Stalin, and Khrushchev.

Stalin's death and its aftermath disclose the jagged course of dictatorial succession. The announcement of his demise was withheld for six hours and ten minutes. A statement accompanying the eventual disclosure declared that the "most important task of the party and the government is to insure uninterrupted and correct leadership . . . the greatest unity of leadership and the prevention of any kind of disorder and panic." As Bertram D. Wolfe has well observed, admonitions against "disorder and panic" are inconceivable in an American transfer.[7] When power passed from Roosevelt to Truman and from Kennedy to Johnson, there were, needless to say, no comparable warnings from high places.

With Stalin's passing, a reshuffling of state and party positions proceeded, with Malenkov, in the intrafactional bargaining, emerging as the head of government and First Secretary of the party. But the bargain did not stick. After nine days Malenkov "asked to be relieved" of his duties as party First Secretary. Two years later, again at his own request, he abandoned the Premiership as well. Malenkov's degradation continued in the Soviet manner when he confessed to "errors" in agricultural policy that could only have been committed by his rival Khrushchev. Another major figure, Lavrenti Beria, head of the secret police, was arrested, shot, and made an "unperson." Meanwhile Khrushchev took over the post of First Secretary and consolidated his power to the point where, in an extraordinary address to the Twentieth Party Congress, he denounced the memory of Stalin, depicting him as a tyrant, a sadist, and a glutton for adulation. Among the interpretations placed upon this grotesque performance is one that Khrushchev, in effect, was pledging not to employ his newly won power according to Stalin's example.

The British Parliamentary System

Many a critic of the Presidency gazes admiringly upon the British Parliamentary system and proposes to engraft upon the American structure some of the better elements of the British. Woodrow Wilson, both as a youthful political scientist and as a practicing President, longed to introduce the British method into American politics. He would greatly have preferred to have been a Prime Minister rather than a President and indeed tried manfully during his incumbency to nudge the office into the ways of the British model. Such legislators as George Pendleton of the nineteenth century and Estes Kefauver of the twentieth doggedly proposed to borrow from British practice to bring executive and legislative effort into purposeful cooperation. A study committee of the American Political Science Association in 1950 emerged with an ingenious plan for adapting the British party system to the circumstances of American parties.[8] Is the British Parliamentary system better for the United States than the existing Presidential system?

The leading attractions of the Parliamentary system are unity and coherence of policy. It encourages the executive to tackle the major problems of the day, to propose bold plans and broad programs. The British executive has every assurance that every major thing he asks for will be enacted, not the 40 or 50 per cent of the important measures that the American President is likely to secure but 100 per cent. The secret weapon of the Parliamentary system is tight party discipline.

The Prime Minister's party, be it Conservative or Labor, provides him with a majority of legislators whose obedience is granitic, "solid masses of steady votes," Walter Bagehot put it, for policy and program. The party leader, who is ordinarily either the Prime Minister or leader of the opposition, possesses powers that are well-nigh autocratic and against which the American President's party powers are limp and pallid. The Prime Minister has the sole ultimate responsibility for formulating policy and an electoral program. The party secretariat or central office is his personal machine. He appoints the principal officers and thereby controls propaganda, research, and finance. He is vested with lordly power over his party followers in Parliament. An M.P. can ill afford to incur his dread wrath by challenging, criticizing, or publicly differing with his party. No M.P. who has crossed the floor, or aligned himself with the opposition, on a major issue has won reelection since 1945.[9] All this, needless to say, is a far cry from the American President's circumstances. Franklin Roosevelt was the only President to launch a substantial purge upon recalcitrant Democrats, with results so inglorious that no successor has dared repeat the venture.

In the selection of candidates for American national legislative office, state and local organizations dominate the decisions. The result is a goodly crop of Senators and Congressmen opposed to the President of their own party on principal policy questions. In Britain the local choice of the candidate must win central approval. The Labor party's constitution provides that a candidate's selection "shall not be regarded as completed until the name of the person has been placed before a meeting of the National Executive Committee, and his or her selection has been duly endorsed." The Labor constitution clearly stipulates the conditions of approval: The candidate must conform to "the Constitution, Program, Principles and Policy of the Party" and "act in harmony with the Standing Orders of the Parliamentary Labor Party."[10] Even if a rebel is backed by his own constituency, the Labor party will enter a candidate against him, thus dividing the party's usual vote and making almost certain his defeat.

British party discipline depends not simply on organization and gadgetry. It also reflects the lesser role of pressure groups in national life. The United States, in contrast, is a land where pressure groups flourish, where regional differences are vast, and their influence is divisive, preventing the tight integration of opinion and leadership in the major parties. Above all, differences between the British and American peoples are an influence, the latter's heterogeneity forcing the parties to be broad and flexible in method. British party methods in the areas of finance, selection of candidates, and platform-development, however, deserve close study for possible borrowings and adaptations to the United States.

The British Prime Minister

Whereas the American President's weakness as party leader earns him un-reliable Congressional support for his program, the British Prime Minister knows the luxury of enduring legislative backing. The President, viewing his ally, the British executive, across the Atlantic, must see him as abiding in a political utopia that assures that whatever he asks for, the legislature will provide.

In theory, the President is more powerful than the Prime Minister in legislation. Head of the executive branch, he is the coequal of Congress. He is not responsible to Congress in the sense that the Prime Minister is to Parliament. To become Prime Minister, Harold Wilson had to be elected to the House of Commons, where he answers daily for the actions of his government. In British constitutional theory he, his cabinet, and other ministers are a committee of the House of Commons.

Although in theory the Prime Minister and his government are the servants of the House of Commons, they are in fact its masters. The govern-ment, not the House, legislates. The government plans and controls the House's time. The introduction of legislation is almost completely the gov-ernment's monopoly. A rule requiring that all legislation involving expendi-ture bear the crown's, or in actuality the government's, approval invests the government with a sweeping control, since virtually all legislation of signifi-cance requires money. This order of things is supported by an implicit democratic rationalization: Parties contest elections on platforms; upon win-ning a popular, and therefore a legislative, majority a party should command priority for its program in the House.

Normally, the British government is certain that any important bill it introduces will pass without significant change, in good time. Although the cannonade of brilliant oratory and merciless jibes may beat upon its program in House debate, the government ultimately prevails. It knows no evil like the committee bottleneck and the crippling amendment that kills or damages beyond recognition the President's requests. At most, Parliament can only influence the government's future course. Flaws exposed in legislative debate presumably will not be prolonged or repeated.

In his daily legislative life the Prime Minister sails a smooth sea com-pared with the American President. Harold Wilson squeaked through the national elections of 1964 with a four-seat margin in the House of Commons. Despite this slim margin, he announced that the bold program promised in his campaign would be fully presented to the House. "Nothing could be worse," Wilson declared, "than failing both at home and abroad because of the Parliamentary balance of power." He brought forward his program, and it proceeded with assurance through Parliament, even when, through attrition, his margin fell to one vote. But Wilson still moved ahead, and the country approved and rewarded his effort by returning him to office in 1966 by a landslide.

The Prime Minister, also unlike the President, shares power with fellow executives, the ministers, and particularly those who comprise the cabinet. The Prime Minister, however, enjoys powers his fellow ministers do not have. In constitutional practice all ministerial offices derive from him and depend upon him, since he can make and unmake ministers. The Prime Minister can prompt the dissolution of the entire government simply by resigning. No minister has such power. The Prime Minister alone can make certain great decisions without cabinet approval. His fellow ministers have small choice but to back him. To repudiate him is to split the party and deliver the government to the enemy.

Yet, in choosing his cabinet, the Prime Minister faces ground rules far more restrictive than any confronting the President. The Prime Minister is literally forced to work with certain associates; the President is not. John Kennedy could choose a cabinet in which not a single major legislative figure of his party was represented. In Franklin Roosevelt's there was only one. The President, it is true, must pay heed to some customary limitations in constituting his cabinet: Give Interior to a Westerner, and Labor, Agriculture, and perhaps Commerce to appointees acceptable to the clienteles of those departments. But these are generalized frameworks within which the President can select among scores, if not hundreds, of individuals. The Prime Minister's choices, on the other hand, are definite and particular. To form a government, the Prime Minister must build upon the support of the principal factions of his party. Factional allegiance requires a *quid pro quo*, a seat for the factional leader in the cabinet. Accordingly, Harold Wilson, in constructing his cabinet, had no choice but to bring his principal opponent, George Brown, into a leading post. This Wilson did by selecting Brown as Foreign Minister.

The Parliamentary System Evaluated

The supreme attractiveness of the Parliamentary system is the ease and assurance with which it produces policy. The executive has charge of legislation, guided by public opinion as it is expressed by interest groups, the press, and in the House of Commons. Administration, whether it concern organizational structure, program, finance, or personnel, is the secure province of the executive. The House votes the funds that the cabinet requests. The House lacks constitutional power to vote more money for any purpose than the cabinet asks for, a situation that is the bane of budget-minded Presidents, who often prefer less money than Congressional Armed Services Committees, goaded by the military, rush to provide. Thanks to iron party discipline, the cabinet can count not only on a majority but regularly on the same majority. Parliament's orientation, like the cabinet's, is national rather than local. The lack of a tradition that the legislator reside in his own district, the common incident of an M.P. elected from a district he has never visited, the party's intolerance of any local deviation from national policy, give Parliament an orientation as resolutely national as the consciousness of Congress, and particularly of the House of Representatives, is local.

But the Parliamentary system, for all its undeniable excellence as a vehicle of national policy, also carries weakness. It is immediately suspect because it is not employed today by any major nation on the rise. Britain's own decline in power and place in the family of nations, although a product of many factors, strongly suggests that the Parliamentary method smacks excessively of the past and has not adjusted sufficiently to modern change. There is indeed much that is anachronistic in the British Parliamentary model, much that once was meaningful but that time and change have reduced to hollow pretense. What was constitutional political fact in that nation in the nineteenth century, as Don K. Price has put it, has become constitutional fiction in the twentieth. The House of Commons in bygone days did control the government and could, when it chose, dismiss it. Nowadays, however, public opinion rather than the House determines cabinet tenure.[11]

The House of Commons has been reduced to a passivity that even the most resolute critic of Congress would not wish upon it. In its tightly restricted capacity, the House resembles the American electoral college, registering the popular will in choosing a government and then automatically ratifying its program and voting the funds it asks for. The House lacks means of initiating policy; unlike Congress, it has no standing committees to investigate and recommend, deprivations that preclude any legislative capacity to take an independent line and exercise meaningful control. More than three decades ago Stanley Baldwin rightly observed that House members widely felt they had "nothing much to do of a responsible nature."[12]

Nowadays outcries are rising in Britain against Parliament's general ineffectuality. In 1963 Brian Chapman of Manchester University voiced the wide concern of responsible Britons when he wrote, "We need a state in which Parliament is an effective partner in the process of government, and not simply an ineffectual appendage employed to make noises of approval or discontent." Seeking a rearranged governmental structure enabling Parliament to "play a vital role in the formulation of policy," Chapman looked admiringly upon the American Congress, with its subject matter and joint committees and urged that the House of Lords be reconstituted by regions.[13]

The administrative features of the Parliamentary system are also questionable. The minister, the equivalent of the American departmental Secretary, is primarily a legislative leader and not an administrator. He is chosen not so much for administrative ability as for his command of House support and his skill in defending party policy. He makes his way by shining in debate and by leadership in party affairs. Accordingly, if Robert S. Mc-Namara, generally hailed as a distinguished Secretary of Defense in the Kennedy and Johnson administrations, were to live and work as a Briton, chances are slight that he would achieve the place and make the contribution permitted him in American public affairs.

Finally, much of the criticism that Britons themselves have levied against their governmental system has fallen upon the civil service. Long and rightly hailed as a model career system for other nations, including the United States, to emulate, the British civil service is handled roughly by its present-day critics. It is viewed as ingrown, uninspired, uncreative, and out of step with the fast pace of Britian's problems. In essence, the administrative class, or policy-making career service, is recruited at a youthful age, when its members complete their university education, after which they pass all their working lives in governmental service. Except for specialized employment, it is difficult, almost unheard of, to bring into the civil service those midway and beyond in a business, academic, or professional career.[14]

The British ministerial system reinforces the tendency of large bureaucratic organizations to be cautious and safe, and therefore unenterprising. A minister progresses in his political career if the civil service keeps him out of trouble. The civil service reads the handwriting on the wall, which instructs that they will gain more by caution (which avoids trouble) than by initiative (which invites it). Furthermore, the civil servant figures that even if the initiative succeeds, the minister will receive most of the credit. Britons looking for reform take their cues from American practice. They propose a generous use of a "brain trust" to be attached to the Prime Minister's and each minister's office, an injection of new blood into the civil service at many levels from the untapped talent of the professions, business, and local government.

The Administrative State

All nations have donned increasingly the trappings of the administrative state. Managing the economy, providing welfare services, and maintaining the military force and weaponry have compounded executive tasks, resources, and power in society. In most of the nations of the world, administration has gained in power and autonomy at the expense of the legislature. The United States, however, for all the expansion of its governmental responsibilities displays far less of a shift of power from the legislature to the executive. The American Congress exerts controls over administration that other legislatures do not possess. Its legislation is more detailed, its controls over administrative structure, finance, program, and personnel are far tighter than those exercised by other legislatures of the world.

In Great Britain Parliament practices a relationship with the executive in matters of administration that, were it followed in the United States, would immeasurably strengthen the President's position as administrative chief. Although Britain has a unified political system, with both legislative and executive power concentrated in Parliament, administration is treated altogether differently. Administration is accorded the full benefit of the doctrine of separation of powers. Paradoxically, the United States claims to observe a separation of powers, but Congress freely breaches it in matters of administration. The British, applying separation of powers, leave to executive discretion the employment of the basic means of administration. The organizational structure of departments, which Congress provides for in close detail, Parliament delegates to executive decision. Personnel policy, for which Congress has compiled a thick volume of close legislation, the British leave to the executive. The executive budget, which Congress can deal roughly with when it chooses, remains fully intact in the hands of Parliament. If even one of these instances of legislative self-denial were adopted by Congress, the President's situation as administrative chief would be vastly improved.

Another British practice equally instructive for the United States is the technique of delegated legislation. Parliament often passes laws in skeletal form, setting forth only major principles and leaving the details to the departments to work out. The practice permits great flexibility in administration. A common additional arrangement is that many administrative rules and orders are not valid until the legislature expresses consent either by positive action or by lack of action. A minority of orders must be affirmed by Parliament; others must lie before the House for forty days and are considered approved if no nullifying action has been taken against them. Delegated legislation specifies the limits of executive discretion, sets forth guiding standards, and requires publicity when the administrative regulations are in preparation. A special House committee investigates such regulation as it chooses and elicits any necessary information from departmental officials.

The British practice might be preferable to the independent regulatory commissions in the United States that trespass so badly upon the President's economic powers. Relative to British practice, the commissions represent a reverse trend by Congress. Whereas Parliament views economic regulation a fit subject for increased executive discretion, Congress resorts to its own commissions, free from ordinary executive control and reporting to the legislature.

The Fifth French Republic of Charles de Gaulle is the ultimate in the democratic administrative state, veering as it does in certain seasons into constitutional dictatorship.[15] As a model of the continuously strong chief executive in a more or less democratic setting, it is too extreme for adaptation to the United States. In the Fourth Republic a well-nigh powerless executive was subordinate to an all-powerful lower legislative house, the Chamber of Deputies. In the De Gaulle republic much of the Deputies' power has been transferred to the executive, chiefly to the President and to a much lesser degree to the Prime Minister in subordination to the President. The President controls policy-making in foreign affairs and national security, and he can, when he chooses, extend his powers by revising constitutional practice at will and ruling under emergency powers for periods extending well beyond the actual emergency. The Prime Minister and his cabinet wield so many powers not subject to the approval of the Assembly, the lower legislative house of the Fifth Republic, that they can confidently anticipate the enactment of most of their vital policies for the low price of occasional minor changes in program and personnel shifts. Parliament's lawmaking powers are limited to specific subjects set out chiefly by the constitution. The administration, in turn, wields a rule-making power over all matters not specifically reserved to Parliament.

French Parliamentary lawmaking is subordinate to administrative necessity. Article XXXVIII of the constitution provides that "for the execution of its program" the executive may ask Parliament for power temporarily to take measures by ordinance that constitutionally are among the subjects reserved to the legislature. The French Senate, which belongs to the administrative tradition of French politics, works as an ally of the executive. A Constitutional Council tests the constitutionality of laws enacted by Parliament. The Council, too, is an auxiliary of executive dominance, watchful that Parliament remains within the confines of its inferior position. De Gaulle conducts his Presidential office as a crisis executive, and under Article XVI, which provides unlimited emergency powers in external and internal crisis, he enjoys authority that largely subjects the government and its policies to Presidential control.

The United States, an executive-legislative state, faces in its great competitor, the Soviet Union, a monolithic administrative state. The Soviet Union is in the hands of party administrators, a political bureaucracy or "new class," as Milovan Djilas terms it. The new class members enjoy special privileges and economic preferences derived from their administrative monopoly. Unlike bureaucracies in the noncommunist world, which are subject to political authorities, "the Communists," as Djilas has written, "have neither masters nor owners over them."[16]

The Soviet Union's top leadership is produced by the party administrative system. Stalin was himself the epitome of the party administrator, rising not as a charismatic leader but as one skilled in the ways of the party apparatus, who outdid competitors who excelled as orators or theoreticians. Stalin neither preached nor inspired but made decisions, spoke without ardor or color, and stressed the concrete administrative tasks of industrializing the Soviet Union and collectivizing its agriculture. To retain power, he incorporated a system of relentless terror into the administrative apparatus.[17]

Stalin's successors, Malenkov and Khrushchev, and their successors, Kosygin and Brezhnev, all were party administrators who climbed the career ladder. The ascent to the top is by apolitical means, accomplished without a struggle for votes or an assertion of new ideas for program and policy but dependent rather upon one's usefulness to the incumbent leadership and upon choosing the right protectors.

Decision-Making Compared

President Johnson's commitment to an eighteen-hour workday, President Eisenhower's extensive overhaul of his top-level staff machinery, and President Kennedy's overhaul of Eisenhower's overhaul evidence a restless dissatisfaction with the means and processes of decision-making. Is the Soviet leadership similarly troubled? Does internal, top-level executive decision-making differ substantially in method in the monolithic Soviet system from that in the pluralistic American system? Is Soviet experience at all relevant and instructive for American needs?

After Khrushchev was overthrown in October 1964, the Soviet Union was governed by a "collective leadership," in which Kosygin as Premier was teamed with Brezhnev, the party's General Secretary. In 1965 Brezhnev added a state post to his party capacity by becoming a member of the Presidium of the Supreme Soviet, or legislature. By serving in the party's Politburo, Kosygin too combines state and party posts.

The top policy organ, over which Brezhnev presides, is the Politburo of the party, which since 1966 has comprised eleven full, or voting, members and eight candidate members, who participate to varying degrees in decision-making. Djilas provided insight into the functioning of a top-level communist policy group when he wrote, "In the Communist system, exclusive groups are established around political leaders and forums. All policy-making is reduced to wrangling in these exclusive groups, in which familiarity and cliquishness flower. The highest group is generally the most intimate."[18]

All members and candidate members of the Politburo are either officials or deputies of the Supreme Soviet. Thus the highest policy decisions are taken in a relatively small group bearing governmental and party authority. The Politburo appears to meet frequently and to work out many decisions on the spot.[19] The American President does not work with any single group as regularly as the Soviet leadership does. The President distributes his consultations among large groups such as the cabinet, the National Security Council, and *ad hoc* groups thrown together for such critical situations as Cuba in 1962 and Panama in 1964. The President, unlike Soviet leaders, may feel behooved to touch base with figures outside the executive branch, such as legislators, private group leaders, and former Presidents. The Politburo seems to have nothing of the elaborately prepared and negotiated papers that characterized Eisenhower's National Security Council. Yet Soviet departments have access to the Politburo through its members and the Secretariat, the party's principal administrative apparatus over which Brezhnev presides. Agencies like the Ministry of Foreign Affairs report to the Politburo directly.

In actual decision-making, the American President is rather more apt to employ competing sources of information and advice than the Soviet leadership. Brezhnev has revealed that an inner cabinet of four members—himself, Kosygin, Suslov, and Podgorny—maintain continual discussions of major policy issues. The other members of the Politburo carry responsibilities for overseeing departments and bring to the Politburo information and recommendations from their departments. The Politburo receives regular reports on scientific and military developments, the economy and foreign policy.

The Soviet administrative system is an elaborate mechanism of control from the top. There are no departmental bureaus with the autonomy of an FBI and an Army Corps of Engineers. In Soviet practice the party, which dominates the government apparatus from top to bottom, leaves nothing undone to assure that the orders of the top command are carried out. The Soviet leader can act with a rigor toward his administrators and ministers that no American President would dare consider even in his fondest dreams. The top leadership must appear infallible despite the treachery of events and human error. If it falters, others must bear the blame.

The Presidency Abroad

The Presidency is America's foremost political export. The Philippines and most of all Latin America have engrafted onto their governments elements of the American Presidential model. At one time or another all the Latin-American countries have adopted the strong Presidency. It is instructive to study what they have borrowed, added, or left out in their adaptation of the American prototype because it reveals what they believe to be the strengths and shortcomings of our Presidential institution.

The powers of the Latin-American President invariably exceed those of the United States Chief Executive.[20] The Latin-American President's appointment power is stronger. He can fill most offices on his own authority, referring relatively few for Senatorial or Congressional approval. He sends messages and appears personally before Congress to request action. In Venezuela he can even introduce bills, a power treated somewhat ambiguously in several other constitutions, which assertive presidents have interpreted to their own advantage. He presents the budget in the form of an appropriation bill, enjoys a broad and strong veto power, including an item veto for appropriations, and has a sweeping power to issue decrees and administrative orders. Laws are passed in far more general terms than the American Congress would ever tolerate, affording the President broad discretion. He enjoys extraordinary powers to cope with civil disorder, invasion, or other crisis and to intervene in the provincial governments.

Latin-American experience abundantly demonstrates, however, that in spite of all his impressive power the President must dominate the army and build a political party or following of "interests," especially the organized urban workers, if he is to succeed. Even the best presidents have indulged in what is termed "exaggerated Presidentialism," by which they assume dictatorial powers for brief or substantial periods. Bolívar, for one, was convinced that exceptional executive powers must be readily available to counter the demagogic exploitation of racial-cultural tensions. The spectacle of the Presidency transformed into an outright military dictatorship is all too common. Although the United States' transplant has not proved to be the means to good government, it is reassuring that each departure from legitimate government for some variant of dictatorship has been marked by an eventual return to the Presidential form.

As is the fate of merchandise, not every potential foreign buyer who has looked at the American Presidential system has bought it. Charles de Gaulle, beholding the American Presidency in 1964, turned aside clamors in certain domestic quarters that France repattern its own Presidency along American lines. De Gaulle would have nothing of it. The American system, he declared in a press conference, was functioning in a limping way, and, if it were applied in France, he foresaw only "a chronic opposition" between the executive and legislature, leading to "general paralysis." Presumably De Gaulle had in mind the breakdowns in Presidential-Congressional cooperation that provide the American nation with a frequent diet of political futility. The American Presidential system, De Gaulle contended, had thrived in the peculiarly favorable environment of the United States:

> it is in a country which because of its technical make-up, its economic riches, its geographical position, never knew invasion, and which for a century has known no revolution; in a country where, moreover, there are only two parties that are divided by nothing essential in any field, national, social, moral, international; in a federal country where the Government assumes only general tasks—defenses, diplomacy, finance—while the 50 states of the union are entrusted with all the rest.[21]

The American Presidency was not transferable, at least not to France.

Epilogue: The Future of the American Presidency

Any organism, including a political organism like the American Presidency, is engaged in continual struggle with its limitations. The Presidency's struggle is intensified by the severity of the problems it deals with, the enlargement of the functions it serves, and the crisis-prone times in which it exists. Whether Charles de Gaulle's dismal estimate of the American Presidential system will be true in the future depends upon our success or failure in dealing with a succession of crises that continue to erupt in foreign and domestic affairs.

If the recent past is a guide, the future President will be faced at one or more places on the world scene with variants of the "limited wars" that have been spawned since World War II: civil wars, wars of "liberation," guerrilla wars, insurrections, infiltrations, and takeovers. He will wrestle with the slippery dilemma of seeking to intervene in such enterprises while avoiding a deep and continuing involvement of his own nation's resources. He may conclude more and more that these military entrapments may be reduced or avoided if local economies are developed faster and if their peoples' aspirations to escape from the bondage of illiteracy, disease, weak agricultural systems, and other shackles are responded to through bigger and better programs of American foreign aid. An economic strategy may gain more satisfying and enduring results than wars of the Vietnam variety.

The President will be forced to keep up with each new turn and twist in the arms race, with the ever burgeoning developments in the nuclear capabilities and defenses of rival nations. But he will also feel increasingly the pressures to effect arrangements for nuclear disarmament. As he has in the past, he will need to strive to forestall the spread of nuclear capabilities among nations and to engage in discussions with the Soviet Union to limit offensive and defensive weapons. Not only must he take up arduous negotiations abroad, but he must develop broader understanding of these approaches at home.

On the American domestic scene, the future Chief Executive will preside over a full cauldron of trouble and woe. Its chief ingredients are the urban crisis and the place of the Negro citizen in a democratic society. For all the public programs and outlays of the 1960's, the cities continue to decay, and white families continue their flight to the suburbs. The President's Commission on Civil Disorders warned in 1968, "Our nation is moving toward two societies, one black, one white—separate and unequal." The commission proposed strategies and programs far beyond anything yet undertaken: the creation of two million new jobs within three years, vast projects of on-the-job training, and enrichment of elementary and high-school education to enable all children to develop their potential and to participate fully in American life. In these and other recommendations, the commission called for outlays whose costs it did not dare to estimate.

The future President will also face a youth crisis of growing magnitude. Increasingly young citizens are vexed by the injustices and the false pieties of the existing order. They see the President both as a vehicle by which oppressive wrongs are committed and an instrumentality by which they can be righted. Youths, with the lofty moral standards they may choose to apply in the sullied marketplace of politics, will articulate and press their demands ever more insistently upon the President.

It is clear enough that if the Presidency is to prevail in the several struggles that lie ahead, if it is to bring domestic society to change its ways, and if the world is to avoid the folly of wars and the danger of arms races, it is imperative that the office be strong and enjoy optimum effectiveness in all its parts. More than ever, the President must be able to extract from Congress appropriations and new laws to sustain the needs of the cities and Negro citizens. The tendency of Congress to reduce appropriations and withhold laws prompted Martin Luther King, Jr., to observe that Congress, rather than the President, is the real power center of the national government.

What can be done to improve the President's position in his transactions with Congress? He and the national majority opinion that he tends to represent are hobbled time and again by the internal organization and working procedures of Congress. The seniority principle that produces excessive numbers of committee chairmen opposed to the President, the subtle devices by which key measures can be bottled up in committee for months and even years, the wealth of procedural maneuvers on the floor that can halt or sidetrack a Presidential measure and prevent it from reaching a vote, should all come under critical scrutiny. An item veto or an "amendatory" veto for the President as well as identical four-year terms for the two legislative houses and their simultaneous election with the President may produce a Chief

Executive and a Congress more attuned in party composition and policy outlook than the present uneven election permits.

The President might fare better in legislation if his position as party leader were strengthened. One of the most promising tendencies afoot is the growing coincidence of the President's legislative program with urban needs. The great urban groups may come to force local party organizations and their Congressional candidates to support the Chief Executive's urban programs. The tendency to vest the management of these programs in local administrative structures involving the groups may provide additional leverage for the President against local party organizations and leaders. The prospects are also good for a national party organization stronger in function and financial power. Gains for the national party are gains for the President.

The strong Presidency will depend upon the Chief Executive's capacity to control and direct the vast bureaucracy of national administration. Ideally, the President should possess administrative powers comparable to those of business executives and the heads of other governments. What the President needs most can be simply formulated: a power over personnel policy, planning, accounting, and the administration of the executive branch that approaches his powers over the executive budget.

In the ultimate analysis the strong Presidency depends upon the quality of the man himself: upon his ability to rally the public behind great goals and upon his judgment, capacity for decision, imagination, initiative, and a score of other characteristics that blend to form the human paragon that the office demands. If a President falls short of some of these uncommon qualities, we may look to his counselors and helpers to prop him up. The President and the American political system must provide conditions of employment that will attract good and wise men to toil along with the President.

For the Presidency to be conducted with competence, wisdom, and strength requires support from many places. It is a struggle that must be waged on many fronts and toward a goal that can never be lastingly won. We can have the kind of Presidency that the nature of this age seems to require only if, and only so long as, the American people are resolved that we shall have it. History has never been inclined to give a people a better government than it wants.

Notes

Presidents of the United States

Constitutional Provisions
Relating to the Presidency

Sources

Index

Notes

Chapter 1 / *Perspectives on Presidential Power*

1 New York *Times*, February 3, 1967.
2 James Reston, "Washington: The President's Prudence on Korea," New York *Times*, January 28, 1968.
3 Tom Wicker, "Two Wars: Can Johnson Win Either?" New York *Times*, September 2, 1965.
4 New York *Times*, August 27, 1967.
5 James MacGregor Burns, *The Deadlock of Democracy* (Englewood Cliffs, N.J.: 1963).
6 New York *Times*, February 3, 1967.
7 Sidney Hyman, "The Qualities that Make a President," *New York Times Magazine*, December 1, 1963, p. 23.
8 William Howard Taft, *Our Chief Magistrate and His Powers* (New York, 1915), pp. 9–10.
9 Woodrow Wilson, *Constitutional Government in the United States* (New York, 1911), pp. 54–55.
10 William Henry Harbaugh, *Power and Responsibility: The Life and Times of Theodore Roosevelt* (New York, 1961), p. 235.
11 Richard E. Neustadt, *Presidential Power* (New York, 1960), pp. 10–12.
12 Wilson, *op. cit.*, p. 59.
13 George Washington to Catherine Macauley Graham, January 9, 1790, J. C. Fitzpatrick, ed., *The Diaries of George Washington*, Vol. 293 (Washington, D.C.: 1931–44), p. 495.
14 Herbert Hoover, *The Memoirs of Herbert Hoover*, Vol. 2 (New York, 1952), p. 293.
15 Neustadt, *op. cit.*, p. 34.
16 Allan Nevins, *Grover Cleveland: A Study in Courage* (New York, 1932), p. 510.
17 *Ibid.*, p. 308.

18   Taft, *op. cit.*, p. 144.

19   Philip Shriver Klein, *President James Buchanan* (University Park, Pa.: 1962), p. 337.

20   Dwight D. Eisenhower, *Mandate for Change* (Garden City, N.Y.: 1963), p. 193.

21   James Bryce, *The American Commonwealth*, Vol. 1 (New York, 1907), p. 58.

22   Taft, *op. cit.*, p. 13.

23   Harbaugh, *op. cit.*, p. 282.

24   In James MacGregor Burns, "The One Test for the Presidency," *New York Times Magazine*, May 1, 1960, p. 102.

25   Theodore Roosevelt, *An Autobiography* (New York, 1920), p. 406.

26   New York *Times*, February 1, 1964.

Chapter 2   /   Creation of the Presidency

1   In Charles C. Thach, *The Creation of the Presidency, Johns Hopkins University Studies in Historical and Political Science*, Ser. 40, No. 4 (Baltimore, 1922), p. 22.

2   Evarts Boutell Greene, *The Provincial Governor in the English Colonies of North America* (New York, 1898).

3   Thach, *op. cit.*, p. 29.

4   *Ibid.*, p. 30.

5   *Ibid.*, pp. 34–40.

6   E. Wilder Spaulding, *His Excellency George Clinton* (New York, 1938), pp. 95–138.

7   George Bancroft, *History of the Formation of the Constitution of the United States of America* (New York, 1885), pp. 326–28.

8   Carl Van Doren, *The Great Rehearsal* (New York, 1948), pp. 88–90, 272–73.

9   *Ibid.*, pp. 91–94.

10   Max Farrand, ed., *The Records of the Federal Convention of 1787*, Vol. 2 (New Haven, Conn.: 1921), p. 135; Max Farrand, *The Framing of the Constitution of the United States* (New Haven, Conn.: 1913), p. 129.

11   Farrand, *Framing the Constitution*, p. 77.

12   Van Doren, *op. cit.*, pp. 59–60.

13   *Ibid.*, p. 145.

14   Farrand, *Records*, Vol. 2, p. 318.

15   *Ibid.*, pp. 59, 100, 105.

16   *Ibid.*, pp. 335, 537.

17   Farrand, *Framing the Constitution*, p. 166.

18   Farrand, *Records*, Vol. 2, pp. 538–39.

19   *Ibid.*, pp. 318, 427, 535.

20   *Ibid.*, p. 318.

21   Van Doren, *op. cit.*, pp. 139–42.

22   *Ibid.*, pp. 292–94.

23   Bancroft, *op. cit.*, p. 208.

24   Douglas Southall Freeman, *Patriot and President*, Vol. 6 of *George Washington* (New York, 1954), p. 117.

25   Thach, *op. cit.*, p. 169.

26   In Leonard D. White, *The Federalists: A Study in Administrative History* (New York, 1948), p. 99.

27   Freeman, *op. cit.*, p. 155.

28   *Ibid.*, pp. 156–57.

29   *Ibid.*, p. 166.
30   *Ibid.*, pp. 191–95.
31   *Ibid.*, p. 252.
32   White, *op. cit.*, p. 103.
33   J. C. Fitzpatrick, ed., *The Diaries of George Washington* (Boston, 1925), Vol. 4, p. 82.
34   Freeman, *op. cit.*, p. 265.
35   John A. Carroll and Mary W. Ashworth, *First in Peace*, Vol. 7 of *George Washington* (New York, 1957), pp. 353–57.
36   Jared Sparks, *The Writings of George Washington* (Boston, 1836), Vol. 10, p. 186.
37   In Freeman, *op. cit.*, p. 226.
38   Carroll and Ashworth, *op. cit.*, p. 154.
39   Freeman, *op. cit.*, p. 209.
40   Carroll and Ashworth, *op. cit.*, p. xxiii.

Chapter 3 / Selection

1   Theodore H. White, *The Making of the President, 1960* (New York, 1961), p. 50.
2   Arthur S. Link, *Wilson: The Road to the White House* (Princeton, N.J.: 1947), p. 405.
3   James A. Farley, *Behind the Ballots* (New York, 1938), p. 101.
4   *Ibid.*, p. 89.
5   Margaret Leech, *In the Days of McKinley* (New York, 1959), pp. 55–57.
6   Malcolm Moos and Stephen Hess, *The Making of Presidential Candidates* (New York, 1960), p. 88.
7   White, *op. cit.*, p. 109.
8   Moos and Hess, *op. cit.*, p. 15.
9   Frank Freidel, *Franklin D. Roosevelt: The Triumph* (Boston, 1956), p. 294.
10   *Ibid.*
11   White, *op. cit.*, pp. 155–57.
12   Theodore H. White, *The Making of the President, 1964* (New York, 1965), p. 202.
13   Freidel, *op. cit.*, pp. 291–93.
14   White, *The Making of the President, 1960,* pp. 158–60.
15   Freidel, *op. cit.*, pp. 308–09.
16   *Ibid.*, pp. 305–06.
17   Link, *op. cit.*, p. 462.
18   White, *The Making of the President, 1960,* pp. 248, 324–25.
19   *Ibid.*, pp. 315, 321–23.
20   *Ibid.*, p. 247.
21   Alfred Steinberg, *The Man from Missouri: The Life and Times of Harry S. Truman* (New York, 1962), pp. 322–24.
22   Leech, *op. cit.*, pp. 83–92.
23   Lucius Wilmerding, Jr., *The Electoral College* (New Brunswick, N.J.: 1958), pp. 46–59.
24   *Ibid.*, pp. 38–42.
25   *Ibid.*, p. xi.
26   *Ibid.*, p. 89.
27   New York *Times,* May 26, 1967.

Chapter 4 / Tenure

1   In Edward S. Corwin, *The President: Office and Powers,* rev. ed. (New York, 1957), p. 35.
2   Richard M. Nixon, *Six Crises* (Garden City, N.Y.: 1962), p. 152.
3   Joseph E. Kallenbach, "Constitutional Limitations on Reeligibility of National and State Executives," *American Political Science Review,* Vol. 46 (June 1952), p. 443.
4   Fred Rodell, *Democracy and the Third Term* (New York, 1940), pp. 13–28.
5   Richard L. Strout, "The Twenty-second Amendment: A Second Look," *New York Times Magazine,* July 28, 1957, p. 5.
6   R. S. Baker, *Woodrow Wilson,* Vol. 6 (Garden City, N.Y.: 1927–39), pp. 438–52.
7   New York *Tribune,* November 5, 1920.
8   New York *Times,* November 7, 1946.
9   New York *Times,* September 13, 1965.
10   Gideon Welles, *Diary of Gideon Welles,* Vol. 3 (Boston, 1911), p. 292.
11   For an account of the Johnson impeachment and its background, see Milton Lomask, *Andrew Johnson: President on Trial* (New York, 1960).
12   *Ibid.,* p. 309.
13   In John F. Kennedy, *Profiles in Courage* (New York, 1955), p. 159.
14   *Ibid.,* pp. 168–69.
15   For extended treatment of disability and succession problems see John D. Feerick, *From Failing Hands: The Story of Presidential Succession* (New York, 1965); Richard Hansen, *The Year We Had No President* (Lincoln, Neb.: 1962); Ruth Silva, *Presidential Succession* (Ann Arbor, Mich.: 1951).
16   Robert G. Caldwell, *James A. Garfield: Party Chieftain* (New York, 1931), pp. 350–52.
17   Theodore Clarke Smith, *The Life and Letters of James Abram Garfield,* Vol. 2 (New Haven, Conn.: 1935), pp. 1194–197.
18   George F. Howe, *Chester A. Arthur: A Quarter-Century of Machine Politics* (New York, 1935), p. 152; David S. Muzzey, *James G. Blaine: A Political Idol of Other Days* (New York, 1934), p. 197.
19   Howe, *op. cit.,* pp. 150–53.
20   *Ibid.,* p. 53.
21   Cary T. Grayson, *Woodrow Wilson: An Intimate Memoir* (New York, 1960), p. 99.
22   Joseph Tumulty, *Woodrow Wilson as I Know Him* (New York, 1921), pp. 446–48.
23   Grayson, *op. cit.,* p. 52.
24   Edith Boling Wilson, *My Memoir* (Indianapolis, Ind.: 1939), pp. 289–90.
25   *Ibid.,* p. 290.
26   Grayson, *op. cit.,* p. 102.
27   Herbert Hoover, *The Ordeal of Woodrow Wilson* (New York, 1958), p. 271.
28   Tumulty, *op. cit.,* p. 443.
29   Hoover, *op. cit.,* p. 275.
30   *Ibid.,* p. 276.
31   Joseph E. Kallenbach, "The New Presidential Succession Act," *American Political Science Review,* Vol. 41 (October 1947), pp. 931–37.
32   David Lawrence, *The True Story of Woodrow Wilson* (New York, 1924), p. 305.
33   See Sherman Adams, *First-Hand Report* (New York, 1961), pp. 181–87; Nixon, *op. cit.,* pp. 144–51.

34   Nixon, *op. cit.*, p. 149.
35   U.S. Senate Subcommittee on Constitutional Amendments, Judiciary Committee, *Hearings,* 88th Congress, 2nd Session (Washington, D.C.: 1964), p. 22.
36   In Clinton Rossiter, *The American Presidency, rev.* ed. (New York, 1960), p. 214.
37   Nixon, *op. cit.*, p. 168.
38   *Ibid.*, p. 179.
39   *Hearings, op. cit.*, p. 14.
40   New York *Times*, February 11, 1967.
41   New York *Herald Tribune,* June 9, 1964.
42   Louis W. Koenig, *The Truman Administration* (New York, 1956), p. 43.
43   Laurin L. Henry, *Presidential Transitions* (Washington, D.C.: 1960), pp. 474–76.
44   *Ibid.*, pp. 484–86.
45   David T. Stanley, *Changing Administrations* (Washington, D.C.: 1965), p. 6.
46   New York *Times*, January 4, 1961.
47   Henry, *op. cit.*, pp. 466, 504.

Chapter 5   /   Party Chief

1   In Clinton Rossiter, *Parties and Politics in America* (Ithaca, N.Y.: 1960), p. 15.
2   In James A. Farley, *Behind the Ballots* (New York, 1938), p. 293.
3   Allan Nevins, *Grover Cleveland: A Study in Courage* (New York, 1932), p. 401.
4   Sherman Adams, *First-Hand Report* (New York, 1961), p. 167.
5   *Ibid.*
6   In George F. Howe, *Chester A. Arthur: A Quarter-Century of Machine Politics* (New York, 1957), p. 254.
7   *Ibid.*, pp. 255–64.
8   Cabell Phillips, *The Truman Presidency* (New York, 1966), p. 195.
9   Hugh Bone, *Party Committees and National Politics* (Seattle, 1958), pp. 167–68.
10   Carl R. Fish, *The Civil Service and the Patronage* (Boston, 1904), p. 82.
11   Nevins, *op. cit.*, p. 199.
12   *Ibid.*, p. 386.
13   Farley, *op. cit.*, p. 267.
14   Arthur M. Schlesinger, Jr., *The Politics of Upheaval,* Vol. 3 of *The Age of Roosevelt* (Boston, 1960), p. 419.
15   Bone, *op. cit.*, p. 169.
16   *Ibid.*, p. 219.
17   In Nathan Schachner, *Thomas Jefferson: A Biography* (New York, 1951), p. 703.
18   *Ibid.*, p. 704.
19   *Ibid.*, pp. 709, 810.
20   William Cabell Bruce, *John Randolph of Roanoke* (New York, 1922), p. 265.
21   Bennett Champ Clark, *John Quincy Adams* (Boston, 1932), pp. 242–46.
22   *Ibid.*, pp. 252–53.
23   Oliver Perry Chitwood, *John Tyler: Champion of the Old South* (New York, 1939), p. 217.
24   *Ibid.*, p. 317.
25   *Ibid.*
26   *Ibid.*
27   Farley, *op. cit.*, p. 231.

28   James A. Farley, *Jim Farley's Story* (New York, 1948), pp. 59–62.
29   *Ibid.*
30   *Ibid.*, p. 96.
31   *Ibid.*, pp. 122–33.
32   *Ibid.*, p. 133.
33   *Ibid.*, p. 144.
34   Schlesinger, *op. cit.*, pp. 409–23.
35   *Ibid.*, pp. 598–99.
36   Adams, *op. cit.*, pp. 25–26.
37   Dwight D. Eisenhower, *Mandate for Change* (New York, 1963), p. 442.
38   Adams, *op. cit.*, p. 21.
39   Eisenhower, *op. cit.*, p. 431.
40   Robert J. Donovan, *Eisenhower: The Inside Story* (New York, 1956), p. 272.
41   Adams, *op. cit.*, p. 166.
42   *Ibid.*, p. 287.
43   New York *Times*, May 1, 1963.
44   New York *Times*, January 30, 1961.
45   New York *Times*, July 26, 1962.
46   *Ibid.*
47   *Christian Science Monitor*, February 14, 1963.
48   New York *Times*, December 26, 1966.
49   New York *Times*, April 3, 1966.
50   New York *Times*, June 8, 1967; London *Economist*, July 30, 1967.
51   See Arthur N. Holcombe, *The New Party Politics* (New York, 1933).

Chapter 6 / Legislative Leader

1   Douglas Southall Freeman, *Patriot and President*, Vol. 6 of *George Washington* (New York, 1954), pp. 162–63.
2   Dwight D. Eisenhower, *Mandate for Change* (Garden City, N.Y.: 1963), p. 502.
3   *Ibid.*, pp. 194–95.
4   *Congressional Quarterly Almanac, 1965*, Vol. 21 (Washington, D.C.: 1966), p. 67.
5   In Ralph K. Huitt, "Democratic Party Leadership in the Senate," *American Political Science Review*, Vol. 55 (June 1961), p. 353.
6   See Joseph S. Clark, *The Senate Establishment* (New York, 1963).
7   *Ibid.*, p. 58.
8   See *Congressional Quarterly Weekly Reports*, January 11, 1963, pp. 31–32.
9   *Congressional Quarterly Weekly Reports*, January 4, 1963.
10   New York *Times*, November 11, 1963.
11   New York *Times*, March 28, 1964.
12   See Richard E. Neustadt, "Presidency and Legislation: Planning the President's Program," *American Political Science Review*, Vol. 49 (December 1955), p. 980.
13   Robert Donovan, *Eisenhower: The Inside Story* (New York, 1956), p. 83.
14   New York *Times*, January 11, 1967.
15   Sherman Adams, *First-Hand Report* (New York, 1961), pp. 25–26.
16   Huitt, *op. cit.*, p. 353.
17   Louis W. Koenig, *The Truman Administration* (New York, 1956), pp. 240–46.
18   Arthur S. Link, *Wilson: The New Freedom* (Princeton, N.J.: 1956), pp. 146–49.

19 *Ibid.*, p. 151; Arthur W. Macmahon, "Woodrow Wilson as Legislative Leader and Administrator," *American Political Science Review,* Vol. 50 (September 1956), p. 656.

20 In Tom Wicker, "The Johnson Way with Congress," *New York Times Magazine,* March 8, 1964, p. 103.

21 See Marshall E. Dimock, "Wilson the Domestic Reformer," *Virginia Quarterly Review,* Vol. 32 (Autumn 1956), pp. 549–50.

22 Helen Fuller, *Year of Trial: Kennedy's Crucial Decisions* (New York, 1962), pp. 255–57.

23 *Ibid.*, p. 97.

24 Koenig, *op. cit.*, pp. 246–47.

25 Neustadt, *op. cit.*, p. 980.

26 New York *Times*, May 15, 1966.

27 Koenig, *op. cit.*, pp. 148–76.

28 Link, *op. cit.*, pp. 146–57.

29 Macmahon, *op. cit.*, pp. 651–56.

30 New York *Times*, July 12, 1965.

31 *Ibid.*

32 *Ibid.*

33 In James MacGregor Burns, "The One Test for the Presidency," *New York Times Magazine,* May 1, 1960, p. 102.

34 Eisenhower, *op. cit.*, p. 286.

35 Adams, *op. cit.*, pp. 25–27.

36 *Ibid.*, p. 9.

37 New York *Times*, March 23, 1966.

38 News conference, New York *Times*, November 14, 1966.

39 Macmahon, *op. cit.*, pp. 652–56.

40 See Edward S. Corwin, *The President: Office and Powers,* rev. ed. (New York, 1957), pp. 250–52.

41 Philip S. Klein, *President James Buchanan* (University Park, Pa.: 1962), pp. 396–97.

42 Koenig, *op. cit.*, pp. 139–40.

Chapter 7 / Administrative Chief

1 Leonard White, *The Jacksonians: A Study in Administrative History, 1829–1861* (New York, 1954), pp. 69–70.

2 William Hillman, *Mr. President* (New York, 1952), p. 14.

3 Lecture, "Training for the Presidency," delivered at New York University, May 2, 1957.

4 White, *op. cit.*, p. 141.

5 President's Commission on National Goals, *Goals for Americans* (New York, 1960), p. 294.

6 White, *op. cit.*, p. 83.

7 Richard F. Fenno, Jr., *The President's Cabinet* (New York, 1959), p. 5.

8 White, *op. cit.*, p. 83.

9 Francis Biddle, *In Brief Authority* (Garden City, N.Y.: 1962), p. 182.

10 In Louis W. Koenig, *The Invisible Presidency* (New York, 1960), p. 308.

11 New York *Times*, December 21, 1940.

12 See Harold L. Ickes, *The First Thousand Days*, Vol. 1 of *The Secret Diary of Harold L. Ickes* (New York, 1954), p. 111.

13 *Ibid.*, p. 147.

14 Rexford G. Tugwell, *The Democratic Roosevelt* (Garden City, N.Y.: 1957), p. 14.

15 Dwight D. Eisenhower, *Mandate for Change* (Garden City, N.Y.: 1963), p. 87.

16 *Ibid.*, p. 135.

17 Sherman Adams, *First-Hand Report* (New York, 1961), p. 51.

18 Koenig, *op. cit.*, p. 338.

19 *Ibid.*, p. 340.

20 Ezra Taft Benson, *Cross Fire: The Eight Years with Eisenhower* (Garden City, N.Y.: 1962), pp. 386–89.

21 See Aaron Wildavsky, *Dixon-Yates: A Study in Power Politics* (New Haven, Conn.: 1962).

22 Joseph Kraft, "Kennedy's Working Staff," *Harper's Magazine*, Vol. 225 (December 1962), p. 35.

23 U.S. Senate Subcommittee on National Security Staffing and Operations, Committee on Government Operations, *Administration of National Security: Basic Issues* (Washington, D.C.: 1963), p. 8.

24 *Christian Science Monitor*, January 12, 1963.

25 Kraft, *op. cit.*, p. 33.

26 U.S. Senate Subcommittee on National Security Staffing, *op. cit.*, p. 6.

27 New York *Times*, June 19, 1962.

28 Kraft, *op. cit.*, p. 33.

29 *Ibid.*, p. 31.

30 *Ibid.*, p. 36.

31 See Charles Roberts, *L.B.J.'s Inner Circle* (New York, 1965), and Joseph Kraft, *op. cit.*, p. 32.

Chapter 8   /   Public Leader

1 The leading general work is Elmer E. Cornwell, Jr., *Presidential Leadership of Public Opinion* (Bloomington, Ind.: 1964).

2 James E. Pollard, *The Presidents and the Press* (New York, 1947), p. 37.

3 See H. C. F. Bell, *Woodrow Wilson and the People* (Garden City, N.Y.: 1945), p. 239.

4 *Ibid.*, p. 113.

5 See Carl J. Friedrich, "Political Leadership and the Problem of Charismatic Power," *Journal of Politics*, Vol. 23 (February 1961), pp. 21–23.

6 Rexford G. Tugwell, *The Democratic Roosevelt* (Garden City, N.Y.: 1957), p. 352.

7 Pollard, *op. cit.*, pp. 557, 796.

8 William Hillman, *Mr. President* (New York, 1952), p. 141.

9 Douglas Southall Freeman, *Patriot and President*, Vol. 6 of *George Washington* (New York, 1954), p. 307.

10 July 20, 1791, J. C. Fitzpatrick, ed., *The Writings of George Washington*, Vol. 21 (Washington, D.C.: 1931–44), p. 317.

11 In Cornwell, *op. cit.*, p. 261.

12 Woodrow Wilson, *Constitutional Government* (New York, 1908), p. 73.

13 See Thomas A. Bailey, *Woodrow Wilson and the Great Betrayal* (New York, 1945).

14 *Ibid.,* p. 29.

15 Frank Luther Mott, *American Journalism,* rev. ed. (New York, 1950), p. 795.

16 U.S. Information Agency, *Cuba Crisis 1962: USA in Action* (Washington, D.C.: 1962), pp. 3–7.

17 Marian Irish, "The Organization Man in the Presidency," *Journal of Politics,* Vol. 20 (May 1958), pp. 262–65.

18 Edward L. Bernays, *Crystallizing Public Opinion* (New York, 1923), pp. 56–57.

19 Irish, *op. cit.,* p. 261.

20 *Newsweek,* Vol. 48 (August 6, 1956), pp. 23–24.

21 See James Deakin, "Hagerty: Voice Behind the Throne," *New Republic,* Vol. 135 (August 27, 1956), pp. 7–9.

22 Pollard, *op. cit.,* pp. 639–40.

23 Leo Rosten, *The Washington Correspondents* (New York, 1937), p. 47.

24 See Cornwell, *op. cit.,* pp. 189–90.

25 New York *Times,* April 28, 1965.

26 New York *Times,* February 28, 1966.

27 New York *Times,* April 20, 1967.

28 Arthur Krock, "Mr. Kennedy's Management of the News," *Fortune,* Vol. 67 (March 1963), p. 82.

29 *Ibid.*

30 New York *Times,* October 31, 1962.

31 James Daniel and John G. Hubbell, *Strike in the West* (New York, 1963), pp. 70–71.

32 George F. Howe, *Chester A. Arthur: A Quarter-Century of Machine Politics* (New York, 1934), p. 173.

33 Ida M. Tarbell, *All in the Day's Work* (New York, 1939), p. 251.

34 Pollard, *op. cit.,* p. 218.

35 Charles Willis Thompson, *Presidents I've Known and Two Near Presidents* (Indianapolis, 1929), p. 122.

36 Pollard, *op. cit.,* p. 376.

37 *Newsday,* September 17, 1965.

38 Reston, *The Artillery of the Press* (New York, 1967), pp. 53–54.

39 *Ibid.,* p. 54.

40 *Ibid.,* p. 55.

41 *Ibid.*

42 New York *Times,* April 21, 1967.

43 See Reston, *op. cit.,* pp. 20–21.

44 James G. Randall and Richard N. Current, *Lincoln the President: Last Full Measure* (New York, 1955), pp. 42–44.

45 News conference, New York *Times,* November 14, 1966.

Chapter 9   /   Chief Diplomat

1 In Clinton Rossiter, *The American Presidency,* rev. ed. (New York, 1960), p. 10.

2 *Ibid.*

3 See Eleanor Lansing Dulles, *John Foster Dulles: The Last Year* (New York, 1963), p. 31.

4   For comprehensive treatment see Sidney Warren, *The President as World Leader* (Philadelphia, 1964).

5   See Louis W. Koenig, *The Invisible Presidency* (New York, 1960), p. 14.

6   New York *Times*, September 12, 1963.

7   Arthur H. Vandenberg, *The Private Papers of Senator Vandenberg* (Boston, 1952), pp. 58, 95.

8   See Alan F. Westin, *The Uses of Power* (New York, 1962), pp. 97–99.

9   Sherman Adams, *First-Hand Report* (New York, 1961), pp. 93–94.

10 For extended discussion see *Congressional Quarterly Guide to American Government* (Washington, D.C.: Autumn 1966), pp. 4–5.

11 In James Grafton Rogers, *World Policing and the Constitution* (Boston, 1945), p. 36.

12 For the resolution's text see Dwight D. Eisenhower, *Mandate for Change* (Garden City, N.Y.: 1963), p. 459.

13 *Ibid.*, pp. 129–30.

14 *Ibid.*, p. 271.

15 New York *Times*, March 2, 1967.

16 New York *Times*, February 18, 1966.

17 New York *Times*, April 20, 1963.

18 Helen Fuller, *Year of Trial: Kennedy's Crucial Decisions* (New York, 1962), pp. 255–56.

19 *Ibid.*, p. 266.

20 In Dulles, *op. cit.*, p. 31.

21 Adams, *op. cit.*, pp. 89–90.

22 *Ibid.*

23 See John Robinson Beal, *John Foster Dulles* (New York, 1957), and Dulles, *op. cit.*

24 In Commission on Organization of the Executive Branch of the Government, *Task Force Report on Foreign Affairs* (Washington, D.C.: 1949), p. 83.

25 *Ibid.*, p. 80.

26 Harry S. Truman, *Year of Decisions*, Vol. 1 of *Memoirs* (Garden City, N.Y.: 1955), pp. 22–23.

27 Dean Acheson, *A Citizen Looks at Congress* (New York, 1956), p. 65.

28 New York *Times*, February 20, 1967.

29 Beal, *op. cit.*, p. 279.

30 New York *Times*, May 21, 1961.

31 New York *Times*, March 5, 1966.

32 Koenig, *op. cit.*, pp. 299–337.

33 New York *Times*, September 4, 1963.

34 New York *Times*, September 17, 1962.

35 Adams, *op. cit.*, p. 101.

36 *Ibid.*

37 Truman, *op. cit.*, p. 242.

38 Fuller, *op. cit.*, p. 236.

39 Truman, *op. cit.*, p. 369.

40 James F. Byrnes, *All in One Lifetime* (New York, 1958), p. 256.

41 U.S. Senate Foreign Relations Committee, *Hearings: Events Incident to the Summit Conference*, May 27 and June 1 and 2 (Washington, D.C.: 1960), p. 232.

42 Truman, *op. cit.*, pp. 411–12, 552.

43 New York *Times*, June 27, 1963.

44 Adams, *op. cit.*, p. 267.

45 *Ibid.*, p. 256.
46 Beal, *op. cit.*, p. 279.
47 New York *Times*, February 11, 1962.
48 New York *Times*, September 21, 1963.
49 New York *Times*, October 23, 1967.

Chapter 10 / Commander-in-Chief

1   Matthew B. Ridgway, *Soldier: The Memoirs of Matthew B. Ridgway* (New York, 1956), p. 191.
2   *Ibid.*, p. 303.
3   *Ibid.*, pp. 288–89.
4   New York *Times*, July 24, 1962.
5   New York *Herald Tribune*, May 8, 1963.
6   Allan Nevins, *The War for the Union* (New York, 1960), pp. 133–59.
7   *Ibid.*, p. 330.
8   Harry S. Truman, *Years of Trial and Hope*, Vol. 2 of *Memoirs* (Garden City, N.Y.: 1956), p. 354.
9   *Ibid.*, pp. 365–83.
10 *Ibid.*, pp. 384–85.
11 *Ibid.*, p. 445; Richard H. Rovere and Arthur M. Schlesinger, Jr., *The General and the President* (New York, 1951), p. 169.
12 Truman, *op. cit.*, p. 356; Walter Millis, *Arms and the State* (New York, 1958), pp. 319–20.
13 Edward S. Corwin, *The President: Office and Powers*, rev. ed. (New York, 1957), pp. 229–32; J. G. Randall, *The President: Midstream* (New York, 1952), pp. 152–53.
14 New York *Times*, March 9, 1962.
15 Randall, *op. cit.*, pp. 132–34.
16 *Ibid.*, p. 168.
17 New York *Times*, June 15, 1965.
18 Dwight D. Eisenhower, *Mandate for Change* (Garden City, N.Y.: 1963), p. 168.
19 See New York *Times*, April 16, 1963.
20 New York *Times*, December 6, 1962.
21 New York *Times*, April 16, 1963.
22 New York *Times*, April 7, 1963.
23 New York *Times*, August 15, 1963.
24 New York *Times*, May 2, 1963.
25 Eisenhower, *op. cit.*, p. 181.
26 New York *Times*, November 30, 1962.
27 See Peter Wyden, "The Chances of Accidental War," *Saturday Evening Post*, Vol. 234 (June 3, 1961), p. 58.
28 New York *Times*, March 29, 1967.
29 New York *Times*, July 6, 1962.
30 New York *Times*, December 10, 1966.
31 Robert Gilpin, *American Scientists and Nuclear Weapons Policy* (Princeton, N.J.: 1962), p. 132.
32 New York *Times*, December 3, 1963.
33 Gilpin, *op. cit.*, pp. 174–264.
34 C. P. Snow, *Science and Government* (Cambridge, Mass.: 1961), p. 1.
35 New York *Times*, January 27, 1964.

Chapter 11 / The Economy

1   Frances Perkins, *The Roosevelt I Knew* (New York, 1946), p. 330.
2   Arthur M. Schlesinger, Jr., *The Coming of the New Deal*, Vol. 2 of *The Age of Roosevelt* (Boston, 1959), p. 567.
3   *Ibid.*, pp. 425, 431.
4   Samuel Eliot Morison and Henry Steele Commager, *The Growth of the American Republic*, Vol. 2, 3rd ed. (New York, 1942), p. 532.
5   Arthur S. Link, *Woodrow Wilson and the Progressive Era* (New York, 1954), p. 236.
6   Robert H. Wiebe, *Businessmen and Reform: A Study of the Progressive Movement* (Cambridge, Mass.: 1962), pp. 45–47.
7   Allan Nevins, *Study in Power: John D. Rockefeller*, Vol. 2 (New York, 1953), p. 363.
8   Edward S. Corwin, *The President: Office and Powers*, 3rd ed. (New York, 1948), pp. 453–54.
9   See Grant McConnell, *Steel and the Presidency, 1962* (New York, 1963).
10   New York *Times*, November 11, 1965.
11   New York *Times*, January 27, 1967.
12   George E. Mowry, *The Era of Theodore Roosevelt, 1900–1912* (New York, 1958), p. 178.
13   Robert Donovan, *Eisenhower: The Inside Story* (New York, 1956), pp. 35, 171.
14   John D. Hicks, *Republican Ascendancy* (New York, 1960), pp. 81, 84.
15   Mowry, *op. cit.*, p. 173.
16   Matthew Josephson, *Sidney Hillman: Statesman of American Labor* (Garden City, N.Y.: 1952), p. 431.
17   *Ibid.*, p. 404.
18   Saul Alinsky, *John L. Lewis: An Unauthorized Biography* (New York, 1949), p. 165.
19   Josephson, *op. cit.*, p. 474.
20   Alinsky, *op. cit.*, p. 189.
21   New York *Times*, February 28, 1961.
22   New York *Times*, May 13, 1965.
23   New York *Times*, March 23, 1964.
24   New York *Times*, February 26, 1967.
25   Alinsky, *op. cit.*, p. 162.
26   Josephson, *op. cit.*, p. 447.
27   New York *Times*, March 16, 1966.
28   James Tracy Crown, "Organized Labor in American Politics: A Look Ahead," *Proceedings of the Fourteenth Annual New York University Conference on Labor* (New York, 1961), p. 261.
29   New York *Times*, December 8, 1961.
30   Josephson, *op. cit.*, p. 618.
31   Crown, *op. cit.*, p. 265.
32   Josephson, *op. cit.*, p. 399.
33   John M. Blum, *The Republican Roosevelt* (Cambridge, Mass.: 1961), p. 59.
34   Perkins, *op. cit.*, pp. 324–26.
35   New York *Times*, June 15, 1962.
36   New York *Times*, August 29, 1962.

Chapter 12   /   Social Justice

1   Louis W. Koenig, *The Invisible Presidency* (New York, 1960), p. 215.
2   John M. Blum, *The Republican Roosevelt* (Cambridge, Mass.: 1961), p. 60.
3   Rexford G. Tugwell, *The Democratic Roosevelt* (Garden City, N.Y.: 1957), p. 153.
4   *Ibid.*, p. 54.
5   *Ibid.*, pp. 153, 215.
6   Blum, *op. cit.*, p. 107.
7   Tugwell, *op. cit.*, p. 151.
8   *Ibid.*, p. 231.
9   George E. Mowry, *The Era of Theodore Roosevelt, 1900–1912* (New York, 1958), p. xii.
10 Henry F. Pringle, *Theodore Roosevelt* (New York, 1931), p. 427.
11 Arthur M. Schlesinger, Jr., *The Politics of Upheaval*, Vol. 3 of *The Age of Roosevelt* (Boston, 1960), p. 29.
12 Arthur M. Schlesinger, Jr., *The Coming of the New Deal*, Vol. 2 of *The Age of Roosevelt* (Boston, 1959), p. 322.
13 Frances Perkins, *The Roosevelt I Knew* (New York, 1946), p. 299.
14 Arthur S. Link, *Woodrow Wilson and the Progressive Era* (New York, 1954), p. 20.
15 See Edwin E. Witte, *The Development of the Social Security Act* (Madison, Wis.: 1962).
16 *Ibid.*, p. 45.
17 Koenig, *op. cit.*, p. 260.
18 *Ibid.*, p. 261.
19 Link, *op. cit.*, pp. 74, 77.
20 Perkins, *op. cit.*, p. 197.
21 Schlesinger, *The Politics of Upheaval*, p. 428.
22 New York *Times*, October 1, 1962.
23 New York *Times*, June 12, 1963.
24 New York *Times*, October 1, 1962.
25 New York *Times*, June 5, 1965.
26 New York *Times*, August 20, 1967.
27 New York *Times*, August 21, 1967.
28 New York *Times*, August 20, 1967.

Chapter 13   /   Political Personality

1   For extended studies of Presidential and related personalities see Alexander L. George and Juliette L. George, *Woodrow Wilson and Colonel House: A Personality Study* (New York, 1956); Erwin C. Hargrove, *Presidential Leadership: Personality and Political Style* (New York, 1966); Arnold Rogow, *James Forrestal* (New York, 1964).
2   Hargrove, *op. cit.*, pp. 12–13.
3   George and George, *op. cit.*, *passim.*
4   Gordon W. Allport, *Personality: A Psychological Interpretation* (New York, 1937), p. 229. See also his *The Nature of Personality: Selected Papers* (Cambridge, Mass.: 1950).

5 Alfred Steinberg, *The Man from Missouri: The Life and Times of Harry S. Truman* (New York, 1962), p. 238.

6 William B. Hesseltine, *Ulysses S. Grant, Politician* (New York, 1935), p. 392.

7 Robert W. Winston, *Andrew Johnson: Plebian and Patriot* (New York, 1928), p. 373.

8 Marquis Childs, *Eisenhower: Captive Hero* (New York, 1958), p. 245.

9 *Ibid.*, p. 247.

10 Emmet John Hughes, *The Ordeal of Power* (New York, 1963), pp. 268–69.

11 Winston, *op. cit.*, p. 342.

12 John S. Bassett, *The Life of Andrew Jackson* (New York, 1925), pp. 448, 486–89.

13 Childs, *op. cit.*, p. 163.

14 *Ibid.*, p. 176.

15 Allan Nevins, *Grover Cleveland: A Study in Courage* (New York, 1932), pp. 214–15.

16 Philip S. Klein, *President James Buchanan* (University Park, Pa.: 1962), p. 331.

17 Arthur M. Schlesinger, Jr., *The Coming of the New Deal*, Vol. 2 of *The Age of Roosevelt* (Boston, 1959), p. 585.

18 James MacGregor Burns, "The Four Kennedys of the First Year," *New York Times Magazine,* January 14, 1962, p. 72.

19 Nevins, *op. cit.*, pp. 631–33, 640.

20 *Ibid.*, pp. 214–15.

21 Burns, *op. cit.*, p. 70.

22 Steinberg, *op. cit.*, p. 250.

23 Harold D. Laswell, *Power and Personality* (New York, 1948), p. 203.

24 *Ibid.*

25 Nevins, *op. cit.*, p. 206.

26 *Ibid.*, pp. 765–66.

27 *Ibid.*, p. 675.

28 Klein, *op. cit.*, p. 285.

29 Schlesinger, *The Coming of the New Deal*, p. 575.

30 Arthur M. Schlesinger, Jr., *A Thousand Days: John F. Kennedy in the White House* (Boston, 1965), p. 674.

31 In Max Frankel, "Why the Gap Between L.B.J. and the Nation," *New York Times Magazine,* January 7, 1968, p. 37.

32 Bassett, *op. cit.*, p. 702.

33 Hesseltine, *op. cit.*, pp. 315–16.

34 Frankel, *loc. cit.*

35 Steinberg, *op. cit.*, p. 256.

36 Childs, *op. cit.*, p. 4.

37 Winston, *op. cit.*, pp. 329–30.

Chapter 14 / Decision-Making

1 Interview televised, December 17, 1962.

2 Roy F. Nichols, *Franklin Pierce: Young Hickory from the Granite Hills* (Philadelphia, 1931), p. 251.

3 William Allen White, *A Puritan in Babylon* (New York, 1938), p. 260.

4 William P. Cresson, *James Monroe* (Chapel Hill, N.C.: 1946), p. 346.

5 Telecast interview, December 17, 1962.

6   Margaret Leech, *In the Days of McKinley* (New York, 1959), p. 176.
7   John Hope Franklin, *The Emancipation Proclamation* (Garden City, N.Y.: 1963), p. 26.
8   Harry S. Truman, *Years of Trial and Hope*, Vol. 2 of *Memoirs* (Garden City, N.Y.: 1956), pp. 332–35.
9   Cresson, *op. cit.*, pp. 449–50.
10 Joseph Alsop and Turner Catledge, *The 168 Days* (Garden City, N.Y.: 1938), pp. 33–35.
11 Cresson, *op. cit.*, pp. 185–86.
12 Albert L. Warner, "How the Korea Decision Was Made," *Harper's Magazine*, Vol. 202 (June 1951), p. 99; Richard C. Snyder and Glenn D. Paige, "The United States Decision to Resist Aggression in Korea," *Administrative Science Quarterly*, Vol. 3 (December 1958), p. 348.
13 Truman, *op. cit.*, pp. 185–86.
14 Hans J. Morgenthau, "The Trouble with Kennedy," *Commentary*, Vol. 33 (January 1962), p. 51.
15 *Newsweek*, Vol. 66 (August 2, 1965), p. 15.
16 White, *op. cit.*, pp. 267–69.
17 Sherman Adams, *First-Hand Report* (New York, 1961), p. 252.
18 Arthur M. Schlesinger, Jr., *The Coming of the New Deal*, Vol. 2 of *The Age of Roosevelt* (Boston, 1959), pp. 528–31.
19 Rexford G. Tugwell, *The Democratic Roosevelt* (Garden City, N.Y.: 1957), p. 546.
20 Schlesinger, *op. cit.*, p. 531.
21 Emmet John Hughes, *The Ordeal of Power* (New York, 1963), pp. 25–27.
22 New York *Times*, July 4, 1957.
23 New York *Times*, July 8, 1957.
24 Sidney Hyman, "The Testing of Kennedy," *New Republic*, Vol. 145 (October 2, 1961), p. 24.
25 Franklin, *op. cit.*, p. 95.
26 *Ibid.*, p. 26.
27 Alsop and Catledge, *op. cit.*, p. 63.
28 Cresson, *op. cit.*, p. 445.
29 Franklin, *op. cit.*, pp. 60–62.
30 Cresson, *op. cit.*, pp. 60–62.
31 Harold L. Ickes, *The Inside Struggle*, Vol. 2 of *The Secret Diary of Harold Ickes* (New York, 1954), p. 339.

Chapter 15   /   Crisis

1   Arthur M. Schlesinger, Jr., *The Coming of the New Deal*, Vol. 2 of *The Age of Roosevelt* (Boston, 1959), p. 15.
2   *Ibid.*
3   New York *Times*, February 16, 1964.
4   Lindsay Rogers, *Crisis Government* (New York, 1934), p. 17.
5   Schlesinger, *op. cit.*, p. 22.
6   *Ibid.*
7   Herbert Hoover, *The Great Depression, 1929–1941*, Vol. 3 of *The Memoirs of Herbert Hoover* (New York, 1952), pp. 2–29.
8   Schlesinger, *op. cit.*, p. 263.

9   Harris Gaylord Warren, *Herbert Hoover and the Great Depression* (New York, 1959), pp. 9–18; Arthur M. Schlesinger, Jr., *The Crisis of the Old Order*, Vol. 1 of *The Age of Roosevelt* (Boston, 1957), pp. 1252–254.

10 Schlesinger, *The Crisis of the Old Order*, p. 82.

11 Warren, *op. cit.*, p. 52.

12 William Starr Myers and Walter H. Newton, *The Hoover Administration* (New York, 1936), pp. 65, 137, 174.

13 *Ibid.*, pp. 35, 199, 354.

14 Warren, *op. cit.*, pp. 142–46, 202–06.

15 *Ibid.*, p. 146.

16 Theodore G. Joslin, *Hoover off the Record* (Garden City, N.Y.: 1934), pp. 5, 14, 77; Warren, *op. cit.*, p. 131; Henry L. Stimson and McGeorge Bundy, *On Active Service in Peace and War* (New York, 1947), p. 161.

17 Joslin, *op. cit.*, p. 18.

18 Schlesinger, *The Crisis of the Old Order*, pp. 184–89; Dixon Wecter, *The Age of the Great Depression* (New York, 1948), p. 46; John Kenneth Galbraith, *The Great Crash, 1929* (Boston, 1954), pp. 190–91.

19 Schlesinger, *The Coming of the New Deal*, pp. 1–3.

20 *Ibid.*, pp. 9, 16, 20–22, 88–94, 319–20.

21 *Ibid.*, pp. 301–02, 440–56; Wecter, *op. cit.*, pp. 70–77.

22 James MacGregor Burns, *Roosevelt: The Lion and the Fox* (New York, 1956), p. 187.

23 Schlesinger, *The Crisis of the Old Order*, p. 482.

24 Burns, *op. cit.*, p. 173.

25 *Ibid.*, pp. 178–80; Schlesinger, *The Coming of the New Deal*, pp. 16–18.

26 Wecter, *op. cit.*, p. 67; Burns, *op. cit.*, pp. 166–67, 184–85.

27 Schlesinger, *The Coming of the New Deal*, pp. 12–13; Wecter, *op. cit.*, p. 65.

28 Schlesinger, *The Coming of the New Deal*, pp. 585–86.

29 Allan Nevins, *The Emergence of Lincoln*, Vol. 2 (New York, 1950), p. 340.

30 See Philip Shriver Klein, *President James Buchanan* (University Park, Pa.: 1962).

31 *Ibid.*, pp. 142–43.

32 Nevins, *op. cit.*, pp. 349–50.

33 Klein, *op. cit.*, p. 355.

34 *Ibid.*, p. 359.

35 *Ibid.*, pp. 361–70; Nevins, *op. cit.*, p. 357.

36 Klein, *op. cit.*, pp. 374–78.

37 Nevins, *op. cit.*, p. 367.

38 Kenneth M. Stampp, *And the War Came* (Baton Rouge, La.: 1950), pp. 82–86.

39 *Ibid.*, p. 80; Klein, *op. cit.*, pp. 391–92.

40 Klein, *op. cit.*, pp. 401–02.

41 For discussions of the crisis see Henry M. Pachter, *Collision Course: The Cuban Missile Crisis and Coexistence* (New York, 1963); Elie Abel, *The Missile Crisis* (New York, 1966); James Daniel and John Hubbell, *Strike in the West: The Complete Story of the Cuban Missile Crisis* (New York, 1963); Arthur M. Schlesinger, Jr., *A Thousand Days: John F. Kennedy in the White House* (Boston, 1965); Theodore C. Sorensen, *Kennedy* (New York, 1965); David L. Larson, *The "Cuban Crisis" of 1962: Selected Documents and Chronology* (Boston, 1963).

42 Kenneth Keating, *Cuba Chronology, 1962* (Washington, D.C.: 1962), mimeographed.

43 Daniel and Hubbell, *op. cit.*, p. 88.

44 For Bundy's own reasons see "Cuba: The Missile Crisis," *NBC White Paper* (NBC broadcast, February 9, 1964), mimeographed transcript, pp. 13–14.

45 Daniel and Hubbell, *op. cit.*, pp. 64–67.

46   For a detailed chronology of the crisis see "The Cuban Crisis: Fourteen Days
      that Shook the World" (New York *Times*, reprint, November 3, 1962), includes
      texts appearing in the *Times*, October 23–November 3, 1962.
47   Daniel and Hubbell, *op. cit.*, pp. 92–93.
48   New York *Times*, October 22, 1962.
49   New York *Times*, October 25, 1962.
50   New York *Times*, October 27, 1962.
51   Daniel and Hubbell, *op. cit.*, pp. 95–125.
52   New York *Times*, April 26, 1963.
53   New York *Times*, October 28, 1962; Daniel and Hubbell, *op. cit.*, pp. 150–53.
54   Kenneth Keating, news release, January 31, 1963, mimeographed.
55   New York *Times*, November 12, 1966.
56   See comment by Theodore Sorensen, *NBC White Paper, op. cit.*, p. 22.
57   *Ibid.*, p. 36.
58   Theodore Sorensen, *Decision-Making in the White House* (New York, 1963),
      p. 36.
59   Frances Perkins, *The Roosevelt I Knew* (New York, 1946), p. 380.

Chapter 16 / The Presidency Compared

1   Coleman B. Ransone, Jr., *The Office of Governor in the United States* (Univer-
     sity, Ala.: 1956), pp. 116–17.
2   Joseph E. Kallenbach, *The American Chief Executive: The Presidency and the
     Governorship* (New York, 1966), pp. 364–65.
3   See Scott Greer, *Governing the Metropolis* (New York, 1962).
4   Francis Williams, ed., *Twilight of Empire: Memoirs of Prime Minister Clement
     Attlee* (New York, 1962), pp. 223–25.
5   New York *Times*, October 16, 1964.
6   London *Times*, October 22, 1963.
7   Bertram D. Wolfe, *Khrushchev and Stalin's Ghost* (New York, 1957), pp. 22–25.
8   American Political Science Association, Committee on Political Parties, *Toward
     a More Responsible Party System* (New York, 1950).
9   R. T. McKenzie, *British Political Parties* (London, 1955), pp. 297–99.
10   In Samuel H. Beer, *et al.*, *Patterns of Government: The Major Political Systems
     of Europe*, rev. ed. (New York, 1962), pp. 183–84.
11   Don K. Price, "The Parliamentary and Presidential Systems," *Public Administra-
     tion Review*, Vol. 3 (Winter 1941), p. 360.
12   *Ibid.*, p. 322.
13   London *Times*, October 22, 1963.
14   *Ibid.*
15   See Roy C. Macridis and Bernard E. Brown, *The De Gaulle Republic* (Home-
     wood, Ill.: 1960).
16   Milovan Djilas, *The New Class* (New York, 1957), pp. 44–47.
17   Boris Souvarine, *Stalin* (New York, 1939), pp. 407–09.
18   Djilas, *op. cit.*, p. 82.
19   U.S. Senate Subcommittee on National Policy Machinery, Committee on Govern-
     ment Operations, *National Policy Machinery in the Soviet Union*, 86th Con-
     gress, 2nd Session (Washington, D.C.: 1960), pp. 36–42.
20   See Charles O. Porter and Robert J. Alexander, *The Struggle for Democracy
     in Latin America* (New York, 1961).
21   New York *Times*, February 1, 1964.

Presidents of the United States

	PARTY	TERM
1. George Washington (1732–99)	Federalist	1789–1797
2. John Adams (1735–1826)	Federalist	1797–1801
3. Thomas Jefferson (1743–1826)	Democratic-Republican	1801–1809
4. James Madison (1751–1836)	Democratic-Republican	1809–1817
5. James Monroe (1758–1831)	Democratic-Republican	1817–1825
6. John Quincy Adams (1767–1848)	Democratic-Republican	1825–1829
7. Andrew Jackson (1767–1845)	Democratic	1829–1837
8. Martin Van Buren (1782–1862)	Democratic	1837–1841
9. William Henry Harrison (1773–1841)	Whig	1841
10. John Tyler (1790–1862)	Whig	1841–1845
11. James K. Polk (1795–1849)	Democratic	1845–1849
12. Zachary Taylor (1784–1850)	Whig	1849–1850
13. Millard Fillmore (1800–74)	Whig	1850–1853
14. Franklin Pierce (1804–69)	Democratic	1853–1857
15. James Buchanan (1791–1868)	Democratic	1857–1861
16. Abraham Lincoln (1809–65)	Republican	1861–1865

	PARTY	TERM
17. Andrew Johnson (1808–75)	Union	1865–1869
18. Ulysses S. Grant (1822–85)	Republican	1869–1877
19. Rutherford B. Hayes (1822–93)	Republican	1877–1881
20. James A. Garfield (1831–81)	Republican	1881
21. Chester A. Arthur (1830–86)	Republican	1881–1885
22. Grover Cleveland (1837–1908)	Democratic	1885–1889
23. Benjamin Harrison (1833–1901)	Republican	1889–1893
24. Grover Cleveland (1837–1908)	Democratic	1893–1897
25. William McKinley (1843–1901)	Republican	1897–1901
26. Theodore Roosevelt (1858–1919)	Republican	1901–1909
27. William Howard Taft (1857–1930)	Republican	1909–1913
28. Woodrow Wilson (1856–1924)	Democratic	1913–1921
29. Warren G. Harding (1865–1923)	Republican	1921–1923
30. Calvin Coolidge (1872–1933)	Republican	1923–1929
31. Herbert Hoover (1874–1964)	Republican	1929–1933
32. Franklin Delano Roosevelt (1882–1945)	Democratic	1933–1945
33. Harry S. Truman (b. 1884)	Democratic	1945–1953
34. Dwight D. Eisenhower (b. 1890)	Republican	1953–1961
35. John F. Kennedy (1917–63)	Democratic	1961–1963
36. Lyndon B. Johnson (b. 1908)	Democratic	1963–1969
37. Richard M. Nixon	Republican	1969–

Constitutional Provisions Relating to the Presidency

ARTICLE I

SECTION 3

6. The Senate shall have the sole power to try all impeachments. When sitting for that purpose, they shall be on oath or affirmation. When the President of the United States is tried, the Chief Justice shall preside; and no person shall be convicted without the concurrence of two-thirds of the members present.

7. Judgment in cases of impeachment shall not extend further than to removal from office, and disqualification to hold and enjoy any office of honor, trust, or profit under the United States; but the party convicted shall, nevertheless, be liable and subject to indictment, trial, judgment, and punishment, according to law.

SECTION 7

2. Every bill which shall have passed the House of Representatives and the Senate shall, before it becomes a law, be presented to the President of the United States; if he approve he shall sign it, but if not he shall return it, with his objections, to that house in which it shall have originated, who shall enter the objections at large on their journal and proceed to reconsider it. If after such reconsideration two-thirds of that house shall agree to pass the bill, it shall be sent, together with the objections, to the other house, by which it shall likewise be reconsidered, and if approved by two-thirds of that house it shall become a law. But in all such cases the votes of both houses shall be determined by yeas and nays, and the names of the persons voting for and against the bill shall be entered on the journal of each house respectively. If any bill shall not be returned by the President within ten days (Sundays excepted) after it shall have been

presented to him, the same shall be a law, in like manner as if he had signed it unless the Congress by their adjournment prevent its return, in which case it shall not be a law.

3. Every order, resolution, or vote to which the concurrence of the Senate and House of Representatives may be necessary (except on a question of adjournment) shall be presented to the President of the United States; and before the same shall take effect, shall be approved by him, or being disapproved by him, shall be repassed by two-thirds of the Senate and House of Representatives, according to the rules and limitations prescribed in the case of a bill.

ARTICLE II

SECTION 1

1. The executive power shall be vested in a President of the United States of America. He shall hold his office during the term of four years, and, together with the Vice President, chosen for the same term, be elected as follows:

2. Each state shall appoint, in such manner as the legislature thereof may direct, a number of electors, equal to the whole number of Senators and Representatives to which the State may be entitled in the Congress; but no Senator or Representative, or person holding an office of trust or profit under the United States, shall be appointed an elector.

3.* The electors shall meet in their respective states and vote by ballot for two persons, of whom one at least shall not be an inhabitant of the same state with themselves. And they shall make a list of all the persons voted for, and of the number of votes for each; which list they shall sign and certify, and transmit sealed to the seat of the government of the United States, directed to the President of the Senate. The President of the Senate shall, in the presence of the Senate and House of Representatives, open all the certificates, and the votes shall then be counted. The person having the greatest number of votes shall be the President, if such a number be a majority of the whole number of electors appointed; and if there be more than one who have such majority, and have an equal number of votes, then the House of Representatives shall immediately choose by ballot one of them for President; and if no person have a majority, then from the five highest on the list the said House shall in like manner choose the President. But in choosing the President the votes shall be taken by states, the representation from each state having one vote; a quorum for this purpose shall consist of a member or members from two-thirds of the states, and a majority of all the states shall be necessary to a choice. In every case, after the choice of the President, the person having the greatest number of votes of the electors shall be the Vice President. But if there should remain two or more who have equal votes, the Senate shall choose from them by ballot the Vice President.

4. The Congress may determine the time of choosing the electors and the day on which they shall give their votes, which day shall be the same throughout the United States.

5. No person except a natural born citizen, or a citizen of the United States

* This paragraph was superseded by the Twelfth Amendment.

at the time of the adoption of this Constitution, shall be eligible to the office of President; neither shall any person be eligible to that office who shall not have attained to the age of thirty-five years, and been fourteen years a resident within the United States.

6.* In case of the removal of the President from office, or of his death, resignation, or inability to discharge the powers and duties of the said office, the same shall devolve on the Vice President, and the Congress may by law provide for the case of removal, death, resignation, or inability, both of the President and Vice President, declaring what officer shall then act as President, and such officer shall act accordingly until the disability be removed or a President shall be elected.

7. The President shall, at stated times, receive for his services a compensation, which shall neither be increased nor diminished during the period for which he shall have been elected, and he shall not receive within that period any other emolument from the United States or any of them.

8. Before he enter on the execution of his office he shall take the following oath or affirmation:

> I do solemnly swear (or affirm) that I will faithfully execute the office of President of the United States, and will to the best of my ability preserve, protect, and defend the Constitution of the United States.

SECTION 2

1. The President shall be Commander-in-Chief of the Army and Navy of the United States, and of the militia of the several states when called into the actual service of the United States; he may require the opinion, in writing, of the principal officer in each of the executive departments, upon any subject relating to the duties of their respective offices, and he shall have power to grant reprieves and pardons for offenses against the United States, except in cases of impeachment.

2. He shall have power, by and with the advice and consent of the Senate, to make treaties, provided two-thirds of the Senators present concur; and he shall nominate, and, by and with the advice and consent of the Senate, shall appoint ambassadors, other public ministers and consuls, judges of the Supreme Court, and all other officers of the United States, whose appointments are not herein otherwise provided for, and which shall be established by law; but the Congress may by law vest the appointment of such inferior officers, as they think proper, in the President alone, in the courts of law, or in the heads of departments.

3. The President shall have power to fill up all vacancies that may happen during the recess of the Senate, by granting commissions which shall expire at the end of their next session.

SECTION 3

He shall from time to time give to the Congress information of the state of the union, and recommend to their consideration such measures as he shall judge necessary and expedient; he may, on extraordinary occasions, convene both houses, or either of them, and in case of disagreement between them with respect to the

---

* This paragraph was modified by the Twenty-fifth Amendment.

time of adjournment, he may adjourn them to such time as he shall think proper; he shall receive ambassadors and other public ministers; he shall take care that the laws be faithfully executed, and shall commission all the officers of the United States.

SECTION 4

The President, Vice President, and all civil officers of the United States shall be removed from office on impeachment for and conviction of treason, bribery, or other high crimes and misdemeanors.

AMENDMENT XII

The electors shall meet in their respective states and vote by ballot for President and Vice President, one of whom, at least, shall not be an inhabitant of the same state with themselves; they shall name in their ballots the person voted for as President, and in distinct ballots the person voted for as Vice President, and they shall make distinct lists of all persons voted for as President and of all persons voted for as Vice President, and of the number of votes for each; which lists they shall sign and certify, and transmit sealed to the seat of the government of the United States, directed to the President of the Senate. The President of the Senate shall, in the presence of the Senate and House of Representatives, open all the certificates and the votes shall then be counted. The person having the greatest number of votes for President shall be the President, if such number be a majority of the whole number of electors appointed; and if no person have such majority, then from the persons having the highest numbers not exceeding three on the list of those voted for as President, the House of Representatives shall choose immediately, by ballot, the President. But in choosing the President the votes shall be taken by states, the representation from each state having one vote; a quorum for this purpose shall consist of a member or members from two-thirds of the states, and a majority of all states shall be necessary to a choice. And if the House of Representatives shall not choose a President whenever the right of choice shall devolve upon them, before the fourth day of March next following, then the Vice President shall act as President, as in the case of the death or other constitutional disability of the President.

The person having the greatest number of votes as Vice President shall be the Vice President, if such number be a majority of the whole number of electors appointed; and if no person have a majority, then from the two highest numbers on the list the Senate shall choose the Vice President; a quorum for the purpose shall consist of two-thirds of the whole number of Senators, and a majority of the whole number shall be necessary to a choice. But no person constitutionally ineligible to the office of President shall be eligible to that of Vice President of the United States.

AMENDMENT XX

SECTION 1

The terms of the President and Vice President shall end at noon on the 20th day of January, and the terms of Senators and Representatives at noon on the 3rd day of January, of the years in which such terms would have ended if this article had not been ratified; and the terms of their successors shall then begin.

SECTION 2

The Congress shall assemble at least once in every year, and such meeting shall begin at noon on the 3d day of January, unless they shall by law appoint a different day.

SECTION 3

If, at the time fixed for the beginning of the term of the President, the President elect shall have died, the Vice President elect shall become President. If a President shall not have been chosen before the time fixed for the beginning of his term, or if the President elect shall have failed to qualify, then the Vice President elect shall act as President until a President shall have qualified; and the Congress may by law provide for the case wherein neither a President elect nor a Vice President elect shall have qualified, declaring who shall then act as President, or the manner in which one who is to act shall be selected, and such person shall act accordingly until a President or Vice President shall have qualified.

SECTION 4

The Congress may by law provide for the case of the death of any of the persons from whom the House of Representatives may choose a President whenever the right of choice shall have devolved upon them, and for the case of the death of any of the persons from whom the Senate may choose a Vice President whenever the right of choice shall have devolved upon them.

AMENDMENT XXII

No person shall be elected to the office of the President more than twice, and no person who has held the office of President, or acted as President, for more than two years of a term to which some other person was elected President shall be elected to the office of the President more than once. But this article shall not apply to any person holding the office of President when this article was proposed by the Congress, and shall not prevent any person who may be holding the office of President, or acting as President, during the term within which this article becomes operative from holding the office of President or acting as President during the remainder of such term.

AMENDMENT XXV

SECTION 1

In case of the removal of the President from office or of his death or resignation, the Vice President shall become President.

SECTION 2

Whenever there is a vacancy in the office of the Vice President, the President shall nominate a Vice President who shall take office upon confirmation by a majority vote of both Houses of Congress.

SECTION 3

Whenever the President transmits to the President pro tempore of the Senate and the Speaker of the House of Representatives his written declaration that he is unable to discharge the powers and duties of his office, and until he transmits to them a written declaration to the contrary, such powers and duties shall be discharged by the Vice President as Acting President.

SECTION 4

Whenever the Vice President and a majority of either the principal officers of the executive department or of such other body as Congress may by law provide, transmit to the President pro tempore of the Senate and the Speaker of the House of Representatives their written declaration that the President is unable to discharge the powers and duties of his office, the Vice President shall immediately assume the powers and duties of the office as Acting President.

Thereafter, when the President transmits to the President pro tempore of the Senate and the Speaker of the House of Representatives his written declaration that no inability exists, he shall resume the powers and duties of his office unless the Vice President and a majority of either the principal officers of the executive department or of such other body as Congress may by law provide, transmit within four days to the President pro tempore of the Senate and the Speaker of the House of Representatives their written declaration that the President is unable to discharge the powers and duties of his office. Thereupon Congress shall decide the issue, assembling within forty-eight hours for that purpose if not in session. If the Congress, within twenty-one days after receipt of the latter written declaration, or, if Congress is not in session, within twenty-one days after Congress is required to assemble, determines by two-thirds vote of both Houses that the President is unable to discharge the powers and duties of his office, the Vice President shall continue to discharge the same as Acting President; otherwise, the President shall resume the powers and duties of his office.

Sources

GENERAL WORKS ON THE AMERICAN PRESIDENCY

Bailey, Thomas A., *Presidential Greatness* (New York, 1966).*
Binkley, Wilfred, *The Man in the White House* (Baltimore, 1958).*
Brown, Stuart G., *The American Presidency: Leadership, Partisanship, and Popularity* (New York, 1966).*
Brownlow, Louis, *The President and the Presidency* (Chicago, 1949).
Burns, James MacGregor, *Presidential Government* (Boston, 1965).*
Corwin, Edward S., *The President: Office and Powers*, 4th ed. (New York, 1957).*
———, and Louis W. Koenig, *The Presidency Today* (New York, 1956).
Finer, Herman, *The Presidency: Crisis and Regeneration* (Chicago, 1960).
Hargrove, Erwin C., *Presidential Leadership: Personality and Political Style* (New York, 1966).*
Heller, Francis H., *The Presidency: A Modern Perspective* (New York, 1960).*
Herring, E. Pendleton, *Presidential Leadership* (New York, 1940).
Hyman, Sidney, *The American President* (New York, 1954).
Kallenbach, Joseph, *The American Chief Executive* (New York, 1966).
Laski, Harold, *The American Presidency* (New York, 1940).*
McConnell, Grant, *The Modern Presidency* (New York, 1967).*
Milton, George F., *The Use of Presidential Power, 1789–1943* (Boston, 1944).
Neustadt, Richard E., *Presidential Power* (New York, 1960).
Patterson, C. P., *Presidential Government in the United States* (Chapel Hill, N.C.: 1947).
Rienow, Robert, and Leona T. Rienow, *The Lonely Quest: The Evolution of Presidential Leadership* (Chicago, 1966).

* Available in paperback edition.

Rossiter, Clinton, *The American Presidency,* rev. ed. (New York, 1960).*
Stanwood, Edward, *History of the Presidency* (Boston, 1928).
Taft, William H., *Our Chief Magistrate and His Powers* (New York, 1916).
Tugwell, Rexford G., *The Enlargement of the Presidency* (New York, 1960).

SPECIALIZED WORKS

Acheson, Dean, *A Citizen Looks at Congress* (New York, 1956).
Ball, George, *Discipline of Power* (New York, 1968).
Berdahl, C. A., *War Powers of the Executive in the United States* (Urbana, Ill.: 1921).
Binkley, Wilfred, *President and Congress* (New York, 1947).*
Burns, James MacGregor, *The Deadlock of Democracy* (New York, 1963).*
Chamberlain, Lawrence H., *The President, Congress, and Legislation* (New York, 1946).
Cornwell, Elmer E., Jr., *Presidential Leadership of Public Opinion* (Bloomington, Ind.: 1965).
Committee on Government Operations, Subcommittee on National Policy Machinery, *Reports* (Washington, D.C.: 1959 and after).
Commission on Organization of the Executive Branch of the Government (Hoover Commission), *Reports* (Washington, D.C.: 1949 and 1953).
Dangerfield, Royden J., *In Defense of the Senate* (Norman, Okla.: 1933).
David, Paul, Malcolm Moos, and R. M. Goldman, *Presidential Nominating Politics,* 5 vols. (Baltimore, 1954).
Davis, James, *Presidential Primaries: Road to the White House* (New York, 1967).
Feerick, John D., *From Failing Hands: The Story of Presidential Succession* (New York, 1965).
Fenno, Richard F., Jr., *The President's Cabinet* (Cambridge, Mass.: 1959).*
Fersh, Seymour H., *The View from the White House: A Study of the Presidential State of the Union Message* (Washington, D.C.: 1961).
Goebel, Dorothy B., *Generals in the White House* (New York, 1945).
Greene, Evarts B., *The Provincial Governor* (New York, 1898).
Hansen, Richard, *The Year We Had No President* (Lincoln, Neb.: 1962).*
Harris, Joseph P., *The Advice and Consent of the Senate* (Berkeley, Calif.: 1953).
Hart, James, *The American Presidency in Action* (New York, 1948).
Hatch, L. C., and E. L. Shoup, *A History of the Vice Presidency* (New York, 1934).
Heller, Walter W., *New Dimensions of Political Economy* (Cambridge, Mass.: 1966).*
Henry, Laurin L., *Presidential Transitions* (Washington, D.C.: 1960).
Hilsman, Roger, *To Move a Nation: The Politics of Foreign Policy in the Administration of John F. Kennedy* (Garden City, N.Y.: 1967).

* Available in paperback edition.

Hinsdale, Mary L., *A History of the President's Cabinet* (Ann Arbor, Mich.: 1911).

Hobbs, Edward H., *Behind the President: A Study of Executive Office Agencies* (Washington, D.C.: 1954).

Holt, W. Stull, *Treaties Defeated by the Senate* (Baltimore, 1933).

Humbert, W. H., *The Pardoning Power of the President* (Washington, D.C.: 1941).

Koenig, Louis W., *The Invisible Presidency* (New York, 1960).

————, *The Presidency and the Crisis* (New York, 1944).

Learned, H. B., *The President's Cabinet* (New Haven, Conn.: 1912).

Longaker, Richard, *The Presidency and Individual Liberties* (Ithaca, N.Y.: 1961).

McClure, Wallace M., *International Executive Agreements* (New York, 1941).

Marcy, Carl M., *Presidential Commissions* (New York, 1945).

Moos, Malcolm, *Politics, Presidents, and Coattails* (Baltimore, 1950).

Nash, Bradley D., *Staffing the Presidency* (Washington, 1952).

Nourse, Edwin G., *Economics in the Public Service: Administrative Aspects of the Employment Act* (New York, 1953).

Overacker, Louise, *Presidential Campaign Funds* (Boston, 1946).

————, *The Presidential Primary* (New York, 1926).

Pollard, J. E., *The Presidents and the Press* (New York, 1947).

Polsby, Nelson W., and Aaron Wildavsky, *Presidential Elections,* rev. ed. (New York, 1968).

Pomper, Gerald, *Nominating the President* (Evanston, Ill.: 1963).*

President's Committee on Administrative Management (Brownlow Committee), *Report with Special Studies* (Washington, D.C.: 1937).

Randall, James G., *Constitutional Problems Under Lincoln* (New York, 1926).

Remini, Robert V., *Martin Van Buren and the Making of the Democratic Party* (New York, 1959).

Rich, Bennett M., *The Presidents and Civil Disorder* (Washington, D.C.: 1941).

Roseboom, Eugene H., *A History of Presidential Elections,* rev. ed. (New York, 1964).*

Rossiter, Clinton, *The Supreme Court and the Commander-in-Chief* (Ithaca, N.Y.: 1951).

Schlesinger, Arthur M., Jr., and Alfred de Grazie, *Congress and the Presidency* (New York, 1967).

Schubert, Glendon A., Jr., *The Presidency in the Courts* (Minneapolis, 1957).

Silva, Ruth, *Presidential Succession* (Ann Arbor, Mich.: 1951).

Silverman, Corinne, *The President's Economic Advisers* (University, Ala.: 1959).

Small, Norman J., *Some Presidential Interpretations of the Presidency* (Baltimore, 1930).

Somers, Herman M., *Presidential Agency: OWMR* (Cambridge, Mass.: 1954).

Sorensen, Theodore C., *Decision-Making in the White House* (New York, 1963).*

Stanley, David T., *Changing Administrations* (Washington, D.C.: 1965).

Stein, Charles W., *The Third Term Tradition* (New York, 1946).

* Available in paperback edition.

Tugwell, Rexford, G., *How They Became President* (New York, 1965).

Warren, Sidney, *The President as World Leader* (New York, 1964).

Waugh, Edgar W., *Second Consul* (Indianapolis, 1956).

White, Theodore H., *The Making of the President, 1960* (New York, 1961).*

———, *The Making of the President, 1964* (New York, 1965).*

Williams, Irving G., *The Rise of the Vice-Presidency* (Washington, D.C.: 1956).

Wilmerding, Lucius, Jr., *The Electoral College* (New Brunswick, N.J.: 1958).*

Young, Donald, *American Roulette: The History and Dilemma of the Vice Presidency* (New York, 1965).

BIOGRAPHIES, PAPERS, AND MEMOIRS OF PRESIDENTS

Adams, Charles Francis, ed., *Memoirs of John Quincy Adams*, 12 vols. (Philadelphia, 1875).

Bishop, Joseph Bucklin, *Theodore Roosevelt and His Time* (New York, 1920).

Blum, John M., *The Republican Roosevelt* (Cambridge, Mass.: 1954).*

———, *Woodrow Wilson and the Politics of Morality* (Boston, 1956).*

Brant, Irving, *Madison the President* (Indianapolis, 1956).

Brown, Stuart Gerry, *The Autobiography of James Monroe* (Syracuse, 1959).

Burns, James MacGregor, *John Kennedy: A Political Profile* (New York, 1959).*

———, *Roosevelt: The Lion and the Fox* (New York, 1956).*

Caldwell, Robert G., *James A. Garfield: Party Chieftain* (New York, 1931).

Carroll, John A., and Mary W. Ashworth, *First in Peace*, Vol. 7 of *George Washington* (New York, 1957).

Childs, Marquis, *Eisenhower: Captive Hero* (New York, 1958).

Chitwood, Oliver Perry, *John Tyler: Champion of the Old South* (New York, 1930).

Cleveland, Grover, *Presidential Problems* (New York, 1904).

Cresson, William P., *James Monroe* (Chapel Hill, N.C.: 1946).

Donovan, Robert J., *Eisenhower: The Inside Story* (New York, 1956).

Eisenhower, Dwight D., *Mandate for Change* (Garden City, N.Y.: 1963).*

Evans, Rowland, and Robert Novak, *Lyndon B. Johnson: The Exercise of Power* (New York, 1966).

Freeman, Douglas Southall, *Patriot and President*, Vol. 6 of *George Washington* (New York, 1954).

Freidel, Frank, *Franklin D. Roosevelt: The Triumph* (Boston, 1956).

George, Alexander, and Juliette L. George, *Woodrow Wilson and Colonel House: A Personality Study* (New York, 1956).*

Geyelin, Philip L., *Lyndon B. Johnson and the World* (New York, 1966).

Harbaugh, William Henry, *Power and Responsibility: The Life and Times of Theodore Roosevelt* (New York, 1961).*

Hoover, Herbert, *The Memoirs of Herbert Hoover*, 3 vols. (New York, 1951–52).

Howe, George F., *Chester A. Arthur: A Quarter-Century of Machine Politics* (New York, 1935).

* Available in paperback edition.

Hughes, Emmet John, *The Ordeal of Power* (New York, 1963).

James, Marquis, *Andrew Jackson: Portrait of a President* (Indianapolis, 1937).*

Klein, Philip Shriver, *President James Buchanan: A Biography* (University Park, Pa.: 1962).

Leech, Margaret, *In the Days of McKinley* (New York, 1959).

Link, Arthur S., *Wilson: The New Freedom* (Princeton, N.J.: 1956).*

———, *Wilson: The Road to the White House* (Princeton, N.J.: 1947).

———, *Woodrow Wilson and the Progressive Era, 1910–1917* (New York, 1954).*

McCoy, Donald, *Calvin Coolidge: The Quiet President* (New York, 1967).

Morgan, Robert J., *A Whig Embattled* (Lincoln, Neb.: 1954).

Mowry, George E., *The Era of Theodore Roosevelt, 1900–1912* (New York, (1958).*

Nevins, Allan, ed., *The Diary of John Quincy Adams* (New York, 1951).

———, *Grover Cleveland: A Study in Courage* (New York, 1932).

———, ed., *James K. Polk: The Diary of a President* (New York, 1929).

Nichols, Roy F., *Franklin Pierce: Young Hickory of the Granite Hills* (Philadelphia, 1931).

Pringle, Henry F., *The Life and Times of William Howard Taft* (New York, 1939).

———, *Theodore Roosevelt* (New York, 1931).*

Quint, Howard H., and Robert H. Ferrell, eds., *The Talkative President: The Off-the-Record Press Conferences of Calvin Coolidge* (Amherst, Mass.: 1964).

Randall, James G., ed., *Lincoln the President,* 2 vols. (New York, 1945 and 1955).*

Roosevelt, Theodore, *Autobiography* (New York, 1913).

Rosenman, Samuel I., *Working with Roosevelt* (New York, 1952).

Schachner, Nathan, *Thomas Jefferson: A Biography* (New York, 1951).

Schlesinger, Arthur M., Jr., *A Thousand Days: John F. Kennedy in the White House* (Boston, 1965).*

———, *The Age of Roosevelt,* 3 vols. (Boston, 1957–60).*

Sherwood, Robert E., *Roosevelt and Hopkins,* rev. ed. (New York, 1950).*

Sievers, Harry J., *Benjamin Harrison: Hoosier Statesman* (New York, 1959).

Sinclair, Andrew, *The Available Man: Warren Gamaliel Harding* (New York, 1965).

Sorensen, Theodore C., *Kennedy* (New York, 1965).*

Stryker, Lloyd Paul, *Andrew Johnson: A Study in Courage* (New York, 1929).

Truman, Harry S., *Memoirs,* 2 vols. (Garden City, N.Y.: 1955 and 1956).

———, *Truman Speaks* (New York, 1960).

Tugwell, Rexford, G., *The Democratic Roosevelt* (Garden City, N.Y.: 1957).

U.S. National Archives, *Public Papers of the Presidents of the United States* (Washington, D.C.: 1957 and after).

White, William Allen, *A Puritan in Babylon* (New York, 1938).*

Williams, Charles Richard, ed., *Diary and Letters of Rutherford B. Hayes* (Columbus, Ohio: 1924).

* Available in paperback edition.

Winston, Robert W., *Andrew Johnson: Plebian and Patriot* (New York, 1928).

COURT CASES

In re Debs (158 U.S. 564, 1895).
Ducan v. Kahanamoku, Sheriff (327 U.S. 304, 1946).
Ex parte Grossman (267 U.S., 1925).
Hirabayashi v. United States (320 U.S. 81, 1943).
Humphrey v. United States (295 U.S. 602, 1935).
Korematsu v. United States (323 U.S. 214, 1944).
Ex parte Milligan (4 Wall 2, 1866).
Mississippi v. Johnson (4 Wall 475, 1867).
Myers v. United States (271 U.S., 1926).
In re Neagle (135 U.S. 1, 1890).
Ex parte Quirin (317 U.S. 1, 1942).
Ray v. Blair (343 U.S. 214, 1952).
United States v. Curtiss-Wright Export Corp. (299 U.S. 304, 1936).
United States v. Montgomery Ward and Co. (58 Fed. Supp. 408, N.D., Ill., 1945; 150 Fed. [2d.] 369, C.C.A. 7th, 1945).
Yakus v. United States (321 U.S. 414, 1944).
Youngstown Sheet and Tube Co. v. Sawyer (343 U.S. 579, 1952).

CHIEF EXECUTIVES OF OTHER COUNTRIES

Adam, Thomas R., *Elements of Government: An Introduction to Political Science* (New York, 1960).
Aron, Robert, *An Explanation of De Gaulle* (New York, 1966).
Attlee, C. R., *As It Happened* (New York, 1954).
Beer, Samuel H., *British Politics in the Collectivist Age* (New York, 1965).
Bulmer-Thomas, Ivor, *The Growth of the British Party System* (New York, 1965).
Carter, Byrum E., *The Office of Prime Minister* (Princeton, N.J.: 1956).
Crankshaw, Edward, *Khrushchev: A Career* (New York, 1966).*
Davis, Harold E., *Government and Politics in Latin America* (New York, 1958).
Deutscher, Isaac, *Russia After Stalin* (New York, 1949).
———, *Stalin: A Political Biography*, 2nd ed. (New York, 1967).*
Djilas, Milovan, *The New Class* (New York, 1957).*
Eden, Anthony, *The Memoirs of Anthony Eden: Full Circle* (Boston, 1960).
Fainsod, Merle, *How Russia Is Ruled*, rev. ed. (Cambridge, Mass.: 1963).
Hazard, John N., *The Soviet System of Government*, 3rd ed. (Chicago, 1964).*
Jennings, Ivor, *Cabinet Government*, 3rd ed. (Cambridge, Mass.: 1959).
MacKenzie, R. T., *British Political Parties* (New York, 1964).*

* Available in paperback edition.

Macridis, Roy C., *The Study of Comparative Government* (Garden City, N.Y.: 1955).

———, and Bernard E. Brown, *The De Gaulle Republic: Quest for Unity* (Homewood, Ill.: 1960).

Morrison, Herbert, *Government and Parliament,* 3rd ed. (New York, 1964).*

Rossiter, Clinton, *Constitutional Dictatorship* (Princeton, N.J.: 1948).*

Rush, Myron, *Political Succession in the U.S.S.R.* (New York, 1965).

Williams, Francis, ed., *Twilight of Empire: Memoirs of Prime Minister Clement Attlee* (New York, 1962).

Wolfe, Bertram D., *Khrushchev and Stalin's Ghost* (New York, 1957).

THE AMERICAN GOVERNOR AND MAYOR

Banfield, Edward C., and James Q. Wilson, *City Politics* (Cambridge, Mass.: 1963).*

Greer, Scott, *Governing the Metropolis* (New York, 1962).*

Jewell, Malcolm E., *The State Legislature* (New York, 1962).*

Kammerer, Gladys, *et al., The Urban Political Community* (Boston, 1963).*

Key, V. O., Jr., *American State Politics* (New York, 1956).

Lockard, Duane, *The Politics of State and Local Government* (New York, 1963).

Ransone, Coleman B., Jr., *The Office of Governor in the United States* (University, Ala.: 1956).

Sayre, Wallace S., and Robert Kaufman, *Governing New York City* (New York, 1960).

* Available in paperback edition.

Index